The BROOKLYNS

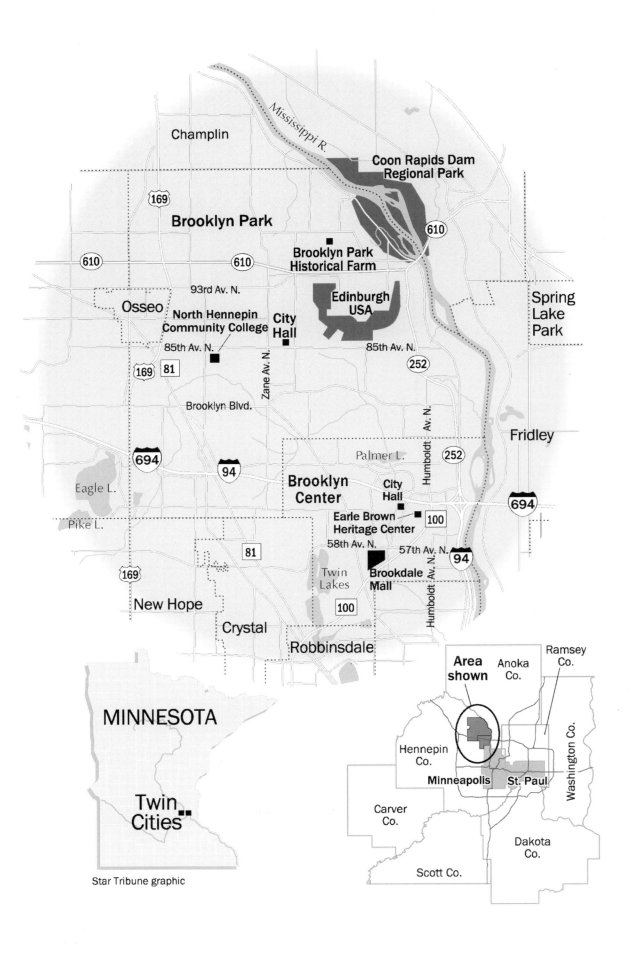

Champlin

Mississippi R.

Coon Rapids Dam Regional Park

169

Brooklyn Park

610

610

610

93rd Av. N.

Brooklyn Park Historical Farm

Osseo

Edinburgh USA

North Hennepin Community College

City Hall

85th Av. N.

Zane Av. N.

85th Av. N.

Spring Lake Park

169 81

252

Brooklyn Blvd.

Humboldt Av. N.

Fridley

694

94

Palmer L.

252

Eagle L.

Brooklyn Center

City Hall

Humboldt Av. N.

694

Pike L.

Earle Brown Heritage Center

100

58th Av. N.

57th Av. N.

94

81

Twin Lakes

Brookdale Mall

100

169

New Hope

Crystal

Robbinsdale

MINNESOTA

Twin Cities

Star Tribune graphic

Area shown

Anoka Co.

Ramsey Co.

Hennepin Co.

Washington Co.

Minneapolis **St. Paul**

Carver Co.

Dakota Co.

Scott Co.

The BROOKLYNS

A HISTORY OF
BROOKLYN CENTER
AND
BROOKLYN PARK
MINNESOTA

Daniel J. Hoisington, Editor

The Brooklyn Historical Society

2001

This book was completed with the assistance of the Community History Program of Edinborough Press.
For more information, contact:

Daniel J. Hoisington
Edinborough Press
P. O. Box 13790
Roseville MN 55113-2293
1-888-251-6336

For more information about the Brooklyn Historical Society, contact:

The Brooklyn Historical Society
P. O. Box 29345
Brooklyn Center MN 55429-0345

PUBLISHER'S CATALOGUING—IN—PUBLICATION DATA
Brooklyn Historical Society
The Brooklyns: A History of Brooklyn Center & Brooklyn Park, Minnesota
International Standard Book Number: 0-9708439-0-9
Library of Congress Card Number: 2001-087195

Table of Contents

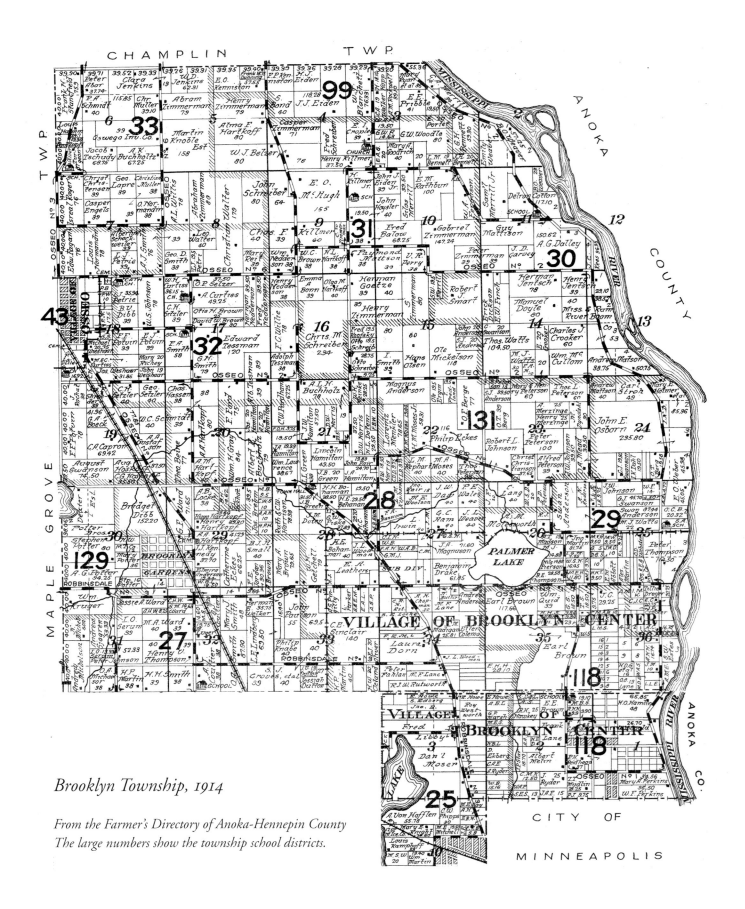

Brooklyn Township, 1914

*From the Farmer's Directory of Anoka-Hennepin County
The large numbers show the township school districts.*

Dedication

WE HEREBY GRATEFULLY ACKNOWLEDGE the assistance of the benefactors who generously funded the development and pre-publication costs of this book through their contributions to the Brooklyn Historical Society. The early support and encouragement of these benefactors made this book possible.

Pacesetter
Brooklyn Center Lions

Patrons

David and Jody Brandvold *on behalf of the Brandvold Family*
Brooklyn Center Rotary
Brooklyn Historical Society
Brooklyn Park Rotary
Cass Screw Machine Products, Inc.
Ron and Betty Christensen
Elaine Tessman Christiansen
City of Brooklyn Center
City of Brooklyn Park
Phil Cohen
Bill and Twila Hannay
Harvey and Marie Johnston
Lynne Johnston
Joyner's Die Casting and Plating, Inc.,

Tony and Joanne Kuefler
Joseph Lampe and Ernee McArthur
Malmborg's Garden Center and Greenhouse
Marquette Bank-Brookdale
Keith and Charlotte Nordby
Dean and Marie Nyquist
Dr. Duane, Karen and Charlie Orn
Roger and Irma Scherer Family
Evelyn P. Schmidt
Vera, William, and John Schreiber
Evelyn Setzler
Alice P. Tessman
Eldon and June Tessman
Edwin and Kathleen Theisen Family,
Wallace and Charlotte Tommerdahl Family

Sponsors

Vernon and Marvel Ausen
Wallace and Elaine Bernards Family
Mary Smith Blesi
Brooklyn Center Fire Dept. Relief Assn.
Brooklyn Center Taxpayers' Assn.
Brooklyn Center Women's Club
Brooklyn Park Lions
Brookpark Dental Center
Bob and Betty Cahlander Family
Phil, Rory and Alex Carruthers
Clarence LaBelle VFW
Ron and Beverly Dow
Gil and Marion Engdahl
Wilbur and Carol Goetze

Ralph and Leone Howe
Don and Sylvia Kramer
Art and Dolores Kvamme
Leonard E. Lindquist
Jim and Marilyn Lindsay
Marquette Bank-Brooklyn Park
North Memorial Health Care
Palmer Lake VFW
Don and Ann Poss
Barbara Sexton
Thomas and Lorraine Shinnick
Earl Simons Family
Mary Ellen Vetter

STATE OF MINNESOTA

OFFICE OF GOVERNOR JESSE VENTURA

130 State Capitol ◆ 75 Constitution Avenue ◆ Saint Paul, MN 55155

Greetings From Governor Jesse Ventura

These past few years have been some of the most interesting, exciting and personally rewarding times of my life. Youth has its time and its special energies. Military service, of course, has its rigid physical and psychological demands, often with only your own personal achievement as compensation for the time and effort. The Office of Governor is truly among the highest of responsibilities, holding some of the heaviest burdens, requiring some of the toughest decisions, yet returning the most unique and heartwarming personal rewards any man could ask for in a lifetime.

We have a beautiful state, clean air, lakes and rivers, many wonderful parks for families to visit or camp in, decent roads and highways to travel, excellent state and local law enforcement agencies to answer the call for help. We have the finest quality homegrown produce as well as dairy products, beef, pork, and poultry from family and corporate farms brought to our kitchen tables. Some of the finest medical services in the world to care for us when we are ill or injured; churches of all faiths providing moral insight, spiritual and worship opportunities to our fast growing, and diverse population.

I am proud to have been Mayor of the fine City of Brooklyn Park, and also very proud and deeply honored to now be your governor.

Sincerely,

Jesse Ventura
Governor

l or (800) 657-3717 ◆ Fax: (651) 296-2089 ◆ TDD: (651) 296-0075 or (800) 657-3598
overnor.state.mn.us   An Equal Opportunity Employer
Printed on recycled paper containing 15% post consumer material

City of Brooklyn Center
A great place to start. A great place to stay.

Dear Friends and Neighbors,

Welcome to our own "Tale of Two Cities," I am very excited about this opportunity to share with you the history of our city and its people.

One of my greatest pleasures as mayor of Brooklyn Center has been the opportunity to meet so many involved citizens of our city. The caring and concern is so evident in each and every one. We are a city of parks, churches, growing commercial areas and wonderful neighborhoods full of people who love this city.

We are indeed an "All America City."

The year 2000 is a special year in many ways, our designation as a Millennium Community is a great honor for us. The theme "Honor the Past–Imagine the Future" is the focus of our year-long celebration. This book is a great part of that theme, and I hope that future readers will appreciate the dedication of the many dozens who worked so very hard for its completion.

My best to you all, with greetings from the city council, city staff and citizens past, present and future.

Myrna Kragness

Myrna Kragness
Mayor, Brooklyn Center

Honor the Past–Imagine the Future

6301 Shingle Creek Pkwy, Brooklyn Center, MN 55430-2199 • City Hall & TDD Number (612) 569-3300
Recreation and Community Center Phone & TDD Number (612) 569-3400 • FAX (612) 569-3494
An Affirmative Action / Equal Opportunities Employer

Dear Friends,

It is indeed an honor to welcome you to the Brooklyn Historical Society's Heritage Book for the Brooklyn Community. This publication's pages hold more than just stories about the area's residents and history — they are truly a guide to where we are headed in the next century.

During my time as a resident and elected official in Brooklyn Park, I have had the pleasure of meeting many of those involved in creating this book. Their dedication, hard work and love of this community should be an inspiration to all who pick up the Heritage Book in the years to come.

Entering my sixth year as mayor of Brooklyn Park, I am very proud of the city I have called home for several decades. Our city boasts of a strong spirit, numerous recreational opportunities, a healthy business community, and outstanding residents who care greatly about where they live.

On behalf of the Brooklyn Park City Council and the entire City of Brooklyn Park, please accept my best wishes and thanks for your interest in our heritage.

Very sincerely,

Grace Arbogast

Grace Arbogast
Mayor of Brooklyn Park

DEAR FRIENDS,

The Brooklyn Historical Society is pleased to present *The Brooklyns: A History of Brooklyn Center and Brooklyn Park, Minnesota*, in celebration of the establishment and growth of our two communities.

Our narrative begins in the 1850s with the stories of the early pioneers, continues with the dramatic changes from a rural to suburban environment, and closes with our own stories written in the year 2000.

The Society members who researched and created this book found inspiration in the zeal and community spirit that shines forth in these pages. We are honored and humbled to dedicate this book to the Brooklyn citizens, past and present.

Mary Ellen Vetter
President

Acknowledgments

IT HAS TAKEN the gifts, hearts and toil of the Brooklyns' people to make this book possible. More than 500 writers are represented in this book. A special "thank you" to all who helped in any way, including those listed:

Daniel J. Hoisington, Editor
Dr. Norene Roberts
Jim Fogerty, Minnesota Historical Society
Oral History Narrators (listed in the Uncommon Lives chapter)
Leone Howe

Showcasing the Cities:
    Mayor Grace Arbogast, Mayor Myrna Kragness, Mary Ellen Vetter, Roxana Benjamin, Pat Milton, Tom Bullington, John Connelly, Sue Lacrosse, Dan Ryan, City staffs of Brooklyn Center and Brooklyn Park

Introduction:	Daniel J. Hoisington
Chapter 1:	Mary Ellen Vetter, Marian Klohs
Chapter 2:	Jane Hallberg
Chapter 3:	Kay Lasman, Howard Heck, Don Davis, Barbara Sexton, Tony Kuefler, Roger Scherer
Chapter 4:	Wallace Bernards, Warren Lindquist, Warren Olson
Chapter 5:	Ernee McArthur
Chapter 6:	Karen Bolstad
Chapter 7:	Lynne Johnston, Evanell Janousek, Dean Nyquist
Chapter 8:	Roxana Benjamin
Chapter 9:	Phil Carruthers, Mary Blesi, Jane Hallberg, Marian Klohs, Cassie Sweeney-Truitt
Chapter 10:	Earl Simons, Wilbur and Carol Goetze, Dr. Bill Dudley, Dale Greenwald, Ernee McArthur, Don Kramer
Chapter 11:	Phil Cohen, Tony Kuefler, Joseph Lampe
Chapter 12:	Phil Cohen, Tony Kuefler, Scott Clark, Ron Warren, Joseph Lampe
Chapter 13:	Neal Bernards, Tony Kuefler, Bill and Lona Schreiber, Phil Cohen, Ernee McArthur, Jane Hallberg, Howard Heck, Kay Lasman, Eileen Oslund, Barbara Sexton, Phyllis Owens
Chapter 14:	Roxana Benjamin
Chapter 15:	Barbara Erickson, Bernice Vaillancourt, Mavis Huddle, Marilyn Barland, Family Writers
Editing:	Charlotte Tommerdahl, Don Kramer, Mary Ellen Vetter, Roxana Benjamin, Donna Laberda
Transcribers:	Linda Eriksson, Donna Laberda
Photographers:	Karen Bolstad, Andrew Von Bank, Mariya Tarasar, Joseph Lampe, Kay Lasman, Helen Jacobsen, Marian Klohs

Fund Raising: Ernee McArthur, Tony Kuefler, Eldon Tessman, Earl Simons, Tom Shinnick, Wilbur Goetze

Book Treasurer: Barbara Erickson

Secretary/Grants: Sandy Cich, Bernice Vaillancourt

Promotion: Don Kramer, Mary Ellen Vetter, Dave Johnson, Roxana Benjamin, Jim Ebert, Gail Baerg

Computer: Dave Johnson, Joseph Lampe, Kathryn Hand

Other Assistance: Brenda Wieland (Callaway, MN, book); Lorraine Berg, Gil Engdahl (Todd County, MN, book); Carol King (Prescott, WI, book); Donna Eddy, Mary Kiffmeyer, (Big Lake, MN, book); Betty Wolfangle (Roseville, MN, book)

Coordinators: Ernee McArthur, Roxana Benjamin, Dave Johnson, Joseph Lampe

Brooklyn Center

A perfect place to start, and a perfect place to stay for a lifetime!

Nestled on the banks of the Mississippi River, just ten short miles from downtown Minneapolis, Brooklyn Center offers all the opportunities of the metropolitan area while priding itself on its small town appeal. From starter homes to gracious homes with lake and riverfront views, to assisted living environments for senior adults, Brooklyn Center is "A Perfect Place To Start, And A Perfect Place To Stay For A Lifetime."

The area that would become Brooklyn Center opened for settlement after the United States signed the Sioux treaties of 1851 and 1852, which opened the land west of the Mississippi.

Brooklyn Center celebrates its heritage as a community each year with a civic festival called "Earle Brown Days." Earle Brown offered his farmland as a training field for pilots in World War I, and a training college for the Minnesota Highway Patrol that he founded in 1929. Today a portion of the farm and many original buildings are home to the Earle Brown Heritage Center, one of the finest convention and hospitality centers in the region.

In the mid–1980s, Brooklyn Center was one of nine U.S. cities that received All-America City Awards sponsored by a Citizens Forum on Self-Government and *USA Today*. Among other things, the awards considered volunteer projects like Brooklyn Center Mediation, Peacemaker Center, and the Brookwood Senior Housing Development.

The Brooklyn Center business community is as diverse as its residents and neighborhoods. Serving as a regional shopping hub for the north metro area, Brooklyn Center is home to Brookdale Center. The Mall is anchored by four major retailers and one hundred plus stores. Brookdale Center was built in 1962, and is presently undergoing an elaborate multi-million-dollar renovation. In addition to Brookdale, nearly five hundred businesses contribute to the economy of the city.

Whether it is the Brookdale Mall, new homes along 53rd Avenue, the new Police and Fire facilities, a twenty-screen theater complex, or a regional furniture distribution facility, residents and businesses are eager to reinvest in their community.

Brooklyn Center is proud of its 522 acres of parks including Central Park and nature centers such as the Palmer Lake Park wilderness area, extensive trail system extending to all neighboring communities and the Mississippi River, city operated Centerbrook Golf Course, recreational activities and facilities. The Community Center features an Olympic sized swimming pool with a 150-foot water slide, a fitness facility, and activity and meeting rooms.

With all of its history and amenities, Brooklyn Center continues to grow, change and revitalize to meet the demands of the new millennium. Brooklyn Center residents enjoy affordable housing, quality education, convenient health care, churches, and volunteer organizations that show a genuine interest in their community. And why not? To them, Brooklyn Center is much more than a place to live, it's home.

Brooklyn Park

Shingle Creek runs through it. Along the eastern border of Brooklyn Park, the Mississippi River gently bends and winds.

Once drawing farmers to its banks, now the river signifies the enviable lifestyle of the area. From pioneer farmers to award-winning developers, the timeless beauty of the land has attracted growth with the promise of prosperity.

It is only natural that a city named Brooklyn Park would emphasize open spaces, nature areas and refreshing waterways throughout diverse housing developments. Wherever you are in the city, a park is only minutes away. The city's Recreation and Parks Department has received the National Gold Medal Award twice for outstanding planning and programming.

Brooklyn Park is home to Hennepin Technical College and North Hennepin Community College, the second largest community college in the state, which serves 6,600 students annually. A community landmark is the North Hennepin Community College's Carillon, a fourteenth-century European style bell tower structure that represents the history of potato growing in Brooklyn Park.

The restored, operating Brooklyn Park Historical Farm of 1900 vintage enriches the lives of children of all ages.

Edinburgh USA Golf Course was ranked one of the best public golf courses in the nation by *Golf Digest*. The golf course is surrounded by upscale residential properties.

The city's prestigious Northland Industrial Park includes the four-star Northland Inn and Executive Conference Center.

New homes are being built in Willows of Aspen, Heritage Farms and Pinebrook Village, and existing homes are being renovated by residents who have put down roots in Brooklyn Park.

The Highway 610 east-west corridor will be the home to the new Target North Office Campus that could eventually employ 4,000 or more in the next decade.

Brooklyn Park has received national attention for planning of its staged development, and this continues with the Master Planning Task Force recommending development of the remaining 4,000 acres in northern Brooklyn Park.

In 1999 Brooklyn Park was chosen as one of thirty cities in the nation to be finalists in the All-America City competition, and has received nine national awards, including being first in Minnesota and fifth in the nation for overall efforts in the 1999 National Night Out event.

In Brooklyn Park, high quality and good value go hand-in-hand. Brooklyn Park is a place where you can feel safe, be healthy, shop, have fun, worship, enjoy life fully, know your neighbors and share your life and gifts with the community.

Brooklyn Center

Proclaimed "The Something More City," Brooklyn Center offers all the opportunities of the metropolitan area while priding itself on its small-town appeal.

Below: From starter homes to gracious homes with lake and riverfront views to assisted living for senior adults, Brooklyn Center is "A Perfect Place to Start, and a Perfect Place to Stay for a Lifetime."

Above: Serving as a regional shopping hub for the north metro area, Brooklyn Center is home to Brookdale Center. The Mall is anchored by four major retailers and one hundred-plus stores. The Brookdale Mall was built in 1962 and is presently undergoing an elaborate multi-million dollar renovation. In addition to Brookdale, nearly five hundred businesses contribute to the city's economy.

Left: The original home of Earle Brown and many of the original farm buildings are now home to the Inn on the Farm and the Earle Brown Heritage Center, one of the finest convention centers in the region.

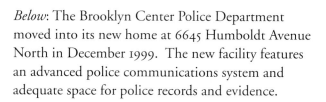

Below: The Brooklyn Center Police Department moved into its new home at 6645 Humboldt Avenue North in December 1999. The new facility features an advanced police communications system and adequate space for police records and evidence.

Above: Dedicated on June 27, 1971, Brooklyn Center City Hall is located at 6801 Shingle Creek Parkway and is adjacent to Central Park and the Community Center Pool.

Below: Brooklyn Center residents are served by two fire stations: East and West. Fire Chief Ron Boman is shown in front of the nearly completed new West Fire Station.

Above: The Community Center Pool and Water Slide opened in 1971 and features an indoor Olympic swimming pool, 150-foot water slide, diving boards, wading pool, sauna, exercise room, game room and meeting rooms.

Left: Opened in 1987, the beautiful Centerbrook Golf Course is a 9-Hole, Par 3 Course offering league play, individual and group lessons, as well as a variety of golf outings.

Below: Over 500 children participate each year in the variety of games and activities offered during the Earle Brown Days Festival which includes an annual Kid's Fishing Contest.

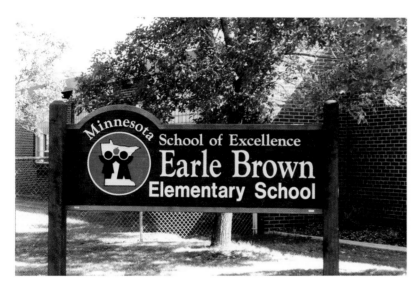

Above: The Earle Brown Elementary School is one of eight schools in Brooklyn Center which encompasses portions of four different school districts.

Left: The Brooklyn United Methodist Church stands today as the first of more than twenty churches in Brooklyn Center.

Left: This view of Brooklyn Center from the Mississippi River shows the Viewing & Observation deck located in the newly renovated North Mississippi Regional Park.

Right: The City of Brooklyn Center prides itself on its 522 acres of parks including Central Park and nature centers such as the Palmer Lake Park wilderness area, as well as an extensive trail system extending to all neighboring communities and the Mississippi River.

Left: Another amenity in the community, Shingle Creek, extends throughout the city and for many years hundreds of volunteers have worked with pride to annually "Clean Up the Creek."

Right: In the mid–1980s, Brooklyn Center was one of nine U.S. cities that received All-America City Awards sponsored by a Citizens Forum on Self-government and *USA Today*. Among other things, the awards considered volunteer projects like Brooklyn Peacemaker Center, Brooklyn Mediation Project, and the Brookwood Senior Housing Development.

Brooklyn Park

Above: The gazebo and rose garden by the Community Activity Center offers a place to relax and enjoy some live music or just take in the great outdoors.

Upper Left: The Brooklyn Park Historical Farm brings visitors back to the way life was in 1900. The farm was renovated in 1998.

Above: Much of the future development in Brooklyn Park will be along Highway 610, an east-west route connecting Interstate 94 with Highway 252. At the beginning of the 21st century, about 35 percent of Brooklyn Park (mainly in the north) remains undeveloped. (shown is W. Broadway overpass)

Above: Wild flowers grow in the warm summer sun. In the background is the city's newly expanded state-of-the-art water treatment facility.

Above: Brooklyn Park residents are served by four fire stations. The newest station, in the north part of the city, was completed in 1999 to respond to additional residential growth.

Above: The Brooklyn Park Community Activity Center is a multi-purpose facility, featuring two sheets of ice, a senior center, community room, weight room, National Guard armory and a beautifully landscaped campus.

Above: Brooklyn Park City Hall, built in 1991, is one of the Upper Midwest's premier government centers. It is located adjacent to the Police Department and Community Activity Center.

Right: Located in western Brooklyn Park, Hennepin Technical College is one of the nation's premier technical institutions.

Left: The Bell Tower (Carillon) stands as a focal point on the campus of North Hennepin Community College, a symbol commemorating our agrarian heritage. It was dedicated on June 21, 1997 and was donated by the Tessman and Setzler families.

Above: Residential life in Brooklyn Park has developed northward over the years. Here, upscale housing blends nicely with golf at Edinburgh USA.

Left: Home to the LPGA Tour for a number of years, the tour-quality Edinburgh USA golf course attracts avid golfers from across Minnesota who enjoy a challenging game mixed with a well-groomed course.

Right: Brooklyn Park neighborhoods are home to many water features. Residents enjoy both the scenic beauty and friendliness of living in our community.

SHOWCASING OUR COMMUNITIES

Left: The West Coon Rapids Dam is one of the city's several recreational amenities. Popular activities along the dam include biking, inline skating, jogging, nature hikes and birdwatching.

Above: On the city's eastern border lies the majestic Mississippi River. Brooklyn Park residents are drawn to its inescapable presence and sense of history and nostalgia.

Above: Business parks have sprung up quickly in Brooklyn Park due to its easy connection to Interstate 694, Highways 81 and 610 and other major thoroughfares.

Right: One of the region's finest executive conference centers and hotels, the Northland Inn brings major events and prestigious guests to Brooklyn Park.

Introduction

BUILDING A COMMUNITY

DRIVING ON I-694, one city blurs into another. You pass one exit with a McDonald's, another with a Perkins. There is a mall — one of the "dales" — with a conglomeration of stores. The stories are often replaceable parts — the early settlers were hard-working immigrants. Most suburban newspapers have carried at least one article about "the last farm" lost to encroaching development. What sets "the Brooklyns" apart? When we read the history of the community, is there something that is ours alone — special, unique, defining?

The Tessmans' Community

The land shaped the settlement and the subsequent economy of the Brooklyns. When vast tracts of Minnesota became available following the Treaties of Mendota and Traverse de Sioux, thousands of prospective settlers headed west to the new territory. As they came to the land north of Saint Anthony's Falls, they encountered four extensive prairies, interspersed with brush and groves of oaks and poplars. Since the open grassland was easily plowed, this land attracted the first settlers. The soil was a sandy loam that provided good drainage, especially suited to early harvests.

August Tessman was among the early settlers. He was born in West Prussia, Germany, in 1838, coming to America at the age of twenty as a stowaway. He settled in Chanhassen, earning a living by transporting bricks on the Minnesota River. On one of his trips to Saint Paul, he met Henrietta Hartkopf, whom he married in 1862. When they learned that Moses Blowers' farm was for sale in Brooklyn Township, they bought it and moved to the area in 1870. The Tessmans' built their home — which still stands — in 1883.

The Tessmans, like their neighbors, were farmers. Of the 132 Brooklyn township names listed in Neill's 1881 *History of Hennepin County*, 118 men gave "farmer" as their occupation. Wheat was the primary crop in the Brooklyn area in those years. The agricultural census for Brooklyn Township show that there were 270 farms producing 46,698 bushels of wheat in 1880. But the growing population of Minneapolis, combined with an increased accessibility, led Brooklyn area farmers to shift production to cater to the city demands for vegetables and flowers.

In the Brooklyns, the local farmers planted potatoes, growing varieties with names like Early Ohios, Rural New Yorkers, Irish Cobblers, Sebagos, Wasecas, and Warbas. Under the guidance of Fred Krantz, the University of Minnesota Horticulture Department developed the "Osseo" in 1954 and "Anoka" in 1965. By 1910, the city of Osseo became the largest potato-shipping point in the United States. For a more complete look at the potato industry, read Norene Roberts' essay, "Growing Potatoes in Brooklyn Park" in Chapter Ten.[1]

It was a tough business, subject to potato bugs and drought. Eldon Tessman wrote, "Potato production was on the decline even when I started farming. The peak years for potato production in Brooklyn Park were in the 1910s and 1920s." Trying to assist nature, farmers introduced irrigation in the 1930s. Tessman noted, "In 1936 my parents used the Skinner system. It's approximately 1½ inches in diameter and has small nozzles every six feet and often they were put on posts to oscillate." The new Norland variety, one farmer said, extended potato growing in the Brooklyns by fifty years, due to its hearty nature.

Who came to Brooklyn Township? As Jane Hallberg notes in Chapter Two, a "colony" from Adrian, Michigan, were among the first landowners. Of the forty-six prominent residents profiled by Edward Neill in 1881, thirty men were from New England (with twenty-one from Maine) and only four were foreign born. In 1932, one writer described the townspeople, stating, "Brooklyn Center Township was settled by New Englanders and Scandinavians. They are the kind of folks who settle on a piece of land and stay there. Many of the old timers live there yet — the Mattsons, the Libbys,

The Howe Store, located at what is now 69th Avenue and Brooklyn Boulevard.

the Hamiltons, the Howes, the Swensons. They are all frugal, thrifty, honest folks. They all used to go fishing in Shingle Creek and go over to Howe's store on Middle Road in the evening and chew the fat. They dropped in at each other's houses for meals and they do it yet."

John Wingard recalled the Scandinavian families, saying, "The Brunsells were the farmers that owned the land where Brookdale was built. Sig Edling was Scandinavian, too. The Bergstrom Brothers always spoke with a Swedish brogue — slow and deliberate."

In Brooklyn Park, however, the families were typically German or Swiss. Keith Caswell noted his family history, saying, "We had Swiss relatives who were truck gardeners and farmers that lived in this area. Some of them homesteaded. Switzerland paid them to come over to the United States because there was no future for them in Switzerland. The Swiss family names were common up in this area. There were Zopfi, Blesi, Zimmerman, and Curtis."[2]

There were tensions between the different nationalities. Glen Sonnenberg recalled,

My mother was Norwegian and she'd say, 'Swedes, *ish*.' In this little area, there was a family called Hartson. That's a German name. [The Sardinskys] were Ukrainian. Across the road were the Stefansens and they were really Danish. They held themselves aloof and they were better than anybody else. That's the way it appeared to us. It took a long time before one family accepted another family, saying, 'I don't want you playing with that boy or I don't want you to be seen with that one.' They never explained why, but they just said, 'No way are you going to have anything to do with them.'[3]

So, the land made a difference. If August Tessman had remained in the Chaska area, he might have worked a small mixed-use farm, with alfalfa or dairy cattle. In Brooklyn Township, however, they became potato farmers.

Creating a Community

The community centered on the rural schools, the churches, and the few crossroad stores. Neill described the township in 1881: "Brooklyn is an exclusively agricultural town. With the exception of Osseo, it has no village. Brooklyn Center is the site of two churches, a store and post office; but its few residences are only a gathering of farm houses."

Howe's Store was an important landmark. Recalling the time before WWII, John Wingard said, "There was a general store on the corner of Osseo Road and what is now 69th Avenue North. As kids, we used to talk about going down there and getting an ice cream cone from Pappy Howe." The store included a soda fountain area. Wingard continued, "Alongside the store, Bergstrom brothers (Arnie, Ted, Carl, Ed, and Phil) built an implement dealership. There was a gasoline pump in front of the building. There was another little store just south of it—a confectionary store which sold groceries, candy, and stuff." Charlie Holmes owned this store.[4]

Students attended local schools until high school. Alice Tessman, for example, attended North High School in Minneapolis with cousins George and Everett Setzler. For medical care, residents visited doctors in Anoka or Osseo. Local farmers joined together and built a community center around 1920, known as "Riverlyn," where they held dances, holiday gatherings, and picnics.[5] The Patrons of Husbandry, known as the "Grange," built a hall in Brooklyn Center in 1876. Settlers organized several churches, including the Methodist Church (1855), First Freewill Baptist Church (1879), the Norwegian Evangelical Lutheran Church (1877). It provided a place for the rural people to gather once a week.

Earle Brown's Village

Sometimes a town's history is defined by one personality—a charismatic leader who acts as a fulcrum. Earle Brown was just such a man. He was wealthy and used his farm as an agricultural showcase with prized Belgian horses. In 1919 he opened an airfield on his land—probably the first commercial airfield in Minnesota. He gained notoriety as a booze-busting sheriff during Prohibition. "He had a reputation," said a friend, "of never asking a person to do any job that he himself would not undertake, which would include risk-of-life."

When he ran for governor in 1932, Brown ran as the apolitical outsider. He would "go through the statehouse and throw out every incompetent man and replace them with the best and most able men obtainable, irrespective of party affiliations." In a campaign biography, the writer described Brown with words that might fit another gubernatorial candidate from the Brooklyns—Jesse Ventura:

> Minnesota has something brand new this year in the way of a candidate for governor. Candidates for political office are pretty well standardized in this reporter's mind. His impression has always been that they are either young men consumed by a burning ambition to get some place or oldish men who have finally despaired of succeeding in business. As the years go by, they acquire all the little tricks and mannerisms of the experienced politician. They have acquired the ability to dodge gracefully any question that might prove embarrassing. There is not the slightest chance in the world of developing Earle Brown into a strutting, hand-shaking, slippery politician.[6]

Still, when the votes were counted, Floyd Olson carried Brown's home town with a vote of 300 for Olson and 246 for Brown.

There are hundreds of "Earle Brown" stories. Donald Weesner, a friend of the Brown family, remembered, "Earle Brown was not too talkative, but he was very interesting and liked to help people, but he wanted to be sure that it was doing some good. Quite often Brown would call on my father and we'd go out to Brooklyn Center in the winter time and take us for a ride in his bobsled."[7]

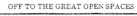

The Star, May 7, 1929.

Earle Brown — farmer, businessman, sheriff, politician — became a legend in Brooklyn Center. This sketch comes from the Minneapolis Star.

Earle Brown's farm was a showcase. Willed to the University of Minnesota, the property was developed over the years.

Garrison Keillor remembered, "We'd hike down to Earle Brown's farm, a thousand-acre ranch that lay along Highway 100, whiteface cattle grazing on a treeless plain, with Mr. Brown's big house, barns, stables, and riding arena in the distance. Earle Brown had been sheriff of Hennepin County and apparently he had the same cowboy fantasies that we had, his farm looked for all the world like a piece of Texas."[8]

A Village

It seems fitting that the village of Brooklyn Center was organized at a meeting in Brown's garage in 1911. Concerned about annexation by Minneapolis, residents voted 69 to 14 to incorporate as a village. Its trustees managed road repair, traffic laws, and preservation of the peace from rambunctious youth and loose farm animals. In 1915, it authorized the General Electric Company to bring electricity into the village.

Baldwin "Baldy" Hartkopf was a common man who made a difference. He grew up in Brooklyn Park, the grandson of German immigrants. Like most of his neighbors, he was a farmer and often got up in the middle of the night to haul potatoes down to the Minneapolis Farmers' Market. His daughter recalled, "My father was sort of like Will Rogers—he never met a man he didn't like. He liked people. He wasn't a rich man—he never was—and that wasn't his goal in life."

Although he was a farmer, he also served his community in government. "I tell you," he said, "government was very important to me, though I couldn't really tell you just why. But there were things that, as a gardener and farmer, I might have a part in deciding." He was appointed to fill a vacancy on the Coulter School Board in 1928. Then, in 1934, Hartkopf was elected state representative, serving for two terms. Baldy remained a "citizen-politician," declaring, "I wasn't really so much of a politician. I was just a young potato picker."[9]

Among his accomplishments, he introduced a bill in the House that enabled Minnesota municipalities to organize planning commissions. In 1940, Brooklyn Township enacted an ordinance regulating land use. To guide its implementation, the board authorized a Planning Commission one year later.[10]

In Brooklyn Township, individuals could make a difference. No historical formula can predict a man like Earle Brown. No clear explanation tells us why a simple potato farmer such as Baldy Hartkopf led Minnesota into the era of community planning.

Garrison Keillor's Town

In 1947 John and Grace Keillor decided to move from south Minneapolis to Brooklyn Park. Their son, Garrison, recalled, "Dad had gotten a G. I. loan to build a house, and he'd found a plan for a Cape Cod bungalow in a magazine." Like many of the neighbors, the Keillors laid their foundation and moved into a "basement" home. He continued, "For five years while he was building the superstructure—it was to take him five years—we would live in the bunker below."[11]

The Keillors were part of a transformation of Brooklyn Township by a single generation—the men and women that grew up in the depression and entered adulthood during World War II. When peace came in August 1945, these young men and women were ready to live their dreams after an enforced interlude. And their dreams took them to the suburbs.

Several key government policies fueled the population shift to the suburbs. First, the Federal Housing Authority made buying a new home an attainable dream by backing long-term mortgages. Phil Cohen recalled, "I learned a lot about housing. Longer-term mortgages back then [during the Depression] were two-year contracts for deed. So every other year, Dad had to go down and negotiate the contract for deed and he'd come home and say, "Well, we've got a roof over our head for another year or two."

In the 1920s, a typical mortgage ran five to ten years, requiring a down payment of forty percent. The FHA payment guarantee, combined with VA benefits to World War II veterans, fueled a steady expansion of new housing. Both programs placed a cap on the dollar amount that a mortgage could be insured—a maximum of $7,500 in 1950—encouraging the construction of small, mass-produced houses that cost just below the limit. This transformed the economy of the suburbs, placing a premium on open land near the highway system.

Benson School, 1953. Students include young Garrison Keillor
Mrs. G. L. Mattson

Glen Sonnenberg remembers, "All of these people who never had anything before now had just a bit of money from the government or from the Army and were going to buy a piece of property. My dad divided his farm into individual lots and he sold to five different fellows that had been in the service and came back and were going to build a house of their own."

Second, the Federal Highway Act of 1957 promised to pay ninety cents for every dollar spent on interstate highways. These new roads made it easier to commute for a long distance and broke the reliance on public transportation. The workplace might be several towns away from home. Highway construction changed the face of the Brooklyns. For example, the construction of I-94 made it a ten minute commute to downtown Minneapolis. As John Wingard recalled, "Roger Scherer and I worked diligently on getting I-94 through North Minneapolis. Our bottleneck was Camden Park, so Roger and I had some meetings with some fellows on the Park Board in Minneapolis and got a bill passed through the legislature for a land exchange. It has done a lot to help Brooklyn Park and Brooklyn Center because we have a major interstate that services the community."[12]

"The Other Side of the World"

Brooklyn Center and Brooklyn Park provided a new life for the postwar generation. Jack Vaughn remembered, "When I moved to Brooklyn Center, I bought my lot in 1946 and built in 1947. When I bought my lot, everybody said, "What are you going out there for? They don't have any street lights or paved roads or nothing."[13]

Phil Cohen had a similar story, saying, "We got married by a justice of the peace down in Iowa in November 1949. We had limited dollars. There was a house in Robbinsdale that was for sale that we could afford but somebody else out bid us. So we found this house in the back of a lot with a cesspool, septic tank, and well. We lived at 5353 Dupont until the house got too small when we had all three kids. We bought a house on 53rd and Humboldt."

Grace Arbogast came to the Brooklyns a decade later. Arbogast remembered, "We felt that we got more value for our money by buying in the northern suburbs than we would have gotten out south. We found a home at the corner of 63rd and Sumter, fell in love with it, purchased it in 1959. At that time, we just thought we were on the other side of world."

Rapid Growth

As more and more homes were built, cracks in the system began to develop. School were inadequate for the baby boom generation. The infrastructure of roads and utilities did not meet the demand. Individual septic systems threatened to overwhelm nature's ability to maintain ecological balance. Keith Caswell, an engineer, recalled, "Brooklyn Park was developing. They did have problems and there was pressure to further develop after World War II and the population explosion that took place in the metropolitan area. The city fathers recognized that and they worked very hard to do it. I was always impressed with the quality of the council people that we had and the leadership. We had Baldwin Hartkopf for instance. We had Red Anderson. We had councilmen that really had an interest in the community."

Threatened with encroachment from Osseo and Minneapolis, the remainder of Brooklyn Township voted to become a village in 1954. Baldy Hartkopf remembered the discussion about a name for the village. He said, "What shall we call this community?" We had to keep the 'Brooklyn' and it occurred to me that families would be coming and bringing children. Well, children need places to play, so we added the word 'Park'."

The new village government established some of Brooklyn Park's most important policies in those early years, notably the postponement of development north of 85th Avenue. "We called it a hop, skip and a jump and we didn't like it, Hartkopf said. "Rudy Peterson wanted to build homes up in the northwest area. But I told him, 'You'd be putting a storm sewer problem on everyone who lives up there." Keith Caswell recalled, "Brooklyn Park, I think, had 100-foot lots. There was a lot of pressure from the outside to go down to 75-foot lots, and so on, but they wanted to get their ducks in order prior to any development. It had a fair population—I think it was 10 to 12,000 people. The council met at least once a month, the planning commission once a month."

In addition, the planning board asked developers to donate parkland. Hartkopf backed up his position. When Orrin Thompson proposed a residential development next to the Hartkopf farm, Baldy said, "I told him I'd give two acres of my land if he'd give five of his." That property is now Baldwin Hartkopf Park.[14]

Building a Community

At the same time, these young men and women built a different kind of infrastructure—social, religious, and educational institutions to serve a growing population. Looking back on those years, Ed Theisen remembered, "Brooklyn Center was an exceptional community in which to raise a family. Burquest Lane was a block long and when our children were small, there must have been fifty little kids in that one or two block area. And the friendships they developed were great. Brooklyn Center really had this neighborhood spirit."

Local clubs and organizations fostered a sense of community. Many civic leaders fondly recall the influence of the Jaycees. Tony Kuefler said, "[The Jaycees] was a pretty good group. I learned a lot about organization and teamwork from them. If I had got into supervision at work before I had that training, I don't think I ever would have made it." Grace Arbogast agreed. "If you look back at the people that were involved in the Jaycees and the Mrs. Jaycees, they were people that went on to be on the council and went on to more political things," she said. "They were very active and committed and dedicated people. They were the real movers and shakers of that time that really made our community known and pulled together." [15]

This network extended to business affairs. Don Rosen, Pilgrim Cleaners, said, "In 1978 when we bought the Phillips 66 station, we needed funds. Jack Bell said to me, "I'm President of Rotary, we'd like to have you join." I thought it over and I said, "Okay, I'll join Rotary." He said, "Okay, then, you've got the money that you need for the station."" [16]

The Brooklyn Park Village Council meets in 1956. Left to right: Hilmer Guntzel, Harry Schreiber, Baldwin Hartkopf Sr., Abe Zimmerman, Al Joyner

Grace Arbogast recalls the camaraderie of those years. Her husband volunteered with the Fire Department. She said, "At that time, they interviewed the wife as well as the husband because it was a family thing. So we went and joined the Fire Department as a family. They had a women's auxiliary, which went to fires, and served food. We'd bring hot cocoa, coffee, sandwiches."

Schools were very important. Phil Cohen first got involved in local politics when his children were ready for school. He noted,

> I started hearing a lot about the School Board. In 1960, I ran for the board and got
> elected. It was my first venture into politics. I remember the superintendent of the
> Minneapolis school system came out and talked to the school board about building a
> high school. He said, "You know, we have the room to take care of your kids in Min-
> neapolis, get them a well rounded education, but you'll never have a school, you'll
> never have a community until you have a Brooklyn Center high school." His words of
> wisdom were what propelled the board and community to build a high school.

Local churches grew as well, adding to the community spirit. Phil Cohen said, "In the churches, you had ministers—the greatest group of ministers you ever had—who would preach from the pulpit about the responsibility of stewards of the community to get involved. St. Alphonsus was the greatest. We had members of the clergy who were members of the Rotary and the Lions."

A Critical Juncture

By the early 1960s, this post-war generation made important decisions. First, the community leaders made critical decisions about a seemingly mundane topic: waste disposal. Although the issue is literally below the surface, development requires a sound infrastructure of roads, water, electricity, and sanitation before construction begins. These long-term investments are expensive. Keith Caswell, the engineer, noted, "Brooklyn Park was going to limit their development to the area south of 85th Avenue. This was a big concern because there were many good successful farmers there. It was excellent land to farm. Brooklyn Park did not want to force those people on to the market."

The proposed plan created a North Suburban Sanitary Sewer District (NSSSD). There was strong opposition from the farmers, who feared higher assessments down the road. Bill Schreiber stated the case, "These supporters were simply stating that we do not want to be beholden to the city of Minneapolis in controlling our growth and development, because Minneapolis exclusively controlled the capacity for sanitary sewer. Downtown Minneapolis interests controlled suburban growth. The alternative was to form your own district, build your own waste treatment plant, and control your destiny." The catch? "You didn't have the downtown Minneapolis banker to help pay for it. That became the controversial part."

The postwar generation developed a leadership network, such as the Brooklyn Center Chamber of Commerce, organized in 1964. Left to right: Phil Cohen, Ed Hamernick, Jack Leary, Carl Anderson, Dallas Lawrence, Tom O'Hehir.

Lyn Joyner, whose brother was village clerk, recalled the bitterness of the debate. "I think several of the people who had honestly supported NSSD really in their hearts felt this was the best way to go." Bill Schreiber recollected, "After Nikita Khrushchev, the head of the Soviet Union, had come to the United Nations and taken his shoe off and pounded the table, [there] was one council member who thought he could do that at a Brooklyn Park council meeting as well."

One primary point of contention was that the sewer system was overbuilt—that it cost too much. Phil Cohen joked, "You could hold Volkswagen races in their sewer system. They greatly oversized it. The only way they could pay for it was by having higher density uses than what was planned, and that's why you have the apartments."

In addition, the relationship between developers and council members raised red flags for many citizens. Ted Willard remembered, "Most of the developers attempted to wine and dine the council members. I remember one of those turkeys delivered to my house. When I got home, there it was, and so what I did was take it to the church and donate it to them. No gratuities. Make that clear to all involved."

Second, Brooklyn Center had to decide what to do with Earle Brown's legacy. In 1949, he left his magnificent farm to the University of Minnesota, retaining the right to live there until his death. In 1954 Brown released some 200 acres of the farm to the University for a model development. With this windfall, the University sought to turn a handsome profit, and used the proceeds to build the Earle Brown Continuing Education Center on the Saint Paul campus.

The project was also an opportunity to set a model for suburban development. Called "Garden City," the University hired Winston Close, University of Minnesota advisory architect, to design the development. Working in partnership with his wife, Elizabeth, Close created plans for a residential community with educational, shopping, housing and recreational facilities. Close said, "This is really something unique. In no similar urban area in American does there exist an undivided tract of this size." Although Winston Brothers, the developer, used the Closes' plans, it eventually became independent of the University.[17]

When he died in 1963, the University sold the 560-acre farm to James and John Sheehan and Deil Gustafson. Gustafson kept the farm buildings for his personal use and proceeded to develop the rest of the property—now the heart of Brooklyn Center. The use of this piece of land would shape the economic development of the city for decades. It spurred Phil Cohen into politics. He recalled, "In 1962, another seat became vacant on the council and I felt I wanted to get involved in that—in the growth, the planning and development of the Earle Brown's farm, so I decided to run for City Council and got elected. Brooklyn Center was the second community in the metropolitan area that had a comprehensive plan developed. This set the stage for the City Council to agree with the University to do a study on how the Earle Brown's farm should be developed. A few changes to the original plan were put in place, principally changing from industrial to commercial, the property below the freeway."

A Legacy

What is the enduring legacy of this generation? When asked, Phil Cohen said, "We had no used car lots. We do not have any corner bars. We have no billboards. We adopted the housing maintenance code and the apartment license. We were one of the first cities to put sidewalks in. We have a good city charter. The greatest sin is to know what's right and not do it."

Ed Theisen spoke proudly of the work of the Capital Improvements Review Board. As they looked into the growing needs of Brooklyn Center, they heard demands for a swimming pool, a civic center, a police station, a fire station, and a city garage. Theisen said, "All of that was put together in one package. A lot of people from Brooklyn Center became involved and became proponents of the facilities, so the Bond issue passed easily. When I look back, it was done at the right time and at the right price."

Jesse Ventura's City

Although he presided over hundreds of city council meetings during his years as Mayor of Brooklyn Park, Jim Krautkremer remembers one evening in particular. Several community residents were opposing the development of a tract of land, concerned especially with the potential damage to a wetlands area. Krautkremer said,

> We were holding this meeting and there was somebody who kept interrupting and finally I took the gavel and I banged down and told this person, I said, "You're going to have time to talk but you're going to have to wait your time. We're going to stay here all night if we need to listen, but we will listen to you." Jerry Marshall leaned over and said, "Do you know who that guy was with the red and green hair that you just gaveled down? You'd better be careful. He's a wrestler, Jesse Ventura."

Although Ventura had a high profile in a profession that rewarded flamboyance, in other ways, he reflected the citizens of the Brooklyns. Raised in Minneapolis, he had taken classes at North Hennepin Community College after his service in the Navy. Like other city residents, he responded to the allure of the suburbs with its new homes, its good schools, and its open space—a quiet community where he could raise his two children. He wrote, "I'd never had any inkling of getting into politics. None. It had never crossed my mind. In a way, you could say that I didn't go into politics; politics came to me. It landed in my lap—or, to be more accurate, in my backyard. That made it impossible to ignore."

Echoing the descriptions of Earle Brown from the 1932 gubernatorial race, Ventura just wanted to clean up the mess in city hall. He recalled,

> In 1990, Terry, Tyrel, Jade and I were living in Brooklyn Park, an older, mostly developed neighborhood in the northern suburbs of Minneapolis. At the time, developers were coming into the area, looking to turn the few remaining potato fields into housing developments. This one particular developer came in and wanted to get the highest buck for what he was about to build, so he demanded that the neighborhood put in curbs, gutters, and storm sewers. We didn't need those things.
>
> The citizens of Brooklyn Park were playing second fiddle to developers. Now remember, the developers put up their projects, and then they're gone; they're on to something else. The citizens lived there year-round. Worst of all, though, was where they planned to put the runoff water: they couldn't drain off into the Mississippi because of pollution laws, so they decided to have a drain right into a local wetland nearby…about a block from my house.
>
> We took a petition up to City Hall and presented it at a City Council meeting. We were voted down seven to nothing. I thought, "Wait a minute. Don't we elect these people to represent us, the populace? It don't seem like they're doing that." And so I started getting more involved and paying more attention.[18]

Jerry Marshall had a different perspective. "All of us came from different walks of life, from different geographical areas certainly. And not knowing one another and coming on the council at relatively the same period of time, it brought together a unique group of people who had the ability to legislate honestly and who had a great sense of camaraderie. We became close friends." As an active member of the Jaycees and then councilman, he learned to work with other leaders—in his view, the seven to zero votes were simply the result of a shared vision. He said, "You [had] a group of people who did get along and wanted to do something for the community. Some people called it the good old boys but most of the people who call people in politics "good old boys" don't do anything. They just call them good old boys."[19]

Ventura challenged Krautkremer in the next election and won all twenty-one of the city's precincts with sixty-three percent of the vote.

The Limits of Growth

In the 1980s and 1990s, Brooklyn Park's growth was dramatic, radically transforming the rural landscape. In 1950, it had a population of 3,065. By 1970 it increased to 26,230. In the 1990s Brooklyn Park became the sixth largest city in Minnesota.[20]

The demand for new housing and commercial space grew unabated. What should be saved? Open space, taken for granted, was rapidly diminishing. As late as 1979, nearly forty percent of the land in Brooklyn Park was used for agriculture. One by one, though, farmers sold off their land to developers. The potato farms came under increased pressure. Finally, potato production ended when Calvin Gray gave up the crop in 1992. Gray said that property taxes were climbing and traffic was "ridiculous." Although some farmers were nostalgic, others recognized that the farms garnered top dollar when sold to developers. Donald Tessman said, "We don't miss farming, we don't miss potatoes, we miss our youth."[21]

Although Eldon Tessman quit raising potatoes in 1976, selling off portions of his fields, he kept the family home and farm buildings. These were threatened in 1991, when Brooklyn Park proposed a widening of 85th Avenue to accommodate new development. Tessman sued to halt construction, and with the help of historian Norene Roberts, gained historic resource status for his farmstead—the first to be protected under the Minnesota Environmental Rights Act. This forced the city to place a curve in the road around his farmstead. His attorney, Mark Anfinson said, "He sees himself as the guardian of a four-generation farm and thought he had lost it all."[22]

The battle that Jesse Ventura joined over the wetlands was not the first intrusion of sprawl into local politics. In the late 1960s, development threatened Palmer Lake. Ted Willard recalled, "They were going to use it as a landfill—fill it up with dirt and trash in layers. I was opposed to it. I didn't want to have a dump under any name across the street from my house." The City Council intervened and bought the land. Even so, many considered it a folly, asking, "Why do you want to buy that swamp?"[23]

The Earle Brown farm raised a different preservation issue: what should we save from our history? Although the State Legislature designated the property as a state historic site in 1974, the honor did not guarantee preservation of the buildings. Indeed, several barns were demolished or moved in 1981. In 1985 the City of Brooklyn Center purchased the remaining farm buildings and authorized the sale of $5.25 million in bonds to develop and restore the Farm. The City, working with Winsor/Faricy Architects, Inc., developed a creative re-use plan that included new construction and modification of the old buildings for business use. In 1990 the Earle Brown Heritage Center hosted a grand opening celebration.

Historic preservation took a slightly different direction in Brooklyn Park. Concerned with the steady loss of farmland, the City purchased the Eidem Farm in 1976. It opened as a "living farm" museum in 1979. Dennis Palm, Recreation and Parks director, said, "I'm hopeful that in this Bicentennial year, we're preserving something of long lasting value for the community."[24]

The Challenge of a Diverse Community

The Brooklyns continued to welcome new families during the 1990s. This included a large Asian population, plus increased numbers of African-Americans, Hispanics, and Native Americans. (Read the moving accounts in *Chapter Five: Social Issues*)

In the late 1960s developers built scores of apartment buildings along the southern border of Brooklyn Park. The city had large tracts of land with all the necessary utilities available to accomodate higher density apartment buildings.

Developers responded to the huge housing demand of the post-war baby boomers as they moved from high school into the work force and began families. Even in the late 1970s, apartment buildings were typically one hundred percent occupied, with some complexes experiencing six-month waiting lists for new residents.

As the baby boomers moved out of the apartments into single family homes, suddenly, there was excess apartment capacity. The decline continued, and by the late 1980s, some apartment complexes experienced occupancy rates of less than sixty percent. These apartments became a magnet for low-income families looking for the piece of the American dream, called the "suburb." Brooklyn Park was the first suburb in the Metropolitan Area to build Section 236 subsidized units.

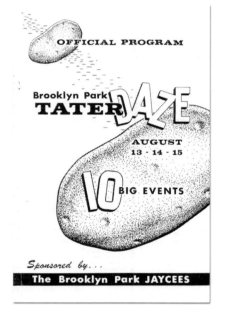

The Jaycees began Tater Daze in 1964.

The new social, racial, and ethnic mix caused some community tension in Brooklyn Center. Howard Heck recalled one incident, saying, "There were a group of people that came to complain…that a black family was moving into their neighborhood and they came in unannounced during a council meeting. All of a sudden, they were out in the hallway and started making noise. Phil Cohen got on the phone and called Vi Kanatz (a member of the Humans Rights Commission) and Vi came down immediately." Ted Willard remembered the evening as well. he said, "She had the facts about housing. One of the rumors is that if these people move in, the value of the housing will go down. They don't maintain their property. Vi had statistics and she spoke very quietly, very calmly. She's standing on the step and they're kind of in a semi-circle, about 15-20 people and she just continued talking about the facts. And one by one, people drifted away and finally there wasn't anybody left."

Looking back, Phil Cohen gives good marks to the people of Brooklyn Center. He said, "I think Brooklyn Center and Maplewood had the two largest black populations. I'm very proud of the community and its race relations." Still, just as the Yankee families were replaced by the Scandinavians and Germans, the changes continue. Ernee McArthur, community activist and former state representative, commented, "We're into this new diversity in the Brooklyns. It's kind of like back in 1852 when the first immigrants came. They came from all different countries. Today we have the same." Phil Cohen remarked, "We have Somalians, Russians, we have everything coming into the community faster than people can understand it. I think there needs to be work in the churches, the civic groups, and the schools."

"Come Home to the Park"

Left to Right: Police Chief Don Davis, Mayor Jesse Ventura, Governor Arne Carlson, Dan Ryan, Terry Troy, Dave Russ, John Herron, Public Safety Commissioner Michael Jordan

Ventura's Legacy

Mayor Ventura's career came to a contentious conclusion. In his best-selling book, *Ain't Got Time To Bleed*, he wrote, "About three years into my term, my mother began to get somewhat frail, so she came to live with us. But our house in Brooklyn Park wasn't really equipped to handle that many people. I knew I had to look for another house." They found a larger home — with land for his wife's horses — in Maple Grove, setting off the controversy.

With only four months left in his term, the city council began to investigate whether Ventura needed to resign if he no longer lived in Brooklyn Park. Ventura recalled, "The good old boys saw this as an opportunity to disgrace me." Claiming that he still lived in the city, the Mayor responded: "It was ridiculous! There's no law that says you can't own two homes. The old boys hired a lawyer to try to find a way to oust me." The judge, after careful review, determined that there was no violation of the law, permitting Ventura to complete his four-year term.

What will be his legacy? More than any single policy, it is that he encouraged new people to enter politics. Grace Arbogast, who succeeded Ventura as mayor, said, "Here's one of the things I liked about Jesse Ventura. They wanted to put sidewalks on 63rd and I was violently opposed to sidewalks. I just could not see it. Jesse came out and walked the neighborhood. He came out with all the other council members and walked. People came out of their houses and talked with him about the issues in our neighborhood. By the time they came to a vote, I wanted them to put a sidewalk in."

Hopes and Dreams

There have been incredible changes in the former Brooklyn Township in the past forty years. As Jesse Ventura said in a speech in 1992, "We're no longer a potato field."[25] The majority of residents have no ties to the community's past. Describing the differences between old and new in 1977, Carol Schreiber said, "We used to have a real sense of the pulse of the community. We, and the others who have been here a long time, knew what was going on. But we're a small percentage now."[26]

As Ventura's life suggests, the bonds to a single town, a single place, are loose — now we live in one town, shop in another, work in a third, and attend church elsewhere. Bill Fignar believes that this makes a difference. As he said, "If our city fathers and the business owners lived here as well as owned the business here, you'd be much better. It's hard for them to be committed."

What bind us now are our stories. As you read this book, you will read the stories of people inspired by hopes and dreams. Early settlers headed into a wilderness with hopes for a piece of land to farm. This land encouraged Earle Brown to dream of his showplace. The postwar generation migrated to the suburbs, looking away from the Depression and World War II to a new vision of community and family. In recent years, a new diverse population moved to Brooklyn Center and Brooklyn Park, searching for a place to call home. This is our common heritage.

Notes

1. Asbjorn Fause and George Corfield, "The Potato Industry in Minnesota," *Economic Geography*, 29 January 1968, 393-401.

2. Keith Caswell, Oral History Interview.

3. Glen Sonnenberg, Oral History Interview with Ernee McArthur, 25 January 2000.

4. John Wingard, Oral History Interview with William Schreiber, ND.

5. Alice Tessman, Oral History Interview with Norene Roberts, 4 May 1994.

6. Alexander Jones, "A Short Biography of Earle Brown," *Minneapolis Journal*, 9 October 1932

7. Donald Weesner, Oral History Interview with Ernee McArthur, 8 July 1998.

8. Garrison Keillor, "My Boyhood Home."

9. Dave Hage, "Tale of two cities: Ex-farmer's life tells Brooklyns' story," *Minneapolis Star*, 6 March 1980, 16-17; Paula Hirschoff, "Baldwin Hartkopf," *Brooklyn Center Post*, 29 January 1976.

10. Dave Hage, "Tale of Two Cities: Ex-farmer's life tells Brooklyns' story," *Minneapolis Star*, 6 March 1980, 16-17; Paula Hirschoff, "Baldwin Hartkopf," *Brooklyn Center Post*, 29 January 1976.

11. Garrison Keillor, "My Boyhood Home."

12. John Wingard, Oral History Interview.

13. Jack Vaughn, Oral History Interview with Ernee McArthur, 28 February 2000.

14. Paula Hirschoff, "Baldwin Hartkopf," *Brooklyn Center Post*, 29 January 1976.

15. Tony Kuefler, Oral History Interview with Ernee McArthur, 18 May 2000.

16. Don Rosen, Oral History Interview, 28 October 1999. BHS.

17. "Earle Brown Farm to get 1,500 Homes," *Minneapolis Sunday Tribune*, 15 August 1954; also see Mary Jane Gustafson, Jane Hallberg, Leone Howe, *History of the Earle Brown Farm* (Brooklyn Center: Brooklyn Historical Society, 1996), 107-117.

18. Jesse Ventura, *Ain't Got Time to Bleed* (New York: Villard, 1999), 137-141.

19. Jerry Marshall, Oral History Interview with William Schreiber, 27 March 1999; "Body Politic," *Minneapolis Star-Tribune*, 29 June 1989.

20. "Suburb restores farm," *Minneapolis Star*, 20 September 1979.

21. "Brooklyn Park's fields growing houses now," *Minneapolis Star*, 17 June 1977.

22. Patt Ligman, "End of an Era: Last Potato Farmer Quits," *Brooklyn Park Sun-Post*, 18 November 1992; Kristine Donatelle, "Judge rules road won't displace BP farmstead," *Brooklyn Center Sun-Post*, 5 February 1992, 2A.

23. Ted Willard, Oral History Interview.

24. Paula Hirschoff, "City purchases old homestead," *Brooklyn Park Post*, 19 August 1976.

25. "City facing up to challenges," *Brooklyn Park Sun Post*, 1 April 1992.

26. "Brooklyn Park's fields growing houses now," *Minneapolis Star*, 17 June 1977.

Chapter One

NATURAL HISTORY

WE NOTICE THE CHANGES in the landscape of our communities as we live in them. Future generations will record and publish today's changes as their history. But today, how do we think of our history? We usually consider the 142 years since 1858 when Minnesota became a state, Hennepin a county and Brooklyn a township. We may consider too, the 300 years since our area became known to European explorers, or even the few thousand years during which it supported Native Americans.[1]

Our real history, however, starts far back in geologic time when the rocks on which Minnesota rests were laid down. The events of that remote period, despite advancing technology, are still debated and only partially understood. In ancient times our area underwent periodic inundation and retreat of giant seas, which deposited the many layers of sand and silt that compacted into the distinct sandstone, limestone, shale and dolomite formations beneath the Twin Cities Basin.[2]

At the end of this era, the climate of the Northern Hemisphere cooled greatly, causing glacial ice to build up thousands of feet thick. As the ice sheet moved slowly across the land, surface pressures up to 400 pounds per square inch scraped off topsoils, tore up underlying rock formations, ground it all up and carried the debris within the ice. Approximately 10,000 years ago the ice sheet melted, depositing the debris as "glacial drift" into outwash plains. Where ice blocks were isolated or buried, water-filled basins were formed as the ice melted, creating lakes. Palmer Lake and Twin Lake are examples of ice block basins. Enormous volumes of water also carved the present day valleys of the Mississippi River and our local streams and creeks.[3]

Sloths, giant beaver, elephants, musk oxen and other animals, are known to have inhabited Minnesota. Fossil finds in the Twin Cities area, now on exhibit in the Science Museum of Minnesota in St. Paul, confirm the presence of giant beaver in our area. This rodent was about the size of a black bear, up to nine feet long, and weighed 500 pounds. As the ice sheet grew larger, animals that inhabited the cold regions were forced ahead of the glacier. Skeletal remains of the mastodon have been found buried in local glacial drift. A mass extinction of these large mammals occurred about 10,000 years ago.

*Wetlands: Palmer Lake Basin
Brooklyn Center*

Continued warming of the climate after the ice melted caused lakes and rivers to shrink, and allowed the growth of birch, pine, maple and oak trees, shrubs and flowering plants. Plants in the warmer lakes and streams provided homes and food for aquatic animals, such as fish, turtles and frogs. Fertile topsoil slowly accumulated during thousands of years of seasonal plant growth cycles.[4]

Differences in soil, slope and moisture eventually created a mosaic of four plant communities—wetlands in depressions, forests where there was adequate moisture, oak savannas in drier areas and prairies in the driest areas. While periodic natural events such as droughts, fires, windstorms and floods created dramatic changes, these plant communities remained relatively stable for thousands of years.[5]

Plants and animals followed the retreating ice, and humans appear to have arrived soon after the ice melted. Wouldn't we like to begin our human story with a written or pictorial record of the landscape at that time? The land's surface probably had not changed a great deal when Europeans first saw it a few thousand years later.[6]

First Human Presence

Archeological evidence reveals that this area supported indigenous peoples. Ours was a hospitable environment, and the natives as farmers and hunters made use of the river, lakes, woods and plains. Plants yielded an abundance of food, giving them corn, beans, squash, pumpkins, potatoes, grapes, plums, blueberries, nuts and greens. Meat was supplied by buffalo, bear, deer, rabbit, birds and other small animals. In addition, many provisions were available from the river and lakes. A variety of herbs served as medicinal remedies. Buffalo, deer, and wolf hides provided clothing, bone tools and other necessities for everyday living.[7]

European Exploration

Our Mississippi River brought European explorers here in 1680, not to settle, but to seek a water route to the Pacific Ocean. By 1700 and into the early 1800s, other visitors were here to harvest a local resource: the fur pelt of the beaver. Fur-trading posts and military forts were established along the Mississippi River. By 1830 small colonies of squatters also dotted the area, forming the beginnings of agricultural settlements.[8]

We are most fortunate to have a description of the natural landscape of our area, albeit from a canoe on the river. When Joseph Nicollet and his party of explorers left St. Anthony Falls in 1836, his quest, on behalf of the King of France, was to reach the headwaters of the Mississippi River. In his journal, he pictures the prairie as:

> …a spreading plain, spreading as far as the eye could see, without any substantial change of level and without woods or even the slightest cluster of shrubs. It is an endless expanse without a single rise, a sea of green, sky and prairie without islands of woods. When passing along the edge of an island, we disturbed some deer, elk, geese, cranes and some swans which were all eating peacefully near the shore.

He tells us that when making camp, little wood was to be found for a cooking or warming fire. Visible were bands of depressions, gullies, small mounds, sand and gravel crisscrossed by lakes, ponds, and swamps, usually bordered by trees. The first spring flower he records as coltfoot and later white anemone (probably pasque flower). His list of vegetation includes herbaceous plants, moss, and some flowering shrubs. Sighted were hawks, gulls, plover and phalaropes.[9]

Blue Heron
Hennepin Parks

Early Settlement

The 1850s brought an influx of settler families looking for good farmsteads. A horticulturalist describes what greeted them: "Two principal plant formations, the forest and the prairie characterize the upper midwest. In this region of extensive sandy and gravely outwash plains are groves of white and bur oak, usually small and scarcely more than large shrubs. Around some of the lakes and along the bluffs of the Mississippi, forest of a better type obtains. On the bottomlands of the river, especially subject to frequent overflow, the chief trees are cottonwoods and several species of willow. On slightly higher land the American elm and soft maple are abundant along with such trees as hackberry, green and black ash, box elder and river birch. Such woody vines as the Virginia creeper, prickly smilax and the frost grape are common on the less frequently flooded parts of the bottom lands, the last often attaining great size."[10]

The native woody vegetation of the prairie region may be considered under three headings: prairie groves, generally detached portions of the deciduous forests (savanna rather than true prairie); bottom land stream forest; and shrubby plants of the open prairie. After the prairie districts were under cultivation, shrubs such as prairie wild rose, wolfberry and lead plant, were found chiefly on fence rows, roadsides and railroad right of way.[11]

Records of mammal populations included opossums, long tail shrews, moles, small bats, rabbits, woodchuck, fox and red squirrel, gopher, vole, field and house mice, wolf, coyote, fox, raccoon, weasel, mink, skunk, and deer. Bison, rare by 1830, were gone by 1880.[12]

In 1881, Reverend Neill describes it thus:

> The surface is very level and consequently nearly destitute of lakes. The few that exist are shallow with low, marshy shores. Palmer Lake in Sec. 26, through which Shingle Creek flows, is the largest. A variation from the uniform level occurs in the southwest, where a small corner reaches on the rolling clay beyond the sandy belt. The extensive marshes yield abundance of good wild hay, most of which can be cut by machines. The timber is small, though a little of the larger growth is found in the northeast near the river, and in the southwest on the clay. The bluffs along the river are low and sandy.

The Mississippi River is navigable here and small steamers ply up and down. Shingle Creek flows across the township from west to east.[13]

As the Mississippi River brought us the early explorers, it brought our European settlers and their households. The river was the transportation route for people, plus the livestock and timber for their farms. It then became the means to export their crops. Commercial enterprises using the river for water power determined the rapid growth of the current Twin Cities. Our history would be entirely different were it not for our navigable river, as all early settlements were within ten miles of the river. The ferry crossing at Dayton/Champlin was the point for bulk transfers from river to road. [14]

One of the early pioneers, George W. Getchell, arriving in 1852, stated that "a good deal of the land is brush with groves of oak and poplar. The soil is warm and fertile throughout, as deep and rich as that of the timbered quarters."[15]

Another pioneer, Chas Bohanon, recorded in 1851, "The countless number of pigeons which migrated here every spring could never be estimated. Anyone could kill hundreds in a day. Ducks and geese are exceedingly plentiful. I remember picking raspberries, blackberries and wild strawberries."[16]

Mrs. Rebecca Plummer stated in 1854, "We did enjoy the game, for we had never had much. Pigeons were very thick. We used to stake nets for them close to the ground. Under these we scattered corn. In the winter when we girls would go to the privy with a lantern, we heard packs of wolves running and howling through the woods. If that wasn't scary."[17]

Irving Caswell's memories of the 1870s relate, "A steamboat made regular voyages along the river from Minneapolis to Anoka. It was named the Monticello and was a side-wheeler. It was often delayed for hours by the rocks of Coon Rapids."[18]

In an attempt to increase timber needed for construction and firewood, the Timber Act of 1873 was enacted whereby "a settler could acquire 160 acres of land by planting ten acres of it in trees. When making a final proof on a tree claim at the end of eight years, there had to be 675 living trees on each of the 10 acres." The entry fee was $14, but no residency was required. One can wonder if this strategy was successful, as prairies by their nature do not support easy or significant tree growth.[19]

The ecological stability changed in these mid–1800s as the early pioneers built homesteads and farms. Trees were cleared, prairie sod was broken and wetlands were filled. As more homesteaders arrived, increasing areas of the original landscape were required for crops, buildings and roads.

Farmyard Landscape: Eidem Farm
City of Brooklyn Park

This period of rapid change had a major impact on native vegetation. New types of vegetation and landscapes were introduced. Lawn and flower gardens became popular. Many flowers, shrubs and trees from other parts of the world were introduced. Over time, most of the natural vegetation in Brooklyn Township was altered or replaced.[20]

The Modern Farming Era, 1900-1950

Types of agriculture differentiated in response to several factors. The move from subsistence farming to market gardening or mixed farming served the rapidly growing city of Minneapolis. Here were the largest dairy farms in the state, shipping their products by railroad from Osseo. Construction of road systems allowed farmers to move inland from the river and transport their produce by truck. A 1914 plat map of Hennepin County shows that most of the farms were small, from 20 to 40 acres. [21]

Brooklyn Center was known as "The Garden City." The marshy land was ditched and drained, resulting in wonderful peat soil. Small family truck farms were supplying Minneapolis with a bountiful supply of vegetables, fruits and flowers.

The northern tier of Brooklyn Township, with easy-to-work flat sandy soil, and adequate rainfall, developed the best potato and onion farms in the state. Peat dredged from swamps was mixed with manure to produce mulch. [22]

This market garden farm economy continued until the land desired for suburban development increased in value to a point that it was more lucrative to sell than to engage in agriculture. [23]

The Urban Landscape Emerges

As the rapid change from wilderness to farm to city swept across our landscape, Joseph Nicollet would search in vain for his woods, wetlands and prairie. By 1970 the land for homes, roads, parks, and for public, institutional, industrial and commercial buildings equaled the land used for farming. Today that balance no longer exists. [24]

Recent field studies have concluded that agriculture and urban development have destroyed or greatly disturbed nearly all of the pre-settlement vegetation in our area. What remains is scattered, and falls into three categories: oak openings and barrens, found along the river and the Southwest corner of Brooklyn Park; wet prairies, marshes or sloughs, primarily in Palmer Lake Basin; and upland prairie, a four-acre remnant, badly deteriorated in the Highway 610 right-of-way. Prospects for restoration are minimal. [25]

Several historic trees from pioneer days have been identified. However, the norm for our groomed, suburban landscape is cultivated trees, lawns, shrubs and flowering plants.

Gone are the bear, buffalo and wolf. We have neighborhood squirrels, rabbits, a gopher or two and birds at our feeders, all wildlife now acclimated to the suburban yard habitat. A greater variety of wildlife will be found in the natural open spaces in our parks: deer, fox, muskrat, mink, skunk, raccoons, snake, rabbit, turtles and toads are commonly observed. Bird life to be seen in the natural areas are ducks, Coot, Common Snipe, Blue Heron, Great Egret, Bald Headed Eagle, Northern Harrier, Ring necked Pheasant, Indigo Bunting, Swamp Sparrow, Western Meadowlark and Red-winged Blackbird. [26]

We have one federally identified "unique natural feature" and that is the scenic bluff shoreline along the river.

Little more than twenty years ago, wetlands were commonly referred to as swamps, bogs or marshes and were considered of little value, if not a simple nuisance. As their ecological and functional values were recognized, new laws have been enacted, old laws enforced, and new policies developed to regulate the alteration of wetlands in Minnesota. Now all units of government, in addition to many natural resource agencies, have become involved with water management. [27]

The oldest Burr Oak, about 300 years

Silver Maple, 110-160 years

A priority in our communities has been an adequate and safe supply of water for our use and an adequate municipal drainage system. Both cities adhere to the primary goals of the preservation and use of natural water storage and retention systems. Because all of our runoff water infiltrates into our groundwater or flows into the Mississippi River, all waters are managed to meet critical standards.

Water for our use is supplied from deep municipal wells in the Drift Aquifer. Permits that control the amount drawn are issued by the Minnesota Department of Natural Resources.[28]

Five watersheds have been identified that define the pattern of stormwater flowage and impoundment:
1) Oxbow Creek Watershed (north of Hwy 610 through Champlin to the river),
2) Riverside Watershed (the banks along the river),
3) West Mississippi Watershed (south of Hwy 610 via Edinbrook Channel to the river at Mattson Brook),
4) Shingle Creek Watershed (southeast from Brooklyn Park through Brooklyn Center to the river),
5) Southwest Area Watershed (through Brooklyn Center into Upper Twin Lake).[29]

Watershed Management, Backyard Holding Pond
City of Brooklyn Park

Artificial drainage systems, both open ditches and subsurface storm sewers, are also in place to move water to treatment basins. These holding ponds are designed to accommodate major storm events, to impound water for natural filtering to improve water quality, to prevent flooding and erosion, to promote groundwater recharge, and to provide fish and wildlife habitat for recreational activities. A neighborhood holding pond is considered a property enhancement.

To protect water quality, streets are swept at least twice annually. Devices called 'skimmers' are installed in holding ponds to prevent floatables from discharging down stream, and abandoned wells are sealed. Since eroded soil can enter the water stream, any construction site more that five-acres or on a slope must have the plan reviewed by the Minnesota Pollution Control Agency. Education materials for citizens encourage the use of non-phosphorus fertilizers and proper disposal of solid, liquid and hazardous wastes.[30]

Water drainage systems are constantly monitored at numerous points because silt and debris collect and the resulting restricted flow can cause occasional minor flooding in a few places. Tests for water pollution are regularly done. Several current water projects include improvements to Shingle Creek near Village North to increase flowage and to provide recreational enjoyment for that neighborhood. The Brookdale Area Ponding Project will divert storm runoff from Shingle Creek into treatment ponds on the Centerbrook Golf Course, and then back into Shingle Creek.

Over time, the impact of increasing flowage has taken its toll on the Palmer Lake Basin. Sediment accumulation accounts for the current lake depth of 1.5 feet as opposed to a historic depth of four feet, causing less effective filtration and a degradation of wildlife habitat. Plans for major reclamation include dredging the 10 channels that accommodate storm sewer outfalls, constructing treatment basins around the perimeter of the lake, and dredging portions of the lake itself.[31]

Floodplain laws prevent construction or any use that would adversely affect the capacity of the drainage system. Farm fields, golf courses, parks, boat launch ramps and such are permitted. Storage or processing of flammable, explosive or potentially injurious materials is prohibited.

A truly natural asset to our community is the Mighty Mississippi, one of the world's great rivers and part of one of the most complex ecosystems on the planet. Beginning as a clear stream in northern Minnesota, the river flows south for 1,336 miles, past forests, farms, small towns and big cities. It widens considerably until it empties into the Gulf of Mexico. It has long been a corridor for fish, wildlife, birds, people and commerce. The river is the major migration flyway in continental North America. Waterfowl, shorebirds and warblers have traveled on this great river for centuries—long before the highway we call "The Great River Road" flanked its waters, islands and backwaters. The river provides food, water and a place to rest for some 320 species of birds.[32]

Coon Rapids Dam
Hennepin Parks

The Annual National Audubon Christmas Bird Count has occurred in Brooklyn Center and Brooklyn Park for the past fifty years. The survey, conducted by the Audubon Chapter of Minneapolis, provides data for national ornithological research. Bird observation sites along our stretch of the river are included in the Great River Bird Trail.

In 1988 Congress designated the Mississippi National River and Recreation Area to manage the river corridor for significant historical, recreational, scenic, cultural, natural, economic and scientific outcomes. The portion of the river below Minnesota has been tremendously manipulated and modified. The need to restore the river to its historic ecological stability has been identified, but the plan will require much effort and oversight.[33]

We have been spared the loss of the beauty and ecological function of the river. Except for the Coon Rapids Dam, our stretch of the river does not contain levees or dikes to prevent seasonally inundated floodplains (we had floodplain laws in place). Nor does channeling or dredging for commercial barge traffic disrupt the normal hydrology, thus maintaining habitat for wildlife.

Proposals to build a dam in this area started in the late 1890s by the Twin City Rapid Transit Company. The main motivation was power for an electric trolley line between Minneapolis and Anoka. The site chosen was the rapids near Coon Creek. Construction began in January 1913, and was completed quickly, with turbines running by August 1914. Eventually, expense of ice damage, cost of manning the powerhouse and the expansion of Northern States Power Company's other generating facilities caused the utility to end power production at the dam in 1965. In 1969 the Hennepin County Regional Park District accepted the dam and powerhouse as a donation from NSP. All generating equipment was removed, and the Coon Rapids Dam Park opened in 1978. After the Visitor Center opened in 1993, the old dam was refurbished and there now is a twelve-foot wide walkway across the river.[34]

The pool behind the dam is approximately 600 acres and extends five miles upstream to the mouth of the Rum River. Since this is a "run of the river" dam, the storage capacity behind the dam is negligible, reducing the amount of reservoir or flood control potential. Maps of the pool area show that relatively little land was flooded up to the Anoka/Champlin area after 1914. Because the pool exists above the dam, the river does not function in that section as a river normally would. Habitats within the river were changed forever when the free flowing river was dammed. Flood surges and changes in flow patterns in channels and backwater areas do not appear in the pool above the Coon Rapids Dam. The river there is effectively a lake.[35]

Despite our urban landscape, there still is a substantial amount of open space preserved for our recreational use and enjoyment. Our two cities are to be commended for the foresight and willingness to provide our citizens and visitors with these amenities, right in our neighborhoods. An extensive trail system stretches across both cities, connecting parklands, especially along Shingle Creek and Edinbrook Channel. A seven-mile trail connects Coon Rapids Dam Park to Elm Creek Regional Park in Maple Grove. A proposed trail along West River Road will connect the North Mississippi Park in Brooklyn Center to Coon Rapids Dam Park. Excellent maps of the Park and Trail systems are available at the Brooklyn Center and Brooklyn Park City Halls.

The Brooklyn's Natural Spaces

Brooklyn Center

Palmer Lake Nature Area: 360 acres of marsh and woods containing Palmer Lake and Shingle Creek. A three-mile dual perimeter trail is usable year round.

North Mississippi Regional Park: Formerly called River Ridge Park, has a boat launch plus wooded trails along the Mississippi from I-694 south, continuing into Minneapolis. A Visitor Center interprets the natural and cultural history of the area.

MAC Environmental Preserve: The buffer zone north of Crystal Airport has a boardwalk through the marsh areas and a trail through the upland oak savanna.

Gene Hagel Arboretum: (at Kylawn Park) A variety of tree specimens and wildflower plantings.

Brooklyn Park

River Park: 46 acres and a 2,000-foot shoreline along the river featuring restored floodplain forest, natural plants communities and an interpretive trail.

Coon Rapids Dam Regional Park: 360-acres. Has a 1,070-foot long walkway on the dam across the river. The West Visitor Center features interpretative displays and programs about the Mississippi and the park's wildlife. Bald Eagle sightings are possible.

Notes

1. *Natural Communities and Rare Species of Carver, Hennepin and Scott Counties Minnesota*, by the Minnesota County Biological Survey; *Vegetation of Hennepin County*, interpreted by F.J. Marschner using Public Land Surveys, 1853-1856; *Map Series 18*, State of MN, Dept. of Natural Resources, 1998.

2. Edmund Bray, *Billions of Years in Minnesota, The Geological Story of the State*, Science Museum of MN, St. Paul, 2nd. ed. 1985, 7-9 and 30-31.

3. *An Inventory of Minnesota Lakes*, Minnesota Division of Waters, Soils and Minerals, Waters Section, Bulletin 25, Minnesota Conservation Department, St. Paul, 6-7.

4. Edmund Bray, 30-31.

5. *Restoring the Past for Our Future*, brochure, Minneapolis Park and Recreation Board, Environmental Operations, Minneapolis, MN, 1997.

6. Edmund Bray, 30-31.

7. Frederick Hoxie, ed., *Encyclopedia of North American Indians*, Houghton Mifflin, Boston MA, 1996, 214.

8. Compiled by Mark J. Kozlak, Hennepin County Property Management Division, *The Preservation of Historic Legacies in Hennepin County*, prepared for the Hennepin County Board of Commisssioners, April 1975, 29-30.

9. *The Journals of Joseph N. Nicollet, A Scientist on the Mississippi Headwaters,* With Notes on Indian Life, 1836-37, trans. by Andre Fertey, edited by Martha Coleman Bray (St. Paul: Minnesota Historical Society, 1970), 244-246.

10. Carl Otto Rosendahl, *Trees and Shrubs of the Upper Midwest* (Minneapolis: University of Minnesota Press, 1975), 12-13.

11. Ibid.

12. Evan Hazard, *Mammals of Minnesota*, Bell Museum of Natural History (Minneappolis: University of Minnesota Press, 1982), 12-14.

13. Rev. Edward D. Neill, *History of Hennepin County and City of Minneapolis*, (Minneapolis: North Star Publishing Co., 1881).

14. Mark J. Kozlak, 29-30.

15. Leone Olive Howe, *Album of Brooklyn Centre— A History of Brooklyn Center*, privately published, 1978, Chapter I, (in files of Brooklyn Historical Society).

16. Ibid.

17. Ibid.

18. "Pioneer Days at Coon Creek*", Anoka County Union*, 1 January 1941.

19. *Timber Culture Act of 1873*, United States Code, Title 43, Chapter 8, Section 311, (verify the Act's title and date, may be 1878)

20. F.J. Marschner, see note 1.

21. Mark J. Kozlak , 29-30.

22. Norene A. Roberts, "Growing Potatoes in Brooklyn Park," *Hennepin History* (Fall 1994), Minneapolis, Hennepin History Museum, 21-24.

23. *History of Brooklyn Center*, Manuscript published by Brooklyn Historical Society, October 1995.

24. Ibid.

25. *Minnesota 610, Supplemental Draft Environmental Impact Statement*, Prepared for MN Dept. of Transportation, Federal Highway Administration, October 1992.

26. City of Brooklyn Park, *Comprehensive Stormwater Management Plan*, Table 3, Section III-27; Sec.III-7; Sec. IV-1; Sec. IV-3, October 1995.

27. *Water Permits in Minnesota*, US Army Corps of Engineers, St. Paul District, brochure July 1991.

28. Ibid.

29. City of Brooklyn Park, see note 26.

30. Ibid.

31. *Brooklyn Center-Brooklyn Park Sun-Post*, May 1999, 26.

32. Dan McGuiness, Writer, Editor, *A River That Works and A Working River, Executive Summary*, Upper Mississippi River Conservation Committee, Rock Island, IL, January 2000, 2-3.

33. *Mississippi National River and Recreation Area, Minnesota, Comprehensive Management Plan, Final Environment Impact Statement*, Vol. US Department of the Interior, January 1995.

34. Thomas F. Waters, *The Streams and Rivers of Minnesota*, (Minneapolis: University of Minnesota Press, 1977) ,328-329.

35. Ibid.

Additional Resources:

Mary Ellen Vetter, Interview with Diane Spector, Director of Public Works, City of Brooklyn Center. Mary Ellen Vetter Interview with Courtney Bednarz, Associate Planner, City of Brooklyn Park.

Chapter Two

HISTORICAL BEGINNINGS

THE OLDEST AND MOST RELIABLE HISTORY BOOK that most of us have access to is the Holy Bible. Deuteronomy 19:15 says: A matter must be established by the testimony of two or three witnesses. This is the rule we have used in this book—to support our historical research with at least two sources whenever possible. Where we have stories by residents, we quote them verbatim, but always we have scanned accounts against known historical facts.

Prehistoric

The American Indian came to North America on a land bridge in ancient times. Recorded history reveals a count of 7,773 Indian mounds in Minnesota in the 1880s, and Brooklyn Township's evidence of such sites is Mound Cemetery (which was named because of Indian mounds in the vicinity) and mounds and two Indian camp-sites found on the south side of Palmer Lake. Some pottery pieces at the campsites point to the Late Woodland period—which could have been as late as the coming of the white man in the seventeenth and eighteenth centuries. As to the mounds, in a geological survey by N. H. Winchell in 1882-5, some of the Palmer Lake mounds were "opened by members of the Minnesota Academy of Natural Sciences, and their contents were described by A. E. Johnson. A fine specimen of a platychnemic shin-bone, considered by him to be characteristic of the mound-builders, was taken from a mound at Palmer Lake."[1]

At some early period, bison roamed the area, as evidenced by the discovery of bison bones at a Township site by John Adler, Crystal. Adler found occidentalis bison bones—a bison which became extinct after the last Ice Age—on the site of the Brooklyn Center City Hall and Community Center during construction in 1970. He also reported finding the tooth of an elephant (woolly mammoth) near Shingle Creek. A bison bone bed was found at the intersection of Eagle Creek and I-694 in Brooklyn Park, but no Indian artifacts were found so it must have been a natural death site.

Explorer Louis Hennepin

Outside of fur traders, it appears that the only early explorer in the Brooklyn Town-ship vicinity was Father Louis Hennepin, a Belgian missionary priest. Hennepin had come to Illinois over the Great Lakes with explorer Sieur de la Salle, who sent him up the Mississippi to explore. He was captured, with two companions, at Lake Pepin and taken to an Issati camp at Lake Mille Lacs. Later, on a hunting expedition, he canoed with the Issati (Dakotas) down the Rum River, from Mille Lacs to the Mississippi in July, 1680. He wrote that the Dakotas stopped in the future Brooklyn area at that time. The Dakotas treated him well. There were 130 families and 250 warriors in the Issati hunting party besides Hennepin and his two voyageur companions.[2]

They traveled in birch bark canoes, which only the northern Indian nations had. The canoes were old, so when they came to a shore opposite the Rum River (no doubt Champlin), the party stopped to build new canoes. Many spread out, searching for

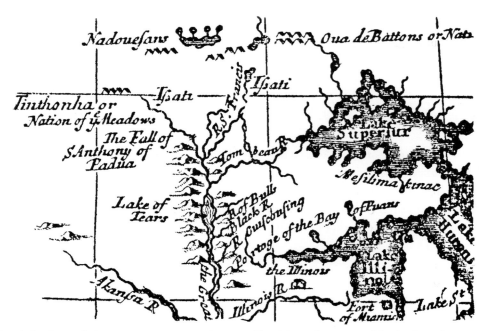

A map from Father Louis Hennepin's A New Discovery of a Vast Country in America, Extending above Four Thousand Miles, Between New France and New Mexico *London, 1698*

birch bark, and the women were in charge of building the canoe "docks," or frames. When finished, the hunting party continued down the Mississippi past the future Brooklyn Township area. (Hennepin called the Dakotas "Issati," and historian Reuben Gold Thwaites translates this to "Isanti" and, later, the name "Santee." Thwaites wrote that they were a tribe of the Dakotas, which meant something like "Confederation."[3]

From the western shore of the River in the future Brooklyn Township, we could have seen Hennepin canoeing with a woman 80-plus years old. She helped him paddle, and now and then she would pat some noisy children who rode in the middle of the canoe. Hennepin said the whole family went on the hunt [for protection]. Jesuit missionary Marquette wrote earlier that the Illinois Indians he dealt with hoped that the missionaries could bring general peace so that they could leave their families at a camp and only the young men would have to go away and hunt.[4]

Hennepin felt that "twas necessary to make a Court to the Women; for the Victuals were all in their Custody, who delivered everyone his Mess." He commented that the American Indians in general were usually strong and not subject to "those diseases which the Europeans fall into for want of exercise." The Indian women bore children silently without obvious great pain, in the woods or lodge. After several misadventures, near Lake Pepin, Daniel DuLuth showed up and took Hennepin and his two companions back to settlements in Canada.[5]

The Attractive New Frontier

Fur traders' claims about the beautiful and bountiful lands and descriptions by American Indians led rugged, brave pioneers to settle in the Brooklyn Township area which today includes the cities of Brooklyn Park and Brooklyn Center, with their eastern borders on the Mississippi. Only the Indians and a few fur traders were here when the first real government was established in 1787 on the east side of the Mississippi and called the Northwest Territory. Acquired by treaty from England, the Northwest Territory included most of the present Minnesota east of the Mississippi. With the Louisiana Purchase from France, by President Jefferson in 1803, future Minnesota lands west of the Mississippi were claimed. The Louisiana Purchase included land that became Brooklyn Township.[6]

Explorers Lewis and Clark, in 1804, did not reach the future Minnesota, but in 1805 Lt. Zebulon Pike came here and purchased from the Dakotas a tract of land for a military reservation described: "From below the confluence of the Mississippi and St. Peter [Rivers], up the Mississippi to include the Falls of St. Anthony, extending nine miles on each side of the river." The reserve was not used for military purposes until 1819, and the present site of Fort Snelling was selected by Col. Josiah Snelling when he arrived here in 1820. The reserve did not include what became Brooklyn Township. In 1820 Missouri Territory was created, and it was required that it be free of slavery. The future Brooklyn Township was in Missouri Territory; and, by 1849, it was in Minnesota Territory, which continued until Statehood in 1858.[7]

Pioneers settled on the military reservation's east side, and did not branch out to any extent to the west side of the Mississippi until the 1851 Treaties of Traverse des Sioux and Mendota, which opened up a large section of Minnesota on the west side of the Mississippi. The law organizing Hennepin County and establishing its boundaries was passed by the Territorial Legislature in March, 1852 — a year that marked the push of pioneers staking their claims in the future Brooklyn Township. The days of the frontier were numbered, and the time of the merchant and homesteader had arrived.[8]

In the 1851 treaties mentioned, the Dakotas signed over to the United States government (in combination with earlier land cessions) most of what is now the southern half of Minnesota, except their reservations — in exchange for certain payments. They were to move to Upper and Lower Sioux reservations along the Minnesota River. After U.S. ratification of the treaties, land claims could be made, but legal titles in Hennepin County did not become available until 1855.[9]

Early Trading

The earliest business in what became Brooklyn Township was fur trading with the Indians, and this trade continued for a while after the new settlers arrived. When the Hiram Smith family came to settle in the "Brooklyn" area, in July, 1854, they had to cross the Mississippi River in a canoe to the trading post of a Mr. Miles, "which was on a high point of land in what is now Champlin," wrote Mary Smith Pribble. (The post was at the mouth of Elm Creek.) Mary said there were Indians gathered at the landing, and they touched her cheek and called her "heap pale face." (Champlin, of course, adjoins what became Brooklyn Township.)[10]

From 1835, Ojibwe people from up the Mississippi traded at Benjamin F. Baker's post on the west side of the River, south of Minnehaha Falls in Section 20. By 1853, the post was made into a hotel, burning in the late 1850s. The Potter family of Brooklyn Park confirm that there was an Indian log trading post, older than 1870, on the North West Trail on their land near I-94 and Boone and torn down circa 1967.[11]

Sometimes it is stated that Minnesota Indians traded their furs only for beads, but from the time fur traders introduced small, colored glass beads as a trading item, the beads were much desired for decorating clothing, moccasins, headdresses, or jewelry. According to a contemporary Ojibwe teacher, the Ojibwe name for the beads "manido-minesag," meant "little berries (beads) with the spirit," conveying a meaning something like "little beads with life in them;" and the beaded art work, such as flowers, leaves, or birds, seemed to come to life even in winter. The Brooklyn Historical Society has three examples of these forest designs on a beaded vest, moccasins, and a wampum bag, from Earle Brown collection.[12]

In 1750, Per Kalm, a Swedish traveling professor, listed some items carried by Canadian voyageurs. Undoubtedly, these items were traded in (the future) Brooklyn Township as the French-Canadian traders operated in what became Minnesota. Among the many items were: muskets, powder, shot and balls; white, blue or red cloth; cloth for leg-wraps "like the Russians" to serve as stockings; hatchets; knives; scissors; needles; steel to strike fire; brass earrings; brass or copper kettles and pots; various paints for the face and body; looking glasses; tobacco; and glass beads and steel wire for various work. Brandy was sometimes traded—although prohibited. Trade items listed in 1855 in the book *Kitchi-Gami* are similar to the 1750 list: beads, shells, blankets, guns, flour and other household items. Even today, the "little beads with the spirit" are popular for the Indian souvenir trade.[13]

Indian People in the Area

During the summer of 1853, a party of men riding horses and in carriages, led by famous voyageur Pierre Bottineau, saw a Winnebago Indian camp three miles above the mouth of the Rum River on the west side of the Mississippi. This camp was roughly three miles from today's City of Champlin, whose land adjoins the old Brooklyn Township and today's Brooklyn Park. There were 100 lodges, made of bark, fastened by strips of buckskin, over arched poles in the shape of a covered wagon. They were eight feet high and ten to thirty feet long. The river bank was lined with canoes, and the village covered about one-eighth mile along the river.[14]

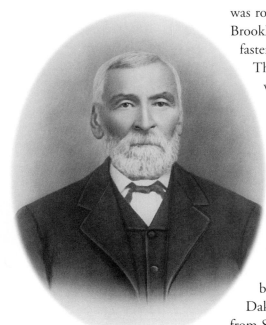

Pierre Bottineau
City of Osseo

The Winnebagoes left, en masse, in 1855 when the U.S. government forced them to move to a reservation near Mankato. Rebecca Plummer, who came to "Brooklyn" in 1854, saw the vast flotilla of canoes traveling down the Mississippi. "There were hundreds of them with their Indian occupants, besides the long procession on foot," as they left their overnight camp on an island in the river.[15]

Several early settlers in the Brooklyn Township area reported seeing native American Indians, quite often the Chippewa (or Ojibwe), on Indian trails; and Levi Longfellow mentions "roving bands" of Indians who camped near his house. One scholar thinks their permanent residence in the area was unlikely because the township was too close to villages of their enemies at the time, the Dakotas. Dakota summer villages were along the banks of the Minnesota River from Shakopee to the river's mouth at Mendota and villages down the Mississippi as far as today's Winona. Dakota chief Good Road's summer village was at the mouth of Nine Mile Creek in today's Bloomington. The "Road of War," where the two tribes could clash, was between the Mississippi (including where it passed Brooklyn Township), the St. Croix, and the Ojibwe villages at Mille Lacs Lake. Other Indian people in the area were the Winnebagoes.[16]

According to Sig Edling, who lived 1903-1979, the present Brooklyn Boulevard was known as Indian Trail because it followed a trail on high ground, surrounded by water from today's Twin Lakes to the area around the present new fire station at 63rd and Brooklyn Boulevard. The Indians and new settlers with oxcarts used to travel the trail, and eventually it became a road. Earl King, in a 1922 Northwestern Bell Telephone Co. commercial survey, recorded: "The first overland roads in Minnesota were the old Indian trails which followed the lines of least resistance and were always the shortest and most practical routes from center to center."[17]

In 1854 there was another Indian trail (mostly along the Mississippi) which led from today's Champlin to the present site of Robbinsdale, according to Mary Smith Pribble. By 1914, this trail was a Hennepin County road. Along the Mississippi, this was also a Red River cart trail. Mrs. Rufus Farnham used to see the carts and drivers go by her farmhouse in 1850 near the present Lyndale. She usually saw them as she was getting water from the well, with a baby tucked under her arm. "Women in those days never had time to look at anything but work," she complained.[18]

Albert Edling told his son-in-law, Bob Clayson, that in 1928 there was an Indian man living in a teepee on Shingle Creek, at the present Xerxes and 69th Avenue North, even after the area was surrounded by farms. Both Earle Brown and the Edlings tried to protect him by trying to get the point of land by the creek (where he was living) for the Native American man.

Land Description

In the early days, Brooklyn Township had small timber generally but had larger trees in the northeast near the River and in the southwest on the clay. Its land surface was level with just a few shallow lakes with marshy shores. Palmer Lake was the largest lake. The Township had four prairies: Getchell to the south, Jenkins to the southwest, Bottineau to the northwest (all named after early settlers) and Long Prairie to the northeast. The latter was four miles in length and one-half mile wide.[19]

James Weaver—First Claimant

James Weaver is credited, by historian Isaac Atwater, with being the first to make a claim in Brooklyn Township because he made a squatter's claim (occupying public land for a number of years, aiming to acquire legal title later), in 1850, by cutting two trees for poles and marking them with his name. He camped on Long Prairie overnight (northeast Brooklyn Park now) and then left his claim for one year. (Note: Claims, of course, were not authorized by the government until the Indian Treaties of 1851.) He returned in 1851 and built a shanty on what became his farm, and he made a living cutting cordwood for two years and worked in lumbering for the next two years. In 1854, he got married, and in 1855, he pre-empted his claim and worked at farming and as a contractor. Weaver's background: he was born in 1823 in the Province of New Brunswick. His father was Dutch. At age 20 James left his home place where he had learned the trade of ship carpenter, and he worked at his trade in Maine for a couple of years. Then he joined the tide of emigrants west, stopping at Chicago, Dubuque, St. Paul, St. Anthony and Fort Ripley (where he helped build the Fort). After these stops, he made his claim in what became Brooklyn Township, and later Brooklyn Park, on Long Prairie where his name appears on an 1874 map.[20]

Getchell and Party

After the Treaties of Traverse des Sioux and Mendota, land on the west side of the Mississippi, including what became Brooklyn Township, was opened for settlers to make squatter's or pre-emption claims. (The latter claim involved driving stakes for boundaries and erecting and occupying a cabin or shack, thus securing the right to purchase the claim before others.) It appears that the first claims after James Weaver were made by Washington Getchell of St. Anthony, his son Winslow, Amos Berry, and Jacob Longfellow—all staked claims on Getchell Prairie in April, 1852. Washington Getchell came from Maine to St. Anthony in 1848 to investigate the abundant pine lumber and agricultural advantages of the area. Getchell's 1852 claim was near today's Palmer Lake in the southern part of the future Township. Of the four new settlers, Winslow Getchell soon went back to St. Anthony, and at the time of Edward Neill's book, published in 1881, Washington and Winslow Getchell and Amos Berry were all in California. That leaves only Jacob Longfellow and family, whose descendants staged a "Longfellow Reunion" on July 4, 1901, at the old homestead claimed by Jacob Longfellow in 1852. The site is now in Brooklyn Center.[21]

Jacob Longfellow

Jacob Longfellow was born in Washington County, Maine on October 6, 1811, and engaged in the lumber trade there as an adult. His daughter, Mrs. Mary Getchell, remembered that her family of six, consisting of father Jacob, mother and four children — Mary, age 8, Levi, age 9, Nathan, age 6 and Seleda, age 6 — all used her

1874 Hennepin County Map

little tin box to save nickels and dimes for three years in order to save for a trip from their home at Washington County, Machias, Maine, to the west and St. Anthony, Minnesota Territory, and eventually Brooklyn Township. In June 1851 they left their hometown with an ox team that took them to a boat in Boston—then a train to Albany, New York—and a canal boat to Buffalo—then a steamboat to Chicago. From there they hired a team and wagon to take them to Galena, Illinois, where they took a steamboat to St. Paul, arriving at St. Anthony on July 2, 1851. They were met at St. Paul by their maternal grandfather, Washington Getchell, who took them to St. Anthony where Getchell had built the second frame house in town. In those days it took a month to make such a journey, compared to air travel today which would be about three actual hours in the air! The Jacob Longfellows lived in St. Anthony for a year and one-half.[22]

Mary wrote: "The summer [actually April] of 1852 father made his claim to this place in Brooklyn, and the next winter built a log house from trees cut from the tamarack swamp about a mile east of here [the farm was northwest of Palmer Lake and near Ezra Hanscom who was just to the east]. In February of 1853 we came here to live [Brooklyn Township]. Father had the oven full of baked potatoes, and even now in imagination I can smell those same potatoes. That winter was a very severe winter with heaps of snow. We had several visits from the Indians, who liked to sit around the stove and get warm.

The next summer we could look across the prairie and see the Indians, with their guns and dogs, hunting prairie chickens." Grandma Getchell named the farm at first 'Crooked Brook' because it was near Shingle Creek and, later, 'Brooklyn.'"[23]

Levi Longfellow

Enlisting at age twenty, Levi Longfellow served in the Dakota vs. United States war and the Civil War. Later on, he became one of the early wholesalers of fruits and vegetables and country produce—at first on a commission basis, and then he became a buyer as well as a commission man. In early days the farm produce business was scattered, but later Longfellow worked through the Minneapolis Produce Exchange which was organized in 1884. The produce business was lucrative, and Longfellow became quite wealthy. In 1916 he challenged Brooklyn (United) Methodist Church: "You raise $10,000 for a new church and I will double it." In 1901 Levi Longfellow was a senior member of the firm of Longfellow Bros.[24]

Ezra Hanscom

In the house of settler Ezra Hanscom, who made a claim near Getchell in July, 1852, the governmental beginnings of Brooklyn Township took place May 11, 1858. At this meeting 128 votes were cast to elect the following: three supervisors—E. T. Alling, Chairman, John Stinchfield and J. P. Plummer; L. T. Andrews, Clerk; Ezra Hanscom, Assessor; James McRay, Collector; James Norris, Overseer of the Poor; H. H. Smith and A. H. Benson, Justices of the Peace; and J. M. Durnam and W. D. Getchell, Constables. The two Justices of the Peace and the two Constables were the first law enforcement run by the Township.[25]

Hanscom's house, completed in July 1853, was on today's Noble Avenue on the southeast side of Shingle Creek. Hanscom's house was probably the town's first frame house because he "immediately" began erecting a house "which was completed the following year," according to Isaac Atwater. At a town meeting in a schoolhouse near the home of Hanscom, on June 7, 1858, the town was named Brooklyn. Hanscom was a town leader in setting up government and taking care of roads and welfare.[26]

Ezra Hanscom's squatter's claim was on Section 27, Town 119, Range 21, west; and he pre-empted the claim when it was possible in 1855. Hanscom had come to Minnesota from Maine in 1850. He was Town Assessor for thirty years and a Supervisor for twelve years. He had married Mary Dow in 1842, and they celebrated their golden wedding on June 26, 1892. They had eight children, among them a teacher, two farmers, a doctor and a druggist.[27]

Pierre Bottineau

In July 1852 Dakota-Ojibwe-French voyageur Pierre Bottineau stepped out of the woods southwest of Osseo, and he said, with his French accent, "Ah, dis is zee plase." He and his companions Pierre Gervais, Pierre Raiche and Joseph Potvin, staked claims and stayed overnight. Bottineau's claim was west of the present Osseo's main street, and the locale became known as Bottineau's Prairie. Thus, Bottineau became the founder of Osseo, which was at first called "Bottineau's Prairie," and the eastern half of it was at one time part of Brooklyn Township.[28] Osseo Road, now known as Brooklyn Boulevard, was one of the Indian trails into the new frontier; and early market gardeners heading for Minneapolis sometimes met wagons, pulled by oxen, carrying families and their possessions enroute to find places to settle.[29]

Mary Jane (Flanders) Smith

Mary Jane Flanders came to Minnesota in 1853. She married Harris Nathaniel Smith whose father, Nathaniel Smith, homesteaded in Brooklyn Township near the present 63rd Avenue North close to today's Crystal airport. Their farm reached almost to today's 68th Avenue North.[30]

The Indians had a trail across one corner of the farm, used when they traveled to Sauk Centre. Mrs. Smith's sister-in-law, also named Mary Jane Smith, taught the first school at Shingle Creek (when she was only age seventeen) in a little claim shanty with three small panes of glass which moved sideways to let in air. To get to the school she crossed the creek on a plank. One day during class the windows were darkened when some unfriendly-looking Indians peered in. They were not friendly like those she knew locally, and they had guns. The children were terrified, but she went on with lessons, and after school, with the children clinging to her, she went outside and showed the visitors pictures from an atlas. After they had enjoyed the pictures for quite some time, "they went away with no harm done."[31]

Besides keeping the home fires burning as a homemaker in Brooklyn Township, Mary Jane (Flanders) Smith conceived the idea of making woolen caps for her two boys, Harris and Oscar. She sent the oldest boy to the city where the fire chief's son and other firemen saw the boy's cap and wanted one. She had compassion for the firemen working in freezing weather and decided to make them caps. The caps were of red and blue wool, with six pieces coming to a point, with a tassel caught at one side. "Before a year had passed, this Betsy Ross of the Minneapolis Volunteer Fire Department saw her ambition realized, and the firemen were clothed in uniformly warm headgear," wrote her granddaughter, Alice Smith Johnson. The latter lady, and Mary Jane (Flanders) Smith, are ancestors of Mary Blesi, a member of the Brooklyn Historical Society from Osseo. Mary once saw one of the wool caps.[32]

Forty years later, on July 31, 1914, Chief Charles Ringer and his men honored the cap donor at the Fairgrounds where she had a special box seat for the occasion. Mary Jane's father-in-law, Nathaniel Smith, a veteran of the War of 1812, is buried in the Brooklyn-Crystal Cemetery (now in Brooklyn Park), and his grave was the first to be marked by the Minneapolis Chapter of the Daughters of the War of 1812.

More Settlers

A week before a colony of fourteen families from Adrian, Michigan arrived (in fall, 1853), in northern "Brooklyn," Alonzo Bragdon and Daniel Chase came to settle. The first settlers on Long Prairie (future Brooklyn Park) were James Weaver, Hiram Smith in 1854, Job Kenneston, Charles Miles, James H.W. Brown, Stephen Howe, William Cate and J. D. Hervey.[33]

Jonathan Estes, J. M. Durnam, N. Crooker, L. R. Palmer and J. P. Plummer came to southern "Brooklyn" in 1853-54. On an 1874 map, an island in the Mississippi, opposite the future Brooklyn Center, shows the owners as "Crooker and Durnam," and it is marked "Durnham's Island." [sic][34]

Nahum Crooker bought his claim in Brooklyn Township when he came here in 1854. In 1853, he had married Esther A. Reidhead. Their children were John and Charles. Crooker's granddaughter, Clara Esther Crooker Green, donated a fine melodeon to the Brooklyn Historical Society a few years ago. It was the property of Nahum Crooker (1825-1899) and Esther Crooker (1832-1934) who came to Brooklyn Center in 1854 and settled by the River. Esther played hymns on it; and their son, Charles Crooker (1862-1957), took lessons and learned to play on the melodeon.[35]

A. H. Benson bought and improved a claim in 1854, moving onto it in 1855. The Benson farmhouse was at today's 70th Avenue North and the River, near Durnam Island. Mrs. A. H. Benson told of the early days when Indians lived, or camped, on Durnam Island. A group of them walked into her kitchen one day while Mrs. Benson was baking cookies. They "said nothing—just devoured the cookies as they came from the oven and departed when the cookies were gone," remembered Grandma Benson.[36]

John Crooker
Minnesota Historical Society

Daily Life of Settlers

Starting in 1853, settlement of what became Brooklyn Township went on rapidly. "Within two years, the town was well settled. Claim jumping was common and led to stirring times and some excitement," according to Edward D. Neill.[37]

Life for the average new-settler family was not easy. Some had small cabins with, occasionally, a leaky roof, and they had to cook and heat with wood-burning stoves. Toilets were outside, as well as their water supply, in the form of hand pumps or wells. They had to lay in supplies for the winter before navigation closed on the rivers and shut off the source of supplies. Mrs. Hiram Smith bought provisions when she came through St. Paul in 1854, enroute to Long Prairie in Brooklyn Township. The rice flour she bought was all the flour in their "colony" until April of the next year. There was great joy when her husband, Hiram, discovered a fine cranberry marsh. The Smiths picked seven bushels but were unable to sell or trade the cranberries in St. Paul as the last steamboat had left, and the town was out of the needed supplies. The neighbor who tried to sell their cranberries in St. Paul lamented, "There is not a yard of cloth or a hank of thread in the town, and I could only get thee three brooms for thy fine cranberries." (As shown in the quote just mentioned, from the book *Old Rail Fence Corners*, at least some of the new settlers were still using the archaic English "thy" and "thee".) A salesman came by and sold the Smiths the new product kerosene for their lamps. The spring of 1855 the Smiths harvested maple sugar and bought a cow and six hens, so they began to live more comfortably. Netting some of the plentiful wild pigeons added to the meat supply.[38]

New settlers' transportation was by boat or on horseback, or with horse and ox carts and buggies. A messenger, going from house to house, was the only method of communication. With no means of calling "911" for emergency help, the settlers purchased tin horns for each family to blast on to call for help. Levi Longfellow tells of an old German man who wanted to test his horn and blew a loud blast in his cellar. Neighbors heard it and rushed from all directions on foot and on horseback, expecting to find a disaster, and soon left, disgusted with the old man and his false alarm![39]

By 1858 new settlers had claimed nearly all the land in Brooklyn Township. Their land was easy to cultivate. Some of the descendants of the early farmers are still on the original land. Farmers in the southern part of Brooklyn Township grew small vegetables for market, and the northern part of the township was mainly into potato growing. Other early businesses were sawmills, the Boom House (where men sorted logs floating down the river), ice cutting and its sale, the West River Road stage, and lumberjack work—with farming as the mainstay which pushed the settlement of the area. The Township remained, basically, a rural farm community until after World War II. Stories about various farms and farm families are included later in this book.[40]

Products Grown Over the Years

Leone Howe, a local historian, remembers some of the vegetables grown in Brooklyn: sweet corn, carrots, onions, radishes, asparagus, potatoes, cucumbers, beets, green and yellow beans, cabbage, peas, and other one-season vegetables. A few vegetables, such as radishes, could produce two crops a season. Some vegetables, like asparagus, carrots, green onions, beets and radishes, had to be bunched and this was mostly done by the women and children. Celery was grown, but was unusual for this area.[41]

Harvesting celery on the Rydeen Farm, Brooklyn Center, circa 1940

Howe says the southern Brooklyn farmers specializing in various vegetables and melons in the horse and wagon days had to leave at 3:00 A.M. to set up at the Minneapolis market. Being so far from the market, the northern Brooklyn farmers started raising potatoes, which they could market at Osseo. Early German or German-Swiss families found the black sandy loam of Brooklyn Township ideal for growing potatoes. Farmers began bringing their potatoes and other products to the spur in Osseo to have them graded, sold and shipped. They had to lease their spur area from the railroad, which came to Osseo in 1881. One broker was Roy Howe, who bought the potatoes from the farmers, graded and bagged them, and often the products were shipped out of state.[42]

Fruits such as apples, rhubarb, muskmelon, watermelon, and some strawberries were grown. Cucumbers were prolific, and local boys took them to the pickling factory at Anoka. There were large cabbage fields on 85th Avenue towards the River. Certain local farmers in the northern Brooklyn Township area did engage in truck farming even in the later years of the Township. Baldy Hartkopf's daughter, Audrey Alford, remembers the Golden Osage melons raised by the Bohanons. Some were one foot in diameter, with two-inch grooves, and they were delicious![43]

Two crops that were relished by local American Indians were strawberries and pumpkins. When pioneer James Gillespie settled in 1853 (before the survey) at his Camden area farm, his first crop was corn and pumpkins. Sometimes Indians would split a pumpkin from the field and eat it like a tasty apple. Some Indians had cultivated a patch of wild strawberries on a eight-acre patch on Gillespie's new farm. The berries were "as large as the small cultivated berries, with a most delicious flavor. Everyone we knew picked and picked but wagonloads rotted on the ground," Gillespie remembered. Also, he recalled that "sometimes Indians would milk a cow on the farm and get creamy milk for their strawberries."[44]

In summary, the northern part of the old township engaged in somewhat more diversified farming than the southern area. Farmers in the northern township area had more dairy cows, and they raised sheep in the winter so that they could get sheep manure for their crops. Later, when farmers began using tractors and commercial fertilizer, they started raising soybeans, corn, as well as potatoes. The small vegetable growers in southern Brooklyn feared the strong winds blowing sand, which could cut off the tops of vegetables. Many farms were ten or twenty acres and rarely forty. This small size enabled farmers to grow hedges around their fields in an effort to stop the wind and sand. Irrigation was important, when it became available, in both north and south Brooklyn Township because the soil drained the water quite fast.[45]

Early Schools

The first school was started in 1854, before the Township was organized. It was on Long Prairie in a board shanty, with two half windows and board roof. Ten pupils were taught by Miss Augusta McLaughlin, from Portland, Maine. She died of consumption the following spring. The next teacher was Miss Amelia Griggs in 1855. Soon a better schoolhouse was built, funded at first by contributions and completed by taxes after the organization of a school district.[46]

In summer 1855 a school was started in the southwest part of the future township by the wife of Reverend Partridge. Mrs. Partridge became ill and the term was completed by Mary Smith. The school building was a straw-covered shed, with the ground for a floor and stalls for horses. Mr. Partridge soon removed the stalls and laid a rough board floor, but the roof was still made of straw. All the early schools were held in similar crude buildings.[47]

In fall 1854 a school was started on Getchell Prairie, taught by Mrs. Mary Huff. The first real schoolhouse building in the Township was a hall erected by the Society of Spiritualists and later purchased by the school district (the latter covered a large section on each side of Osseo Village). In summer, 1855 or 1856, this school began near Osseo on Section 18, and it was called the Smith District. Miss Sylvia Rowe taught, and her successor as a teacher was H. H. Smith, who taught for several years—three months in the summer and three months in the winter.[48]

Captain John Martin Arrives in 1855 at St. Anthony

Steamboat captain John Martin of Peacham, Vermont, had acquired capital from going to the 1849 California gold rush—$15,200. In 1853 he made a trip to Minnesota Territory and saw the opportunities in steamboating, railroads, and lumber; so he came to St. Anthony in 1855 with his wife, Jane, and young daughter, Jean (the future mother of Earle Brown, prominent citizen of Brooklyn Center). By selling his Vermont property and having his gold rush bonanza, plus Minnesota enterprises, Martin became one of the richest men in Minnesota. He bought 100 acres of the site of the Earle Brown Farm from his daughter's husband, Cyrus Elwood Brown, in 1875, for $6,000. The farm became a sanctuary from the city for the Martins and Browns. After his daughter's death, he "sold" the farm—then 420 acres—to his grandson, Earle Brown, for consideration of one dollar. Martin died in 1905.[49]

Territorial Days Change to Minnesota State Government
Notices were posted for a special Town Meeting to be held on May 27, 1858.

Town Meeting
Notice is hereby given that at a legal call of Freeholders there will be a town meeting held at the School-House in district No. 4 near Ezra Hanscom's on the 7 of June at 2 o'clock (P.M.) for the purpose of taking into consideration the raising of money to defray the Town expenses and to determine the running at large of Horses, Cattle, Sheep, and Hogs. Also the naming of the Town.[50]

Town Meeting Minutes record "that the name of this town be Brooklyn."

Minnesota changed from a Territory to a State in May, 1858.

At their June 7, 1858, town meeting, the freeholders voted to raise $300 to defray the town expenses and that hogs and sheep could not run at large; but the motion was made, seconded and carried that horses were permitted to run at large except unruly and stud horses of two years old and upwards — also all peaceable, orderly cattle were permitted to run at large. This was the meeting that officially named the Township. "Motion made, seconded and carried unanimously that the name of this Town be Brooklyn." From its status as a Territory, Minnesota had just become a State on May 11, 1858. Statehood perhaps was the catalyst, but it was also on May 11, 1858 that Brooklyn Township had its political beginnings at Ezra Hanscom's house. Before the Township was named "Brooklyn," it was usually referred to as Getchell's or Bottineau's Prairie.[51]

The Colony That Brought the Name Brooklyn

The name "Brooklyn" was chosen for their new settlement by pioneers who came from Adrian, Michigan and its vicinity to the future Brooklyn Township in the fall, 1853. The name came from a township and railway village in southern Michigan which was named "Brooklyn" and was near their former home location. Allen B. Chaffee led a colony of fourteen families from Adrian and its vicinity to the future Brooklyn Township in the fall, 1853. Besides Chaffee, family names of those in the colony were (according to Edward D. Neill): H. H. Smith; Thomas Keeley; D. B. Thayer; Otis H. Brown; Seneca Brown; Jeremiah, John and Job Brown; Homer, Rowell and Stephen Roberts; Stephen Caner; John Fogerson; and John Clark.[52]

Some new settlers, John Fogerson, Job Brown and others, drove a team and stock for the leaders, Chaffee and Smith, and traveled for about seven weeks. Others took about two weeks to travel by Rock Island railroad, a boat to St. Paul, and a ferry across the Mississippi. They could not even buy sugar or nails in the first store, still under construction, on the river's west side. When they reached their claims, Smith, Keeley and Thayer built a shanty, with such a bad roof that they had to catch rainwater in tin pans. Soon they each had their own better-built house. All the Brooklyn, Michigan pioneers settled within three or four miles of Osseo. An 1855 survey put some of the settlers in Maple Grove and some in Brooklyn (in the future Brooklyn Park).[53]

After the 1855 survey, Osseo was part of both Brooklyn and Maple Grove Townships. In the spring of 1875, by an act of the State Legislature, Osseo was incorporated with a president, three councilmen, a recorder and a treasurer.

Warren Sampson, Isaac LaBissoniere, Clark Ellsworth, Seneca Brown, D.B. Thayer and James McRay all settled on Bottineau's Prairie in 1854. In 1856 Sampson and LaBissoniere platted the village; and soon after that A.B. Chaffee (of the Adrian, Michigan colony) laid out a village to the southeast of what became Osseo, and he called it "City of Attraction." Although the latter has been called a ghost town, it is now part of the city of Osseo.[54]

Settlers in and around Osseo could go to Warren Sampson's general merchandise store and post office, opened in 1855 in the settlement then called Palestine. People could also visit the saloon of a Mr. Gagnon. Sampson started a wood market at which he bought green wood from the farmers and shipped it to Minneapolis mills after drying it for one season. This wood market soon became the community's chief source of revenue. The land was covered with timber and brush, with the grub hoe their main tool to clear for a small crop of grain. The first of five blacksmith shops was started in 1855 by Clark Ellsworth, and Rudolph Niggler started the first hotel. Mail was carried on foot for 70 miles from St. Paul to St. Cloud by a man named Joseph Labonne. People walked long distances to church, school and town. In the earliest years of settlement, there was little money circulated, and everything was done by trade. There was much growth in the little town in 1855-56, and the settlement was named "Osseo" after it was platted.[55]

In the Osseo area, some pioneers made mattresses out of corn husks, and the Osseo area women, especially, were skilled in making straw hats by hand from wheat straw. After grain was cut with the cradle scythe, women and children would gather the remaining spears, cut the heads for the farmer, and use the straws to make hats. One family could make dozens of sun protector hats in the winter and trade them for clothing and groceries. Most had sheep but never sold the wool, preferring to spin it into yarn to knit mittens, stockings or caps. In early spring they tapped maple trees for sugar and syrup.

Indian Battle

In the midst of efforts to get settled and clear the land and plant, there was a disturbing Indian battle to the south of Brooklyn Township. In May, 1858, in retaliation for continuing hostilities between the Dakota and Ojibwe tribes, the Ojibwes from Mille Lacs came down the Rum River and, leaving their canoes and ponies at Coon Rapids, they went overland down the Indian trail in Champlin and Brooklyn Township and cut over to the woods opposite a Dakota village at Shakopee where a fierce battle took place. The battle was on May 29, 1858 and was the last important battle between these two Minnesota Indian tribes. Minnesota became a state 18 days before the battle, and Brooklyn Township was formally named just 9 days after the battle.[56]

Rumblings of Trouble

Minnesota's Dakota Indians found themselves driven by treaties out of their old hunting grounds. They were still permitted to hunt to the north and west of their reservations, but game was scarce as settlers and their civilization had driven away the game. Also, in 1861, the corn crop of the Dakotas who farmed was destroyed by cutworms, and even with food provided by their Indian agent, about 4,000 Dakotas eagerly awaited the government's yearly payment in order to buy provisions. However, the payment was late because of the Civil War, and although the local agency's food was distributed, the traders refused to sell any more goods on credit to the Dakotas. A Dakota leader, in council, reluctantly made the decision to attack the Redwood Agency to obtain goods.

Dakota-U.S. War

The 1862 Dakota-U.S. conflict was a terrifying time. It occurred while some of the local defense forces were engaged in the Civil War. The spark was an argument over the theft of eggs which resulted in some renegade Indians killing five people at Acton. If caught, there would have been harsh punishment. Although Brooklyn Township was far from the area first attacked, people were edgy, and some settlers fled to St. Paul for refuge. It was not known whether or not the Ojibwe nation would join the war.[57]

A fort built at Osseo was 30 by 30 feet in size, and the men took turns as watchmen at night. Nearly all left in town took refuge at the fort at night. Father Boerboom, wrote: "The Indian, however, never brandished his tomahawk in the moonlight of

Osseo; although a terrible scare was thrown into the dwellers one night when the watchmen raised the cry of: 'The Indians are coming!' Everybody ran hatter-scatter screaming with fright, seeking a place of refuge or hiding, whilst the brave men prepared their weapons for the fight, when the glimmering light of the moon revealed the approach of a small and strictly peaceful herd of young cattle." Besides the fort, the fact that Dakota-Ojibwe-French Chief Pierre Bottineau lived at Osseo has also been cited as a reason the area was not attacked. Bottineau's three nationalities made him a walking peace pipe. By December, 1862, the bloody war was over, with General Henry Sibley's army the victors.[58]

Levi Longfellow Enlists

Like many of his compatriots, Levi Longfellow, at age 20, enlisted in the Army, thinking his regiment would be ordered to join the Army of the Potomac and the Civil War; but within a week, they got news of the Dakota-U.S. outbreak of war. They were ordered to report to St. Peter, where they arrived August 24th. Four days later they hurried forty miles to Fort Ridgely because it was in a state of siege. After a fight, they drove off the Dakotas by September 2nd. Then the regiment was sent sixteen miles away to Birch Cooley where the Fifth Minnesota troops had been surprised by the Indians. They helped stop that attack. The regiment had several other assignments, including burying the dead sometimes, until the war ended. After his local Army service, Levi enlisted in Company B of the Civil War forces in October, 1862. He was a private in the Civil War and transferred to be principal Musician on a noncommissioned staff. Levi was discharged from the U.S. Army on March 1, 1865. In his later years, Levi Longfellow used the title "Colonel." Records show that Levi was discharged as a "private," so his title would have come from his post-military service as a department commander of the Grand Army of the Republic organization.[59]

Levi Longfellow

Other Civil War Soldiers

"Brooklyn furnished its full quota of men for the [Civil] war, some of whom won distinction and promotions, and a few sleep on southern battlefields," wrote Isaac Atwater. A few who served were:

Alva Getchell—enlisted August 4, 1862 at age 19.
Nathan G. Longfellow—enlisted at age 16, served with the First Mounted Rangers, was wounded and discharged a year later. (He re-enlisted eight months later.)
Levinne Plummer—enlisted in 1862 and discharged in 1865 with the rank of Captain in the artillery.
George Pomeroy served three years, with seven months of that time spent in the infamous Confederate prison at Andersonville, Georgia.
James H. Brown enlisted in the First Minnesota Infantry. He had both legs and one arm broken in battles. He was taken prisoner and exchanged after three months and never returned to Brooklyn Township to stay. [60]

Early Post Offices

Early post offices were established in Brooklyn Township at Palestine (Osseo)—1855, Harrisburg—1858, Industriana—1860, Warwick—1869 and Brooklyn Centre—1873.[61]

'Ghost towns' and Paper Cities

The West River Road was the location of early townsites that are commonly called 'ghost towns' today. Another, more accurate name is 'Paper cities,' because plats were made showing lots and blocks in the enthusiastic days of the 1850s which came to nothing. Their existence was on paper only. *The Minnesota Republican*, September 18, 1856, noted a 'New Town', called Harrisburg, located ten miles above Minneapolis on the west side of the river. The article described the area; "At this point, it is said, the river is particularly well adapted to holding logs—from ten to fifteen million feet can be boomed by the aid of a large island. The projectors of the place are said to be 'solid men,' and the mills and a hotel, together with dwelling houses, are to be commenced immediately." Harrisburg was located in Section 11 between 93rd and 96th avenues north in Brooklyn Park. The townsite was platted as 160 acres, and had a hotel, a post office, a sawmill, and several dwellings. Eventually, the sawmill was torn down, one house burned, and the rest of the houses were removed. The townsite was located near the Riverview School house in Brooklyn Park today.

Another 'paper city' was Industriana. It was established as a post office and sawmill on May 12, 1860, and its name was changed to 'Brooklyn' on February 15, 1869, according to post office records at the Minnesota Historical Society. The 'Brooklyn' post office was discontinued on March 26, 1877. Industriana was located on the west side of the Mississippi at the east end of 69th in Brooklyn Center.

Another settlement, never platted, was at Warwick, around 200 76th Avenue N. in Brooklyn Park. Warwick was centered around the Fischer House at 77th and West River Road. Apparently, this was sometimes a stop on the Camden-Anoka stage line between 1874-1912. Warwick had a house, store, and post office. The post office was established on June 30, 1891, and discontinued August 31, 1901. The first postmaster was John B. Johnson in 1869 (Minnesota Historical Society post office file). The Brooklyn Historical Society has a 1932 map which still shows Warwick as a place.

Formation of Two Cities

Crystal Lake and Brooklyn Center split off from the Township in 1860 and 1911, respectively; however, Brooklyn Center was composed of southeastern Brooklyn Township and eastern Crystal Lake when incorporated in 1911. A news article explained the latter changes: Largely farming districts, both the village of Brooklyn Center and the village of Crystal Lake incorporated in 1911. They covered an area of 20 square miles of Hennepin County land. Reasons were: to facilitate public business, better police protection, speeding automobiles and to avoid annexation by Minneapolis. In 1966 Brooklyn Center adopted the Council/Manager form of government and became a city.[62]

Brooklyn Township board members began hearing rumors, in 1954, that their neighbor city, Osseo, wanted to annex part of the Township. Because cities were allowed to annex territory from townships, "We agreed unanimously that we must do something and do it fast," said Baldy Hartkopf, who was township clerk at the time. The township's 3,368 voters agreed to support incorporating; so the Village of Brooklyn Park came into being on May 5, 1954—created out of the large area remaining of Brooklyn Township. Baldwin Hartkopf was the first Mayor of the new village. Brooklyn Park became a Charter City in 1969. A 1996 study stated that Brooklyn Park was the sixth largest city in Minnesota.[63]

The Eidem House

Productive Land

After the prairies were cultivated, they yielded good crops of corn and wheat, and by 1895 Brooklyn Township was "an exclusively agricultural town," according to writer Isaac Atwater. Where there was brush, there was good pasture, and the meadows produced luxuriant crops of grass. Drained land became rich farm land. Dairying was a popular occupation, and raising cattle and horses was a profitable business. Farms gradually became market gardens that produced wagon loads of vegetables that were quickly absorbed by the produce buyers in Minneapolis or Osseo. Osseo served northern Brooklyn Township for shopping, and the Brooklyn Centre store and post office, opened in the southern part of the Township in 1875, served its surrounding area.[64]

The Eidems

This farm is a ten-acre living record of farm life in Minnesota during the years of 1890-1910. The earliest Eidems here were John J. Eidem, Sr., and his family. Born in Norway in 1842, John, Sr., came to America in 1866, at age 24. At age 22, he had married Isabel (or Ingaborg) Hanson in Norway. The couple came to Brooklyn Township in 1877 and built a house west of Noble and 105th and engaged in general farming. Of fourteen children, nine survived.[65]

Their first child born in America was John Eidem, Jr. He married Electa ("Lectty") Cotton April 29, 1892, and in 1894 they moved into what was destined to be the Brooklyn Park Living Farm. They farmed there from 1894 and 1956.

The City of Brooklyn Park acquired the farmhouse, outbuildings and acreage in 1976. The Recreation and Parks Department schedules events so the public can transport themselves back to the turn of the century by viewing the restored farm buildings, tours, displays, pioneer crafts and old-time activities. The current address of the farm is 4345 101st Avenue North.

Earle Brown Acquires Farm in 1901

The red and white landmark in Brooklyn Center, known as the Earle Brown Farm, was sold to Brown in 1901 for consideration of one dollar by his Grandfather John

Martin. Over the years Brown increased the size of his farm from 420 acres to 750 acres. The farm is visible from Highway 100. Its gentleman farmer, Earle, became famous when he served as Hennepin County Sheriff, trained and founded the Minnesota Highway Patrol, and ran for Governor. He began Minnesota's first commercial airport on his land when he invited WWI military pilots to train there, and Earle's collection of antique vehicles and a model lumberjack display enriched life on the farm. Earle Brown and his wife, Gwen, involved many people in their good works, making the Brown name famous statewide. Today the farm, a State Historic Place, has become a Bed and Breakfast Inn and Heritage Center for conferences, with the renovated barns housing successful business tenants. Annual Brooklyn Center "Earle Brown Days" are currently a reminder of Brown and his accomplishments.[66]

Earle Brown's relatives entrusted his extensive diaries to the Brooklyn Historical Society the summer of 1999. Some Brown diary entries: November 12, 1921, Brown gave all his Sheriff's Deputies a fur coat; in September, 1933, he went to Europe to get horses; in February, 1935, he bought a stagecoach for $173.50; March, 1935, he sold his covered wagon and oxen; in 1939, he bought the horse "Temptation" for $175; in October, 1939, he bought four yearling mules at $90 each, adding, in November, nine head of mules, and in 1942 he started a mounted Guard School at his Brooklyn Farm, opening a second class of mounted guards on April 1st.[67]

This history book covers stories of Township days and the growth of the suburbs of Brooklyn Park and Brooklyn Center. These early settlement stories have emerged mainly from history books and the precious stories of old and new settlers in what was once called Brooklyn Township. The stories of their descendants and newer settlers are told in the last half of this book. The book is like a jigsaw puzzle whose parts join to solve the puzzle of the "who, how, why and when" of the two Brooklyn towns.

Notes

1. Theodore C. Blegen, *A History of the State*, 1963, 17-21 Hennepin County Library. Robert G. Thompson, Phase III Archaeological Investigation of the Palmer Lake Site, Brooklyn Center, MN. Brooklyn Historical Society. Scott Anfinson to Nina Archabel (a letter), 14 November 1997, Indian History of Brooklyn Center, MN. Historical Society State Historic Preservation office. Mary Jane Gustafson, *"Bison Bones Found on Brown Farm," Brooklyn Center Post*, 18 June 1970. N.H. Winchell, *Geologic and Natural History Summary of Minnesota*, Volume 2, 1882-5, Chapter XI. Brooklyn Historical Society. "Boys, Workers, Scientists Have Hand in Fossil Find," *Sunday Tribune*, 24 August 1958.

2. Father Louis Hennepin, *A New Discovery of a Vast Country in America*, London, 1698. Reuben Gold Thwaites, interpretation of Hennepin's book with the same title, *A New Discovery of a Vast Country in America*, 1903, Minnesota Historical Society.

3. Ibid.

4. Ibid.

5. Ibid.

6. Mary Jane Gustafson, "City of Brooklyn Park, Past to Present," circa 1973, Brooklyn Historical society. Edward D. Neill, *History of Hennepin County and the City of Minneapolis*, 1881, Brooklyn Historical Society. Mary Jane Gustafson, "A Glance at History," 1970s, Brooklyn Historical Society. Ford and Johnson, *Minnesota, Star of the North*, 1961, Brooklyn Historical Society. Daughters of the American Revolution, *Old Rail Fence Corners*, 1914, Minnesota Historical Society. Poatgieter and Dunn, *Gopher Reader*, 1966, 7. Ibid.

8. Hennepin County Library. William Mace, *A School History of the United States*, 1904, Jane Hallberg. D.H. Montgomery, *Leading Facts of American History*, 1910, Jane Hallberg. Works Progress Administration Federal Writer's Project, *Guide to Minnesota*, Minnesota Historical Society Press, 1985, 50, 51.

9. Ibid., W.P.A. Writer's Project, 50, 51. Ford and Johnson, *Minnesota, Star of the North*, 1961, 350.

10. D.A.R., *Old Rail Fence Corners*, 1914, 186-188, 219, MHS.

11. Dr. Norene Roberts, "Early Transportation Routes in Brooklyn Park," 24 April 1995, BHS. 1870 Potter Log Cabin File, BHS.

12. Mizinokamigok, or Liz, Interview by Jane Hallberg, 1979, BHS.

13. Per Kalm, *Travels Into North America; the America of 1750*, 1937 English version based on 1770 version, MHS.

14. Jane Hallberg, "The Story of Pierre Bottineau," 1979, BHS. Bottineau files, BHS.

15. D.A.R., *Old Rail Fence Corners*, 186-188, 219, MHS.

16. Ed Letterman, "Looking Back—Indians 1820-1850," Ramsey County Historical Society.

17. Sig Edling, Speaker at Brooklyn Historical Society, 14 January 1971, BHS. Earl King, Northwestern Bell Telephone Co. Commercial Survey 1922, BHS.

18. D.A.R., *Old Rail Fence Corners*, 186-188, 219, MHS.

19. Neill, *History of Hennepin County*, 25.

20. Isaac Atwater, *A History of Minneapolis and Hennepin County*, 1895, 1475-76.

21. Ibid., 1470. Neill, *Hennepin*, 255.

22. Ibid, 1470. Edward D. Neill, *History of Hennepin County*, 255.

23. Ibid., 1470; Mrs. Mary A. Getchell, "The Longfellow Reunion, 1901," BHS. D.A.R., *Old Rail Fence Corners*, 1914, MHS.

24. Ibid., 1470; Mrs. Mary A. Getchell, "The Longfellow Reunion, 1901," BHS. D.A.R., *Old Rail Fence Corners*, 1914, MHS.

25. Atwater, *A History of Minneapolis and Hennepin County*; Neill, *History of Hennepin County*.

26. Atwater, *A History of Minneapolis and Hennepin County*; Neill, *History of Hennepin County*.

27. Atwater, *A History of Minneapolis and Hennepin County*; Neill, *History of Hennepin County*.

28. Father Henry J. Boerboom, *Historical Sketch of Osseo and The St. Vincent de Paul Parish*, 1922, BHS. Jane Hallberg, *The Story of Pierre Bottineau*, 1991; Atwater, *A History of Minneapolis and Hennepin County*; Edward D. Neill, *History of Hennepin County;* Bottineau file at Brooklyn Historical Society. D.A.R., *Old Rail Fence Corners*.

29. Earl King, Northwestern Bell Telephone Co. Commercial Survey, 1922, BHS. Sig Edling, speaker at Brooklyn Historical Society, 14 January 1971, BHS. D.A.R., *Old Rail Fence Corners*, 1914, MHS, 57.

30. Alice Smith Johnson, *Pioneer Chronicles*, 18-20, Mini Print, Inc., BHS.

31. Ibid.

32. Ibid.

33. Neill, *History of Hennepin County*, 286,

34. Ibid.

35. Ibid.; BHS Acquisitions.

36. Ibid. Mrs. John Thompson, Journal 1970, BHS. "Mrs. John Thompson story," *Brooklyn Center Post*, 30 April 1970, BHS.

37. Neill, *History of Hennepin County*, 286;

38. D.A.R., *Old Rail Fence Corners*, 1914, 186-188, 219, MHS. George Phillip, Ltd., *Oxford Family Encyclopedia*, 1997.

39. Ibid.

40. Atwater, Volume II, *History of Hennepin County*, 1471, BHS. Dr. Norene Roberts, *"Growing Potatoes in Brooklyn Park," Hennepin History Magazine*, Fall, 1994, BHS. Leone and Ralph Howe, "Farm Produce Information," Interview by Jane Hallberg, 1999.

41. Leone Howe, Brooklyn Township and Brooklyn Park, Interview by Jane Hallberg, 1999. James Gillespie II, Brooklyn Park, Interview with Jane Hallberg, 1999, BHS. D.A.R., *Old Rail Fence Corners*, 75.

42. Ibid.

43. Ibid.

44. Ibid.

45. Ibid.

46. Neill, *History of Hennepin County*, 287-288.

47. Ibid.

48. Ibid.

49. Jane Hallberg, Leone Howe and Mary Jane Gustafson, *History of the Earle Brown Farm*, (BC: Brooklyn Historical Society, 1996), Chapter 1. Earle Brown's Gilfillan family Bible history article, Mrs. Jean Grothem and family, 1999, BHS.

50. Brooklyn Township Minute Book, 1850, Brooklyn Park City Hall. Ford and Johnson, *Minnesota Star of the North*, 1961, 145; Neill, *History of Hennepin County*, 286.

51. Ibid.

52. Atwater, *History of Minneapolis and Hennepin County*, Volume II, 1895, 1470; Neill, *History of Hennepin County*, 286.

53. Ibid.

54. Ibid.

55. Father Henry J. Boerboom, *Souvenir of the St. Vincent de Paul Church*, 1852-1922, BHS. *The One Hundred Year History of the City of Osseo*, 1875-1975, City of Osseo.

56. "Battle Between the Sioux and the Chippewas," Library of the Curator, Hennepin History Museum, 18-20. Orange S. Miller, *History of Champlin, Minnesota*, 1958, BHS; Ford and Johnson, Minnesota Star of the North, 1961, 157-169, BHS. Poatgieter and Dunn, *Gopher Reader*, 1966, 26-28, HCL. Mrs. Cecelia Schilling, "A Nine Year Old Girl's Experience in 1862 Massacre," *The Southern Minnesotan magazine*, BHS.

57. H. Boerboom, *Souvenir of St. Vincent de Paul Church*, 1852-1922, 25, 29, BHS.

58. Ibid.

59. D.A.R., *Old Rail Fence Corners*; Isaac Atwater, *History of Minneapolis and Hennepin County*, Volume II, 1183, BHS. Hennepin History Museum, *Men of Minnesota*, 1915.

60. "First Settlers in Brooklyn Township Came in 1852," *North Hennepin Post*, 25 October 1962; Neill, *History of Hennepin County*.

61. Ibid, 288. Father Henry J. Boerboom, "History of 100 Years of Osseo," 1952, BHS. Dr. Norene Roberts, "Early Transportation Routes in Brooklyn Park," 1995, BHS. Minnesota Republican, 18 September 1956, BHS. Dana Frear, "Ghost Towns of Hennepin County," Minnesota Historical Society.

62. Dr. Norene Roberts, "A Short History of Brooklyn Township Town Hall," *Minneapolis Journal*, 19 February 1911, 10, Column 5 "Two Villages Created." "Baldwin Hartkopf," 6 March 1980, 16, 17, *The Minneapolis Star*, BHS. "City of Brooklyn Park Past to Present", *North Hennepin Post*, circa 1969, BHS. "Brooklyn Center is 65 Years Young on February 18, 1976," *North Hennepin Post*, BHS. Ernee McArthur, "History of Brooklyn Center, MN., October 10, 1995," BHS. Mary Jane Gustafson scrapbook, BHS.

63. Ibid.

64. Atwater, *History of Minneapolis and Hennepin County*; Leone Howe, *Album of Brooklyn Centre*, 1978, BHS.

65. Ibid.

66. *History of Earle Brown Farm*, BHS.

67. Earle Brown diaries, BHS.

The Brooklyn Township Hall

by Norene Roberts

BEFORE TWO VILLAGES WERE INCORPORATED, Brooklyn Center in 1911 and Brooklyn Park in 1954, township supervisors constituted the governing body in rural Brooklyn Township. The town hall became the place for annual township meetings. Early suburban residents of Brooklyn Park will recall that they voted at the town hall until it closed in 1961 because it lacked space to accommodate the growth needs of the village. The half acre site was too small for expansion of the town hall. The site was sold to Skelly Oil Company for a gas station, then became a site of a series of restaurants. Finally, in the mid-1990s, it returned to public ownership as the "Old Town Hall Square" park at the northeast corner of Zane Avenue and Brooklyn Boulevard.

The Town Hall history is interesting. From the time of its construction in the 1870s until 1911 when the Village of Brooklyn Center was incorporated, all male citizens of Brooklyn Township voted there (women did not get the vote until 1920). According to WPA files dated 1941 at the Minnesota Historical Society, the Town Hall was built in 1874. It was a white frame building measuring 26 x 28 feet and looked very much like a one-room schoolhouse, but was never used for that purpose.

Brooklyn Township was first settled in 1852 and organized May 11, 1858, the same year Minnesota became a state. The first township meeting was held April 19, 1858 at the home of Ezra Hanscom who lived on Noble Avenue. Subsequent annual meetings of the township were held in school houses and homes around the township, such as the District 4 school house near Hanscoms, E. T. Alling's house, the District 6 school house near Industriana (an early townsite southeast of Palmer Lake), the school house in District 2 on Bottineau Prairie, the school house on Long Prairie, the school house on Getchell Prairie, and the Howe school, "a house on the Industriana cross road on the west side of Palmer Creek," and William Fisher's house.

At the Annual Meeting on March 12, 1872, a committee of John N. Durnam, N. H. Getchell and Horace H. Smith, was reaffirmed as the building committee for the "Town House." These men had been elected on May 2, 1871, to oversee the building of the township hall. At the annual town meeting on March 11, 1873, the location of the new "Town House" was discussed. Chris Schreiber offered land near his farm (in Section 16 on the east side of Zane Avenue N. north of 85th). Ezra Hanscom offered a motion to build at once. John Hechtman offered a motion to locate the site near Fishers Corner (probably in Brooklyn Center near the West River Road). The size of the new building was also discussed, Asa Howe suggested 36' x 40' which lost. It was moved and seconded to build 26' x 26'. Brooklyn Township bought a half acre of land at Zane Avenue and Brooklyn Boulevard from Martha Jane Longfellow for $25.00 on June 10, 1873 for the new township hall.

At the March 3, 1874, meeting of the town supervisors, an audit was done of the township accounts, including those of the building committee. They show that almost $400 had been spent on the construction. N. G. Abbott bought $279 for lumber and was paid $38 for labor on the "Town House." W. H. Getchell, William A. Fisher, Nahum Crooker, J. P. Conary and W. H. H. Taylor, all local landholders, were paid for labor. A. H. Benson and H. P. Whitney were paid for labor with their teams. Horace H. Smith was paid $30 for the land survey and plat. The next week, the Annual Town Meeting was held at the old Howe school, which had just been purchased by the Bohannon Grange of the Patrons of Husbandry. This and the new "Town House" appear on the 1874 Andreas' Atlas of Minnesota in Section 28. The Grange Hall was at the intersection of Noble and what is now Brooklyn Boulevard. As the Howe school, this building had been used for township meetings most of the previous ten years, 1864–1874. At this March 10, 1874 meeting, an additional $400 was voted to finish the "Town House."

Brooklyn Park Village Hall

The first annual township meeting was held in the new, but apparently uncompleted, "Town House" on March 9, 1875. N. G. Abbott was reimbursed for "work on the town house shingles and nails" he did on March 23, 1875. At the March 14, 1876, annual town meeting, a resolution passed to get "sealed proposals also for finishing the town house in Brooklyn." The building needed #2 wood siding and "two coats of paint and oil" on the outside and matched four inch wide flooring on the inside and coat of paint to finish the door and window trim. On March 13, 1877, minutes of the annual meeting show that the building was still not completed to everyone's satisfaction. The township supervisors recommended that the township hall be "underpinned with stone" (receive a stone foundation), that exterior shutters be added to the windows. Those in attendance voted to put three inch flooring in the interior, build a raised platform and railing, buy "suitable seats," a "suitable stand and table, and half a dozen chairs."

The building became the Brooklyn Park Village Hall from 1954 until 1961. By the time the original township hall was razed, a concrete block addition had been built on the rear. The Brooklyn Historical Society has the front door, the large key to the door, and one of our members has a long oak bench from the building which she donated to us and is in the Brooklyn Park City Hall.

Finding the early history of Brooklyn Township is not easy. The City of Brooklyn Park has the surviving records of the township. The Minnesota Historical Society has township records deposited in their archives section with a few years missing between 1858 through 1917.

Chapter Three

GOVERNMENT

TO THE CASUAL OBSERVER it would seem that Brooklyn Center and Brooklyn Park have much in common. They were both carved out of Brooklyn Township (the southern part of Brooklyn Center was carved out of Crystal Lake Township). They both have "Brooklyn" in their name, but that is where the similarity ends. Brooklyn Center was settled by pioneers of mostly Scandinavian descent. The pioneers of Brooklyn Park were mostly of German descent. Brooklyn Center was incorporated in 1911 and Brooklyn Park was incorporated forty-three years later. Brooklyn Center is much smaller in area than it's neighbor to the north; therefore, the Brooklyn Park population may ultimately be more than four times more numerous. There have also been some very apparent differences, and also some similarities in the path taken by their city leaders to reach their present state of governance. These commonalties and differences will be discovered in this chapter.

Brooklyn Center Government

Formative Years

Brooklyn Center's beginnings were more a matter of self-preservation than anything else. Town Board President P.W. Reidhead attended meetings in Minneapolis, and feared annexation of the land north of the Minneapolis border. In response, Reidhead and other residents (many of whom were small farmers) began the process of incorporation into a village on February 11. This was completed, by village election, on February 14, 1911. The election was held in Earle Brown's garage. The newly born village had a thriving population of 500 citizens. P. W. Reidhead became the first president of the village, along with J. P. Crooker, S. E. Locke, and F. M. Libby as trustees. The terms of office were one year, until 1939, when they became two-year terms.[1]

Some of the early ordinances dealt with restriction of filth, and littering (including dead animals) on highways. Speed limits were set at 20 miles per hour, and no hunting or shooting was permitted within the village. General Electric Company was given permission to bring electricity to the village in 1915.[2]

As time went on, issues and concerns changed, along with a change of leadership. F. M. Libby became president; J. P. Crooker, J. Ryden and M. F. Lane were trustees. A lot of attention was given to restriction of juveniles going into pool, bowling and billiard halls without a parent, as well as regulation of hours of operation of such places. Ice houses were declared a nuisance and a license became required to operate one. It was the opinion of some that this ordinance was put into place to enable a person (unnamed), who had an ice delivery service, to "fatten his pocket". Farmers feeding their hogs garbage now faced new regulations.

Brooklyn Blvd. and Noble Avenue North in the 1920s

Speed limits within the heart of the village were decreased to 10 miles per hour, and "keep to the right" at intersections became the law for all vehicles. These ordinances were enacted under the leadership of M.F. Lane, president, J. P. Crooker, J. Ryden, A. J. Larson, and W. Brunsell, trustees.[3]

In the late 1920s the leadership shifted from farmer oriented to blue collar worker. W. G. Gallien was elected president, J. J. Wheeler, N. Jensen, J. Ryden, were trustees. The stock market crashed in 1929, and the Great Depression began.[4]

After the Prohibition Act was lifted in 1933, ordinances reflected regulation of behavior in public places, as well as regulations on serving non-intoxicating malt beverages. No spiking of beverages with alcohol was allowed, and there were fines of up to $100 or 90 days in prison if caught. The president of the village at this time was W. Brunsell; at various times over several years the trustees were A. J. Larson, J. J. Wheeler, J. Ryden and W. Miller and the clerks were H. Waldron, H. C. Kitcherer and M. F. Lane.

By 1940 the village saw the need for more organized planning, so an ordinance was enacted regulating zoning and land use. The first comprehensive plan, which provided for organized and orderly development, was created. It was very farsighted and thorough for its time, and issues such as sewage were included. Traffic law obedience was an issue. The building or changing of structures was regulated. This was the beginning of the planning and zoning functions of city government. The first actual Planning Commission was formed in 1942. This was under the leadership of then president M.F. Lane and trustees J. Bigelow, N. Jensen, and J. Ryden.[5]

Municipal Liquor Store and Fire Department at 6445 Lyndale Avenue North. Originally, it housed the BC Village offices.

World War II brought about some new issues. In 1942, an ordinance was drafted providing for civilian defense and public safety during blackouts and air raid signals.[6]

In 1947, Minneapolis Gas Light Company was given permission to bring gas to the village for the purposes of lighting and heating. In this same year, the village electorate established a municipal liquor store operation.[7]

Rapid Development Era

By 1950, with a population of about 5,000, Brooklyn Center was about to grow at a rate unprecedented in any prior decade. The volunteer fire department was the only organized political faction and was quite powerful. The formation of the Planning and Zoning Commissions in the 1940s was invaluable as a response to this growth, as decisions became increasingly complicated. Soon there was a need to regulate truck traffic weights on village streets. Regulation of dump grounds became an issue, and subdividing land became a frequent topic at City Council meetings. As more and more people moved into the village, water well depth requirements were increased, especially if used for consumption. An ordinance regulating sanitary sewer systems, and the creation of an operating fund to pay for them, became necessary.

In May 1955 Art Lee was brought before the village council to be hired as the village engineer. The process was overseen by village attorney, Don Fraser, (who later went on to become the 5th District Congressman and later Mayor of Minneapolis). The council hired him. Art Paulson was mayor at the time. The population had grown to

Left: Art Lee, BC Village Administrator; Right: Mayor William Super; Center: Unidentified.

Garden City Development streets were named for authors and poets.

about 8,000. The first two council meetings, with Art Lee as engineer, had two very significant issues to deal with. At the first meeting, Daytons announced the building of a major shopping mall, and at the second meeting, the Winston Brothers developers announced the development of the Earle Brown Farm area—and both wanted sewer and water! This was quite a challenge for the village government to take on.[8]

William Super became the next mayor. The total budget in 1955 was $60,000 and was reported on two single sheets of paper. Things "blossomed" from there. Several developers were working within the village, and many streets got their names in interesting ways such as developers or property owners family members' names. Janet Lane and Joyce Lane were named after Andrew Wangsted's granddaughters; Amy Lane was named after builder Norm Chazin's youngest daughter; Eckberg Drive was named after a teacher who owned the property; Ericon Drive was named after a Swedish truck farmer and Judy Lane and Burquest Lane also were named after farm family members. Howe Lane was named after property owner Frank Howe; Wingard Lane was owned and named after farmer Art Wingard. Some streets had an area theme, such as the Northport area had a "port" theme, which may have had something to do with the fact that at one time there was a "lake" there, created by storm sewer runoff. Eventually it was eliminated, to the dismay of property owners there, who thought this was a natural lake, and that they, therefore had lake shore property. Thus, streets in this area had names like Sailor Lane, Admiral Lane, and Commodore Drive. The Garden City area had a theme that used authors' and poets' names, so streets had names such as O'Henry, Poe, Quarles, Nash, and Thurber. Pearson Drive was named after Pearson Builders, who did a lot of development in Brooklyn Center. Paul Drive was named after developer Vern Donnay's son.

The first infrastructure improvements were water and sewer. In 1954, the Park Board and Recreation Commission were established by ordinance. They were later combined, and Gene Hagel was hired as Director of the Parks and Recreation Department. The council met every week and the Planning Commission met every week. Long hours and hard work were the order of the day.[9]

By the early 1960s, racial problems surfaced, when a black family wanted to move into the Palmer Lake area. Many white residents packed the council chambers to protest. Mayor Gordon Erickson advised the city not to make a big fuss over it. About the same time, a black family was not allowed to purchase a home in the Garden City area. However, another black man who worked at the Joslyn Pole Yard bought land in the Twin Lake area, and sold parcels to black families. More information on this can be found in the portion of the book that discusses social issues.[10]

Political power was shifting to an urbanized power structure. Phil Cohen was elected mayor. In 1966, by charter amendment, trustees became known as council members. The rush to develop continued. Interstate highways, and the constant need for platting requirement changes for building and subdivision of land, were often the business of the village staff and council.

In the mid-1960s, a study was done to convert some of the Earle Brown Farm into a tax generating commercial area. This became a major attribute to the city in the form of the present day City Hall, Community Center and Central Park complex, the Target Store area development and adjacent office buildings. During the mid-1970s and into the 1980s many options were considered to utilize the farm buildings. In 1974, there was a "Town Farm" commercial area considered with a live dinner theater, grocery store, hardware store and others businesses. By 1976 a shopping market area with 175-200 small shops in a frontier style motif was being looked at. Much controversy was involved, and the future of the farm at times seemed uncertain. In an attempt to preserve the buildings and grounds of the farm from being commercialized for private purposes, at the urging of the local newspaper editor and the Brooklyn Historical Society, the city council took the action to have the farm listed as a State Historic Site on the State Historical Site Registries. In 1974, through legislative action, the State Legislature designated Brooklyn Farm/Earle Brown Farm a State Historic Site. In 1993 the Legislature reclassified the farm as a State Historic Place).

In 1985 the city HRA (Housing Redevelopment Authority) bought the farm for $2,100,000. In 1988 plans were drawn up for the present day use of the farm as a conference center, with office and meeting space, a bed and breakfast, and a restaurant (which has since closed). The City Council wanted to maximize quality, the Sheehan Brothers (part owners along with Deil Gustafson) wanted to maximize profits. City infrastructure had to be relocated around the farm due to the plan to bring the freeway through the area. With the rapid growth and development came many problems, such as traffic, freeway noise, and congestion. The young bustling community accepted these problems as part of progress. [11]

Brooklyn Center was very proactive in preserving a high quality of life by enacting certain ordinances to keep the city beautiful. One such ordinance is the sign ordinance. It was said that we did not want to become another Lake Street or Central Avenue with billboards obscuring the view and cluttering the freeways and main roadways, so signage was tightly regulated. Around that same time, other ordinances were passed which also protected the integrity of the city. Some examples of this were prohibiting used car dealerships, unless the dealer also had a new car franchise, housing maintenance codes were established, and Minnesota State Aid (MSA) funded sidewalks (no assessed cost to property owners) were created.

Four BC Mayors. Left to right: Arthur Paulson, Gordon Erickson, Phil Cohen, William Gallien

In 1969 Brooklyn Center was a key player in legislation that changed the face of liquor licensing in the state of Minnesota. In 1966 Split Liquor Legislation, that is, municipal off-sale coupled with private on-sale licensing, became an issue. Brooklyn Center Councilman Howard Heck, State Representative Roger Scherer, the Jaycees and the Chamber of Commerce combined forces to bring about legislation that would permit Split Liquor licensing. By 1969 their efforts paid off, and the Split Liquor licensing bill was signed into law. Also, no on-sale liquor establishments were allowed unless food was served (more on this is contained in the Brooklyn Historical Society document entitled "Brooklyn Center's Role in Split Liquor Licensing"). All of this was the result of foresight and planning [12]

In 1966 government organization faced a change, as the village moved into the status of a city. This action actually began in 1959, when the League of Women Voters completed their "Study and Evaluation of Forms of Local Government" report. There were two political factions involved. The League of Women Voters ("Plan B Girls") favored Optional Plan B, the "council-manager" form of village government, and the Citizens for Better Government group favored a city charter. The League supported the distinct separation of policy and administration. Some residents were concerned that certain offices would become appointed positions, not elective, and that the city manager would have too much power. The Village Council was split on the issue. In 1961, the issue was placed on the November ballot, and 2,950 voted "no", while 1,689 voted "yes". The Charter Commission submitted the City Charter issue to the voters November 8, 1966, and it passed. The Village Council membership had changed, and the new council favored city, rather than village status. The City Charter council-manager form of government was approved with the modification that the department heads appointed by the city manager required confirmation by the city council. This structure of government continued until the city charter was amended on November 12, 1996 (effective February 8, 1997) after which the city manager was allowed to appoint department heads without the approval of the City Council.[13]

Karl Schuller, Ernee McArthur, and Rep. Roger Scherer are recognized for their work on the Split Liquor issue by Brooklyn Center Councilman Howard Heck.

In 1968, under the leadership of City Manager Don Poss and Mayor Phil Cohen, a capital improvement bond issue passed with over a 70% approval and the project came in with a "...shining light—on time and under budget." Prior to this, the city's park facilities, village hall, fire stations and public works building all were very inadequate. This bond issue was said to be like a Christmas package sending the city into the future. It was a major thrust into becoming an urbanized community. During this time, the city bought all forfeited properties, and purchased remaining parcels, until it owned all of the Brooklyn Center portions of the Palmer Lake Basin, and turned it into the premier open space it is today. During this time, properties were also acquired on North Twin Lake, as well as the Twin Lake Island and peninsula.[14]

During this era, local officials believed that the northern suburbs were not getting their fair share of funding for roadway improvements. While urban sprawl was officially discouraged by the Metropolitan Council, Poss, Cohen and others thought the southern suburbs were receiving road funding that encouraged sprawl, while northern highway projects were repeatedly delayed.[15]

During the Don Poss years, there was a challenge concerning the Volunteer Fire Department. The main issue was whether to have a full time fire chief hired by the city manager, which Poss wanted, or a part time, elected fire chief, which was what the Department wanted. Control over the appointment was the area of contention. The city was pulled in two different directions. The problem was resolved by rewriting the city charter provisions and the Department elected a new part time fire chief. A decade later, at the department's request the chief became a full time position, with hiring done by the city manager.[16]

Poss left his position as city manager in 1976 to work as first executive director of the Stadium Commission, and 1976 was Phil Cohen's last year as mayor. The focus changed in the 1970s and 1980s, with Dean Nyquist as mayor and Gerald Splinter as city manager. The city was in good fiscal condition and the energy and attention shifted to social issues. Housing for seniors and the Peacemakers/Mediation program were examples of issues on the "front burner" during these years. In 1986, Brooklyn Center was presented the coveted "All America City Award" and was one of only

10 cities to receive this award that year. Mayor Nyquist also had the honor of being invited to a White House Luncheon and a NASA Shuttle landing, during his time as mayor, putting Brooklyn Center in the public eye on a national level.

The annual Prayer Breakfast, initially sponsored by the Jaycees, was again held in Brooklyn Center. This Prayer Breakfast enjoys a long 22-year history with Nyquist as one of its primary organizers. In 1978 Celia Scott was the first female elected to the City Council and served for a total of 16 years. At one point during Nyquist's time as mayor, a group of agnostics appeared at the open forum portion of a council meeting and requested that the practice of invocation be discontinued at city council meetings. He asked them not to come back again, and they didn't. On February 24, 1986, the City Council approved the addition of a nine-hole golf course to the city. Nyquist did not accept a salary during his time as mayor of Brooklyn Center.[17]

Difficult and Challenging Years

The 1990s brought a new decade and a new mayor, Todd Paulson. This was a troubling time for Brooklyn Center. There were concerns about the city's image. Much negative press was being written, and it looked like a downward spiral at times. Much of this was perception rather than reality. There were concerns from citizens about the presence of crime in their neighborhoods, as well as in the commercial areas. Mayor Paulson presented a controversial "State of the City" address. Some of the proposals that were troubling were: combining of departments, freezing of department heads' salaries until changes outlined were completed or until the salary survey was completed, and a moratorium on development and redevelopment for six months. Many people were offended by this. Some other issues at the time were the widening of 69th and connecting it to the Shingle Creek Parkway industrial/commercial area, the council's consideration of banning all advertisement of tobacco products within the city, and the live broadcasting of City Council meetings.[18]

Brooklyn Center, All-America City

Redevelopment Years

The first all-female sweep in a Minnesota City Council election took place in 1994 in Brooklyn Center, with Myrna Kragness as the first woman to be elected as mayor of the city. An all-female council was big news statewide. Early in her term, the decision to reconstruct Humboldt Avenue was made, after an 18-month battle rehashing the various demands of citizens in the project area. An attack on blighted apartments was begun in an effort to "stay ahead of urban blight". The council had difficulty operating, in part due to the frequent unexcused absence of Council member Barb Kalligher. Kalligher eventually resigned in December 1995, due to personal issues, and a special election was held in March of 1996, in which the "all female council" ended, as Charles Nichols won the seat. Once again, Brooklyn Center had a gender mixed as well as racially mixed council.

The 1995 resignation of long time City Manager Jerry Splinter, and the hiring of his replacement, presented a challenge to the council. After much interviewing and processing, Michael McCauley, a man who had

All-woman Council. Left to right: Barb Kalligher, Debra Hilstrom, Mayor Myrna Kragness, Kristen Mann, Kathleen Carmody

spent his boyhood years in the area, was hired as City Manager. The next few months were alive with politics. Between the Primary and General elections, the invocation issue came to the forefront. The Council decided by a 4-to-1 vote to discontinue the practice of invocation at Council meetings, and in its place had a "Moment of Silence." Mayor Kragness was the only one who voted to retain invocation. This was a very controversial move on the Council's part. Although he placed first in the Primary, Charles Nichols finished third in the General Election, with Kay Lasman finishing first and Robert Peppe coming in second. After the election, the new Council reinstated invocation as a part of the order of business, but the invocation is delivered prior to calling the business meeting to order, and its content is defined by Resolution 98-28 adopted February 9, 1998. Additional information is available in the Brooklyn Historical Society's file on the invocation issue.[19]

Brooklyn Center Staff, 2000
Left to right: Patty Hartwig, Brad
Hoffman, Diane Spector, Jim Glasoe,
Michael McCauley, Charlie Hansen.

The present council, Mayor Myrna Kragness, Council members Debra Hilstrom, Kay Lasman, Robert Peppe and Ed Nelson, have worked well together, putting personal agendas aside, to move forward toward a better tomorrow for Brooklyn Center, as we enter the new century and new millennium. Some of the key programs this council has dealt with are: the code enforcement program, the street and sewer improvement program (twenty-five-year program to add new curb, gutter and sewer (where needed) to all neighborhoods in the city), and the 53rd Avenue project (for which the city won an Honorable Mention Award for housing redevelopment, at the League of Minnesota Cities Conference in 1999).

Brooklyn Center has a bright future ahead as plans move ahead on widening and beautifying Brooklyn Boulevard, redevelopment and renovation of Brookdale, reclaiming the use of the Joslyn Pole Yard area with a new industrial/commercial area, Highway 100 improvement and reconstruction, as well as the redevelopment project (Cub Foods) at Bass Lake Road and Brooklyn Boulevard.

Brooklyn Center, officially designated a Millennium Community, is very much a key player in the metro area's tomorrow. As a strong inner ring suburb, with the trend becoming popular to get rid of the commute—in other words move in, not out—one could say we are on the cutting edge of a new tomorrow![20]

Brooklyn Center City Council, 2000
Left to right: Robert Peppe, Kay
Lasman, Mayor Myrna Kragness,
Debra Hilstrom, Ed Nelson

Notes

1. Mary Jane Gustafson, "In 75 Years," *Brooklyn Center Post*, 2 June 1986.

2. Ibid; *Brooklyn Center Post*, July 16, 1981; History Presentation of Brooklyn Center Police-2-15-83, BHS; "Brooklyn Center, Minnesota–50 Years of Progress," 1911-1961, BHS; Mary Jane Gustafson, *History of Brooklyn Center*, 1971, BHS.

3. Article on prices of produce, *Brooklyn Center Post*, 16 June 1977; Article on streets, *Brooklyn Center Post*, 16 July 1981; Art Lee, telephone interview by Ernee McArthur, 25 February 1999 BHS; Don Poss, videotape interview, by Ernee McArthur, tape 1, 12 September 1998, tape 2 14 October 1998, BHS; Philip Cohen, videotape interview, by Eileen Oslund, 20 February 1999, BHS; Marge Dupont, videotape interview, Ernee McArthur and Kay Lasman, 14 July 1999, BHS.

4. Ibid; Myrna Kragness, Video taped interview, by Bill Schrieber, 21 March 1999, BHS; Brooklyn Center City Ordinance 1, Abatement of Nuisance; Brooklyn Center City Ordinance 4, Regulating plowing and defacing highways.

5. Brooklyn Center City Ordinance 21, Traffic Laws; Brooklyn Center City Ordinance 24, Ordinance relative to misdemeanors, breach of peace, and disorderly conduct.

6. Brooklyn Center City Ordinance 27, Providing for civilian defense, etc, during war emergencies; Brooklyn Center City Ordinance 28, Ordinance relating to air raid precautions.

7. Brooklyn Center City Ordinance from 1947; Tony Kuefler, article, "Brooklyn Center's Role in Split Liquor Licensing," BHS.

8. "Brooklyn Center, Minnesota— 50 Years of Progress"; Mary Jane Gustafson, "In 75 Years"; Art Lee, telephone interview.

9. "Brooklyn Center, Minnesota— 50 Years of Progress"; Article on streets; Art Lee, telephone interview; Conversation with Philip Cohen, Kay Lasman November 18,1999, BHS.

10. Art Lee, telephone interview.

11. Conversation with Philip Cohen, BHS; Don Poss, videotape interview; Minnesota Statutes, Chapter 138.664, Subdivision 11; "Earle Brown Farm Town plan will incorporate old barns, buildings," *Brooklyn Center Post,* 6 June 1974; "Earle Brown Farm may be going, going," *Minneapolis Star-Tribune,* 21 May 1981; "HRA buys historic Earle Brown Farm," *Brooklyn Center Post*, 25 July 1985; "Earle Brown Farm: A New Chapter in History," *Brooklyn Center Post,* 13 May 1988.

12. Don Poss, videotape interview; Conversation with Philip Cohen; Tony Kuefler.

13. Don Poss, videotape interview; Philip Cohen, videotape interview; Brooklyn Center City Council minutes for 12 November 1996: Amendment of Ordinance 96-16 (department head appointments).

14. Don Poss, videotape interview; Philip Cohen, videotape interview; Conversation with Philip Cohen; History of Brooklyn Center, BHS.

15. Don Poss, videotape interview;

16. Ibid; Philip Cohen, videotape interview; Conversation with Philip Cohen.

17. Ibid; Dean Nyquist, videotape interview, by Eileen Oslund, 7 April 1999, BHS; City Council Resolution 86-30 and 86-31: Approval of plan for 9-hole golf course.

18. "Council considers ban on tobacco advertising," *NorthWest News*, 6 December 1993; "Cops: Partners take a proactive approach to crime," *Brooklyn Center Post*, 29 December 1993; "Watchful suburbs giving themselves a night out," *Minneapolis Star and Tribune,* August 1993; "Looking for trouble," *Brooklyn Center Post*, 29 December 1993; "Marketer hired to promote city," *Brooklyn Center Post*, 21 April 1993; "Council to meet in closed session", *Brooklyn Center Post,* 9 November 1994; Philip Cohen's reply to the "State of the City Address".

19. Brooklyn Center City Ordinance 21; "Marketer hired"; "Women will be at the helm", *Minneapolis Star and Tribune,* 17 December 1994; "Humboldt Avenue will be rebuilt in 1995", *Northwest News*, 5 December 1994; "The walls will crumble on Willow Lane," *Northwest News*, 29 August 1994; "Barb Kalligher resigns from City Council, *Brooklyn Center Post*, 20 December 1995; "Interim manager selected," *Brooklyn Center Post*, 2 June 1995; "Council members seek Splinter's ouster," *Brooklyn Center Post*, 17 May 1995; "City Council says 'amen' to invocation", *Brooklyn Center Post*, 4 September 1996; "Council refused to reconsider invocation," *Brooklyn Center Post*, 16 October 1996; City Council meeting minutes, 26 August 1996-resolution 96-162; "Peppe/Lasman win Brooklyn Center Council seats," *Brooklyn Center Post*, 13 November 1996; Conversation with Michael McCauley with Kay Lasman, November 1999, BHS.

20. "Cops: Partners take...."; 1999 Brooklyn Center City Council Goals; "City gets tougher with codes," *Brooklyn Center Post*, 7 May 1997; " Discovering Brooklyn Center good news," Brooklyn Center Post, 13 August 1997; "Work begins this November on Shingle Creek Pond project," 1 January 1997. Documents acknowledging Brooklyn Center as a Millennium Community, Mayor Kragness, Philip Cohen.

Brooklyn Park Government

THE FIRST MEETING of the Brooklyn Park Village Council was May 5, 1954. The village operated under the standard form of government established by the State Legislature. It consisted of a Mayor, a Clerk and three Trustees who each had one vote. The first Mayor was Baldwin (Baldy) Hartkopf, the three Trustees were Abraham C. Zimmerman, Donald Anderson and Hilmer Guntzel, and the Clerk was Al Joyner. Also elected was R. L. Krienke as Assessor. The official population of the new village was 3,868. The total property valuation was $5.8 million.[1]

The mayor's first action was the appointment of a cleanup committee composed of Roy Krienke, Don Anderson and himself to paint the Village Hall and "not to spend more than $25 for paint." Other council actions were of a more serious nature. The following appointments were made in the first month: George Hedlund, attorney; Russ Stetler, building inspector; Lyle Jenkins, marshall, and Harry Robertson, deputy police officer. In June and July a zoning ordinance was adopted, the mayor and clerk salaries were set at $40 a month and trustees at $30. An 18-member planning commission was established. In September, Keith Caswell was hired as village engineer, and the 1955 budget was set at $22,000.

The first village election was held on December 7, 1954, with 151 votes cast. Those re-elected were Hilmer C. Guntzel, Trustee, Al Joyner, Clerk, and R.L. Krienke, Assessor. Harry Robertson was elected Constable, and Frend Hamilton was elected Justice of the Peace.[2]

The little one room Town Hall at 7640 Osseo Road became the Village Hall. It stood where Town Square now is on Brooklyn Boulevard. The wood frame building quickly proved too small to serve the growing Village. On August 3, 1961, the Village Council accepted a bid for the purchase of the building and land from the Skelly Oil Company for $35,000.

Having served on the township board, Mayor Hartkopf and Abe Zimmerman provided a smooth governing transition. Farms began disappearing along the border with Brooklyn Center and Crystal, and the fields were producing a crop of new homes mostly purchased by World War II veterans and financed with four percent loans backed by the Federal Government. This meant endless meetings of village staff with land brokers, real estate agents, housing developers and contractors. Council meetings frequently included plat approvals for housing projects.[3]

Rapid development meant that the Council was hard pressed to plan and construct services to meet the needs of the many new residents. The population mushroomed by 1960 to 10,197. Modern police and fire departments, a planning commission, and public works and recreation and park departments were needed. Consultants were retained to plan and design streets, water systems, and sanitary and storm sewers.

Brooklyn Park was slow in developing, compared to many other second ring suburbs. The farmland was productive and farmers could make a living while they waited for development to reach them. Also, the high water table made irrigation for farming inexpensive, but installing utilities for new homes expensive. Developers found cheaper buildable land in other suburbs. When land prices elsewhere increased, the village slowly became more attractive, making it feasible for developers to recoup the higher cost of utilities.[4]

In the early years, the village was completely dependent on "ad valorem" taxes

Baldwin "Baldy" Hartkopf, first Mayor of Brooklyn Park, 1954 to 1957

(property taxes levied across the entire community) to fund its services. In 1959 the State Legislature passed the Municipal State Aid Act to provide funds for maintenance and upgrading of collector streets that connected to Federal, State or County designated roads. Brooklyn Park designated its first streets to receive State Aid designation on November 3, 1960. But the village soon learned that as Federal and State funded programs increased in number, the ability of the Council to chart its own destiny would gradually diminish.[5]

The village did not have a water system or sanitary and storm sewer systems. Houses in the early subdivisions, such as the large Orrin Thompson subdivision in the southwest corner of the village, had their own wells and septic systems. Storm water in these subdivisions drained into ditches along the village streets and county and state highways, and from there into Shingle Creek, wetlands or the Mississippi River. The Federal Housing Administration stepped up their requirements for community water and sewage systems. The Village Council realized it must soon develop central storm and sanitary sewers and water systems.

The residential area along and adjacent to the West River Road was rapidly growing by the late 1950s, along with pressure to serve that area with utilities. Storm sewer projects are always the bane of local governments. Residents on high ground see no need for storm sewers and do not want to pay for them. Residents living in low areas demand that sewers be installed to prevent flooding of their property. Public improvement hearings on storm sewer projects attracted a large turnout of affected citizens. These contacts with "city hall" caused some homeowners to get involved in local government. Art Kvamme and his wife moved to Brooklyn Park in 1956. Art became involved in local politics because of the storm sewer issue, ran for a seat on the council in 1960, and won. In 1961 Art ran unopposed for mayor. Wilbur Goetze, who was serving on the planning commission at the time, was appointed to serve out Art's remaining two years as trustee.[6]

The Village Council approved two major improvement projects in 1961 and 1962 that would divide the community and become burning issues in future local political campaigns. The first was the Shingle Creek Storm Drainage Project. The second, more divisive issue was the establishment of the North Suburban Sanitary Sewer District (NSSSD) and the accompanying Sanitary Sewer System that was to serve the area south of 85th Avenue.

The high water table in the Village was a hindrance to development. Some of the land had standing water after the spring thaw because there were many areas of peat that overlaid the generally sandy subsoil. The proposed solution was to lower Shingle Creek through Brooklyn Center and Brooklyn Park, allowing more ground water to drain into it. The water table could be lowered further by constructing a storm sewer system draining into the Creek. Lowering the level of Shingle Creek became an issue between the two Brooklyns, and the first meeting of the two Villages to discuss it was held in 1957. Brooklyn Center paid a consultant to study the effect of lowering the Creek. The study inferred that if the Creek were lowered, the water level on Twin Lake also would be lowered, so Brooklyn Center balked at the proposed dredging.[7]

Storm sewers were built in Brooklyn Park but their outlets into Shingle Creek were buried and plugged. The FHA delayed the financing of additional housing projects in both communities until this problem was resolved. A new study was made by the Brooklyn Center consultant. The result was that the Creek could be lowered somewhat without affecting Twin Lake.[8]

Arthur E. Kvamme, Mayor of Brooklyn Park, 1962-1963

A hearing was held on January 5, 1961, by the Brooklyn Park Village Council on the first storm sewer project in the village and the deepening and straightening of Shingle Creek. The dredging would increase its capacity, drain nearby wet areas, and use dredged material to raise the elevation of adjacent land, increasing its value. Most of the affected growers and many homeowners opposed the project, and there were a number of settlement claims negotiated between landowners and the village. Much of the subsequent development of Brooklyn Park would have been drastically limited if it had occurred during the current age of wetland protection laws.[9]

A sanitary sewer system was also on the minds of the Village Council. The Minnesota Health Department became concerned with the pollution of private wells by septic systems. The sewage also contaminated individual shallow wells. Brooklyn Center was adjacent to Minneapolis and connected to the Minneapolis-Saint Paul Sanitary District (MSSD). Brooklyn Center and other first ring suburbs of the Twin Cities entered into a contract with the MSSD for sewage service. The Brooklyn Park Council met with officials of the MSSD on October 20, 1960, to explore the possibility of connecting to MSSD. The MSSD was not interested in allowing a connection because their interceptor system was not sized large enough to accept sewage from second ring northern suburbs. The sewer district, by its power to decide where and when it would extend sewer service, could decide the timing of development in the Metropolitan area.[10]

Communities across the Mississippi River from Brooklyn Park were in the same stage of development. They also realized that they would eventually need sanitary sewer systems. They too were rebuffed by the MSSD. In 1959 the first meeting was held between elected officials from Brooklyn Park, Fridley, Coon Rapids, Blaine, Mounds View and Spring Lake Park to discuss the possibility of creating a sanitary sewer district that would serve all six villages. The proposed sewer district would come to be known as the North Suburban Sanitary Sewer District (NSSSD).[11]

The Brooklyn Park Council held a public discussion on the proposed creation of the NSSSD on February 24, 1961. An NSSSD study committee was formed, with representatives from each of the six municipalities, and its first meeting was held on May 19, 1961. City Clerk Al Joyner was an early proponent of the NSSSD and represented Brooklyn Park.[12]

The next step was to get an enabling act through the State Legislature. The Minneapolis and St. Paul legislative delegations actively opposed the bill. The DFL party in the Twin Cities also opposed formation of the NSSSD. However, DFL Governor Rolvaag supported the NSSSD. The six municipalities, with the help of their legislative delegations, gained the support of out-state lawmakers. The bill creating the Act was passed by the 1961 Legislature and signed by newly elected Governor Anderson. [13]

The goal of the new district was to construct a primary trunk sewer system and connect to a MSSD interceptor in northeast Minneapolis. Each village would construct their own sanitary sewer system connecting to the NSSSD system. The NSSSD district would fund its system by user fees from the six member communities. A trunk line, sized large enough to serve all of the future needs of Brooklyn Park, would be constructed in the village to a pumping station near the Mississippi River. Then a pipe would be built under the river, connecting to the NSSSD primary trunk system in Fridley. The pipe under the river would be installed, paid for and owned by the NSSSD.[14]

It would take some time before the NSSSD system was in place and ready to accept sewage from the six sponsoring communities. The village needed immediate relief or development would be held up indefinitely. So, in 1961, Caswell, the Village engineer, was asked to determine if the Brooklyn Center sanitary sewer system had any unused capacity that Brooklyn Park could use. Brooklyn Center's system was in place up to its border with Brooklyn Park. Caswell's review of Brooklyn Center's design data indicated that there was excess capacity in their trunk system. Don Poss, Brooklyn Center City Engineer, was approached and he made an independent calculation of the sewer capacity that concurred with Caswell's.

The first negotiation between the two village officials took place on September 21, 1961, and an agreement was signed the following month. Brooklyn Park could now go ahead with the construction of their sanitary sewer system. The sewage would be pumped into the Brooklyn Center system on a temporary basis. The sewage cost to Brooklyn Park's residents would be at the same rate as Brooklyn Center was charged by the MSSD, plus a small fee to cover Brooklyn Park's administrative cost.[15]

A public informational meeting was held on January 5, 1962, to inform residents about the first phase of a village sanitary sewer system, designed to serve the village south of 85th Avenue. The total cost for the trunk and lateral pipes, plus a hook-up charge for an average lot, would be $950. The financing plan called for the developed land to start paying on its assessment immediately. The assessment against the vacant land was to be deferred until it was developed. The Village Council voted unanimously to proceed with the sewer project.[17]

A consultant was hired by the village to formulate a prospectus for a bond issue to pay for the village sewer system. The bond issue, at $ 4,151,233, was at the time the largest municipal issue in the history of Minnesota. The sale was successful and the bonds were sold on June 5, 1962, at an average rate of 3.82 per cent, payable over a 20-year period. The bond consultant told the Council that the low interest rate on the bonds meant that the assessments levied would produce a surplus in the bond account. He claimed this surplus would be a hedge if the planned rate of future hook ups did not meet expectations.[18]

The Contentious Years

Opposition to the NSSSD grew in Brooklyn Park. Charges began circulating in the village that the trunk sewer was over designed by Caswell Engineering, resulting in a much higher cost than was needed to meet Brooklyn Park's future needs. There was a proliferation of privately published newsletters in which unsubstantiated denunciations and charges were made.[19]

The landholders decided to protect their interests. In 1962 the farmers in Brooklyn Park were invited to a meeting to discuss how the NSSSD and the bond payments on the village sanitary sewer system would affect their livelihood. The bonds were to be paid off in twenty years but those present believed that the south half of the village would not be fully developed by then. To make the payments, the village would be forced to start assessing the undeveloped land. The farmers would be forced off their land. They formed the "Brooklyn Park Landowners Association" to oppose the inclusion of the city in the NSSSD. Eldon Tessman was elected secretary. Bill Schreiber, only twenty-one years old at the time, was selected to serve on the committee.[20]

In 1962, Flora Rogge, a schoolteacher, was elected to the council and replaced John Tierney. Al Joyner lost his re-election bid for a fourth term as village clerk to Gail Bakken. Gail was the community affairs reporter for the *Brooklyn Park Post* and was well-known in the village. Rogge and Bakken were opposed to the NSSSD and were highly critical of Caswell's design of the sewer and the way the bond issue was handled. Wilbur Goetze, who voted in 1962 in favor of joining the NSSSD and for the bond issue, changed his position. The power on the Council in 1963 now shifted away from support for NSSSD, and open criticism of the financing of the sanitary sewer system came to the fore.[21]

John Wingard, a former farmer and Justice of the Peace in Brooklyn Center, was a member of the State Legislature. He was asked to sponsor a bill to allow Brooklyn Park to withdraw from the NSSSD. John was successful in getting the bill passed. The village council, by a three-to-two vote, withdrew from the NSSSD in March 1963. The NSSSD system design, without provision for sewage from Brooklyn Park, was approved by the Minnesota Water Pollution Control Commission in December 1963. A federal grant was received by the district to assist in paying for the construction of the system. Brooklyn Park now found itself as the only developing northern suburb without a permanent sanitary sewer outlet.[22]

The council did not renew Caswell Engineering's contract in 1963. Flora Rogge and Gail Bakken were not happy with Keith Caswell and his engineering firm because of his support for the NSSSD and his design of the village sanitary sewer system. Wilbur Goetze joined them in the vote. Kvamme and LaRose voted against the motion. Cal Brown was hired as the first full time Village Engineer.[23]

Mayor Kvamme was opposed by Trustee Flora Rogge in the hotly contested 1963 election. Her campaign criticized the design of the trunk sewer. Rogge supported a full time Village Engineer and wanted the zoning map updated. Both she and George Samardich, who ran for Trustee and supported Rogge, won in a landslide.[24] Mayor Rogge's council seat was vacated by her election as mayor. Supporters of Ray Skinner, who was defeated by Samardich, presented a petition with over 1,000 signatures requesting he be appointed trustee, but the council selected Lawrence Kochevar.[25]

Differences among the council members soon surfaced in council appointments, styles of conducting council meetings and the continued rehashing of the sanitary trunk sewer and its design. Accusations among the council members at the council meetings became commonplace over NSSSD, the sanitary sewer and other issues.[26]

It became evident that the sanitary sewer hook-up rate was not occurring as planned. Funds collected from assessment payments were not sufficient to meet the bond payments. In March 1964, the council agenda included a resolution increasing the special assessment levy to repay the sanitary sewer bonds sold in 1962. Curt Pearson, the Village Attorney, explained that the construction cost exceeded funds in the bond issue by $350,000. Village Clerk Gail Bakken stated that the additional cost was caused by the addition of the 60-inch trunk sewer, extending north near the West River Road to 87th Avenue to serve the village north of 85th Avenue when that area started to develop. The council voted to increase the general levy to pay the additional cost. Keith Caswell, in a recent interview, contends that the 60-inch sewer was included in the original bid package. He also stated that the low bid was under the estimated cost. He also said he was taken off the project while it was under construction and was not responsible for the final cost.[27]

In 1964, the Council retained the engineering consulting firm of Orr, Schelen, Mayeron to review the design of the sanitary sewer system. The consultants prefaced their August 1964 report by stating that they were constrained by a tight time limit. Based on the report the council voted to sue Caswell's firm for $500,000.[28]

Flora Rogge, Mayor, 1964-1965; Trustee, 1963

Caswell defended his design in a letter to the *Brooklyn Park Sentinel*, saying that he sized the pipe to include future sewage from Maple Grove and Champlin. The Village Council and the State regulatory agencies approved the decision. The Minnesota Department of Health called the sizing for other municipalities an example of good planning. He noted that the other engineering consultant considered only Brooklyn Park in its design, which resulted in a smaller pipe. Former mayor Kvamme wrote a letter in the *Sentinel* in defense of the Caswell design. He said that most trunk sewers are over designed to accommodate future growth. Art noted that because Brooklyn Center's trunk was over designed Brooklyn Park was able to use the excess capacity.[29]

The council retained Black and Veatch Consulting Engineers to review solutions to the sewage disposal problem. They determined that the extra Brooklyn Center trunk sewer capacity would be used by 1975. The hoped for connection to the MSSD was rejected because of the high cost of extending a trunk sewer into north Minneapolis. The engineers recommended that joining the NSSSD would be the most feasible alternative, but the council made no move to adopt the recommendation.[30]

Brooklyn Park, in the late 1950s and early 1960s, was a hodgepodge of residential neighborhoods in the southern half of the village. Homeowners in these new neighborhoods soon became aware that the young village was experiencing problems during its rapid growth. In order to seek redress and protect their interests, the new residents formed neighborhood associations and became involved in local issues and elections. The Brooklyn Park Landowners Association (1962), the North Towne-Lynbrook Association (1965), the Brookdale Estates Civic Association (1963), and the Brooklyn Park Taxpayers Club Inc. (1965), were the most successful organizations. Richard J. Myshak was the first president of the Brookdale Estates Civic Association. Ron Dow was the first president of the North Towne-Lynbrook Association.[31]

Edward Shimek, Mayor of Brooklyn Park, 1959-1961; Trustee, 1957-1959

Edward Shimek served the city in three roles during this period. He was elected to the Council in 1956 and served two and one half years. Ed was appointed Mayor by the Council in 1959 to fill out the unexpired term of Theodore Miksza, was re-elected to a two-year term, and did not run for a third term. He was Mayor when construction started on the sewer and was opposed to the NSSSD. Ed was appointed administrative assistant in 1963, and manager when the village voted for a Council-Manager form of government. The village voted for a Home Rule Charter government in 1969 and Ed was appointed City Manager. He served in that capacity until 1971.[32]

Some of the developers of the early large housing subdivisions installed their own water systems. The village required the system to be maintained until a certain number of houses were sold, and then be turned over to the village. In March 1962, Keith Caswell proposed Phase 1 of a village water system, including a one-million-gallon storage tank.. Phase 1 was in place and operating by the end of 1963. The council required that all new homes be connected to city water if available. Existing homes were required to connect if a well required re-drilling. Phase 1 served only a small area of the village, so development was stymied because village water had to be available before new subdivisions could be approved. To get development back on track, a master water distribution plan was authorized in 1965.[33]

The village had rented the old Benson School, located at 73rd Avenue and West River Road, for $75 a month, with a right to purchase. The staff overcrowded the building, so the council voted to build a new village hall on city-owned land at 85th and Zane Avenues North. On December 6, 1966, the voters approved bonding to build a new village hall, after rejecting three previous construction bond issues.

Miles Coleman, Mayor, 1966-1967

The village had established a municipal liquor store in 1954, but it was not profitable until 1963. The council decided to get out of the liquor business and issue licenses to private operators. In November 1964 the voters confirmed the council's position, and the municipal liquor store closed.

The December 1964 village election was an endorsement of Mayor Rogge's programs and a victory for the candidates who supported the programs.[34]

A problem with the administrative line of authority suddenly broke onto the scene and became an embarrassment for the village. In January 1965, a petition signed by over 1,000 registered voters, requesting the establishment of a charter commission, was presented to the Village Council. In May, the District Court appointed a 15-member Charter Commission, which recommended that the voters approve a changeover to the Plan B "Council/Manager" form of government. The voters approved the change in a special election on September 13, 1966. This transferred the council's day-to-day management responsibilities to a manager appointed by the council.[35]

The sanitary sewer and the NSSSD issue continued to dominate the political scene in the village. Charges made by a local public official about the issue caused a Hennepin County grand jury to investigate the allegations in 1965. The Grand Jury found "that the records and accounts of Brooklyn Park are very detailed and complete. According to these records and our interrogations, all expenditures appear to be made in compliance with the law."[36]

The 1965 election reflected a change in how the voters viewed the activities of the Council. The voters were starting to tire of the sanitary trunk sewer, NSSSD and Caswell issue. Miles Coleman defeated Mayor Rogge in a close race.[37]

The 1966 election brought about another step in the realignment of the Council. Paul LaRose and Bob Kottke were elected. Former Clerk Gail Bakken came in third and Flora Rogge was fourth out of a field of ten candidates.[38]

An emerging issue was the increasing assessed value on the farmland as housing development approached. The Brooklyn Park Landowners Association asked their State Representative, John Wingard, to carry a bill for them in the Legislature that would keep the increasing land values in check until the growers were ready to sell. The Legislature passed the "Green Acres" law in 1967. The land would be classified as agricultural for tax purposes as long as the owner cultivated it as his primary source of income. No special assessments could be levied against the land until it was sold for development, and taxes were paid on the gain in value for the previous three years when the land was developed. The law is still in effect.[39]

The village accepted a gift of parkland donated by Baldy Hartkopf, the first Mayor of Brooklyn Park, and named it Hartkopf Park. Baldy promoted a policy requiring developers to donate some land for park purposes. The Village required five percent of development land to be deeded to the village for parks (later changed to 10%). The zoning ordinance was changed again to require land for pathways where designated. A Park Department was established by the Village Council in May 1964. Dennis Palm was hired by the City in 1965 as director of the Recreation and Parks Department, and voters approved a $600,000 bond issue in a special election on September 7, 1967. Additional land was purchased and development of the parks began.[40]

In 1967 Bjorn Rossing was elected Mayor and William "Bill" Schreiber was the newly elected member on the Council.[41]

A headline in the October 12, 1967, issue of the *Brooklyn Park Post Sentinel* stated, "Village Lawsuit is Settled." The settlement involved complete settlement of the lawsuit and all issues were settled "once and for all." Settlement came after Charles Hvass, the trial attorney hired earlier by the village, strongly recommended that the village accept settlement rather than go to court. Well-intentioned people were divided and it is obvious that both camps were honest in the stands they took.

A Coming Together of the Community and Government

James Krautkremer replaced Lloyd Belford on the Council in 1971. Krautkremer was elected Mayor in 1972 and served in that office for eighteen years. Brooklyn Park experienced twenty-three years of steady growth and continuity in philosophy under the leadership of Rossing and Krautkremer.

A group of citizens thought the village had developed to a point where it should be governed by a more sophisticated "Home Rule" form of government. The voters approved the charter in an election in September 1969. The population in 1970 was 26,230. The new City was divided into three voting districts called East, Central and West. Bjorn Rossing was the village mayor when the City Charter was approved. He served two years as city mayor and retired.[43]

Bjorn Rossing, Mayor, 1968-1972
Tom Ewer Photography

In 1968 the city applied to the Metropolitan Council for funding to develop a "701" comprehensive plan for the community. The plan was completed and adopted by the city in 1971. [44] The salient feature of the 701 plan was called "staged development." The first geographical limit for development was 85th Avenue. "Staged development" had evolved beginning in 1962. The storm sewer work and dredging of Shingle Creek at that time improved drainage south of 85th Avenue. The sanitary sewer trunk system also was designed to serve the area south of 85th Avenue. The Village Council had adopted a policy of allowing development to occur only where storm and sanitary sewer service were available. Limiting growth to the southern half of the village also was an economic necessity. Village finances were stretched thin in the 1960s and early 1970s because utility hook-up fees were used to make the sewer bond payments. So growth was directed to where hookups were possible. The 701 plan called for this limit to remain until all of the land south of 85th Avenue was platted and development was under way. When that point was reached, the 701 plan was amended to allow developments north of 85th Avenue.[45]

The Legislature established the Metropolitan Council in 1967 to act as a coordinating agency in the seven county metropolitan area. The Metropolitan Council now requires all comprehensive plans to include the "staged development" concept.[46]

The 1969 Legislature established the Metropolitan Sewer Board. The new Board was charged with managing all of the metro area's sewage treatment plants. The NSSSD was abolished and the city's sewer trunk system was purchased by the new commission for $1,081,847. The Commission paid for it by issuing credits to the Village to be applied against future sewage fees.[47]

The council was concerned about Champlin Township developing land without municipal utilities, and considered it a threat to the Brooklyn Park staged development policy. Brooklyn Park petitioned the State Municipal Board to annex the township. The Village of Champlin became aware of the petition and quickly submitted its own annexation petition. The Board ruled in favor of Champlin.[49]

James Krautkremer, Mayor, 1973-1990; Trustee, 1971-1972

Much of the area in the eastern portion of the City was developed before sewer and water were available. City staff recommended that the roads and utilities should be installed as soon as possible in this area and designed to fit the anticipated development of the open land to the west. It was a very difficult plan to sell. But the utilities

1979 Brooklyn Park City Council. Standing (L-R): Wesley Long, City Clerk; Neil Johnson, Director of Public Works; Ron Dow, East District; Delos Webster, Central District; Curtis Pearson, City Attorney. Seated (L-R): Gerald Marshall, East District; E. Jack Umland, Central District; Jim Krautkremer, Mayor; R. M. Henneberger, City Manager; Rick Engh, West District. Absent: Clarence Small, East District.

and streets were installed and the affected residents started to pay their share in installments. Years later many residents told Ron Dow, representing the East District, they were thankful the Council went ahead with the project because the cost of construction in later years would have been much higher.[50]

Brooklyn Park was concerned about the shortage of north-south access routes from the City to I-694 and wanted a Xerxes Avenue access to I-694. The Brooklyn Center Comprehensive Plan, adopted in 1965, did show an interchange there. However, the Brooklyn Center staff realized if Xerxes Avenue was extended into Brooklyn Center there would be a major intrusion in the residential neighborhood west of Palmer Lake and it would destroy much of the Palmer Lake wetlands. The Brooklyn Center Conservation Commission strongly objected to the Xerxes extension and the council went on record in opposition. In the end, I-694 did not include a Xerxes Avenue interchange. The Metropolitan Council presently requires that such issues between communities be referred to them for resolution.[51]

The 1970s ushered in the era of federal and state funded programs that restricted the autonomy of municipalities. As aid from the State and Federal Government grew the lobbying by the cities became more sophisticated. By 1999, local governments in the state spent $1,172,494, protecting their interests and seeking more aid.[52]

Brooklyn Park was the fastest growing municipality in Hennepin County in the 1970s. This fast growth outpaced the city's ability to finance needed services such as police, fire, water, sewers, health services, park programs and street maintenance. The State Legislature passed a levy limitation law in 1972, limiting yearly property tax increases to six per cent per capita.[53]

A bond issue was proposed in 1981 to acquire 100 acres for park purposes, develop 600 acres of existing parkland and construction of phase one of a community activities center in Central Park. The Federal Open-Space Program would provide matching funds for land acquisition. The park bond issue passed in a special election.[54]

The 701 comprehensive plan provided for an extensive industrial park near Boone Avenue. The City took the first step in 1966 to ensure that MnDOT included a bridge for Boone Avenue in the design of I-694. They were successful in their effort, but the City had to pay for it. Mayor Krautkremer wrote the following: "I worked for over twelve years to get approval for the Boone Avenue interchange. Initially the Metropolitan Council turned down the request, but reversed their position when we showed them that their policy of having interchanges one mile apart did not work since over

85% did not meet this criteria and more than 50% were closer than the Boone Avenue site. I then worked with the MnDOT Commissioners to get financing. Four different MnDOT Commissioners told me 'no problem,' but nothing happened. Finally Commissioner Dick Braun said 'no,' and when asked what was needed to get approval, he outlined the needs. We met those needs and finally received approval. The interchange was built with Tax Increment Funds, using only local funding." The City paid to remove the existing bridge and construct the new one.[55]

The apartment boom, starting in the late 1960s, was a financial godsend for the City but it eventually turned into a major headache. Apartments were taxed at a much higher rate than single family houses and many more could be constructed per acre, so the city readily approved applications for multi-family housing projects, which generated significant sewer hookup and property tax revenues.

Century Courts on Brooklyn Boulevard was constructed in 1967 and phase 2 was constructed in 1970. The complex consists of one and two bedroom apartments. The city council placed restrictions on them in order to ensure quality construction and prevent property values from decreasing. Within a period of four years, all of the many apartment complexes in the City were built.

The Congress passed laws shortly after the apartment boom to provide affordable housing for low- income families. The Department of Housing and Urban Development (HUD) established guidelines that abolished the City restrictions.[56]

The first phase of the Century Courts deteriorated to a point where it had as little as 50% occupancy by 1997. The property was sold to the Dominion Group and renamed Huntington Pointe. Dominion was serious in its plan to upgrade the complex but they faced a daunting task. In the end, Dominion obtained the financing to rehabilitate the buildings without EDA participation.[57]

"Problem tenants" was another issue the apartment owners had to grapple with. Mayor Krautkremer initiated a program in 1990 whereby the city staff brought the apartment managers together. The "Property Managers Coalition" developed a program in which they shared information on troublesome tenants. The program was a success and most managers participated.[58]

About 1973 the City Council awarded a contract to Black and Veatch, a renowned national engineering consulting firm, to prepare a study of the city's water distribution system and recommend the most feasible source of supply. The consultants recommended that the city draw its water from the Mississippi River and construct a treatment plant on the river. Later estimates indicated the future population for the city as less than the earlier estimates, making the treatment plant not feasible.[59]

The Minnesota Department of Transportation (MnDOT), decided to design and construct the long awaited Trunk Highway 252, and it opened in 1986.[60]

The first mention of TH 610 was in a November 30, 1966, article in the *Brooklyn Park Sentinel*. The MnDOT long range plan called for a bridge across the Mississippi River in Brooklyn Park. The city council became concerned with MnDOT delays in funding the North Crosstown Highway and the included bridge. Councilman Ron Dow proposed a publicity stunt that he hoped would bring attention to the need for the bridge. "I wrote a tongue-in-cheek memo to the city council encouraging the preparation of a feasibility study concerning costs of teardown, transportation, rebuilding, toll charges and other methods of financing and a schedule of events to purchase the Brooklyn Bridge from the city of New York. Brooklyn Park/Brooklyn Bridge sounded good to me. A known worldwide historical structure in a city that needs a bridge! The council agreed and Mayor Bjorn Rossing wrote a letter to Mayor John Lindsay of New York. The press picked it up and we were in the news around the world. A bumper sticker was printed, 'BUY THE BRIDGE OR MOVE THE RIVER'. We publicized our problem and we had fun in the process."

It was not until 1986 that the city and the other cities in the north corridor finally realized their goal of a bridge across the river as the first phase of the North Crosstown Highway 610.[61]

The city was the first in the State to use "Tax Increment Financing" (TIF) for economic development. TIF districts were established throughout the City. The Boone Avenue industrial park was the first use of TIF. The city's share of the reconstruction of 85th Avenue was financed using TIF funds.[62]

Brooklyn Park was one of the first Minnesota communities to use Industrial Revenue Bonds to spur development. The Cornelius Company was the first to use them.[63]

Richard Henneberger was city manager from 1973 to 1987. Charles Darth was the finance director and the two of them improved on a method of internal financing adopted by the city just prior to Henneberger's employment. This method, called the Investment Trust Fund, would provide fiscal stability for the Park that still exists today. It allowed the city to be its own banker. Money from the Trust Fund is allocated back to each line item in the budget as needed.[64]

Money in the Fund was used to build the present city hall, the previous city hall annex, the operation and maintenance facility and the police building. Because it used its own funds, the council was not required to get approval from the voters to construct these facilities.[65]

The 1980s ushered in an era of great change in the Park. All of the vacant areas south of 85th Avenue were developed or platted for development. A regional commercial center was starting to grow in the area of Brooklyn Boulevard and Zane Avenue. Utilities were in place, parks were improved and a new administrative campus was unfolding just east of the city hall. The Community Center, National Guard Armory and the Police Building were in place. A new City Hall and Water Treatment Plant would soon follow. Administrative staff was greatly expanded. Brooklyn Park's population had grown to 43,332 in 1980 and it was one of the largest cities in the State.

Over the years, Fred Seed, working with Evelyn and Bob Schmidt of Brook Park Realty Company, had gradually purchased land for development. Most of the land purchases included a clause that allowed the growers to live on the property, and work their land until the start of development. James Seed took over his father's business after Fred's death and the James Seed family with Evelyn and Bob Schmidt helped develop the Edinburgh Golf Course area. Land around and within the golf course was set aside for upscale mixed housing. The city paid for the construction and operated the golf course. A clubhouse designed to resemble the Edinburgh Golf Course clubhouse in Scotland was owned and operated under a public and private partnership. The course and clubhouse opened in 1987.[66]

Edinburgh USA Clubhouse

The clubhouse experienced financial difficulties and in 1989, the city's Economic Development Authority (EDA) purchased the clubhouse for $1.8 million dollars. The EDA hired Clubhouse Associates, a management group, to run the clubhouse. It continued to lose money, so the EDA terminated its contract in November 1991. The Recreation and Park Department managed the property from 1991 to 1997.

In 1991, the City Council approved the upgrading of 85th from Zane to Highway 169. There was one problem. One of the barns on the Eldon Tessman farm intruded into the widened right-of-way and it would have to be demolished. The Tessmans proposed that a slight bend to the south in the alignment would save the barn and not cause a traffic safety problem. After a two-day trial in January 1992, the court decided in favor of the Tessmans.[67]

A Political Shift

The 1990s arrived and Brooklyn Park was about to be thrust onto the national scene. Mayor Krautkremer ran for re-election in 1990 for a seventh term. Jesse Ventura, a newcomer to local politics, also filed for the office. Ventura became interested in local government because of an issue in his neighborhood. He and some of his neighbors, who lived on or near the West River Road, were opposed to a proposed subdivision that would encroach on a wetland. This issue would become one of his campaign pledges to become the "environmental mayor."[68]

The Ventura camp labeled their opponents as "the good old bunch." The campaign became fierce with both sides filing charges of campaign violations with the Hennepin County Attorney's office. Ventura won the election with 65% of the vote and carried every precinct. Ventura had the honor of being the first Mayor to conduct the City's business in the newly constructed city hall located at 85th and Regent Avenues.[69]

The Edinburgh clubhouse was a campaign issue in the 1990 election between Mayor Krautkremer and Ventura. In 1992 Mayor Ventura asked the State Auditors office to review the clubhouse books. The State Auditor submitted a report in February 1993 exonerating CA of wrongdoing. In 1997 the EDA hired Lancer Food Service to manage the clubhouse. Under Lancer, the clubhouse operation has been profitable since 1998. The golf course operation was profitable from the beginning.[70]

Mayor Krautkremer worked tirelessly during his term to get support and then financing for Highway 610. By 1990 the Congress was considering whether 610 should be included in a special funding bill. Mayor Ventura and Charles Darth, the city director of inter-governmental affairs, traveled to Washington DC to lobby for 610. His "presence" and connections were instrumental in obtaining the federal funds necessary to construct the first phase of the highway through Brooklyn Park. He jokingly said that section of the highway should be named "Ventura Highway."[71]

Mayor Ventura created a predicament for the Council halfway in the last year of his term when he moved his family to a ranch in Maple Grove. The City Council requested an administrative law judge to investigate the facts of Ventura's residency and make a ruling. City Attorney Curt Pearson was concerned that all actions taken by the council and signed by the mayor would be subject to litigation if the mayor were found to be holding office illegally. Ventura represented himself before the judge and won the case.[72]

During Ventura's four-year term the crime rate in the city dropped dramatically because of crime prevention programs, such as National Night Out. Brooklyn Park's image as a good place to live greatly improved. He put Brooklyn Park on the map.[73]

Along with growth came big city problems. A task force made a presentation to the City Council on January 11, 1993. The efforts of the task force resulted in the formation of a community-wide civic promotion called "Come Home to the Park".

Mayor Ventura poses at the groundbreaking ceremony for a new Post Office building

Brooklyn Park City Staff, 2000
Front row, l-r: Greg Andrews, Marian
Mortsensen, Linda St. John, David
Sebok; Back row, l-r: Curt Boganey,
Steve Schmidt, Jon Thiel, Wade Setter

In the 1990s, recreation and park needs again were a concern for the City. A bond issue failed on September 13, 1994. On September 30, 1997, a park bond referendum that included a senior center was successful.[74]

Grace Arbogast, elected to the Council in 1992, filed for mayor in 1994. She said her priorities as mayor would be public safety, expansion of the business base and improving the city's parks. Grace won the election and became the tenth Brooklyn Park Mayor; she was re-elected in 1998.[75]

In 1998 the Minnesota Orchestral Association petitioned the city for rezoning a parcel of land near the intersection of highways 169 and 610 for a controversial Performing Arts Center. As this book neared completion, it was unclear whether all of the issues concerning it had been resolved.[76]

The present council faces a situation that is unusual for most suburbs. It is involved with redevelopment in the older areas of the city such as apartments and the upgrading of parks, utilities and streets. At the same time, it must plan for development north of 93rd Avenue. A major Target Corporation office complex will be located north of Highway 610 and is projected to house over 4,000 employees.[77]

In 1999 Brooklyn Park was one of thirty finalists for the title of "All America City." The Park was not one of the ten cities awarded the title, but Mayor Arbogast declared, "Brooklyn Park is still a winner."[78]

Should the Two Brooklyns Become One?

A merger of the cities certainly has been contemplated by many citizens of the two Brooklyns, past and present. Two of their favorite sons, Phil Cohen of Brooklyn Center and Bill Schreiber of Brooklyn Park, were willing to be quoted on this subject. When asked, Bill listed a few reasons why it could be desirable. He then speculated if the two cities were in the same school district that would make a "joining together" possible. Brooklyn Park Mayor, James Krautkremer once broached the possibility of a merger of both Brooklyns to then Mayor Cohen. Phil replied, "any politician who brought this up would lose the next election."

Notes

1. Brooklyn Park Village Council Minutes, BP City Hall.

2. Brooklyn Park Village Council Minutes; Baldy Hartkopf, audio interview, 21 May 1982, BHS; League of Women Voters of Brooklyn Park brochure, "The Mushrooming Community, 1965, BHS.

3. Brooklyn Park Village Council Minutes.

4. Wilbur Goetze, videotape interview, 6 February 1999; William "Bill" Schreiber, videotape interview, 23 August 1999, BHS.

5. Brooklyn Park Village Council Minutes.

6. Art Kvamme, videotape interview by Howard Heck, 26 August 1999, BHS.

7. Brooklyn Park Village Council Minutes.

8. Ibid.

9. Ibid.

10. Ibid; William "Bill" Schreiber; Lyn Joyner videotape interview, 23 August 1999, BHS; Keith Caswell, videotape interview by Howard Heck, 10 February 2000, BHS.

11. Brooklyn Park Village Council Minutes.

12. Ibid.

13. Ibid; Keith Caswell.

14. Ibid; Darrell Schneider, Caswell Engineering employee, videotape interview by Howard Heck, 10 February 2000, BHS.

15. Brooklyn Park Village Council Minutes.

16. Don Poss, audiotape interview by Ernee McArthur, 12 September 1998, BHS.

17. Brooklyn Park Village Council Minutes.

18. Ibid; Keith Caswell.

19. Art Kvamme.

20. William Schreiber.

21. Lyn Joyner; *Brooklyn Park Sentinel*.

22. Ibid; John Wingard, videotape interview, 21 March 1999, BHS.

23. *Brooklyn Park Sentinel*.

24. Ibid.

25. Ibid.

26. *Brooklyn Park Sentinel*.

27. Keith Caswell; *Brooklyn Park Sentinel*.

28. Ibid.

29. Ibid.

30. Ibid.

31. League of Women Voters of Brooklyn Park; Brooklyn Park Taxpayers Club newsletter, March 1967, BHS.

32. Ed Shimek, videotape interview, 6 February 1999, BHS.

33. Brooklyn Park Village Council Minutes; 1979 Brooklyn Park Budget, BP City Hall.

34. *Brooklyn Park Sentinel*.

35. Ibid.

36. Ibid.

37. Ibid.

38. Ibid.

39. Ibid; John Wingard; Eldon Tessman, videotape interview by Howard Heck, 17 August 1999, BHS.

40. Brooklyn Park Village Council Minutes; Ed Shimek; Recreation and Park bond referendum brochures, BHS; *Brooklyn Park Sun Post*, 1998.

41. Brooklyn Park Village Council Minutes; *Brooklyn Park Sentinel*; Brooklyn Park Taxpayers Club.

42. *Brooklyn Park Sentinel*.

43. Ron Dow, videotape interview by Howard Heck, 27 March 1999, BHS.

44. Tater Daze program for 1968 and 1969, BHS; Brooklyn Park Comprehensive Development Plan, 1970, BP City Hall.

45. Scott Clark, Brooklyn Park Planning Dept. telephone conversation Howard Heck.

46. *Brooklyn Park Sentinel;* Ed Shimek

47. 1979 Brooklyn Park Budget; Tater Daze program for 1968 and 1969, BHS; Ron West, former city planner, Report to City Council, History of Timed Development in Brooklyn Park, Minnesota, BHS; Metropolitan Waste Control Commission, "The MWCC and the Mississippi: 50 Years of Stewardship" 1998, BHS; Gary Defries, Assistant City Engineer, telephone conversation with Howard Heck.

48. *Brooklyn Park Sentinel*; Gary Defries, Assistant City Engineer, telephone conversation with Howard Heck.

49. *Brooklyn Park Sentinel*; Ron West; John Rohe, former Councilman, Brooklyn Park City correspondence and news clippings, BHS.

50. Jerry Marshall, videotape interview, 27 March 1999, BHS; Ron Dow; Ron West.

51. Ron Dow.

52. 1979 Brooklyn Park Budget; Richard Henneberger, former City Manager, telephone conversation with Howard Heck; *Minneapolis Star Tribune*, 30 January 2000, 15, BHS.

53. 1979 Brooklyn Park Budget.

54. Recreation and Park bond referendum brochures, BHS.

55. *Brooklyn Park Sentinel*; James Krautkremer, videotape interview by Howard Heck, 27 March 1999, BHS; Ron Dow.

56. Wilbur Goetze; Ron Dow.

57. Scott Clark.

58. Jerry Marshall.

59. Ron Dow; Ron West.

60. Ron Dow.

61. Ibid.

62. James Krautkremer; Scott Clark.

63. James Krautkremer; Charles Darth, former Finance Director and later Director of Inter-Governmental Affairs, Brooklyn Park.

64. Richard Henneberger.

65. J. Krautkremer; R. Dow; Charles Darth.

66. Jack Umland, videotape interview, 27 March 1999, BHS; Evelyn P. Schmidt, owner of Brook Park Realty, videotape interview, 16 February 1999, BHS.

67. Eldon Tessman.

68. Lyn Joyner.

69. *Minneapolis Star Tribune*, 30 January 2000, 15, BHS. Jesse Ventura, Minnesota Public Radio interview, 28 May 1999, BHS.

70. Jack Umland; *Brooklyn Park Sun Post*, 1998, Brookdale Hennepin Area Library.

71. Charles Darth; *Brooklyn Park Sun Post*, 1998, Brookdale Hennepin Area Library.

72. Ibid; Jesse Ventura, Minnesota Public Radio interview, 28 May 1999, BHS.

73. *Minneapolis Star Tribune*, 30 January 2000, 15, BHS; Jesse Ventura, Minnesota Public Radio interview, 28 May 1999, BHS.

74. Recreation and Park bond referendum brochures, BHS.

75. *Brooklyn Park Sun Post*, 1998; *NorthWest News*, November 1994,

76. *Brooklyn Park Sun Post*, 1998.

77. Ibid; *Park Pages*, Brooklyn Park city newsletter, September/October 1999, BHS.

78. Ibid.

Earle Brown and the Founding of Minnesota Troopers

by John R. (Jack) Morrison, Class of 1930 – Badge #32,

WHY a capitalist–banker–board director–philanthropist–farmer and horse breeder would want to become a cop will forever be a mystery. Enter Earle Brown: He began his career in police work as Sheriff of Hennepin County. During the terms he served, he had the reputation of never asking a person to do any job that he himself would not undertake, which would include risk-of-life.

The origin of the Minnesota Highway Patrol began in the late twenties between two old friends who hatched the idea that the State of Minnesota needed a State Police Force. Charles (Charley) M. Babcock was the Commissioner of Highways, and father of the old Jefferson Trunk Highway Systems. He and Earle were close friends. Charley's home was in Elk River, which was the town which may have been the place the seed was planted that finally turned out to be the "Highway Patrol."

One afternoon after a trip to his cabin near Garrison on Mille Lacs Lake, Earle stopped in Elk River to met with Mike Auspos, the Sherburne County deputy sheriff. While they were meeting a bank was robbed so Earle and Mike made chase and during the chase, gun fire was exchanged. The robbers were apprehended.

A bill was passed in 1929 providing 35 men to become Minnesota Highway Patrol officers. This bill was not exactly the way Earle wanted it to be. He wanted a bill passed that would include full State Police powers. At the time there were two political parties — Republican and the Farmer-Laborite Party. The Farmer-Laborites strongly objected to such a broad mandate. The Labor portion of the Party feared that with full police power, they would risk strike breaking authority. Consequently the bill was watered-down limiting the police powers to the State Highway only.

Earle Brown

There was a rub, however; no provision was made financially by the State to pay for the training and lodging or various supplies needed for the recruits. Therefore, Earle dug down in his pockets and provided the necessities — building conversions and other expenses. He paid for the whole works.

January 1, 1930, the first class of recruits arrived — the barracks were a converted horse barn (stable) with a show area between two wings — north and south. The wings were where the horse stalls had been — Earle had them converted into rooms (with bars) no privacy between quarters. Instructors quarters were in the converted hayloft above the class area which had been altered for night duty.

Our classes were held in the center of the building, which had been the show area. We even had the horses' trough for water — plus a monkey for a mascot.

Earle chose four of his talented deputies, and one deputy from Sherburne County, to become instructors for the class. He sent them to be trained as instructors to the Pennsylvania State Police at Harrisburg, Pennsylvania. These officers were of the highest stature, strict, knowledgable, and fair — everything was business. At 10:00 P.M. the lights went out and the quarters became stone quiet. The duty officer would check every stall periodically to see that everyone was in bed and silent.

Four instructors came from Hennepin County and the fifth was from Sherburne County, and was Mike Auspos who was with Earle when they apprehended the Elk River bank robbers. The deputies he chose were: George Koch (our nickname for him

Earle Brown put the Training Class to work on his farm, chopping wood.

was "King Fish")—the others were Paul Ryden, Glen Dahl and "Cat" Ralph Potvin. We couldn't even hear Potvin's footsteps.

The morning bell rang at 6:00 A.M. At 6:30 we were doing calesthenics—at 7:30 we were running to Earle's mess hall converted from his farmhouse a quarter mile down the road for breakfast. At 8:30 classes began. We were kept busy. We even had a Drill Instructor who happened to be one of us. His name was Earl Larimer, an ex-marine sergeant. He did his best to make us look like a drill team. Earl later became Chief of the Patrol. He was a natural-born leader.

Outside of class they had other plans to see what kind of timber their recruits were made of. Earle had a large acreage of hardwood trees—and it seemed the worse the weather got the more they wanted the recruits to chop down trees and bucksaw them into one foot pieces of logs. Mrs. Brown brought bags of popcorn and cookies to our barracks every Sunday night. We never knew when the Chief would show up; however he did some checking on his own periodically.

Because Earle was so popular as the sheriff of Hennepin County, he made a bad decision. Some Republican friends talked Earle into the race for Governor in 1932. Floyd B. Olson, the former Hennepin County Prosecutor and County Attorney, was very popular and Earle lost the election. A big bang followed a short time later when about half of the Patrol were fired on the same day—myself included—July 1, 1933. A movement began within the remaining members to form a Troopers Association and pass laws that would give them protection and offer benefits to insure their safety without political influence. I returned to the Patrol in 1939.

My wife, Isabel, and I visited Earle in 1957. He was then 83 years of age. We sat in his study, which had not changed in decor all those years. In keeping with his love of animals, Earle had two most beautiful Dalmatian dogs at his feet. It is my fond recollection that he was always flanked by his "friends" wherever he went. Also, he had a private pet cemetery for his faithful beauties located by the south end of his home.

Earle returned to private life and built an office building on his property. He hired the nephew of his good friend Charley Babcock—Mahlon Babcock—of Anoka as his personal secretary. Mahlon, a Minnesota University graduate with law and accounting degrees was well qualified for the job. He also was President of the First State Bank of Anoka. The two of them shared the new building. Earle willed the whole shebang to the University of Minnesota after his demise.

I'm dead sure tears would come to Earle's eyes if he realized what happened to the eggs he hatched 70 years ago—to the splendid and most efficient, educated and talented police force in the entire country. An organization for Minnesotans to be proud of, and thankful for.

Municipal Law Enforcement

THE CITIES OF BROOKLYN CENTER AND BROOKLYN PARK are today served by law enforcement agencies which are highly regarded and professionally staffed, and they have been well supported by their respective city councils. Also important in the success of the departments have been the contributions and involvement of citizens and civic organizations.

Early Beginnings

Municipal policing emerged in Brooklyn Park in 1954 with the appointment of Harry J. Robertson as the first full-time police employee and chief. He retained this position until his retirement in 1978. Robert Cahlander, Sr. was appointed Brooklyn Center's first police chief in 1953, and he served in this capacity until 1962. Prior to his appointment, he functioned as a part-time elected constable for twenty-one years.[1]

Early policing in Brooklyn Center and Brooklyn Park was typical of smaller communities which were evolving from rural settings to urban environments. Patrol services were provided by Chiefs Robertson and Cahlander during the afternoon and evening hours. They drove their own vehicles. Today's modern two-way radios, mobile digital terminals, cellular telephones, and sophisticated medical emergency devices were definitely not found in the early patrol vehicles. However, the dedication to duty by the original police officers was well known.

A subtle contributing influence on the image and style of policing may have been the high standards established by one of Brooklyn Center's most famous residents, Earle Brown. A man of varied interests and recognized integrity, he served as Sheriff of Hennepin County from 1920 until 1929, and he would serve again 1943-1947. His leadership of the Sheriff's Department was one of the factors which resulted in his being appointed as the first Chief of the Minnesota Highway Patrol in June of 1929. He participated in the selection of the first group of thirty-five troopers and personally provided much of the equipment they utilized in performing their duties. Additionally, he converted buildings on his Brooklyn Center farm to serve as training barracks for the Highway Patrol. The organization's name was later changed to the Minnesota State Patrol.

The original police officers had virtually no formal training. They learned "on-the-job" and often received assistance from the sheriff's department or the neighboring communities of Minneapolis or Robbinsdale. They were rather successful in preventing criminal behavior due to the fact that they personally knew the area farm families, often on a first name basis, and the residents in the sparsely populated neighborhoods. High numbers of arrests were not recorded in the early years, however, the officers were aggressive in issuing citations to speeders, stop sign violators, and the teenage "hot rodders." They responded to occasional acts of vandalism or thefts, medical situations, and motor vehicle accidents.

Brooklyn Center and Brooklyn Park's first officers enjoyed positive working relationships with the local justices of the peace, or "JP's," and often had input in determining the sanctions or punishments to be imposed upon any individual found guilty of violating local ordinances. They would hardly recognize the state mandated court system of today. It evolved from the JP concept, to city courts, to municipal and district courts, to the current structure of the Hennepin County District Court with

Robert Cahlander, Brooklyn Center's first police chief

its various geographical divisions which hear misdemeanor, gross misdemeanor, and felony level cases.

The early peace officers could perhaps, by today's standards, be regarded as publicly paid community watchmen. The positive rapport they established and maintained with citizens in their respective jurisdictions would indeed serve as a model for modern day police departments which advocate a community oriented policing philosophy.

Crime Trends

As builders acquired and developed tracts of farmland, Brooklyn Center and Brooklyn Park began to change. The tranquil rural settings evolved into vibrant urban neighborhoods. The growth of the 50s and 60s resulted in increased demands for all governmental services including law enforcement. New housing, apartment complexes and expanding commercial development resulted in more traffic concerns and increased conduct requiring police intervention. Vandalism, shoplifting, check forgery, residential burglaries, auto theft, and theft from vehicles were regularly recorded.

The changing demographics resulted in more serious criminal behavior in the 70s, 80s, and 90s. Crimes against persons, narcotics violations, and gang activities became serious challenges for the communities. Some high profile, stranger-on-stranger homicides in the late 80s and early 90s confirmed the fact that Brooklyn Center and Brooklyn Park had indeed "lost their innocence." Another factor impacting upon the social reality of crime at this time was the increased involvement of juveniles.

Early police officers supplied their own cars.

Responses

Both Brooklyn Center and Brooklyn Park initiated professional proactive responses to the changing crime trends. In addition to the highly visible patrol divisions, each agency created investigative units, canine units, school liaison and youth oriented programs (such as DARE), special response teams, support services units, detention services, and community based crime prevention programs.

The crime prevention endeavors resulted in successful and highly regarded neighborhood organizations being implemented. In Brooklyn Park, for example, the Crime Prevention Association was established in 1990, and the first neighborhood crime watch was formed. By the end of 1999, over 250 groups existed throughout the city. Initially, they were a reactive response by citizens to crime. Today, they have expanded their mission to a proactive one impacting many aspects of the community. The Crime Prevention Association has been the catalyst for the city's coordinated involvement in the annual National Night Out celebration. For nine consecutive years, Brooklyn Park has won national awards for this effort.

Brooklyn Center's Neighborhood Crime Watch was formed in 1983. Today, there are in excess of 150 units in the city.[2]

Both organizations combined efforts during the 1994 National Night Out celebration to host an event which came to be known as "Light Up The Boulevard." At the conclusion of the various neighborhood gatherings, all citizens were invited to stand on Brooklyn Boulevard and, with flashlights in hand, "Light Up The Boulevard." This very high profile event received a great deal of media attention including live telecasts by area television stations.

Involvement by citizen and business volunteers working with the police department has proven to be a significant factor in confronting and reversing crime trends.

The two departments have regularly cooperated in the delivery of services. For example, in 1979 and 1980, in response to increasing numbers of parties involving large numbers of people, Brooklyn Center, Brooklyn Park, and Crystal deployed officers on an overtime basis to handle the calls. Officers from the three cities were teamed up to respond to the calls. By doing this on an overtime basis, regular patrol services were not reduced. This approach was successful and issues related to loud, out of control parties were eliminated.

In 1993 the two departments, together with three others, created one of the first regional drug task forces to respond to increasing illegal drug and gang activities. Partial funding for this endeavor was initially received from the state, and it became a model for other communities confronting similar issues. This joint approach was most successful, and the task force has been expanded to include additional communities from both Hennepin and Anoka Counties.

The agencies were also participants in creating a police cadet program in 1993 with other area departments. This endeavor, coordinated by the Northwest Hennepin Human Services Council, provided career opportunities within law enforcement agencies for qualified minority candidates. In 1997 the program was recognized by the Minnesota legislature in authorizing funds for the concept to be applied statewide. Departments receiving funding had to adopt the model created in the Northwest Hennepin suburbs. Brooklyn Center and Brooklyn Park have also cooperated in training and recruitment activities.

Personnel

In July of 1978 Minnesota became the first state in the nation to license peace officers. The legislation, which is administered by the Peace Officer Standards and Training (POST) Board, mandates that prior to being licensed as an officer, individuals must be a graduate of a recognized two or four year college program, complete a "skills" course, undergo psychological and physical evaluations, partake in written and oral examinations, and pass a comprehensive background check. Most agencies also require newly appointed officers to complete an extensive field training orientation (FTO) program.

Prior to the implementation of the POST Board licensing standards, agencies would typically hire individuals in compliance with local policies and then send the new officer to a basic 240-hour training course offered by either the Training Division of the Minnesota Bureau of Criminal Apprehension or the Suburban Police Academy. Indeed, the recruitment, selection, and training of police officers has changed significantly since the appointment of Chiefs Robertson and Cahlander.

Both the Brooklyn Center and Brooklyn Park Police Departments have been rather sophisticated in selection of new officers. Each has also been committed to enhancing the professional skills of personnel by providing quality in-service training on a variety of public safety and criminal justice topics.

It is interesting to note that before the adoption of the POST Board Rules and Regulations, Brooklyn Center became one of the first cities in the state to implement a college incentive program. Through the program, the city paid a portion of tuition and fees. Upon successful completion of a class, an officer would also receive additional salary compensation. A number of personnel participated in and benefited from the program. Additionally, it served as a model for other municipalities considering a similar program.

National Night Out Award presented to Chief Setter

Facilities

As previously denoted, both police departments have been well supported by their respective city councils. This is particularly evident with regard to physical facilities. During the early years, both agencies shared buildings with other city services. Often the structures had been built for another purpose and were remodeled or modified to accommodate the governmental departments. Again, this was typical of developing communities or suburbs.

The trend, however, changed significantly in the summer of 1971 when the Brooklyn Center Police Department moved into space specifically designed for police operations. The area was in the lower level of the City Hall which, together with the Community Center, was constructed in the area of 63rd and Shingle Creek Parkway.

In the ensuing years remodeling and modification were made to the facility, however, by the late 1990's a decision was made to construct a new, free standing building. In 1998 ground was broken for a facility in the area of 67th and Humboldt, and in December of 1999, police operations moved to it. The new police facility should serve the city well as it enters the new millennium.

Crime Watch Captains Meeting

The Brooklyn Park Police Department also functioned from a variety of locations. However, a rapidly expanding agency with significant space needs resulted in the city council in 1985 authorizing construction of a new building. This facility, located at 5400 85th Avenue North, became operational in August of 1986. Continued growth of the department resulted in remodeling and an addition in 1997 and future expansion is anticipated. It is interesting to note that following construction of the police station, the Community Activity Center was expanded; and in 1991, a new City Hall was constructed. All of these facilities are located in close proximity to the police department and the result has been the creation of an attractive, functional state of the art civic complex.

Summary

The citizens of Brooklyn Center and Brooklyn Park can view with pride the professional services provided by the two police departments. They work well with each other in responding to certain situations, and they are well supported by the Hennepin County Sheriff's Department at the county level and the Bureau of Criminal Apprehension at the state level.

Both agencies have adopted a strong community policing orientation in the delivery of the varied services and both long ago realized the benefits of working with citizen and business organizations to achieve mutually beneficial goals.

The cities first two Police Chiefs, Harry Robertson in Brooklyn Park and Bob Cahlander of Brooklyn Center, are to be commended for the agencies they created and the emphasis each placed on community support and participation in addressing crime and other social issues. Both agencies have been served by successor chiefs who subscribed to the same standards. In Brooklyn Park, they are: Don Davis, 1978-1995 and Wade Setter, 1995 to present. In Brooklyn Center, Thomas O'Hehir, 1962-1978; James Lindsay, 1978-1992; Trevor Hampton, 1992-1994; Scott Kline, 1994-1998; and Joel Downer, 1998 to present.[3]

Notes

1 James P Lindsay in a prepared historical outline of the Brooklyn Center Police Department, February 1983, BHS.

2. Chief Joel Downer, interviewed by Don Davis in December 1999.

3. Ibid.

Chapter Four

EDUCATION

NO SEGMENT OF BROOKLYN TOWNSHIP SOCIETY has undergone more change in the past one hundred fifty years than education. With this daunting task in mind, the writers have tried to do justice to education in a limited number of pages. The emphasis—right or wrong—is on public education, grades K-12, although other topics are discussed. A "long version" of this chapter is in the archives of the Brooklyn Historical Society, containing extensive information on "education then and now" and "educational mandates," subjects not covered here for lack of space.

Just defining the geographical area served by education in Brooklyn Township was a challenging task. The authors did the best they could with the information available, with no slights intended to any school district, person, area or institution.

Throughout the past one hundred fifty years, public education in Brooklyn Township has not been without some controversy, perhaps more so in the last forty years as the federal and state governments, and the courts have become more involved in the schools. Topics such as sex education in schools, the place of religion in the school, civil rights legislation, book censorship, prayer in school, banning the Bible from the school library (1992), to name a few, had an impact on education for good or bad, depending upon your point of view. The writers of this chapter are aware of some of the controversial issues that have surrounded public education in Brooklyn Township. Are, or were, these issues important, and have they had an impact on education? The answer is "yes," but time, space and resources do not permit the exhaustive research needed to do justice to them. For these reasons, the writers chose not to deal with these issues in this chapter.

The concentration for the chapter is on what happened early on in education in the township, with some cameos of what the authors considered well known early schools and then more emphasis on where education is today in the Brooklyn Center-Brooklyn Park area. The middle years during this period are slighted somewhat. The writers hope that by contrasting the early days of education in Brooklyn Township with today, readers will get a flavor of what has happened in one hundred fifty years, and perhaps agree that education has changed significantly.

School District Organization

The method of organizing education by having a local school district evolved out of the New England Township unit of self-government.

The citizens living in a specific area could create a legal unit for school governance. By the time Minnesota became a territory, and then a state, these so called common school districts with a one room rural school dotted the American landscape. In Minnesota, these small units were governed by an Annual School Meeting (the local patrons) and a three-person school board.

Hennepin County had over 140 of these common districts at one point. A number of these districts and parts of others were included within the boundaries of old Brooklyn Township. These schools became centers of activity for the surrounding locale in both a social and civic sense. Often they carried the name of a nearby family; proximity or fame brought about name usage.[1]

The "high" school movement began in the last half of the 1800s. The earliest high schools in the Brooklyn area were at Anoka (1880) and in the rapidly growing City of Minneapolis. Osseo High School (1920) and Robbinsdale High School (1936) were created in later decades.

After World War II, societal changes and the beginnings of urban sprawl changed the rural landscape in ways that led to present population patterns. In the late 1940s under legislative impetus, school district consolidation began. The small rural school districts were attached to nearby high school districts. The result of this complex and emotional consolidation movement is the four independent districts that serve the Brooklyn area today.

More than thirty districts in Anoka and Hennepin counties were involved in the creation of Anoka-Hennepin #11. Thirteen small common school districts formed District 43 (Osseo #279 in 1957) by 1953. District 24 (Robbinsdale #281) was created in a like manner with common districts joining the existing high school district. Only Brooklyn Center #286 was not part of the final consolidation movement. Within the 2.8 square mile district, education evolved from the one room rural setting in 1877 to Brooklyn Center Junior-Senior High School in 1961.[2]

The large size of the 175 square mile Anoka-Hennepin School District #11 is often a point of question, according to Mr. Erling Johnson, Superintendent of District #11 from 1964-1975. At the funeral of Mr. Morris Bye, the Anoka School Superintendent at the time of consolidation in the early 1950s, the topic was broached in a humorous fashion. The story was told that Mr. Bye went to the top of the Anoka water tower with a telescope. He established the district boundaries where the range of the telescope ended. In a sense humorous, but the strong leadership of school superintendents during the consolidation years should not be underestimated.[3]

Smith School Students, 1919
Alice Tessman

The part of District #11 which now runs down the west bank of the Mississippi River in present Brooklyn Park and Brooklyn Center was originally served by three common school districts from north to south: Dunning #99, Riverview #30 (on present school site), and the southern most Benson #29 which extended into the Village of Brooklyn Center.

The historical record indicates that the large Independent School Districts of today were formed by the consolidation of the antecedent rural districts. The present boundaries, especially in the metropolitan area, are almost absolutely secure. However, inside these large districts that contain multiple elementary, middle, and high schools, the question of where area attendance lines are drawn will be a constant issue. These areas will always change to reflect the current demographic needs of the respective place within the Independent Districts. Rapid student population growth early in a district's history probably means both a stable and declining enrollment will be part of any future.

Brooklyn Township Education

The school district called #2 was formed in 1853 by early rural settlers of Brooklyn Township who thought education was important. While the boundaries of this District were uncertain, the creation of a school district allowed the settlers to build schools through an education tax. However, the first school created in 1854 was funded by local contributions and held in a wood shanty. With a board roof and two half-windows, it housed ten students, taught by Augusta McLaughlin. At the time Brooklyn Township embraced almost half of the northern portion of Hennepin County.

In the fall of 1854, school was also held in a temporary building on Getchell Prairie just west of Palmer Lake. This school was taught by Mary Huff and later by Mrs. Joel F. Howe. A school near Osseo in Section 18 was built in 1855.

During the summer of 1855, a shed with a straw-thatch roof and a packed dirt floor was made into a school by the wife of Reverend Partridge. She removed the existing horse stalls in the shed and installed a rough board floor. In the winter of 1855-56, school was also held in the home of Mr. J. Reidhead as well as in the various private homes in the area. This continued until 1859 when the first schoolhouse proper was built. Eventually, seven schoolhouses were built from 1859 to 1880.[4]

An early teacher in Brooklyn Township describes the Spartan accommodations: "I taught the first school at Shingle Creek when I was a girl of seventeen. My school house was a claim shanty, reached by a plank from the other side of the creek," said Mary Harrison, who arrived in 1850. "My boarding place was a quarter of a mile from the creek. The window of the school house was three little panes of glass which shoved sideways to let in air."[5]

In its formative years, Brooklyn Township was part of the American Frontier. Part of frontier tradition was that people of a certain area had the right to organize their own school districts. So from District #2 sprung four Hennepin county school districts: #25, #26, #28, and #29. These districts were formed in the 1860s and 1870s. In 1877, District #118 was created out of parts of all four districts. Over the next 70 years students attended rural grade schools in Twin Lake District #25, Brooklyn Center District #28, Benson District #29, and Earle Brown District #118.

Between 1945 and 1958 school district reorganization was carried on throughout Minnesota. In Brooklyn Township, four school districts ultimately emerged from this period. Twin Lake #25 joined Robbinsdale District #281, Brooklyn Center #28 joined Osseo District #279 and Benson #29 was attached to Anoka-Hennepin District #11. Earle Brown #118 remained unchanged, and its small size became anachronistic in the midst of the massive neighboring school districts. In 1958, Earle Brown #118 elected to become Brooklyn Center Independent School District #286. District #286 encompassed the same boundaries set by the local pioneers in the spring of 1877.

In an interview with Doug Germundson of the *Brooklyn Center Post* in January 1976, Florence Street spoke of her 61-year teaching career, most of which was spent at the Dunning School. She later taught at the Corcoran School. Street's experience in education was probably typical of teaching in the late 19th and early 20th centuries.[6]

The curriculum covered the three R's (reading, writing, and arithmetic), along with history, geography, and penmanship. All levels of students grades 1-6 or 1-8 were in the same room. Street taught each level in fifteen-minute sections while the rest of the students studied. Brighter young students sometimes studied with the older students.

State boards were taken after 8th grade if you hadn't missed 30 days of school. Older students who were needed at home or were bored came to school just enough to

Cora Lane Hunt attended Dunning School from 1890 to 1895.

qualify for the exams. Because poor attendance often led to poor performance, some 16 year-olds were classified as fourth graders. Unlike today, there were no social promotions to advance students despite poor work.

Most parents took care of discipline at home. Rowdy kids were kept after school to memorize geography. Home visits to student's families seemed to help with discipline problems. Street used a little slap, which often met with little result, so she found other ways to discipline students. Spit balls were a big problem in her day. She made offending students chew newspaper after school, which solved the problem. Today, educators are still looking for parental involvement in education but would frown on the discipline Street used, even if effective.

Baseball was a popular sport back then. Students would rush outside at recess so they could bat first. The older kids won this race so Street had them file out single file to give the younger students a chance.

Overcrowded classrooms are not unique today. One year Street had fifty-four students in grades 1-8, and no place to seat the twenty-five new kids. The kindergarten class sat at two tables all year long. That year the teacher had fifteen kids to get ready for state boards. All this for $65.00 a month and driving five miles to school in a horse and cutter.

The early boards maintained a simple elementary, ungraded school for a term as short as three months. By levying taxes, boards could build these "little red school houses." The system also provided for two terms in a year, a winter term for the older boys and girls who needed to work in the spring, summer, and fall, and a summer term for younger children. The winter term started after harvest and continued to January. Summer term began after spring planting, each term lasting from three to five months as determined by the board. Although year-round schools were held for different reasons back then, they are not a modern concept. By the later 1800s, this two-term plan gave way to the present nine-month school year.

Riverview Schoolhouse, School District #30
Minnesota Historical Society

Although the first teachers were female, male teachers later took over. Perhaps this was in response to discipline problems with the older boys in class. The pointer or the French twist was used on boys as punishment and unruly girls were made to sit in the corner wearing a dunce cap. This discipline seems demeaning by today's standards but probably proved very effective then.

School generally started at 8:00 A.M. and lasted until 4:00 P.M. The school children all walked to school since there were no buses, although sleighs were sometimes used in the winter for transportation. There was a short recess in the morning and afternoon when the students played ball or tag games. Everyone brought a lunch to school in a pail. Sometimes a hot dish was sent to school by one of the families. The students ate right at their desks. There were no lunchrooms or free milk. Children had to supply their own books and buy a slate on which to write. Subjects taught mainly encompassed the three R's in grades 1-8. The teacher sometimes boarded with a local family, a practice that continued until the early 1900s.

During the 1930s, the county superintendent of schools voiced a concern about maintaining a healthy school environment. Measles, mumps, scarlet fever, whooping cough, colds, and influenza caused numerous absences. Since there were no school nurses to address these problems, the parents and teachers had to handle them. Eventually, the school nurse program evolved out of these health issues.

Most teachers received only a two-year certificate to teach or were products of "Normal Training Schools." There was no salary schedule and wages and living expenses varied from school to school. In 1935 rural school teacher salaries ranged from $47.50 to $160.00 per month. The average salary for the year was $710.00. One can only imagine the level of teacher salaries in the 1800s.

Some Well-Known Early Schools

Abraham Lincoln School

The portions of present Brooklyn Park and Brooklyn Center served by Robbinsdale School District #281 can be traced back to two rural districts, Twin Lake District #25 and Abraham Lincoln District #27. The District #281 portion of southwestern Brooklyn was part of the northern portion of Abraham Lincoln District #27. Its origins go back to one of the first schools in this section of Hennepin County, located at the present corner of County Road 81 and Bass Lake Road.

What became District #27 was organized in September 1860. A building was quickly erected and the school term began in December with a male teacher presiding. Two hundred fifty dollars had been assessed against the taxable property in the newly formed district. Taxpayers could give labor for one-third of their tax if they wished. Taxpayers were allowed $1.00 a day for labor and $2.00 a day for a man and a team of horses. This District #27 schoolhouse burned in 1895.

In the summer of 1895, a new one room school was built at the present Lincoln School site at 6200 West Broadway. The school was known as the Coulter School from the nearby and active Coulter family. In 1915, a one room addition was added and in 1926 a four room building was constructed and named Abraham Lincoln School. In the post World War II baby boom years enrollment increased rapidly, with a ten-room wing being constructed in 1950. In 1953, during the controversial school consolidation period throughout the state, the southern part of District #27 became part of what is now Robbinsdale District #281, and the northern portion joined Osseo District #279. Renovation and remodeling have kept Lincoln school functioning.[7]

Benson School

The original one-room Benson School was named after the A.H. Benson family and was built around 1872 on a donated piece of property on or near their property on the River Road (at what is now 73rd Avenue). This school became Hennepin County District #29. The original white schoolhouse was replaced by a brick building around World War I, as the original building was moved back from the River Road. After numerous improvements, the original school was converted into a single family home, which now stands at 1302 73rd Avenue North.

In 1952 the Benson School District #29 merged with Anoka District 11. The brick schoolhouse remained in use until October 1957 when a new wing was completed at Riverview School to accommodate the grade 1-3 Benson students. The old schoolhouse became the Brooklyn Park City Hall during the 1960s. The building stood vacant in 1967 after completion of the new Brooklyn Park Municipal building. The Anoka School District authorized the building to be torn down in 1974. However, developers purchased the building and two-acre site for office building use. Later the brick building was demolished. Riverview School now serves this area.[8]

Diane Mattson remembers her school days at the Benson School very well. Her first grade teacher, Estelle Shaver, hid her in the clothes closet before school because the principal would not have allowed her to come to school early. Diane's parents both worked and there were no close neighbors or Day Care to leave her with before school hours. Diane said there wasn't much to play with at recess but the girls chased the boys and tried to kiss them. In sixth grade, Connie Guntzel, Gary (Garrison) Keillor, and Diane had a newspaper and started a chorus. Gary always liked to write and sing. As we all know, he went on to do this professionally.

Upper grades at Benson School,
September 1926
Paul Kopacz

The fifth and sixth graders were sent to Sunnyvale School by way of Champlin in the transition from Benson School to Riverview. After the Benson and Riverview Schools the pupils were sent to Anoka for junior and senior high. Many of them were called, "The West River Gang." They were very active in all activities at school. "A small school didn't hurt us. We didn't have all the extras some students have now", Diane says. Years later Gary and Bill planned a grade school class reunion. Diane said, "It seemed like we were still family." With a bit of nostalgia, they visited the site where Benson School had been.[9]

Berg School (District #131)

The Berg School was located on the west side of Xerxes Avenue North at about 81st Street. The attendance area was generally west of Humboldt Avenue, east of Regent Avenue, south of 85th Street, and north of 75th Street. The last students attended Berg School in 1953. The area then became part of the Osseo School District. The school was rented as a house for some years and was ultimately razed when the area was subdivided for homes in the late 1960s and early 1970s.

George Lazaroff attended Berg School for all eight grades during the 1930s. He recalled coal in the basement with Mr. Fair coming in each morning to stoke the fire. A Mother's Club rotated going to school to cook one hot lunch item each day, such as soup, stew, or a hot dish. Doris Pavloff Chestuik recalled water in the school basement during wet 1940 springs. She said the Mother's Club women carried everything outside from the basement for a Hy-lex washing to kill the mildew.

Berg School Mothers' Club
20th Anniversary Party

Brooklyn Center School (District #28, Later Joined To Osseo District #279)

The Brooklyn Center School was located on the west side of Brooklyn Blvd. at 71st Avenue. Albert Purdham thinks the brick school building was built about 1924 to 1926, and was the third school built by District #28. A wooden schoolhouse had been built on the same site about 1871, and the original school may have been built across the street. When Willow Lane School was built on the east side of Brooklyn Blvd. in 1955, Brooklyn Center School was renamed the Willow Lane Annex, and classes were held in both buildings. The Annex was sold to the Village of Brooklyn Center in 1959 and the village, and then city, offices were located there from March 1960 to June 1971. The building stood vacant for six years until it was renovated for CEAP, the Community Emergency Assistance Program. The building was gutted by fire December 31, 1977, and was demolished in May 1978.

All of Roy and Myrtle's children attended the Brooklyn Center School, sometimes called the Howe School. "During World War II," Ruth Howe remembers, "the Brooklyn Center ladies met in the school lunch area to roll bandages. Eighth graders were excused from class an hour each week to help in this war effort project. It was under the capable supervision of Anne Hamilton."

Cap Martin and Earle Brown Schools

According to a study of Brooklyn Center Schools done by Warren Olson, the "Cap Martin" School was District #118's first school. It bore the name because Captain John Martin was the closest and most famous resident near the school. The first classes in the school were probably held in the summer of 1878. At that time, two terms made up the school year—fall to early winter and the summer term. This accommodated children who stayed home and helped on the farm, and also because of the fiercely cold winters in Minnesota.

The Cap Martin Schoolhouse was located approximately a block south of the barns on Martin's farm and faced west. The schoolhouse was white, of frame construction. Ike Anderson, who attended the school, said it was a long walk to school in -40 degree weather from 54th and Emerson Avenue North across the fields. Sometimes he would rest in the corn shocks to get warm when he faced a cold northwest wind.

Anderson's first teacher, a woman, took the streetcar to 51st and Lyndale Avenue North and then someone gave her a ride by sleigh in the winter to the school. The school had a potbelly stove and usually only three to five boys would show up in very cold weather. School was from 9:00 A.M. to 4:00 P.M., five days a week. Students brought lunch in a tin syrup pail, and milk or coffee in a whiskey bottle. Students had two recesses, one in the morning and one in the afternoon. The outside toilets back of the schoolhouse were a considerable distance. The pump was close to the school. A man replaced the woman teacher because the boys were so wild. The little one-room school was later moved to the site of the present Earle Brown School at 59th and Humboldt Avenue North, where it was destroyed by a tornado in 1929.[10]

The small Cap Martin School became inadequate as attendance increased. In 1884, 32 students attended summer sessions. In 1912-1913 fifty-four students attended the nine-month session. Bond issues to build new and larger quarters were turned down by voters in 1913 and again in 1915.

During the winter of 1915, Earle Brown bought the land surrounding the Cap Martin School. When additional farm buildings were built around the school, the school seemed part of the farm, but it remained school district property. A clause in the original deed stated that if the one acre where the school stood ever ceased to be used for school purposes, ownership of the acre would revert to the owner of the property from which it was taken. This made Brown favor a new school site.

The school board approved the purchase of two acres of land at what is now 59th and Humboldt Avenue North. The cost was $700.00 and two days later voters approved a $7,500.00 bond issue. Construction of the new school was completed in 1917. The Cap Martin Schoolhouse was moved from Brown's farm and placed next to the new two-room school. The Martin School was moved in the old customary way—on skids and pulled across Earle Brown's pasture by a team of horses.

Earle Brown claimed that the village school district was mistakenly named for him. "The school is on 59th Avenue and that used to be called Brown's Crossroad—but after a farmer who lived up the road—not after my family," Earle explained to a reporter. "When the school was built, they named it after the road—Brown. They eventually got Earle Brown's first name in there. But he was the wrong Brown." Brown let the school district park its school bus in his barn. He was very surprised when he saw printed on it: "Earle Brown School District #118." However, this followed the custom of naming a school after the largest landowner or most famous person in the area.

Earle Brown School, 1st and 2nd grades, October 6, 1926
Dolores Duoos

A fire in February 1967 destroyed fourteen Earle Brown classrooms. Facilities were rented at Spring Lake Park and other places as a bond issue for new classrooms was passed and building began.[11]

The present trees along 59th by the school were planted by the school children after the two-room unit was built. There was no graduation ceremony until 1929, but that year a severe tornado blew the top off the schoolhouse canceling the ceremonies. Earle Brown allowed the school board to use a house he owned as a temporary school.[12]

Dunning School

A prominent early school was the Dunning School at 10980 West River Road. It was an example of the one room, one teacher school of common district #99, serving students in grades 1-8. Built in 1860 it was named after J. B. Dunning, who served as school treasurer from 1877 to 1885. Cora Lane Hunt, a student in the school from 1890 to 1895, said the school had double-seated desks so that every child had a partner, with boys on one side of the room and girls on the other. The January 29, 1976, *Brooklyn Center Post* contains an interview with Mrs. Florence Street, who began her sixty-one year teaching career at the Dunning School. The School eventually became part of the Anoka-Hennepin School District. In 1932 Consolidated District #42 was formed, which is the area west of Dunning School. In the early days, this district consisted of a high school (Osseo) and the elementary grades in the same building.[13]

Schreiber School

The red brick schoolhouse known as the Schreiber School (Hennepin District #31) was built in 1910 at 99th and Regent Avenue North in Brooklyn Park. According to Norene Roberts, who researched the school, the building may have been a one or two-room school. Local residents referred to the building as the Schreiber School, perhaps because two early 1860s settlers, Frederick and Christian Schreiber, owned about twenty percent of the property within District #31. Maps from the 1880s show a school located at this site. The school was renovated in 1975 into a beautiful home now owned by Rick Ketzback.

Students would walk to school, or in bad winter weather get a sleigh ride to school. Some students would even skate to school with their clamp-on skates. There were thirty-five students in grades 1-8. Students being disciplined would sit up front. Books were furnished at the school and the desks had inkwells with separate pens. Students brought their own lunches and sometimes mothers would supplement this with a jar of hot dish, soup or cocoa. The wood burning furnace was in the basement and later coal was used for fuel. A kerosene stove in the hall was used for heating lunches.

The bathrooms were outside. The school bell wasn't used too much because it pulled too hard and came off the pulley. Water came from an outside hand pump. If it was frozen, pails of water were hauled in from the Hoysler Farm just south of the school. Students in grades one through eight attended District #31 until the spring of 1948 when consolidation occurred with the Osseo School District. The school was closed for two years, then re-opened in the fall of 1950. The school was used for three years until construction of the Osseo School [14]

Smith School

An article in the April 12, 1973, *Brooklyn Park Post* describes the "Skunk Hollow School" that stood at 89th and West Broadway, and originally was known as the "Smith School." In this school children learned the three Rs for over seven decades. In later years Brooklyn Park policemen battled with skunks in the school, hence the nickname of the once Smith School. Former Mayor Baldwin Hartkopf believed the school was built around 1880 after its predecessor, a log cabin school, burned to the ground. Hartkopf attended the school in 1908 as a six year old. Effective use of the school ended around 1950 according to Hartkopf.

The Brooklyn Park Police Department was housed in the building in the 1960s. In the later 1960s and early 1970s the school sat vacant and its windows boarded with its floor buckling. In April 1972 the Brooklyn Historical Society, through agreement with the Brooklyn Park City Council, started housing artifacts from the building and began restorating it. This pleased former Mayor Hartkopf, who wanted to make a historical landmark out of the building. Because the school was located on valuable property, the Brooklyn Park Recreation and Park Department proposed a plan to move it to the Historical Farm. This never materialized and the school building apparently was just burned to the ground.[16]

Smith School, District #32
Minnesota Historical Society

Twin Lake School

The District #281 section of southwestern Brooklyn Center was once a part of the Twin Lake District. In the summer of 1945, the three-person school board of District #25 passed a resolution to dissolve the district. Rapidly increasing enrollments, lack of matching facilities, and the difficulty of arranging education for grades 9-12 at nearby Robbinsdale or Patrick Henry high schools, were cited as the reasons. Previously, Robbinsdale-Crystal Independent District #24 agreed to join the Twin Lake District. At the annual school meeting of district patrons on July 16, 1945, the vote was 103 to 13 in favor of dissolution and joining Robbinsdale. However, this action was quickly declared illegal by the Hennepin County Attorney because a local district could only dissolve, but could not vote to join another district; this power was reserved for the Board of County Commissioners. Another favorable vote was held in August and by mid September the County Board acted favorably to attaching Twin Lake to Independent District #24 (the core of modern District #281). The building still stands.[17]

Schools Serving Brooklyn Township Today

Today's schools bear little resemblance to the schools of the 19th century in terms of numbers, size, educational opportunity, ages served, programs, etc. The Benson, Schreiber, and Cap Martin Schools were rural, one room schools with a simple 3 Rs curriculum serving students in grades 1-8. Pictures of Abraham Lincoln and George Washington were generally found in front of the classroom, along with a chart illustrating the Palmer Method of Handwriting. The United States Flag could also be found, which was used for the Pledge of Allegiance.

Today, Anoka-Hennepin School District #11 has three elementary schools serving the northeast section of Brooklyn Township: Evergreen, Monroe, and Riverview. Brooklyn Center District #286 has the Earle Brown Elementary School serving students in southeast Brooklyn Township, while Osseo School District #279 has eleven elementary schools serving students in northwest Brooklyn Township: Birch Grove, Crest View, Edgewood, Edinbrook, Fair Oaks, Garden City, Orchard Lane, Palmer Lake, Park Brook, Willow Lane and Zanewood. Robbinsdale District #281 serve students in Southwest Brooklyn Township via Northport and Lincoln elementary schools.

Earle Brown School, early 1960s

The same districts serve secondary students in Brooklyn Township—Anoka Hennepin District #11: Jackson Junior High in Champlin; Champlin Park High School in Champlin; Osseo District #279: Brooklyn Junior High in Brooklyn Park, Northview Junior High in Brooklyn Park, Osseo Junior High in Osseo, Park Center High School in Brooklyn Park, Osseo High School in Osseo; Robbinsdale District #281: Hosterman Junior High in New Hope, Cooper High School in New Hope; Brooklyn Center District #286: Brooklyn Center Junior and Senior High School.[18]

The compulsory instruction law was rewritten in 1997 to explicitly authorize home schooling for students in the compulsory school age. There was home schooling prior to this but it was not specifically addressed by statute. Home schooling is growing in the state but in Brooklyn Center #286, only twelve students are home schooled in grades K-12 and most are elementary students.

Open Enrollment allows students to attend other school districts of their choice under certain conditions and is open to students K-12. Some districts lose or gain students through this program. As an example, Brooklyn Center #286 has 29% of its high school students in open enrollment and 12% of its elementary student body.

Pre-school and nursery schools for pre-kindergarten students are sponsored or run by schools and other private agencies to accommodate parents who desire their children to have this experience or need to do it because both parents work outside the home. Some schools and private parties provide day care programs for even younger children for the same reason.[19]

No private or parochial high schools are to be found in Brooklyn Center and Brooklyn Park but many high school age students elect to attend private schools outside the area, such as Totino Grace in Fridley. There are some parochial schools (grades 1-8) serving students in the area, most prominent of which is St. Alphonsus Catholic School at 7025 Halifax Avenue North in Brooklyn Center. St. Vincent de Paul School in Osseo and St. Elizabeth Ann Seton School on the Mineapolis/Brooklyn Center border are available for students grades 1-8. There is a Step By Step Montessori School in Brooklyn Park for parents who subscribe to that approach to education.

Hennepin Technical College

Hennepin Technical College, with campuses in Brooklyn Park and Eden Prairie, is the community's technical college providing technical education in over 45 career fields. In response to the economic and educational needs of the community, the Minnesota legislature in 1968 passed legislation that allowed the formation of Joint Independent School District 287. The mission of the district was to provide vocational education for post high school students seeking career education and high school students attending the thirteen suburban Hennepin school districts. Before the buildings were constructed, classes were held in area high schools. The two campuses officially opened in 1972 with over 1,900 students enrolled in forty-five career programs.

Since 1972 the college has undergone numerous remodeling and building projects to respond to enrollment growth and the changing needs in training. Many changes have been made in career offerings. In addition, changes occurred in the governance of the college. In 1995 as a result of legislative action, all public two-year and four-year colleges, with the exception of the University of Minnesota, were merged under one state governing board. The new system is known as Minnesota State Colleges and Universities (MnSCU).

North Hennepin Technical College

Responding to the changing needs of the community, the college offers greater flexibilty in course offerings and scheduling which allows students to fit college work into their busy work and family schedules. While many students are entering a career for the first time, an equal number of students with four-year degrees are attending Hennepin Technical College to enhance their career opportunities. In 1999, full-time enrollment was 3,651 with a head count of over 7,000. In addition, Customized Training Services provided industry-specific training for over 10,000 students. Eleven hundred students attended from the area high schools.[o]

North Hennepin Community College

The 1965 Minnesota State Legislature enlarged the junior college system by adding two more in the Twin Cities—one in Northwest Hennepin County and the other in the Anoka/Ramsey County area, serving students in the Brooklyn Township area. North Hennepin Junior College, as it was known then, opened its doors in a former Osseo Junior High in 1966 and moved to its new campus in Brooklyn Park three years later. Chancellor Philip Helland appointed Dale Lorenz as the school's first president. He and a small staff and faculty started NHS (North Hennepin School) in Osseo in 1966. North Hennepin State Junior College eventually became North Hennepin Community College through the work of school officials and legislators.

A interesting story surrounds the debate as to the permanent location of North Hennepin Community College. Some Osseo officials wanted the school located in Osseo while many Brooklyn Center and Brooklyn Park officials wanted the school in Brooklyn Park. The latter won out and the school was built at 7411 85th Avenue North in Brooklyn Park and opened for classes in 1969.

North Hennepin Community College

The college is an active community college with classes for two-year degrees and continuing education. The first catalogue for North Hennepin Junior College listed seventeen lower-division and pre-professional curriculums, leading to an associate of arts degree. Students seeking a Bachelors Degree transferred to a four-year college or university. North Hennepin Community College is an outstanding two-year public institution that had a student body of 6,622 in the fall of 1999, more than fifteen times larger than the humble start in Osseo in 1965.[21]

Conclusion

This chapter hopefully tells you where we have been in education in the past 150 years in Brooklyn Township, and where we are today. But what will education be like in the next millennium? Will educators be so preoccupied with mandates and security concerns that they lose sight of what education is all about? Already there is public concern about where we are headed, Some ask if we should return to simpler times and focus on the 3 Rs once again? The controversy over the present "Profiles in Learning," and the Graduation Standards proposed by the State, are typical of this debate.

Can and should the public education focus be cradle to grave educational programs and services? What will the public treasury permit? How much accountability can be or should be put into the system? Can technology solve all education problems? Some educators believe education is cyclical. Will we come back to where we started or will the public always demand more? The key to good education has always been a caring teacher, concerned parents and willing and motivated students. The writers believe a good public education system is and has been the backbone and strength for people in Brooklyn Township. The writers hesitate to predict the future in education, but after reviewing education in the past 150 years, they remain optimistic.

Reflections of a Superintendent

Dr. LeRoy Norsted, Superintendent of Osseo Independent School District #279 from 1958-1984, was interviewed by the writers on October 17, 1999 about his experiences as Superintendent in District #279. He saw enrollment in the district increase from 1,800 students K-12 in 1958 to 18,000 in 1984 when he retired. Only a couple of bond issues for buildings were defeated during his tenure. Most of them passed as Superintendent Norsted, his staff and the community had a vision for the future. Boundary lines for attendance purposes were another thing, and always were subject to controversy. Park Center High School opened in 1971 and Brooklyn Junior High on the same site at 73rd and Brooklyn Boulevard initially took care of the secondary school students living in the north west corner of Brooklyn Township. Both schools were named without much controversy.

Osseo High School, founded in 1924, originally held all the students grades K-12 in the district. Eminent domain was often used by Superintendent Norsted and the school board to secure school sites for future schools as they saw the potential growth for the area. There was some controversy — the Community College site. Should it be in Osseo or Brooklyn Park? It ended up in Brooklyn Park.

The Osseo District always contracted for private transportation for their students. The board had to approach the State Legislature for building construction help. Attorney and legislator Peter Popovich helped in this respect.

When asked what his most satisfying accomplishment was, Superintendent Norsted replied, "Providing quality school buildings for an ever increasing student population. Some of his frustrations settled on committee work, teacher degrees, and inability to get rid of incompetent teachers."[22]

Brooklyn School students, 1936

Reflections of a Student at Benson School, 1940-1948

by Mavis V. Fiebiger Huddle

NOT ONE, but a big two-room school, grades 1-8, a neat red brick building with a wide center stairway leading to Mrs. Olson's "big room" for grades 5-8, and Miss Steinke's "little room" for grades 1-4 (she was a spelling tigress!). First time you missed words, write them 25 times; 2nd, 50 times; 3rd, 100 times. We studied (for tests anyhow) or penmanship practice. Twice blessed!

Each grade had reading, writing, and arithmetic, geography, history—grade one began with Leif Erickson; Mrs. Schmitt came Tuesdays for music, no piano, just a pitch pipe and sing loud! Fridays was art, new masterpieces each weekend. Also, the *Weekly Reader* newspaper designated by grades, informed us on world events, especially World War II. What a thrill to seeing the "Movie Man's" brown panel-job truck at school once each month as we arrived from our long walks (many way over a mile), no buses! Films were black and white, of course.

Playground equipment: four old-style swings, boards on chairs—you quickly learned to stand clear. We had two great lo-o-o-ng teeter-totters, many a sliver in the buns here! And space to play softball! We really went "big time," getting a new steel slide and monkey bar (ladder over two supports)! Great youthful adventures were sneaking around "pirate trails" in huge lilac bushes at front corners of the playground almost year-round, and run-sliding (no sled) on icy wintertime sidewalks!

Rainy days we would play "tame" games in the basement recreation room. Another indoor privilege—looking at our teacher's wonderful View Master disks with pictures from all over the world. They were 3-D and in color.

The basement housed "biffies," a furnace/coal/maintenance room (where sweet Ole Anderson was always there to fix most anything), plus a food storeroom stocked with canned goods prepared each summer by school mothers. Also, the kitchen and lunchroom was decorated for holidays by Mrs. Palmquist (Palmy), a wonderful cook. She even made clever holiday tray favors. And heavenly brownies. Hot lunches (meal, milk, dessert) were 25 cents weekly; later they jumped way up to 50 cents.

There was a teachers' lounge, and a library with a hectograph that made purple copies of pictures or materials the teacher prepared for us, lots of "art." Some of us (our work finished) got to operate this magical copy machine.

The "Benson Men's Club" sponsored at least one dance a year at Riverlyn Inn (95th at West River Road), as well as plays and musical programs to raise money for the necessary extras. PTAs couldn't sponsor functions where liquor was sold. Dances were great family fun, and many kids came. Jimmy Werner danced a great waltz and schottische at age eight, and he taught me. At the age of seven, I thought he was fantastic.

Grade 8, Class of 1948, was booted mid-year to Anoka; our eight seats were needed for others. We missed our 8th grade graduation, a big event back then.

The community grew. Benson School, now three rooms by using the teachers' lounge, became impractical. Riverview put on a big addition, and Monroe and Evergreen Park Elementary Schools were built. Benson School, named for the man who donated the property, went dormant until its quiet, almost unnoticed demolition.

Notes

1. Warren H. Olson, "A Historical Study of Independent School District #286, Brooklyn Center, 1877-1967." Research paper in partial fulfillment for the degree of Master in Education, Macalaster College, 1967, 11-16.

2. Ibid, 82-97.

3. Erling Johnson. Interview by Wallace Bernards, Warren Lindquist, and Warren Olson, tape recording, 20 September 1999, Brooklyn Historical Society.

4. Avis Nelson, "History of Brooklyn Schools." Handwritten six-page manuscript. Early history of Brooklyn Township, especially Brooklyn School, District #27; Rev. E. D. Neill, *History of Hennepin County*. Minneapolis: North Star Publishing Company, 1881, 285-293; Township History, Brooklyn, 1469-1470.

5. Mary Harrison, "Reminiscences of Early Settlers," Brooklyn Historical Society.

6. Doug Germundson, "She Recalls the one-room Schoolhouse Days," *Brooklyn Park Post*, 29 January 1976.

7. "Lincoln Elementary School, 1860-1985; Serving our Community for 125 years." District #281 archives, Robbinsdale, Minnesota.

8. Harry Kopacz, Letter, not dated, reminisces about Benson School, Brooklyn Historical Society; Paul Hirschoff, "History of Benson School spans over a Century," *Brooklyn Park Post*, 29 January 1976; Gail Bakken, "Closing of Benson School Ends Years of History for Structure." *Brooklyn Center Press*, 26 September 1957.

9. Diane (Dee) Mattson, Article on Benson School, Brooklyn Historical Society.

10. Jane Hallberg, Leone Howe, and Mary Jane Gustafson, "History of the Earle Brown Farm". Brooklyn Center Historical Society, 1983, 15-16.

11. "14 Classrooms are Destroyed by Fire," *Brooklyn Center Post*, 23 February 1968.

12. Hallberg, Howe and Gustafson.

13. Doug Germundson, "She Recalls the one-room School House Days," *Brooklyn Park Post*, 29 January 1976.

14. Norene Roberts, letter dated 12 November 1995 to Jane Hallberg and Roxana Benjamin, about Schreiber School, Brooklyn Historical Society; Jane Hallberg, miscellaneous notes on the District #31 Schreiber School, 9900 Regent Avenue North, 20 November 1995, Brooklyn Historical Society.

15. Eldon Tessman. Interview by Jane Hallberg, date unknown. Brooklyn Historical Society.

16. "'Skunk Hollow' School gets a new Lease on Life," *Brooklyn Park Post*, 12 April 1971, two sections.

17. C. M. (Clark) Ostrum, "Minutes of Twin Lake School Board 1945-19. District #281 archives, Robbinsdale, Minnesota.

18. Brooklyn Park, Brooklyn Center, Maple Grove, Osseo phone book, August 1998-99, by GTE Sun Community Directories.

19. Minnesota Statutes, "Compulsory Instruction Law. Health Standards for School Children. Non- Public Pupil Aids." Includes laws as amended during the 1999 Legislative Session, MN Revisor of Statutes; Department of Children, Families, and Learning. Memo to "Individuals Interested in Home School Information" from Traci LaFerriere, dated May 1999, Brooklyn Historical Society.

20. Carole M. Carlson, Hennepin Technical College, one page history of Hennepin Technical College, 9 June 2000, Brooklyn Historical Society.

21. John Reilly, "Origins of the Two Year Public College in Minnesota, 1914-1970." Chapter Two of five-chapter manuscript with notes, Brooklyn Historical Society.

22. Leroy Norsted, interview by Wallace Bernards, Warren Lindquist and Warren Olson, 14 September, 1999, Brooklyn Historical Society.

Chapter Five

SOCIAL ISSUES

THERE ARE A WHOLE LOT OF STORIES to be told to each other in the Brooklyns as we continue to celebrate our growing diversity, and this is what this book is all about, telling, listening to and learning one another's stories.

The Brooklyns area people began with the first generation Native Americans. The second-generation settlers on the land were of various nationalities that on the census would be categorized as the "white" race.

There was "ethnic" and "class" discrimination among the nationalities as evidenced by restrictions on where Norwegians could be buried in Mound Cemetery and statements about the people who settled in the area bordering on Minneapolis: "That's where the Bohemians lived and we didn't talk to them." A "Bohemian" in the dictionary is described as "one who lives unconventionally." Some of the people in Bellvue Acres, Brooklyn Center's first neighborhood, did live unconventionally: in underground, chilly, capped basements.[1]

In 1913 was the beginning of a good-sized Black community that was centered around 50th and Humboldt, but reached north only to the Minneapolis city limits.[2]

The Brooklyn Center 1960 federal census of 24,356 included twenty-four Negro, forty-seven other, and the balance white. The 1970 census population of 35,173 represented 1% minority, 4% in 1980 of a census population of 31,230, and 10% of a population of 29,079 in 1990. The Black population increased from twenty-four in 1960, 182 in 1970, 530 in 1980 to 1502 in 1990. The Native American population was 201 in 1980 and 271 in 1990. The Asian population had increased from 296 in 1980 to 668 in 1990. And the Spanish/Hispanic/Latino population was 367 in 1990.[3]

The story is told of the Black pole yard employee who purchased land near Twin Lake in Brooklyn Center and in turn sold land to the Black community in the mid and late 1950s when the Maurice Britts, Ulysses Boyd and Charles Nichols families built their homes. Maurice Britts and Charles Nichols are both former educators. Nichols was not permitted to buy a house in Garden City when that subdivision was built in the 1950s because he is Black. Maurice Britts is a writer of books and poetry including *I Will Survive*. Maurice was Brooklyn Center's first Black Council person in the 1970s. Charles Nichols is also a former Brooklyn Center Council member and in 2000 is the appointed chairman of the Metropolitan Airports Commission. Ulysses Boyd served on the Brooklyn Center Community Prayer Breakfast Committee for many years.[4]

I Will Survive *by Maurice Britts*

The Brooklyn Park League of Women Voters government study in 1965 gave an overview of the 1960 federal census on population characteristics: "with a population of 10,197, most are white, there is one Negro, four Indians, eight Japanese, and one of another race."[5]

The Brooklyn Park 1970 federal census population of 26,230 represented less than

1% minority races. In 1980 the minority population was 4.3% of 43,332 and in 1990, 10% of 56,778. The Black population had increased from 840 in 1980 to 2,785 in 1990. The American Indian census count was 170 in 1980 and 348 in 1990. The Asian population was 614 in 1980 and 1,916 in the 1990 federal census. The Spanish/Hispanic/Latino population was 650 in the 1990 census.[6]

In 1967 a Community and Human Resource Development Forum moderated by Vi Kanatz, executive director of the State Commission Against Discrimination, was sponsored by the Brooklyn Center Chamber of Commerce. Rev. Carl Groettum, pastor of Cross of Glory Lutheran Church, (Charles Nichols' family pastor) called for "open housing" and "equal opportunity in employment." Pastor Groettum said; "We teach that all men are the children of God by creation through faith in Jesus Christ, but we don't treat all men as brothers. There is a great contradiction between [church] leaders and what the people who are the church say and do. We can't legislate. We can't pass laws to make men free. We have to change the hearts of men."[7]

Bob Larsen, then president of Brookdale Ford, said: "Character, industry, self discipline are needed. We must re-affirm faith in the dignity of individual man."[8]

Mary Jane Gustafson, newspaper editor, writing an editorial about the Forum said: "Dr. Duane Orn perhaps best hit the nail on the head, offering one solution to many of today's ills, Dr. Orn said: "We parents must open up our hearts, look at ourselves and set good examples."[9]

The Brooklyn Center Human Rights Commission was created by the City Council in 1968. The Commissions name was changed to Human Rights and Resources Commission in 1987, and in 2000 is inactive. In 1998 Brooklyn Center joined with nine other cities to form a Northwest Hennepin Human Rights Coalition. The Coalition hosted the March 2000 Heritage Festival. The Heritage Festival began in 1992 to help area citizens understand and welcome the increasing diversity.[10]

The Brooklyn Park Human Relations Commission was formed in 1994 to achieve the goals of the City to provide equal opportunities and fair treatment for all people. Brooklyn Park is one of the ten cities in the Northwest Hennepin Human Rights Coalition.[11]

Native Americans

Until the 1851 treaties opened the land for settlement in 1852 the first generation Native Americans were camped in the Brooklyns and had contact with the land by walking the trails. What must have been the Indians' understanding as squatters were claiming land ownership, a concept foreign to their own culture?

A corollary could be made to another land area with the same distinctive dates of 1851 and 1852:

Chief Seattle, born in 1786, was chief of the allied tribes of Puget Sound when white settlers arrived in that area in 1851. In 1852, Chief Seattle wrote in a letter to the U.S. government:

"We love this earth as a newborn loves its mother's heartbeat. So, if we sell you our land, love it as we have loved it. Care for it as we have cared for it. Hold in your mind the memory of the land as it is when you receive it. Preserve the land for all children and love it, as God loves us all.

As we are part of the land, you too are part of the land. This earth is precious to us. It is also precious to you. One thing we know: There is only one God. No man, be he Red or White Man, can be apart. We are brothers after all."[12]

So the second generation of people moved onto the land in Brooklyn, and there is evidence they heeded Chief Seattle's message without hearing or knowing it, as have the generations who followed in the last 148 years.

On June 15, 1924, the U.S. Congress approved a Law making all Indians citizens. [13]

But what has happened to the American Indians with the settlers coming onto the land? Indian Reservations were established where the natives were forced to live. There are reservations today, but some of the people have moved out, bringing their traditions and values with them. Natives will tell you they return to a home on the Reservation to find peace, to share and experience Native family values and traditions. Among them are their deep respect for their elders, the children, the drums, their music, the dances, their healing ceremonies, their love of the land and their people. [14]

In 2000, the Native Americans are sovereign nations within the United States, and the debate continues about the land, fishing rights and other issues. Gambling and other business establishments have provided employment and a source of income for the people.[15]

Chippewa spiritual leaders from four Minnesota Indian reservations and one from Canada met on April 13, 2000, at the Leech Lake powwow grounds in Cass Lake, Minnesota for an unprecedented ceremony during which they asked forgiveness for humankind's disrespect of the Earth and its creator. The spiritual leaders said they've recently had dreams and visions that indicate the Great Spirit is using floods, catastrophic winds, snowless winters and drought to warn Indians and non-Indians alike to return to simpler and more spiritual lives. The leaders normally work alone, but they said the situation is so grave they joined forces for the special ceremony that included singing and praying in their native Ojibwe language. [16]

Mah-Gos-Equay, a descendant of Minnesota's Chief Whitefisher, grew up on the White Earth Indian Reservation and has lived in Brooklyn Park for 49-years. We share her Native American life story:

Eva Whitefisher

Being Native American by Mah-Gos-Equay

I am a proud Native American of one-third Ojibwe (Chippewa) Indian descent.

"Chippewa" is a white man's word. Long ago, when he asked the Indian what tribe he belonged to, the Indian said "Ojibwe," and the white man thought he said "Chippewa."

"Indian" also is a white man's word. Christopher Columbus was off-course when he landed in America. He thought he was in West Indies; thus, he called us "Indians." In grade school we were taught (because the history books said so) that Columbus discovered America, and I used to sit and ponder that because I knew we were already here when Columbus arrived! Which gives you an insight into how little we counted—how unimportant we were.

I grew up in Callaway on the White Earth Indian Reservation in northwestern Minnesota. There are still many, many Indian reservations all over the United States, places hand-picked by the government, many of them on the most desolate land that could be found, and originally guarded by Army soldiers to be certain that the Indians stayed on the reservations. Food supplies were provided by the government, issued from the Army outposts, much of which never reached the Indians.

My great grandmother, Eva Whitefisher, was the daughter of a famous Ojibwe Indian Chief. I am proud to be the descendant of a chieftain, Chief Whitefisher. Eva was an interpreter for Bishop Whipple, the first Episcopal bishop of Minnesota. She lived in the Crow Wing area near Brainerd, on Gull Lake, where a reservation had been established for the Indians.

The lumber barons decided that the timber land was too valuable for Indians to live on, so a new reservation was established for them at White Earth, which at that time was a very remote area. The time was the early 1860s. In the spring, the entire band of Gull Lake Indians were uprooted and marched all the way to White Earth. My grandmother Emma (Eva Whitefisher Beaulieu's daughter), was very young at the time, but was told that the Indians were starving, so at night some of the Indian men would leave the reservation and take vegetables from gardens. When a member of the tribe did not return, they knew he had been caught and hanged or shot.

For years the Indian HAD TO live on the reservation — he could not move from it. My grandmother had a picture, "End of the Trail," hanging on her living room wall. She told me one time that the picture tells the whole story of the Native American. His land had been taken from him, he had been stripped of his hunting and fishing grounds, and he had no place left to go."[17]

Mii-gwetch! Thank you!

Being Black by Dr. William Dudley

My name is Bill, and my skin is black, so is my son's. This is our heritage.

My grandfather, born into slavery, taught himself to read and write. He could read the Bible better than I could. I grew up, the second oldest in a family of eleven children, on my father's tobacco and cotton farm in Aurora, North Carolina. My grandfather moved in with our family when he was eighty years old and I was eight. He taught Sunday school when he was age one-hundred, and was responsible for my basic philosophy of life. These are some of his philosophies:

1. Hard work never hurt anyone.
2. If anyone can, I can.
3. Nothing beats a trial but failure.
4. There is always room for improvement.
5. The old "can't," never gets anything done.

Dr. William Dudley and his son, Ballam

My father lived education. He was always reading. His life style was characterized by his respect for God's law, respect for human beings, respect for man's laws expressed through the virtues of honesty, justice, temperance, fortitude and prudence. He left a legend of parental success.

My mother's prudence was demonstrated by her philosophy — never hate because the hater is the loser. Education is something that cannot be stolen—. She rewarded us for honesty. There was no drinking, gambling, swearing, cursing or dancing in her house by anyone. Love was a good word, but rarely used except in the biblical context. Yet, the sincerity in words, deeds and actions made love a media for our family lives. By the time I was five-years old I knew education was man's acquired asset.

This was my beginning! We prayed the Bible together. I learned the Scriptures that Christians know in Galatians 3:26, 28 from granddad's King James Version: "For ye are all the children of God by faith in Christ Jesus. There is neither Jew nor Greek, there is neither bond (slave) nor free, there is neither male nor female: for ye are all one in Christ Jesus." I learned from the Bible book of Philippians not to be intimidated by my opponents in any situation not only to believe in Christ, but to suffer for Him.

Is it not surprising then, grounded in the Word and knowing our true identity, that all but one, and he is a traveling minister with the Evangelical Church, have

William Dudley with his family

graduated from college? Among seven brothers and three sisters, we have fourteen college degrees.

In 1957, after seven years at Tuskegee College in Alabama, and receiving my Doctor of Veterinary Medicine degree, I came to Minnesota from the deep south with a keen understanding of being treated as a second class citizen. I have learned that prejudice is a liability that must be treated as any other liability in order to succeed in the north or south. Driving through South Dakota, I stopped at a motel for a room, only to have the attendant turn the lights on, see me, and then turned the lights off. The next motel I stopped at the attendant gave me a room, asked if I needed a wake-up call, truly a different experience from the south. During internship training, I learned what happened to me in situations was an organized process to keep Blacks ignorant. My first job in Minnesota was working for the federal government as a meat inspector in St. Paul.

In December 1958 I learned that Dr. Lyle Spake, the veterinarian in Brooklyn Center, wanted to sell. I learned that the telephone was an asset, but my face was a liability. Nobody wanted to lend me the money and I so informed Dr. Spake. The next day Dr. Spake had me call a loan officer with TCF to inquire about a loan he had arranged for me. The banker asked about my credit and I told him I had none because I had just finished college. Two weeks later the loan was approved and I had never met anyone at the Minneapolis TCF Bank.

Recognizing my facial liability, I permitted Dr. Spake and the realtor to process the building acquisition through Village Hall. Everything went well until I visited Village Hall upon the insistence of my attorney, then I was turned down. A Mr. Abraham took my case, and I was allowed to operate my business.

I joined Trinity Church, married, but it took eighteen months before we could find a place to live in the area. We purchased land to expand the business and I credit Ed Hamernick at Brooklyn Center State Bank who had faith in me. Mr. Hamernick wanted the land loan paid before I would build a new structure. I paid the loan earlier than scheduled, built our new building and we moved into the adjoining apartment. We were able to buy a lot on Medicine Lake in Plymouth by buying it through another person, after we were told it was sold. Because of the sloping lakeshore lot we needed an architect to design our home. In 1970, we moved into our new home and I still reside there with my son, Ballam, age 14, named after my grandfather.

I am a charter member of the Brooklyn Center Chamber of Commerce and was president in 1970-1971; a member of Toastmasters: past YMCA Board of Management, the Plymouth Human Rights Commission, and Jaycees and Lions Club.

I, too, like Martin Luther King, have a dream, that my son will be judged not by the color of his skin, but by the content of his character.

I end my story with a humble prayer for forgiveness: "Ask and you shall receive..." I ask forgiveness for the crimes and sins of my Black brothers and sisters toward humanity, and in the name of my Black brothers and sisters give forgiveness to others for the crimes and sins against us.[18]

Being White by Lynne Johnston

In 1951 the Tousignaut family, a family with eight or ten kids, were chicken farmers at the location that is now Brookdale Ford (Bass Lake Road and Highway 100) in Brooklyn Center. The Tousignaut children attended Our Lady of Victory School in North Minneapolis.

Joanne Tousignaut and I were friends from school. I don't know why, but we loved to spend time at the chicken farm. My family lived at 46th and Camden in North Minneapolis, then moved to Brooklyn Center in 1954.

It was Joanne's tenth birthday. Mrs. Tousignaut loaded us girls in the back of their family pick-up truck for a birthday swimming party at Twin Lake in Brooklyn Center. We were stopped at the gate with the message that the white girls could come in, but the Black girl could not come in. Joyce Bush, our friend who was Black. encouraged us to leave her behind to wait outside the gate. Mrs. Tousignaut was having none of this. We girls were loaded back into the pick-up truck and we proceeded to Camden pool for our birthday party.[19]

Being Hmong by Mylee Xiong

First we want to tell you that the original Lee family is Hmong and we came from Laos. My husband's name is Chang Lee and my name is Mylee Xiong.

I was born in Thailand in 1975, during the Vietnam War. My mother was pregnant with me while walking from Laos to Thailand. If I had been born on the way, I would have been killed to protect all the others because the enemy would have heard me cry as a baby. I was born the first night we arrived in Thailand. I am very thankful to be alive and here in Brooklyn Center today.

A Lutheran Church in Huron, South Dakota sponsored my mother, myself and my three sisters from Thailand. We were the only Asian family in Huron. When I was in the second grade we moved to California. I found I had lost my original language and had to learn it all over again.

My brother came to the United States in 1976. I didn't know I had a brother until I got here. He is a police officer in Merced City, California. My mother died in a car accident in 1997. My sisters still live in California.

I met my husband at the library in Merced City. We married a short time later and have four children: Kurtys, Kathlene, Austin and Alisha.

When we first moved to Minnesota from California, we lived in North Minneapolis but in 1998 had the opportunity to purchase our home on 55th Avenue North in Brooklyn Center.

It is our tradition that the oldest son care for the family, so we have an extended family living with us. It is also a tradition that the older parents care for the children. When the youngest son marries, the parents then live with him and his family until they pass away.

In school, our kids take ESL (English as a Second Language) because they did not speak English. At a teachers conference recently we were told our son is the top pupil in the ESL program. Our first son already knows computers and is even teaching me on our computer. Education is important to us, as is being responsible. Some of our family members attend the University of Minnesota and Brooklyn Center Junior and Senior High School.

My husband and I are both employed and other members of the family also contribute to the family's needs. I was "Employee of the Month" at a large International Corporation, and am given a lot of trust and responsibility. I am a hard worker and want to excel.

Chang loves to fish and his dream of owning a boat has become a reality. We enjoy growing our own vegetables and eat traditional and American foods.[21]

Mylee Xiong, Chang Lee and family

Notes

1. *The Brooklyns: History of Brooklyn Center and Brooklyn*, Chapter 9, Cemeteries; Chapter 12, Housing.

2. Roy and Karol Arneson, Edythe Scheidegger, Historians for Olson PTA, *Floyd B. Olson Jr. High School and the History of Camden*, Spring 1974, 30.

3. 1960s Census of Population, Volume I, Characteristics of the Population, Part 25 MN, 25-88, Hennepin County Library; 1970 Census Characteristics of the Population, Vol. 1 Part 25 MN; Hennepin County Census Analysis Center, 1980 Census Report; Hennepin County Census Analysis Center, 1990 Census Report November 1991; County and City Data Book, U.S. Department of Commerce, Bureau of the Census 1994.

4. Conversations with Maurice Britts, Ulysses Boyd, Charles Nichols by Ernee McArthur, 10 February 1999, BHS.

5. Brooklyn Park League of Women Voters, *The Mushrooming Community*. Brooklyn Park, Minnesota, 1965, BHS.

6. 1960's Census of Population.

7. Mary Jane Gustafson, "Pastor Carl Groettum Calls For Open Housing, Equal Opportunity," *Brooklyn Center Post*, 26 January 1967, BHS.

8. Ibid.

9. Ibid.

10. *The Brooklyns: History of Brooklyn Center and Brooklyn Park*, Chapter 7, Organizations.

11. Ibid.

12. Chief Seattle, 1852, Letter to the U.S. government, BHS.

13. *The World Almanac and Book of Facts 1998*, *United States History*, 503, Hennepin County Library.

14. Conversation with Charlotte Tommerdahl and Leona Raisch by Ernee McArthur, BHS.

15. Ibid.

16. "Indians see hand of Great Spirit in weather," *Minneapolis Star Tribune*, 14 April 2000, BHS.

17. *Being Native American*, Mah-Gos-Equay's story.

18. *Being Black*, Dr. William Dudley.

19. *Being White*, Lynne Johnston.

20. *Being Hmong*, Mylee Xiong.

Chapter Six

CHURCHES

The First Churches

THE BEGINNINGS of the Methodist-Episcopal Church took place here in the spring of 1854, with the formation of a class. The first preaching took place in two residences: that of Elder J. W. Dow, who lived in a log shanty, and the 12 by 16 foot cabin of J. P. Plummer. The church was at the same location as today—7200 Brooklyn Boulevard. The Brooklyn Baptist Church was built in 1868 at a cost of $2,200 and a size of 25 by 38 feet, with a six-foot vestibule. It was on the northwest corner of the Brooklyn Boulevard and 69th Avenue North intersection.

St. Vincent de Paul Church

The beginning of the first Catholic church is described by Father Henry Boerboom of St. Vincent de Paul Church, Osseo. "The pioneers here… were religiously inclined." In 1855 Father Keller, who spoke German and French, "said the first Holy Mass in the first frame house of Osseo (owned and occupied by Pierre Bottineau) which stood three-quarters of a mile west of the present site of the village." (Bottineau's old 1854–built house was discovered by a member of the Brooklyn Historical Society. It has been moved by the City of Maple Grove with the intent to renovate it, so it is still in existence today.) One hundred families attended the mass. The priest remarked, "You people should have a church here." That remark caused Bottineau to organize the building of the first church in Osseo, using the finest timbers from the woods. Within a few months a log church which measured about 30 by 50 feet was built on his father-in-law's farm (Pierre Gervais). Called the "Church of St. Louis," it was about forty rods west of the St. Vincent de Paul Church which was torn down circa 1997. Steeple Point senior housing is now on the St. Vincent de Paul Church site, and the new Catholic church is to the northeast of the old location in Brooklyn Park. Apparently the architects for the new senior housing wanted to preserve history, so they saved the old church steeple and made the front of the building slightly resemble the old church; and in the lobby they have hung a huge light fixture from the old church.

—*Jane Hallberg*

THE MINNEAPOLIS APOSTOLIC LUTHERAN CHURCH NORTH became part of Brooklyn Center, MN, in July 1986, when its members purchased the Faith Community Church Of God building at 6630 Colfax Avenue North. In the early years, the group had met in homes and then in rented facilities.

The ALCN held its dedication services October 18th and 19th, 1986. During the first few years in our Brooklyn Center church, the congregation was pastored primarily by a member, Donald Bisila, and visiting speakers from other areas of this region. Richard Barney was pastor from 1990 to 1995. Jim Maunu became pastor in 1997.

We believe: "Stand fast therefore in the liberty wherewith Christ hath made us free, and be not entangled again with the yoke of bondage." We are still a small congregation, endeavoring to worship and serve our God as we continue on our journey to that blessed home above. All are welcome to join us in worship.

The Apostolic Lutheran Church North is a branch of the Apostolic Lutheran Church of America. Originally this church group was started in the United States by the Finnish/Swedish/Norwegian immigrants who came to the U.S. in the late 1800s, who were believers in this Christian faith. The Apostolic Lutheran church is primarily Finnish in heritage and Lutheran in doctrine. Many of the members still have Finnish roots.

Apostolic Lutheran Church North

6630 Colfax Ave. N.
Brooklyn Center, MN 55430

IN 1954 AMOS AND NORMA LEVANG felt a burden from the Lord to pioneer a church in Brooklyn Center. The site chosen was Twin Lake School at 4938 Brooklyn Boulevard. The first service was held on Sunday, July 22, 1956, with an attendance of twenty-seven. The organizational meeting of Brooklyn Center Assemblies of God Church was held on November 1, 1956. Property was purchased at 60th and Xerxes Avenue North, the present site of the church. Volunteer labor and the dismantling and salvaging of parts of the original Brooklyn Center Baptist Church building, purchased for $100.00, helped to make an educational unit possible. Dedication took place on October 18, 1959.

In 1964 the parsonage was built. The present sanctuary dedication took place on October 25, 1970.

King's Academy Day Care building was purchased in 1976, providing additional Sunday School and day care space.

In 1977 an Accelerated Christian Education School, grades K-12, began. Five young people graduated in May 1986.

Pastor Levang left in June 1979, Robert Cilke became senior pastor. He and his wife, Barbara, continued the vision of the Levangs with the construction of a Family Life Center. Ground was broken on June 30, 1985 and the dedication was part of the 30th Anniversary. On July 14, 1996, Brookdale Christian Center celebrated the 40th anniversary of the Church. Pastor and Mrs. Robert H. Cilke continue to serve the congregation and the community.

Brookdale Christian Center Assembly of God

6030 Xerxes Ave. N.
Brooklyn Center, MN 55430

Brookdale Covenant Church

5139 Brooklyn Blvd.
Brooklyn Center, MN 55429

TWENTY-TWO PEOPLE GATHERED on November 28, 1899, at the home of Gust Peterson, 4100 Dupont Avenue North. These friends agreed to and signed the charter establishing the Swedish Evangelical Mission Church of Camden Place. The church grew from twenty-two charter members to a membership of 250 in 1954 and a Sunday School consisting of over 450 students of all ages.

The church outgrew the building on 42nd and Emerson Avenues north, and the decision was made to relocate to the Brooklyn Center area and build a new parsonage and church.

In 1949 the church purchased a tract of land at the busy intersection of Hwy 100 and Osseo Road for future use. In 1951 the new parsonage was built on this land. A chapel was built in the basement that became the home of the Community Covenant Sunday School of Brooklyn Center. Groundbreaking services were held for the new church in June of 1955. The cornerstone was laid in October of that year. Brookdale Covenant Church was dedicated in June 1956.

Over the next forty-three years, the church experienced growth and a large variety of ministries, even sending twenty-five of its members to begin a daughter-work in Brooklyn Park, which eventually became Redeemer Covenant Church at 78th and Brooklyn Blvd. In 1999 we observed our centennial with a year-long calendar of events ending on New Year's Eve.

Brooklyn Center Church of Christ

6206 North Lilac Dr.
Brooklyn Center, MN 55430

ON AUGUST 6, 1961, thirty-two people met in the basement of a Dairy Kwik Store to form the Brooklyn Center Church of Christ. In November 1961 the church moved its meeting place to the Brooklyn Center Police, Court and Firehouse building at 65th and Lyndale Ave. N. The congregation grew to an attendance in the eighties and property was acquired at 6206 North Lilac Dr. in Brooklyn Center. Before construction on a new building was completed, the City of Brooklyn Center remodeled the Police, Court and Firehouse building; consequently, the congregation met in the Columbia Heights Field House on Mill St. in northeast Minneapolis from January 1963 through October 1963. When the Field House was unavailable the congregation met in the Columbia Heights VFW Hall. On November 3, 1963, the Brooklyn Center Church of Christ met in its new facilities on North Lilac Drive

By the mid-1960s, the Brooklyn Center Church of Christ had become self-supporting, and in 1969 the first elders were appointed. The Brooklyn Center congregation has been served by six pulpit ministers. Other ministers who worked with the congregation include personal workers, campus ministers, a family minister, a missionary, a youth minister, and a counselor. As of August 31, 1999, the Brooklyn Center Church of Christ included 160 members.

BROOKLYN CENTER LUTHERAN MISSION held its first church service on February 1, 1959, at the Willow Lane Elementary School Annex.

Wilbur F. Dorn was installed as the first resident pastor in November 1959. Shortly after his arrival the congregation was organized. At that time the name of Brooklyn Center Lutheran Mission was changed to Brooklyn Evangelical Lutheran Church, which it is called today. In March 1959 land was purchased at 5840 69th Avenue North in Brooklyn Park. A building was built and used as a chapel and then later converted into a parsonage.

The present church building was dedicated on November 19, 1961. Shortly thereafter, the previous chapel was converted into the parsonage. Since that time, additional acreage has been purchased, so the congregation now rests on a plot of approximately six acres. Brooklyn Evangelical Lutheran Church was a mission church until it became self-supporting as of January 1, 1969.

In 1977 Pastor Wilbur Dorn resigned and Pastor Michael Mulinix was installed in July 1977. Pastor Michael Mulinix resigned in 1998 and Pastor Curtis Holub was installed as the present pastor on March 28, 1999.

An addition to the educational unit of the church was added in the spring and summer of 1983. Members volunteered their time and talents to complete the addition and it was dedicated in October of 1983.

Brooklyn Evangelical Lutheran Church

5840 69th Ave. North
Brooklyn Park, MN 55429

THE BROOKLYN PARK ASSEMBLY OF GOD CHURCH is located in the "Bragdon Memorial" building. This building is currently used for church office and small meetings.

The church meets at the Edinbrook Elementary School on Sunday mornings. They have a 10:00 A.M. service with Sunday School for all ages at 9:15 A.M. A prayer group meets Friday evenings at 7:30. Ken Plaisted is the pastor.

Editor's Historical Note: "Bragdon Memorial" building was the home of the First Freewill Baptist Church of Brooklyn which was incorporated March 5, 1885. The first religious services started in 1879 when they met at the Dunning school house. Elected trustees were Alonzo Bragdon, J.B. Dunning, W.H. Gaslin, Silas Merrill and George W. Pomeroy. The church building was called "Bragdon Memorial" named for Ebin Bragdon, a Christian soldier who died in the Army during the Civil War. He had left a small sum of money, which he wished to be used for Gospel purposes, and it was in the hands of his brother, Alonzo Bragdon. Emmett Rathburn was chosen solicitor for additional funds. Contract for the building was let in June 1885 and completed in September 1885. The cost of the church was $1,250. Church parlors were added in 1910, and the church was stuccoed in 1924.

The "Bragdon Memorial" building was substantially modified circa 1943 during renovation. For a while, the city parked snow plows in the building. In 1988 it was observed the church had pointed arched windows and the exterior walls were covered with siding. New doors, windows, roof and the interior was remodeled with lowered false ceiling and oak beam construction.

Information from the WPA written by Mrs. Edward Neill, Osseo, MN, June 1934. and from Minnesota Historical Properties Inventory, 1988 by Dr. Norene Roberts.

Brooklyn Park Assembly of God

10255 Noble Ave N.
Brooklyn Park, MN 55443

Brooklyn Park Evangelical Free Church

7849 West Broadway
Brooklyn Park, MN 55445

In June 1956 a group chartered as the Brooklyn Center Evangelical Free Church met at the Willow Lane School on 71st and Brooklyn Boulevard. The future building site was on land that had been the home of the first church chairman, John Soderholm. It was their desire that a testimony of the saving power of Jesus Christ be erected on this corner. The building was completed in 1957 at 69th and Quail Avenue North.

By 1968 the congregation had outgrown its facilities, so an auditorium to seat 300, as well as a lower fellowship hall and Christian Education space were added. In 1978 the congregation purchased ten acres of land in Brooklyn Park.

In 1983 the congregation sold the building at the corner of 69th and Quail Avenue North to the Korean Presbyterian Church. Church was then held at Park Center High School. In 1984 the church moved to its present location in Brooklyn Park and changed its name to Brooklyn Park Evangelical Free Church. Nine-hundred people currently attend the services. In 1996 the structure in Brooklyn Park was severely damaged by fire. The congregation met at Osseo Senior High School until May 1998 when the enlarged facility was completed.

Senior pastors who have served our congregation are: founding pastor, A.G. Sandberg; Ed Groenhoff; Merle Christensen; Carl Backie; Gilbert Maple; and our current pastor Richard Ensrud. We praise God for lives that have been changed because of Jesus Christ.

Brooklyn Park Lutheran Church

1400 81st Ave. North
Brooklyn Park, MN 55444

Brooklyn Park Lutheran Church (BPLC) has served the Brooklyn community for nearly forty years. In its humble beginning it was a little church off a crushed rock road surrounded by vast open fields at the corner of Humboldt Avenue and 81st Avenue North. Presently it is located at the busy intersection of a four-lane highway at Highway 252 and 81st Avenue and is surrounded on all sides by well-established neighborhoods. BPLC became easy to identity when three large crosses were installed on its southwest corner.

Its first services were held in Riverview School on November 29, 1959. It was formally organized in April 1960 with ninety-eight charter members. The groundbreaking for the first section of the building was September 25, 1960. A sanctuary was added in 1973. In 1978 ground was broken for an educational wing which was completed in 1979. A large multi-purpose addition was added in 1995.

The church has had only three senior pastors since its beginning. Pastor Delmar Gusdal was its founding pastor and served from 1960 to 1966. Dr. Harley Schmitt was installed as pastor in 1967 and served the congregation until October 1995. During his twenty-eight year ministry the church steadily grew and underwent three building expansion projects. Pastor Todd R. Wallace became senior pastor in July 1996. Nearly five hundred people attend three weekly worship services and the congregation is studying the feasibility of adding a new sanctuary.

BROOKLYN METHODIST CHURCH had its beginnings in 1854 when two mothers knelt in prayer for guidance. Gathering their children, they then began teaching Bible lessons. Though seventy-five men from this community left for the Civil War, the people who were left kept their meetings and the Sunday School alive in homes, granaries, and later in the Howe School. Hiram Bohanon donated the land for the first church building. On September 16, 1866, the first meeting was held in the new church. A second building was added in 1916 under the challenge of Levi Longfellow.

World War I took its toll of youth again, and once more a depression came to the community. For economy, the forty-five member Baptist Church voted to join the fifty-five member Methodist Church in alternating Sunday Services in each building. Finally, the Baptist church was closed and its members joined the Methodists, bringing with them their church bell, which is presently installed in the bell tower of our sanctuary.

In the 1920s a large recreation hall was built under the direction of Reverend Henry Soltau, which served as a true community center. Plays, athletic events, and the "Harvest Home Festivals" were held there for many years. Its use and maintenance became an increasing problem and the building was torn down in the early 1940s. In October 1958 ground was broken for the new educational wing. In the 1960s two houses east of the church were bought for the parking lot.

Brooklyn United Methodist Church

7200 Brooklyn Blvd.
Brooklyn Center, MN 55429

Courtesy of the Minnesota Historical Society

THE FIRST MEMBERS of The Church of Jesus Christ of Latter-day Saints (LDS/ Mormons) arrived in Minnesota in 1847. Shortly after the turn of the century, national Church leaders began discouraging converts from emigrating to Utah, counseling them instead to lay the foundation of the Church in their own communities. Since then, the Church has steadily grown throughout the Twin Cities.

Historically, the Church has had a strong missionary effort. More recently, missionaries are young men and women who are financially supported by their families or personal savings. One can frequently see them walking from one appointment to another or knocking on doors to share a message of Jesus Christ.

For many years, members of the LDS in Brooklyn Park and Brooklyn Center traveled some distance to attend their church meetings. The Church did not own any buildings in the Brooklyn Park and Brooklyn Center area and membership was small. The members traveled to Anoka and Minneapolis for their meetings. It was not until the fall of 1992 that members had a chapel in Brooklyn Park. At the present time, there are about 400 members of the Church living in the Brooklyn Park and Brooklyn Center areas. The Edinbrook chapel houses a Family History Center where members and non-members alike are welcome to research their family history. The Edinbrook Chapel also supports a deaf congregation.

Church of Jesus Christ of Latter-day Saints

4700 Edinbrook Terrace N.
Brooklyn Park, MN 55443

Church of Saint Gerard

*9600 Regent Avenue, North
Brooklyn Park, MN 55443*

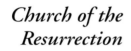

THE CHURCH OF SAINT GERARD was established in 1970. The parish was founded by the Redemptorist Fathers and Brothers of the St. Louis Province and was built on the momentum of the Second Vatican Council. Reverend Robert Oelerich, C.Ss.R. was the first pastor. The original facility was dedicated on May 21, 1971.

In 1990, due to a reconfiguration of their apostolic commitments, the Redemptorist Fathers and Brothers relinquished the pastoral care of St. Gerard's to the Franciscan Friars of the Third Order Regular, Province of the Immaculate Conception. On July 1, 1990, Reverend James Keena, C.Ss.R., the last Redemptorist pastor, bid farewell to the community and Reverend Anthony M. Criscitelli, T.O.R. became the first Franciscan pastor.

The worship space and other areas of the parish center were already beginning to prove inadequate for the 1,600 families that now called St. Gerard's their spiritual home. After extensive research and planning, ground was broken for a new church and addition to the parish center on October 4, 1997. Exactly one year later, the growing community celebrated its first Mass in the new church. The solemn dedication took place on October 18, 1998.

As we prepare to enter a new century, St. Gerard's looks forward to a future filled with growth and possibilities. Faithful to our founding, we strive to be a faith community who takes seriously its baptismal vocation to continue the mission of Jesus Christ.

Church of the Resurrection

*7600 Humboldt Ave. N.
Brooklyn Park, MN 55444*

CHURCH OF THE RESURRECTION'S FIRST SUNDAY SERVICE was held on July 28, 1985. The first months we met in community rooms and schools. On November 15, 1985, Pastor Jim prayed, "Father, you have called us to an important work. Could we please have a permanent home in one year?"

In February 1986, the Rickard children rented the building at 76th and Humboldt Avenue North for their parents' 25th anniversary celebration. It was then the home of Brooklyn Park Wesleyan and had originally been built in 1960 as Emmanuel Baptist Church. The Wesleyan congregation found smaller quarters and we moved in on November 15, 1986 — one year to the day after Pastor Jim made his request of the Lord!

We officially dedicated our building on June 7, 1987. We were bowed with humility as we looked back over the previous twenty-three months. God had given us a beautiful building that seats over 200 and will expand to seat over 550. "This place is to be a launching pad for ministry."

Beginning in 1990, Resurrection Church has been the birthplace for several original Christmas musicals.

The story of Church of the Resurrection continues. We have an awesome respect for the call of God upon us, and believe that we are called to be a church on fire, where the presence of God is so powerfully manifest that people run here to be saved, healed, and set free to love and serve Him!

CROSS OF GLORY began as a mission church of the Evangelical Lutheran Church. The first unit was constructed at 5929 Brooklyn Boulevard in 1955. Pastor Carl Groettum was called in January 1956 to serve the new church. The first service was held on March 31, 1956. The formal organization of the church occurred May 26, 1956.

In the fall of 1956 a second unit was built, since education facilities were inadequate. By 1960 the baptized membership had risen to almost 2,400 and Sunday School enrollment soared. This led to the planning and construction of a new sanctuary. The service in the new sanctuary was held March 18, 1962.

Pastor Groettum retired in 1987. Bruce Kjellberg was called as the senior pastor on January 1, 1988 and retired December 1998. Steven Nelson served as interim senior pastor until Pastor Jerry O'Neill was called in May 2000.

In January of 1989 a decision was made to pursue the building of a pipe organ. The Rutz Organ Company was contracted to build a 33-rank, three-manual organ. It was completed early in 1991. In 1996 a remodeling program was approved, which added a large fellowship hall and kitchen and upgraded the entire building. In 1998 the fellowship hall became the site of a weekly low-cost lunch for senior citizens. Seven churches, including Cross of Glory, provide the volunteers.

Buildings, activities and outreach point to a church, congregation and community looking forward to the 21st Century, led by the cross.

Cross of Glory Lutheran Church

5929 Brooklyn Blvd.
Brooklyn Center, MN 55429

IN 1978 ELM CREEK CHAPEL (ECC), began as a daughter church from Northbrook Alliance Church in Brooklyn Center. We met at Osseo Senior High School. Bob St. Cyr was our founding pastor. In 1979 we purchased twenty acres of land at our present site and in 1983 we completed and dedicated our construction phase one.

In 1986 a daughter church of ECC was started in Champlin called Champlin Community Church (CCC), and construction phase two was built.

In November 1992 ECC and CCC consolidated to become Crossroads Alliance Church (CAC).

In 1999 Jeffrey Jarvis joined the CAC staff along with Senior Pastor Paul Ratzloff and the minister of youth John Byrne. CAC has begun the process of a facility expansion that includes hiring an architectural firm to draw up a master plan for the future.

Crossroads Alliance Church

9000 101st Ave. N.
Brooklyn Park, MN 55445

Edinbrook Church

4300 Edinbrook Pkwy. N.
Brooklyn Park, MN 55443

IN 1948 SEVERAL FAMILIES joined together to start a Baptist church in Brooklyn Center. They held their services in the Earle Brown School. Their student pastor, Don Gold-smith, was attending Bethel College at the time. The church grew in numbers, so all was in order to build a small church building on 57th and Morgan Avenues north. The congregation began using it in 1953. services were held there until it was sold in 1955 to the Northbrook Shopping Center developers.

The congregation moved back to the Earle Brown School until land was purchased to build a church right across the street from the school. In 1957 the congregation moved into the church, which was called the Brooklyn Center Baptist Church. John Breitholz was the pastor.

The church was sold in 1991 to the Korean Presbyterian Church of Minnesota, and it was back to attending church in a Brooklyn Park school for a couple of years.

Land was purchased in Brooklyn Park and another church was built called Edinbrook Church. Ivan Veldhuizen is pastor. The church seeks "to inspire religious people to develop a meaningful relationship with God one person at a time." Church attendance has grown and there are three services on Sunday morning to accommodate all who wish to attend.

Eternal Hope Lutheran Church Missouri Synod

10508 Douglas Drive
Brooklyn Park, MN 55443

MT. OLIVE LUTHERAN CHURCH OF ANOKA established a satellite mission church in the Champlin/Brooklyn Park area in 1971. Eternal Hope Lutheran Church held its first worship service on Palm Sunday, March 26, 1972, in the gymnasium of Jackson Junior High in Champlin. The first church Constitution and the name were adopted on December 22, 1974.

The last service at Jackson Junior High was held on February 25, 1974. Dedication of the building at 10508 Douglas Drive was held on June 2, 1974.

Deacon Austreng served as laypastor until May 1977. the first "official" pastor, The Rev. Gary Ludholz, was installed on May 15, 1977, and served until November 1980. The Rev. Jack E. Jacobsen was installed on January 10, 1982 and served until his retirement on June 20, 1993. The Rev. Tim Booth served as interim pastor 1993–1995. Pastor Roger Dramstad has served Eternal Hope since March 1995.

As the congregation has changed over the years, so has the building. In 1983 the first addition and remodeling of the original "house-church" was begun and was dedicated on October 21, 1984. In 1988 a second addition was built.

Eternal Hope is a small church in the big cities. With a small congregation of about 300 people, it has a very friendly atmosphere. We are looking ahead to celebrating our 30th anniversary in the year 2002.

FAMILY OF GOD LUTHERAN CHURCH is the result of a mission effort begun in this community by the Lutheran Church in America. The Rev. Leroy Pillman was the pastor-developer assigned to the Brooklyn Park area. In September 1970 a meeting was held in the Council chambers of Brooklyn Park Municipal Building and the first worship service was held at Crest View Elementary School, on September 27, 1970, with 154 persons present. On February 7, 1971, the congregation was formally organized. At the first congregational meeting Pastor Leroy Pillman was called as its first pastor.

Family of God Lutheran Church

8625 Zane Ave. N.
Brooklyn Park, MN 55443

During the second year after organizing, Family of God outgrew Crest View and rented the facilities of Our Saviors Reformed Church on Zane Avenue. Worship services and Sunday School were held there until a church building could be completed

On September 24, 1972, groundbreaking ceremonies were held at the Zane Avenue site, and construction was begun shortly thereafter. The building was ready for occupancy early in 1973.

Pastor Pillman resigned on December 31, 1977. Pastor Mark Hallonquist was installed as the second pastor on October 8, 1978. In 1982 Family of God began a campaign to finance the expansion of the church building, which was dedicated March 3, 1985. Family of God approved another capital funding appeal and plans for a new sanctuary which was dedicated on March 5, 1995.

FELLOWSHIP BAPTIST CHURCH organized in September 1993. In April 1994 the former Northbrook Medical Clinic located at 5840 North Lilac Drive in Brooklyn Center was purchased for the home of the Fellowship Baptist Church. The focus of the ministry is to meet the spiritual needs of the residents in the North Metro area. This is a multicultural church, with people of several ethnic backgrounds attending.

Fellowship Baptist Church

5840 N. Lilac Drive
Brooklyn Center, MN 55430

The Pastor ministers weekly to the inmates at the Anoka County Jail. The Church has been instrumental in helping former inmates and their families in putting their lives back together.

There are Sunday School classes for all ages, and a puppet ministry for children. Sunday School meets at 10:00 A.M. The morning worship service is at 11:00 A.M. and the evening service at 6:00 P.M. Wednesday evening at 7:00 P.M. there is a Bible study and prayer time for all ages.

Dr. Keith Hedges has been the pastor of the Church since the beginning. Our future is that of walking in faith and continuing to tell the good news of the gospel and how it can change lives.

First Lutheran Church of Crystal

7708 62nd Ave. N.
Brooklyn Park, MN 55428

IN THE SPRING OF 1951 Rev. J.T. Quanbeck, Executive Director of the Board of Home Missions of the Lutheran Free Church, was authorized to organize and develop a Lutheran church in the Crystal area. Rev. Clarence J. Carlson conducted the first service in the Abraham Lincoln School on August 26, 1951.

On September 16, 1951, Professor George Soberg of Augsburg College became the first part-time pastor. Students from Augsburg started and ran the Sunday School with about fifty students until June 1952. Sunday, May 4, 1952, the First Lutheran Church of Crystal was organized with 20 charter member families. In 1953 a church building was purchased and moved to the current property and was dedicated on May 11, 1954.

Pastor John W. Steen became the first full-time pastor May 31, 1956. Rev. Clarence Framstad became Assistant Pastor in 1957. Other staff assistants have been Pastor William Rosenow, Pastor Kenneth Marquardt, Pastor Lester Dahlen, Pastor Stanley Olson and Pastor Larry Meyer. The first youth pastor was Larry Meyer who was installed August 22, 1976.

Space became a continuing problem throughout the 1950s and 1960s so additional construction was required. An educational building was dedicated May 3, 1959. A new parish house at 8180 62nd Ave. N. was dedicated May 1, 1960. A new church sanctuary was dedicated October 29, 1963. A new Administration Building also was built. A bell tower and elevator were dedicated in 1995.

Grace Fellowship

8601 101st Ave. N.
Brooklyn Park, MN 55445

GRACE FELLOWSHIP began with a Dream, a clear and simple vision in the hearts and minds of a group of Christians. A Dream being built by faith and supported with prayer. What is this Dream? To reach lost and hurting people in our community with the Good News that "You matter to God."

We use music that is contemporary. We speak to issues that relate to daily life in language that is fresh, and with a content that is Biblical. Our slogan is "Come as you are... You'll be loved". Ministering in the 1990s means using cutting edge and contemporary methods to present with excellence the ageless truths of the Bible.

At Grace, Sunday morning worship is only half the story! Friendships begin. Stories are told. Laughter is shared. And people get better acquainted with God.

We will be creative and innovative. We will seek to reach beyond ourselves, caring for the community and the world we live in. We will invest no more than is necessary on buildings. We will invest in outreach and multiplication, seeking to increase the ministry of this church through starting other churches.

We surround all that we do in prayer. If it is in our own power and wisdom that we work, all will be in vain. As we seek and serve our God, our plans shall succeed. We will be a church whose foundation is Prayer!

HARRON CHURCH began in 1914 when Dr. Frank Harron and laypersons from North United Methodist Church came to Brooklyn Center and held Sunday School meetings in various places. In 1927 the land was purchased and a basement was built, with most of the work donated. Paris Reidhead was in charge with his services donated. Ted Nordquist was the only skilled worker on the payroll. Frank Smith dug the basement with his team of horses. The bishop came up one Sunday afternoon and the cornerstone was laid. When they found they were running out of money Mrs. Perkins loaned them $1,500.

In 1932 the dining room and kitchen were added to the basement and the upper structure was built. The first service to be held was Mrs. Perkins' funeral. In her will she canceled the loan and added $500 more.

In 1941 Harron Church was dedicated with a big celebration and the burning of the mortgage. In 1950 the parsonage was built. Rev. Warren Nyberg was it's first full time minister. In 1959 an educational wing was added to the church.

We are helping another church at present. Today we are a church with a small membership, but we are big in spirit! The Kenyan Community Seventh Day Adventists meet in our sanctuary every Saturday, and occasionally we have services together.

Harron United Methodist Church

5452 Dupont Ave. N.
Brooklyn Center, MN 55430

REVEREND RUDOLPH PETERSON, vice-pastor of the newly formed Hope Evangelical Lutheran Church in 1929 wrote in the first annual report "that there was room for and need of a Lutheran Sunday school in this part of the city." Mr. and Mrs. Walter Smith opened their home temporarily for this purpose. So began the mission of what is now Hope Lutheran Church serving the needs of numerous residents of Brooklyn Center for the past seventy-five years.

Pastor Peterson continued in his report: "...in the spring of 1926 the mission board bought a school house located on the Brooklyn Center road just outside the city limits. The schoolhouse was moved to 52nd and Dupont Avenues north. The Sunday school met in this building for the first time on Sunday, May 2, 1926 with seventy-four children in attendance." The congregation was officially organized on December 18, 1928.

During the 1930s and 1940s the congregation grew under the leadership of various pastors, including Melvin Hedin, Kenneth Larson, C.O. Nelson, E.T. Smith, and Carl A. Zimmerman. In 1954 Pastor Zimmerman resigned and Roger E. Carlson became pastor and served for thirty-three years.

A new sanctuary was built in 1957. The former sanctuary was presented to the Pilgrim Rest Baptist Church and moved to 51st and James Avenues North in 1968. Hope helped establish a sister congregation in Brooklyn Center by assigning 100 of its members to join Lutheran Church of the Master. Thomas J. Brock is the current senior pastor.

Hope Lutheran Church

5200 Emerson Ave. N.
Minneapolis, MN 55430

Jehovah Jireh Church of God in Christ

6120 Xerxes Ave. N.
Brooklyn Center, MN 55430

ON MAY 17, 1992, Jehovah Jireh Church of God in Christ held its opening service. There were eighteen people in attendance, twelve of whom signed on as charter members. On July 12, 1992, Elder McKinley Moore was officially installed as pastor of Jehovah Jireh by Jurisdictional Bishop Stanley N. Frazier. On Sunday August 23, 1992, God opened a door in the city of Brooklyn Center, and Jehovah Jireh held its first service at the Brookdale Christian Center Assembly of God.

It was the vision of Pastor Moore that Jehovah Jireh would have its own building in four years. Trusting just as our name says that "The Lord will provide"; Jehovah Jireh moved to our new location in Brooklyn Center on September 3, 1995, just three years and three months after our opening service.

We have since learned that the original congregation which built this building broke ground on October 2, 1960.

We are now in our sixth year of existence. Our membership has continued to grow. In November 1998 we had the official opening of the "Bishop C.H. Mason Institute of Child Development." In 1998 God blessed Pastor Moore to leave his secular job, and minister full time at Jehovah Jireh. On December 30, 1998, we fulfilled our lease option and closed on the purchase of our building. To God be the glory for the things He has done!

Living Word Christian Center

9201 75th Ave. N.
Brooklyn Park, MN 55428

IN NOVEMBER 1980 Mac and Lynne Hammond stood before a gathering of twelve individuals in a meeting room at the Radisson Hotel in Plymouth, Minnesota. There Mac shared his heart, a vision and the Word. On that day, Living Word Christian Center was born. One year later, church attendance had grown to 150 and meetings were moved to North Hennepin Community College. In 1983 the congregation moved to the site that would be its home for the next fifteen years—an office park on Aspen Lane in Brooklyn Park.

In the Spring of 1998, after much prayer, effort and corporate sacrifice, Living Word Christian Center moved into its present home—a beautiful facility at 9201 75th Avenue North in Brooklyn Park. A church body of more than 7,000 members made that glorious move.

The broad vision Pastor Mac Hammond articulated on that Sunday morning in 1980 has changed very little in the eighteen intervening years. Many parts of it have been realized. Other parts are now coming into manifestation. Much remains to be prayed out and walked out.

At the core of that vision is a heart to reach the Twin Cities and beyond with the life-transforming love of Jesus Christ. It's a vision more and more individuals each week are making their own by becoming a part of the exciting and close-knit family at Living Word Christian Center.

Lutheran Church of the Master (LCM) has been part of Brooklyn Center history for thirty-nine years. In that time the congregation has grown from 203 members worshipping at Garden City School to more than 3,000 members who worship at its present 69th Avenue location. Pastor Paul Swedberg organized LCM as "mission developer" under the Board of American Missions, Augustana Lutheran Church.

From its first sanctuary built on five acres that had once been the potato farm of Theodore Bigelow, sold to the church for $7,500, it has grown to today's campus which includes three apartment buildings and connecting walkways sitting on seven acres of land with buildings worth more than two million dollars.

At LCM we are aware that God has not called us to build buildings, but people. Our primary focus is never on our facilities, but on our ministry. We believe God calls us to minister to the needs of our community. Lutheran Church of the Master has mirrored this since its earliest years when we were actively involved in the organization of CEAP (Community Emergency Assistance Program) and Mary's Place (with Mary Jo Copeland) to today's "Life House Program".

LCM's community is like most late 20th century urban communities. It is never static; it is ever-evolving, ever-changing. We are proud to be members of this great community and strive to continue to work with and bless all of our neighbors.

Lutheran Church of the Master

1200 69th Ave. N.
Brooklyn Center, MN 55430

In 1953 Rev. Wenger called for a meeting to be held in September for those people interested in starting a new church north of Victory Memorial Drive and west of the Mississippi River. In September 1953 Sunday services started in the Earle Brown School. In December 1953 this group elected their first officers and filed Articles of Incorporation with the State. The congregation chose "The Lutheran Church of the Triune God" as its official name. The name was chosen by a church member as he laid in the hospital. Rev. Brauer was appointed as the church's vacancy pastor.

January 1954 the Minnesota District of Missouri Synod agreed to purchase property between Humboldt and Irving Avenues for the parsonage and first church unit. Groundbreaking and construction of the new church began in June 1954, finishing in November with a dedication of the Chapel. Rev. Rosenau was called to be pastor. The main sanctuary was dedicated in January 1962.

The congregation is forty-six years old. It has been served by Rev. Rosenau, Rev. Fehrmann, Associate Pastor Rev. C. Thompson and Assistant Mission Pastor Rev. M. Thompson. Twelve of the church's men have studied and become pastors and are now serving in locations worldwide. Fourteen Vicars have concluded their training under Pastors of the church. Four Deaconesses and numerous other men and women have gone on to be teachers and church workers.

Lutheran Church of the Triune God

5827 Humboldt Avenue North
Brooklyn Center, MN 55430

Northbrook Alliance

6240 Aldrich Ave. N.
Brooklyn Center, MN 55430

THE CHRISTIAN AND MISSIONARY ALLIANCE has its origin in the New England states. There was a Bible study group in a Presbyterian church that decided they would like to sponsor missionaries in the foreign field. This required becoming organized. Those being sent had to have a formal education. The first school was in Nyack, New York. Others have been added, not the least of which is Crown College in St. Bonifacious, Minnesota.

Northbrook Alliance started as Northside Chapel at Fremont and Lowry Ave. in North Minneapolis in 1945. The congregation rapidly outgrew the facility and obtained the land at the present location. The Earle Brown School served as a stepping stone until the contemporary Gothic structure was built in 1956. Later the Educational Unit and Gym were added in 1974.

Many missionaries have been sent all around the globe from this vibrant congregation. There is outreach for every age group. We desire to be a friend and helper to those in the community who probably do not have a church affiliation. The need for prayer with a purpose can be a catalyst to keep Brooklyn Center the best place to maintain good family values.

North Center Baptist Church

6606 68th Ave. N.
Brooklyn Park, MN 55428

NORTH CENTER BAPTIST CHURCH had its beginning as a mission church of the Southtown Baptist Church of Bloomington, MN. In its infancy, worship services were held in various homes. In May 1960 the congregation purchased 9.6 acres of land at 68th Ave. N and Georgia to be the site of their future church building, which is still its present location. As construction progressed, its present name was chosen.

From its inception, North Center was affiliated with the Southern Baptist Convention and the Northland Baptist Association (currently called the Twin Cities Metro Baptist Association.) John Swartz was called to pastor the church. The church was constituted as a church March 7, 1962, with forty-five charter members. The first service in the new building was in May 1963. Five men were ordained as deacons at the time—Elif Norberg, Ralph Tebbenberg, Don Farley, Virgil Wells, and Francis Brands.

The pastors who have served North Center over the years, in addition to Pastor Swartz, are Pastors Harold Warwick, Richard Wohler, C. J. Langton, and Stan Weese, currently serving since January 1989.

Construction of an auditorium and remodeling of the original structure was completed in 1980.

While the North Center congregation is diverse racially, socially, and generationally, the church is united in its purpose to reach the unchurched and lead them to become passionately committed followers of the Lord and Savior Jesus Christ.

"FOR GOD SO LOVED THE WORLD, that He gave His only begotten Son, that whoever believes in Him should not perish, but have eternal life." God so loved the people of Brooklyn Center and north Minneapolis that, in 1945, He called His shepherd, Archbishop Murray, to ask Father Joseph Musch, a Chaplain in World War II, to organize a parish. Father Musch called that parish "Our Lady of Victory" in gratitude for America winning the war. Jesus' mother was very popular among the Catholic servicemen when asking for intercessory prayer. Father Musch was on the front lines with the troops, praying and giving the last Sacrament under the noise of the big guns, and this contributed to his loss of hearing.

The parish evolved from the Camden Theater, to the quonset huts moved from San Francisco docks to 53rd and Colfax Avenues in Brooklyn Center, to the newly built school, to the present church in 1953.

Fr. Musch retired in 1974 and he died in 1988. In 1974 Fr. George Kovalik as pastor and Fr. Donald Salt as his assistant were called to shepherd the people. In 1984 Fr. Vincent Colon became our shepherd pastor.

In 1992 parochial schools in north Minneapolis consolidated. OLV School was renamed St. Elizabeth Seton School.

When Fr. Colon retired in 1993, Fr. Terrance Hayes was appointed pastor. In addition to his pastoral duties, Fr. Hayes has been chaplain to the Minneapolis Police Department for twenty-eight years.

Our Lady of Victory Catholic Church

5155 Emerson Avenue North
Minneapolis, MN 55430

A LITTLE OVER THIRTY YEARS AGO a small group of people had a dream: to form a new Reformed Church in America family in the Brooklyn Park area. That dream became a reality on November 26, 1967, when Our Savior's Church was officially organized by the Classis of Minnesota. Through the years, those who worshipped at Our Savior's have been led and nurtured by four pastors: Berend Vander Woude (1968-74), Forrest Harms (1976-89), Leon Fikse (1991-95) and Lori Walber (1996-present).

The desire of the congregation has always been to worship in the Reformed tradition, gather together for education and fellowship, and be actively involved in community service. Its mission statement, adopted in 1998 reads "Together in Christ—gathered to worship, united to care, inspired to serve—Growing in faith." As the community of Brooklyn Park has changed from potato fields to high rise apartments, Our Savior's has remained steadfastly committed to being a witness to its community of the love of Jesus Christ.

Our Savior's Reformed Church

8209 Zane Ave. North
Brooklyn Park, MN 55443

Prince of Peace Lutheran Church

7217 West Broadway
Brooklyn Park, MN 55428

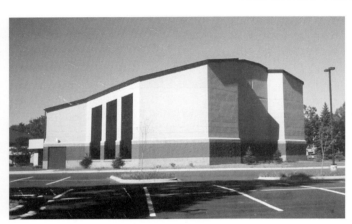

THE YEAR 2000 means "Happy 40th Birthday" to Prince of Peace Lutheran Church, affectionately known as POP. It became a vital part of the city of Brooklyn Park on February 21, 1960, when Reverend Norman Landvik led 153 people in worship at Park Brook Elementary School.

The first official sanctuary opened its doors on April 10, 1960, at 7217 West Broadway. The first sanctuary is now being used as a chapel and Sunday school rooms. The second sanctuary, which was dedicated on December 11, 1977, is now known as the Christian Life Center (CLC).

We worship in a new sanctuary, seating 750, which was dedicated in October, 1997. Pastors are Ronald Prasek, Roger Herfindahl, and Heidi Caldwell.

It is not the building that makes POP an integral part of Brooklyn Park, but it's the spirit and enthusiasm of its people. Several community groups use the facility on a weekly basis.

Music and education have always had a high priority at Prince of Peace. There are opportunities for ages 5 to 105 to participate in the music program, and over 600 are enrolled in the Sunday school, confirmation classes and adult Bible studies.

An important part of POP is its outreach ministry, as identified in the church's Mission Statement: "Our purpose is to carry out the Great Commission (Matthew 28: 19,20) of making all people followers of Jesus Christ.

Redeemer Covenant Church

7801 Brooklyn Blvd.
Brooklyn Park, MN 55445

AT THE CLOSE OF THE LAST CENTURY, in November 1899, Swedish immigrants settled in Brooklyn Township. They dreamed of having a church in their own community, but they helped establish the Swedish Evangelical Mission Church of Camden Place. This congregation thrived and grew, and in 1956 they moved into a new church in Brooklyn Center, the Brookdale Covenant Church. In 1962 a daughter church was established in Brooklyn Park.

On Sunday, March 4, 1962, forty-four enthusiastic people gathered in the Park Brook School to sign the charter. The dream came alive and became the Redeemer Covenant Church of Brooklyn Park. The pattern was set for the Redeemer Covenant Church: children, young people and music are always important.

On Sunday, August 26, 1962, the first service was held in the new church building. Five building programs have added onto and changed the look of the original little church.

The vision for Redeemer Covenant Church in the hearts of the founding members was to hold up Jesus Christ as Lord and Savior in the community of Brooklyn Park and beyond. Out of Redeemer have come many young men and women who now serve as pastors and missionaries. God has brought Redeemer through some wonderful times and He has been faithful through some dark times. The vision of the founding members remains the same in the hearts of the members today at the close of this great century.

RIVERVIEW ELEMENTARY SCHOOL at 93rd Avenue North and West River Road was the first meeting place for the Riverview Methodist Church. The Brooklyn Methodist and Anoka Methodist Churches held commissioning services and sent out some of their members to start this new congregation. Eighty-nine people appeared for the first service on September 11, 1966. Reverend Frank DeCourcey served as the first pastor. On November 6, 1966, the Church was officially organized with sixty-five charter members. The name has since been changed to Riverview United Methodist Church, the word "United" being added to symbolize the union of the Methodist and the Evangelical United Brethren Churches.

Riverview United Methodist Church

2100 93rd Way North
Brooklyn Park, MN 55444

The first service in our new church building held on April 7, 1968. The building became a "multi-use facility" in 1970 when it was rented to the new St. Gerard's Catholic congregation. Since then the building has rented space to the Anoka-Hennepin School District for kindergarten classes and later for its Early Childhood Family Education program. A Russian-language speaking congregation began renting space for services in 1995. The building has also been used as a voting place and meeting place for many community events.

Members of the congregation met in January 1996 to vote on a building program with the theme "Lift High the Cross" to help the Church remain visible after the completion of the nearby interchange of Highways 610 and 252. Construction was completed during the summer of 1997 adding needed space and "Lifting the Cross High."

THE ARCHDIOCESE purchased twenty acres of land at 70th and Halifax as a parish center. When Archbishop William O. Brady established the parish in 1959, he assigned pastoral duties to the Redemptorist Congregation, and St. Alphonsus became the first Redemptorist parish in Minnesota. Fr. Roger Godbout was given the task of building the new parish. In January 1959, assisted by seven young priests from St. Louis, he conducted a door-to-door census. This census identified over 1,100 Catholic families living within the assigned parish boundaries.

St. Alphonsus Catholic Church

7025 Halifax Ave. N.
Brooklyn Park, MN 55429

Parishioners used neighborhood public schools for weekend masses. St. Alphonsus church was completed in 1960 and the first mass celebrated on May 8, 1960. A new parish school opened to 177 students in September 1961. The Sister Servants of the Holy Heart of Mary staffed the school for many years. A new church was completed in 1969 to accommodate continued growth, with the first mass in the new church celebrated on May 25, 1969. The original church was then converted into a gymnasium. In 1997–98 St. Alphonsus undertook more major construction. Although professional builders were contracted to do the main construction, many parishioners also volunteered their time and talent in many of the renovation aspects of the project.

St. Alphonsus pastors have been Fathers Roger Godbout, Thomas Morrissy, William Broker, John Dowd, Daniel Lowery, James Shea, Harry Grile, Tom Donaldson and Patrick Grile. St. Alphonsus (1999) serves some 3,200 parishioner families.

St. Vincent De Paul Catholic Church

9100 93rd Avenue N.
Brooklyn Park, MN 55445

THE FIRST CATHOLIC CHURCH in Osseo/Brooklyn Park/Maple Grove area was a log cabin built in 1856, which was dedicated to St. Louis. The second church, a frame structure, was built in 1864 and dedicated to St. Vincent de Paul. The third church, a brick structure, was built in 1922.

Our current church (the fourth), now located in Brooklyn Park, was dedicated on June 10, 1989. As a special memorial to the first patron of the parish, the chapel in the present church is dedicated to St. Louis.

The St. Vincent de Paul Religious Education Center and gym was opened in January 1999 and has a current enrollment of 320 students in day school, 260 children in pre-school on Sunday morning, and 1,500 in evening Religious Education.

Regan Hall was opened in 1999, and can accommodate 300 people for weddings, anniversaries, and parties. We have our own catering service for these events.

We have many groups, programs, and activities involved in our parish life. These include the Council of Catholic Women, Knights of Columbus, Youth Ministry, Parents Morning Out, Singles Group, Music Ministry, Funeral Lunch Ministry, Senior Outreach Ministry, Fun Fest, and Auction for Education.

St. Vincent de Paul parish is composed of 3,300 families (11,500 people) drawn mainly from Brooklyn Park, Champlin, Maple Grove and Osseo.

The Salvation Army

2300 Freeway Blvd.
Brooklyn Center, MN 55430

THE SALVATION ARMY is a community of helping hands ready to lift up those in need. It is a Church offering a message of love, and a service agency that reflects the community it serves. Often, it is a last resort for those who need its services. The Salvation Army is a solid, reputable symbol of hope in the face of adversity, tragedy and disaster. The Salvation Army was founded in 1865 by William Booth in the streets of London. Since the commencement of the organization, officers, soldiers, and volunteers have formed a continuous "blue line" of ministry and compassion. The Salvation Army came to America in 1880, organizing corps in Philadelphia and New York.

The Salvation Army has been present in the northwestern portion of the Twin Cities since 1886. Area residents have access to community centers, food pantries, thrift stores, rehabilitation programs, shelters, self-sufficiency programs, camps, youth programs, churches, and after school programs.

A new Corps facility, to be built at 101st Avenue North and Noble Parkway, will provide an array of programs particularly focused on youth. After-school activities are the focus of the Northbrook Corps. In a fast paced society, both parents generally hold full-time jobs, leaving many children looking for after school activities that offer a safe and friendly environment for their children.

Volunteers help The Salvation Army collect and distribute winter jackets during the Army's annual "Coats for Kids" program. The Army's "Childspree" program provides back to school clothes for the area's disadvantaged children. Many more volunteers gather toys and help The Salvation Army disperse them to children who otherwise would go without a gift during the Christmas season.

SPIRITUAL LIFE MINISTRIES was founded in 1985 by its current Senior Pastor, Judy Fornara. The fledgling congregation began meeting in a borrowed room of a local church. In May 1987 the Church had its first service at a leased facility at 6500 Shingle Creek Parkway with a congregation of over 100 people. In July 1999 ground was broken for a new building at 6865 Shingle Creek Parkway. On January 17, 1999, the first service was held in the new building with a congregation of 400 people. The Church is independent with no denominational affiliation. The Church sanctuary has seating for approximately 900.

Pastor Judy Fornara graduated from Oral Roberts University with a B.A. in Education, and an M.A. in Theology from Bethel Theological Seminary in St. Paul, Minnesota. Pastor Fornara is the founder and director of Spiritual Life Training Center, a two-year Bible school affiliated with the Church. The Bible school teaches students leadership skills with an emphasis on service in the mission field. Students participate in foreign and local crusades, retreats, seminars and conferences throughout the two-year course, learning both to minister and administer.

The Church is also the sponsor of the "Covenant Life Ministerial Organization," which sponsors approximately seventy-seven churches and over 100 licensed and ordained ministers seeking to foster unity among churches, establish new churches and provide fellowship, direction and counsel to individuals and churches throughout the world. The Covenant Life Ministerial Organization extends membership to individuals and churches.

Spiritual Life Church

6865 Shingle Creek Parkway
Brooklyn Park, MN 55430

WEST RIVER ROAD BAPTIST CHURCH came into being in early 1973 when a group of North Suburban residents gathered for prayer and fellowship to discuss the organization of a new congregation. On March 4, 1973, the first worship services were held in the home of one of the members.

Shortly following organization, the church purchased five acres of land on West River Road and the first phase of building was completed in May of 1976. God continued to bless the work and in 1985 a new addition was added to the original structure. Our most recent addition provided additional classrooms, restrooms, a new fellowship hall, expanded the auditorium and parking lot. This phase was completed in September of 1993. To God be the Glory!

As we have been excited about the growth of our building, we are excited also about the growth of our congregation. We want to be of service to our community, to our members and to YOU. If there is ever a way we can be of help to you, please do not hesitate to call on us. It would be a pleasure to serve you.

West River Road Baptist Church

9901 West River Road
Brooklyn Park, MN 55444

Chapter Seven
COMMUNITY ORGANIZATIONS

THROUGH THE YEARS, the people of Brooklyn Center and Brooklyn Park have joined together in community organizations and clubs. These groups help to train leaders, assist those in need, and provide an outlet for recreation and artistic expression. They lay a foundation for community activism and neighborly concern that extends beyond the immediate activities of the group.

Wendell Berry wrote, "When a community loses its memory, its members no longer know one another. How can they know one another if they have forgotten or have never learned one another's stories? If they do not know one another's stories, how can they know whether or not to trust one another? People who do not trust one another do not help one another." In one sense, these community organizations are the means by which a community shares its stories.

Alcoholics Anonymous, Al-Anon, Alateen

Alcoholics Anonymous (AA) is a fellowship of men and women, founded in 1935, who share their experience, strength and hope with each other that they may solve their common problem and help others to recover from alcoholism.

Al-Anon Family Groups, founded in 1951, is a fellowship of relatives and friends of alcoholics who share their experience, strength and hope in order to solve their common problems. Alateen, part of the Al-Anon Family Groups, is a fellowship of young people whose lives have been affected by alcoholism in a family member or close friend. They help each other by sharing their experience, strength and hope.

American Legion Brooklyn Center Post #630

The American Legion lost its last founder on June 4, 1999. George Washington Bentley died at Minneapolis Veterans Medical Center at the age of 101 years, eight months short of his 102nd birthday. In 1919 George was in the Paris meeting hall when the original Legion was organized. On October 8, 1947, the Duoos Brothers American Legion Post #630 received a temporary charter and on January 15, 1948, they received a permanent charter with fifty members and Roy Peek as first commander. The Post is a member of the tenth District of the Minnesota State American Legion Organization. The Post started by meeting in board members' homes. In the mid-1950s they purchased land at 4307 70th Avenue North in Brooklyn Center, the present site of the Legion Club House. The ground breaking for the new clubhouse was in October 1957. The first Legion clubhouse was small, with a small bar and a dirt floor. Later, additions were made and a cement floor was poured. *Darrel Fehrman, Legion Historian.*

American Legion Brooklyn Center Post #630 Auxiliary

The American Legion Brooklyn Center Post #630 Auxiliary was chartered in February 1948 with a membership of forty-eight. The Auxiliary supports Americanism by donating flags to the local schools, by supporting the Girls State, and the Poppy Program. It also helps with the "Drop In" service men's club at the airport, the gift shop at the Veteran's Administration Hospital. The Auxiliary helps with the family picnic in the summer, the children's Christmas Party, the annual Senior Citizen Dinner. They also pack and deliver Thanksgiving and Christmas Baskets to residents of the area. The Auxiliary has donated to the Palmer Lake School playground, to Minnesota Home School and the local emergency fund. They hold fund-raisers for local sports in the community. *Submitted by Rita Ascher*

The Foundation was established in 1988 to provide a means by which Brooklyn Center residents can make contributions to a community organization whose primary focus is addressing some of the community's unmet needs. Since 1989 the Foundation has granted awards totaling $33,000. Those funds have been derived mainly from the interest income of its endowment fund. The Foundation's main grants have been to address the unmet needs of children of low-income families in Brooklyn Center, and to target Foundation resources to persons aged 18 and under. The Foundation Board, responding to needs of school children unable to afford basic school supplies, has authorized the allocation of its available investment funds be directed to the school districts serving Brooklyn Center students. The school officials then re-allocate the funds where they determine the greatest need to be. *Submitted by Phil Cohen*

Brooklyn Center Charitable Foundation

The Citizens for Better Government (CBG) was born because of the outcome of the 1959 Brooklyn Center city election. For the first time, a candidate for Mayor and a candidate for Trustee were endorsed by a major political party. The DFL endorsed Stuart Buck for Mayor and Howard Heck for Trustee. Both DFL candidates lost, due in large part to the concern of many voters that partisan politics had no place in local government. The following summer, Phil Cohen, Bill Arrell and Howard Heck met and endorsed the idea of organizing a non-partisan local political group. The only request made of candidates it supported was that they strive to represent all the people of the city of Brooklyn Center on a non-partisan basis. Subsequently, Heck was endorsed for Trustee, Henry Dorff for City Clerk and John Nordberg for Assessor. All three CBG candidates won handily and CBG became a major political force in Brooklyn Center for the next thirty years. In 1992 Citizens of Better Government disbanded and re-incorporated as the Brooklyn Center Taxpayers Association. *Submitted by Tony Kuefler*

Citizens For Better Government Brooklyn Center

Brooklyn Center Civil Defense was founded in 1946 by Harold Hannay. Harold was the Director, and in the early 1950s Doris (Mrs. Jim) Vaughn served as secretary. Civil Defense was organized to protect and assist people in times of emergency, natural disaster, and possible nuclear attack during the Cold War years. The 1968 Civil Defense report to the City Council by Ed Coleman, Director, listed the fallout shelters that met Federal guidelines: Brooklyn Center State Bank, Cross of Glory Lutheran Church, Earle Brown School, Lutheran Church of the Triune God, Sears Automotive Center and Sears retail outlet at Brookdale. The Emergency Operating Center and Office was located at City Hall.

Harold Hannay organized the first parades in Brooklyn Center, which included other volunteer fire/civil defense departments, and a Miss Brooklyn Center queen contest. The parades began on the Earle Brown Farm and ended at the fire station on 65th and Lyndale. Fundraisers to buy equipment included pancake breakfasts held at the old log cabin on the Earle Brown Farm.

Brooklyn Center Civil Defense

During the 1965 Fridley tornado, the roofs fell in on Fridley's emergency equipment, leaving the City without vehicles. Brooklyn Center's Civil Defense Operations Officer, Jack Vaughn, and others found their World War II crisis situation training helpful during this 48-hour rescue mission. Civil Defense was discontinued in the late 1970s, and its functions were assumed by the Fire and Police Departments.

Discover the Center Community Connections

Discover the Center is a community-wide effort to facilitate, bridge organizations and encourage collaboration, while informing and educating both residents and non-residents of the quality of life within Brooklyn Center.

Discover the Center began as an image campaign to celebrate the positives of the community of Brooklyn Center. It has evolved to become an organization that strives to celebrate the positive things that happen in Brooklyn Center and an umbrella organization designed to unite the community. We want to bring together individuals and organizations in order to better communicate and collaborate on efforts to improve the quality of life in Brooklyn Center. Some of the projects we have initiated are: We the People Rallies; Organizational Summits; *Realtor Day;* Youth Initiatives; 10K Runs (part of Earle Brown Days). We see a bright future as we continue to work with different organizations promoting the quality of life here in Brooklyn Center. The Community of Brooklyn Center has been identified as a Community of Promise for Youth by the Minnesota Alliance With Youth in conjunction with the President's Summit for Youth. We believe Brooklyn Center is a Community of Promise not only for youth, but for all our citizens.

Earle Brown Days Festival

The Earle Brown Days Festival (named after the late Brooklyn Center resident Earle Brown) has been an annual event in Brooklyn Center since 1982. Prior to 1982, the city's annual festival was called Early Bird Days. Early Bird Days was begun in 1975 by Arnie Mavis of the Brooklyn Center Park and Recreation Department and consisted mainly of athletic events. Some key festival events held over the years include a Circus and a Hot-Air Balloon Show with Rides.

Arnie Mavis, Jerry Pedlar, Tom Slupske, Myrna Kragness, Phil Cohen and Henry Dorff have each chaired the festival committee, for one or more years. Some other folks who have been active in several festivals include Larry Roen, Ron Christensen, Judith Bergeland, Pat Holcomb, Joelien Zastrow, Karen Youngberg, Tony Ditty and Tony Kuefler. *Submitted by Tony Kuefler, Phil Cohen and Sue LaCrosse*

Brooklyn Center Family Resource Center

The Brooklyn Center Family Resource Center is a safe and friendly place where people in the community can connect to information about and referrals to programs and services that can benefit them and their families. In 1994 the State of Minnesota looked at the way that communities were being served. They decided that communities themselves should identify what the needs are and take ownership in deciding what services should be provided to meet those needs. Northwest Hennepin Human Services Council received a Planning Grant from the State in January 1994. They facilitated bringing together three of the four school districts to form the Northwest Hennepin Family Service Collaborative.

The Collaborative was initiated to redesign the way that schools, humans services, public health, county, and various other entities worked together to better serve individuals, families and children. The Brooklyn Center Advisory council began meeting in August 1994. The Resource Center opened its doors in March 1996 and was initiated by an Open House on April 27, 1996. *Submitted by Linda Hanka*

Brooklyn Center Fire Department Auxiliary

The Brooklyn Center Fire Auxiliary membership consisted of wives of the Brooklyn Center firemen. We were organized in the early 1950s to support the firemen when needed. In the event of a big fire, the Auxiliary gathered at the fire station to prepare food and coffee for the firemen although our primary role was that of a social organization. The Auxiliary met once a month at the fire station. A business meeting was conducted and chaired by an elected president. Our planned social events were a big part of our lives. Many "500" card parties took place along with square dances, Halloween costume parties and sometimes a dinner party that might include a pig roast and all the fixings. Everyone looked forward to the annual Firemen's Dance in October and every summer a family picnic was enjoyed by young and old. Another annual event was our family Christmas party. The Brooklyn Center Fire Auxiliary existed until the mid 1980s in a formal sense. Lifestyle changes such as increased activity in jobs, children in sports, band, etc., caused a membership decline and a vote to disband. *Submitted by Betty Cahlander, Shirley Bentzen and Midge Eggert*

Brooklyn Center Volunteer Fire Dept.

Prior to 1949, fire protection was supplied under a contract with the City of Minneapolis Fire Dept. (MFD), who, when the alarm sounded, responded with two engines, one hook and ladder and a small tanker. Minneapolis wanted $8,000 for the 1949 contract, triggering the formation of the Brooklyn Center Volunteer Fire Department. In September 1949 the State of Minnesota chartered the department, and in December 1949, the Relief Association was chartered with thirty-seven members. Dan Elmer was elected as the first fire chief and founded the Mutual Aid Agreement with neighboring suburbs. Brooklyn Center did not renew its contract with Minneapolis.

The first fire station was a bay in Gilbertson's Garage at 65th & Lyndale. In 1950 the station was moved to the old municipal building which housed the city offices, police department, and garage. The department built a couple of tanker wagons for hauling water. In 1956 the department acquired its second engine, a new Pirsch 750 gpm pumper and Carl Anderson was elected as the new Fire Chief, serving through 1966. In 1959 the West Station was built. Don Mason was elected Fire Chief in 1967 and served as Chief until 1974. A new East Station was added in 1971. Bob Cahlander served as Acting Fire Chief from 1974 to 1976.

In 1975 City Manager Don Poss proposed making the Fire Chief position a full-time paid position. However, Poss would not assure the members that he would select the full-time Chief from within the department. The proposal was strongly opposed by the Volunteer Department members and became a hotly contested political issue, with the Volunteer Fire Department position prevailing. Interestingly, a few years later the Fire Department itself recommended to make the Fire Chief a full-time paid position. Current Chief Ron Boman was elected Fire Chief in 1976. Under Chief Boman, the East Station was remodeled and the West Station was replaced with a totally new station in 1999. Brooklyn Center now had two ideally located, state-of-the-art fire stations. A volunteer fire department saves the Brooklyn Center taxpayers an estimated $1,500,000 annually. *Submitted by Tony Kuefler*

Brooklyn Center Jaycees

The purpose of the Jaycees is to offer leadership training through community development for young people between the ages of 18 and 35. The groundwork for organizing a Jaycee Chapter in Brooklyn Center, was started in November 1955, by Dr. William Taylor and Ed Hoffman. Twenty-eight young men joined forces, and the Brooklyn Center Jaycees became a reality when they received a charter on February 29, 1956, with Al Kattar elected as their first president. The Brooklyn Center Jaycees held a membership count of over 100 members for several years. They lost their charter in 1986, when their membership fell below the required twenty-five member minimum. In the late 1980s there was an unsuccessful effort to resurrect the Brooklyn Center chapter. Jaycees had an affiliate organization called the Mrs. Jaycees. Mrs. Jaycees organized and ran community projects of their own, as well as worked cooperatively with their affiliate Jaycee chapter. In the early 1980s the Jaycee organization opened membership to both men and women. Many men and women put their Jaycee leadership experience to work for their community by providing leadership in church, community and political organizations and by serving on City Commissions, City Council, and in the State Legislature. *Submitted by Tony Kuefler*

League of Women Voters of Brooklyn Center

The League of Women Voters is a nonpartisan political organization. It encourages the informed and active participation of citizens in government and influences public policy through education and advocacy.

The League of Women Voters of Brooklyn Center became a provisional league in 1958. The work of the League divides into two parts, program and voters' service. In 1959 the League of Women Voters of Brooklyn Center studied and evaluated forms of local government. They supported the Optional Plan B (council-manager) form of village government. The village Plan B issue was placed on the ballot in November, 1961 and it lost. The League continued to support council-manager form of government through the approval of the city charter in 1966.

Men have been members of the League of Women voters since 1974; however, the name of the organization was not changed. Presidents, in order of service, include: Vi Kanatz, Dee Nelson, Mabel Berg, Martha Pryor, Doris Pederson, Dolores Hastings, Barbara Sexton, Phyllis Plummer, Eileen Oslund, Barbara Jensen, Nancy Tanji, Lois Moeller and Barbara Sexton. *Submitted by Barbara Sexton*

Brooklyn Center Leisure Time

Brooklyn Center Leisure Time began after June 1971 when City Hall employees moved to the current location on 6301 Shingle Creek Parkway. The Civic Center Complex housed City Hall and the Community Center. The Recreation Department moved into the community center. Leisure Time began as a jointly sponsored club with CEAP volunteer Dorothy Alley and staff advisor Kathy Flesher from the Parks and Recreation Department. Mrs. Alley found it necessary to resign after a couple of months, and Jan Benson another CEAP volunteer took her place. CEAP provided transportation through volunteer drivers for individuals who needed transportation. For a while, a different church each month would provide cakes for refreshments.

The current club leader, Ruth Geissler began as volunteer driver and meeting helper in January 1974. Sometime in 1974-75, the city assumed the full sponsorship of the club. Participants bring their lunch, coffee and tea are provided by the funds from the "kitty." *Submitted by Kathy Flesher*

Hennepin County Library was created in 1922 to serve county residents outside of Minneapolis. The earliest library service was a deposit collection established in 1925 or earlier in the Gadow Store. Another later deposit collection was located at the Brooklyn United Methodist Church. By the 1940s, a bookmobile served residents.

In 1962 a survey sponsored by the Brooklyn Center Jaycees noted substantial interest in a library. As a result of this survey, Mayor Gordon Erickson appointed a 10-member study commission that submitted a final report with recommended action in 1964. Residents through a referendum approved by more than a 2-1 margin, the sale of Village obligations to finance the construction of the first library in Brooklyn Center. Brooklyn Center qualified for assistance under the Library Services Act of 1964, and received $60,000 toward the construction of a library. Ground was broken on February 13, 1965, at 5601 Osseo Road and the library opened December 29, 1965.

In 1975 planning began for the Brookdale-Hennepin Area Library, which opened in 1981. It was incorporated into the Brookdale Regional Center at 6125 Shingle Creek Parkway that includes District Court, Service Center and Social Services.

Brooklyn Center Libraries

The Brooklyn Center Lioness were organized jointly by the Brooklyn Center Lions and the Brooklyn Park Lioness in 1979. Membership is by invitation to people over eighteen years of age. We have one social dinner meeting and one business meeting each month. Our purpose is to carry out service programs and activities and to unite members in friendship and mutual understanding. Some Lioness projects over the years have been a fashion show and luncheon in the spring, monthly bingo for nursing home residents, craft bazaar, bake sales, working at the Camp Courage Halloween party each fall, pumpkin sales, adopt a park semi-annual cleanup, packing Christmas orders at the Diabetes center, working a concession trailer at the Dudley softball tournament, collecting food for the Lions world service Food Drive Day in October; raffle sales, paint-a-thon and sorting glasses for Volunteer Optometrics Serving Humanity (VOSH). The Lioness work jointly with the Brooklyn Center Lions on many projects. We donate to Leader Dogs for the blind, Diabetes programs, Eye Banks, scholarships, crime prevention, and many other worthwhile things. Lioness and Lions clubs are very involved in sight projects. *Submitted by Lorraine Shinnick*

Brooklyn Center Lioness

Chartered May 12, 1955 with forty-four members, Norris O. Johnson was Charter President. Charter member Larry Roen is an active member in 2000. In the summer of 1956 the club participated in the first of many parades. We are now the sponsor of one the largest parades in Minnesota: The Earle Brown Days parade held annually in June. This was the first of many civic betterment projects including building Lions Park at 55th & Russell Ave. No., dedicated in May 1968.

The Brooklyn Center Lions have been heavily involved in this community over the past forty-five years including sponsoring a program Entertainment in the Park, donated thousands of dollars for crime prevention and drug awareness programs, $55,000 to a scholarship fund for high school seniors, collected over 30,000 pairs of used eye glasses, built handicap ramps, and contributed thousands of dollars to the BHS for pre-publishing costs of this book.

We are involved in many humanitarian projects sponsored by Lions Clubs International Foundation such as Campaign Sight First for the eradication of preventable blindness, Hearing Dogs for the hearing impaired, Leader Dogs for the visually

Brooklyn Center Lions Club

impaired, and Youth Outreach, Minnesota Lions Eye Bank and Children's Eye Clinic and Lions Hearing Foundation. In 1992 we sponsored a project to raise money for a van to be used by the International Diabetes Center for training doctors in rural Minnesota in the proper diagnosis of Diabetes. Our club raised $20,000 for Diabetes research since 1986. *Submitted by Tom Shinnick*

Brooklyn Center Police Association

The Brooklyn Center Police Association is a non-partisan corporation organized under the Laws of the State of Minnesota. The Association was formed in 1959 as a social organization for police officers at the time when there were only nine officers.

In 1960 the Association formed together over an issue of wages, and by 1963 the Association assumed the bargaining and negotiating duties for the patrol officer membership. In 2000 the officers are members of Law Enforcement Labor Services (L.E.L.S.) Local #82. The Association members pay dues, have a dinner social once a year and support youth programs and activities such as Drug Abuse Resistance Education (D.A.R.E.). The Association became involved early on with the school patrol program. Annual school patrol picnics have been sponsored by the Association over the years. The Police Department has grown from one full-time officer and chief in 1956 to forty-three police officers and a chief in the year 2000.

Brooklyn Park Police Association

The Brooklyn Park Police Association was incorporated as a Minnesota nonprofit corporation on December 13, 1972. The objectives and purposes of the Association are to promote good will between the police department and the community, to foster and maintain fond and enlightened public relations, and to promote, secure and advance the City of Brooklyn Park as a whole. Membership is restricted to full time sworn police officers employed by the Brooklyn Park Police Department. The Association was originally funded by the dues of its members. Some projects included a fund to pay for information leading to the arrest of persons responsible for crimes committed in Brooklyn Park and the purchases of AM radios in squad cars.

After twenty-eight years the Police Association is as strong as ever. The Association has given thousands of dollars to youth sports organizations, children with special needs, and continues to sponsor a youth firearms safety course. The Association sponsors a Christmas party for the children of all police department employees and volunteers, and a party for all civilian support personnel as a thank you from the officers for the outstanding work they do. *Submitted by Lieutenant S. Pearson*

Brooklyn Center Community Prayer Breakfast

For many years there has been a national prayer breakfast in Washington DC and likewise a state prayer breakfast in Minnesota. The idea for a local annual prayer breakfast was conceived in 1979 by then Mayor Dean A. Nyquist. Brooklyn Center is believed to have the longest continuing run of annual prayer breakfasts in Minnesota with its 22nd annual in 2000. The breakfast was referred to as the Mayor's Prayer Breakfast until 1985. For the past nine years the breakfast has been held at the Earle Brown Heritage Center.

The speaker at the first breakfast was Al Palmquist and the theme was "It Only Takes A Spark To Get A Fire Going." Governor Al Quie was the second breakfast speaker and spoke about "In God We Trust." Subsequent speakers included Senator Dave Durenberger, John Staggers, Jeff Siemon, Esther Olson, Bill Bontrager, Dr. James Mason, Kurian Parayil, Al Quie (Prison Ministry), Rick Beggs, Richard J. Allison,

Linda Rios Brook, John Campbell, Pat Hurley, Bob Stromberg, The Refreshment Committee, Chris Carter, John Crudele, Jim Murphy, and in 1999, Leith Anderson speaking on "Our Millennium Mindset." The speaker in April 2000 was Evelyn Christenson, author of "What Happens When Women Pray."

The Brooklyn Center Rotary Club is a chapter of Rotary International. There are approximately 1.2 million Rotarians, members of more than 29,000 Rotary clubs in 161 countries. The object of Rotary is to encourage and foster the ideal of service as a basis of worthy enterprise. In 1977 several Brooklyn Center businessmen gathered to discuss the establishment of a Rotary Club. In 1978 the Rotary Club of Brooklyn Center received its charter from Rotary International. Don Borrell was elected president. Since that time hundreds of men and women have gathered weekly for lunch, fellowship, and community and international service. Rotary Club projects include: Crime Prevention Fund and programs; Peacemaker Center; Camp Enterprise, the club sponsors two BCHS students to this annual camp devoted to teaching students about entrepreneurship; Earle Brown Days Family Fun Games; STRIVE, a mentorship program at BCHS; Service Above Self and Volunteer of the Year Awards for the community; Banking on the Poor, a bank to provide small loans to persons in Solia, Mexico, who wish to start a small business; Well drilling in a town in rural India which had minimal water; Tanzania dental office and generator. With other clubs we sponsored the equipping of a dental clinic in Tanzania, and the purchase of a backup generator for a hospital. *Submitted by Diane Spector*

Brooklyn Center Rotary Club

The Brooklyn Center Taxpayers Association (BCTA) is a successor organization to Citizens for Better Government (CBG). The BCTA was issued its Minnesota Certificate of Incorporation on July 15, 1992, and held its first general membership meeting on July 19, 1992. The BCTA is based on the same non-partisan government principles as was the CBG. BCTA is a citizen organization which provides oversight of city government spending and activities. The BCTA works to assure that the city financial condition is kept strong by monitoring the city council's fiscal decisions; insisting on ethics and integrity in governing our city; and supporting candidates for city council who share its concerns and principles. BCTA is incorporated as a non-profit corporation with the state; however, dues and contributions are not tax deductible. BCTA has two types of voting membership: General Member (resident); Associate Member (non-resident property owner). Beginning with the 1992 City Council elections, the BCTA became heavily involved in seeking out, endorsing and supporting qualified non-partisan candidates. *Submitted by Tony Kuefler*

Brooklyn Center Taxpayers Association

The Brooklyn Center Women's Club was organized in January, 1966, with a membership of thirty-nine women. As of today the club has grown to about 200 members. The purpose of the Brooklyn Center Women's Club is to promote social, cultural, and civic activities. Each year the Brooklyn Center Women's Club awards one or more college scholarships, each one given to a deserving senior girl selected from one of the northern suburban high schools. Also an annual donation is made to Brooklyn Center Crime Prevention and to Brooklyn Center Recreation Division. In addition, the club helps support the Community Emergency Assistance Program (CEAP) with a food drive in November, toys in December, and a baby shower in May, all donated by

Brooklyn Center Women's Club

the club members. In December the club also helps with the Kids' Shopping Korner, at which time many youngsters do their Christmas shopping for their families. The club's income is derived from the annual dues each member pays, plus any member contributions. Other funds are obtained through various fund raisers which the club holds. Membership is open to all women twenty-one years of age or older. Brooklyn Center residency is not required for membership. *Submitted by Bea Humbert*

Brooklyn Center Year 2000 Celebration Committee

In 1998 the Earle Brown Days Committee recommended the City Council form a Steering Committee to initiate community interest in a "Year 2000 Celebration." The City Council approved the concept and formally recognized the Celebration by Resolution in November 1999. In December 1999 the "Brooklyn Center Year 2000 Celebration Committee" was organized under Minnesota law as a non-profit corporation. Seventeen community organizations participate in the Committee, as well as the City of Brooklyn Center and Independent School Districts 279 and 286. Phil Cohen chairs the Committee, which planned activities for 2000. The Celebration recognized older residents and long-term businesses, including an All-Class Brooklyn Center High School Reunion. A time capsule from 1976 was opened on July 9, 2000. Historic preservation activities include an open house and tour of the Earle Brown Heritage Center. A new time capsule will be assembled to be opened at Brooklyn Center's 100th Birthday Celebration in 2011, including a book written in by young people. *Submitted by Phil Cohen*

Come Home to the Park: A Proud Community in Action!

In 1992 a group of residents and community leaders decided Brooklyn Park needed a boost in its self-esteem and formed Come Home to the Park, an organization of residents, business people, church leaders and members of the city's staff who promoted the "good news" of Brooklyn Park. During the previous three or four years, the community experienced a number of high profile crimes which brought a great deal of negative attention to the city in both the print and electronic media. Come Home to the Park was formed to bring attention to the good things that go on in the city and the people who do them. Come Home to the Park has been the recipient of many awards such as the "Hometown Pride" award given by Midwest Living Magazine as one of only sixteen cities out of 650 entries from across the nation. As a result of the program, Brooklyn Park was named the winner of the "Most Innovative City" Award by the Association of Metropolitan Municipalities in 1995. In 1999 Brooklyn Park was one of only thirty cities nationwide to be named as a finalist in the National Civic League's "All America City" competition. *Submitted by Dan Ryan*

Brooklyn Park Community Organization

Formed in 1980, the Brooklyn Park Community Organization, Inc.(BPCO), is a private, non-profit, volunteer group. Any individual or organization can become a member. The BPCO's mission is to provide a networking system for community groups working together to make Brooklyn Park a quality place in which to live. The BPCO Bylaws state that its purposes are to develop a sense of community awareness and spirit among residents, organizations and businesses in the community; promote harmony and public involvement in community activities; promote communication and cooperation within the community, among residents and between organizations; and to plan events, activities and programs to accomplish these purposes.

In 1965 the Brooklyn Park Jaycees started Tater Daze to highlight Brooklyn Park's potato growing heritage and ensure that it doesn't fade from memory. In 1980 the event's sponsorship was taken over by the BPCO. Tater Daze is a four-day event, and includes entertainment, sports, carnival, fireworks and a premier parade. In conjunction with the Brooklyn Park Recreation and Parks Department, BPCO sponsors the Shingle Creek Cleanup. Two other Recreation and Parks Department programs are supported by BPCO: Spooktacular and the award-winning Children's Art Festival.

In 1957 a committee consisting of Ray Nordberg, Earl DeBoer, Don Krienke, George Lorsung and Richard Martin petitioned the Brooklyn Park Village Council for an ordinance creating the Brooklyn Park Volunteer Fire Department (BPVFD). On April 10, 1957, the Village Council approved the establishment of the BPVFD and accepted the committee's offer to raise funds for equipment. Brooklyn Park was contracting with the City of Osseo for fire protection.

Brooklyn Park Volunteer Fire Department

The first meeting was held with 140 interested and potential fire fighters present. Orris Aldrich was elected the first Fire Chief. Funds were needed for equipment, so a donation dance was held at the Riverlyn Club. A 1949 GMC truck chassis and an 800-gallon Standard Oil tank truck were purchased for $200. All equipment was housed at various members' homes and garages. The first annual benefit dance was held in 1957 at Ryan's Bass Lake Ballroom in Plymouth. The voters in 1958 approved a $100,000 bond issue to furnish the BPVFD with trucks, two stations and equipment. In 1960 the State of Minnesota certified the fire equipment and recognized the BPVFD. The East and West Fire Stations were completed in 1960, and in 1968 Jerold Almer was elected Fire Chief.

In 1969 a full-time Fire Chief was recommended by the City Manager to the City Council. The Fire Chief would be an administrator and the assistant chiefs would direct fire fighting in the field. The firemen voted for Jerold Almer to be Fire Chief.

In 1970 Lyle Robinson, a charter member of the Department, was named Fire Chief. In 1971, James Driste, a member of the Department was named full-time fire inspector. The East and West Stations were enlarged in 1972, and in 1973 the North Suburban Fire Training Tower was completed on the North Campus of the Hennepin Vocational Technical School. In 1984 Lyle Robinson resigned after thirteen years as Fire Chief and seventeen years with the Department. James Driste was named Fire Chief on September 1, 1984. He had been the fire inspector for twelve years and with the Fire Department for twenty years.

In 1990 the Northwest Fire Chiefs organization was formed with eight fire departments. In 1994 a Juvenile Firesetter Intervention Program began. James Driste retired as Fire Chief on April 31, 1999. The City ordinance was changed in 1999, permitting the appointment of a chief from inside or outside the Fire Department. The City Manager appointed Steve Schmidt, a BPFD firefighter for twenty-three years. In 2000, there are four fire stations: East, West, Central and North. The department has thirteen emergency vehicles with Engine 41 on order, a rescue boat, a hazardous materials trailer, four officer vehicles and sixty-six volunteers.

Brooklyn Park Volunteer Fire Department Women's Auxiliary

The Brooklyn Park Volunteer Fire Department's Women's Auxiliary was formed in 1958/1959. The first president was Alvera Nordberg. The Women's Auxiliary was formed by firefighters' spouses to support the department through fundraising activities, support at fire scenes and support members' families in times of need. Funds were raised to purchase firefighting equipment, as well as provide flowers and/or gifts to sick members or members who had lost a loved one. This was the beginning of the Sunshine Program. The Women's Auxiliary assisted firefighters at large or prolonged firecalls by providing refreshments and food. The Women's Auxiliary assisted at training sessions involving structure burns. They brought their families and provided a picnic for everyone in attendance. The Women's Auxiliary developed a support system by holding monthly meetings and attending seasonal luncheons with other fire departments. The Women's Auxiliary became part of the fire prevention program for pre-school children by providing educational programs. As more and more families became dependent upon two incomes, the Women's Auxiliary ceased to function in 1986 or 1987 and the Woman's Auxiliary became a function of the Fire Department's full-time administrative staff.

Brooklyn Park Firefighter's Relief Association

The Brooklyn Park Fire Department, chartered in April 1957, formed the Brooklyn Park Firemen's Relief Association (BPFRA) on August 25, 1960. The BPFRA was established to provide benefits for the firefighters, including a retirement fund, and provide uniforms and equipment. Several fund raising activities, including the annual Fire Department Dance, were developed to raise funds. Active members of the Fire Department elect six members to govern the Relief Association. The City Manager, Finance Officer and the Fire Chief are ex-officio members of the nine-member board. All funds and investments are approved by the Board of Trustees.

The Retirement Fund was funded by the State of Minnesota's 2% Fire/Police Fund. The money came from the insurance industry (auto and structure insurance). The city also contributed to the Retirement Fund from the annual budget.

On April 9, 1984, the BPFRA negotiated with the City Council to move to a defined contribution retirement program, whereby each member receives a portion of the Relief Association funds. Funds were prorated by years of service, with annual increases by the city, and the state 2% Police/Fire Fund. Members started a scholarship program for members and retired members' families. Any family member was eligible who was attending a post-secondary school full time. The scholarship was named the "Douglas B. Conner, Jr. Memorial Scholarship". Douglas Conner was the first member to die while he was an active member of the Fire Department. In 1997 the name was changed to the Brooklyn Park Firefighters Relief Association.

Brooklyn Park Jaycees

In February 1964, with the help of the Minneapolis Jaycees, twenty young men met at the Octagon Restaurant and decided to form a Jaycee Chapter in Brooklyn Park. We took the Jaycee Creed as an opportunity to make this area a better place to live, work and play. Members were from Brooklyn Park, Brooklyn Center and Osseo. No one age 21 to 35 with a commitment to the organization was turned away.

The Jaycees were prime sponsors of the first Tater Daze Celebration held in 1965 between the grounds of Brooklyn Jr. High and Donnay Estates Cul-de-sac. Home-owners, renters and business people all joined in to celebrate Brooklyn Park's heritage. The Jaycee sponsorship of Tater Daze continued for fifteen years. Now it is sponsored by the Brooklyn Park Community Organization. Jaycees also were involved in internal character building programs such as "Speak Up" and "Spoke." Bob Kottke was the first president in 1964.

The Chapter no longer exists, because it dropped below the minimum requirement of twenty-five members. *Submitted by Jerry Marshall*

League of Women Voters of Brooklyn Park, Osseo, Maple Grove

The League Of Women Voters of Brooklyn Park (LWVBP) was founded April 1964, with Audrey Humphreys as president. The Minnesota League of Women Voters recognized Brooklyn Park as a provisional League in December, 1965, with Mary Hansen as president. In April 1966 Brooklyn Park became a fully recognized League with Anne Lee as president. To be a recognized League, State League of Women Voters required a survey of our city and publication of the information in a booklet: "Brooklyn Park, The Mushrooming Community."

LWVBP first studied the government of the then village which was operated under a state code as "Plan A." In 1966 Brooklyn Park citizens petitioned for a change to council-manager form "Plan B" and approved the change by voting in the fall of 1966. In a special election in September 1969, citizens voted to become a city, retaining the council-manager form of government.

In 1984 LWVBP officially changed its name to the League of Women Voters of Brooklyn Park, Osseo, Maple Grove, recognizing that one third of its members lived in Osseo and Maple Grove. *Submitted by Marilyn McAlpine*

Brooklyn Park Libraries

Brooklyn Park's first public library located at 8600 Zane Ave. N. opened April 26, 1976, in a brand new building. Fran Jones was the first head librarian. Robert Rohlf served as Hennepin County Library Director. Prior to the opening, the area had been served by a series of bookmobile stops in what was largely a farming community. The Brooklyn Park facility was one of several libraries built as part of a long range construction program authorized by the 1969 State Legislature and implemented by the Hennepin County Board of Commissioners. The official public dedication ceremony was on September 26, 1976. The program included U. S. Congressman Bill Frenzel as keynote speaker, Hennepin County Commissioner John Derus, Brooklyn Park Mayor James Krautkremer and the unveiling of a Brooklyn Park time capsule by the city's bicentennial task force.

The first year's circulation totaled 228,923. Twenty years later the circulation for 1997 was 453,228. Community partnership is a large part of the library's focus. The staff continues to work with a number of groups like Early Childhood Family Education, Headstart, Kindergarten Connection, Brooklyn Park Partners, Northwest Hennepin Human Services Council and the local schools. Children's programs and storytimes attract large audiences from a growing population of young families.

Brooklyn Park Lioness Club

The Brooklyn Park Lioness Club was started in 1962, one year after the Brooklyn Park Lions Club was organized. The Club was started by wives of the Lions with about 20 members. Sue Brodin was the first President of the organization then known as the Lionettes. Of the original members, Dolores Kvamme and Shirley Seid are still with the Club and very active in the ongoing commitments of the Club.

Goals of the Club have been to assist the Lions Club in their Service projects including Tater Daze, Smelt Fry, Safety Camp, the Lions Eye and Hearing projects,

Diabetes, Courage Center, Friendship Ventures and Homeward Bound. We held style shows, Pampered Chef shows and a steak fry and auction to raise funds to return back to the community. Other past activities have included the Jr. Queen and Commodore from Brooklyn Park, we've made quilts, sewed vests for our Brooklyn Park Lions as well as made batches upon batches of cole slaw and hot sauce for the Smelt Fry as well as baked goods for our Bake Sales held along with the Lions pancake breakfasts and fish fries. We have sponsored five Lioness Clubs: Robbinsdale, Maple Grove, Wayzata, Coon Rapids and Brooklyn Center. *Submitted by Eleanor Warian*

Brooklyn Park Lions

The Brooklyn Park Lions Club was chartered July 6, 1961, with twenty seven members of which only one is still active—Art Kvamme, who this year became a life member. At one time, eighteen of the thirty Past Presidents were still active members in the club. Three of the past presidents have become District Governors. They were Lions Howard Givens, Tony Brunello, and Bob Bayard. The annual Smelt Fry fund raiser has been held for thirty-seven years. Pancake Breakfasts are held annually. The major fund raiser has been the Pull-Tab Gambling Operation at the Northwest Inn. The operation was started in 1988, and over a half million dollars in profit has been given for hundreds of different charitable events and projects. Service projects of the club are: Christmas Baskets, Boy Scout Troop Sponsors, Eye Glasses for Needy, Camp Courage, Courage Center Golf Tournament, Brooklyn Park Police, Fire, Parks & Recreation, Tator Daze Community Celebration, College Scholarships, CEAP, University of Minnesota Lions Eye Bank, Childrens Eye Clinic and Hearing Clinic, Leader Dog for Blind, Hearing Dog for Deaf, Lions World Service Day, Drug Awareness, Diabetes Awareness Program and other worthwhile projects. *Submitted by Art Kvamme*

Brooklyn Park Mrs. Jaycees

In 1964 twelve women, wives of Jaycees, gathered at Carol Kottke's home to form the Brooklyn Park Mrs. Jaycees. The Brooklyn Center Mrs. Jaycee chapter assisted us to fulfill membership requirements in the Mrs. Jaycees of Minnesota in 1964 with Carol as our first president. Our major purpose was to assist our Jaycee husbands in developing the community as they developed their leadership abilities. We assisted the Jaycees in their two-year door-to-door Attitude Survey, and the first Tater Daze celebration. On the state level we contributed to Cystic Fibrosis and Aid to Retarded Children. We sent campers to Camp Courage and to Camp Friendship. Brooklyn Park's Recreation and Parks Department received a puppet wagon designed by Mrs. Jaycees and built by the Jaycees. Voter registration had our volunteer services, and the police department received a new resuscitator. Our baby-sitting clinics taught young people how to care safely and responsibly for babies and children. Women's roles changed over the years, and the Mrs. Jaycees disbanded. *Submitted by Ardis Hopps*

Brooklyn Park Police Association

The Brooklyn Park Police Association was incorporated as a Minnesota nonprofit corporation on December 13, 1972. The objectives and purposes of the Association are to promote good will between the police department and the community, to foster and maintain fond and enlightened public relations, and to promote, secure and advance the City of Brooklyn Park as a whole. Membership is restricted to full time sworn police officers employed by the Brooklyn Park Police Department. The Association was originally funded by the dues of its members. Some projects included a fund to pay for information leading to the arrest of persons responsible for crimes committed in Brooklyn Park and the purchases of AM radios in squad cars.

After twenty-eight years the Police Association is as strong as ever. The Association has given thousands of dollars to youth sports organizations, children with special needs, and continues to sponsor a youth firearms safety course. The Association sponsors a Christmas party for the children of all police department employees and volunteers, and a party for all civilian support personnel as a thank you from the officers for the outstanding work they do. *Submitted by Lieutenant S. Pearson*

Brooklyn Park Mayor's Prayer Breakfast

The Brooklyn Park Mayor's Prayer Breakfast was first held in 1991 and 1992 while Mayor Jesse Ventura was in office. The groundwork was laid in the early 1960s and 1970s when individuals from various Brooklyn Park businesses and churches were challenged to form an independent committee similar to the Anaheim, California concept of having a mayor's prayer breakfast.

The 1991 and 1992 programs included leaders from the city, state and nation. Keynote speakers were Adolph Coors and Colonel Nimrod McNair. Unfortunately, leadership did not step forward and the breakfast was not held during the years 1993 to 1995. Then under the strong encouragement of Mayor Grace Arbogast and the leadership of other individuals in the community, the vision was re-cast and the breakfast was again held beginning in 1996. The breakfast has been strongly supported and well attended over the past four years. Keynote speakers have continued to be the highlight of the morning, including nationally recognized speakers, such as Bob Weiland (1996), Doug Mazza (1997), Russell Quinn (1998), Don and Barbara Hodel (1999) and Andrew Wyatt (2000). *Submitted by John D. Sutherland*

Brooklyn Park Rotary Club

During the summer of 1980, a group of civic-minded business and professional men who lived or worked in Brooklyn Park became interested in forming a service club in the community. They wanted opportunities to serve others, frequent and regular meetings, and a diversity of members. Rotary International with a motto of "Service Above Self" became the obvious choice for the framework within which to establish such a club. By the Winter of 1981, the requisite number of twenty-five men had been recruited to become charter members of the new club. The Rotary Club of Brooklyn Park was chartered in March 1981 under the sponsorship of the Rotary Club of Brooklyn Center. The initial executive committee was President Richard Mueller, Vice President Richard Edlund, Secretary Roger Uglem, and Treasurer Richard Gunderson.

In March 1987 the Rotary Club of Brooklyn Park held its first Annual Wild Game Dinner. The amounts raised by the event for charitable projects and purposes have increased from approximately $4,000 in 1987 to approximately $26,000 in 2000.

In 1987 Judith Lamp, Principal of Park Center High School, was the first woman to be inducted as a member of our club and one of the first in Minnesota. In 1997-1998, President Pamela Nei was our club's first woman chief executive officer.

At the present time, our club has approximately fifty members, five of whom are among the original charter members: Gordon Jensen, James Klecker, Gary LaPalme, Thomas Stewart and Eldon Tessman. *Submitted by Donn N. Peterson*

The Brooklyn Park Seniors Citizen's Club

The Brooklyn Park Seniors Citizen's Club was chartered in 1974. A small group of individuals (approximately seventeen) organized the group. The first meeting site was in the home of Vera Schreiber and then moved to the Prince of Peace Lutheran Church and later to St Gerard's Catholic Church. In 1975 the Central Park Community building was constructed and the group moved there, and finally to the Zanewood Community building in 1980. The Community Activity Center has also been home for the club's monthly luncheons and social activities. The Brooklyn Park Senior Center was completed in 1998 and is the permanent home for senior adult recreational and social activities. The new facility is attached to the south side of the existing Community Activity Center, 5400 85th Avenue, Brooklyn Park. It consists of a members lounge area, the Club Coordinator's office, a meeting room capable of seating 450 persons and a complete kitchen. Our first meeting in our new home was held January 14th, 1999, almost twenty-five years to the exact day of our first meeting in the Schreiber's home. *Submitted by Louise J. Leninger*

The Brooklyn Park Women of Today

The Minnesota Women of Today became an organization on July 1, 1985. It started in September 1950, when the Mrs. Jaycees of Minnesota was chartered. In May 1979 the name was changed to Minnesota Jaycee Women. They voted to become members of the U.S. Jayceettes as a state, requiring each member to belong to the U.S. Jayceettes. Affiliation was a big issue in 1982-1983. The U.S. Jaycees said there had to be a Jaycee chapter in order to have a Jaycee Women chapter in the community. On July 3, 1984, the Supreme Court ruled that the women must be granted full membership in the Jaycees. That winter, three options were discussed: 1) to merge with the Jaycees; 2) to disaffiliate from the Jaycees; 3) to remain the way they were. In March, the membership voted to disaffiliate from the Jaycees. On July 1, 1985, the Minnesota Women of Today was established with 184 chapters, including the Brooklyn Park Women of Today. The Women of Today have a mission statement in which we state that our main focus is on service, growth and fellowship. *Submitted by Bonnie Braasch*

Brooklyn Senior Adult Supper Club (Brooklyn Twins Club)

The Brooklyn Senior Supper Club began as the Brooklyn Twins Club in 1958. The Brooklyn Twins Senior Club was one of the first senior clubs in the Northwest Hennepin area. The first meetings were held at Al and Eva Brueninger's home in the village of Brooklyn Center. The name of the club was chosen because there were many Brooklyn Park residents as members and wanted a name to represent everyone.

The club met on the first and third Friday of every month, September–May. Membership was open to persons 55 years and over, single or married. As the membership grew, the club moved to the Brooklyn Center Fire Station, then to Earle Brown School. For three months, February–April, 1988, the club met on a trial basis at the lovely new Earle Brown Commons. The club returned to the school and in September of 1989 moved to the Brooklyn Center Community Center.

Initially, the club was sponsored by the United Way through Suburban Recreation Association. In January 1976 the club sponsorship was undertaken by the City of Brooklyn Center. In September 1991 the club changed to a supper club and began meeting on the third Friday of the month, September–May. The twins name is being phased out of the club name. (Some people think it is a club for twins.)
Submitted by Kathy Flesher

The Brooklyn Community Chamber of Commerce had its beginnings in 1964 when it was called the Brooklyn Center Chamber of Commerce. According to Earl Simons, a meeting was held with Dallas Lawrence and Ed Hamernick from the Brooklyn Center State Bank, Phil Cohen and me. At this meeting we discussed forming a Brooklyn Center Business Association which led to a meeting with Ed Hogan, of the Minneapolis Chamber of Commerce, who encouraged us to form a Chamber of Commerce. Bill Hannay was the organizing chairman and Jimmy Johnston was the first president. Ernee McArthur was the first Executive Secretary and for seven years the office was in the McArthur home. In 1972, when Ernee was elected State Representative, Barbara Sexton became the full time Executive Secretary.

In 1978 Lonnie McCauley became the Executive Director and worked with the City staff to obtain Industrial Revenue Bond funding to aid businesses faced with interest rates of more than 20%. In 1985 Julie Vreeland became the Executive Director and was the catalyst for the All America City Award. In 1990 Mary Welch became the Executive Director, and with her heart and the support of Chamber members the Heritage Festival was born. In 1995 the Brooklyn Center Chamber expanded to include Brooklyn Park and changed its name to Brooklyn Community Chamber of Commerce. In 1996 Kent Campbell became the Executive Director. With his hard work, membership grew from 115 to 280. In 2000 Leatha Lemmer was named Executive Director. *Submitted by Dale Greenwald*

Brooklyn Community Chamber Of Commerce

The Brooklyn Community Band began as the Brooklyn Center Community Band in 1963 with twenty-four members. Dick Papke was the organizing director and they met at the Brooklyn Center High School. Their debut concert was held at Brookdale Center in 1963. Don Molde was named director in 1968. Riggs Opland became director in 1970, followed by Woody Hoiseth and then Paul Schierenbeck from 1986-1999. In 2000, Jane Ruohoniemi is the director. In the late 1980s the band became the Brooklyn Community Band, sponsored by the Park and Recreation Departments of Brooklyn Center and Brooklyn Park. Other sources of support are membership dues, fund raising, and concert honorariums.

The Band plays about ten concerts in June and July, including civic celebrations, concerts in the Park and at senior care centers. The Band has a legacy of ending most concerts with "Stars and Stripes Forever," a march by John Philip Sousa. Three charter members of the original 1963 band continue in the Band in 2000. They are Jim Stumpfa, Carol Abild and Joan Wikstrom. *Submitted by Paul Schierenbeck*

Brooklyn Community Band

"A Major Event of Great Historical Significance," an open house on the Earle Brown Farm, was held September 27, 1970, with 3,000 in attendance. This high-visibility event kicked-off the formation of the historical society. Judge James H. Johnston, master of ceremonies, summed up the meaning of the day when he said: "History, in illuminating the past, illuminates the present and in illuminating the present, illuminates the future. A page of history is worth a volume of logic."

At its first formal meeting on October 8, 1970, the organization chose the name Brooklyn Historical Society and Mary Jane Gustafson was elected the first president In 1997 Dean and Marie Nyquist invited the BHS to open an office in their Brooklyn Peace Center Building, allowing the gathering of history files from many sources.

BHS has published numerous pamphlets documenting local history. In 1983 a BHS

Brooklyn Historical Society

book, "History of the Earle Brown Farm," was published, updated in 1996. Major initiatives included advocacy for restoration and preservation of the Earle Brown Farm and other local historic sites. The Hall of Fame program recognizes residents who made significant contributions to Brooklyn Center and Brooklyn Park. The Society is a 501(c)(3) tax-exempt organization. The Society's presidents have been: Mary Jane Gustafson, Vern Ausen, Dr. Norene Roberts and Jane Hallberg, Madeleine Roche, and Mary Ellen Vetter. *Submitted by Jane Hallberg and Leone Howe*

The Brooklyn Peacemaker Center

In 1984 a community mediation project was developed in the vacant parsonage of the Brookdale Covenant Church for the purpose of providing a vehicle to resolve neighborhood disputes. In the early 1980s, it had become popular to experiment with victim-offender mediation. A criminal offense was handled outside of the court system, giving the opportunity for the offender and the victim to meet and discuss the event. As an extension to the victim-offender mediation, juvenile offenders were also referred to the program. The Brooklyn Peacemaker Center, in a ten-year time period, has offered alternatives to criminal prosecution for nearly 3,000 young people. The consistent annual success rate (less than 6% re-offend) has generated support from State and County agencies for this small private organization, which had previously been (and continues to be) supported by the community. *Submitted by Pat Milton*

Camp Fire and Bluebirds

Once upon a time there were no Bluebirds or Camp Fire Girls. In fact it wasn't until 1910 that a man and his wife decided to do something about this. They had a family camp. Their girls and the girls' friends spent many wonderful hours together. All agreed that they should have a camp just for girls. This became Camp Fire Girls, ages ten years, or fifth grade to ninth grade. When the girls reached ninth grade they became Horizon Club Girls. These girls learned to do more mature, more professional duties and projects. But the little girls ages seven to ten were left out until 1913, when the Bluebird Groups were started. One of the main fund raisers of the Camp Fire, and Bluebird Groups was to sell candy. This was a big project, with all of the candy being stored in one of the parents' basement. The money was used to pay national dues, or to do something special for someone in need, for their parents, or their leader. In later years boys were allowed to join these groups. *Submitted by Barbara Erickson*

Community Emergency Assistance Program

Brooklyn Center resident Madeleine Roche founded Community Emergency Assistance Program (CEAP) in April 1970 to respond to the need for human services in Brooklyn Center and Brooklyn Park. With other citizens, she joined with local churches to bridge the gap in assistance for those in need. In 1971 CEAP was incorporated as a tax-exempt charitable organization and elected its first Board of Directors. CEAP's first office was located in St. Alphonsus's rectory.

With the help of the Brooklyn Center Jaycees and the Bicentennial Commission, CEAP moved into the old Brooklyn Center City Hall until it burned New Year's Eve 1977. CEAP then operated temporarily out of two houses until it moved into a building built for CEAP in 1980 on land donated by Bob Johnson, located behind the Red Lobster on Brooklyn Boulevard. For the next seventeen years CEAP occupied that building until it moved into its current location in Brooklyn Park in February 1997. *Submitted by Sarah Henfling*

Brooklyn Center's Neighborhood Crime Watch was formed in 1983. In 1999 their numbers boast in excess of 150. The Brooklyn Center Crime Prevention Program has been the major sponsor of neighborhood watch groups and the National Night Out celebration. The group sponsors an annual awards program, a crime tips reward program, and youth crime prevention programs.

The Brooklyn Park Crime Prevention Association was formed in 1990 to reduce crime in the city. Our first crime watch was on 81st Ave. east of Xerxes. Crime was at an all time high and violent crimes were escalating. Neighbors joined with the Police department to take back their neighborhoods. In 1990 we started with twenty crime watches and our first National Night Out celebration and received our first national recognition for our efforts with the Rookie of the Year award. Our crime watches have spread to apartments and businesses and we have now reached over 250. Our involvement with the community and the Police Department has resulted in nine straight national awards and a first place ranking in Minnesota every year in our population category with the National Association of Town Watches. In 1999 we placed 5th in the nation. We received recognition from former Gov. Carlson for our Police Community Partnerships. Today we have our own newsletter, *The Nosey Neighbor Newsletter*, a crime tip reward fund, Santa Cop, neighborhood alert programs, an active partnership with the city, nine national awards and recognition for our efforts, and a National Night Out celebration that is second to none. In 1995 the B.P.C.D.A. and B.C.N.C.W. joined for a joint celebration of National Night Out at the Village North Shopping Center. *Submitted by: Peg Snesrud, President, BPCDA*

Brooklyn Center Neighborhood Crime Watch and the Brooklyn Park Crime Prevention Association

The Virginia Dare Chapter, Daughters of the Revolution (DAR), held its first meeting in October 1906. The program committee decided to have programs on Minnesota history its first year. The six charter members were Bertha Kneeland, Annabelle Painter, Anna Satterwaite, Ruth Starr, Helen Tanner, and Marion Tuttle. On April 14, 1934, twelve members of the Virginia Dare chapter disbanded and organized as the John Witherspoon Chapter of the DAR. Esther Barnum was the first regent of the new chapter. Members are directly descended from a Revolutionary veteran, or someone who supported the revolutionary side. *Submitted by Barbara Sexton*

Daughters Of The American Revolution John Witherspoon Chapter

The DFL Party began in the Brooklyns in the late 1950s. In 1960 Richard Parrish of Robbinsdale, was one of the first DFLers to win elected office from the area. He served in the House of Representatives and the State Senate representing Brooklyn Center and adjacent suburbs.

In 1971 Maury Britts was the first DFL endorsed candidate elected to the Brooklyn Center City Council and was the first black council member. Others who won city elections include Gene Lhotka, Todd Paulson, Dave Rosene, Barbara Kalligher and Debra Hilstrom. Todd Paulson was elected Mayor in 1990. DFL endorsed candidates for the State Legislature include: Senators Hubert H. (Skip) Humphrey III, Bill Luther, Ember Reichgott Junge, Linda Scheid and Don Betzold, and State Representatives Lyn Carlson, Bill Luther, Bob Ellingson, Linda Scheid, Darlene Luther and Phil Carruthers.

Phil became the Speaker of the House in 1997-1998. In 2000 he chose not to seek reelection.

Submitted by David Kanatz

DFL Party

4-H Clubs of Brooklyn Park and Brooklyn Center

4-H Clubs were an integral part of rural life in the Brooklyns, and in 2000 one small community club exists as part of a neighboring suburban club. The 4-H Emblem is a four-leaf clover. An H on each leaf stand for pledging "Head, Heart, Hands and Health to better living for my club, my community and my country." Minnesota added "Home" to the pledge, and in 1973 national action was taken to add "my world" to club, community and country. Volunteer leaders of the Benson School 4-H Club (1943-1982) were Grace Bennett Johnson, Ardis Fiebiger and Mavis Fiebiger Huddle. The Pete and Ardis Fiebiger softball team earned the Hennepin County 4-H Club Softball traveling trophy permanently after five consecutive wins. The Earle Brown Gophers 4-H Club met in the homes of members. Elaine Tessman Christiansen was "Minnesota Vegetable Queen" and "National Vegetable Queen" in 1951. *Provided by Minnesota 4-H Foundation and local residents*

Fraternal Organizations

These Fraternal Organizations that were active in the Brooklyns include:
Order of the Eastern Star is a fraternal organization of Master Masons to which men and women may belong. They work to promote charity, good will, and social enjoyment and support social and charitable projects. The chapter met twice a month at the Winslow Lewis Lodge Hall in Osseo during the 1930s, according to Alice P. Tessman. The Masons spend millions of dollars annually for hospitals, homes for widows and orphans, and the aged, relief for people in distress and scholarships for students.
Shriners is an organization related to the Masons. Shriners are noted for the hospitals they have established. The Shrine has the same aims and ideals as the Masons. It admits men who are at least 32nd-degree Masons in the Scottish Rite or Knights Templar in the York Rite.
Independent Order of Odd Fellows' chief purpose is to give aid, assistance, and comfort to its members and their families. It is a secret society and has its own system of rites and passwords.
*Benevolent and Protective Order of Elk*s is a fraternal and charitable organization. Elks Lodge 44 is relatively new to Brooklyn Park and is located at Xerxes Avenue and Brookdale Drive. The lodge serves lunches and has rental rooms for receptions. The Flag Day ceremony at the Community Activity Center was sponsored by the Elks.

Friendship Quilters of Brooklyn Center

The Friendship Quilters was founded in February 1974. Kathy Flesher arranged for a meeting room. Mary Jane Gustafson wrote a feature article and the group was launched and has continued these twenty-five years with a membership of twenty or more. Joanne Holzknecht is the only member left from the original group. The quilters work on their own projects, but also do community service such as last year making 80 hats for women having chemotherapy; and making ABC quilts for babies. *Submitted by Joanne Holzknecht*

The Gardenaires Club

The local Gardenaires was started in 1960, and joined the Federated Garden Clubs in 1961. Several of our members are master gardeners. We have called our club "The Flowering Crabs," "Club of Brooklyn Center," "Home and Garden" and the "Gardenaires." We planted flowerbeds at the BC Community Center and in 1978 we spent $2,000 for a fountain at Central Park. Every spring we plant at the Brooklyn Park Historical Farm. The club sponsors a scholarship to a local student. We volunteer at the State Fair and help at the Renaissance Festival. Every fall the Brooklyn Park Historical

Farm holds an open house. Our members cook on the old fashioned wood stove. We decorate the house throughout with garlands at Christmas time and have a huge tree with all Norwegian decorations. At Christmas time we have a tree at the Arboretum and decorate with homemade natural articles. *Submitted by Novella Zimbrick*

The Harmonettes began as the Earle Brown Mother Singers (EBMS). They have entertained in the community since September 1949, under the direction of June Scofield, accompanied by pianist Alpha Carlson. They sang at civic affairs, schools, nursing homes and hospitals, just to name a few. In 1953 the Hamilton School Mother Singers joined the group and the name was changed to The Harmonettes. Dorothy Dale became their accompanist and the Harmonettes entertained throughout the area at many community events. *Submitted by Karen Carlson Bouley*

The Harmonettes

The Heritage Festival began in 1992 as a business/school/community partnership. It was initiated by the Brooklyn Community Chamber of Commerce to help area citizens understand and welcome the community's increasing diversity. The Festival aims to foster deep respect for the heritage of everyone, but the central theme is celebrating our common American heritage. Over 2,000 people have attended each year since 1993. *Submitted by Mary Welch*

The Heritage Festival

Two organizations of church congregations, the Joint Ministry Project (JMP) in Minneapolis, and the Suburban Ecumenical Action Coalition (SEAC), laid the foundation for Interfaith Action. The two groups had similar goals and each had become increasingly aware that the problems they were attempting to address did not stop at the city's limits. In 1995 JMP and SEAC concluded that the best option was to sponsor the creation of Interfaith Action and then dissolve their separate organizations. In this way, they could create something new that would capitalize on the strengths of each organization while sharing the lessons learned from past history. We are presently a part of ISAIAH, which has groups active in the Twin Cities and in St. Cloud. ISAIAH is affiliated nationally with the Gameliel Foundation. At a January 1996 ecumenical convocation in honor of Rev. Dr. Martin Luther King, Jr., 700 people witnessed the covenant to create Interfaith Action. We hold an annual Martin Luther King event to review our accomplishments, and to educate members of our Congregations about current issues. In the late 1990s, on the regional level, affordable housing for working families became a vital issue. *Submitted by Barbara Sexton and Sylvia Winkleman*

Interfaith Action

The Walter J. Breckenridge Chapter of the Izaak Walton League of North America organized in 1922. Four men began this chapter in Camden, in north Minneapolis, located on the Mississippi River. In 1932 they purchased a piece of property with 290 feet of frontage on the River in Brooklyn Park. Four years later they built the chapter house, largely with volunteer labor. Its fireplace is distinctive with stones from the forty-eight states that comprised the United States at that time. Dr. Walter Breckenridge joined this chapter about 1940. Always a faithful member, he became increasingly active during his retirement. To honor him as a "defender of soil, woods, waters and wildlife," this organization changed its name to the Walter J. Breckenridge Chapter. *Submitted by Charles Purdham*

Walter Breckenridge Chapter of The Izaak Walton League of North America

The Kiwanis Club of North Suburban Minneapolis

This club was chartered on September 29, 1973. It was established as a breakfast club and had its first meetings at the Holiday Inn in Brooklyn Center. There were twenty-five members in the original group and they came from Brooklyn Center, Brooklyn Park and surrounding area. Kiwanis is an International service organization with more than 320,000 men and women in 8,500 clubs in 82 different geographic areas.

Our own North Suburban Club serves the community through support of other organizations such as Earle Brown Days, Boy Scouts, Courage Center, U of M Children's Cancer Research, High School Scholarships, Community Emergency Assistance Program (CEAP), Southern Anoka County Assistance (SACA), The Salvation Army, Brooklyn Center Fire and Crime Prevention Programs, Youth Leadership Training, and other miscellaneous projects. The Club, together with students from Brooklyn Center High School, annually clean a two-mile section of Highway 100 in the Brooklyn Center area. To raise money to support these projects, the Club has an annual peanut sale in September and sells poinsettias at Christmas time. Also during Christmas, the Club rings bells for the Salvation Army. *Submitted by Roger A. Johnson*

Knights of Columbus

The Knights of Columbus are a Catholic, family, fraternal and service organization founded by Father Michael J. McGivney, a young Catholic priest in New Haven, Conn. The Knights of Columbus charter was issued by the Connecticut State Assembly on March 29, 1882. In Brooklyn Center/Brooklyn Park the Father Donald Schumaker Council #6772 was started on February 29, 1976. There were 113 charter members with programs such as Ad-Altari-Dei for the Boy Scouts, Pennies for Seminarians, Prolife, Christmas Mass and Dinner. By the second year the St. Alphonsus School participated in the annual Marathon for Non-Public Schools and the Knights help sponsor that program with finances and volunteer resources. One continuous program the Knights have carried on for over twenty years is the annual Tootsie Roll Drive for the benefit of people with mental retardation. Some of the programs the Knights started are the following: Spring Flings, Moonlight Bowling, Back to the Fifties, Summer Camporee at Serres, Ladies Auxiliary cookbook, Keep Christ in Christmas, Mississippi River Boat Cruise, Old Log Theater, Golf tournament, Softball team and tournament and Living Stations of the Cross. *Submitted by Don Carson*

North Hennepin Business and Professional Womens Organization

After enjoying five years of membership in the St. Louis Park Business and Professional Womens Organization (BPW), Mary Hawkins noted that business women in the North Hennepin area, did not wish to travel to St. Louis Park for meetings.

In August 1970 sixty business women in the North Hennepin area were invited to an organizational meeting. Forty-five women attended the first meeting and thirty-six signed as Charter Members. They were helped by Jule Ann Johnson, a past State President, and her St. Louis Park Club as sponsor. Since 1971 North Hennepin BPW has organized and chartered nine BPWs in Minnesota.

North Hennepin BPW provides financial aid to women wishing to return to school for training to advance in their careers and to members to attend seminars, workshops or evening school classes. In the last few years, profit from silent auctions was donated to a single mother and four children, Caring and Sharing Hands, Battered Women's Shelter and Good Samaritan Care Center. North Hennepin BPW sponsored two young women to vie for Young Careerist, with one winning competition at State level and an expense paid trip to the National Convention to join young career women from around the United States. One of our members won in the Individual Development Program at State level and was sponsored to attend a National Convention in Boston. *Submitted by Mary L. Hawkins*

The Brooklyn Park Commercial Club was chartered on May 6, 1971, which in turn became the Brooklyn Park Chamber of Commerce, November 3, 1972, which merged with the Osseo-Maple Grove Chamber of Commerce (which began September 10, 1975) to form the North Hennepin Area Chamber of Commerce on May 4, 1983. *Submitted by David Looby*

North Hennepin Chamber of Commerce

The North Metro Minneapolis Convention & Visitors Bureau is a destination marketing organization whose mission is "to promote economic growth for its members as a preferred destination for events, meetings and tourism." The Bureau is a private non-profit organization founded in 1987, and is governed by a Board of Directors whose members represent the cities, business and hoteliers. The Bureau is managed by a paid Executive Director, currently John Connelly. Funding for the Bureau's operations derives from a 3% lodging tax assessed by hotels and motels on rented rooms. Funding cities currently include Anoka, Blaine, Brooklyn Center, Brooklyn Park, Coon Rapids, Fridley and Maple Grove. *Information submitted by the Bureau*

North Metro Minneapolis Convention & Visitors Bureau

In 1998 a group of City Council members, City Managers and City staff members of various cities met to discuss joining together in an area-wide human rights effort. The effort would extend beyond individual city Human Rights Commissions to provide the resources, creativity, and capacity for the region as a whole to address human rights issues. Meetings led to the formation of the Northwest Regional Human Rights Coalition. This group meets on a quarterly basis at the Crystal Community Center. The Cities involved in the coalition include: Brooklyn Center, Brooklyn Park, Champlin, Crystal, Golden Valley, Maple Grove, New Hope, Plymouth and Robbinsdale.

Northwest Hennepin Human Rights Coalition

Meetings during the first full year of the Coalition's history have included a range of speakers addressing such topics as diversity issues in the region's schools, reports on outreach activities being undertaken in other metro area communities, a report on the activities of the State of Minnesota League of Human Rights, and a report on mediation as a tool to address human rights concerns.

Staffing is provided for by the Northwest Hennepin Human Services Council, through funding by the CO-OP Northwest Project. The Coalition hosted the Heritage Festival in March 2000. Brooklyn Center folded its Human Rights Commission into the Coalition. Brooklyn Center has been an active participant in the Coalition's activities since its formation, supplying a liaison to the City Council, a commissioner, and City staff support for Coalition activities. *Submitted by City of Brooklyn Center*

Northwest Hennepin Human Services Council

Created in 1972, Northwest Hennepin Human Services Council (NWHHSC) is "a joint venture of the northwest municipalities and Hennepin County." NWHHSC is responsible for the overall research, planning and coordination of human services for the northwest Hennepin area, which represents fifteen cities. The Council provides research, planning and coordination in many areas of human services including family issues, community health issues, emergency services, senior services, domestic violence prevention, transportation, housing initiatives, services for people with physical and developmental disabilities, jobs and training services, and diversification efforts. NWHHSC staff established a set of organizational values in order to provide quality services to the northwest Hennepin community. We value advocating for human services needs, respecting diversity and different perspectives, and collaborating using a team approach. *Submitted by NWHHSC*

North Hennepin Leadership Academy

Since 1989 the North Hennepin Leadership Academy (NHLA) has provided the North Hennepin community with a strong and progressive leadership program for "building the leaders of tomorrow." NHLA provides local employers with an opportunity to invest in their workforce, by increasing their employees' knowledge of community issues and leadership skills and to make a significant contribution to the north west suburbs. The NHLA is sponsored by Brooklyn Community Chamber of Commerce, North Hennepin Chamber of Commerce and North Hennepin Community College. The NHLA is a dynamic and integral asset of this community. This interactive program provides community members with valuable insights into both the positive and negative aspects of our society. Participants also learn how to step up to the opportunities of leadership in their community/organizations and to develop the crucial tools needed to deal with the multitude of leadership challenges today.

North Hennepin Mediation Program

North Hennepin Mediation Program is a community based non-profit organization offering dispute resolution services to residents and businesses of the North and Northwest Suburban Hennepin County area. Established in 1983, North Hennepin Mediation Program is one of only six certified programs in the state of Minnesota.

North Hennepin Mediation Program handles disputes between neighbors, businesses and consumers, landlords and tenants, family members, juvenile cases of shoplifting, vandalism, harassment and truancy, offenders and victims, citizens and agencies, divorced people and others. Mediation is also offered to Housing, Family, Juvenile, Harassment and Conciliation Court disputants. Mediation is free to users except in Post-Divorce cases. Post-divorce cases are handled on a sliding fee scale with a $70 maximum cost shared by the parties.

Community volunteers are the backbone of the organization. All mediators are volunteers who have participated in forty hours of intensive initial training and participate in continuing education for each year they mediate. The Board of Directors and all committees are staffed by volunteers. The program operates with three paid staff, two part time and one full time.

North Hennepin Mediation Program is funded, by the state of Minnesota, Hennepin County, municipalities, foundations, corporations, individuals and social, civic and professional organizations. *Submitted by Janet Mauer*

In 1966 a few people gathered and started the North Hennepin Pioneer Society. They elected Victoria Joyner, President; Frend Wadsworth, Vice President; Dean Tripp, Secretary; and George Reinking, Treasurer. The first project of the society was the Brooklyn Park Potter log cabin, which was in the path of a highway. We paid $1.00 for this building. The men moved it and replaced rotted logs with logs from an old trading post nearby. The Burschville School, west of Corcoran, was acquired a few days after the last class left on May 31, 1967, upon the event of consolidation with Buffalo. We paid $1,000 for the land and received a deed and abstract. In July 1967 the cabin was dismantled, and the logs were hauled to the school site for reconstruction in October 1967. In August 1968 we were ready to show the reconditioned school to our neighbors. The Buffalo School District presented the Burschville School and bell to us, led by Hennepin County School Superintendant Mr. Cummings. Among the many who came was a teacher and her pupils of 1897 of this same school: Teacher: Lydia Krienke who is now Lydia Ziebarth. Pupils: Emma Roehlke Pagenhopf, Walter Roehlke and Elsie Roehlke Schendel. During 1969, the school was opened to the public for tours. *Submitted by Dorothy Schoenmann*

The North Hennepin Pioneer Society

In working with families who are going through divorce, the mediators discovered that children are often the victims. They are victims because the parents have separated geographically so as to make visitation with the child difficult. To meet this need, the P.O.P. Visitation Center was established, a 501 (c)(3) organization. The demand for services exceeded all expectations many times over. In 1999 volunteers performed more than 1,048 hours of visitation. Another need was a place for the parents to exchange the children, in situations where the court has ordered the parents to refrain from any kind of contact or discussion with the other parent. In 1999 there were 1,262 exchanges performed by volunteers. In areas where a visitation center does not exist, the supervised visitation ordered by the court is often times carried out in the sheriff's office. *Submitted by Dean and Marie Nyquist*

Parents Opportunity for Peacefulness (POP) Visitation Center

In 1965 James H. Johnston, President of the Brooklyn Center Chamber of Commerce, invited the various organization presidents to join in forming a President's Roundtable. The idea for a Roundtable came from Allen G. Erickson, a Chamber board member. The purpose of the President's Roundtable was to cooperate with one another in the matter of setting dates for various functions so as not to conflict with one another and to promote each others' programs and to consider other areas of mutual interest for the betterment of the organizations and community as a whole. The Roundtable served its purpose well for a number of years, then was discontinued by the Chamber in the late 1970s when assumed by another organization.

President's Roundtable

Project P.E.A.C.E stands for Protect, Educate, Advocate, Comfort, and Empower. It is a 501 (c)(3) community-based domestic abuse intervention project staffed by advocates who are available to offer support, information, referrals, and options for ways to help women deal with their situations. Each woman is assured complete confidentiality. It is not a part of the court system. Services include a 24-hour Crisis Line, Legal Advocacy, Educational Support Groups and Community Outreach and Volunteer Opportunities.

Project PEACE

Republicans in the Brooklyns

The Minnesota Republican Party began as a third party in 1855 when 200 former Democrats and Whigs met at St. Anthony to form a new party opposed to slavery. In the late 1950s Annece Johnson and others knocked on doors while pushing their babies in strollers, asking; "Are there any Republicans living here?" Thus began the Republican party in the Brooklyns. Elected Republican standard bearers include Hennepin County Sheriff Earle Brown; State Senators Dean Nyquist, Al Kowalczyk and Don Kramer; State Representatives Baldwin Hartkopf, Leonard Lindquist, John Wingard, Roger Scherer, Bill Schreiber, Ernee McArthur, Richard Krambeer and Bill Haas; and Brooklyn Center Council members Vern Ausen, Tony Kuefler, Bill Fignar and Bob Peppe. In the 1990s the "Political Pages" newspaper was published to inform local residents of Party positions, candidates and activities. *Submitted by David Johnson*

Boy Scouts of America

On February 8, 1910, Mr. Boyce and a group of businessmen, educators, and political leaders founded the Boy Scouts of America. Boys who join BSA understand and agree to live by the Scout Oath or Promise, Law, Motto, Slogan, and the Outdoor Code of Ethics: as an American, I will do my best to be clean in my outdoor manners, be careful with fire, be considerate in the outdoors, and be conservation-minded. Service to others has always been a central part of Scouting. Scouts today carry on this tradition of service in their homes, communities, and nation by gathering food and clothing for needy neighbors, building playgrounds, repairing parks and public buildings, and cleaning up after storms, etc. Brooklyn Center and Brooklyn Park in 2000 have twelve Boy Scout Troops and sixteen Cub Packs.

Girl Scouts in Brooklyn Park and Brooklyn Center

In 1981 the greater Minneapolis Girl Scout Council purchased the building which had been the Brooklyn Center Hennepin County Library. Brookdale Shopping Center and Brooklyn Center Civic Center were the scene for gatherings of hundreds of Girl Scouts ages 7 to 17 for celebrations of the anniversaries of the founding of the national Girl Scout movement. Individual troops performed songs and folk dances on a stage in the atrium as troops displayed art and crafts in booths set up around the sidelines. A display tent and campsite were erected to demonstrate the girls' skills in many areas of Scouting. As leaders retired, they missed the camaraderie, so they began the "Alumnae Friends of Girl Scouts of the Greater Minneapolis Council." Eileen Casey wrote the organization's by-laws and was the first secretary, and Marilyn McAlpine was the first president in 1972. The group meets at the Brooklyn Center Girl Scout Council office building and one of its projects is to preserve and exhibit memorabilia of the Girl Scouts in the Greater Minneapolis Area. *Submitted by Marilyn McAlpine*

Twin Lakes Alano Society

In 1974 the Robbinsdale School District 281 sold its Twin Lakes Elementary School at 4938 Brooklyn Boulevard to the Twin Lakes Alano Society. The Society manages the business affairs of the Alano building, in which the AA (Alcoholics Anonymous) Squad meetings and Al-Anon meetings are held.

Clarence LaBelle VFW Post #217

The Veterans of Foreign Wars Post was organized on November 21, 1930. It was named after Clarence R. LaBelle, a soldier from North Minneapolis, killed during World War I at the age of nineteen. He had recovered from his wounds and gone back into action when he was killed. The first commander of the Post was P. A. Bowers. In 1940 the VFW Post #217 moved into their new accommodations at 2201 51st Avenue

North, the former Reed School. The Post sold its real estate and now rents space at the Palmer Lake VFW in Brooklyn Park. The Post sponsored many activities: Buddy Poppy sales, many Pancake Breakfasts, Bingo Games, and dances. The Post sponsored Ice Fishing Contests, boxing matches that included champion boxer, the late Arnie Nyberg, owner of Christy's Auto Repair at 53rd and Dupont. The Post sponsored basketball teams, softball teams, gun safety training for young people and Boy Scout Troops. Proceeds from the various fund raisers were used to help needy veterans and their families. *Submitted by Barbara Erickson*

Clarence LaBelle VFW Post #217 *Auxiliary*

The Clarence LaBelle VFW Post and the Auxiliary were founded in 1931. In 1996, the Auxiliary was recognized "For providing sixty-five years of patriotic and community service to America" by the United States VFW Auxiliary organization. The Auxiliary assists the Post fulfill its obligations. Funeral luncheons, teen dances, Halloween parties for children, Junior Girls Auxiliary, flags, layettes for needy moms, sewing pajamas, scuffs, laundry bags, Memorial Services, rolled bandages to help with the war effort, blood donors, Civil Defense training, Poppy Sales, sewing items for the cancer foundation, reading to the blind at the MN Veterans Home and the VA Hospital, are just many of the ways we have been called to serve. The veterans and their families take priority. When the Post moved to Palmer Lake VFW in Brooklyn Park we moved with them in the early 1990s.

School District 279 *Wastebasket Revue*

In 1967 Duane Malawicki, a music teacher in District 279, brought with him from a previous teaching experience at Virginia, MN the idea of a variety show to raise money for student scholarships and to provide an opportunity for all the new teachers to meet employees in other school buildings. Ideas for the show were generated by fifteen to twenty teachers, and they literally collected the ideas in a wastebasket, and that was the birth of the name Wastebasket Review. Approximately 300 staff members participate in the Revue each year.

The theme of the first show was "Miss Newteach." The theme of the 2000 Revue is "It's About Time." Eight performances of the variety show are scheduled in 2000. Since its inception, the Wastebasket Revue has awarded more than $530,000 in scholarships and is organized with a board of directors.

Excerpted from Lauri Winters article, *Brooklyn Center SunPost,* March 29, 2000

Chapter Eight

Sports in the Brooklyns

The residents of Brooklyn Park and Brooklyn Center have been fortunate to enjoy a variety of organized sports for as many years as they have been organized cities: from the structured programs of two very active Park and Recreation departments to the many volunteer run programs, prompted by parents' desire to occupy their children with good healthy fun.

During the years of the two cities' existence, the cities, schools and communities have offered the opportunity for youth and adults to participate in baseball, basketball, bowling, football, soccer, volleyball, swimming, hockey, archery, softball, skiing, ice skating, golf and any and every other sport that could be considered a "game," or provide a bit of competitive spirit to the community.

There are not enough pages in this book to mention the number of winning teams, medals and honors won by area teams and players. Many residents also proudly reside on State Hall of Fame lists of sports such as softball and bowling.

A brief mention of some of the activities follows, including national sporting events held in our communities, which have inspired participation in sports and some local beginnings of long running programs.

Dudley Classic

Perhaps the longest running national affiliation with sporting events has been Brooklyn Center's sponsorship of the Dudley Classic Men's slow pitch softball tournament. In 1984 the Minnesota Recreation and Park Association (MRPA) approached Brooklyn Center's Park and Recreation department asking if they would help host a major men's slow pitch tournament. The tournament was to feature Howard's Furniture from North Carolina with Dudley Sporting Goods sponsoring Howard's trip to Brooklyn Center and the balls for the tournament. Because of their involvement in the tournament, it was then named the "Dudley Classic." With the renowned team of Howard's being in the tournament, Brooklyn Center was able to attract many teams

Dudley/ Budweiser Men's Major NIT. This national tournament is hosted by the City of Brooklyn Center every year. Local state teams compete against national powers for a berth in the USSSA World Series.
City of Brooklyn Center

from out of state. The tournament became very popular with metro slow pitch players and fans that turned out in large number to watch this intense competition.

In 1986 MRPA decided to drop out as a sponsor of the tournament. At that time it became a Brooklyn Center Park and Recreation Tournament. Another change was Budweiser Beer became a major sponsor, which then changed the name of the tournament to the Dudley Budweiser Classic. It was also at this time that Warren Bellon became the tournament director. Under his direction, along with the Brooklyn Center Park and Recreation staff, led by Arnie Mavis, the tournament grew with teams entering from all over the nation.

The tournament is limited to twenty-six teams with over half of them from out of state. The tournament is sanctioned by the United States Slow-Pitch Softball Association (USSSA). The Dudley Budweiser Classic is rated the number one men's slow pitch tournament in the nation with at least three-fourths of the top teams playing.

The main playing fields are at Brooklyn Center's Central Park. The tournament traditionally starts the third Friday in June and lasts through the weekend. In addition to top-notch talent, the tournament consistently draws more than 8,000 fans. Over the years the Dudley Budweiser tournament has benefited local programs such as the Brooklyn Center Crime Prevention Fund, the Brooklyn Center Fire Department, Brooklyn Center Youth Hockey and Swim Club, not to mention thousands of dollars in revenue to area businesses. This tournament has brought the city of Brooklyn Center a great deal of positive publicity, helping to put it on the map.

Brooklyn Center/ Brooklyn Park baseball team, circa 1915. On the left is Joe Holmes. Second player on left is Earl Dorn.

Submitted by Arnie Mavis

LPGA Golf Tournament

In 1990 Brooklyn Park was first exposed to the LPGA ladies professional golf tournament at Edinburgh USA Golf Course. This tournament not only brought prestige to the community and golf course, but with 144 of the best women golfers in the world, it brought inspiration to thousands of women and girls. It also brought wonder to the men in the audience at the power and perfection of the pro game.

The excitement of having a professional tournament in our back yard spread throughout the city. The effects were far-reaching from over a million dollars in added revenue for businesses each summer, to the community coming together in friendship volunteering to help make it happen. The 800 plus people working behind the scenes signed up each year to be a part of this event. Volunteers and a well run Recreation and Park Department, led by Denny Palm, gave the city and golf fans for miles around something to look forward to for many years.

The tournament purse, as well as the attendance, grew each year. Visitors from all over the United States attended the tournament. In 1990 the purse was $375,000. It grew to over $550,000 and was considered a prime stop for many top golfers year after year, drawing names like Betsy King, Pat Bradley, Laura Davies, Beth Daniel, Nancy Lopez, Liselotte Neumann and Michelle McGann.

During the first five years the tournament was held at Edinburgh USA in Brooklyn Park, the City generated over $75,000 for charitable organizations and special activities supporting park department programs. Some of the benefiting organizations were, the Arts Council, Community Resource Center, Northwest Trails, Babe Ruth and BPAA Baseball, BPYHA, and many others.

In 1997 International Management Group (IMG), who owned the rights to the tournament, announced that they were moving the tournament to Rush Creek Golf Course in Maple Grove. The move was economical for IMG. They were pursuing increased sponsorship sales in order to increase the purse for the tournament. The increased purse would consistently attract bigger names to the tournament, which in turn meant more ticket sales. Rush Creek is also a privately owned public course — the Edinburgh is owned and operated by the City of Brooklyn Park. IMG had an agreement with Edinburgh to pay for a portion of the golf fees and revenues lost during LPGA week. Being privately owned, Rush Creek could offer their course free and with additional incentives that Brooklyn Park could not.

Submitted by Brooklyn Park Recreation and Park Department

Brooklyn Center Little Leagues

Little League Baseball came to Brooklyn Center in 1958 as the Brooklyn Center Little League Inc. playing at the old Dayton Field, land now occupied by the water tower across from Brookdale Center. In 1961 another Little League organized due to the growing population in the northern part of the city. So, two leagues were formed, the Brooklyn Center American and the Brooklyn Center National Little League.

The Brooklyn Center American Little League began playing at Evergreen Park, moving in 1969 to their new facility at 61st and Vincent Avenue North. The fields were built with an initial contribution from Roy Iten. He was called the financial pioneer who got things started for the teams to have a new home. This move was necessary due to the building of Evergreen Park Elementary School.

With the building of Brookdale Center, and the widening of Highway 100, the Brooklyn Center National Little League had to move. A new field was built in 1963 on 2½ acres of land now occupied by Center Brook Golf Course. With the coming of the golf course, the Little League moved to its present location, on what is now part of Lions' Park on 54th and Russell Avenue North.

In 1994 the Brooklyn Center American Little League went to Williamsport, PA to participate in the Little League World Series. This was a tremendous accomplishment, bringing a lot of recognition and pride to the community.

The two Little Leagues have provided a summer sports program for the youth of Brooklyn Center and surrounding communities for more than forty years. Both Little Leagues have touched the lives of many kids. Some have gone on to play professional baseball, such as Tim Laudner who played for the Minnesota Twins. Tim came from the Brooklyn Center American Little League. Many local high school teams had their players come through these two great programs. *Submitted by Tom Shinnick*

Brooklyn Park Athletic Association (BPAA)

Volunteer community athletic associations have played a major role in the development, instruction and organization of youth athletics in the City of Brooklyn Park.

The Brooklyn Park Athletic Association (BPAA) was the first organized association to address the issues facing a young and growing community. The BPAA was recog-

Swedish-born Liselotte Neumann won the Minnesota LPGA title in 1994 at Edinburgh USA Golf Course.

nized by the State as a legally organized corporation on March 9, 1965. The original officers were: Howard Clune, John Crunstedt, Virgil Sellhelm, James Greenwood and Robert Almer. A 1960 newspaper article written by then BPAA Treasurer, Bob Longson, tracks the beginning of the group.

The Mission Statement of BPAA is to benefit the physical, mental, moral and character development of its members and of the youth in our community by providing major sports programs and activities for boys and girls regardless of ability or financial status. Many of the specialized athletic groups that exist today began under the umbrella of BPAA and branched off as size or specialization warranted.

The Brooklyn Park Youth Hockey Association (BPYHA) was organized in 1969. The organization branched off from the BPAA as a specialized athletic group, focusing on the sport of ice hockey for those between the ages of 5 and 15 years of age in the city of Brooklyn Park. Most of the ice time used by the organization in its early years were outdoor rinks within the city's park system. As indoor ice became more available in the 1970s, they skated a majority of the indoor ice time at the newly built Northland Ice Arena, located in the Industrial District off Boone Ave. The BPYHA has now grown to 550 player members and skates predominately at the two sheets of ice at the Brooklyn Park Community Activity Center. It was due to the popularity of the sport of hockey, addition of a strong girls hockey program and active ice skating clubs, that a second sheet of ice was added to the community center in 1998.

1994 Central Region Little League Champions. The Brooklyn Center American Little League team participated in the 1994 Little League World Series in Williamsport, PA. They were 1994 State Champions and 1994 Midwest Champions.

The girls hockey program grew in the early 1990s under the wing of BPYHA. By the mid-90s the Brooklyn Area teams were serious competitors. This can be attributed to a decision to enter the teams into an accelerated category of competition rather than into more instructional league play. BPYHA made sure their girls teams had all the skills to play with the best. All youth sports teams are for fun at the time they are playing, but the inevitable happens, that the youth teams grow up to be the high school, college and even professional players. The Brooklyn Park and Brooklyn Center Youth programs were proudly reminded of this as they watched the Park Center Girls Hockey Team win the Girls State Hockey Tournament in the year 2000.

Maplebrook & Kickers Soccer

Maplebrook and Kickers Soccer have provided soccer programs for children interested in developing their soccer skills. These groups are open to players from the surrounding communities. The Maplebrook Soccer Association hosts an annual soccer tournament that attracts over 200 teams to the community. Over the years the number of soccer players has continued to increase and is one of the fastest growing sports for boys and girls in youth athletics. The challenge for 2000 and beyond is to accommodate the many interested participants by creating enough soccer fields.

Submitted by Brooklyn Park Recreation and Park Department

BPAA Youth Baseball & Babe Ruth Baseball

Brooklyn Park Babe Ruth Baseball started with a national charter in 1961. For various reasons, the charter went dormant for a time. In the meantime, BPAA continued to serve youth in their baseball program, which was for 8 to 12 year olds. Players also joined the Brooklyn Center Babe Ruth program, which had a charter since 1959. Younger children joined Park and Recreation programs such as T-Ball. BPAA baseball, at its peak in the early 90s, registered 1200 plus players for their program each summer. Higher registration was often attributed to the success of the Minnesota Twins with the 1987 and 1991 World Series wins.

In 1988 Brooklyn Park's Babe Ruth Charter was activated once again. It continued separately from Brooklyn Center, until declining numbers in the Brooklyn Center Program suggested a merge of the two charters. In May 1998 a celebration was held reuniting the two baseball communities and forming the Brooklyn Area Babe Ruth League for 11 to 18 years olds. During this same celebration, Phil Cohen was honored for his commitment and contributions to area baseball, by dedicating the baseball diamonds at Grandview Park, as Cohen Field.

In 1999 the Brooklyn Area Babe Ruth baseball program registered 350 players at three levels of competition — City Leagues, B-travel Teams and A-travel teams. With a renewed competitive spirit the league qualified five teams for the state Babe Ruth Championship titles, four won state championships and the fifth placed in the top four. This is the first time a community has done this in the state of Minnesota.

Submitted by Ron Ostendorf

Roy Iten, Iten Chevrolet, was a major sponsor of sports in the Brooklyns.

Brooklyn Park Traveling Basketball

During the early 1980s traveling basketball teams were playing as individual teams that were not part of an association. In the late 1980s these individual teams formed the Brooklyn Park Traveling Basketball Association.

A group of Brooklyn Park residents, lead by Bill Dubois, started BPAA basketball in 1970 for grades 3 through 6. In the summer of 1983 resident traveling basketball team coaches and volunteers formed the Brooklyn Park Traveling Basketball Association. In 1983 there were teams of boys and girls from grades 6–9. In 1991 the program expanded to include 5th grade. The BPAA expanded in 1984 to include grades 7 through 9 for boys and girls, for the house league program.

Gender Equity in Sports

In the early 90s the state mandated that sports programs being offered to boys had to also be offered to girls if there was an interest. This famous document, Title 9, affected school funding of programs and many young lives took a different direction. The predominant sport where this has exploded onto the front of sports pages is girls hockey. In 1995 a task force was commissioned to study the need for additional sheets of ice. The shortage of ice time was a statewide problem due to the fast expanding girls hockey programs. The task force stated there was a "massive shortage," and recommended twenty new sheets of ice. The plan included a statewide grant program.

Planning for the Future

In 1999 the Brooklyn Park Recreation and Park Department created an Athletic Facilities Task Force to examine the use of current facilities and make recommendations for the future. This task force comes at a time of the city's next expansion beyond 93rd Avenue. This area, famous for its new 610 highway, has also opened up new neighborhoods full of families and children in need of new park facilities.

Reflections on Brooklyn Center Centaurs Football

by Ron Stave, Former Coach

I RECALL MANY HUMOROUS INCIDENTS connected with putting together a sports team in a new school. That first season, with no home field, the football team sometimes crossed Earle Brown's farm, past Carl Swing out cultivating, to get to a practice field at Garden City Park. The gates had to be closed behind us so that the horses wouldn't get out. There were a few times the gates were not closed and some of the horses did get out. You can imagine how that upset Carl Swing and he threatened the boys that if they continued to be so undisciplined about the closing of the gates they would not be allowed to come that way anymore.

Because the newly laid sod on the Brooklyn Center High School field could not be played on, the Centaurs played all their games away.

The team scored its first touchdown in the fourth game of the season against Elk River; the Centaur fans cheered as if we had won the state tournament.

There was a builders' strike and the new high school on 65th and Humboldt was not completed when school was to open. The team dressed in the basement of Earle Brown Elementary School. Huge cardboard boxes served as lockers—four guys to a box. The players hung their uniforms and towels to dry over the water pipes. There were only two showerheads for fifty-five players, and they were upstairs – that meant quick dashes up and down the steps wrapped in a towel.

Students came from Minneapolis North, Henry and Marshall High Schools, and most of them had not played football before, so they had to learn the game from scratch—where the line of scrimmage was, what the neutral zone was and where to line up. The Centaurs were winless the first seven games while playing an independent schedule, but later went on to win conference titles. Many fine young men have worn the purple and white of Brooklyn Center High School.

Sports bond a community together through retelling of the stories of great games and through the memories of shared moments between teammates and coaches.

1982 State Champions, Class A
Post Publishing

Chapter Nine

HISTORIC HOMES AND CEMETERIES

"If buildings present an occasion to study the past, what happens when the structures which reflect that past are obliterated? We have no point of departure, no way to measure from where we have come and where we are going." — Norene Roberts [1]

Two Indian campsites were found in 1990 by a Minnesota Historical Society highway survey done in conjunction with the expansion and rerouting of 69th Avenue. These sites are on the south side of Palmer Lake near the Shingle Creek outlet. The survey found evidence of repeated use of the campsites, including stacked stones for a sweat lodge. The sweat lodge is thus the oldest known structure in what became Brooklyn Center and Brooklyn Park. [2]

The Brooklyn Center/Brooklyn Park area was largely agricultural during its first 100 years. Two "Century Farms" — those owned by the same family for at least 100 years — still are being farmed: the Vera Schreiber family farm and the Eldon Tessman and Alice Tessman farms, both in northern Brooklyn Park.

5748 Humboldt Avenue North, Brooklyn Center

Some homes and buildings remain from this agricultural period. Among the especially notable farm homes in Brooklyn Center are 6001 Fremont Avenue North, 3318 50th Avenue North, 1912 55th Avenue North and 160 55th Avenue. Brooklyn Park has a significant number of such homes, among them 7833 Noble Avenue North, 7308 West Broadway, 8735 North Brook Circle, 8101 Zane Avenue North and 6516 West Broadway Avenue North. Several buildings on the Earle Brown Farm date from 1895 and may have been built by Capt. John Martin, grandfather of Earle Brown. Other buildings at the Farm date from the early 1900s, including the cottage (called the Earle Brown house), a two-story gable-roofed, frame construction building. The bedrooms on the second floor were added after Brown's marriage in 1921. The pump house and water tank date from approximately 1910. The Earle Brown Farm is designated as a State Historic Place. [3]

Brooklyn Center and Brooklyn Park were known for their truck farms — smaller farms that raised produce for market. An example of a former truck farm home is 5748 Humboldt Avenue, Brooklyn Center. The two-story Homestead Style house was part of a 40-acre vegetable farm that operated until the early 1960s. [4]

Unfortunately, many old homes of Brooklyn Center and Brooklyn Park have disappeared as a result of development. Road construction caused demolition of many old houses. The Crooker House, formerly located at 6725 West River Road, was demolished when Highway 252 was constructed. The house was built about 1880 by Nahum Crooker, who homesteaded in 1856 some forty-four acres of land along the Mississippi

River near 67th Avenue North and West River Road.[5] The Magnuson Farmhouse, at 4014 69th Avenue North, dates from 1880, and was removed in 1991 during the reconstruction of 69th Avenue North. The 1870s J. L. Woodman/W. W. Wales House at 6505 Brooklyn Boulevard, was removed during construction of a Metro Transit Lot in 1995.[6]

A substantial number of homes in Brooklyn Park have been demolished to make way for Highway 610, among them the ornate American Foursquare-style home at 7440 93rd Avenue, which dates to about 1900-05, and the Homestead-style house at 1805 93rd Avenue, dating to about 1898-1914.[7]

Not only have many old homes been lost, but early business buildings as well. The Slaughterhouse, dating from around 1880, located in Brooklyn Center at what is now 5637 Brooklyn Boulevard, burned in 1978 before it could be redeveloped into a new use. The Brooklyn Center Store (formerly the C.R. Howe Store) located on the southwest corner of 69th Avenue and Osseo Road — the "Centre" of Brooklyn Township – was torn down many years ago.[8]

A few of the old one-room schoolhouses of rural Brooklyn Township remain. The old District 29 Benson School, located at West River Road and 73rd Avenue North, still survives. Moved a block east to 224 73rd Avenue in Brooklyn Park, it is still being used as a home. The building was extensively remodeled and converted to two stories. The brick Schreiber School was converted with major alterations to a lovely residence, which stands at 9900 Regent Avenue North. At 9024 101st Avenue North is the brick District 33 "Zopfi" school built in 1910 that was converted into a dramatic home and business. What may be an old schoolhouse is at 827 57th Avenue North, Brooklyn Center.[11]

The old Benson School House is now a private residence.

Urbanization

The first portion of Brooklyn Center to urbanize was the southeast portion, just north of 53rd Avenue. A number of homes in this area date from 1900 through the 1940s. Urbanization first occurred along main roads, such as 53rd and 55th Avenues in Brooklyn Center, West Broadway and Noble Avenue in Brooklyn Park, and along county roads, such as County Road 131 (now 69th Avenue North) and County Road 109 (85th Avenue North).[12]

Particularly significant was the development along West River Road in both Brooklyn Center and Brooklyn Park. According to a 1936 WPA survey, the front side-gabled portion of the house at 8540 West River Road property was constructed by homesteader Andrew Rixon around 1859. The house was added to in 1873 by Andrew Mattson. Starting in 1874, Mattson used the house as a "halfway house" for the stagecoach between Anoka or Champlin and Minneapolis. Later changes to the structure included a front porch, stucco siding and foundation. After 1912, the Mattson family ran the property as a truck farm.[13]

The neighborhoods adjacent to West River Road now are fully developed, and contain many upscale homes. The style of homes along West River Road varies greatly, from stately colonial, to 1950s ramblers, to 1960s and 70s modern. Two of Brooklyn Park's best known former residents, Garrison Keillor and Jesse Ventura, both lived in the neighborhoods around West River Road (Keillor while growing up, Ventura while Mayor of Brooklyn Park).

Rixon–Mattson House, 8540 West River Road

The area near West River Road also includes a wonderful ethereal architectural creation: the three-story blockhouse-like cabin built on a small island on the Missis-

Earle Brown Farm House

sippi River between Willow Lane and Durnam Island. This seasonal home, which was owned by former state legislator and prominent attorney Leonard Lindquist, is now owned by his son, Larry. It was built in 1928 by Harry E. Wilcox, who founded Wilcox Trux Company, a truck and bus manufacturer later purchased by General Motors. Around the exterior of the cabin are quotations from Omar Khayyam. [14]

The neighborhoods around West River Road contain many well-built, attractive homes. A charming example is the modified Cape Cod home at 501 69th Avenue North in Brooklyn Center, built in 1941.

Rapid Development

In the 1950s and 1960s, Brooklyn Center expanded rapidly, as did the southern portion of Brooklyn Park. Many of the homes built in the 1950s were ranch-style homes, by such builders as Vern Donnay and Orrin Thompson. These "ramblers" as they are also known, were inexpensive to construct but well built. Brooklyn Center and the older parts of Brooklyn Park contain literally thousands of these homes, which were part of a nation-wide trend after World War II to construct inexpensive homes. Houses were built quickly, almost on an assembly-line basis. They are now highly affordable for young families and other first time homebuyers. [15]

The Challenge

The historic homes and buildings of Brooklyn Center and Brooklyn Park are under ongoing assault. As growth occurs in new areas, and as renovation and renewal takes place in the aging parts of the cities, older buildings continue to be torn down. Both cities have purchased old farms for preservation: Brooklyn Center with the Earle Brown Farm, which was converted into a convention center, and Brooklyn Park with the Eidem Farm, now known as the Brooklyn Park Historical Farm.

The continuous aging of these two communities provides an historic preservation challenge. The cities must maintain their housing, industrial and retail stock so that people want to live, work and shop in our communities. The goal should be to upgrade and improve Brooklyn Center and Brooklyn Park while not destroying their historical and architectural charm.

As the cities age, what is considered older buildings will change. Homes built in the 1930s, 1940s and even 1950s are starting to be of historical interest. With the popularity of the 1950s — its music, cars and fashion — the "ramblers" and split-levels of the 1950s can easily be an asset. At least one restaurant in Brooklyn Center — the 50s Grill — trades on the appeal of the 1950s.

Notes

1. Dr. Norene A. Roberts, "Reconnaissance National Register Survey of 26 Municipalities in Hennepin County," State Historic Preservation Office, Minnesota Historical Society, September 1988, 147-8.

2. Robert G. Thompson, Phase III Archaeological Investigation of the Palmer Lake Park Site, Brooklyn Center, Hennepin County, Minnesota, prepared for the City of Brooklyn Center and Short, Elliot, Hendrickson, Inc., January 1992 (HGS No. 88-1147), 20-37, 40-45; 1990 Annual Report, Minnesota Municipal and County Highway Archaeological Reconnaissance Study, Minnesota Historical Society, 185-188; 1991 Annual Report of same title, Minnesota Historical Society, 141-47.

3. Norene Roberts and Brad Hoffman, Minnesota Historic Properties Inventory Form, "Earle Brown Farm," Form BCC-12, 1985, 1988. Minnesota Statutes Section 138.664, subd. 11 designates the Brooklyn Farm as a State Historic Place. Statute authored by Rep. Ernee McArthur.

4. For a complete description of the house and farm, see BHS house files.

5. Mary Jane Gustafson, "Owner fights to save 100 year-old home," Brooklyn Center Post, 13 August 1981, 1.

6. "Brooklyn Historical Society to Replicate Second Oldest House in Brooklyn Center," NorthWest News, 23 September 1991; Roxana Benjamin, "What Has Become of This Historic House?," NorthWest News, 13 January 1992; Norene Roberts, "Two Old Houses in Brooklyn Center Torn Down," Brooklyn Historical Society Newsletter, March 1995, 5.

7. List of properties and map obtained from Mr. Keith Slater, Right-of-Way Manager, Minnesota Department of Transportation, 10 May 2000, Brooklyn Historical Society.

8. Mary Jane Gustafson, "New Mini-Courthouse in Slaughter House?," Brooklyn Center Post, 3 July 1975; Minnesota Historic Properties Inventory Form HE-BCC-13; Leone Howe, Album of Brooklyn Centre: A History of Brooklyn Center, Chapter VI, "Businesses of Brooklyn Centre" (self-published, 1978).

9. Id. at Chapter IV, "Education"; (writer states that the District 29 school was built in 1872); Gail Bakken, "Closing of Benson School Ends Years of History for Structure," Brooklyn Center Press, 26 September 1957, 1. (author states that the old school building was converted to a residence owned by the Arnold Richardsons; it has square headed nails, boards as wide as almost two feet, and actual 2"x 4"s); Paula Hirschoff, "History of Benson School spans over a century," Brooklyn Park Post, 29 January 1976.

10. Dr. Norene Roberts, Reconnaissance National Register Survey, op. cit., "Brooklyn Park," 33; Norene Roberts, Minnesota Historic Properties Inventory Form No. BPC 15, May 1988, Minnesota Historical Society, Historic Preservation Office; City of Brooklyn Park, "Historic Property/Site Map," 2 November 1999, provided by Marjorie Mangine; interview with David Strootman, current owner; notes of interview with Alice P. Tessman by Norene Roberts on 4 May 1994, Brooklyn Historical Society; Neal Gendler, "One-room school graduates to three-bedroom home," Minneapolis Tribune, 28 June 1981, 7E.

11. See discussion of this home in Appendix.

12. Dr. Norene Roberts, Reconnaissance National Register Survey, op cit., "Brooklyn Center," 24; Brooklyn Historical Society, "History of Brooklyn Center, Minnesota," 10 October 1995, 2-3; letter of Mary H. Simmons to Jane Hallberg, 24 April 1997, Brooklyn Historical Society.

13. U.S. Work Projects Administration, Historic Building Survey (for Hennepin County), 1936, Boxes 313 (a-g) and 314 (h-z); Ike Anderson, edited by Jane Hallberg, "The Camden-Brooklyn Township-Anoka Stage, circa 1904," Brooklyn Historical Society, 1978; Dr. Norene A. Roberts, "Reconnaissance National Register Survey, op cit. 33; Paula Hirschoff, "River Road Weaves Tale of City's Oldest Home," Brooklyn Park Post, 29 January 1976, 1.

14. "Obituary of Harry E. Wilcox," Minneapolis Star, 30 October 1954, 4; "Mississippi River Hideaway: 'Lost Week-end' House," newspaper clipping from undated, unknown paper, Brooklyn Historical Society; Garrison Keillor, "My Boyhood Home," Brooklyn Park (magazine published by Brooklyn Park Economic Development Authority), 1994, 42 (discusses childhood memories of the island house).

15. Dr. Norene A. Roberts, Reconnaissance National Register, op cit., 32; Jennifer McMaster, "Ranch Houses Reconsidered," The Minnesota Preservationist, Vol 2, No. 2, March-April 1999; Ann Baker, "Quaint Cape Cods, Ramblers Receiving New Status as Future's Historical Homes," St. Paul Pioneer Press, 18 February 1999; Richard Lacayo, "Suburban Legend William Levitt," Time Magazine; Jerry Adler and Karen Springen, "Back at the Ranch," Newsweek, 12 October 1998.

The writer thanks the staff of the Minnesota Historical Society for their help. In addition, the assistance of Ms. Cassie Sweeney-Truitt of the Minnesota House of Representatives is greatly appreciated.

Historic Homes and Buildings of Brooklyn Center

5501 Lyndale Avenue North

4702 69th Avenue North

5501 Lyndale Avenue North. Built in 1878, this Italianate home is considered the oldest remaining house in Brooklyn Center. It is called the "Mikkelson House" after its original owners, Ole and Mary Mikkelson. The lot purchased by Ole was part of the Isaac Garcelon Addition. Ole came to Minnesota from Selbu, Norway with his mother and two brothers. He was a painter and he farmed with his two brothers on 85th Avenue and Xerxes in Brooklyn Park. The house, unlike many of the early homes in Brooklyn Center, was not a farmhouse. Mary and Ole once rented rooms upstairs to loggers working on the Mississippi. Ole died in 1935 and Mary in 1939. Their adopted grandson Floyd inherited the home, then sold the house in 1950 or 1951 to Bruce M. and Doris P. Hendry, who liked the high ceilings, walk-in attic, three bedrooms and large lot (one-half acre). They raised their four children there, among them Bruce E. Hendry, a well-known stockbroker and businessman.

Sources: Mary Jane Gustafson, "Oldest BC home built in 1878," Brooklyn Center Post, May 21, 1981; Doris and Bruce M. Hendry, article submitted to the Brooklyn Historical Society; Rhonda Evenson and Norene Roberts, Minnesota Historic Properties Inventory Form on the Ole Mikkelson House, Form No. BCC 7, prepared in June 1988 for Hennepin County Inventory of Historic Properties, Minnesota Historical Society (hereafter "Minnesota Historic Properties Inventory").

4702 69th Avenue North. A wood frame, two-story home, it was built in 1888 by John Watson and served as a farmhouse for a large farm first owned by Hiram Bohanon. Bohanon gave 8 acres to the Brooklyn Methodist and Episcopal Church in 1872. The original part of the house is L shaped with an enclosed porch. It has square cut nails, 23 inch roof planks, and had basement water cisterns (at least one of them was connected to the roof to capture run off)and a coal chute. The home now is owned by David and Tammy Earley.

Sources: abstract of property; interview with David A. Earley.

1019 73rd Avenue North. Built in 1890, this house has been extensively remodeled, so that little of its original appearance is visible. It is owned by Patrick Ready, who purchased it from his grandmother, Lillian Eisenbrand, who is now 93 years old and lives in Dayton. Lillian and her husband Harold bought the house in 1937 and lived there until 1964, the year Harold died. Lillian does not remember the name of the prior owner, but her neighbor, Mavis Huddle, consulted with some longtime residents and they believe it was owned by the Lehmans and perhaps before that by Carl Anderson, who owned a farm in the area. Mrs. Eisenbrand remembers that the prior owners were vegetable farmers, raising crops such as asparagus and potatoes on the 10 acres. There was a long shed on the property used for preparing and cleaning the vegetables for sale. The Eisenbrands sold the shed to the Brooklyn Center building inspector. The Eisenbrands were not farmers but they had a large garden and about a dozen wild plum trees (planted by a prior owner). Over time they sold off most of the land.

When the Eisenbrands bought the house it had no basement except for a small root cellar, and no bathroom. The house originally had a kitchen, a living room (part of which they used as a dining room) and two small bedrooms, all on the main floor, with an attic upstairs. The house was rented out from 1964 to 1991 or 1992, when Pat Ready bought it from his grandmother.

Sources: Interviews with Pat Ready, Lillian Eisenbrand and Mavis V. Huddle.

5510 Emerson Avenue North. It is known as the Boyson House, for Hans Boyson, who built the house in 1893. The two-story, wood frame Queen Anne style home has some geometric decorative elements on the gables and a small front porch which faces 55th Avenue North. Part of the wood apparently came from an 1867 schoolhouse, called the "Red Schoolhouse," which was torn down in 1889 and was located at what are now the tennis courts in Webber Park, near 44th in Minneapolis. The home was remodeled in 1976 with a two-story addition parallel to Emerson Avenue that creates an L shaped house. In 1900 the home and eleven acres were purchased by Jane Withrow Dunn and her husband from Mr. Boyson. Their daughter Alberta (Bertie) Dunn inherited the house and lived her entire life there. She passed away in 1986. Until recently the house was numbered 5500 Emerson, but a new house was built on the corner. The home is currently owned by Carl A. (Al) and Wendy Linder.

Sources: Newsletter of the Brooklyn Historical Society, August, 1994, p. 6; Mary Jane Gustafson, "It was a time for reminiscing," Brooklyn Center Post, April 17, 1975; obituary of Alberta Dunn, Brooklyn Center Post, February 12, 1986; interview with Carl A. Linder.

5510 Emerson Avenue North

6100 Fremont Avenue North. One of the nicest old homes in Brooklyn Center. This large, two story Queen Anne style home was built in 1895. It sits on a large lot and served as a farmhouse. In reviewing the abstract, it appears the house was built by the Mendenhall family. In 1862, the land was owned by Richard Mendenhall and passed to Nereus Mendenhall in 1865. He died in 1894 and his daughter Gertrude Mendenhall then inherited the property. In 1904 the property was conveyed to the Garrett family. A tornado in 1923 or 1925 destroyed all of the out buildings and barns.

In the neighborhood the home is still called the Lund House, after Floyd T. and Grace Lund who purchased the home in 1936. The current owners are Brian and Linda Hultquist, who purchased it from the Kline family. The Hultquists are deeply interested in the history of the house and its prior owners. They have a wonderful set of old photos of the house, including pictures of Denman and Lily Garrett and of a preschool run by Grace Lund.

Sources: Lauri Winters, "New BC residents search for history of this old home," Brooklyn Center Sun-Post, February 26, 1997; Minnesota Historic Properties Inventory Form on a house on 61st Avenue in Brooklyn Center, form No. BCC 11, June 1988, on file with Minnesota Historical Society; interviews with Linda and Brian Hultquist.

5556 Emerson Avenue North. Shirley A. Leopold, the current owner, has lived there since 1965, when she and her husband bought it from a bank. It was built as a farmhouse and is cross-gabled. Brooklyn Center Assessor records put its date of construction as 1895. It has two stories and was stuccoed in 1970. Before that it had asphalt siding which looked like bricks. Interesting features are the notched corners of the house with windows in the notch; such corners were a fairly common element in Shingle and Queen Anne style homes.

Source: Interview with Shirley A. Leopold.

5556 Emerson Avenue North

6844 Colfax Avenue North (formerly 110 69th Avenue). This former farmhouse, built in 1895, is now owned by Lonney and Joanne Eckenrode. It is cross-gabled, with two stories and a windowed attic. Based on their study of the abstract, the Eckenrodes believe it was built by John and Axelia Werner, who passed it to John E. Werner, Jr. and his wife Rosella. Peter (Gus) and Anna Lindgren bought the home in 1955. In the neighborhood, the home is still known as the Lindgren House. Across the street, at 6839 Colfax, is a home that was developed out of one of the outbuildings of the farm, they believe. That house dates to 1926, according to City Assessor records.

Sources: Interviews with the Eckenrodes, Joseph and Madeleine Roche, Walt and Sandra Weinholz; abstract of property.

1912 55th Avenue North

1912 55th Avenue North. Built in 1898, its current owners are Ed and Peggy Lynn, who purchased it in 1987. It was built by John Ryden, a potato and vegetable farmer whose brother, Erick Rydeen, lived at 5601 Logan Avenue North. The home stayed in the Ryden-Edling family until the Lynns purchased it. Brookdale Shopping Mall now sits on part of the substantial Ryden farm. The house sits on a large lot at Morgan Avenue and 55th Avenue, and juts out into Morgan. The house is two stories, stuccoed, with a three-season porch on the west side. It is an L-shaped structure, of gable-front-and-wing style, with a number of additions over time. A kitchen was added in approximately 1910 and an addition to the east in the 1930s or 40s.

Sources: Interview with Ed Lynn.

5325 Humboldt Avenue North. This front-gabled house dates to 1900, according to City Assessor records. It is a very small one-story house, with perhaps two bedrooms, which has had a front porch and aluminum siding added. It is similar to many houses in this part of Brooklyn Center, adjacent to the Minneapolis border.

5818 Emerson Avenue North

5818 Emerson Avenue North. The City Assessor lists this house as having been built in 1900. The current owners are Mary and Scott Thornton, who purchased it in 1995. Scott's understanding is that two additions were added to the house. New wood siding was added that gives it a more contemporary look. The oldest part of the house is 1½ stories and its master bedroom was remodeled into a loft-like room. This part of the house has a limestone foundation and a five foot high basement.

Source: Interview with Scott Thornton.

6125 Camden Avenue North. Dating from 1900, the house was moved from across the street, where it served as the farmhouse for the Sonnenberg farm. This part of Brooklyn Center is known in abstract records as the Sonnenberg Addition. Members of the family still live across the street, in a newer house built when the original farmhouse was moved. The farmhouse has had at least four additions, many of them with used brick as the facade.. The original part of the house was L shaped, with 9 foot ceilings on the main floor, a 12 inch by 12 inch centerbeam, as well as 8" x 8" beams.

Source: Interview with the current owner, Corey Lerbs.

5455 Humboldt Avenue North. According to City records, this house was built in 1900. For many years it was owned by the Carlson family. Paul Carlson, a history professor at Texas Tech University who was raised in the house, states that his grandparents bought it when they immigrated from Bodafors, Sweden in 1928 or 1929. Their names were Karl Albert Johansson and Akevilina Albertina Johansson.

Karl's son Howard was Paul's father. Howard was born in Sweden and emigrated with his parents to America. In the Swedish style, he took his father's name as his surname, so he was Howard Karlsson, later Americanized to Carlson. Howard and his brother had a vegetable farm, with most of the vegetables raised on their land in

Johnsville, 12-15 miles north of Brooklyn Center on Highway 65. According to Paul's sister Jean Forrest, eventually Howard gave up farming, sold off parts of the land and worked as a carpenter. Howard and his wife Alpha expanded the house as their family grew. The attic upstairs was converted into bedrooms. In doing so, a brick sun parlor with exposed rafters was removed. Howard and Alpha Carson owned the house until 1988, when it was sold. Currently it is owned by Craig LaBelle and Mary Wheelright.
Sources: Interviews with Craig LaBelle, Paul Carlson, Karen Carlson Bouley and Jean Carlson Forrest.

5221 63rd Avenue North. An American Foursquare two-story built in 1900, the house is currently owned by Robert Stark. It has a hipped-roof dormer and a new brick veneer. The back of the house is stuccoed and there is a small rear addition.

5456 Emerson Avenue North. Now owned by Barbara Ploumen, the 1¾ story home was built in 1900 by the Hanchett family. It has a cross-gabled roof and Colonial Revival elements. The original clapboard siding is under slate siding. There are four entries to the home, which probably had additions added over the years in classic farm style as the family grew. Barbara Ploumen's husband Richard was the City Public Works Superintendent until he passed away eight years ago, and her father Wally Bursch is a former Brooklyn Center School District Board member.
Source: Interview with Barbara Ploumen.

5456 Emerson Avenue North

5748 Humboldt Avenue North. A former farmhouse, it dates from 1901 and is currently owned by Richard and Lydia Norberg. It is two stories, front-gabled with a windowed attic and narrow wood siding. The Norbergs bought it in 1965 from Vern and Mary Perron, who operated a truck farm of approximately forty acres. At about the time the Perrons sold their house, they subdivided their property, which stretched to Fremont Avenue. The Perrons' daughter, Darlene More, who now lives in Andover, grew up in the home. Her father Vern worked nights at Minneapolis Moline and then each morning would sell vegetables at the downtown Minneapolis Farmers' Market. The farm had a small barn (later torn down and the lumber used for the garage on the property), plum and apple orchards and a chicken coop. A work horse was used for farm work. The Perrons purchased the farm in 1944 or 1945.
Sources: Interview with Richard Norberg; interview with Darlene More.

827 57th Avenue North. Built in 1901, this front gabled 1½ story house is owned by Les Duoos, who grew up in Brooklyn Center on Emerson. Dan Larson, the prior owner, was told that it was once a one room schoolhouse. The exterior is stucco, and there are two bedrooms on each floor. The house has horse hair plaster walls, old interior gas lights and wooden shakes under the asphalt shingles. Sawdust was used to insulate some of the walls, which makes Les believe that a previous owner renovated the home during WWII, when sawdust was commonly used as insulation.
Source: Interviews with Les Duoos and Dan Larson.

827 57th Avenue North

1300 55th Avenue North. This Craftsman style farmhouse was built in approximately 1904. Now stuccoed, it was remodeled to add dormers, two bedrooms and a bath to the second floor. It has a fine gabled roof, with exposed wooden rafters and braces. An orchard apparently once surrounded the house. Its current owner is Constance Besaw, who moved there in 1991. Source: Interview with Constance Besaw.

5357 Emerson Avenue North. Built in 1905, it was used for many years as a corner grocery store, as can be seen from its large front window and storefront appearance. The living quarters apparently were in the rear. It was purchased in 1956 by Karl (deceased) and Margarete Rosenow. It has a decorative concrete block foundation, and is now sided with aluminum and with faux brick in the front.

1600 55th Avenue North. This two story duplex dates from 1905. It features an intersecting gable roof with a cornice and wide frieze. The windows have cornices or pediments. There is a large bay window. It was stuccoed in 1975 and the original windows are under the aluminum storms. $20,000 was spent to bring the house up to code in 1995. Paula and Rodger Brodin bought the house in 1961. It was sold to the current owners Ake and Carole Hallman. According to the abstract, the land was once owned by the Reidheads, a prominent local farm family. At one point it was willed to Holiness Methodist Church in North Minneapolis to be used as a parsonage but was later sold. In the 1930s it was part of a 40-acre truck farm.
Sources: Article submitted by Paula Brodin to the Brooklyn Historical Society; Minnesota Historic Properties Inventory Form, no. BCC 6, June 1988.

1600 55th Avenue North

6337 Bryant Avenue North. This stucco, two-story Queen Anne farmhouse was built in 1908. It currently is owned by Naomi Eastman, who bought it in 1966 from Ralph Dobeling. The property consists of two lots and Naomi believes at one time it may have stretched to the Mississippi River, as there was a barn there. Naomi has modified the home over time. There were four bedrooms upstairs, now there are three. She took out a wall to make a living room out of the dining room and the porch, and added patio doors to the backyard.
Source: interview with Naomi Eastman.

5105 North Lilac Drive (also known as 5105 Brooklyn Boulevard). Built in 1908, the house is part of the property of Malmborg's Garden Center and Greenhouse. It was built by the owners of Rice Brothers Wholesale Florists, which built the adjoining greenhouses in approximately 1906. The style of this two story rectangular house is based on Colonial Revival. It has a large front porch with Doric columns and its roof has a raking cornice line with returned eaves and corner boards. The windows are corniced and some still have their detailing, while others are now aluminum.
Sources: Andrew Schmidt, The 106 Group, Minnesota History/Architecture Survey Form, inventory no. HE-BCC-004, prepared August 1994; Rhonda Evenson, Minnesota Historic Properties Inventory Form, no. BCC 4, prepared June 1988; interview with Mr. George Lucht of Malmborg's.

5105 Brooklyn Blvd. North

6520 Brooklyn Blvd. Originally a farmhouse, the square, two story home is of a style called "American Foursquare." It features an interesting roof called "gable-on-hip": a small decorative peak is on the roof where the roof types intersect. City Assessor records date the house to 1908. Stuccoed with concrete block construction, it and the Malmborg House (described immediately above) may be the only remaining farmhouses of what once were many along Osseo Road, now Brooklyn Boulevard. On a large corner lot, with its imposing size, the house marks the rural, agricultural past of our city as it watches over our busy main street. State Senator Gen Olson, who grew up across the street at 6505 Brooklyn Boulevard (since torn down), remembers that this house changed hands many times during her youth. The Madigans, Helleruds and Aguilars were owners at various times, she states. Martha Weber, age 90, who still is active in running Weber Greenhouse on Brooklyn Boulevard with her son, remembers this as the "Madigan House." Mrs. Weber moved into Brooklyn Center in 1926. The current owner is Phyllis Owens, who purchased it in 1962.

Sources: Interviews with Phyllis Owens, Gen Olson and Martha Weber.

5432 Bryant Avenue North. This 1½ story house dates to 1908 and is now owned by Dennis Johnson, who bought it around 1981. Originally the type was "Hall and Parlor," that is, two rooms wide and one room deep. The previous owner, says Johnson, made extensive renovations, including adding a dormer, two bedrooms and a bath in the upper story, and rearranging rooms on the main floor. The Madsen greenhouse once stood across the street. A former neighbor, Evelyn Berry remembers that the house was owned by Katherine Sward. The abstract shows that she purchased it in 1946 from Oscar T. and Anna M. Nelson, who had bought it from Hjalmar and Jennie Johnson in 1934. The prior owners were John Fredjahn Johnson and Anna I. Johnson who bought it in 1927. Before that it was in the Perkins family. Ephream and Nancy Perkins owned the land in the 19th century and passed it to Mary Perkins in about 1903 (she was unmarried), who passed it to William F. and Marianna G. Perkins in 1925. Taxes were $35.65 in 1926, $36.94 in 1929 and $65.10 in 1950.

Source: Interviews with Dennis Johnson and with Evelyn Berry, who reviewed the abstract.

5432 Bryant Avenue North

5414 and 5416 Girard Avenue North. These are two adjacent front-gabled homes that were built around the same time on small 40 foot lots. 5414 Girard dates to 1909, while 5416 Girard to 1910. These, together with homes such as 5325 Humboldt (described above), 5333 Camden, 5407 Fremont, 5553 Emerson (see all three described below), 5338 Logan and 5340 Colfax, all probably are some of the first homes built for blue collar families, as opposed to the many farmhouses in Brooklyn Center. These homes thus represent the early suburban housing phenomenon, as families moved out of Minneapolis to find less expensive lots. The current owner of 5414 Girard, Dorayne Ganzer, bought the house in 1965 and states that there are three different kinds of foundation blocks, indicating at least two additions. Her parents moved to Brooklyn Center in the 1950s to a house at 5340 Emerson. Another neighbor, Diane Holborn, remembers that the prior occupants of 5414 were the Rasmussens. The Gates were longtime owners of 5416 Girard. The current owner of 5416 is Richard Mikulak.

Source: Interviews with Dorayne Ganzer, Diane Holborn.

5416 Girard Avenue North

5601 Logan Avenue North. A large 2½ story stucco house sitting on a big corner lot, it is cross-gabled with wooden ornamental braces under the wide, overhanging eaves. Originally a farmhouse, it dates to 1909. Robert A. Tessman, who lives at 1900 Brookview Drive in Brooklyn Center, states that in about 1952 the house was moved west a few hundred feet from what is now his lot to its current location on a new foundation. The Rydeens were the original owners, he says. The current owner, Gregory Johnson, found in the house a 1936 Swedish version of a Chicago newspaper with Erick Rydeen as the name of the subscriber. The construction is clay tile, that is, the walls were made from baked clay blocks which were stacked and then concrete and stucco applied over them. The resulting exterior walls are eight inches thick. Attractive

features of the interior include oak floors, oak and maple woodwork and a built-in buffet (which was moved but preserved).
Sources: Interviews with Gregory Johnson and Robert A. Tessman.

5333 Camden Avenue North

5333 Camden Avenue North. A front-gabled house with some Craftsman-style elements, it dates to 1910. It is one story plus an attic. Alice Opsahl, now 94 years old, and her husband Henry (deceased) bought it in March 1947 from the Gustafsons. She remembers that their first year property tax (called a farm tax even though the house was not part of a farm) was $64.00. They replaced the stucco exterior with asbestos or slate siding and added a sun porch in the rear. The property was made up of three lots, two of which they sold to the city for Bellvue Park.
Source: Interview with Alice Opsahl.

5407 Fremont Avenue North. A 1910 cross-gabled house that has been substantially remodeled by the current owners, Lloyd and Mary Thorson, who purchased the home in 1975. Additions to it include a new room in the front, an additional partial basement and aluminum siding. Sources: Interview with Lloyd Thorson.

5327 Bryant Avenue North. An attractive home with Colonial Revival elements, built in 1910. The main part of the house is Foursquare type with a hipped roof, while the front of the house is gabled. The entrance has Doric columns and a pediment roof.

627 58th Avenue North

627 58th Avenue North. Dating from around 1910, the one and a half story former farmhouse has a gabled roof over the front and the wing, corner boards, exposed eaves and clapboard siding. An interesting detail is the small ribbon of windows on the front. A review of the abstract shows that the land was first homesteaded in 1856 by Andrew McCuan. Jumping ahead to 1905, the land was sold by Paul Soro to Henry McAllister who in turn sold it to Walter H. Gould in 1909. The lot was part of the Gould Riverview Addition. Ernest and Martha Johnson bought the house in 1923 and lived there until they sold it in 1966 to Duane and Rosemary Borg. The Johnsons also built a number of homes in the area for their children. The current owner is Judith Paurus, who bought it in 1971. She was told that the house was built in 1907.
Sources: MN Historic Properties Inventory Form, no. BCC 10, June 1988; interview with Judith Paurus.

6425 Fremont Avenue North. This 1910 stucco house is somewhat unusual in that it has a roof called "hip-on-gable." There is a dormer on the second floor.

5338 Logan Avenue North. Also hip-on-gable roofed, this is a one-story, stucco, L-shaped house built in 1910.

1821 55th Avenue North. Sitting at the corner of 55th and Logan Avenues, this cross-gabled 1910 house has brick around the bottom, stucco on the remainder. Owner Tom Zettervall believes it was a farmhouse that was remodeled around 1926, based on dates of 1926 stamped on the bathtub and the coal chute. The house is in the John Ryden Addition, and may have been a Ryden family home at one time, he believes. Ray and Mary Hanson owned the home from 1964 until he bought it in 1988.
Source: Interview with Tom Zettervall.

5553 Emerson Avenue North. This 1910 house has been the home since 1927 of Bob Cashman, 73, who served as the State Fire Marshall in the 1960s and before that as the Brooklyn Center Fire Marshall. He investigated the fire that destroyed the Earle Brown School that had been built by the WPA in the 1930s. Born in Robbinsdale in 1927, he moved with his parents to this house that same year. His mother, Iva, has her maiden name on the cornerstone of Harron Methodist Church. There was one prior owner before his family purchased the home. The house is part of the Bert Reidhead Addition. Reidhead was a prominent local farm family.
Source: Interview with Robert Cashman.

5553 Emerson Avenue North

3318 50th Avenue. An especially beautiful home with long, clean lines. Built by the Palmers, this Colonial Revival farmhouse dates to 1912. Porches in the front and rear have been removed. There is a limestone foundation and cross gabled roof on this one and a half story building, which features corniced windows, an oculus window in the front and an attractive pediment over the front door.
Source: MN Historic Properties Inventory Form, no. BCC3, June 1988.

5321 Penn Avenue North. A former farmhouse built in 1913, this two-story rectangular home has a steep cross gabled roof, clapboard siding and corniced windows. The roof has a prominent cornice and large overhang. There is an enclosed front porch.
Source: Rhonda Evenson, Minnesota Historic Properties Inventory Form, No. BCC5, prepared for the Minnesota Historical Society, June 1988.

3318 50th Avenue North

5451 Lyndale Avenue. Owned by Gale Finstad, this 1920 Craftsman style house is 1½ stories, stuccoed, with gabled roof and exposed eaves and brackets in the gable ends. It has a brick foundation. It was not a farmhouse but served as a residence.
Source: MN Historic Properties Inventory Form, no. HE BCC8, June 1988.

5049 Brooklyn Blvd. A classic Craftsman style house, this dates to 1920. It features a low-pitched gable roof with wide, unenclosed eave overhangs, exposed beams under the gables, and column piers on the enclosed porch. There are decorative planters under the main front windows, and ribbon windows (four contiguous windows) on the second floor. An attractive, distinctive home.

5950 Beard Avenue North. This modest 1920 stucco home has some Prairie School elements: the ribbons of geometric windows with small panes, the geometric panes of glass in the door, the flat roof over part of the porch, the low pitched roof (made flat in the front by the hip on the gable) and wide overhanging eaves.

630 58th Avenue. A 1927 farmhouse, it is a two story rectangular home with a gabled roof, corner board windows corniced, exposed eaves, clapboard siding and enclosed front and back porches. Some of the windows have vertical muttons.
Source: MN Historic Properties Inventory Form, no. HE BCC 9, June 1988.

Weber's Greenhouse and House, 5040 Brooklyn Blvd. While not especially old, this greenhouse and adjoining home represent the greenhouse business which was common in Brooklyn Center but which is now almost gone. The home was built in 1938 and the greenhouse in 1940 by Martha Weber and her husband Alfred L. on what was then

5040 Brooklyn Blvd. North

Osseo Road. Martha Weber was born in Sweden in 1909 and grew up in north Minneapolis. In 1926 she moved into the Rice Brothers' Florists house at 5105 Lilac Drive in Brooklyn Center. Her father-in-law, the chief grower at Rice Brothers, lived in the house. She cleaned the house and worked at Rice Brothers. She and her husband built their one and a half story home in 1936 for $2,500.00. The greenhouse was built in 1940 and expanded in 1945-46; the latter part was an old greenhouse that was purchased from the University of Minnesota and reconstructed. Martha and her son John still run the business, which sells spring flowers and vegetables to the public.
Source: Interview with Martha Weber.

Twin Lake Alano, 4938 Brooklyn Blvd. Formerly Twin Lake Elementary School, this brick building with stone finishing was built in 1945, closed as a school in 1972 and sold in 1974. Previously a white wooden schoolhouse stood on the site. Many of the windows have painted boards over them, for energy conservation. The tower-like main entrance and parapet-type detailing on the roof line give this building a castle-like appearance.
Sources: Robbinsdale School District; interview with Martha Weber.

Endnotes

This summary of historic and significant buildings is not meant to be exhaustive. The discussion of architectural styles is largely based on Virginia and Lee McAlester, *A Field Guide to American Houses*, Alfred A. Knopf, 1984. Photographs of Brooklyn Center homes and buildings are by Andrew Von Bank, except for 4702-69th Ave. N.; and 4938, 5105, 5040 and 5415 Brooklyn Blvd.

Historic Homes and Buildings of Brooklyn Park

6325 West Broadway Avenue North. Known as the Henry Smith Thompson Farmhouse, it is an old frame house with angled window lintels and a wide frieze. There is a wide overhung eave on the gables. Much of it has been modified through large additions. The farm was homesteaded in the mid-1850s by Henry Smith Thompson and was rebuilt after an 1884 fire.
Sources: Minnesota Historic Properties Inventory Form No. BPC27, which in turn references Lauraine Kirchner, Pioneer Chronicles, 1976, pp. 168-70.

8540 West River Road. Sometimes called the Rixon-Mattson farmhouse, this home was built in part by a homesteader named Rixon around 1859, and in 1873 Andrew Mattson added to it when he bought the property. The home was a Halfway House, a stopping place for the stagecoach which ran, circa 1904—and an unknown period before that—between Camden and Anoka. At 4 P.M. each day the stage left Camden and arrived at Anoka about 7 P.M. and stayed overnight. At 7 A.M. the next morning it returned to Camden and made the 4 P.M. trip to Anoka again. Each trip took about three hours. At the Halfway House rest stop, passengers could stretch and the lead horses drank at a wooden trough by the wooden windmill, while the pole team drank from buckets. The main use of the house in the old days was as a farmhouse. The current owner, Paul Cook, is the fourth owner. He pointed out the old carriage house behind a house to the north, and an old metal windmill, both of which were part of the Mattson property. Dr. Norene Roberts in 1988 wrote that this Rixon–Mattson house is eligible for National Register status.

8540 West River Road

Sources: U.S. Work Projects Administration, Historic Building Survey (for Hennepin County), 1936, Boxes 313 (a-g) and 314 (h-z); Ike Anderson, edited by Jane Hallberg, "The Camden-Brooklyn Township-Anoka Stage, circa 1904" (Brooklyn Historical Society, 1978); Dr. Norene A. Roberts, "Reconnaissance National Register Survey, op cit., P. 33; Paula Hirschoff, "River Road Weaves Tale of City's Oldest Home," Brooklyn Park Post, January 29, 1976, p. 1.

10311 Noble Avenue North. Mr. Emelio and Mrs. Barbarra Munoz purchased their 18 acre farm at 10311 Noble Avenue North in 1994. Their home was rebuilt in 1984 around the original home built in 1862. It features a steep side-gabled roof. A very handsome home.

The Isaac Potter Log Cabin. Now located west of Corcoran on Bass Lake Road, this log cabin was formerly in Brooklyn Park at Boone Avenue and I-94. It was built after the Potters arrived here from North Carolina in 1870. It is one of the oldest standing Brooklyn Township/Brooklyn Park houses. The Potters built their cabin beside a busy trading post. It used to be on the Potter farmstead at Boone and I-94; however, in 1967 it was moved by the North Hennepin Pioneer Society to a lot west of Corcoran on Bass Lake Road. By 1970 it was reconstructed, using logs from the old trading post at its original site to replace deteriorating logs. It is a one-room log cabin with chinking and a low loft for sleeping quarters. The Potter's farming operation in Brooklyn Park grew over time, requiring large crews to help with crops and livestock; it became a showplace for students of farm progress. The last occupants of the farm were the

Isaac Potter Cabin

families of Peter Potter and Victor Gervais (his wife was Stella Potter). The Potters moved in 1959 to Wright County to farm, thus making way for the encroaching city.

Sources: 1999 Potter Reunion writings; North Hennepin Pioneer Society, Dorothy Schoenmann, contact; "Historical Group Seeks Aid in Log Cabin Project," North Hennepin Post, August 2, 1967.

10317 Jefferson Highway North. An 1875 two-story front and wing gabled home, it has a one-story side addition. Mr. Douglas B. and Mrs. Diane H. Hasner have owned this home since 1988.

10600 Winnetka Avenue North. City records show this home was built in 1878. The date of 1868 is inscribed on the interior basement wall. It is front gabled with side additions. Mr. Elmer Ohlhauser purchased this home in 1972.

10856 Noble Avenue North. This house was built between 1875 and 1880 by Seth Pribble, a Civil War veteran who was born in Maine. He and his wife Mary are buried in the Champlin Cemetery. It is currently the home of Bill and Lynn Sullivan, who purchased it in 1985. The house has pine floors, high ceilings, china door knobs and windows that extend almost down to the floor. The yard has beautiful old oak trees which must be nearly as old as the house. The Sullivans found pieces of old china and glass and an old cobalt blue Bromo Seltzer bottle on the grounds. There is a rumor that there are several old graves in the yard as well.

Source: Memories submitted by Bill and Lynn Sullivan.

7833 Noble Avenue North

7833 Noble Avenue North. The land upon which this handsome house now stands is part of an eighty-acre parcel purchased by Amos Berry from the United States government in 1856 — two years before Minnesota was granted statehood. Early documents reveal the main part of the house was built in 1900 by David Hamilton (the City says it is as old as 1880). Before construction began, many horse-drawn wagon loads of limestone (likely quarried from the banks of the nearby Mississippi River) were hauled to the site to lay a sturdy foundation, one that has settled remarkably little in nearly a century. The house was raised over heavy notched beams and all building materials were secured with square nails. It features patterned shingles in the gables, a cross gabled roof, cornerboards and corniced windows. The house continued to be a farm until 1961 when Earl Dorn, its last farmer/owner, sold most of the land to a developer. Restored extensively in 1974 and again in 1996, this house survives as a unique reminder of Brooklyn Park's early rural past.

Sources: Article submitted by current owners; Norene Roberts, Historic Properties Inventory Form BPC-5.

6633 West Broadway Avenue. Known as the Ward Farmhouse, it is an L-shaped Homestead-style house with a cross-gabled roof and a front porch. The window frames are tabbed. The City's Economic Development Authority bought the house from the Slothoubers. The EDA heard that the house was a regular stop on a stagecoach line.

Sources: Historic Properties Inventory Form BPC-30; interview with Stacy Kilvang of the EDA.

7557 Noble Avenue North. Known as the Lawrence Homestead House, it dates from about 1880, according to the city. It is Colonial Revival style with a cross gabled roof.

There are Tuscan columns on the porch and it has corniced windows. Some sheds still remain on the property. Lawrence married a Getchell, from the same family that was the first to homestead in the area. Getchell Prairie was named after the family.

Sources: Minnesota Historic Properties Inventory Form BPC-006; Leone Howe, Album of Brooklyn Centre, Chap. I, 1978.

9941 Zane Avenue North. This is part of the Vera Schreiber Farm. Fredrick and Mary Ann built the brick farmhouse at 10232 Zane Avenue, in 1865, across from Oak Grove Park. Eventually their farm holdings would total 320 acres. The farm is now 143 acres. Fredrick purchased 78 acres in 1867 and another 65 acres in 1890. It had a small house located on it. This became John and Eda's home where Harry was born in 1898. They also had three daughters, Nora (Schwappach), Marion (Paul) and Irma (Rochat). A substantial addition was constructed in the early 1900s resulting in the white farmhouse that is 9941 Zane Avenue today. The two-story house has the original wood detail on the eaves, a cistern in the basement, and attached summer kitchen. The house is cross-gabled, Queen Anne-style, with gingerbread in the gable ends.

9941 Zane Avenue North

Harry and Vera Schreiber lived in the home south of the farmhouse, where Vera still lives. Harry and Vera purchased the farm in 1947 and expanded the potato production. Harry's parents, Eda and John, lived in the old farmhouse until the mid-50s when they passed away. Harry died in 1958 and his sons, Gerald, Jack and Bill, continued the potato operation. Vera Schreiber has lived on this land for nearly 75 years and is grateful that the farm has been preserved in family ownership for more than 130 years.

Source: Article submitted by Vera Schreiber; Historic Properties Inventory Form BPC-002.

8708 Green Haven Drive. Mr. Forrest D. and Catherine J. Ward have lived at this address since 1946. Their children are Daniel, Kathleen Berglund, Mary McHugh, Ellen Fischbach, John, Maureen Ward, Pegeen Ward and Eileen Lundgren. This home was built in 1880. It is an attractive side gabled home with a large gabled dormer.

6508 85th Avenue North. The Eldon and June Tessman home is one of four Tessman family homes located on 85th Avenue, which was known as Tessman Crossroad (so described in the 1920 census), between Zane Avenue North and Broadway Avenue North. This, the original Tessman farmstead home, was built in 1883 by August Tessman. It has remained in the Tessman family to the present time. August Tessman's eldest son Albert F. Tessman and his wife Dena Kimmerle Tessman lived in the home from 1895 to 1927. Their second son, Bert E. Tessman, and wife Esther Hildebrandt Tessman lived in the home until 1942 and 1950, respectively. Their son Eldon A. Tessman and wife, June Oswald Tessman, and their family have lived in the home from 1950 to the present time. The home is a two-story frame house with Chaska brick for the exterior. Bert and Esther Tessman did an extensive remodeling of the kitchen area in 1937 with new birch cabinets installed and the pantry was converted to a bathroom. The home also was stuccoed at that time.

Source: Article by Eldon Tessman.

6508 85th Avenue North

5032 101st Avenue North. A brick Italianate farmhouse, it has two stories with an intersecting hip roof. It is cream-colored brick with concrete windowsills and a rusticated concrete block foundation on the porch. There are segmented, arched windows, ornamental brackets at the eaves and a large wooden frieze. There is decorative brick in the front gable end. It dates to approximately 1885.

Source: Minnesota Properties Inventory Form BPC-016.

10541 West River Road. This Homestead-style, cross gabled home was built by the Bennet Family. It dates to 1886, according to the City of Brooklyn Park. Purchased by Martin and Deloris Countryman in 1949, it was an old farmhouse with an outside toilet and water from an outside pump.

Source: Article submitted by Martin and Delores Countryman.

5032 101st Avenue North
Above: House
Below: Barn

6108 85th Avenue North. In 1888, two more Tessman homes were built which were identical in floor plan. August Tessman's son Adolph Tessman and wife Mollie Peterson Tessman and members of their family lived in the home at 6108 85th Avenue North until 1950. Jim and Elaine Gibson and family moved into the house in 1950 and did an extensive remodeling of the home. In 1964, the Don and Jean Hoglund family moved into the home and reside there to the present time.

Source: Article by Eldon Tessman.

6717 85th Avenue North. The other 1888 Tessman home was built for August Tessman's youngest son, Ferd, who never married. It is located at 6717 85th Avenue North. When Ferd moved away, the George Rochat family lived in the home for some time. In 1932, Albert and Dena Tessman's son Donald E. Tessman and wife Alice Stevenson Tessman and their family lived in the home and remained until 1988.

Source: Article by Eldon Tessman.

9248 West Broadway Avenue. This L-shaped farmhouse has original wood siding, Tuscan porch columns, a wide frieze and cornerboards. There are leaded glass bay windows on the front porch. Quite a large house, it has several intersecting gable roofs. City records show that it dates from 1890.

Source: Minnesota Historic Properties Inventory Form BPC-011.

8400 93rd Avenue North. This cross-gabled, stucco house has a gabled dormer and front porch. There is a one-story addition with a flat roof. The house incorporates an old Osseo jail that was moved to the site, according to Nellie Fischbach, the owner. The City of Brooklyn Park dates the house to 1890. Nellie Fischbach lives next door at a newer house at 8300 93rd Avenue North. The two houses are at the corner of Highway 169 and 93rd Avenue (County Road 30). Nellie and her husband, Wayne, were potato farmers. Wayne was born in 1922 and died in 1982. Before them, Wayne's parents, Peter and Lulu Fischbach, owned the property and lived in the house at 8400 93rd. Lulu's parents, Leo and Fannie Walter, owned the farm before them. The farm has been in the family for over 100 years.

Wayne and Nellie farmed potatoes until about 20 years ago. Their two sons (Peter and Charles) raised potatoes for about another five years. Now Charles has a successful garden store where he sells produce (mostly sweet corn) that he raises. The farm is now about thirty acres but it was approximately 80 acres. They sold some of it to St. Vincent's Catholic Church for a cemetery.

Source: interviews with Nellie Fischbach.

9008 93rd Avenue North. Mr. Wayne D. and Mrs. Anna R. Printz purchased this home in 1963. Built in 1890, it is a stuccoed Homestead-style home with an enclosed front porch.

9309 Winnetka Avenue North. Mr. Paul N. and Mrs. Susan D. Bromen purchased the home in 1984. Mr. Bromen states it appears as though the home was added onto, and refurbished two or three times prior to their purchase of the property. Built in 1890, it is stuccoed with a gabled roof.

Brooklyn Park Historical Farm, 4345 101st Avenue North. This farmhouse, on ten acres, is a living record of Minnesota farm life during the years 1894-1910. John Eidem, Jr. married Electa Cotton in 1892, and they moved into the farmhouse in 1894. The Eidems farmed there from 1894-1956. The house faces north and is a two-story, Queen Anne-style, three-bay farm building built circa 1894. The foundation is fieldstone, and there is a high, hipped roof. The gables have diamond-patterned siding and decorative gingerbread millwork. There is a kitchen addition from the early 1900s and a hipped porch with classical columns. A second partially-screened porch adjoins the kitchen. The house has weatherboard siding and two interior brick chimneys, with a third chimney partially intact. A barn and four outbuildings are on the property. Special events, tours, displays, crafts and old-time activities are scheduled by the City's Recreation and Park Department during the four seasons.

Sources: National Historic Register submission by City of Brooklyn Park, October, 1990; Historic Properties Inventory Form BPC-018.

10225 Winnetka Avenue North

9801 Xerxes Avenue North. Built in 1895, it is a Homestead-style home with wood siding, an enclosed porch and a side addition. Nickolas A. and Rosa M. Lazaroff purchased this home in October 1984. They have three children, Nickolas, April, and Christopher.

10225 Winnetka Avenue North. This house is remembered by the grandchildren of prior owners, Mr. and Mrs. Herman Schmidt, who described it in their own words: "When we were young children, we played in the house on Road 103 (now Winnetka). It was the home of our grandparents, Mr. and Mrs. Herman H. A. Schmidt. The home had previously belonged to our grandmother's parents, named Buchholz. The house was built in the late 1890s or very early 1900s.

"As one entered the back door into the kitchen, on the right was the cream separator. Straight ahead was the door to the main room of the house, and in the kitchen, to the right of this door, was a wood-fired range. To the right of the stove was a small table for food preparation, and along the wall were shelves for storage of pots and pans. Meals and other family activities took place in the main room of the house. The focal point of the main room was a large table around which family and guests sat to eat, talk and enjoy the wonderful meals prepared by our grandmother. Grandpa always read from a German devotional book before each meal. Besides the roast chicken, the best part of the meal was the freshly baked corn bread, spread with gobs of melting butter and covered with white gravy which was flavored with the cracklings from rendering the fat from freshly-butchered hogs.

"There were three bedrooms upstairs, only two of which were completely furnished. The third one was used for storage and the pressure tank for the lighting system. Our mother, Tillie, was born in this house."

Source: Story courtesy of the Ebert family via Wesley W. Ebert, Penngrove, California and Jim Ebert, Brooklyn Park, Minnesota.

4201 101st Avenue North. This is the Silas Merrill Farmhouse and is east of the Brooklyn Historical Farm. It is owned by the City of Brooklyn Park. An L-shaped, Homestead-style house, it has gingerbread bargeboard in the gables. It probably dates to about the 1890s.

Source: Norene Roberts, Minnesota Historic Properties Form BPC-019, 1988.

7633 West River Road. At a spot on West River Road called Warwick, after an early settler, there is a historic house that could be called the Johnson-Fischer place. A man named J.B. Johnson came to Brooklyn Township in about 1868 to live and he ran a mercantile business at Warwick. The following year he was appointed postmaster and held the office until 1873, when a post office was started at Brooklyn Centre (located at 69th and the present Brooklyn Boulevard).

The Warwick store, house and outer buildings all burned in 1894, but Mr. Johnson rebuilt with $4,000 in insurance money. William and Emma Fischer moved into this farmhouse in 1903. The house was a big, old white house "on the corner." It was a stagecoach stop and grocery store. Sometime in the ensuing years, the porch was torn off. A stone foundation on the north side of the farmhouse is a remnant of the old post office. Mail wagons on the way to Anoka would stop at Warwick. Russ Mozey, a later owner, treasures mementos from the Warwick store such as coffee bins, bread boxes and an old wooden Wisconsin Peerless refrigerator.

This handsome house is a two-story Queen Anne-style home. The windows are of an interesting geometric design and there is a windowed attic. There are lightning rods on the roof and the house is now sided in aluminum.

Sources: Interview with Eunice Fischer Masica, June 1994; Noralee Taylor, "Landmarks: Brooklyn Park Then and Now: Stagecoach Days and Farm Families," Brooklyn Park Post, May 19, 1988, p. 9A; Minnesota Historic Properties Inventory Form BPC-033.

7633 West River Road

6716 85th Avenue North. The fourth Tessman home was built for August Tessman's son Edmund Tessman and his wife Louise Setzler Tessman in 1897 and is located at 6716 85th Avenue North. They and their children, Raymond and Alice, have resided in this house until the present time. Raymond passed away in 1993 and Alice still sleeps in the same bedroom she was born in. The home and farmstead suffered extensive damage from a tornado in 1925.

Source: Article by Eldon Tessman.

8900 West River Road. This is one of a few old homes that still stands from the early days of the West River Road. Before being acquired in the 1940s by Arthur and Josephine Blesi, the land was owned by the Mississippi and Rum River Boom Company. In 1974, the land and house owned by the Mrs. Josephine Blesi Estate was sold to Joe and Judy Klohs, who currently live here. The house has gone through many stages of improvement since the Klohs' purchase in 1974, which makes the original age of the building unrecognizable at the present time.

5816 101st Avenue North. Mr. Timothy J. and Mrs. Lauri J. Wollenzien purchased the home in October of 1997. It was built in 1900 and has been extensively refurbished on the interior. It is a side-gabled home with a front addition.

8900 West River Road

8900 Zane Avenue North. This handsome house was recently purchased by Mr. Elliot and Mrs. Carrie Reed. It was built in 1900 by Christian Schreiber, who homesteaded the property in 1856, as recorded in the first recorded plat of Brooklyn Township in 1860. It is a Homestead-style, wood-sided home with front and side porches. The land was actively farmed until the 1980s when it was sold by Mr. and Mrs. Jim Schreiber.

10725 Noble Avenue North. On January 11, 1856, Mr. Lewis Atkinson acquired this piece of property as a result of a Federal Land Grant to him by the U.S. Government. In April 1955, Mr. Cyrus and his wife Ruth Beck purchased the property from Mr. Myron H. Maher. An Italianate-style two-story of brick construction, it is L shaped with a gabled front and side roof. It dates to 1900.

6661 68th Avenue North. Mr. Richard and Mrs. Nadean Rudolph purchased their home in 1980. Built in 1900, it is an L-shaped Homestead-style house with wood siding.

9204 West River Road. This dates to about 1900, according to the city. The land was purchased before the Civil War by a Swiss family, the Jentschs. The house originally was a farm home for a farm of 100 acres. Mr. Harold Shimek lived at this house for 25 years and every Christmas and Easter decorated his home. In the summer his yard was a piece of art, with beautiful flowers. In the fall of 1998, Mr. Shimek sold his home and moved to Champlin, where he now resides. The house is cross-gabled and has a long columned porch.
Source: Article submitted by Edward Shimek.

6516 West Broadway Avenue. An American Foursquare-style residence, it was built in approximately 1910. It has three-inch lap siding and corniced window moldings. The porch has newer columns. It is a very handsome house with a beautiful porch. One of the most attractive homes in the city.
Source: Minnesota Historic Properties Inventory Form BPC-028.

8101 Zane Avenue North

8101 Zane Avenue North. The house dates to 1910 and has Queen Anne and Victorian elements. Most notable are the cupolas and octagonal towers. Mr. Emmet W. and Lori G. Sims and their daughter Dannielle moved here from California in 1995.

9900 Regent Avenue North (The Schreiber School). This former red brick schoolhouse was built in 1910 and it is pictured about that time, with no trees around it. Note the pump in the front yard. It was named after the Schreiber family who had a farm nearby. The east side had long, eight-foot windows that were used in a 1975 renovation. The former one-room school is now two stories, with a basement. It has

9900 Regent Avenue North

an open ceiling with sparkle plaster. The upstairs rooms are to the side on a balcony system with an open, banistered stairway leading upstairs. The roof was not changed except that the belfry is now a hipped-roof dormer window on the second story of the house. Current owners are Jo Dee Hagstrom and Rick Ketzback.

7949 Zane Avenue North. Known as the John A. Hamilton House, it dates from 1910, .according to city records. Of Homestead Style and L-shaped, it is a small, one-story house with clapboard siding, with a front porch and a shed addition in the back.
Source: Minnesota Historic Properties Inventory Form BPC-004.

5808 80th Avenue North. This is a second John A. Hamilton House, which according to city records dates to 1912. It is an American Foursquare home with Colonial Revival styling. There are pilasters, a wide frieze under the eaves and a stained-glass transom. The porch has been removed.
Source: Minnesota Historic Properties Inventory Form BPC-004.

6348 West Broadway Avenue. This attractive house dates to 1915, according to the City of Brooklyn Park. It is a Colonial Revival-style home with a front gabled porch and two large gabled dormers. It is square and served as a farmhouse for the Luger Farm. It has a wide frieze, cornerboards and lap siding.
Source: Minnesota Historic Properties Inventory Form BPC-035.

8808 101st Avenue North. Mr. Kevin A. Thurs purchased this home in 1987. Records show this home being built in 1915. It is stuccoed, with a front bay window and a front and side gabled roof. There is a decorative bracket on the front gable.

"Riverlyn," 9510 West River Road. Though not a house, this building at 95th Avenue and West River Road — now known as Rum Runners Bar and River Grill—is of considerable historic interest. The building originally was known as Riverlyn and was built around 1919 by a local improvement association in connection with upgrading West River Road. It served as a social center for the rural community, with picnics, plays, receptions and dances held there. In 1957, the new Village of Brooklyn Park bought the building for use as a municipal on/off liquor store and bar. The original Craftsman-style building was extensively remodeled at that time. It was not a commercial success and the Village sold the building in the late 1950s. Thereafter it became a dance hall and then a series of restaurants.
Sources: "Riverlyn," Brooklyn Historical Society Newsletter, August 1994, p.2, citing North Hennepin Post, May 30, 1957.

5909 Bethia Lane

5901–5909 Bethia Lane North. The significant building on this property is the dairy barn, which dates from approximately 1920. It may be the only dairy barn still standing in Brooklyn Park. It replaced one destroyed by fire. An interesting feature is the cupola on the barn, which has a cow on the top. It has a double-pitched gabled roof and the main part of the walls are from rusticated concrete block. On the same property is an outbuilding which was originally a garage and has been converted to a house. Also nearby is the original farmhouse, which was extensively renovated in 1947.
Source: Minnesota Historic Properties Inventory Form BPC-025.

7306 Noble Avenue North. This is known as the Hanscom House. Pioneer Ezra Hanscom's house was built on today's Noble Avenue on the southeast side of Shingle Creek in 1853. Former state representative Alpha Smaby lived here. It is a two-story bungalow with dormers, and according to city records, dates to 1922. The styling is reminiscent of American Craftsman but without some of the detailing.
Sources: Minnesota Historic Properties Inventory Form BC-008.

7548 Noble Avenue North. This is known as the Dow House, after the family of the first minister in the area. A stucco house, it is two stories with cross-gabled roof, returned eaves and a box-shaped bay window. It dates from 1925.
Source: Historic Properties Inventory Form BPC-7.

2601 Brookdale Drive (Lazaroff Nursery). This perhaps is the last remaining truck farm in Brooklyn Park. The house dates from 1930 and is front gabled. There is an addition with a hipped roof. Source: Minnesota Historic Properties Inventory Form BPC-032.

10500 Noble Avenue North

7826 Brooklyn Boulevard. Known as the Aaron and Lydia Tessman House, it dates to 1930. It is a stucco, English Cottage-style home with lancet arched windows. The foundation is stone. There is a bas relief tree motif on the front chimney. Originally it was a farm residence.
Source: Minnesota Historic Properties Inventory Form BPC-034.

10500 Noble Avenue North. The original land was purchased in 1856 from the United States government. It is believed the first permanent residence was built around the turn of the century. The original house may have been a two bedroom farmstead. It had a very small kitchen and living room. The basement had a root cellar and was very small with a low ceiling. The little back porch is original and has been attached to an addition. The Mottaz' bought the home in 1972 when they fell in love with the house and its 6½ acres. The original old barn and carriage house are still standing and the carriage house is now a workshop. The home has had some improvements and has become the first Bed and Breakfast in Brooklyn Park, called "The Meadows."
Source: Article submitted by Lynn and Del Mottaz.

200 Brookdale Avenue North. This is the home of John and Grace Keillor, where Garrison Keillor was raised. It was built by the Keillors beginning in 1947 and for a while was a basement home. It was completed in 1952. It is an attractive Colonial Revival/Cape Cod-type home with shutters, gabled dormers and a large picture window. Six children were raised in this home—four boys and two girls. In 1972 the home was sold and the Keillors moved to Florida for twenty years. But Brooklyn Park beckoned them back and in 1991 the Keillors repurchased the home. Before John Keillor retired, he worked as a Railroad Post Office employee.
Sources: Interview with Grace Keillor; Noralee Taylor, "Lake Wobegon: Garrison Keillor's boyhood home," *Brooklyn Park Post*, May 19, 1988, p. 9A; Garrison Keillor, "My Boyhood Home," *Brooklyn Park* (magazine published by the Brooklyn Park Economic Development Authority), 1994, p. 42.

200 Brookdale Avenue North

The Second Time Around: 10225 Noble Avenue North.

by Darla Jordeth

Our homes become an integral piece of our lives — holding our hopes and our memories. This is the story of one woman's love affair with a house.

MY FIRST ENCOUNTER with the Noble House was mid-summer 1980. An intriguing ad in the *Trib* boasted of a vintage home with acreage, just twenty minutes from downtown Minneapolis. What more could an antique lover with a green thumb and a husband with a knack for carpentry desire? We drove out to take a look. The hobby farm had a house with a simple old-world charm that endeared it to me instantly. The yard appeared to be never ending; it connected to twenty-six miles of Hennepin County Park trails. We seemed to have found the ideal place to raise our son.

Although the house was showing its age in some rather unflattering ways, it was irresistible nonetheless. We looked past its sorry condition, completely ignoring the poorly done remodeling. We saw in it what other old house lovers see in their restoration projects: the latent beauty of past splendors hidden under layers of paint, paneling, dirty carpet and outdated drapes. We took joy at the thought of reclaiming the maple floors, the wide oak woodwork, the built-in china closets and leaded windows. Lost beneath unsightly screening were huge pillared porches. I fell instantly in love.

I was 28, the house was 65. It was a May/December romance that some said wouldn't last but it has endured eighteen tumultuous years. We spent the first six years renovating, restoring, planting and pruning. In 1986 the unexpected happened: my husband left. As my divorce approached I was forced to sell our lovely country home.

Twelve years would pass before I saw the inside of my home again. I consider it a miracle that in the spring of 1997 I was offered the chance to buy back my house on Noble Avenue. In prior years it had been on the market but I had not been able to afford the purchase price. I knew this could be my last chance, expediency called for a budget stretch. In its precarious condition developers would, most likely, tear it down. Too many uncaring occupants had reduced it to the look of an inner-city crack house. Entire rooms had been destroyed. Of twenty-eight windows, over half were cracked or broken. The house was unlivable. We worked three more months before we could even "camp out" in it. A year and a half has gone by and the "to do" list is shrinking.

I have resurrected this home twice now, and though I will eventually see the acreage succumb to oncoming development, I plan to grow old here. My son insists that the house stay in the family. It has become like a long-lost friend to us, we care about its future. Here's what little we know about its past: It was built in 1901. It is an orphan seeking its roots. No abstract is currently available to verify its early history. The Schreiber family once owned the land, possibly building at this location.

Exploration of the attic and basement reveal the use of "recycled" timbers from a pre-existing structure. Old nails found embedded in those timbers are a type used widely in the late 1800s. We doubt that stucco is the original exterior, though the earliest known photo (circa 1950) shows it as such. That photograph also pictures the original barn. The gambrel roof (originally of cedar shakes) lends a casual Dutch Colonial styling, but it is the open pillared porches that give it character.

The house sits on eight and a half acres. It was part of a much larger vegetable farm in the first half of the century. In the 70s the Dorn brothers grew corn, asparagus and pumpkins. In the mid-80s we planted apple trees and berries, but it was Arlo and Shiela Carpenter who ran it as Applebrook Farm in 1987-1993. I just grow flowers. The orchard is overgrown now. The search for its pre-Dorn history continues.

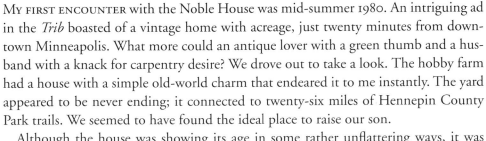

Cemeteries

Mound Cemetery (Brooklyn Center)

On May 2, 1862, a group of men met to establish a cemetery in Brooklyn Township. The cemetery was started when two acres of land was purchased at 69th Avenue North near Palmer Lake for $48 from James Henderson and his wife. Thirty-three names were on the list of donors, workers and original owners.[1]

On May 31, 1862, the Association was registered with Hennepin County. Ezra Hanscom was elected President, A.H. Benson Secretary, Hiram Bohanon Treasurer, and John Durnam, George Plummer, J. C. Post, Asa Howe, James Henderson, J. W. Wales and James Ham, Trustees.[2]

The Association chose the name "Mound Cemetery" because Indian mounds were located at the south end of Palmer Lake. The Cemetery was dedicated "to God as a holy burial place for His children and was sacred to the community," according to Ellen Bohanon, wife of an Association Treasurer.[3]

In 1873 another piece of land, a little over two acres, was purchased for $30. The Association was incorporated in May 1875 and Asa Howe was elected President. In 1883 a second two acres was purchased for $300. The latter parcel was purchased from James and Pearl Hendrickson with the stipulation it must always be used for "God's Acres." The last piece of land was purchased from Frank Howe in 1956.[4]

Mound Cemetery, founded 1862

During World War II, when most able-bodied men were in uniform, Mrs. Everett Sandahl, mother of six, took up the pick and shovel and dug over 100 graves. Later she became Secretary of Mound Cemetery Association.[5]

Ellen Bohanon, referring to the Association minutes, said, "We forget how prejudiced people were. Listen to this from the June 8, 1876, minutes: 'The secretary is instructed not to sell to Norwegians except the west tier.' All the Norwegians were buried on the west side of the cemetery, in an area known as Potter's Field." According to Leone Howe, wife of the current president, this policy was rescinded two years later, and the fence eventually was moved to include this area.[6]

In January 1970 the City of Brooklyn Center executed an agreement with the Mound Cemetery Association, paying $15,000 to lease four acres for Freeway Park for seventy-five years, much against the Association's will. "We figured we had land for 100 years," Ellen Bohanon said. "This may crowd us. You wonder what the world is coming to."[7]

The Mound Cemetery Board of Directors in the year 2000 includes Ralph Howe, (President), Ed Ham, (Secretary), Gayle Redmann, (Treasurer), Kenneth Bohanon, Rex Dorn, Bruce Erikson, Jerry Lane, Robert Miller, David Purdham, Michael Rose and Gordon Sandahl, who also is the caretaker of the 17-acre cemetery.[8]

The current cost of a 4-ft by 8-ft lot is $400, sold in full lots only, with a maximum of twelve lots per family in a designated area. Cremations may have two burials in a lot.[9]

Brooklyn and Crystal Lake Cemetery (Brooklyn Park)

A group of citizens from the Brooklyn and Crystal Lake Townships met November 20, 1863, at the old District #27 schoolhouse and "took into consideration the propriety of forming an Association for the purpose of a Cemetery." Thomas R. Hill was chairman of the meeting and Josiah Dutton, secretary. Warner Willey, Elisha McCausland and Josiah Dutton were chosen to ascertain whether proper lands could he had and at what price. [10]

On December 4, 1863, the name Brooklyn and Crystal Lake Cemetery Association was selected, with DeWitt C. Crandall, William Stinchfield, Charles H. Warde, Henry S. Thompson, Gilbert J. Merritt, and James H. White as trustees.

On December 11, 1863, the formal organization was perfected and the By-Laws adopted. Charles H. Warde was elected president; William Stinchfield, treasurer; and James H. White, secretary.

A tract of land was purchased from William G. Jaques. Members were assessed $45 to pay for the land and $37.50 to pay for the cedar posts, and the two Townships each paid $5. But, the land was too low, so it was sold and a tract of land was bought from Thomas P. Hill and wife for $30. This tract consisted of "one acre of land, square in form, fenced on two sides, lying east of the highway" (southeast corner of present-day West Broadway Avenue and 73rd Avenue North). On September 1, 1896, approximately one additional acre to the north was purchased from Adolph A. Hartkopf.

In 1927 sixty years had passed since the sale of the first lots, and all original founders of the Association had passed away. A group of those interested felt the necessity of an assurance that the graves should be adequately protected and cared for during the years to come. Accordingly on May 15, 1928 a meeting was held with the twenty-five lot owners present. The Association was incorporated and By-laws were adopted on June 1, 1928.

Walter P. Quist was instrumental in compiling cards showing a plat of the land in the cemetery and the names of those resting in it. The card file is now one of the most treasured possessions of the Association.

The Association established a Trust Fund by resolution on May 15, 1928, and the agreement with the Trust Company was signed on April 25, 1929. The revenue is devoted exclusively to the permanent care, improvement and beautification of the Cemetery. The present Rules and Regulations were adopted on March 22, 1932. In 2000, the Board Members are Roland Wenz (President), Mary Blesi (Vice President), Lola Sletten (Secretary), Scott Bartlett (Treasurer), Bill Sampson and Dave Sorenson (Trustees). [11]

Brooklyn and Crystal Lake Cemetery

St. Vincent De Paul Cemetery

St. Vincent De Paul Church was originally known as St. Louis Catholic Church. The St. Louis Catholic Cemetery was organized in 1853, located in Brooklyn Township, Section 18, Township 119, Range 21 West. Today this is 93rd Avenue North and Highway 169. When the town of Osseo was incorporated in 1875, the cemetery was within its boundaries. The first recorded meeting of the cemetery board was May 10, 1920. At that time, the cemetery paid $12 to cut 3½ acres of grass. The cemetery was not incorporated until 1950. [12]

The first burial in 1856 was Emanuel Reighe, born June 15, 1823, died September 22, 1856. At the entrance to the cemetery, three priests are buried in the mound in front of the statue of the Crucifixion, apparently because their families also are buried in the cemetery. They are: Rev. Francis Savey, born in France, July 13, 1862, died September 13, 1914 (Rev. Savey was the parish priest from 1903 to 1914); Rev. Raymond Aubert, 1905-1985; and Rev. Edward M. Clemens, 1905-1993. [13]

Today, the cemetery has grown to 18.05 acres. The land is owned by St. Vincent De Paul Church. There are approximately 3,000 burials in the cemetery.[14]

St. Vincent dePaul Cemetery

Notes

1. "Mound Cemetery Was Old When State Was Born," unidentified newspaper article with text and logo "Minnesota Centennial 1858-1958," possibly from North Hennepin Post, in BHS cemeteries file; Leone Olive Howe, *Album of Brooklyn Centre: A History of Brooklyn Center*, privately published, 1978, Chapter IX.

2. "Mound Cemetery Association family affair," Brooklyn Center Post, 8 May 1975.

3. Ibid.

4. Ibid; Telephone interview with Leone Howe, by Ernee McArthur, 31 May 2000.

5. "Brooklyn Center Cemetery Once Had A Lady Gravedigger, "North Hennepin Post, Anniversary Edition, 25 October 1962, 9.

6. "Mound Cemetery Association family affair"; Leone Olive Howe, *Album of Brooklyn Centre*, Chapter IX.

7. "Mound Cemetery Association family affair".

8. Telephone interview with Leone and Ralph Howe, by Ernee McArthur, 31 May 2000.

9. Telephone interview with Mrs. Gordon Sandahl, by Ernee McArthur, 31 May 2000.

10. Brooklyn and Crystal Lake Cemetery Association, Hennepin County, Minnesota, 1936, 3, (the Association's official informational brochure), copy in BHS files.

11. From Mary Blesi, Vice President, Brooklyn and Crystal Lake Cemetery Association BHS

12. Edward D. Neill, *History of Hennepin County and the City of Mineapolis including the Explorers and Pioneers of Minnesota*, (Minneapolis: North Star Publishing Company, 1881), 294; 100 Year History of the City of Osseo – 1875-1975, Osseo Lionettes and North Hennepin Pioneer Society 1975; Peter Phenow, Cemetery caretaker, document regarding St. Vincent De Paul Cemetery, 1999, in BHS files.

13. Alfred J. Dahlquist, *The Grave Markers of Hennepin County MN* Volume 2 (Park Genealolgical Company, Brooklyn Park, 1992), 13; Peter Phenow.

14. Assessor's Office, City of Osseo, 1999; Peter Phenow.

Chapter Ten

BROOKLYN TOWNSHIP BUSINESSES

Brooklyn Township — 1851 to 1900

Following the opening of the area to settlement, the availability of land through the United States government's Pre-emption Act of 1841 resulted in nearly immediate claim to all of the area that became Brooklyn Township. The Township was organized on May 11, 1858, the same day Minnesota became the 32nd State.[1]

Because they grew, harvested, packaged, priced and sold their potatoes, vegetables and other produce, the early settlers of Brooklyn Township were truly business people. They delivered their produce to homeowners, grocers, wholesalers and shippers who distributed this produce throughout the United States.

The sale of their farm produce supplied money to provide for their families' welfare while they cleared the balance of their land and brought it into production. Brooklyn Township and the surrounding Anoka Sand Plain area was recognized nationally as the leading producer of early season potatoes. Traditional businesses located in nearby Camden, Osseo, Robbinsdale, Minneapolis and St. Paul provided the early settler families with groceries, clothing and other necessities of life.[2]

Brooklyn Township — 1901–1920

During the first two decades of the 1900s the farm families continued to expand their production of vegetables, potatoes, and other farm crops.

On February 14, 1911, the village of Brooklyn Center was organized in the southeast portion of Brooklyn Township. Brooklyn Center consisted of approximately 3,040 acres. The rest of Brooklyn Township then consisted of approximately 12,087 acres.

In 1913 construction began on the Coon Rapids Power Dam—sometimes called the Northern States Power Dam. It was originally planned to provide power for an electric transportation system between Minneapolis and Anoka. When that project was dropped, the dam ended up providing four megawatts of power daily to the north suburban area for fifty-two years. The power producing turbines shut down in 1966.[3]

The Yaklich family operated a grocery store on West River Road and 79th Avenue North during this time. Libby's Garage opened at 93rd Avenue North and West River Road. The Riverlyn Community Center was built at 9510 West River Road and various restaurants have since operated in this location. This period was generally prosperous as the businesses and agricultural production continued to flourish in the area.

Brooklyn Township — 1921-1940

"The Roaring Twenties," "Boom To Bust"—whatever term one used to describe this era would probably not be the correct overall description of our community during this time. As a rural community consisting of mainly small family farms, the hard working people of Brooklyn Township seemed to go about their lives as usual. They adjusted to change when necessary to maintain themselves and their families.

The end of the 1920s began a very trying time for Brooklyn families. The decade started with businesses and farmers prospering, until the stock market crash of 1929 and the worldwide depression which followed. The depression was devastating for the entire nation, as well as Brooklyn Township. Many families were without jobs, banks were forced to foreclose mortgages on many businesses, and the drought years caused terrible hardships for farm families.

The Crash of 1929 and the onset of the Depression affected almost everyone. Our area seemed to survive better than most, however. A good question is, why? Some feel it was the resourcefulness of the people and their will to keep going forward. As Roger Scherer said, "The Howes, the Scherers, Earle Brown and others developed ideas that created jobs and opportunities for people." Irrigation saved crops and enabled farmers to continue to grow food. New sources of lumber kept people working in the lumber industry. The creation of the Minnesota Highway Patrol meant opportunities in law enforcement for others. The people of Brooklyn Township struggled, but survived.

Louie Killmer of Kilmer Electric, circa 1923

In these early days, the farms were not large. Some families lived on 20 acres of land growing vegetables. The average was 40 to 60 acres with the largest at 200 acres. Twenty acres of hand-harvested land is a lot of ground to cover. With farms near to Minneapolis markets, the Brooklyn Center and northern Brooklyn Township truck farmers loaded their trucks the night before so they could be at the market by at least 5 A.M. Grocers came to buy their produce early to get the best vegetables. At home, the family prepared vegetables, for example, they would cut asparagus, bunch it and prepare it for loading the next day.[6]

Some old families of Brooklyn Center who were growers were Ralph, Stan and Sig Edling; George, Walt, Ernest, and Roy Brunsell; and Al Rydeen. Their farms later were to become Brookdale Center. Across Osseo Road to the west were Arden Burquest, George Grim, Adolph Boyson and Paul Pearson. Near the 63rd Avenue North area were Frank and Roy Howe, and Mert Lane. Going north, were Dan Lane, Dave and Del Magnusson, Richard Pengilly, Frank Locke, Stanley Leathers and the Larsons. On 69th Avenue North, near Palmer Lake, were Ed Ham and George Keefe.

Elaine Tessman Christiansen — 1951 American Vegetable Queen

The railroad tracks at the Minneapolis-Brooklyn Center border were a center for potato and onion growers of Brooklyn Center to ship their produce by the boxcar to Chicago. Because of the easy access to Minneapolis, there were numerous greenhouses in Brooklyn Center. Henry Nelson, father of Marv Nelson and the grandfather of Steve Nelson, the last owner of Lynbrook Bowl, started Malmborg's at 5120 Brooklyn Boulevard in 1906. It was sold to the Rice family, later to Lloyd Malmborg and then George Lucht and two partners. Weber's at 5040 Brooklyn Boulevard, began in 1926. The Hans Rosacker greenhouse was on the northeast corner of 57th Avenue North; Miller's on 59th and Brooklyn Boulevard; and the Brooklyn Center Greenhouses at 61st Avenue North. Madsen's started at 5501 Aldrich Avenue North in 1925, and is still located at 49th Avenue North and Brooklyn Boulevard.[7]

In the early years, the flat, sandy soil was ideal for fast growing. But the 1934-1936 drought was very difficult for Brooklyn farm families. With their crops totally devastated by the drought, they turned to developing irrigation. From primitive pumps and gasoline engines along with heavy steel pipes, they started to improve their systems with better wells and pumping equipment. A real milestone occurred around 1950

Aerial view of Madsen Floral Company, built in 1925.

Branding calves in the late 1930s at the Earle Brown Farm

when lightweight aluminum pipes began replacing the heavy steel pipes used before.

Al Rydeen's family was first to irrigate with small pipes built up on a frame. Roy Howe was among the first growers to irrigate large acreages of potatoes. Roy had 200-foot deep wells drilled on each of his farms, with 30 horsepower electric motors and pumps installed for a reliable supply of water. The heavy galvanized six inch steel irrigation pipes had to be moved every 3 hours around the clock to get the necessary one-inch of water per acre. Farmers without irrigation systems suffered from limited yields in those dry years.[8]

The beginning of this period predated the more sophisticated potato products such as french fries, potato chips, and the hundreds of potato products, frozen or dried, that fill our many grocery store shelves today. Brooklyn Township was an ideal area for growing potatoes, having sandy soils and being next to the large populated area of Minneapolis and St. Paul. This gave the growers a ready market for their crop. The frost came out of the sandy soils early in the spring, enabling the farmers to get their crops planted early. While the plows got the fields ready for planting, the women and children cut the certified seed potatoes with a sharp knife fastened to a table or chair, leaving at least one eye on each potato piece. The seed potatoes were brought in from the Red River Valley in the fall and stored in root cellars all winter.

Planting was done with four horses pulling a two-row planter. The horses also were used for weeding and harrowing. Leone Howe said "The wind cut young plants off to the ground. The solution was to plant hedges around a field. It was rare to see any field over thirty acres without a hedge of trees. Brooklyn Center then was rows and rows of hedges, rows and rows of vegetables." Many fields were spread with manure hauled from the stockyards in South St. Paul to fertilize the soil and prevent wind erosion.[9]

A dredge machine from the Howe's farm was brought to the Sinclair farm to dredge peat soil from the swampy areas. Manure spreaders spread it on the high sandy knolls to improve moisture-holding capacity and reduce wind erosion.[10]

In the winter, farmers would cut ice or lease their horses to the lumber industry in northern Minnesota. Some farmers cut and sold Christmas trees at the market. Some had a contract to clean out railroad boxcars, used to haul animals, so they could use the manure to spread on their fields. Brooklyn Center was charming during the truck farming era with its main street lined with huge elm trees, fields with plants of every color and many rows of water sprinklers.[11]

The Earle Brown Farm, which sits in the heart of Brooklyn Center, is historically significant for many reasons. The farm was an early settlement and landmark, the location of some government functions, and the site of the old Captain Martin School. Used for pilot training toward the end of World War I, the Earle Brown Farm was the first commercial airfield in Minnesota and later the training ground for the Minnesota Highway Patrol founded by Earle Brown. In addition to raising sheep, cattle, and registered pigs, Earle Brown had registered Belgian show horses. Some were riding horses and some were workhorses.[12]

During this era, Nick Lazaroff was an active vegetable grower with his farm located in Brooklyn Park at 2601 Brookdale Drive. His son George and wife Harriet are active in their large commercial vegetable growing business in Brooklyn Park.[13]

Farm machinery businesses at that time included Bergstrom Brothers in Brooklyn Center as well as implement dealers in Osseo, which included Heinen Brothers and Syverson Brothers. Later Carl Bergstom started his own farm machinery business on his Brooklyn Park farm.[14]

Harvest time on the Bergstrom farm, early 1940s

The A.J. Spanjers Company has been operating continuously in Brooklyn Township for the past seventy-five years. They opened for business in 1925 on West River Road near the old Lynbrook Bowl location in Brooklyn Center. In 1984 they moved to Brooklyn Park. The company started with weather stripping and caulking of windows for homes, businesses and structures of all types. Three generations later the Spanjers Company's main business is the restoration of historic buildings. Robert Spanjers is its President. He and his two sons, along with a partner, operate the company.[15]

The Howe Store on 69th and Osseo Road was a general store that served the people of the area. Elfreda Ploof (Richard) a longtime resident of Brooklyn Center writes, "Often our parents would drive us to 69th and Osseo Road to a corner store and shop. We were five children and had double dip ice cream cones for $.05 each." Elfreda is the daughter of Oscar and Hilda Peterson. Oscar purchased the Wilcox farm in 1927 and was a truck farmer for many years on West River Road land. Elfreda said, "Because of a dry summer, potatoes did not grow very big. One summer my father gave 2,000 bushels to the Salvation Army."[16]

Prior to the commercial and residential use of refrigeration, ice from lakes was the only source of coolant available to preserve food. In "The Ice Man Cometh and Then He Fadeth Away," by Mary Jane Gustafson, Brooklyn Center resident George Nassig is quoted as saying "I spent eleven years cutting ice on Twin Lake in Brooklyn Center. One year we cut 75,000 tons on Twin." George worked for Cedar Lake Ice Company from 1922 to 1936.[17]

It took until the late 1930s and early 1940s for a recovery to begin from the depression and drought.

Brooklyn Center Store (formerly the Howe store) SW Corner of 69th & Brooklyn Blvd. Owners are Bill and Doris Gadow in the 1930s

One of Brooklyn Center's first "Super Markets" owned by Cliff and Gen Lane (late 1950s)

Brooklyn Center — 1941-1960

Then came World War II! The War years were dedicated to "giving one's all" to the efforts of winning the War. Everyone responded to the call and victory was achieved.

Once the war was over, the population of Brooklyn Center increased at a very rapid pace. After World War II, the housing boom came to the suburbs and land values began to increase. Rising property taxes made continued use of the land for farming difficult. Farmers began to look for other places to farm. The population of Brooklyn Center increased to over twenty thousand people during that period. In fact, "The Growth in Brooklyn Center, percentage-wise, during the decade of 1950-1960 was the largest of any municipality in Minnesota."[18]

With the tremendous growth in population came the opportunity for business growth. Several developers presented plans for shopping centers. There was also an influx of independent businesses waiting to open their doors. Customers wanted to do "one-stop-shopping."

Cliff and Gen Lane owned a grocery store on the northeast corner of 69th Avenue and Osseo Road. The Lane family lived in a large farmhouse at the same intersection. They had one of the largest Red Owl agencies, which carried a full line of groceries, produce and fresh meats. They offered free delivery and charge accounts. In the late 1950s it became Lane and Ernst Big Ten Store. In the same area there was a pharmacy run by Florence and Dick Johnson, Crystal Brook Dry Cleaners owned and operated by Bill Boettcher, a barber shop run by Warren Graber, and the Roland Martini paint and wallpaper store. Dr. Arthur Jaeger was the first dentist to locate in Brooklyn Center in the same area. Les Todd owned and operated a Pure Oil Station directly across Osseo Road.[19]

Richard and Florence Johnson decided to go into business in the fall of 1955 as Brooklyn Center Pharmacy. There was a soda fountain in the store. This became a popular hangout for families with children and also for teenagers. There was no Dairy Queen or McDonalds in the area yet. The store also carried a large assortment of Hallmark greeting cards, sundries and, of course, prescriptions. It was open from 8 AM to 10 PM seven days a week with prescriptions delivered as late as 2:00 AM in case of emergencies. The delivery service was a big asset to many of the young mothers in the area who were unable to drive or didn't have a car during the day. There was no bus service yet.[20]

The first shopping center in the Northwest suburban area was Northbrook Shopping Center at 57th and Logan Avenue. Some of the tenants were Ideal Drug,

Richard and Florence Johnson at work in the mid-1950s.

Northbrook Clinic, Northbrook Hardware, Cook's Paint, Home Bakery, Pilgrim Cleaners, and Country Club Market. Another shopping center was in the making at 67th and Osseo Road, but plans fizzled with only a National Tea Store built on the site.[21]

Plans for additional shopping centers were being discussed at council meetings. One proposal was from Dayton's for a 10 million dollar Northdale Shopping Center (now Brookdale), and there was a proposal for a Garden City area development. The Dayton proposal was on property that had previously been proposed for a center by a group called The Northern Lites. That proposal was turned down by the council and was opposed by the Garden City Group. The council was also informed by the University of Minnesota that "they would drop their Garden City Plans and make the farm a tax-exempt experimental plot — if the Northern Lites project was approved." Was this a power play?[22]

Roy Howe added a third business that was incorporated as Howe, Incorporated on January 25, 1940. In addition to farming and operating his potato broker business, Roy was now manufacturing and distributing fertilizer. In 1943 Roy Howe rented a basket manufacturing plant on Raymond Avenue in St. Paul. He took a truckload of fir logs to a logging facility in northern Minnesota and had the logs made into slats and lath, then brought them back to St. Paul to be made into 60-pound bushel baskets. After the baskets were assembled, they were hauled back to Brooklyn Center. They were either used on his farm or sold to other growers.[23]

Anderson Automatics was one of the first new businesses to locate in Brooklyn Center during this period. During the early 1940s, Anderson Automatic Screw Machine Products, as it was called then, began with its founder Carl E. Anderson and wife Genilla with three machines purchased for $500. Carl Sr. liked the idea of staying at his location in Brooklyn Center because of its close proximity to the railroad, to other developing businesses, and to home. In addition, the taxes paid from the business would help his tax structure at the homestead. "Carl Anderson Sr. wanted Brooklyn Center to be the finest growing community in North Minneapolis," says Carl Anderson Jr.[24]

Anderson Automatic. Carl Anderson, founder, stands in the white shirt at the front.

In 1954 Sig Edling showed Carl Anderson Sr. a French Potato Cutter owned by Bud Howe. Sid wanted Carl to make it faster and more efficient. So, Carl traveled to Grafton, North Dakota to see the inventor, Damon French, and came back with permission to remodel and manufacture new machines. By the time Carl was done with it, the cutter was recognized as one of the best in the business. Carl has many inventions to his credit, but his remodeled potato cutter became his pride and joy.[25]

With the need for automobile transportation increasing, the need for auto service increased with it. Two businesses that fulfilled that need on the East side of Brooklyn Center were Bill West's Service Center and Christy's Service Center. Both served their customers so well that each had their own followers saying theirs was the best.

Brooklyn Park — 1941-1960

World War II had revived the world economy and Brooklyn Township was beginning the conversion from farming to home building in earnest. Thompson Homes was actively constructing residential homes on the Henry Engvall farm, Associated

Contractors and Dietrich Brothers were building in the southwest area of Brooklyn Park. Other home-building sites were the Marvella and Ziegler additions in northern Brooklyn Park.

The Starlite Outdoor Movie Theater received its license in 1958. It was located on West Broadway where Target and Cub Foods are now located. The Starlite was an entertainment center enjoyed by many patrons of the north metro area for years.

The Joyner family completed the first building of the Joyner Silver Shop located on Lakeland Avenue and Brooklyn Boulevard in 1947.[26]

One of the first traditional commercial businesses to operate continuously was Tony Renko's garage. Tony's Garage was opened in 1948 and remains in operation after a number of expansions. In 1972 Tony and his wife Adell sold their business to two of their employees. The garage on West River Road is now called Complete Auto and Truck Service.[27]

Another long-time family business in Brooklyn Park was Veit and Company, which began operations in southwestern Brooklyn Park in the 1940s. It moved its expanding operations to 7900 Lakeland Avenue in 1958 and became a diversified excavation, construction and demolition firm. Arthur Veit's son, Vaughn, purchased the company in 1975 and moved it to Rogers in 1981 to have direct freeway access and larger shop facilities for heavy equipment.[28]

Dr. William Funk established his animal hospital and clinic in 1957, which is still in operation and is run by his children at 7425 Jolly Lane.[29]

This was a time of great change in Brooklyn Park—the beginning of the decline in potato and vegetable farming and rapid urbanization of Brooklyn Park.

Brooklyn Center — 1961-1980

There was a lot of commercial building going on in Brooklyn Center during this period. There was re-development of some of the area and the remaining undeveloped land quickly filled in with industrial, commercial, and retail buildings. These developments made Brooklyn Center the commercial hub of the north suburban area.

Pilgrim Cleaners provides a good example of how businesses stimulated re-development at that time. In 1960, Pilgrim Cleaners moved a complete dry cleaning plant and its corporate offices into an old building at 6846 Osseo Road. In 1978 Pilgrim Cleaners purchased the Phillips 66 station next door to its plant and provided its customers with a canopy drive through. The new structural design and overall look established by Pilgrim Cleaners on the corner of 69th and Brooklyn Boulevard (named Osseo Road until October 17, 1970) was recognized by the Brooklyn Center Chamber of Commerce with it's "Beautification of the Year" award.[30]

A tremendous amount of new development occurred. A number of small industrial buildings were built along 48th Ave North in 1960 and 1961. France Avenue in the 4700 and 4800 block became the homes of Cass Screw Machine, Anderson Automatics and Brooklyn Pet Hospital in 1965. Dale Tile was added in that area in 1973.

Retail outlets were rapidly appearing in Brooklyn Center in the early 1960s. The Brookdale Center project was planned with unusual care. A nationally known economic and real estate consultant company was hired to conduct an economic survey to determine the best possible site selection to supplement the Southdale Center in Edina with another suburban center in the metro area. The conclusion was that the Brooklyn Center area offered the most advantages. The location selected was the triangle formed by 57th Avenue North, Highway 100, and Osseo Road (Highway 152)—

Opening of Brookdale Center (1962)

Brookdale Center

with 268,000 people living within a 15-minute drive. It was readily accessible from any direction. Equally important as an asset of the site was the fact that 200 acres of land were available so that a transitional zone of office buildings and other recreational and commercial buildings could be developed in complete harmony with existing adjacent farm and residential properties.[31]

Brookdale Center's two stage construction started in September of 1960. With J.C. Penny and Sears as the first stage anchors, it opened on March 6, 1962. Some of the first merchants included a full-line grocery store, meat market, drug store, liquor store, cleaner, barber shop, pet shop, photo store, variety store, gift shop, two shoe stores, men's store, record shop, four women's stores, millinery shop, hobby shop, children's wear store, beauty shop, restaurant, candy shop, utility company sales and service office, savings and loan association branch office, and other offices. It grew to 45 stores in stage one.[32]

In a region often beset by inclement weather, Brookdale Center offered shoppers the advantages and attraction of a perpetual springtime. For the first time shoppers could enjoy the comfort of having every foot of the Center, including all shops, arcades and public areas, air-conditioned and completely free of snow, dirt, or excessive heat. Merchants too, were excited about this shopping center. Brooklyn Center's Bill Hanson was the owner and manager of the Brookdale Barber Shop. Bubbling with enthusiasm Hanson is quoted as saying, "Isn't it a beautiful spot? Imagine working in such beautiful surroundings?" He added, "And we're going to give certificates with a gold seal to the parents commemorating a child's first haircut."[33]

In 1966 Daytons and in 1967 Donaldsons were added as the second stage anchors. Brookdale was one of the first developments to bring four major competing chains together under one roof. With all the other tenants that joined them in the mall, Brookdale Center became the second largest shopping center in the state with a total of around 72 stores. In 1976 sales at Brookdale Center were approximately $90 billion with 78 stores. Sales at Brookdale Center increased every year for at least the first 15 years of operation. The opening of other large regional shopping centers had little effect on Brookdale's sales. The year one opened during an economic downturn, sales at Brookdale increased four percent.[34]

The philosophy of the shopping center when it opened, was to offer "one stop shopping" where the customer could purchase everything. Merchants soon learned that when mom did her shopping, she liked to purchase her groceries and services elsewhere, separate from her fashion purchases. Fashion then became the focus at

Brookdale. Super Valu, one of the original tenants, moved into the periphery area in 1968. Promotions at the Center changed too. In the early years major promotions took on a carnival and circus atmosphere with elaborate fashion shows, big name bands and talents. By 1975, community events had the highest priority when 110 community events were held at Brookdale Center. It hosted notable events like 'Dinner for a Dime' sponsored by the Brooklyn Center Lions; the Brooklyn Center Fourth of July celebration; and the Charity Ball for CEAP, which raised thousands of dollars.[35]

The area around Brookdale Center filled in after it started attracting traffic. Some of the businesses in the area that were added on Xerxes Avenue included: Jay's Drive-in in 1965, Goodyear in 1966, Firestone in 1968, Midwest Federal Savings and Loan in 1969, McDonald's in 1973, and Westbrook Mall in 1975. Shoppers City opened in 1962 on the Northeast corner of 63rd Avenue and Osseo Road (which was widened in 1964). In later years K-Mart, Red Owl Country Store, and Builders Square occupied some portion of the site. Today it is the home for Rainbow Foods and Walgreens. Northbrook Shopping Center gained Country Club Market in 1963 and Bill West's new Service Station in 1965. Between 1965 and 1969 Osseo Road became the address for additional businesses like Bridgeman's, Boulevard Center, Brookdale Car Wash, Kentucky Fried Chicken, Marc's Big Boy, and Farrell's Ice Cream Parlor.

In the midst of this activity several community leaders formed the Brooklyn Center Chamber of Commerce in 1964. It promoted Brooklyn Center in many ways and influenced the direction of the city and the expansion of commerce and industry.[37]

Brooklyn Center was on the move. Why else did it attract six auto dealerships in just five years? Brookdale Ford opened in 1964 at 2500 County Road 10. Iten Chevrolet opened in 1965, Brookdale Chrysler in 1967, Velie Olds (later became Bob Ryan Oldsmobile) in 1968, Brookdale Pontiac also in 1968, and North Star Dodge in 1969. All were located between 61st and 69th Avenue North on Osseo Road.

In the 1960s and 1970s, parts of the Earle Brown farm along Freeway Boulevard and Shingle Creek Parkway saw construction for Northwestern Bell, Medtronic, Holiday Inn, State Farm Insurance, the Brooklyn Center City Garage, the MTC Bus Garage and Palmer Lake Plaza. Many other companies occupied industrial buildings that were built in the area.

In 1974 the Brooklyn Center Branch Regional Post Office was announced, becoming the largest branch in the Twin Cities. Dallas Lawrence of the Brooklyn State Bank had worked hard for a new Post Office since the mid-1960s.[38] Office buildings also joined the landscape near the Earle Brown farm in the 1970s on John Martin Drive and Earle Brown Drive.[39]

Brooklyn Chamber of Commerce Organizational Meeting — 1964

Brooklyn Park — 1961-1980

The transition from agriculture to urban growth accelerated early in this period. Of the more than fifty commercial potato growers in 1960, only eighteen remained by 1968. This era saw Brooklyn Park become a city on October 9, 1969, with an estimated population of 22,000.

The Jaycees were a very important part of the business community in Brooklyn Park during the 1960s and 70s. A membership list shows 79 active members. The

Jaycees sponsored the first Tater Daze celebration an August 14-16, 1963. The Jaycees sponsored this event annually until 1970, when the Brooklyn Park Community Organization took over sponsorship. Tater Daze has been celebrated annually ever since. [40]

About one hundred years after Brooklyn Township was founded, the agricultural economy was converting into an urbanized area with the construction of many single family homes and apartment complexes. In the mid 1950s Brooklyn Park had about 25 conventional businesses. Now there are 40 to 50 times as many. This growth was spurred by an outstanding group of young business families in the 1960s and 1970s. Some of these are still very active today with many having expanded nationwide.[42]

Tony Brunello established his State Farm Insurance Agency in 1959 and exemplifies the young business owners of that time. According to Tony, an organization of business owners was needed to show Brooklyn Park they were united in purpose and had an organization to speak for them. The Brooklyn Park Commercial Club organized because they did not have the number of members necessary for Chamber of Commerce status. Within two years Commercial Club membership had increased sufficiently to organize the North West Chamber of Commerce in November 1972. Later they changed their name to North Hennepin Chamber of Commerce. The Chamber has remained a very positive influence ever since. Tony operated his insurance business until 1995 when he sold his business and closed his office.[43]

In November 1971 Brooklyn Park's first bank opened its doors. Three local businessmen, Arthur Veit, Eldon Tessman and Wilbur Goetze, along with Vic Jude, the area's State Senator, and Harold Pohlad, a banker from New Brighton, founded the Brooklyn Park State Bank.

On December 27, 1972 a very significant grand opening occurred when Jim Stuebner opened his Northland Industrial Park. Consisting of 156 acres, Northland Park is located at the intersection of I-94 and Boone Avenue.[44]

The changes from agriculture to residential dwellings, along with numerous commercial and industrial developments, changed Brooklyn Park forever. The business community, along with its residents of the 1960s and 1970s are owed a big thank you for their participation in a critical time of change. The changes and adjustments made during this time prepared a solid foundation upon which Brooklyn Park has grown.

Brooklyn Center — 1981-2000

The country was in a recession. Could business survive? This was the big question as the 1980s began. And if they survived, who would still be working?[45]

In 1980 the City of Brooklyn Center approved the very first Industrial Revenue Bonds. This helped several companies to stay in business. This was a turning point and could not have happened without the hard work and help of Jerry Splinter, City Manager and his staff; the City Council; and Lonnie McCauley, the Executive Director of the Brooklyn Center Chamber of Commerce, and its members.[46]

In the 1980s the city of Brooklyn Center changed from a developing community to one of redevelopment because almost all of the land had been developed. This was quite a change, and Brooklyn Center city staff worked very hard to help with redevelopment needs so businesses could stay in Brooklyn Center. The pole yard at 49th and France was closed and cleaned up in the mid 1980s. In the late 1980s Center-Brook Golf Course opened. The city realized a dream when the Earle Brown Farm was transformed into the Earle Brown Heritage Center. Motels were built to accommodate the conference center activities and the needs of business people and visitors.

This effort was recognized in 1986, when Brooklyn Center was named an "All America City." In the late 1990s the Brookdale Water Ponding Project helped clean up Shingle Creek and take care of runoff in the area surrounding Brookdale Shopping Center. The development of 500,000 square feet of office and warehouse space began in 1999. Brookdale Shopping Center is to be redeveloped starting in 2000. The upgrading of Highway 100 to freeway status is slated to start construction in 2001.

Brooklyn Park — 1981-2000

In Brooklyn Park, this era is noted for the fast growth of commercial and industrial businesses and the construction of upscale housing as a result of the influence of Edinburgh USA. The I-94 interchange and freeway access at Boone Avenue continues to provide easy access to the business community and has allowed industrial development in that area. The expanded Highway 610 river bridge and the completion of Highway 610 across northern Brooklyn Park will provide similar freeway access to an even larger area of the community and will bring similar positive results. This long awaited highway is resulting in a surge of industrial and commercial development, evidenced by the Target North Office Campus and the industrial growth between 89th Avenue and 93rd Avenues and adjacent to West Broadway and Highway 169.

A list of businesses assembled by the Economic Development Office of Brooklyn Park totals 1,132 as of October 1999. The business development staff at the City of Brooklyn Park has developed a report regarding the Xylon-Wyoming Avenue Industrial Park. This report shows nearly 29 million dollars of new construction in the last two years and reflects the positive effect of the new Highway 610.[47]

Edinburgh USA Golf Course under construction in 1985.

Outstanding growth of industrial companies and commercial office buildings continues in the Stuebner Properties within the Northland Industrial Park, located at I-94 and Boone Avenue. In April 16, 1987, Stuebner was awarded "The National Developer of the Year" award by the National Association of Industrial and Office Park Association. Northland Park is now home to over 150 businesses, which employ more than 16,000 people. Stuebner stated that Northland Properties anticipates paying 12 million dollars in real estate taxes in the year 2000. This represents the tremendous benefit Brooklyn Park is receiving from Stuebner's presence in our community.[48]

The Edinburgh USA Golf Course is another outstanding accomplishment. The upscale housing surrounding this championship course constructed on approximately 850 acres is a benefit to the whole community. This land was primarily swamp land, "too wet to plow but not wet enough for ducks." With the help of the storm water disposal system designed by Westwood Engineering, the James M. Seed family and Evelyn and Robert Schmidt, developers of Edinburgh USA, transformed this liability into a very prestigious amenity.[49]

The portion of northern Brooklyn Park now being opened for development consists of approximately 4,000 acres. This potential for high quality industrial, commercial and residential development promises a bright future for the City of Brooklyn Park in the new millennium. But, "Where Have They Gone?" asks John Wingard, referring to the potato growers of Brooklyn Center and Brooklyn Park. What happened to them as this development occurred? Some farmed until they retired, while others moved their operations farther out to places like Elk River and Big Lake.[50]

With its sewer, water, and highway infrastructure in place, northern Brooklyn Park is attracting high quality commercial, industrial and upscale housing to the 4,000 acres of its relatively undeveloped land. This growth began in earnest several years ago when the Highway 610 construction received its approval. Brooklyn Park has overcome the serious problems it faced in the past 40 years. The 1981-2000 era has been very significant in Brooklyn Park's history. Its long list of accomplishments can be expected to continue as plans for the future unfold. Now, it's "Full steam ahead for the new millennium."

Notes

1. *The World Book Encyclopedia*, "Pre-emption" (Field Enterprises Educational Corporation, 1974), 659; "Imagine" Brooklyn Historical Society, Brooklyn Center, MN, (hereafter cited as BHS), Spring, 1999, 4; "Sectional Map of Hennepin County, 1860," Brookdale-Hennepin Area Library.

2. Norene Roberts, "Growing Potatoes in Brooklyn Park," *Hennepin History*, (Fall 1994): 16-27.

3. Karen Kobe and Chris Gellerman. Interview by Wilbur Goetze, 9 March 2000.

4. Peter Jennings and Todd Brewster, *The Century*, (New York: Doubleday, 1998), 100, 102.

5. Roger Scherer, "Scherer Brothers Lumber Co—50th Anniversary," newsprint, BHS, 1980, 2.

6. Mary Jane Gustafson, "Historic Brooklyn Center, 75th Anniversary Supplement," *Brooklyn Center Post,"* 6 February 1986, 1.

7. Betty Hajder and Dolores Kvamme, "The Madsen Business Story," BHS, 3 April 1999.

8. Dorothy Howe Munkberg, et al., "Howe's Best Bet—The Life and Times of the Roy and Myrtle Howe and Their Family," BHS, December, 1996, 60.

9. Ibid., 59.

10. Ibid., 59.

11. Mary Jane Gustafson, "Historic Brooklyn Center (75th Anniversary Supplement)," *Brooklyn Center Post,"* 6 February 1986, 12.

12. Jane Hallberg, Leone Howe, and Mary Jane Gustafson, *History of the Earle Brown Farm* (Brooklyn Center: Brooklyn Historical Society, 1996), vii, 17, 83.

13. Harriet Lazaroff. "Lazaroff Family History," BHS, 12 October 1999.

14. Adele Bergstrom, "Carl Bergstrom Family History," BHS, 6 October 1999.

15. A. J. Spanjers Company, Inc. *Twin Cities Metro Report*, 1999 Millennium Edition, 79.

16. Elfreda Ploof, "Elfreda Ploof Family Story," BHS, August, 1999.

17. Mary Jane Gustafson, "The Iceman Cometh and then He Fadeth Away," BHS, 1980, 1.

18. "Brooklyn Center — 50 Years of Progress 1911-1961," September, 1961, inside cover.

19. Gen Lane, "Cliff and Gen Lane Business Story," BHS, April, 1999.

20. Richard Johnson, "Brooklyn Center Pharmacy 1955-1967," BHS, August, 1999.

21. Don Rosen, "The Heritage of Pilgrim Cleaners in Brooklyn Center," BHS, 27 October 1999, 1.

22. *North Hennepin Post*, 21, 28 October 1954.

23. Dorothy Howe Munkberg, et al., "Howe's Best Bet — The Life and Times of the Roy and Myrtle Howe and Their Family," BHS, December 1996, 66.

24. Dennis Anderson, "Anderson Automatics Business Story," BHS, October 1999.

25. *Brooklyn Center Press*, 19 December 1957, 1, 5.

26. Orlyn and Gwen Joyner, "Joyner Family History," BHS, 15 August 1999.

27. Tony Renko, "Tony Renko Family History," BHS, 12 January 2000.

28. Veit Family, "Veit Family in Brooklyn Park," manuscript in BHS files, 12 October 1999.

29. William Funk, DV, "Dr. William Funk Family History," BHS, 1999.

30. Don Rosen, "The Heritage of Pilgrim Cleaners in Brooklyn Center," BHS, 27 October 1999, 1.

31. Ann Kaufmann, Editor, "Daytons News," March 1962.

32. Ibid.

33. "Brookdale Bulletin – Special Section for Brookdale Center, Part I," *Brooklyn Center Press*, 8 March 1962.

34. Mary Jane Gustafson, "Sales at Brookdale Shopping Center increase every year," *Brooklyn Center Press*, 27 January 1977.

35. Ibid.

36. "Leg-it at Brookdale Kicks off this week," *Brooklyn Center Post*, 6 September 1979.

37. Duane Orn, MD, "Fifteenth Anniversary Celebration Address," BHS, 1980.

38. "BC Post Office, largest branch in Twin Cities," *Brooklyn Center Post*, 2 May 1974.

39. Ron Warren, "Notes on Brooklyn Center Industrial Development," BHS, 11 March 2000.

40. Brooklyn Park Jaycees, Membership Roster, BHS, 1960; *Tatar Daze Official Program*, BHS, 1963.

41. Harvey H Goetze, Brooklyn Park's History of Growing Commercial Potatoes, *Tater Daze Official Program*, BHS, 1963.

42. Wilbur Goetze, "Early Business in Brooklyn Park," BHS, 13 January 2000.

43. Tony Brunello, "Tony Brunello Business History," BHS, October, 1999.

44. Wilbur Goetze, "Grand Opening Northland Industrial Park," BHS, December, 1999.

45. Mary Jane Gustafson, "Help of God needed in recession time," *Brooklyn Center Post*, 26 June 1980, 1.

46. Mary Jane Gustafson, *Brooklyn Center Post*, 1980.

47. "Brooklyn Park Business List," City of Brooklyn Park, October, 1999; Jason Aarsvold, "Xylon/Wyoming Avenue Industrial Park," BHS, 17 November 1999; Brett Johnson, "Brooklyn Park Council Finalizes Dayton Hudson Plan," *Brooklyn Park Sun Post*, 17 November 1999, 1.

48. James Stuebner. Interview by Wilbur Goetze, October, 1999.

49. Evelyn Schmidt, "Evelyn Schmidt Family Business History," BHS, July, 1999.

50. John Wingard, "Where Have They Gone," BHS, 6 October 1999.

Working on the River

by Roger Scherer

This story gives one example that illustrates the ingenuity and perseverance of some of Brooklyn Township's people.

BACK IN 1929 several weeks of heavy May–June rain put a crimp in the Scherer Brothers hay baling business, so Clarence and Munn went over to the Mississippi River to watch some of the old timers snagging deadheads up from the muddy bottom of the river bed. They learned that a twenty mile stretch of the Mississippi, north of Minneapolis, was loaded with valuable sunken logs. These logs were the remnants of the great river drives of the last century. Thousands of the logs — mostly white and Norway pine — had been forced to the bottom, covered with sand, and abandoned when the sawmills gradually faded away in Minneapolis. Clarence chanced to ask a pair of old river rats working logs from a scow how much they wanted for half interest in the operation. The price was $250, which happened to be Clarence Scherer's total net worth, the Scherer Brothers bought in at $240. Four years later, at the depth of the depression, the brothers bought out their partners, bought a little saw rig on the river bank north of the city and moved their milling operations to the present site at Ninth Avenue Northeast, Minneapolis.

Deadheading logs was a dangerous job that took special skill and knowledge. The deadheaders, mostly old river-wise lumberjacks, cruised along the river currents probing the bottom with long iron poles. They studied the currents and carefully recalled the spots where the big log jams had clogged the river. When the logs were found, the men pushed a hook and chain under one and hauled it up with a winch on the scow. One particular jam was so rich it came to be known as White Pine Island. Here, twenty feet below the surface, was a buried pile of fine white pine totaling one and one-half million board feet. As the men worked this bonanza, the logs popped to the surface like corks.

In the years from 1930 to 1950, deadhead logging in this stretch of the Mississippi River produced about twenty-two million board feet of lumber, of which Scherer Brothers accounted for about fifteen million. After twenty years, the time had come to write finis to Mississippi River logging.

Scherer Brothers' crew at work in 1932. Clarence and Munn are seated at the center, rear of photo.
Greg Scherer

Health Care

In earlier times only Minneapolis and St. Paul had hospitals. Maternity Hospital was an exception when it opened in 1886. It was a new concept for a suburb to have a hospital when North Memorial Health Care (formerly Victory Hospital) opened in 1939. Maranatha Ministries (1959) is the oldest facility for the care of the elderly in Brooklyn Center. There are other senior residences, including Earle Brown Terrace, whose entrance building is Earle Brown's former office on the Farm. The Crossings is also owned by Lang-Nelson Associates. The Alterra residence is located adjacent to the Earle Brown Terrace. The Shingle Creek high rise building, across Shingle Creek from Brooklyn Center City Hall, was built in the 1960s.

Maternity Hospital 1886-1956

Dr. Martha Ripley graduated from Boston University Medical School in 1883 at the age of forty. That same year her husband suffered a severe injury in a mill accident and she had to support the family. They moved to Minneapolis and she began a medical practice. Her interests were in reducing deaths of women in childbirth and of infants. Delivery of babies in hospitals was uncommon until the 1910's. In 1886 Dr. Martha Ripley founded Maternity Hospital. It expanded in 1887 to an 18-room house and in 1887 a small band of women under Ripley's leadership bought a bigger house.[1]

In 1896 five acres of land was purchased at Glenwood and Penn Avenues North with a still bigger house. This was the hospital's location for 20 years. The specialized hospital pioneered in such techniques as natural childbirth, allowing mothers and babies to room together, and to offer women privileges unusual for the time, such as showering during labor and even giving fathers access to the delivery room. Women were taught sewing, cooking; personal hygiene, housekeeping and care of babies. Some learned stenography so they could get jobs. No patient was turned away.[2]

North Memorial Hospital, 1955

In 1911 there was public support for an even larger building. Dr. Ripley died in 1912 at the age of 68. In 1915 the hospital's name was changed to Ripley Memorial. It closed in 1956.[3]

Dr. Ripley had been president of the Minnesota Women's Suffrage Association from 1883-1886.[4]

Barbara Sexton of Brooklyn Center said she gave birth to her youngest daughter, Lynn Sylvia Sexton, at Maternity Hospital in 1956. The cost was $100 for the delivery and five days in the hospital.[5]

North Memorial Health Care

North Memorial Health Care, (Formerly Victory Hospital) located in the northwestern Twin Cities suburb of Robbinsdale, is a full-service not-for-profit medical center with 518 licensed beds, 5,000 employees and 850 physicians. Its mission is to provide both primary and tertiary level health care services to meet the total health care needs of people residing in the northwest quadrant of the metropolitan area, and to meet the referral needs of the people in greater Minnesota and western Wisconsin. North Memorial provides quality services to nearly 400,000 patients annually. [7]

North Memorial Health Care

In 1939 Dr. Samuel Samuelson built Victory Hospital on property he owned in Robbinsdale. In a time when the only hospitals were located downtown Minneapolis and St. Paul (to be closer to physician's offices), building a facility in the suburbs was a bold step. Dr. Samuelson could envision the health care needs of a growing community, and the first suburban hospital in Minnesota was admitting patients. Dr. Samuelson was born in 1900 and died in a plane crash in 1957. [8]

Victory became North Memorial Hospital in 1954, when it was organized as a private, non-profit hospital. Vance C. DeMong became administrator, and three years later, North Memorial received accreditation by the Joint Commission on Accreditation of Hospitals. During DeMong's 27 years of leadership, he witnessed the completion of several expansion projects, taking North Memorial from a 30 bed facility to a 518 bed medical center. Vance died at the age of 75, at North Memorial of pneumonia. [9]

North Memorial's early leadership in emergency care has catapulted into a successful emergency and trauma services center. The first totally integrated hospital-based medical transportation system in the state of Minnesota began at North Memorial, and now includes two helicopters, 100 ambulances, and 575 employees. [10]

North Memorial provides centers of excellence in primary care; cardiology through North Heart Center; obstetrics, perinatology, gynecology, neonatology and pediatrics through North Women's and Children's Center; oncology and hospice care through North Cancer Center; and rehabilitation through North Rehabilitation Center. North Memorial is a leader in microvascular surgery and limb replantation. It serves as a teaching affiliate of the University of Minnesota in family practice and surgery. [11]

North Residential Hospice

North Residential Hospice is part of a program of services offered by North Hospice, a service of North Memorial Health Care. It is a specially constructed residence on over two acres of land on Upper Twin Lake in Brooklyn Center, opened in June 1997. This 5,900 square foot rambler, with eight private rooms, offers panoramic views

North Residential Hospice

of the lake and nature. It is a welcoming home in the community for hospice patients who need 24-hour care and prefer an intimate home-like setting.[16] Those who have experienced North Residential Hospice describe it as a peaceful and loving environment. It is a place where they feel welcome, heard, attended to, cared about and loved. Most important, North Residential Hospice is described as a place like home.[17]

The Brooklyn Park Medical Center

The Brooklyn Park Medical Center at 5805 74th Avenue North, built in 1975, is one of four Columbia Park Medical Groups (CPMG). The other three Medical Centers are in Columbia Heights, Fridley and Andover, Minnesota.[18] The origin of CPMG dates back to 1959, when two physicians joined together in the practice of medicine in Columbia Heights. They believed by practicing with other physicians in a group setting, they could practice better medicine and service to their patients and the community. The four Medical Centers are staffed in 2000 by a total of 70 doctors.[19]

Brookpark Dental Center

The Brookpark Dental Center located at 6415 Brooklyn Blvd. has been serving the dental needs of Brooklyn Center area residents since 1963. It opened shortly after founders Dr. Gregory T. Swenson and Dr. Brian Murn met at a dental conference. Dr. Swenson said, "I grew up in a farm community. While I learned to work hard and take nothing for granted, maybe the most important thing I learned is if neighbors are to truly be neighbors, they must need each other and they must help each other. In a way we learned to see value in a common dependence on a common life and a common ground. And we've tried to carry those understandings of community and our place in it through to how we practice our profession."[20]

The original Brookpark team had the equivalent of three full-time dentists, three assistants, three hygienists and a support staff of five. As Brooklyn Center grew, so has the dental center, which has a 70 member staff that includes twelve doctors.[21]

The ParkDental Health Centers, and its flagship Brookpark Dental Center, are the first and only Minnesota dental practices to receive accreditation with the American Academy of Dental Group Practice. They were the second practice nationwide to receive the AADGP accreditation.[22]

HealthPartners Brooklyn Center Clinics

Located at 6845 Lee Avenue North (across the street from the Brooklyn Center U.S. Post Office), the HealthPartners Brooklyn Center Medical Clinic opened in January of 1976 with three doctors and thirteen staff members. After two expansions through the years, the building is now 26,500 square feet and houses 25 doctors and midlevel care providers as well as 100 support staff. The clinic serves the primary care needs of 18,000 patients covered by HealthPartners insurance.[23]

The HealthPartners Brooklyn Center Dental Clinic is located two miles from the medical clinic at 5901 John Martin Drive. This facility opened in the fall of 1985 and provides general and pediatric dental services. The clinic sees patients covered by most major dental plans and on a fee-for-service basis.[25]

Hennepin Care North Clinic

Hennepin Care North is a Family Practice Clinic at 6601 Shingle Creek Parkway, Suite 400. It began in 1993 and is affiliated with Hennepin County Medical Center.[26]

Maranatha Ministries

In 1950 the need of a home for the aged was brought to the attention of the Board of the Conservative Baptists of Minnesota. By common consent, it was decided such a home should be built in the Twin City area.[27]

After much prayer, and a period of time for research of feasibility, finance, location and legal procedures, construction of Maranatha Baptist Care Center started in 1959. It was completed in 1962 and dedicated in 1963. The first stage was a facility of forty beds.[28] By 1968, the funds were available to complete Wing III and the Chapel. This increased the number of beds to ninety-eight and gave the residents a place for worship.[29] In 1985, several private rooms were converted to semiprivate rooms, which increased the number of beds to 108. Also in 1985, an addition at the front of the building was constructed. This was done to gain adequate office space and free other areas for storage and resident services.[30]

In 1987, Maranatha Ministries was expanded to include a new senior apartment complex, Maranatha Place, owned by Center Park Senior Apartments. This complex is linked to the nursing home, and offers fifty-eight independent apartments and seven assisted living units. Construction was completed and the apartments were occupied in the fall of 1988. In 1996, a new thirteen bed rehabilitation unit was added to Wing II to aid residents who have short-term rehabilitation needs, e.g., post-stroke, post fracture, wound care, respite care.[32]

Northbrook Clinic

Dr. Robert Shragg opened his Brooklyn Center practice next to the drug store in the Northbrook Plaza Shopping Center in 1955. In 1958, Shragg asked his friend Dr. Michael Kozak to join him at the Brooklyn Center location. Two years later, they purchased a small house on Lilac Drive. The house was converted into a clinic, and Dr. Ralph Papermaster joined the pair in 1960. The three doctors worked together for thirty-eight years. The third location of Northbrook Clinic is their present location at 8559 Edinbrook Parkway In Brooklyn Park.[34]

Dr. Shragg, when he retired in 1997, said, "In the early days, doctors were gods, everything was dependent on you. Now you have to practice defensive medicine." Shragg remembers taking a nurse from the office with him to make house calls. "Making house calls was just part of the practice. We didn't have throat cultures and blood counts then. We listened to the patient and the patient told us what was wrong. Now we do all the tests and then we see the patient." Shragg literally practiced cradle-to-grave medicine. For Shragg, attending a patient's funeral is a routine part of his medical practice. He said, "It's part of caring for the family."[35]

When Dr. Shragg retired in 1997, he left a practice which included caring for family members of five generations and being the longest-practicing doctor on the staff at North Memorial Health Care.[37]

Dr. Mark DePaolis, author and physician who practices in Brooklyn Center at Park Nicollet Clinic-Brookdale, wrote about his doctor, Dr. Kozak of Northbrook Clinic. He said, "He was my doctor, he was always my doctor, from the time I was born until I grew up and went to medical school." Dr. DePaolis said, "People don't usually get to have a doctor of their own anymore. . . new rules force people to look for new doctors whether they want to or not."[38]

Northport Medical Center, Ltd.

Northport Medical Center, Ltd. is a primary health care clinic that is family practice oriented. In 1960 Dr. Emer Monson and Dr. Rene Braun started its operations at 5415 Brooklyn Blvd., where it still remains. The current principals are Dr. Duane Orn, Dr. John Muesing, David Collins, PA-C and Elizabeth Neels, PA-C.[39]

Northport Medical Center's principal service is health care within a family mode. Hospitalization of patients is usually done at North Memorial Health Care and Abbott Northwestern, and in the past has included Lutheran Deaconess Hospital and Methodist Hospital. Northport Medical Center physicians have served as physicians to Brooklyn Center High School and its athletic teams. Dr. Orn has served as Brooklyn Center City Health Officer. Northport providers care for nursing home patients in most of the local area nursing homes.[40]

Park Nicollet Clinic-Brookdale

The Park Nicollet Clinic-Brookdale opened at 6000 Earle Brown Drive in Brooklyn Center in August 1983 as an urgent care, walk-in clinic. Their primary care departments were pediatrics, internal medicine, and family practice. In 1989 they expanded to include one-third of the building and in 1999 expanded to include the entire building, and became a full facility that includes mental health and ophthalmology/optometry.[41]

Notes

1 "Childbirth Pioneer," *Star Tribune*, 14 March 1999, BHS.

2. Ibid.

3. Ibid.

4. Ibid.

5. Ibid.

6. Ibid.

7. "History" North Memorial Health Care, 21 October 1999, BHS; Seymour Handler, MD, Historian, North Memorial Health Care, BHS; "New Name, New Administration, Staff of 45 Doctors at North Memorial Hospital," *North Hennepin Post*, 12 January 1955, BHS; "Vance DeMong, ex-hospital CEO, dies" *Star Tribune*, 11 September 1999, BHS; "Just for Women," *The Health Resource for Replenishing Yourself*, a publication of North Women's Center, Fall, 1999, BHS; "Men's Health 1999 offers free education sessions" *Brooklyn Center SunPost*, 15 September 1999, BHS; North Residential Hospice, North Memorial Health Care, BHS; Conversation with Barbara Sexton by Ernee McArthur, BC Hall of Fame, BHS.

8. Ibid.

9. Ibid.

10. Ibid.

11. Ibid.

12. Ibid.

13. Ibid.

14. Ibid.

15. Ibid.

16. Ibid.

17. Ibid.

18. "Columbia Park Medical Group Employees Handbook," BHS.

19. Ibid.

20. "Brookpark Dental Clinic celebrates 25 years" Brooklyn Center, *Brooklyn Park Sun-Post*, 26 August 1998, BHS; "We've Been In Brooklyn Center Since 1963 Serving Your Dental Needs" *Brooklyn Center 75th Anniversary, 1986*, BHS.

21. Ibid.

22. Ibid.

23. Patsy Kuentz, Health Partners Brooklyn Center Clinics, BHS.

24. Ibid.

25. Ibid.

26. Hennepin Care North Clinic, Affiliate Hennepin County Medical Center, telephone interview, BHS.

27. Larry Peterson, Maranatha Ministries, BHS

28. Ibid.

29. Ibid.

30. Ibid.

31. Ibid.

32. Ibid.

33. Ibid.

34. "Family doctor reflects on 44-year career," *Brooklyn Center SunPost*, 9 April 1997, BHS.

35. Ibid.

36. Ibid.

37. Ibid.

38. "A doctor you could count on for the long haul," *Star Tribune*, Mark DePaolis, writer and physician who practices in Brooklyn Center, BHS.

39. Northport Medical Center, Ltd., Dr. Duane Orn, BHS.

40. Ibid.

41. Park Nicollet Clinic–Brookdale, Carol Greenland, BHS.

Newspapers

THE FIRST NEWSPAPER in Brooklyn Center was *The Sun*, a 9 x 6 inch four-page monthly paper introduced on October 21, 1898 by its owners: editor Richard E. Knight and publisher F. D. Huff. The paper was printed in Camden Place and sold for three cents until January 1899, when the price dropped to a penny. Twice in the first five months, the paper ran apologies for offending readers. One issue stated, "Not any news was to be found in Brooklyn Centre."[1]

SunPost

The first weekly newspaper arrived in the North Hennepin area some 88 years ago, evolving into the present day *SunPost* newspapers. From 1912-1928, the weekly carried various titles, including *The Searchlight* and *The Voice of Robbinsdale*. In 1928 John Suel moved his *Hennepin County Enterprise* to Robbinsdale, and in 1937 changed the name to the *Robbinsdale Post*. A sister paper, started in 1946, was the *North Minneapolis Post*. In 1950, the *Robbinsdale Post* was renamed the *North Hennepin Post*.[2]

In 1951 Post Publishing Company was purchased by six employees: Edward L'Herault, Carrold Johnson, Willard Sehnert, Richard Germundsen, Wayne Nelson and H.O. Sonnesyn. L'Herault was publisher for 32 years until his son, Gary, assumed those duties in 1983. Sonnesyn was editor from 1937 to 1941 and 1945 until 1969. Gary L'Herault, owner LeRoy Westerland and Germundsen continued to run the paper until 1986. Bob Bork wrote his first story for the *Robbinsdale Post* in 1943 when he was a junior at Robbinsdale High School. In February 1963, he was named managing editor; he retired in 1988.[3]

In 1955 Clint Folin started the *Brooklyn Center Press*. The first issue of the tabloid four-page newspaper made its appearance on February 16, 1955. Four thousand copies were mailed to residents, with the promise of a second edition in two weeks.[4]

On November 29, 1956, the *North Hennepin Post* took over the *Press*. The paper changed from a tabloid size to a standard eight-column newspaper, with Folin as editor for about a year. Gail Bakken Andersen was editor for eighteen months before Mary Jane Gustafson became editor, a position she held until her retirement in 1987. Subsequent editors were Betsy Dick, Rita Seymour, Jon Kerr, Lisa Legge, Karl Puckett, Sheila Knop, Greta Bendtsen and Lauri Winters.[5]

The name change from *Brooklyn Center Press* to *Brooklyn Center Post* took place when the *Brooklyn Park Post* began publication in 1966. *Brooklyn Park Post* editors have included Kay Olson, Paula Hirschoff, Carol Braun Shukle, Marilyn Roth, Noralee Taylor, Carolyn Thompson, Patt Ligman, Mike Garlitz and Brett Johnson.[6]

The *Brooklyn Center/Brooklyn Park Sun* Newspaper was published by Sun Newspapers in the early 1970's. Nancy Fellger was one of the editors.

In 1987 the Post Publishing newspapers were purchased by Guy Gannett Publishing, and in 1991 merged with Sun Newspapers. The *Brooklyn Center Post* was renamed the *Brooklyn Center Post News* in 1989, and the name was changed again in 1991 from

Post News to *Brooklyn Center SunPost*. In July 1998, the *Brooklyn Center SunPost* and *Brooklyn Park SunPost* newspapers were included in a sale to Lionheart Newspapers, LLC.[7]

Osseo Review, Osseo Press, Osseo-Maple Grove Press

What began as the *Osseo Review* newspaper founded in 1920, became the *Osseo Press*, then the *Osseo-Maple Grove Press*. Over the years, the paper included stories about the people in Brooklyn Township, but never covered Brooklyn Park government, according to one of the former owners. There have been four owners, three of whom are Helmuth and Werner Schultz, Don and Carol Larson and presently Lionheart Newspapers, LLC.[8]

The Brooklyn Park Sentinel

In 1956 Al and Orlyn Joyner believed that the local news in Brooklyn Park was not being adequately represented to the people by the media in Brooklyn Park, so they founded *The Brooklyn Park Sentinel*. At the time, the Minneapolis newspaper had a metro section, which featured local community news. Orlyn said, "It was two plus years of hard work; as an economic venture it was premature, but it was a successful venture in readership and was the legal newspaper in Brooklyn Park." After operating the newspaper for over two years, the paper was sold, and two years later it was sold again and became the *Post Sentinel* and then the *Post* again, now the *Brooklyn Park SunPost*.[9]

Post Publishing Company on Corvallis.

NorthWest News

NorthWest News began publishing 39,000 newspapers weekly on April 2, 1990 and produced six issues in six weeks. In September 1990, the free distribution newspaper for Brooklyn Park and Brooklyn Center resumed publication on a bi-monthly schedule. The newspaper was started by four Brooklyn Park residents, Pat Milton, Roxana Benjamin, Kathleen Pierce and Val Iverson.

Mary Jane Gustafson, the former "first lady of news" for Brooklyn Center, was a feature writer and mentor for the newspaper until her death in late 1990. The newspaper published for nearly five years. Much to the communities' sorrow, the main investors closed *NorthWest News* for tax purposes in February 1995.

For a short time, our communities enjoyed what most never have: the benefit of three papers for their reading enjoyment. When asked if they would ever start another newspaper, Milton and Benjamin replied, "We have learned to never say never."[10]

Political Pages

In the 1990s local Senate District 47 Republican leaders felt that existing media did not adequately provide information on party activities and candidates, so in election years they published free distribution tabloid newspapers called *Political Pages* to inform local residents.[11]

Northwest Community Television

In 1982 Storer Cable was granted the franchise for nine northwest suburbs, including Brooklyn Center and Brooklyn Park. Northwest Suburbs Community Access Corporation was formed as a nonprofit corporation to serve the nine suburbs. A studio was opened at the Northbrook Shopping Center in Brooklyn Center and the first workshop was for a senior citizens group. In 1982 there were ten channels for community programming; in 2000 there are five. In 1983 Brooklyn Park and New Hope studios opened. The New Hope studio was closed in 1998.

In 1986 Northwest Community Television moved to a new building at 6900 Winnetka Avenue in Brooklyn Park. In 1998, their Internet web site went online, and on March 1, 1999, the new public access center opened.

Channel 35 started in 1990 with local community news and information, and programming was scheduled 24 hours a day on Channels 32 through 37. In 1994, Channels 32 through 37 were moved to Channel 12 and Channels 34 through 37 and "News 35 Northwest" were renamed "Cable 12 News." In 1996 "Community Journal" debuted, receiving national "Hometown Award for Best Newscast" that year, and a live morning news program began. In 1997 an evening newscast debuted, along with a weekly sports show called "SportsJam." Also in 1997 Northwest Community Television received a "Hometown Video Festival Award for Best Local Election Coverage."

From 1982 through 1999, Northwest Community Television trained 6,000 area residents in the use of television production equipment and over 27,000 programs were produced.   *Information submitted by Northwest Community Television*

Notes

1. "Way Back in 1898 Sun Was First Paper In Brooklyn Center," by Nancy Fellger, *Brooklyn Center/Brooklyn Park Sun*, Wednesday, July 22, 1970; See also "William Knight" in Brooklyn Families chapter of this book.

2. Lauri Winters, manuscript titled "History of *Sun-Post* Newspapers," 1999, in BHS files. "*BC Post* begins 20th year today", *The Brooklyn Center Post*, 16 February 1976. "A 15-year love affair — the *Post* and BC," *The Brooklyn Center Post*, column by Mary Jane Gustafson, 13 February 1975.

3. Ibid.

4. Ibid.

5. Ibid.

6. Ibid.

7. Ibid.

8. Wilma Schultz and Carol Larson, 1999 telephone interviews regarding *Osseo Review/Osseo Press/Osseo-Maple Grove Press*, summary in BHS files.

9. Orlyn Joyner, oral history interview by Bill Schreiber, 23 August 1999, in BHS files.

10. Pat Milton and Roxana Benjamin, "The Never-Say-Never Newspaper," 16 March 2000, manuscript in BHS files.

11. "Republicans in the Brooklyns," in Organizations chapter of this book.

12. Newspaper microfilm cataloged at Brookdale/Hennepin Area Library:
North Hennepin Post, August 1950-May 1967 and January 1968–December 1988
NorthWest News, April 2, 1990–December 21, 1992 and January 25, 1993–June 20, 1994
Robbinsdale Post, 1939–1950
Robbinsdale Times, March 1912–August 1912
Osseo Review, March 1906–February 1918
Osseo Press, November 1923–February 1966
Osseo/Maple Grove Press, February 1966–December 1992 and January 1993–present
Brooklyn Center Press, August 1957–April 1966
Brooklyn Center Post, April 1966–January 1989
Brooklyn Center Post News, January 1989–July 1991
Brooklyn Center SunPost, July 1991–present
Brooklyn Park Sentinel, November 1963–February 1967
Brooklyn Park Post, March 1966–December 1967
Brooklyn Park Post Sentinel, January 1968–December 1971
Brooklyn Park Post, January 1972–1989
Brooklyn Park Post News, January 1989–July 1991
Brooklyn Park SunPost, 1991–2000

Growing Potatoes in Brooklyn Park

by Norene A. Roberts

SINCE 1965 the potato has been celebrated each summer in Brooklyn Park at the city's annual Tater Daze festival. Little wonder—the potato was a major agricultural product in Brooklyn Park and the area around Osseo for 111 years.

A 1937 article described Minnesota as having three major potato growing regions: the Sandland area, the Hollandale district in Freeborn County, and the Red River Valley region. The Sandland area, north of the Twin Cities, was defined as a concentration of potato production in Hennepin, Ramsey, Anoka, Isanti, Chisago, and Washington counties. As in other parts of this area, Brooklyn Park had the right combination of temperature and light sandy soils with good drainage and rainfall to grow excellent crops of potatoes. And, although potatoes are no longer grown in the city, the area is still remembered in two potato varieties developed at the University of Minnesota: the Osseo (1954) and the Anoka (1965).[1, 2]

The Rails Reach Osseo

Successful commercial potato production in northern Hennepin County began after the construction of the St. Paul, Minneapolis and Manitoba Railroad, which reached Osseo in 1881. This line was later taken over by James J. Hill and renamed the "Great Northern." After 1900 long lines of farmers and wagons loaded with potatoes were commonly seen in late summer along the main street in Osseo, where the crop was weighed, bought, and shipped out by rail.

Like other parts of Hennepin County, the potato-growing area was initially settled in the early and mid-1850s, attracting many German and ethnic German Swiss families. Early settlers grew wheat, Indian corn, oats, barley, and hay and practiced mixed farming. By 1900, northern Hennepin County was known for its many potato farms. And, while mixed farming, including dairying, was always practiced on Hennepin County Farms, after 1900 the concentration of potato production north of the Twin Cities around Osseo made that area famous for its potatoes.

Osseo was the potato-marketing center of Hennepin County. It had through rail facilities and a depot close to the potato farms. To get the potatoes to market, families such as the Tessmans of Brooklyn Park dug them up with pitch-forks. Alice Tessman's father Edmund could flick the fork deftly with his wrist, popping the potatoes to the surface. Once the potatoes were out of the ground, the entire family and the hired hands picked them up and loaded them into bushel baskets for the trip to Osseo.

At the turn of the century, the Tessmans drove potatoes by horse and wagon to the Minneapolis Farmers' Market via Osseo Road (now Brooklyn Boulevard). At the market they sold their potatoes from booths. Most of their crop, however, went to

Loading potatoes on the Earle Brown farm, cica 1905
Minnesota Historical Society

the Osseo potato market. They also delivered potatoes, eggs, butter, and wheat to local markets and to neighbors. Potatoes brought to Osseo came in by wagonloads in bushel baskets to be weighed at the scales in front of the International Hotel, where most of the buying and selling occurred. The buyers sent bulk shipments out by rail immediately because neither the farmers nor the buyers had local storage facilities.[3]

Feeding Sheep in the Off-season

Raising sheep provided a collateral industry for growing potatoes in Brooklyn Park and the Osseo area. By the turn of the century, the area had established a pattern of raising potatoes during the growing seasons and feeding sheep through the winters. Sheep provided "free" fertilizer that was spread on the fields in the spring before seed potatoes were planted. This cheap soil amendment involved labor rather than a large cash outlay. The sheep were shipped from Montana by rail to Osseo in the late fall. Osseo residents became accustomed to the lines of potato wagons giving way to herds of sheep being driven down the streets of the town after the crop was in. Before there were good roads and trucks, driving sheep through the streets was the most practical way to move them from one place to another.

Sheep at the Edmund Tessman farm, 1932
Alice Tessman

The sheep were sometimes owned by others and simply "boarded" with area potato farmers for the winter "when the families were less busy farming," according to Alice Tessman. Screenings (hulls from wheat, or rye grain) were shipped by sheep-owners to Osseo, where the farmers would pick them up. At the end of the 1906 year, 140 rail cars of screenings were unloaded at Osseo to feed the animals over the winter. Often the feed was hay and grain.[4,5]

The sheep industry around Osseo began in 1893 when a local man, Edward Egan, bought 100 native sheep from a farmer north of Anoka. He fed them screenings during the winter, for which he paid four to seven dollars a ton. He lost money the first year but persisted anyway. The next year, he took on a partner and brought 1,000 sheep from Miles City, Montana. Word spread, and by 1899 sheep-feeding was practiced by many farmers in northern Hennepin County.[6]

In 1907, some 25,000 sheep were being fed each winter by twenty-eight farmers living principally in Brooklyn Park. An average lamb arrived weighing between 65 and 70 pounds and was shipped out in the spring weighing 100 to 105 pounds. During the 1930s, Aaron Tessman trucked sheep to the stockyards in South St. Paul at the end of the winter for sale and slaughter. Before roads and trucks were improved, however, the sheep were simply herded back to Osseo for shipment by rail.[7]

According to Alice Tessman, her family never ate mutton: "Didn't care for it much." She also remembers taking care of lambs inside the family farmhouse when they needed care they could not get in the herd.[8]

The 1910s and 1920s

Between the coming of the railroad in 1881 and World War I, the potato industry was oriented exclusively to the rails and to Osseo. There was no refrigeration, so potatoes had to go to market promptly to minimize losses from spoilage. The potato farmers of Brooklyn Park hauled their crop to the scales at Osseo, sold to the buyers who stayed in Osseo hotels, and loaded the produce on rail cars. This was the quickest, most profitable way to market. The farmers tolerated the long lines waiting at the scales so they could sell their potatoes as soon after they were dug as possible. The higher moisture content of freshly dug potatoes made them heavier, and thus worth more when they were weighed. As the potatoes dried out, they lost value.

By 1912 the *Osseo Review* boasted that the city had "become known far and wide as the potato center of the state." The potatoes grown in Brooklyn Park made a signifi-cant contribution to Osseo's fame. During the 1912 harvest season, the Osseo potato market opened on July 22. In the first twenty-one days, seventeen buyers stayed at the Osseo hotels as the harvest arrived at the scales. Between July 22 and August 15, 1,821 wag-onloads of potatoes were brought into the city and shipped out in bulk in 410 rail cars. At this time, a single rail car normally held 400 to 500 bushels of potatoes. The total harvest that year was much higher because the market lasted until the last potatoes came in early in October.[9]

By the mid-teens and throughout World War I, Osseo potatoes were in high demand, and the city of Osseo became the largest potato-shipping point in the United States. Sometime after 1914, the scales that had stood in front of the International Hotel in Osseo were moved. Loads of potatoes were then brought to the Osseo Elevator for weighing and shipping. The rails took potatoes to distant points, where they were packaged and forwarded to various destinations.[10]

Baskets of potatoes being loaded on boxcar, Osseo, cica 1925
Minnesota Historical Society

As early as 1920, some of the Osseo buyers began to use a mechanical grader to separate potatoes into batches of similar size. The grader was mounted on a truck that could be moved from one rail car to the next during loading. This preprocessing saved a step for the bagging operation farther along the rails."[11]

Local growers often bought seed potatoes at a reasonable price in the Red River Valley in the early fall. Fields were fertilized in the fall or spring and late potatoes were harvested generally between mid-to-late July and early October. As the potato market continued to expand during the 1920s and early 1930s, as many as 20 to 25 buyers would arrive in Osseo, sometimes making bids on the spot in the middle of the street.[12]

Beginning in the mid-1920s, improved trucks and roads began the slow decline of the railroad-based market system in Osseo. Improvements in farm technology also made potato-growing easier. Farm families were happy to give up the digging pitch-fork in the 1920s. The Edmund Tessman family bought a single-row digger, pulled by two horses in 1920. This mechanical digger had a Cushman engine run by gasoline (a great improvement over picking potatoes by hand digging with a fork). The Tessmans also switched from wagons to trucks in 1921, greatly reducing the amount of time it rook to transport the crop from the fields.[13]

The Tessman's single-row digger was replaced by a double-row digger, pulled by four horses. Still, the potatoes had to be picked up and loaded into baskets. Calvin Gray recalls that after his father began to grow potatoes in Brooklyn Park in 1929, it was a child's job to walk behind the potato digger, pulled by the tractor his father drove, and to put the newly dug potatoes into bushel baskets by hand.[14]

The 1930s

In the Sandland Area, potato production peaked in 1931, when 96,500 acres were planted in potatoes, producing over 7,000,000 bushels. Hennepin County had 17,923 acres, 1.26 million bushels, planted in potatoes, of which Brooklyn Township, the area that is now Brooklyn Park, grew 4,678 acres, 38 percent of the potatoes grown in the county.[15, 16]

Harvesting potatoes at Edmund Tessman farm, Brooklyn Park
Alice P. Tessman

Popular varieties of potatoes included the Early Ohio, Rural New Yorkers, followed by Bliss Triumphs, Irish Cobblers, and Burbank Russets. During the drought that plagued the 1930s, the Early Ohio, long a favorite with area farmers, became distorted in shape. Its poor appearance caused it to be replaced by the other varieties. Under the direction of potato breeder and faculty member Fred A. Krantz, the University of Minnesota's Horticulture Department developed the Warba in 1933 and a red-skinned Warba in 1939. The Warba was a high-quality potato with deep eyes, but it never became a favorite with area farmers because they thought it "ugly."[17, 18]

Several factors put an end to the busy summer street scenes in Osseo by the close of the 1930s. Drought caused yield-per-acre to drop. Some farmers switched to other crops and other family farms in the area went bankrupt. But many Brooklyn Park farmers continued in the potato business until suburban development finally forced them to quit. Most of these hold-out farms were located north of 85th Avenue North where, until the past ten years, the city of Brooklyn Park remained substantially rural.[19]

With the increasing reliance on trucks, the railroad and depot in Osseo became less important, and the Osseo potato market collapsed.

While the drought caused hardship in the 1930s, electricity and irrigation made life easier for those local growers who continued raising potatoes. Although Edmund Tessman electrified his farmhouse in 1920 with a battery-run generator, many farm chores were still done by hand. In 1931 Northern States Power Company put the "high line" (power line poles) through the area. By the end of the 1930s, area farms could run pumps for potato-washing operations, and those who survived the drought could pump water to their fields.[20]

The Irrigation Era

The advent of irrigation made it possible for many area farmers to remain in business during and after the 1930s. Irrigating potatoes began as a response to severe drought in the early 1930s, but continued until the last farmer, Calvin Gray, gave up growing potatoes in Brooklyn Park in 1992. Edward "Sandy" Arnlund was the first to irrigate potatoes in what is now Brooklyn Park, in 1934-35. His farm was east of Brooklyn Boulevard, just south of Zane Avenue North, about where a Dunkin' Donuts stands today.

By 1936 Aaron Tessman had fifty-five of his eighty acres under irrigation on his farm along the banks of Shingle Creek at 7826 Osseo Road. He began to phase out asparagus, watermelons, muskmelons, and onions when he saw the benefits of irrigating potatoes. Tessman's initial investment was a (then-staggering) figure of $4,300. The money went into motors, pumps, pipes, wiring, and a half-mile of poles and water lines. Gas, oil, and electricity cost him $200 per month. Nonetheless. in 1936, he estimated that his forty acres of potatoes would yield 200 bushels per acre, a fourfold increase over non-irrigated fields. Soon, most area farmers took up the practice.[21]

In 1937 Edmund Tessman dug a water hole a quarter-mile north of his farmhouse at 6716 85th Avenue North and installed a gasoline motor to pump the water. Other farmers used point wells, or shallow wells, from which water was pumped by gasoline engines to the potato fields.[22]

In 1935 the Edmund Tessman family had bought new and larger trucks, which altered the way they bagged, sold, and transported their potatoes. Next door, Albert Tessman started to use tractors, rather than horses, but he kept the animals around as a novelty until 1938.[23]

While much of the potato-growing equipment of the 1930s has been replaced, there are some survivals from its companion industry (sheep-feeding). Eldon Tessman's farm still has a ca. 1936 screening house that was used for feeding sheep when they overwintered on the farm. It is a small structure, only 12 by 24 feet, with two 8- by 2-foot "screening" doors on one side. These doors were used to pour the screenings into the building. This farm also has a 30- by 120-foot sheep shed, built in 1936 of tamarack poles for $600. It is a shed roof building, enclosed on the west, north, and east, but open on the south where the sheep were sheltered during the winter.[14]

The 1940s

Despite the drought of the 1930s, in 1941, Brooklyn Township, most of which is now Brooklyn Park, produced thirty-seven percent of the potatoes grown in Hennepin County. The farmers benefited from improvements in potato breeding during this time. The Pontiac variety, developed in Michigan, was introduced during the early 1940s. It replaced some of the earlier varieties because it was winter-hardy.[25,26]

Of material benefit to the families growing potatoes commercially in the 1940s was a mechanical potato harvester developed in Minnesota by Peter Dahlman of Grandy. Located east of Highway 65 and north of Cambridge in Isanti County, Grandy is considered part of the Sandland area. Dahlman opened a factory in nearby Braham to manufacture his machines. Aaron Tessman of Brooklyn Park helped finance development and distribution of the Dahlman harvester, and eventually had dealerships in Minnesota and Hastings, Florida. The Edmund Tessman farm bought a Dahlman harvester around 1949. As it became popular, the Dahlman harvester was used by Minnesota–growers in all three major potato-producing areas, as well as in other states from Maine to Florida.[27]

In the 1940s many Brooklyn Park potato farmers became their own marketing and distribution centers. Eldon Tessman converted the large English-style, side-gabled wheat barn, built ca. 1882-1886 by his great-grandfather August, into a potato-processing and storage facility in 1940.

Originally, the barn was divided into three sections—the end bays stored grain and hay and the middle section was a wagon run. After the conversion to potatoes, one end-section of the barn was used for unloading, washing, grading, weighing, and packaging potatoes, which then were stored on wooden racks in both end-sections of the barn. The racks held the potatoes off the floor and allowed for ventilation around the bags until they were shipped. In the center section trucks came in for loading.

From 1940 the processing that had been done somewhere else along a rail line took place on the Tessman farm itself. Potatoes were sized under a canopy built in 1940

Elfreda and Clifford Petersen loading potatoes on parent's farm
Earl Simons

outside the barn. Next they were put through a washer and sponge dryer located in an open doorway. They were then brought inside, where they went to a picking table to be graded into batches of similar quality. Next they were sent to an electric dryer, a packaging table, and then to two scales. At the end of this process, the bags, weighing from 10 to 100 pounds, were stored on wooden floor racks.[28]

Growing Potatoes in the Suburbs, 1950-1992

In 1954 Brooklyn Park became a village, and developers started to build along West Broadway north of Crystal. Soon, the village began to fill with new homes south of 85th Avenue North. With the economic boom that followed World War II added to on-farm processing and better trucks, the potato farmers of Brooklyn Park sold into a more varied market. The rise of the supermarket provided new outlets to go along with the traditional farmers' markets.

Between 1950 and 1976. Eldon Tessman sold part of his potato crop locally to Red Owl and some to Northwest Produce in northern Minnesota and Canada. He also shipped south to Des Moines, Iowa, and as far away as Schmeiding's, a distributor in Arkansas. His cousins, Raymond and Alice Tessman, sold part of their crop to Applebaum's, but Raymond also delivered potatoes to St. Paul. After World War II, Brooklyn Park potato-growers sent trainloads of potatoes to the Fleming Company in Topeka, Kansas, in 100 pound sacks in as many as twenty semi-trailer-loads at a time.[29] Another Brooklyn Park grower, Wilbur Goetze, sold his potatoes to chain stores and wholesale distributors and individuals, who sent them throughout the Midwest, the southern United States, and Canada.[30]

The food processors also needed potatoes. In the mid-1960s, Goetze notes that "the vast majority of potato chips sold in the Minneapolis area from mid-July to October [were] from potatoes grown in this area.[31]

When the Tater Daze celebrations began in 1965, there were at least five families in Brooklyn Park who had been growing potatoes for four generations; two lines of the Schreiber family, the Gray family, the Goetze family, and the Tessman family. In that year, Brooklyn Park was only about 15 percent developed. and the population was around 15,000. A short five years later, in 1970, the city's population had doubled to 30,000, but the number of active potato-growers in the city had fallen 50 percent, from around 50 growers in 1965 to around 25 in 1970.[32]

Eventually, potato farmers in Brooklyn Park quit for the same reasons they had in Brooklyn Center to the south: suburban development. Eldon Tessman, who still lives with his family in his great-grandfather's 1883 farmhouse, retired from potato farming in 1976, citing the danger of pulling onto the road and out of his fields as development encroached. In 1992, when Calvin Gray gave up potato farming, development pressures had also reached his farm at West Broadway and 87th. Gray described the traffic at his door as "ridiculous," but development pressures and the construction of water and sewer lines in northern Brooklyn Park were even more telling. The property taxes for these "improvements" made a 175 acre farm like Gray's far too expensive to be profitable.[33]

The potato era in Brooklyn Park ended in the fall of 1992 when Calvin Gray, the last commercial potato-grower in the city, gave up raising red and white russets on his Brooklyn Park farm. "It's progress, I guess," he commented.[34]

Hauling potatoes to market, circa 1925. Left: Raymond Tessman; Right: George Setzler
Alice Tessman

Members of the August Tessman family have lived in Brooklyn Park since 1870. They have seen the entire spectrum of changes in potato growing, production, and marketing in the area. Most of the photographs and much of the information for this article came from Alice P. Tessman, whose father, Edmund, built the 1897 house in which she lives today. She is a granddaughter of August Tessman. Eldon Tessman is a great-grandson of August Tessman. He and Alice live next door to each other on 85th Avenue North. Information from Alice Tessman is taken from an oral history project commissioned by the North Hennepin Community College Foundation.[35]

Notes

1. Asbjorn Fause and George S. Corfield. "The Potato Industry in Minnesota," *Economic Geography*, (October 1937): 395-97.

2. Leon Snyder, *History of the Department of Horticultural Science and Landscape Architecture, 1849-1982* (St. Paul: University of Minnesota, 1982), 24.

3, Harvey H. Goetze, in "Brooklyn Park's History of Growing Commercial Potatoes," Official Program, Brooklyn Park Tater Daze, Brooklyn Park: N.P., 1965, 15.

4. Alice P. and Eldon Tessman interview with the author, 14 June 1994.

5. Ibid.; "Sheep Industry Growing Rapidly," *The Osseo Review*, 16 January 1907, 1.

6. "Sheep Industry Growing Rapidly," 1.

7. Ibid.; Alice P. Tessman interview, 14 June 1994.

8. Alice P. and Eldon Tessman interview.

9. "Osseo-Home of the Early Ohio Potato," The Osseo Review, 15 August 1912, 1.

10. Alice P. Tessman interview; Osseo Lionelles and North Hennepin Pioneer Society, *100 Year History of the City of Osseo, Minneapolis*: Merit Printing, 1975, 8.

11. Harvey Goetze, in "Brooklyn Park's History of Growing Commercial Potatoes," 15.

12. Ibid.; Wilbur Goetze, in "Potato Growing in Brooklyn Park," Official Program, Brooklyn Park Tater Daze, Brooklyn Park: N.P., 1965, 14.

13. Alice P. and Eldon Tessman interview.

14. Patt Ligman, "End of an Era: Last Potato Farmer Quits," *Brooklyn Park Post*. 18 November 1992.

15. Fause and Cornfield, "The Potato Industry in Minnesota," 396.

16. Department of Agriculture, State Farm Census Bulletin, 1931, township summaries, State Archives, Minnesota Historical Society.

17. Fause and Cornfield, "The Potato Industry in Minnesota," 396; Eldon Tessman interview, 1991.

18. Eldon Tessman interview; Snyder, *History of the Department of Horticultural Science and Landscape Architecture*. 1849-1984, 24.

19. Harvey Goetze, in "Brooklyn Park's History of Growing Commercial Potatoes," 15.

20. Alice P. and Eldon Tessman interview.

21. "Aaron Tessman Has Largest Water System in County," *North Hennepin Post*, Robbinsdale Anniversary, Section D, 25 October 1962 (reprinted from *Hennepin County Enterprise*, 20 August 1936; Eldon Tessman interview.

22. Alice P. and Eldon Tessman interview.

23. Ibid.; Harvey Goetze, "Brooklyn Park's History of Growing Commercial Potatoes," 15.

24. Eldon Tessman interview.

25. Department of Agriculture, State Farm Census Bulletin, 1941, township summaries, State Archives, Minnesota Historical Society.

26. Eldon Tessman interview.

27. Alice P. and Eldon Tessman interview.

28. Eldon Tessman interview.

29. Alice P. and Eldon Tessman interview.

30. Wilbur Goetze, in "Potato Growing in Brooklyn Park," 14.

31. Ibid.

32. Harvey Goetze. in "Brooklyn Park's History of Growing Commercial Potatoes," 15; Stan Maslowski, "Life on Growing Edge: City Status Reflected in Disappearing Farms," *Brooklyn Center Brooklyn Park Sun*, 20 May 1970, 1.

33. Ibid.; 35. Ligman. "End of an Era; Last Potato Farmer Quits," 1.

34. Ibid.

35. Alice P. Tessman, "August and Henrietta Hartkopf Tessman Family History," unpublished typescript, 25 June 1983.

Presentation of a potato planter. Left to right: Vern Ausen, Jim Tuzinski, Mary Jane Gustafson, Warren Lindquist

Chapter Eleven

TRANSPORTATION

Native American Travel Routes

During the 19th century there were no Native American settlements in what is now Brooklyn Township because this area of northern Hennepin County was contested by the Dakota and Ojibwe and was not safe for settlement by either tribe. However, historic accounts mention Indians passing north and south through the area. Thus, the earliest land transportation routes in northern Hennepin County were trails and paths used by the Native Americans. Few were ever mapped.

According to Sig Edling, a truck farmer in Brooklyn Center, the route of present day Brooklyn Boulevard was originally known as "Indian Trail" because it followed an old trail on high ground.[1]

Another well-travelled north-south path, used by both Dakota and Ojibwe, followed the west bank of the Mississippi River. Several independent fur traders in the area traded with the Ojibwe from northern Minnesota. One of the independents, Benjamin F. Baker, had a small string of posts, most of them among the Ojibwe farther up the Mississippi. Baker's main camp was about a mile north of Ft. Snelling on the west side of the Mississippi. Anecdotal reminiscences from early settlers of Brooklyn Park during the 1850s mention the travels of Ojibwe down the west side of the river, a movement that probably was reinforced when the Ojibwe began trading at Baker's post in the 1830s.[2]

Earliest Roads in Brooklyn Township

The three most important early roads through Brooklyn Township in the 1850s settlement period were those known during most of the 20th century as West River Road, Osseo Road and West Broadway. Early maps and narratives used assorted names for these roads. West River Road was sometimes called "Mississippi and Crow River Road" or "Minneapolis Champlin Dayton Road;" Osseo Road was called "Middle Road;" and West Broadway was called "Robbinsdale Road," "Crystal Lake Road," or even "Osseo Road" on the pre-1910 P.M. Dahl Road Map.[3]

The Dahl map also clearly shows the northern portion of Crystal Lake Township, four sections of which are now in southern Brooklyn Center. Bass Lake Road (County Road 10) was an important east-west road through sections 3-6.[4]

The Mississippi and Crow River Road began in the Camden area of North Minneapolis. It roughly followed Lyndale Avenue through Brooklyn Center and West River Road through Brooklyn Park. It continued up the west side of the Mississippi River to a point across from the City of Anoka, crossed Elm Creek at Champlin, and headed northwest to a point near where the Crow River empties into the Mississippi.[5]

A second early road, recorded by government surveyors in 1853, roughly corresponded to Osseo Road, and led from Minneapolis through Bottineau Prairie, then to present-day Osseo. Originally, Osseo Road turned north toward 85th Avenue at what is now the corner of Zane Avenue and Brooklyn Boulevard, then headed west.[6]

West Broadway in southwest Brooklyn Township leading into Osseo also was an early north-south route. West Broadway was sometimes referred to as the Robbinsdale Road or the Crystal Lake Road, and the portion between Robbinsdale and Champlin became known as Jefferson Highway before 1920.[7]

Early Governmental Involvement

The first roads built in what is now Minnesota were government military roads. However, funding was fitful and uncertain for road surveys and construction. In the early 1850s the Territory of Minnesota turned to its own coffers to provide monies for road construction, but never expensed more than a few hundred dollars for all roads in the territory. Pre-territorial routes in Minnesota (before 1849) did not include the West River Road through Brooklyn Center and Brooklyn Park. As early as the late 1840s or early 1850s, a path or unimproved road along the west bank of the Mississippi River may have been used occasionally as a tote road by early lumbermen traveling between St. Anthony and the mouth of the Rum River.[8]

What is now West River Road was surveyed in April 1855 by Campbell Beall. The River Road surveyed by Beall may have been one of the 38 roads authorized by the Territorial Legislature to meet the demand for roads as new settlers poured into the territory. The Trygg map, recording the Brooklyn Park area at the time of the original government land surveys between 1853-55, shows West River Road as the "Minneapolis and Crow River Road."[9]

The early 1850s were the boom years of first settlement and settlers found virtually all the roads in the territory in pitiful condition. In 1856, the Territorial Legislature of Minnesota asked Congress for an appropriation to build a road west of the Mississippi River from Fort Snelling to Pembina in the Red River Valley. Congress did not specifically grant a road appropriation, but did find money for the removal of timber along the Red River road from old Crow Wing (now in Wadena County) and the Red River.[10]

By the mid-1850s Minnesota's counties assumed the greater portion of the expense of laying out and constructing roads. Almost immediately after Brooklyn Township was organized in May 1858, the township supervisors began to address the crucial need for roads. The first road petition by the supervisors was for a road west from the river toward the mouth of Bass Lake Creek and then to the township line near Eagle Lake Creek (today's 69th Avenue). This petition was dated July 15, 1867 and referred to West River Road as "the state road leading from Minneapolis to the Crow River." The second road petition, signed July 17, 1867, was for a road running east on the boundary between sections 4 and 9 in northern Brooklyn Park and connecting "to the river road near the town site of Harrisburg." The fourth road was petitioned to run south from 69th through the east half of Section 35 which became the John Martin farm and later that of his grandson, Earle Brown. This road became known as a portion of the "Hopper Road," and it followed present day Logan and Humboldt Avenues North.[11]

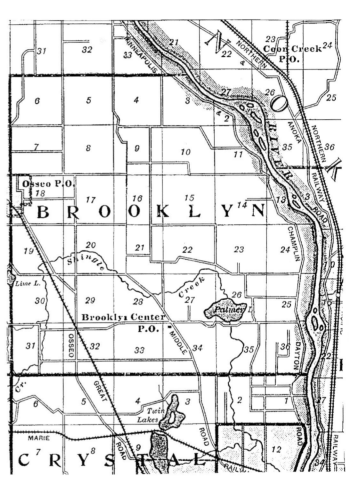

Pre-1910 Road Map by P. M. Dahl. Note Osseo Road, Middle Road, and Minneapolis-Champlin-Dayton Road

The Camden-Anoka Stage Line

One of the first houses built on the river road is still standing at 8540 West River Road. It is the Andrew Rixon House, built between 1859-1865, and sold in 1872 or 1873 to Andrew Mattson, a Swedish immigrant. Mattson opened the house to the public as a halfway house on the Camden-Anoka stage line in 1874 and put a sign over the front door reading "Half-Way House," presumably because it was halfway between Minneapolis and Anoka or Champlin. It continued until 1912 as a stopover place for passengers to stretch and horses to be watered. The stage stop in Anoka was at Bridge Square, and it took over three hours to make a one-way trip. The stage is said to have carried newspapers as well as passengers.[12]

Later History of West River Road

After 1910 automobiles began to travel along West River Road, although people in Brooklyn Township began to buy cars as early as 1908. Because the hauling of material for construction of the Coon Rapids Dam in 1913 had worsened the condition of West River Road, a West River Road Improvement Association was formed. Members of the Association, made up of local farmers, graded, rolled and oiled the road and constructed a community center, which they named "Riverlyn," later known as "Kixx's" and "Rum Runners."[13]

The Minnesota highway system was established in 1920. West River Road became County Road 12 (a state aid road) in 1926. In 1936, it was designated US 169. In 1959 it was designated the "National Route, Great River Road." In 1988, Congress created the Mississippi National River and Recreation Area, administered by the National Park Service. West River Road through Brooklyn Park now lies wholly within the new recreation area.[14]

Evolution of the Modern Transportation System

Pre-1950

The primary method of transportation that evolved in Brooklyn Center/Brooklyn Park after about 1910 was the automobile and/or truck. At certain contract stops, Greyhound buses dropped off and picked up passengers coming from or going to the city of Minneapolis. The Mineapolis streetcar line terminated at 42nd and Washington Avenue North in Camden, eleven blocks south of Brooklyn Center. Thomas H. Girling, a Robbinsdale newspaperman, who also served on Robbinsdale's city council and was its second mayor, started the first bus line into Robbinsdale from the Radisson Hotel in Minneapolis with a route extension into Anoka.[15]

The main roads in this time period were Lyndale Avenue, which paralleled the Mississippi River through Brooklyn Center (Old US 169), Osseo Road, a north/south roadway about two miles west of the Mississippi River, West Broadway in southwest Brooklyn Township, and Highway 100, which cut through Brooklyn Center diagonally, southwest to northeast. The few main east/west roadways all were county roads.

Post-1950

With the development of the suburbs after World War II and the National Highway Act during the Eisenhower Administration in the 1950s, freeways started to edge their way towards Brooklyn Center.

For many years Highway 100, a segment of which still runs through Brooklyn Center, was the beltway perimeter road circling Minneapolis and St. Paul. The north and east segments of Highway 100 were replaced by I-694, and the south segment by I-494. However, the west segment of Highway 100 remains today because the west segment of I-494/694 was located approximately 6-8 miles west of Highway 100. In the early 1960s, I-94 came from Hudson, Wisconsin, went westward through downtown St. Paul, on through downtown Minneapolis and up as far as Plymouth Avenue North in Minneapolis. Construction of I-94 stalled there for many years.

The I-94/I-694 route in Brooklyn Center is slightly confusing because there were two major construction phases. The first being in 1964-65, and the second in 1980-82. The 1964 construction was the east/west construction of I-694 through Brooklyn Center, while the 1980 reconstruction made changes to several I-694 interchanges when the I-94 link from downtown Minneapolis was finally completed. Since late 1982, the east/west freeway segment through Brooklyn Center is actually both I-94 and I-694, while the north/south segment of freeway in Brooklyn Center is I-94, connecting to downtown Minneapolis and St. Paul.

Construction of I-694 *Cuts Through the Heart of Brooklyn Center*

The 1964 construction of the first interstate highway through Brooklyn Center split the Village practically through the middle. It had a major impact on neighborhoods, and especially school districts, because Brooklyn Center is a small community of only 8½ square miles that was already dealing with the issue of being split among four school districts. Because the I-694 project was such a disruptive event, Mayor Gordon Erickson mailed a detailed Highway Improvement Report to every resident.[16]

Connecting *I-94 in Minneapolis to I-694 in Brooklyn Center*

In the early 1970s plans were unveiled to connect I-94 from Plymouth Avenue North in Minneapolis to I-694 in Brooklyn Center. Much of the right-of-way along old Lyndale Avenue had been purchased, cleared and taken off the tax-rolls several years earlier, working a hardship on the city and school district. A construction bottleneck developed when the Minneapolis Park Board refused to give up so-called "park land" in the Camden area, near the Mississippi River. And, according to federal law, there was no way that the Interstate Highway could be built on the "park land" unless the Park Board approved its taking for highway purposes.[17]

However, an eventual political power play by Minneapolis Mayor Al Hofstede, Council President and 5th Ward Alderman Lou DeMars and 3rd Ward Alderman Joseph Strauss threatened to cut off parks financing. The Park Board saw the wisdom of approving the plan for I-94 to go through the "park land," which was marginal at best for park development.[18]

The construction plans for I-94 and I-694 were brought before the Brooklyn Center City Council for preliminary review and conceptual design approval, and were adopted. After the Council held informational meetings and public hearings, it gave final approval for construction. This segment of I-94, the final missing link between the east coast and Montana, was finally completed and opened for traffic in the late fall of 1982.[19]

November 1982 opening of I-94 connection to I-694

Old Highway 100/Dupont Avenue Bridge

In the early 1960s Old Highway 100 was re-routed north to link with I-694, leaving abandoned right-of-way which eventually became the site of the "Crossing at Brookwood" housing development southeast of Highway 100.

During the same time, School District #286 was developing the site between 65th and 67th Avenues and Dupont and Humboldt Avenues for the new Brooklyn Center High School. It became evident that a bridge was needed to provide access to the school from the area south of Highway 100 and I-694. After months of unsuccessful negotiations with the Minnesota Highway Department, State Senator Richard Parish arranged a meeting with newly elected Governor Elmer L. Anderson for the School District officials to present their case. Within a few days after the meeting, Governor Anderson announced that the Highway Department would build a Dupont Avenue bridge as part of the I-694 project to replace Highway 100 to the east. That caused great concern among the residents living on Dupont Avenue south of the proposed bridge. In defense of the residents south of the bridge down to 57th Avenue, Dupont did become a raceway that still today has to be constantly patrolled for speeders.[20]

Bridges at Shingle Creek Parkway and John Martin Drive

The development of I-94, along with the sale of the Earle Brown Farm by the University of Minnesota, opened the Farm for commercial and industrial development. This development required better access to the businesses moving in. Therefore, a bridge over I-94/694 at Shingle Creek and a bridge over Highway 100 at John Martin Drive were installed as part of the I-694/94 construction project in 1980. In conjunction with the installation of the Shingle Creek Boulevard interchange, the I-694 interchange at Xerxes was eliminated for safety reasons, while the freeway overpass at Xerxes Avenue was left in place.[21]

Metropolitan Transit Commission

In the mid-1970s Brooklyn Center asked the Metropolitan Transit Commission (MTC) to help subsidize a "Brooklyn Center Circulator Bus Route" within the community to provide transportation for low-income and elderly residents. This was started, but after several months the needed subsidy kept increasing while ridership was limited. With the subsidy nearing four dollars per rider, it was felt that cabs could provide a better service and the program was terminated.

Also in the 1970s, the MTC was looking for a site in the northern suburbs to build a badly needed bus garage. They were turned down by cities east of the river. After pleading with Brooklyn Center officials, the city agreed that it was good public policy to have the site located in Brooklyn Center, thinking that it also would bring better public transit service to Brooklyn Center and the northern suburbs.

At the same time, Brooklyn Center was concerned about the loss of tax-base, as other facilities owned by the MTC were tax exempt. The MTC then agreed to have the facility built and owned by a private party, who would then lease it to the MTC, thereby alleviating the loss of tax revenue. This promise lasted for just a few years, after which the MTC reneged on their promise by purchasing the bus garage property and having it declared tax-exempt.

The MTC has sometimes not been the best of citizens, and bus service in Brooklyn Center has always left much to be desired. The MTC's last act of snubbing their nose at the city was in the mid-1990s, when the MTC refused to pay its share of a street improvement assessment, citing its tax-exempt status. Finally, after appealing the matter to the Metropolitan Council, our area Met Council Members Bill Schrieber and Roger Scherer persuaded Met Council Chairman Curt Johnson to support their proposal to pay a portion of the assessment and the Metro Council, on an 8 to 7 vote, then ordered the MTC to pay.[22]

Highway 100 Reconstruction

Highway 100 north of France Avenue was upgraded to freeway standards at the time of the 1-94 connection with 1-694. However, Highway 100 to the south of France is still the 'ancient' Highway 100, with five traffic lights in the segment between France Avenue and 36th Avenue North in Crystal/Robbinsdale. This, along with crumbling bridges and insufficient lanes, demanded action on upgrading, which had been deferred since the mid-1960s.

In 1994 the cities of Brooklyn Center, Crystal, New Hope and Robbinsdale, later joined by Golden Valley, assisted by the North Metro Mayors Association, organized into what is now the North Metro Highway 100 Council. Through their efforts, and many others, the construction project was finally funded by the Met Council and MnDOT. The result will be a new Highway 100 from Glenwood Avenue in Golden Valley to 50th Avenue in Brooklyn Center. Ground breaking took place in April 2000, with completion scheduled for 2003.[23]

Osseo Road/Brooklyn Boulevard

On January 14, 1971, lifetime Brooklyn Center resident Sig Edling related some history of Osseo Road to members of the Brooklyn Historical Society. Mr Edling reported that in 1908 the Minnesota State Legislature passed a bill providing that Osseo Road was to be a "State legislative road" and instructed the State Highway Department to complete its improvements. Mr. Edling stated that the original trail along the route was used by oxcarts following the high ground and thus it developed into an actual road. In springtime it was surrounded by water to approximately today's 63rd Avenue North.[24]

1-694, *looking east. Note the Humboldt, Hwy. 100, and Dupont Avenue bridges.*

Mr. Edling further recalled that in the development of Osseo Road, Mr. Jacobson owned a store on Osseo Road and 69th and he had the only truck in the area in the early 1920s. About this time, the city purchased a snowplow, which took sixteen teams of horses to handle. Four horses in the front to steer and twenty-eight horses behind to push it. In the early 1930s a caterpillar tractor was bought and operated by the Chief of Police at that time, to clear the snow off the roads. The equipment was barely sufficient to keep the road open and the frequency of snowstorms required almost constant plowing. Edling said that farmers in the area were not too keen on the idea of the snowplowing, because they used sleighs drawn by horses as their means of transportation and preferred the snow-covered road as opposed to plowed roads.[25]

Here are a few excerpts from "What is Osseo Road?" a narrative written by Ted Willard, a Minneapolis native and long-time Brooklyn Center resident. Mr. Willard states that Osseo Road is "the name of a nine block-long segment of street running from

44th and Penn Avenues in Minneapolis to the border of Brooklyn Center and the beginning of Brooklyn Boulevard. A four-lane roadway traversing Brooklyn Center and Brooklyn Park to Highway 81. For many years, a two-lane blacktop road. A dirt and gravel road used by farmers to haul their produce to Minneapolis. A buffalo trail used by Indians and early settlers to reach the rich farmlands of the northwest. A focal point of history for Brooklyn Township."[26]

Ted goes on to say, "one of my childhood recollections is going for a Sunday afternoon 'drive in the country', a trip from north Minneapolis to the farm of Israel Rougier on Osseo Road just north of the Village of

Osseo Road at 69th before 1926. Howe Store and Baptist Church in background. (West side looking south)

Osseo, after stopping to visit one or more of the many relatives in Osseo. My grandparents used to come from their home in Osseo, down the rutted dirt Osseo Road to see us in Minneapolis. They sometimes came in the winter for a few days in a small sleigh, pulled by one horse, the little bells on the harness and sleigh jingling cheerfully as they drove into our yard, and they would be all tucked in with fur robes. They were in their early eighties when they made their last visit together."[27]

In 1960 Ted and his wife Sylvia moved their family from north Minneapolis to Brooklyn Center, where Ted became active in his new community. Ted shared his mixed feelings when in the late 1960s it was proposed to change the name of Osseo Road to Brooklyn Boulevard. Ted stated, "after being elected Treasurer of the village for two terms, then to the village and city council, I was faced with an uncomfortable decision. Osseo Road, both in Brooklyn Center and Brooklyn Park, was no longer a two-lane roadway. After construction of Brookdale Mall, the traffic load required an upgrade to a four-lane highway, plus shoulders and turning lanes. Many businesses had Osseo Road addresses, and were receiving complaints from customers who thought they were located in Osseo. A study committee recommended renaming to "Brooklyn Boulevard." The Brooklyn Park city council had agreed to the renaming, and so, somewhat reluctantly, Ted concurred with his colleagues and the new name was adopted unanimously for both "Brooklyns." Fortunately for history's sake, the Minneapolis council did not agree, so the nine-block stretch from the road's beginning at 44th and Penn Avenue north to the Brooklyn Center border remains Osseo Road, to remind us of the one-time buffalo trail, Indian trail, settlers trail, farm-to-market dirt road, country blacktop road and now urban highway."[28]

"Study will focus on improving Brooklyn Blvd," proclaimed a May 1992 newspaper headline: "Plans to improve Brooklyn Boulevard in Brooklyn Park are being discussed, said James Winkels, community development director. Plans are to survey Brooklyn Boulevard businesses and residents as to how they view the street, especially in the Village North area. Residents along the boulevard will be asked what opportunities they see, as well as the problems they witness. A graduate intern, yet to be hired, from the University of Minnesota will help with the project. Winkels said he expects a variety of answers to the survey. 'We've had a lot of people say...the boulevard doesn't look as good as it used to,' he said. Once the information has been gathered, Winkels said the city plans to work with the Brooklyn Park Business and Community Development Association to improve the area."[29]

On August 2, 1993, after seven months of study, including citizen input at several public forums Scott Clark, Director of Planning for Brooklyn Park, announced goals for the redevelopment project, with the overall goal being community betterment. Redevelopment of Brooklyn Boulevard in Brooklyn Park was approved and construction was completed in 1996.[30]

The City of Brooklyn Center, in conjunction with Hennepin County, has a major redevelopment project on Brooklyn Boulevard from 65th Avenue to 73rd Avenue, with construction slated to start in the summer of 2000 with completion in 2001.[31]

Highway 10/610

In the 1990s a second river crossing north of I-694, along with a "North Crosstown Highway," became necessary to serve the developing areas in the Northern Metro Suburbs and to alleviate traffic congestion on I-694. The Highway 10/610 connection had been planned since the late 1960s, but funding was long delayed.[32]

In the 1980s reconstruction of US Highway 10 east of the river was scheduled and funded. The new river crossing, which was the first segment of Highway 610 built, was completed in late 1987. The Transportation Act of 1991 earmarked $45 million for construction of the 610 bridge and highway west to US 169. The Transportation Act of 1998 earmarked $24 million for the Hwy 610 development from US 169 to I-94 in Maple Grove.[33]

The 1992 January/February issue of the *Brooklyn Park City Newsletter* cited progress on the Highway 610 project: "A recent victory for transportation in Brooklyn Park and all of Minnesota showed what can happen when property owners, community representatives, business owners, elected officials, legislators, county commissioners, and mayor and city council members join together to work for a single purpose. Residents can participate in a public hearing to discuss the proposed construction of Highway 610 on November 19, 1992. Engineers and consultants from the cities and Minnesota Department of Transportation will be at the public hearing to answer questions about Highway 610's construction. Residents will be able to attend informal, small discussion sessions. "It will give everyone an equal opportunity to speak and ask questions," says Brooklyn Park City Engineer Gary Brown."[34]

The Hwy 610 (Richard Braun) Bridge was constructed to provide an intermediate river crossing between Anoka and Interstate 694. An Environmental Impact Statement and cooperation between local, county and state agencies ensured that the design of the bridge minimized impacts on the natural features of the river corridor and provided mitigation for areas that were disturbed during construction. The bridge will begin to see increased traffic as Trunk Highway 610 officially opens in late 2000. Construction of a second bridge, immediately south of the existing bridge is underway. The new bridge will be designed to match the existing bridge and include trail access across the river to link Hennepin County and Anoka County trail systems.[35]

West River Road/Highway 252

When Highway 252 was completed, it replaced the West River Road as the main thoroughfare through Brooklyn Park on the west side of the Mississippi River. Then in 1986, Highway 252 was relocated outside the Mississippi River Critical Area. In 2000, a pedestrian bridge over Highway 252 at 85th Avenue is scheduled for construction.[36]

1960s construction of Osseo Rd. bridge over Hwy. 100 near Brookdale

Hwy. 610 ramp signs at Zane Avenue interchange.

West River Road is a state Constitutional highway in that it is mentioned in the Minnesota Constitution. After a period of time, the roadway was to revert to the community. Although no official state action to revert ever occurred, the State's position is that West River Road has reverted to Brooklyn Park. Consequently, in 1994 a Brooklyn Park Task Force was appointed to recommend the future of West River Road. Two residents on the task force were in favor of reopening West River Road. Affected residents responded with a petition signed by over 120 residents opposing the reopening of West River Road.[37]

Travelers along West River Road will have to continue to negotiate the sharp left turn at 97th Avenue indefinitely. The Brooklyn Park City Council voted to vacate street easements for the section of West River Road between 97th and 101st avenues at its June 28, 1995, meeting. At its height, West River Road carried about 14,000 cars a day. Today, about 4,000 traverse the scenic route. Since 1987, travelers have had to make a sharp left turn at 97th Avenue, then a hard right on Russell Avenue before returning to West River Road.[38]

Relocation of Highway 252 has allowed West River Road to revert to a collector street for the residential neighborhoods of the corridor. A street reconstruction project will convert approximately 4 miles of West River Road from rural to urban street design with curb and gutter. The project begins at Brookdale Drive and ends at 97th Avenue and includes a 3.6-mile section of the Great River Road. Construction is expected to begin in 2000 with an estimated project cost of $4,000,000. A ten-foot wide bituminous trail will be constructed west of the roadway. The trail will connect to existing trails south of Brookdale Drive to allow access through Brooklyn Center to the Minneapolis trail system.[39]

The Future

Highway traffic in the area at certain times of the day is at a standstill, especially west of Brooklyn Boulevard where westbound I-694 traffic is funneled from three lanes down to two. This is due in part to extensive development beyond the original seven-county metro area. People who get on the "mainline" thirty miles out can move through to their destinations, while "locals" are annoyingly slowed by metered ramps. Congestion will only get worse in the years ahead.[40]

Because endless highway expansion is not possible, any serious long-term reduction of metro-area congestion will require diverting a significant portion of automobile trips into transit. Traditional transit such as buses or electric streetcars (LRT) are too costly and/or cannot attract enough riders to reduce congestion and meet the needs of the northern suburbs.

A technology "paradigm change" is required to construct a transit system at a low enough cost to be widely deployed, with service characteristics that will attract sufficient riders to alleviate road congestion. One such technology that will be available within a few years is Personal Rapid Transit (PRT). The question is, will our transportation planners have the foresight and leadership to implement a 21st century solution to urban congestion?[41]

Notes

1. Norene Roberts, "Early Transportation Routes in Brooklyn Park," 24 April 1995, BHS.

2. Ibid.

3. P. M. Dahl, Civil Engineer, "Road Map of Hennepin and Ramsey Counties," pre-1910, Hennepin History Center.

4. Ibid.

5. J. William Trygg, *Composite Map of the United States Land Surveyors' Original Plats and Field Notes*, (Ely, MN: J. W. Trygg, 1964), Sheet 7 shows Brooklyn Township in 1855.

6. P. M. Dahl.

7. *The Osseo Review*, 9 August 1916; "Neighboring Towns Join Osseo Gladly," *The Osseo Review*, 19 September 1917.

8. Norene Roberts, citing Steven, 1891:134-135.

9. Norene Roberts, citing Larson, 1966:150.

10. Norene Roberts, citing Larson 1966:161.

11. P. M. Dahl.

12. Ike Anderson, "The Camden-Brooklyn Township-Anoka Stage," edited by Jane Hallberg, 1978.

13. Norene Roberts.

14. Ibid.

15. "T.F. Girling First Editor," *The North Hennepin Post*, 3 April 1952, 2.

16. *Highway Improvement Report*, by Brooklyn Center Mayor Gordon Erickson, undated, BHS.

17. "Proposed Link of I-94 in North Minneapolis"; *Brooklyn Center Post*, 24 April 1980.

18. Phil Cohen, "Evolution of the Major Transportation System in Brooklyn Center," 16 May 2000, BHS.

19. Ibid.

20. *Brooklyn Center Post*, 17 January 1980.

21. *Brooklyn Center Post*, 24 April 1980.

22. Phil Cohen.

23. Ibid.

24. Sig Edling, presentation to Brooklyn Historical Society, 14 January 1971.

25. Ibid.

26. Ted Willard, "What is Osseo Road?" 28 June 1999, BHS.

27. Ibid.

28. Ibid; "Osseo Road Once a Cattle Road," *Brooklyn Center Post*, 15 October 1970.

29. "Study will focus on improving Brooklyn Blvd," *Brooklyn Park Sun-Post*, 13 May 1992.

30. "Redevelopment Plan for Brooklyn Blvd," *NorthWest News*, 23 August 23 1993.

30. "Proposed Link of I-94 in North Minneapolis," *Minneapolis Star Tribune*, 17 July 1974.

31. *City Watch*, a newsletter for residents of the City of Brooklyn Center, January 2000.

32. Phil Cohen.

33. Ibid.

34. "Funding comes through for Highway 610," *Brooklyn Park City Newsletter*, Jan/Feb 1992; "Public forum to air Hwy 610 design," *Brooklyn Park City Newsletter*, Nov/Dec 1992; "Highway 610 Map," *Brooklyn Park Sun-Post*, 10 February 1993; "Public Hearing for New Highway 610," *NorthWest News*, no date, BHS.

35. *Mississippi River Stewardship Plan*, City of Brooklyn Park Community Development Department, draft document, May 2000.

36. Ibid.

37. "Task Force on Future of West River Road," *NorthWest News*, 25 April 1994.

38. "Council makes West River Road detour permanent," *Brooklyn Park Sun Post*, 5 July 1995.

39. *Mississippi River Stewardship Plan*.

40. Phil Cohen.

41. See Internet Web site, www.taxi2000.com.

Chapter Twelve

HOUSING

Pre-1950 Brooklyn Center Housing

Prior to the 1950s, Brooklyn Center was primarily occupied by a number of garden farms. Therefore its residential housing consisted of farm houses, plus a scattering of houses along its major thoroughfares, such as Lyndale Avenue and Osseo Road. Also, some cottages, as well as estate type homes were built along Lyndale Avenue, the Mississippi River and Twin Lakes. Some residential housing began to develop in the southeast neighborhood in the 1920s, bordering Minneapolis. However, it was really more of an extension of Minneapolis than it was the start of Brooklyn Center, with its occupants utilizing Minneapolis schools, churches and services.[2]

1950–2000 Brooklyn Center Housing Development

Beginning in the 1950s, Brooklyn Center's residential growth greatly accelerated, with the progression of housing development going pretty much by neighborhood,

in a clockwise fashion starting with the Southeast neighborhood (reference the map of Brooklyn Center Neighborhoods). Initially, the housing development was primarily single family homes with a few duplexes and a scattering of four-plex apartment units. Following development and adoption of the City's Comprehensive Plan in the 1960s, development of major apartment complexes, low income apartments, senior apartments, and townhouses all became part of what we now have in the year 2000 — a balance of various types and cost ranges of housing.[3]

Typical 60s ranch-style house

Brooklyn Center Population Statistics 1920–1990

The numbers in the following table show the growth in population for Brooklyn Center and reflect the tremendous demand for new housing in the period from 1950 to 1970.[4]

1920	788
1930	1,344
1940	1,870
1950	4,284
1960	24,356
1970	35,173
1980	31,230
1990	28,793

CITY OF BROOKLYN CENTER

Northwest

Northeast

West Central   Central

Southeast

Southwest   Neighborhood Map

July 2000

Southeast Neighborhood

The southeast neighborhood is Brooklyn Center's oldest residential neighborhood, where development began with Bellvue Acres, as described later by Mary Simmons. The neighborhood is bordered by I-94 on the north, Mississippi River on the east, 53rd Avenue on the south and Shingle Creek Parkway on the west.[6]

The primary builder of single family homes in the southeast neighborhood, other than Bellvue Acres, was Marvin Anderson Builders. The southeast neighborhood expansion began soon after the end of World War II and the area was pretty well developed by the end of the 1950s. The initial development phase was primarily made up of single family homes, some duplexes and a few 4 and 8-plex apartment units.[7]

Southwest Neighborhood

Nearly all of the western boundary of the southwest neighborhood is shoreline of middle and upper Twin Lakes. This presents the opportunity for families to live year-round on a lake, yet be within eight miles of downtown Minneapolis. Housing along the Twin Lakes shoreline in the pre-1950 era was primarily of the lake cottage variety. Then as Brooklyn Center's housing development growth moved into the southwest neighborhood, many of the cottages were upgraded to or replaced with prime lake-shore homes. Today, because of their access to the lake, many of the Twin Lakes area

Willowbrook Apartments — A typical 60s apartment complex

homes rival the Mississippi riverfront homes in the northeast neighborhood as the most upscale homes in Brooklyn Center.[9]

The primary builder of single-family homes in the southwest neighborhood was Pearson Construction Company. The southwest neighborhood is dissected by the only railroad in Brooklyn Center, by Highway 100, and by Brooklyn Boulevard. It includes the land east of Brooklyn Boulevard, which became Brookdale Mall in the early 1960s.[10]

Central Neighborhood

The central neighborhood, which is perhaps better known as the Garden City area, is bordered by 1-94 on the north, Shingle Creek Parkway on the east, County Road 10 on the south and Brooklyn Boulevard on the west. Some of the Shingle Creek area was developed into Brooklyn Center's primary park (Central Park) in the late 1970s and is a nice amenity and very positive recreation attraction for the entire community, but particularly so for young families in the central neighborhood.[12]

The primary builder in the southern third of the central neighborhood was Hipp Homes, with several other builders involved in developing the remainder of the central neighborhood.[13]

West Central Neighborhood

The west central neighborhood is bordered by 1-94 on the north, Brooklyn Boulevard on the east, County Road 10 on the south, and Crystal and Brooklyn Park on the west. The primary builder of single family homes in the west central neighborhood was Pearson Construction Company. The west central neighborhood contains two nature areas that are unique in Brooklyn Center—the MAC Environmental Preserve and the Gene Hagel Arboretum.[15]

Northwest Neighborhood

The northwest neighborhood is bordered by 73rd Avenue and Brooklyn Park on the north, Palmer Lake on the east, 1-94 on the south, and Zane Ave. and Brooklyn Park on the west. One of the primary builders in the northwest neighborhood was Hipp Homes.[17]

Northeast Neighborhood

The northeast neighborhood is bordered by 73rd Avenue and Brooklyn Park on the north, the Mississippi River on the east, I-94 on the south and Palmer Lake on the west. Prior to the 1950s, much of the housing along the Mississippi river was primarily of the lake cottage variety. Then as Brooklyn Center's housing development moved into the northeast neighborhood, many of the cottages were upgraded to or replaced with prime riverfront homes. Today, because of their access to the river, many of the northeast neighborhood riverfront area homes rival the Twin Lakes lakeshore homes in the southwest neighborhood as the most upscale homes in Brooklyn Center.[19]

Although the northeast neighborhood vies with the southeast neighborhood for being the largest neighborhood on a square mile basis, it contains a disproportionately high number of townhouse and apartment units compared to the other neighborhoods.[20]

Some Housing-related Issues.

Development and adoption of a Comprehensive Plan for Brooklyn Center in the mid-1960s has played a significant role in guiding housing development in Brooklyn Center. Zoning for housing developments—townhouses, walk-up apartments, high-rise apartment buildings, etc., was set forth as part of the first Comprehensive Plan that the city adopted. There was a need to provide apartment living for young families who could not afford to purchase homes right away. Four and eight-plex apartment buildings were the norm before adoption of the Comprehensive Plan. Also, at this time townhouses were being built, and the new federal housing programs provided housing assistance subsidies for low-income families and seniors. The first rent-subsidized high-rise for seniors was built on the site next to Brooklyn Center City Hall in the 1970s.

Melrose Gates Apartments

Brooklyn Center and Columbia Heights were among the first suburban communities to take the initiative in providing low-cost housing for low income families and seniors. Mayor Phil Cohen of Brooklyn Center and Mayor Bruce Nawrocki of Columbia Heights used this to their advantage in the early days of the Metropolitan Council, when suburban communities were accused of not providing their fair-share of low-cost housing for low-income families and seniors. Brooklyn Center's Comprehensive Plan addressed this issue years before the Metropolitan Council existed.[22]

The City of Brooklyn Center and the Brooklyn Center School District were negatively affected by the Interstate Highway 94 extension from downtown Minneapolis. This happened when the Minnesota Highway Department bought and removed the homes in the proposed I-94 route in the 1960s, but didn't build the I-94 link until the late 1970s. The delay was primarily due to a land exchange dispute between the MN Highway Dept. and the Minneapolis Park Board. The impact on Brooklyn Center was not only the loss of many much needed quality homes during our period of high housing growth, but also the premature loss of property taxes by the city and school district for several years.[23]

David Brandvold, a Brooklyn Center resident and home builder, had a unique approach to his profession. It allowed him to earn a living by working near his home, while also greatly benefiting his community. Mr. Brandvold had a passion for finding lots in the various neighborhoods of Brooklyn Center, that were sitting vacant for whatever reason. The lots were smaller or larger than normal for the neighborhood, odd shaped, or for various reasons left vacant in a built-up neighborhood, some for many years. Mr. Brandvold had a knack for designing and building new homes on these odd lots that not only fit the lot, but the neighborhood, as well. David Brandvold had a reputation for being a quality builder, and received a Distinguished Service Award from the Metropolitan Council in 1978 for sharing his approach and expertise while serving on their Housing Design Competition Committee.[24]

Crossing at Brookwood, a complex of apartments and occupant owned condominiums, was Brooklyn Center's initial involvement in promoting, as well as participating in, the development of a particular type of housing for a particular demographic group. The city identified a number of parcels of land along the east side of Highway 100 that could be acquired, attracted a willing developer and used city monies to provide front-end funding for land purchase and installation of utilities. The city also worked with the developer to attract older city residents, who wanted to continue living in Brooklyn Center, but were looking for an alternative to living in and maintaining their own single-family homes. Completed in 1984, this turned out to be a very successful venture, accommodating senior residents, while freeing their single-family homes for younger families. The impact of younger families moving into the freed up single-family homes, was another benefit to our community, in that it helped stabilize school enrollments. Brookwood is located in the northwest corner of the southeast neighborhood.[25]

Soderberg Apartment Specialists (SAS) to the rescue! In 1995 Jim Soderberg, president of SAS received a call from TCF National Bank officials offering to sell him the Timber Ridge apartment complex in Brooklyn Center. The complex had gone back to TCF through foreclosure. Timber Ridge had previously had at least five different owners since it was built in 1969. Timber Ridge had been a neglected property for several years, and was attracting the worst of tenants and became a very troubled and failing apartment complex. Over 700 emergency 911 calls were received by the Police Department the previous year. The stack of city housing code violations issued in the previous year was as thick as a phone book. City officials were skeptical about the odds of anyone being able to turn around the property.

Soderberg's first reaction was, "This one is right up our alley, and I can't think of anyone else who would be more qualified for it. I always get excited; the more beat up I see the buildings the more excited I get about it." SAS had experience in this type of project, having done four similar apartment renovations in Minneapolis and other suburbs. "I think it's so much fun to take an awful, awful place and really make it nice. And this one is going to be a huge transformation," Soderberg said at the time.

The rest is history. Soderberg gave notice to all existing tenants; then he and his staff went about cleaning up and fixing up the 216-unit apartment complex, with haste. They filled 10 roll-off dumpsters with the trash from the apartments. They installed 20,000 yards of new carpeting and five semi-truck loads of new Kenmore appliances, put a fresh coat of paint on every wall and ceiling, installed ceramic floors in kitchens, installed new window blinds and fixtures, rebuilt all elevators, replaced all stairwell treads, upgraded the security system and re-roofed all of the buildings.

The amazing thing is that SAS was able to completely renovate the entire complex and fill the entire complex with new well-screened tenants in just four and a half months. Brad Hoffman, Brooklyn Center's community development director was quoted as saying, 'The project is like night and day from what it was a few months ago. I think Jim has accomplished an awful lot in a short period of time."

Through the efforts of a new owner who has a commitment to owning a high quality facility filled with quality tenants and the cooperation and support of city staff, Brooklyn Center regained 216 quality housing units. Equally important it removed a blighted property with troubled tenants from the northeast neighborhood.[26]

A 53rd Avenue Development Project was undertaken by the city in 1996. Beginning in October 1996, the Economic Development Authority (EDA) undertook a housing project along two blocks of 53rd Avenue, which borders Minneapolis. Land acquisition started in November 1996. The cost of acquisition, relocation, clearance and site development was $2.8 million. The city hired a construction manager in the summer of 1998 to build fifteen new single family homes and hired a real estate broker to market the homes. The purpose of the project was to replace old, blighted housing with new modern homes and with some special landscaping treatment to enhance the southeast gateway to Brooklyn Center. This project, like the Brookwood venture, not only accomplished its original goal but actually turned out to be a tremendous success, with more buyers than homes and all buyers coming from within a one-mile radius of the project. Like Brookwood, this project is also in the southeast neighborhood, only in the opposite corner.[27]

53rd Avenue Housing

Brooklyn Park Housing Development

Scattered farm homes were built in the 1800s, but the modern history of Brooklyn Park's housing starts in the 1950s. The shape of the City's housing was driven by the demand of the post World War II generation, the proximity of Brooklyn Park to downtown Minneapolis, and the fluctuating financial conditions over a 30-year period of time that included interest rates ranging from 7 percent to 18 percent.

The City officially adopted its first Comprehensive Plan in July 1970, but the Plan was not done on a blank slate. From 1966 to 1970 over 3,200 housing units were constructed in the City, these were mostly apartments along the Zane Avenue corridor, including the 1,140-unit Century Court complex, which remains one of the largest in the entire Twin Cities. These multi-family facilities met the need for low-cost housing fueled by the baby boomer generation. By the mid-1980s, the City had approximately 6,100 market rate units.

After this time, market rate apartment construction was halted throughout the metropolitan area due to a series of market considerations. During the 1990s, a selected number of multi-family projects were constructed to fill certain market niches (i.e., a luxury complex at Edinburgh USA, conversion of market rate housing to senior facilities, senior cooperative housing, and a handicap-accessible facility).[28]

The demand for apartments was the first step in the baby boomer housing cycle. By the mid-1970s the apartment boom had started to wane and the next cycle centered on the demand for starter homes. Brooklyn Park was strategically located as it both served as the outer ring of suburban development and all of its properties were within the Metropolitan Council's Municipal Urban Services Area (MUSA). This allowed the City the option of selecting what properties should be opened for development based on a growth management policy that dated from the mid-1960s. The challenges to the City to promote higher-end housing was, in part, due its lack of desirable features such as wooded areas, rolling hills, wetlands and lakes.

During the 1970s and well into the 1980s, the shape of housing in the entire Twin Cities area was severely affected by high interest rates, which caused homeowners' mortgage payments to be consumed by financing costs. The opposite situation occurred in the mid to late 1990s when historically low interest rates allowed homeowners to drastically increase the size of their homes for the same amount of money. The high inflation rate in the 1970s and 1980s forced the type and price of new housing built in not only Brooklyn Park but in the majority of like situated communities to offer the majority of new homes in the 900 to 1,200 square foot range. Despite escalating interest rates, the late 1970s saw rapid growth in Brooklyn Park and in 1977 almost 1,000 single family homes were built.[29]

Edinburgh USA

By 1983 almost all of the land area south of 85th Avenue had been developed, and serious policy questions arose regarding the need of the City to diversify its housing stock towards a higher end market. The outcome of these discussions was the plan to construct a championship golf course, to be designed by a nationally recognized firm, that would serve both as a regional recreational amenity and as an asset to the Brooklyn Park housing market. The ability of the City to construct a links style course, which would maximize the amount of linear footage available for housing, became a joint partnership between Gracelyn Development (a partnership between the James Seed Trust and Mattson's Landing comprised of members of the Schmidt family) and the City. The Gracelyn Development obligation was to assemble approximately 160 acres of property, and the City would pay for a golf course plan designed by Robert Trent Jones Jr.[30]

Upscale housing at Edinburgh USA Golf Course

In 1984-85 a series of development agreements were generated resulting in construction of the golf course. One of the interesting stipulations was contractual park credits for the land dedicated for the golf course. This prepayment of credits resulted in the golf course being the open space for the Edinburgh area. Eventually, the developers renegotiated to provide additional land for neighborhood parks. The other essential element was the creation of a new "golf course" zoning district (Planned Community Development District) that had open standards for development. Effectively, the developer and the City Council negotiated everything from the size of the house to roof pitches. After several of these negotiations, standards for the Edinburgh area were established with housing minimums ranging from 1,000 square feet to 2,400 square, depending upon the style of the home and its geographical proximity to the golf course. Other requirements that became standard were 7:12 roof pitches, mandatory homeowners associations and trees, shrubs and the entirely of the lot being sodded. Gracelyn Development's initial concept contained a master plan that covered 1,000 acres and served as a framework for development.[31]

The Edinburgh area became a radical departure from the majority of the housing stock found throughout the rest of the City but the pace of development was slower than anticipated and the last properties were being finalized in 2000. Despite a slower growth rate, the goals of raising the City's housing values and styles and creating an area unique to Brooklyn Park were accomplished. A significant number of new owners within the first five years were previous Brooklyn Park homeowners. According to Bob Schmidt, during the first five years 80 percent of the new owners came from within the community and helped create the success of the Edinburgh concept. The completion of the Edinburgh vision was a significant step for the City as it now had an area where homeowners who had either outgrown their homes or had secured sufficient equity could purchase move-up housing within the community.

The Multiple-Family Dilemma

During the late 1980s, the City's apartment stock started to deteriorate due to a complex array of conditions: 1986 Federal real estate tax amendments; regional changes in social and demographic trends; stagnant rental rates caused by a lack of demand for the style of apartments located in the City; and the natural aging process of a community.

In 1990 the community began public dialogue to both acknowledge the severity of the problem and the negative regional perception it produced, and to identify what level of political will existed for change. Since 1990, the electorate of the City has established a strong and straightforward policy: "Use all available resources, be courageous and investigate and initiate strategies in all phases of community rejuvenation, whether it be in public safety, physical housing rehabilitation or constructing programs that bolster social needs."[32]

Waterford Apartments, an EDA rehab project

The initiation of community and political will occurred in 1990 when Mayor Jesse Ventura, a former professional wrestler, met with the owners of an apartment complex that had become a source of major public safety issues and rapid physical deterioration. At the meeting, he pounded his fist on the table and ordered the problem to be corrected. This attitude, along with $16 million dollars of public financing infused into limited partnerships and loans, catapulted the City to a regional leader in apartment-solving issues.

The community not only addressed the physical issues associated with apartment rehabilitation but also public safety, recreation and social service issues. Their collaborative efforts with other public and private organizations resulted in successful strategies that totally rejuvenated the perception of the community. The community's success story has been memorialized in the document "Concentrated Residential Area Action Plan."[33]

On January 18, 1995, Governor Arne Carlson acknowledged in his "State of the State Address" the initiatives that Brooklyn Park developed. In 2000, the City has fully transformed its apartment community so that private reinvestments are occurring and the fruits of the past decade of community input can be seen.[34]

Single-Family and Beyond 2000

In 2000, the City's Master Plan is being reviewed for possible adoption of the remaining 4,000 undeveloped acres stretching from 93rd Avenue north to the City's border. The two key policy questions for the Plan were how to maintain the higher-end housing achieved in the Edinburgh golf course area and what land use and design considerations were needed for the Highway 610 corridor.

Regarding housing, the City initiated a Planned Unit Development zone regulating all phases of design including house values and minimum size requirements. As of April 2000, over 410 new single-family homes have been built in this new planned development area, and it is anticipated that housing will continue to grow at a rate of 400 single-family homes per year. In order to create definable neighborhoods, all subdivisions are designed with interconnected trail systems that lead to strategically located central parks. To date, the area's housing size and values have been equal to that of the Edinburgh area. It is important to remember that the low interest rates throughout much of the 1990s helped create a strong housing market resulting in larger house sizes and unprecedented demand.

In summary, after thirty years of housing development the City finds itself with an extremely wide range of housing choices, strong neighborhoods and a place where people want to invest in a community.

Notes

1. Mary Simmons, lifetime resident, manuscript on Bellvue Acres, 2000, BHS.

2. Ron Warren and other Brooklyn Center City staff members, consulted by Tony Kuefler; Phil Cohen, manuscript on "Housing in Brooklyn Center," 13 July 1999.

3. Map of Brooklyn Center Neighborhoods; *Annual Report of Statistical Facts*, City of Brooklyn Center; *Comprehensive Plan*, City of Brooklyn Center; *Report on Housing Opportunity in the Twin Cities Area*, Metropolitan Council, October 1978; *Apartment Directory*, City of Brooklyn Center, December 1999.

4. *Annual Report of Statistical Facts*.

5. *Apartment Directory*.

6. Mary Simmons; Map of Brooklyn Center Neighborhoods; *Annual Report of Statistical Facts*.

7. Ron Warren et al; Phil Cohen; Map of Brooklyn Center Neighborhoods; *Annual Report of Statistical Facts*, City of Brooklyn Center.

8. *Apartment Directory*.

9. See note 7.

10. Ron Warren; Phil Cohen; Map of Brooklyn Center Neighborhoods.

11. *Apartment Directory*.

12. See note 7.

13 Ron Warren.

14. *Apartment Directory*.

15. See note 7.

16. *Apartment Directory*.

17. See note 7.

18. *Apartment Directory*.

19. See note 7.

20. *Apartment Directory*.

21. Ibid.

22. Phil Cohen; *Report on Housing Opportunity in the Twin Cities Area;*

23. Phil Cohen.

24. Ibid; Metropolitan Council letter and Certificate, 27 October 1978.

25. Ron Warren; Phil Cohen; *Apartment Directory.*

26. *Minnesota Real Estate Journal,* 10 July 1995.

27. Ron Warren; Phil Cohen; *Brooklyn Center Sun-Post,* 5 April 2000.

28. Building Division records, City of Brooklyn Park.

29. Ibid; National Association of Realtors.

30. Series of documents from the Brooklyn Park Recreation and Parks Department.

31. Conditional Use Permits from the Planning Division, City of Brooklyn Park; Marketing map brochure from Brook Park Realty.

32. Concentrated Residential Area Action Plan, April, 1995, City of Brooklyn Park.

33. Ibid.

34. Ibid.

35. Draft Plan from Planning Division, City of Brooklyn Park.

Bellvue Acres, Brooklyn Center's First "Neighborhood"

by Mary Hovey Simmons

EIGHTY YEARS AGO, in 1920, the Village of Brooklyn Center took its first baby steps toward "cityhood." Until then market gardens covered the entire village, and farmhouses were scattered along dusty gravel roads. By 1920 the World War I had been over for more than a year, and throughout the country new families were being formed, optimistic about the future and eager to set up homes of their own.

In April of that year, a small parcel of land in the southeasternmost corner of Brooklyn Center, running from the Mississippi River on the east to Dupont Avenue on the west, and from 53rd to 55th Avenues North, was platted as "Bellvue Acres" and subdivided into acre lots of 126 x 300 feet. There were already a few houses scattered across this flat, treeless corner of Brooklyn Center, but it wasn't until the advent of Bellvue Acres that the village's first "neighborhood" was born. Because most of the potential buyers worked in downtown Minneapolis, one of Bellvue Acres' selling points was that it was within walking distance of the end of the Minneapolis streetcar line.

My parents, Bill and Signe Hovey, were among the first young "settlers" on Bryant Avenue. They bought a tiny house on a big lot at 5418 Bryant, and lived there until their second child was born, when my father built a house across the street at 5405 Bryant. Not all of the new settlers were young couples. Some were immigrants, mostly Swedish, who had come to America at the turn of the century hoping to make a living by farming in Minnesota and Wisconsin. Many of them had failed, my mother's parents, John and Agnes Peterson, among them. At my father's urging, the Petersons bought two back-to-back lots, facing Bryant and Dupont Avenues.

It is difficult today to believe the primitive conditions under which those first homesteaders lived, worked and raised their families. Like "sodbuster" pioneers, who lived underground in sod houses because there were no trees with which to build houses, many Bellvue Acres homesteaders spent years living underground in chilly capped basements, until they saved enough to build an "upstairs." Most basement-dwellers were of the immigrant generation, grown cautious after past financial failures. But the younger couples, with growing families, needed real houses. (So many young wives were pregnant that local jokers called the neighborhood "Bellyview Acres").

My father, a journeyman printer who had lived all his life in Minneapolis and had no construction experience at all, built his own Craftsman-style house at 5405 Bryant, using plans he had ordered through a magazine. My dad didn't have to learn plumbing though, because the house plans didn't assume that the house would have any. But like most other new houses on our street, water for washing, cooking, and drinking was pumped by hand from the well out back to a cistern in the basement, and from there up to the kitchen with a small hand pump fitted beside the kitchen sink. Water for Saturday night baths and Monday clothes-washing was heated in big teakettles on the kitchen stove. The privy in the back yard took care of our other needs.

Indoor darkness came early in the winter, with few electrical outlets for floor lamps. We children spent the evening reading and drawing pictures (two of us would grow up to be commercial artists) and listening to records played on the wind-up phonograph. At bedtime my mother read us a story, and my father went down to the basement to shovel coal into the octopus-armed furnace, to keep the house warm until morning.

Old snapshots show my young parents as rail-thin but smiling, proud of their accomplishments. They and their Bellvue Acres neighbors deserved to feel proud!

Brooklyn Stories

The "people next door" are the beginning point for any community. As the Brooklyns grew, neighbors connected with neighbors to build a sense of community.

Chapter Thirteen

UNCOMMON LIVES

THE TERM "uncommon" refers to persons whose lives have been in some way unusual, persons who have made a difference, or made a unique contribution, or have been involved in a "cutting edge" project, people who have set themselves apart. Tim Laudner, the former Minnesota Twins baseball player, recalled a quote that summed up the essence of an uncommon life.

It is not the critic who counts,
not the one who points out
how the strong man stumbled
or how the doer of deeds
might have done better.
The credit belongs to the man
who is actually in the arena,
whose face is marred
with sweat and dust and blood;
who strives valiantly;
who errs and comes short again and again;
who knows the great enthusiasm,
the great devotion, and spends himself in a worthy cause;
who, if he fails,
at least fails while daring greatly,
so that his place shall never be
with those cold and timid souls
who know neither victory nor defeat.

—*Theodore Roosevelt*

WALTER "BRECK" BRECKENRIDGE is a pioneer in nature filmmaking, a respected wildlife author, and prolific painter of birds in their natural setting. Breckenridge, a longtime Brooklyn Park resident, also served as the director of the University of Minnesota's Bell Museum for twenty-three years (1945-1968).

Walter Breckenridge

Breckenridge's interest in nature began early one summer day in his hometown of Brooklyn, Iowa when his father showed him a dead prairie chicken. Young Walter was fascinated. "I was so taken with that bird and that I hated to just strip the feathers off and eat it."[1]

Since there was no taxidermist in Brooklyn, Walter learned the art by correspondence. "By the time I graduated high school I had a little museum of about 60 specimens of birds and small mammals." He donated the collection to his high school's biology department.

Breckenridge's hobby led him to the University of Iowa, where he worked as an assistant to the university's museum of natural history. He moved to the University of Minnesota in 1926 and soon expanded his talents to film. "We used a 35-millimeter hand-crank camera, exposure depended on how fast you turned the crank."

He filmed nesting cranes, ruffed grouse drumming, prairie chickens on their booming grounds, and sharp-tailed grouse strutting. He captured some rare species on film that few had ever seen before. Audiences loved the films. For twenty-five years he narrated his nature films to enthusiastic National Audubon Society members around the country.

On a July afternoon in 1933 Breckenridge married Dorothy Shogren and immediately took her on a seven-day expedition to Hudson's Bay to study disease in grouse and rabbits. For fifty-six years the couple lived on a sprawling 2½ acre lot on the Mississippi River in Brooklyn Park where they raised three children and logged 180 species of birds in the fertile flyway that was their backyard. They moved to a retirement community in 1996.

The Breckenridge apartment now contains dozens of paintings that Walter has done over the years: loons at sunset on Great Bear Lake in the Northwest Territories, bison in the Black Hills, and a canvasback that won second place in the 1965 federal duck stamp contest.

His understanding of nature, art, and sense of natural history allowed Breckenridge to create the wonderful dioramas on display at the Bell Museum. "The diorama halls representing pre-European Minnesota habitats remain some of the best in the world," said Bell Museum director Scott Lanyon.

Breckenridge operated with a simple goal, "I want to teach people how interesting wildlife is and how we should preserve it. Building these (dioramas) at the museum attracted attention to wildlife and birds in the field."[2]

"Breck's knowledge and commitment to education has made him an outstanding Minnesota naturalist," write Gayle Crampton and Don Luce. "His love for nature and his dedication to seeing it preserved have inspired educational projects that continue to reach thousands of Minnesotans."[3]

1. Winegar, "For the Love of Nature," *Minneapolis Star Tribune*, March 11, 1998.

2. Ibid.

3. Gayle Crampton and Don Luce, "A Life in Natural History," James Ford Bell Museum of Natural History Imprint, Winter 1987.

Mary Jo Copeland

MARY JO HOLTBY was born on October 23, 1942 in Rochester, Minnesota to parents Woody and Gertrude Holtby. She graduated from Holy Angels Academy in 1960 and married Dick Copeland in April 1961. The Copelands settled in Brooklyn Center, attended St. Alphonsus Church, and raised twelve children.

When her youngest child, Molly, started pre-school in 1981, Copeland was encouraged by her husband Dick to share her love with the outside world. The outside world has never been the same.

Copeland became frustrated by the bureaucracy involved in charity work. She says, "People in need shouldn't have to fill out forms and go through interviews. If they are hungry, you feed them. If they are dirty, you clean them."[1]

Copeland started Sharing and Caring Hands in 1985, an all volunteer organization, to serve the needy of north Minneapolis. The program began modestly out of a 2,000 square foot storefront on Glenwood Avenue with a $2,000 a month budget. Copeland put a sign in the window and welcomed anyone who walked through the door.

"When someone walked in I would say, 'What can I do for you today?' If they needed socks, I gave them socks; if they were hungry, I fed them. I didn't care why they needed help. I just helped them."[2]

Copeland raised $7.5 million to build Mary's Place, a transitional apartment complex for women and children in poverty that is named for the Virgin Mary. Initially, Minneapolis city officials opposed Mary's Place, contending that the area was zoned for industrial use, not residential. That fact didn't stop Copeland. As *St. Paul Pioneer Press* columnist Joe Soucheray wrote, "These characters who populate City Hall in Minneapolis have never been up against anything like Mary Jo Copeland. They do not have a clue to what lies in store for them." Soucheray was right. Mary's Place was built and opened in 1995.[3]

Despite her hectic schedule, or perhaps because of it, Copeland rises at 3:45 am each morning to pray the rosary at St. Al's. She enjoys living in a quiet Minneapolis suburb, "I have found peace and feel safe in Brooklyn Center."[4]

On the national front, Copeland remains a visible figure in the belief that publicity generates additional contributions. Her many honors include the Norman Vincent Peale Unsung Hero Award, the Pax Christi Award, Person of the Week on NBC's Nightly News, and having feature articles written about her in Parade and People magazines.

"They (the poor) simply need to know that they are not alone in the world. To be a great leader, you must be a great servant, and that's what I do. I serve. I catch souls here."

1. From "Soul Catcher", date, author, and source unknown.

2. Ibid.

3. Joe Soucheray, "Mary Jo Copeland Will Win This Battle," *St. Paul Pioneer Press*, 23 May 1993.

4. Mary Jo Copeland, Response to a questionnaire by Neal Bernards, 3 April 2000.

LAWYER, BANKER, ECONOMICS PROFESSOR, casino owner, sportsman, father, convicted felon. Deil Gustafson was many things during his complex, fascinating life. Boring he was not.

Deil Gustafson

Born in Chicago in 1932, Gustafson grew up on a farm in Iowa before attending Carleton College in Northfield, Minnesota. He served in the U.S. Army from 1953 to 1955, graduated from the University of Minnesota, earned a master of science degree from the University of North Dakota, and a degree from the William Mitchell College of Law. Gustafson taught economics at the University of Minnesota, practiced law, developed the Earle Brown Farm, and owned the Summit Banks.[1]

Gustafson ascended to the rarefied height of political power where the confluence of money and politics often becomes entangled. He became a favored aide to Hubert Humphrey, whose 1960 campaign for president he helped run. *St. Paul Pioneer Press* columnist Nick Coleman wrote, "Deil Gustafson was a wealthy power broker who wielded a strong, behind-the-scenes influence in DFL Party circles in Minnesota."[2]

Gustafson's downfall came when he bought into the Tropicana Hotel in Las Vegas. Gustafson became involved with the Kansas City and Chicago underworld, who were reported to own a half-interest in the Tropicana and allegedly skimmed millions in profits from the hotel/casino.[3]

"This man was at the center of a huge bank fraud related to the Mafia," wrote John L. Smith of the *Las Vegas Review-Journal*. For his crimes, Gustafson spent forty months in prison from 1984 to 1987.[2, 4]

Smith remains incredulous that, despite his conviction, Gustafson retained a positive image in Minnesota. "He was a man who bragged about his Mafia connections. In Minnesota he may have been a member of the boys' choir. But in Las Vegas we have a much different view of him."[5]

Political allies from his Minnesota DFL days remain loyal. Longtime Minneapolis politico John Derus recalls, "Gus was a very sophisticated man, a brilliant man. Gus wasn't a perfect man, but he took whatever he had to face and overcame it and handled it with great grace and dignity."[6]

Gustafson's daughter, Kristina states that he was a great father, "He came home every day and helped me with my homework. There was never a time in my life when we weren't together."[7]

Critics and supporters agree on Gustafson's intelligence. Minneapolis prosecutor Doug Kelley says, "He was a brilliant man, but the mob got the best of him. In the end he was a smart guy who outsmarted himself."[8]

Deil Otto Gustafson died Friday April 2, 1999, and was laid to rest in an old Swedish cemetery on a hill overlooking the Cannon River valley. Buried with him were the secrets of a complicated, conflicted life.[9]

1. Funeral Notices, *Star Tribune,* April 4, 1999, B-8, BHS.

2. Nick Coleman, "A One-of-a-Kind, Gustafson Took his Secrets With Him," *St. Paul Pioneer Press,* 7 April 1999; Jane Hallberg, Leone Howe, and Mary Jane Gustafson, *History of the Earle Brown Farm,* (Brooklyn Center: BHS, 1983), 119.

3. Ibid. 4. Ibid. 5. Ibid. 6. Ibid.

7. Andrew Telljohn, "Deil Gustafson, 67, Former Real Estate Magnate, Dies," *Star Tribune,* 15 April 1999.

8. Nick Coleman.

9. Ibid.

Jimmy Johnston

Hennepin County District Judge James Johnston was a fair-minded, courteous judge who gave each case, no matter how trivial, his full attention. Athlete Jimmy Johnston is a passionate skier, golfer, and lifetime advocate of outdoor activities.

Born February 13, 1928, Jimmy Johnston compiled a list of firsts in his law career. He became the first lawyer to open an office in Brooklyn Center and the city's first municipal judge (1962-64). He later became a Hennepin County municipal judge, retiring in 1993.[1]

Johnston installed the first rope tow at Wirth Park in 1957 to assist his ski school students. In 1961 he co-founded the Professional Ski Instructors of America and later founded the Midwest Ski Area Operators Association. "Active nationally as well as locally, Jimmy Johnston's list of skiing activities is like a railroad track in the prairies, so long it disappears in the distance before you can see it," read an article in Skiing New Magazine in 1968.[2]

His love of skiing extended to the written word. Johnston started the Minnesota-Wisconsin Ski News in 1953 as its first editor. The Minneapolis Star named Johnston their ski editor for the Sunday edition. He also originated the first 24-hour telephone snow report line in the Twin Cities.

Johnston's love for golf and skiing came at an early age. His father managed Minneapolis golf courses and young Jimmy began skiing on the snow-covered hills there in 1936 at age eight. With practice, and the grace of a good natural athlete, he won the city slalom championship his senior year of high school.

After a two-year stint in the Air Force, Johnston returned to Minnesota for law school. While still a student, the Minneapolis Park Board asked him to head their ski school program. From this modest beginning with twelve kids and 86 adults learning to ski the snow plow on Wirth Hill, Johnston oversaw the instruction of 30,000 children and 120,000 adults in thirty years of ski instruction.

Johnston succeeded by applying the same level-headed, calm rationale to skiing as he did to law. Fellow judge William Christensen believes Johnston succeeded marvelously, "He's friendly, fair-minded, likable. He treated everyone with respect and concern whether it was a high visibility case or an ordinary one."[3]

Johnston applied the creative aspect of ski instruction to his approach to life as a judge. In 1980 he co-initiated a program to sentence defendants to community service rather than jail. He was an early proponent of merging the municipal and district courts to improve efficiency and expedite the court process.

Judge James Johnston was regarded highly by his peers on the bench and those who stood before him. Ski advocate Jimmy Johnston is held in such esteem by his fellow ski instructors that he was presented a lifetime achievement award at the annual Veteran Professional Ski Instructors Reunion in Park City, Utah in December 1995.

Johnston now lives in Naples, Florida where his golf game gets constant attention but his slalom technique suffers.

1. Margaret Zack, "Judge James Johnston Hangs Up Gavel After Distinguished Career," *Minneapolis Star Tribune*, 1994.

2. Edna Dercum, Max Dercum, Doug Pfeiffer, Sponsorship Letter to the National Ski Hall of Fame, February 1996.

3. Zack, 1994.

Kimm Julian is a world-renowned operatic baritone who has performed with opera companies around the world. Julian was born April 14, 1954, to Mae and John Charles Julian and attended Park Brook and Edgewood Elementary schools while growing up at 66th and Quebec Avenue North.

Kimm Julian

His parents divorced in 1962 and moved to Crystal in 1968. There he attended Hosterman Junior High where Diane Ristrom was his vocal teacher. Encouraged by Ristrom to join a barbershop quartet, Julian got his first taste of theater performance by singing at a Sweet Adelines convention 1970.[1]

At Cooper High School Julian was cast as Huck Finn in the school's production of Tom Sawyer by Harold Wildung, who Julian calls "a tremendous influence" for giving him a chance to perform.

Tragically, Julian's mother died in a car-train accident in 1970, sending Kimm and his brother Kirk to live with his mother's twin sister Ethel Holmes' family in Brooklyn Park. Since Kimm was a varsity swimmer and involved in his school's music program he stayed at Cooper High.

Julian studied music at Simpson College in Iowa and earned his masters and doctorate degrees in Musical Arts from the University of Iowa. From academia he made his professional opera debut with the Des Moines Metro Opera and has gone on to international critical acclaim. The London Financial Times writes, "The American Kimm Julian is a mature Onegin, a stiff avuncular figure, perhaps a foretaste of one of Henry James's more icy creations, finely sung, intelligently acted."[2]

Julian currently lives in Brooklyn Park with his wife, Judy. They have two children, son Courtney and daughter Britanny. While remaining grounded in Minnesota, Julian travels the country to sing roles for companies including the Washington Opera, the Seattle Opera, the New York City Opera, and the Opera Theater of St. Louis.

Asked why he lives in Brooklyn Park while many opera singers call New York home, Julian bluntly states, "I do not like New York. Brooklyn Park is home to me. There's a support system for my wife and family here that I don't have elsewhere."[3]

That support system is especially important to Julian since his brother Kirk was killed in a car accident in 1977. Julian and his best friend since childhood, Craig Swanson, still talk almost daily on the phone.

Lest one think that performing opera is all jet setting, Perrier, and pampered living, Julian relates the story of a 1998 rehearsal gone bad. "Another actor and I were rehearsing a scene with a knife we were both uncomfortable with. The actor went to stab me and the switch (to release the blade) failed and the knife went three inches in to my abdomen. I had major surgery and it took me 11 months to recover."[4]

Julian stays fit through swimming, carpentry, and singing. He is known to take his full dress Harley-Davidson motorcycle out for a spin. But his real passion is cooking. Claims Julian, "If I weren't a singer I'd be a chef."[5]

1. Kimm Julian, response to questions asked by Neal Bernards, 9 February 2000.

2. From a Trawick Artists press packet.

3. Julian interview by Neal Bernards, 8 March 2000.

4. Ibid.

5. Ibid.

Garrison Keillor

GARRISON KEILLOR is the writer, composer, and long-time host of Minnesota Public Radio's wildly popular Saturday afternoon program, *A Prairie Home Companion*. His cast of characters, including Pastor Ingqvist, Norwegian bachelor farmers, and the Tolleruds are derived largely from a childhood spent in and around the truck farms of Brooklyn Park, circa 1955.

Keillor, born August 7, 1942, in Anoka, Minnesota moved with his family from south Minneapolis to West River Road and 77th Avenue North in Brooklyn Park in 1947. He and his siblings were educated in a three-room brick school house called the Benson school.

"It was a small, beautiful school, run by the local school board," writes Keillor. "We were awfully lucky to attend there. And that's exactly how I feel about Brooklyn Park in the Fifties. It was a good place to grow up."[1]

Keillor began broadcasting *A Prairie Home Companion* on July 6, 1974, on KSJN from Macalester College. The eclectic radio host based his show loosely on Nashville's Grand Ole Opry, though focusing on American music like jazz, gospel, hymns, and folk rather than country.

Longtime regular Vern Sutton likens Keillor's structure for the show to that of a worship service. "It has a very similar liturgical structure," claims Sutton. "It's a two-hour worship service where all the hymns and the readings and everything go to the sermon and then we conclude."[2]

By May 1980 *A Prairie Home Companion* gained national syndication. On November 4, 1985, Keillor made the cover of *Time* magazine and by 1987 his weekly radio audience had hit three million listeners. But by then Keillor had tired of the weekly grind of writing and composing a two-hour show himself so he moved to Denmark.

Keillor, whose relationship with local media has often been contentious, returned to New York in 1989 and launched a new variety series called *The American Radio Company of the Air*. By 1993 Keillor returned to St. Paul and changed the name of his show back to "A Prairie Home Companion."

The success of Keillor's radio programs lies in his ability to recreate a small-town feel for those who grew up in rural America and to create a longing for such a childhood for others who did not. His monologue, "News from Lake Wobegon," comes directly from his experiences growing up. "The pastoral qualities of Lake Wobegon—the innocence and freshness—really stem from Brooklyn Park, my boyhood home, writes Keillor."[3]

Keillor reminisces about scenes many long-time Brooklyn Center and Brooklyn Park residents can relate to, "We'd bike down to Earle Brown's farm, a thousand-acre ranch that lay along Highway 100, whiteface cattle grazing on a treeless plain, with Mr. Brown's big house, barns, stables, and riding arena in the distance."

Keillor can still be heard each Saturday afternoon spilling tales on public radio from his childhood experiences in Brooklyn Park.

1. Garrison Keillor, "My Boyhood Home," source and date unknown.

2. Noel Holston, "Longtime Companion," *Minneapolis Star Tribune*, 4 July 1999.

3. Keillor.

TIMOTHY JON LAUDNER, a 6' 3," 214-pound right hander, played catcher for the Minnesota Twins during their World Championship season in 1987.

Tim was born June 7, 1958, to Marvin and Eileen (Oswald) Laudner in Mason City, Iowa. Tim has an older brother, Randy, and a younger sister Joan. In 1965 the Laudner family moved from Iowa to Woodbine Lane in Brooklyn Center, and in 1967 they moved to 69th and Halifax, where they lived until 1976.

Tim said Brooklyn Center had a wonderful sports program. He played Little League at ages 10, 11 and 12 for the Malmborgs Orioles. John Polomny continued to be his coach when he played for the Babe Ruth team, the Charlie Construction Company White Sox, at ages 13, 14 and 15 and in Senior Babe Ruth, at ages 16, 17 and 18 when he played for the Iten Chevrolet Novas. They competed in the State and Regionals, and went to North Carolina to play in the Nationals when he was 18.

Laudner said Phil Cohen was a better person than a politician, that Phil was a fabulous human being and a wonderful person in youth baseball, along with his son Steve.

Tim attended Willow Lane, Palmer Lake, Brooklyn Junior High schools and graduated from Park Center High School in 1976. Math and sports were his interests in high school. He played tight end on their winning football teams and they took third place in the State High School Baseball tournament in the 1975–1976 season. Tim attended the University of Missouri for three years on a baseball scholarship, making the All-Big 8 team in 1979.

In high school Tim had been scouted by the Twins' Angelo Guiliani, but it wasn't until 1979 that he was the Twins third round draft choice and was sent to the Orlando Twins farm team. Tim had forty-two home runs, 100 runs batted-in and was the Southern League's Most Valuable Player, Tom Kelly was his coach.

Tim said he was shocked, excited, and had mixed emotions when told "you are going to Minnesota," because his team was in the playoffs. He felt loyalty to his team members Randy Bush, Gary Gaetti and Franky Viola.

Tim spent three years in the minor leagues before making his major league debut with the Twins on August 28, 1981. He singled and homered in his first game and homered again the next day. Tim was very popular with Twins' fans. Tom Kelly came to the Twins 1983, and became manager in 1986.

In 1990 Tim retired. He now works for Kleve Heating and lives with his wife, Tammy and children Samuel and Sarah, in Medina, Minnesota.

What did he learn playing baseball all these years? A whole lot of people gave him the opportunity to compete. It is a wonderful thing to be given an opportunity to win and to lose. He learned to be humble, to gain self-confidence. He believes in Theodore Roosevelt's message: "The credit belongs to the man who is actually in the arena."

Tim Laudner

Kirby Puckett

To Minnesota baseball fans, Kirby Puckett is synonymous with the hometown team. Former Twins general manager Andy McPhail conveys the depths of Puckett's popularity, "There was a long line in front of the (Twins) store one day, and this little girl— she couldn't have been more than four—walked past everyone, went up to the Twins' logo, pointed at it and said, 'Kirby Puckett.'"[1]

Kirby was born March 14, 1961, to William and Catherine Puckett, their ninth and final child. The large, loving family lived in the Robert Taylor Homes on Chicago's rough south side where Kirby was sheltered from negative influences by his older siblings, a protective mother, and a love for baseball that kept him playing rather than looking for trouble.

Kirby graduated from Calumet High School in 1979 as an All-American baseball player and attended Bradley University in Peoria, Illinois on a baseball scholarship. After one year at Bradley he transferred to Triton Junior College in River Grove, Illinois. Puckett led Trition to the national Junior College baseball finals and was drafted in the first round of the 1982 free agent draft by the Minnesota Twins.[2]

The small (5'9") outfielder with the bubbly personality, quick swing, and great leaping ability made a big impression in his first major league game. Puckett smacked four hits in his major league debut on May 8, 1984, against the California Angels.

From that fast start Puckett took off running as a Twin. His evident love of the game, happy demeanor, and good citizenship won over fans young and old as his baseball skills continued to develop. In a short time Puckett became the most popular Twin during autograph signing sessions and at public speaking engagements.

On November 1, 1986 (after the baseball season), Puckett married Minnesota native Tonya Hudson and moved into their new house in Brooklyn Park on the Edinburgh golf course. They have two children, Catherine and Kirby Jr. and now live in Edina.

"Maybe he wasn't born here," gushes one long-time Twins' fan, "But try to convince anyone that Kirby Puckett is not a Minnesotan through and through."[3]

Puckett's storied career was tragically cut short in 1996 by glaucoma in his right eye. He struggled in the beginning of the year to regain his hitting form while trying to see through the blur of a damaged retina. Numerous operations by the world's best eye surgeons only confirmed that Kirby would never play baseball again. He is now completely blind in that eye and serves as a vice president for the Twins' front office.

Despite his shortened career, Puckett entered baseball's Hall of Fame with statistics that include six Gold Gloves, 2,304 hits, 1,071 runs, 1,085 runs batted in, 207 home runs, and .318 batting average.

Rather than being embittered about his shortened baseball career, Puckett is thankful, "I just thank God that I got the chance to live out the dream that I had since I was five years old."[4]

1. Chuck Carlson, *Puck! Kirby Puckett: Baseball's Last Warrior*, Addax Publishing: Lenexa, KS, 1997.

2. 1997 Minnesota Twins' Media Guide.

3. Carlson; Steve Rushin, "A Bright Outlook," *Sports Illustrated*, 26 May 1997.

BORN AT ASBURY METHODIST HOSPITAL in Minneapolis to parents Glen and Evelyn Sonnenberg, mezzo soprano Melanie Sonnenberg has solid roots in both Brooklyn Center and Brooklyn Park.

Melanie Sonnenberg

Ms. Sonnenberg's childhood was spent along the banks of the Mississippi River in Brooklyn Center, where she attended Earle Brown Elementary School. In 1962, the Sonnenberg family settled further north along the Mississippi in Brooklyn Park. There, Melanie attended Riverview Elementary School and later graduated from Anoka Senior High.

An exceptional musician and versatile actress, Melanie Sonnenberg is well known in the music world for her impressive interpretations of roles ranging from the "bel canto" repertoire to the mezzo soprano heroines of Russian opera. Cited by the New York Times as "a rich and fluent mezzo and...an outstanding singer", she has performed throughout the United States and Europe to critical acclaim.[1]

She credits Sim Varner at Anoka Junior High and Joyce Paul at the Senior High with developing her interest in theater and numerous voice coaches, piano teachers, and orchestra leaders for honing her talents in music. Of particular note are Kenneth Davenport, head of the orchestra and string instruction in the Anoka school system, Bonita Melting and Ruth Hallenberg at Anoka Senior High, and her long-time piano teacher, Irene Anderson at the MacPhail school of music, who "provided an enormous foundation for my present career."[2]

Ms. Sonnenberg studied voice and theater at the University of Minnesota and appeared in roles with the Minnesota Opera, the St. Paul Opera, and was the first prize winner of the Metropolitan Opera Auditions. A great influence at the University of Minnesota was Dr. Vern Sutton, who Sonnenberg calls her greatest mentor and influence. To this day she and Dr. Sutton discuss stagecraft and the future of the arts.

The operatic talents of Ms. Sonnenberg have allowed her to perform title roles in the United States, Germany, Italy, Austria, and Japan. In New York alone she has appeared as leading artist at Carnegie Hall, Town Hall, Alice Tully Hall, and the New York City Opera. Sonnenberg's recording of Brahms' Alto Rhapsody with the Fort Worth Symphony can be heard on the Reference Records label. She has appeared on television in Europe and on PBS as Lola in the City Opera's production of "Cavalleria Rusticana" on "Live from Lincoln Center."

Sonnenberg's rich voice and stage presence add spark to whatever production she leads. Wrote one New York critic, "At about the three-hour mark mezzo Melanie Sonnenberg...spun around to the audience and let loose a barrage of performing temperament and endless roulades which stirred the stolid proceedings into vibrant life."[3]

Though now a resident of New York City, Sonnenberg attempts to return to Brooklyn Park every Christmas and summer to visit her immediate family who still live in the area.

Presently, Ms. Sonnenberg sits on the National Board of Governors for the American Guild of Musical Artists. She has given masters classes at universities in the United States and in Russia.

1. Will Crutchfield, "Opera: Rossini's 'Journey to Rheims' in St. Louis," *The New York Times*, 15 June 1986; Peter G. Davis, "Opera: Bel Canto Sings 'La Pietra del Paragone,'" *The New York Times*, 16 January 1979.

2. Melanie Sonnenberg, Response to Questionnaire from Neal Bernards, 11 April 2000.

3. Bert Wechsler, "Soaring Soprano's Carry 'La Donna,'" *New York Daily News*, 3 February 1992.

LaVyrle Spencer

FROM BROWERVILLE TO BROOKLYN PARK, LaVyrle Kulick traveled a long psychological distance to become LaVyrle Spencer, leading romance novelist. Born to an alcoholic father and a mother who later divorced him, young LaVyrle was moved from town to town across Minnesota while her family searched for a "new start."

From Browerville the Kulicks moved to Alexandria, then Mankato, and finally Staples. These frequent, disruptive moves made LaVyrle "bold and aggressive." She states, "I was a cheerleader in all three towns, which tells you something about how I had to push my way in."[1]

In Alexandria LaVyrle discovered music, in Mankato she met Inella Burns, her 10th grade English teacher and mentor. Ms. Burns encouraged Kulick's writing, taught her of rhythm in the written word, and inspired LaVyrle to become an English teacher. Burns was not surprised to see her student succeed in writing. "I noticed she had a more extensive vocabulary than most sophomores. She had a way with words." [2]

Uprooted from Mankato, LaVyrle moved to Staples, a smaller town with much less to offer, except Daniel Spencer. LaVyrle Kulick met Dan Spencer at a gathering where they did a bit of vocal harmonizing. LaVyrle said, "You're pretty good." He said, "You're pretty good, too." They've been in love ever since.

LaVyrle and Dan married, moved to Brooklyn Park and raised two daughters, Amy and Beth. While busy raising a family, Spencer could not shake visions of a book. "It was driving me crazy. It would wake me up," she recalls.[3]

Finally, at 4 A.M. on a July morning in 1976 she began writing. Though the outline of a book swirled in her head, Spencer knew she needed something more. That something was background and research. Armed with a tape recorder and a lot of questions, she visited her grandmother, Bessie Adamek in Staples. "If I set the scene in April, I would put in what Grandma said happened in April."

The end result was *The Fulfillment*, which Spencer asked Princeton, Minnesota romance author Kathleen Woodiwiss to read. Woodiwiss forwarded it to her publisher, Avon, and they put it out in 1979.

Since then Spencer has won the Romance Writers of America Golden Medallion Award for historical romance for her books, *The Endearment*, *Hummingbird*, and *Twice Loved*.

She credits much of her success to her three goals in writing, "Make 'em laugh, make 'em cry, make 'em wait. Dickens said that first," notes Spencer. "Of course, when you're writing romance, you have to turn 'em on somewhere along the way." Turn them on she did—to the tune of 1.5 million-copy press runs for her most popular books.[4]

Janet Baughman, Spencer's mother, recalls that LaVyrle was always at the library, "so I wasn't really surprised that she became a writer. I never went to high school— my parents were too poor—so I'm really proud of LaVyrle."

LaVyrle Spencer has retired from the romance novel business and is believed to be enjoying life in Stillwater, Minnesota.

1. Kim Ode, "Romance Writer Turns to Mainstream," *Minneapolis Star and Tribune*, 23 March 1986.

2. Ibid.

3. Ibid.

4. Ibid.

JAMES GEORGE JANOS. A Slovak no different from any other of a thousand who grew up in south Minneapolis in the 1950s and 1960s. Only this Janos is more widely known by his wrestling name: Jesse "The Body" Ventura.

Jesse Ventura

Born July 15, 1951 to parents Bernice and George Janos, Ventura took to organizing wrestling matches between neighborhood kids at an early age. He recalls serving as promoter, ringmaster, referee, and ultimately, performer in a makeshift wrestling ring in his parents basement. This flair for self-promotion served him well as a professional wrestler, movie actor, radio personality, mayor of Brooklyn Park, and as governor of Minnesota.

Ventura graduated from Roosevelt High School in 1969 and drifted for a while, until a friend, Steve Nelson, talked him into joining the navy. Ventura followed his older brother Jan into the Navy's Underwater Demolition Team. That decision shapes Ventura's thinking to this day. "Once a SEAL, always a SEAL," writes Ventura.[1]

After Ventura's stint with the UDT's (now part of the Navy SEALs), he grew his hair long and joined a motorcycle gang. James Janos quickly tired of the aimless life and became the pro wrestler Jesse "The Body" Ventura. Ventura switched from pro wrestling to acting in 1986 with a role in Arnold Schwarzenegger's movie Predator where he uttered the now-famous line, "I ain't got time to bleed."

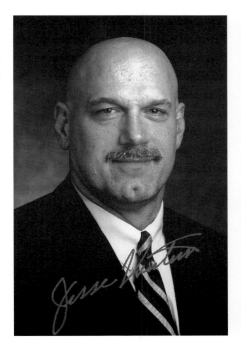

Ventura, his wife Terry, son Tyrel, and daughter Jade settled into a home along the Mississippi River in Brooklyn Park. It was here that his political career began. He defeated Mayor Jim Krautkremer and served as Brooklyn Park's leader from 1991 to 1995. The flamboyant mayor was still as much wrestler as he was politician, often attending city council meetings wearing a bandanna around his head and a chip on his shoulder.

Animosity between Ventura and much of Brooklyn Park's city council ran so deep that the council tried to oust their mayor by questioning his residence. In June 1994 Ventura had purchased a home in Maple Grove and the rest of his family lived there. An administrative judge ruled in Ventura's favor, but the experience squelched any desire to run for re-election.

Ventura turned to talk radio to air his views and listeners loved his outsider, anti-establishment attitude. In an election that shocked and surprised political observers around the country, Ventura defeated Democrat Hubert "Skip" Humphrey III and Republican Norm Coleman in the Minnesota gubernatorial election of 1998.

Governor Ventura's tenure in office has been marked by controversy. During his first year in office, the Governor came under intense fire for calling organized religion a "sham and a crutch for weak-minded people" and speculated that St.Paul's confusing street design had been laid out by "drunk Irishmen."[2]

Despite the controversy, or perhaps because of it, Ventura remains in the national spotlight for his rags to riches story. In a 1999 address to students at Roosevelt High School, Ventura said, "The American dream is still there. I'm living proof that dreams can come true."[3]

1. Jesse Ventura, "I Ain't Got Time to Bleed," Villard Books: New York, 1999.

2. Adam Fisher, "When Ventura Speaks, Consider Source," *Daily Hampshire Gazette*, 9-10 October 1999.

3. Ventura.

Jon Vezner

SINGER. SONGWRITER. HUSBAND to country star Kathy Mattea. Jon Vezner grew up in Brooklyn Center with modest plans to become a music educator, but a few good songs, a marriage to country star Kathy Mattea, and a conviction to move to Nashville allowed him to become one of country music's most successful modern songwriters.

Born on June 6, 1951, to Harriet and Kenneth Vezner, Jon faced a difficult childhood. He was born with growths in his throat and stomach and with club feet. By age 2 Jon had already endured nine surgeries to correct these problems.

Despite his physical difficulties Jon played high school football and wrestled. In fact, Vezner cites Al Johnson, his wrestling coach, as one of the Brooklyn Center people who most influenced him. He also cites Brooklyn Center High School educators Leo Verrett (art), Roger Dick (English), and Warren Olson (social studies teacher and football coach).

"Although it was a suburb of Minneapolis, Brooklyn Center still had a small feel to it," write Vezner. "I believe our graduating class of 1969 was the largest ever and that was only about 205 people. So you at least knew everyone on a first name basis." [1]

Along with the sporting activities Vezner served as lead singer and bass player in various bands, developing a love for music that would serve him well later in life. Vezner, however, admits, "I wasn't very good." [2]

He earned a degree in music theory after attending North Hennepin Community College and Southwest State University in the mid-1970s. He and fellow Brooklyn Center grad John Kokesh then set up a studio to record Vezner's songs.

In 1984 Vezner and Kokesh got Wrensong, a song publisher in Minnesota to sell some of Vezner's songs to country acts Dave & Sugar and Mel McDaniel. In 1986 Vezner made the commitment to full-time songwriting by moving to Nashville. Upstairs from his apartment lived a former waitress and demo singer named Kathy Mattea. [3]

"Her car battery went dead one day, so I 'jumped' her," states Vezner. The two struggling artists became friends, dated, and finally married on Valentine's Day in 1988. [3]

Mattea initially resisted recording any of her husband's music fearing claims of nepotism. So Vezner's songs wound up on recordings by Reba McEntire, Ronnie Milsap, and Lorrie Morgan. In 1990 Mattea broke down and recorded her husband's song "Where've You Been" (co-written with Don Henry). The song propelled Mattea to her second consecutive Country Music Association (CMA) female vocalist award, a Grammy, and to gold record sales. "Where've You Been" also garnered Vezner a CMA song of the year award for 1990.

Since then Vezner has had songs recorded by Janis Ian, John Mellencamp, Steve Wariner, Faith Hill, and Diamond Rio. Clay Walker's version of Vezner's "Then What" became a number one hit country single in 1998.

Vezner still composes songs for Warner-Chappell Music and lives with his wife in Nashville, Tennessee.

1. Jon Vezner, response to questionnaire by Neal Bernards, 11 April 2000.

2. Mary Jane Gustafson, "Four Vezner Songs Are Recorded by Nashville Stars," *Brooklyn Center Post*, date unknown.

3. Press release from Warner-Chappell Music, author and date unknown. 4. Ibid.

More Uncommon Lives

Ike Anderson – A local lumberjack who was a walking history book.

Vern Ausen – A rock of strength in the Brooklyn Historical Society and the community.

Roxana Benjamin – On the cutting-edge in publishing NorthWest News.

Wallace and Elaine Bernards – 50 years in education, volunteer in Criminal Justice System; prayer breakfasts and "giving kids a second chance" program.

Janis and Sue Blumentals – Architectural team that transformed the historical Earle Brown Farm buildings into a useful and functional complex.

David and Jody Brandvold – Passionate developer of Brooklyn Center's Southeast neighborhood; a voice for children.

Byron Brekke – Lifetime commitment to leadership in the school district and vocational/technical college in his area.

Bob Cahlander Jr. "The Bear" – Went out of his way, above and beyond the call of duty as a public servant for 41 years.

Phil Carruthers – The Brooklyns own "Speaker of the Minnesota House of Representatives."

Beverly Ann Cohen – A master cook, a great listener.

Don Davis – A police officer who was "Mister Communicator" focused on prevention.

Jim and Rose Denn – A compassionate couple to all in their time of need.

Dr. Bill Dudley – He believes in himself and he believes in others.

Julia Dussault – "The Angels came and took the pillow lady, no more trick or treat pillows."

Jim and Rose Ebert – "I hope that I helped someone each day of my life and made them smile" – "The most loving, caring, cooperative and encouraging person."

Donn Escher – Respected public servant with a lifetime commitment to volunteer leadership in his community.

Arnie Foslien – Great mentor of community, industry and church lay leaders.

Father Roger Godbout – Census taker, founder and organizer of St. Alphonsus Catholic Parish.

Pastor Carl Groettum – Census taker, founder and thirty-one year pastor of Cross of Glory Lutheran Church.

Eugene Hageman – Toils in the vineyard of volunteerism.

Jane Hallberg – Preserver of history, author, historian.

Harold Hannay – He saw what needed to be done, and did it, founder Brooklyn Center Civil Defense.

Baldwin Hartkopf – First Mayor of Brooklyn Park, he had a passion for grassroots politics.

Del Holmin – Shoppers City general manager who figuratively embraced those considered unemployable and turned their lives around by offering them meaningful employment with advancement.

Ralph and Leone Howe – History makers and history preservers.

Frank Irvin – He helped those who couldn't help themselves.

Roy Iten – An auto dealer who established a legacy of community involvement.

Mel and Helen Jacobsen – Documented history through photo journalism.

Vi Kanatz – Voice of reason and human decency.

Al Kattar – Man of great faith and dedicated leader and worker in church and community.

Dawn Keifer – Volunteer organizer and leader in her community and church.

Marian Klohs – A Brooklyn Park living historian, preserver and nature lover.

Dick Koop – Held up a standard for youth accountability. An original "Come Home to the Park" enthusiast.

Jim and Dorothy Knuckey – Mentors of young residents on what community involvement is all about.

Don and Sylvia Kramer – A team whose hearts and home have an open door to the needy and hurting.

Cliff and Gen Lane – Hometown team who treated their customers like family.

Dallas Lawrence – Pioneer in business development, champion of Brooklyn Center's Post Office.

Warren Lee Lindquist – Elementary school principal, "would love doing it all over again, it's been a wonderful ride."

Pat Milton – On the cutting-edge in publishing NorthWest News.

Keith and Charlotte Nordby – Two great humanitarians.

Arnold Nyberg – Honesty in auto repair, and his family follows in his footsteps.

Ron Ostendorf – In twenty years has volunteered thousands of hours to youth basketball and baseball programs.

Dennis C. Palm – Pioneer in excellence in Recreation and Parks management.

Curt Pearson – Brooklyn Park City Attorney 1963-1999, architect of staged development policies, instrumental in city bonding and financing programs.

Dick Peterson – Invented the Peterson Bluebird House, credited with helping to save the species.

Richard Risley – Law enforcement with community understanding, a lion with a Lions heart for diabetes education.

Dr. Norene Roberts – Made the history book complete, gifting others with her gifts.

Jon Rohe – Long time community leader, a model of commitment.

Bjorn Rossing – Mayor who led in a new, positive beginning for Brooklyn Park.

Dan and Karen Ryan – Commitment and personal involvement go hand in hand, Come Home to the Park enthusiasts.

Roger Scherer – Legislator and successful businessman, generous with his life for the benefit of his community and church.

H. A.(Lex) Schoonover – "Don't send a boy to do a man's job," Sears' manager in the beginning days of Brookdale.

Carol Schreiber – Tireless leader and worker for charitable and political causes in our communities.

Fred and James Seed – Fred had a dream to create a city, James followed his father, in addition he helped develop Edinburgh USA Golf Course.

Barbara Sexton – From an Ensign in the Navy during the Korean War to a genealogist and community leader.

Earl Simons – If there is something to be done to better the community, he gets involved.

Peg Snesrud – A model of commitment to keeping neighborhoods livable and safe.

Jim Soderberg – In only four and a half months and without any government subsidy, rehabilitated and filled with new occupants a very troubled, failing, 216 unit apartment complex.

Bud and Barbara Sorenson – His avocation is parks; love and service to the mentally challenged.

Carol Starner and Jean Knapp – A calling: to meet the needs of terminally ill babies.

James C. Stuebner – Brought class and distinction to Brooklyn Park with construction of the Northland Inn.

Gene Sullivan – Successful businessman, passion for cooking which he donated for church and community benefits.

Cecilia Scott Svardal – First woman to serve on the Planning Commission and also the first woman on the City Council in Brooklyn Center.

Les Thurs – Dedicated Little League Baseball promoter, sponsor, and worker.

Mary Ellen Vetter – Dedicated to preserving history and the environment.

Barbara Wacek – A role model for volunteers, and a dedicated Camp Fire leader.

Barney Wilson – The something more printer for the Something More City, "if you wait a day, I'll get you a good deal."

Uncommon Lives and Oral History

Oral history is one of the most exciting tools available for collecting and preserving history. By conducting oral interviews with narrators, we document and capture people's memories. The memories of those interviewed, when used as a source of information, are endnoted in this book. The transcripts are being edited and approved by those interviewed, and the collection will be available for access by the public.

Audrey Hartkopf Alford, daughter of Baldwin Hartkopf, first Mayor of Brooklyn Park (1954-1957), Interviewer: Ernee McArthur.

Grace Arbogast, Mayor of Brooklyn Park 1995 to present, Council member 1993-1994, Interviewer: Bill Schreiber.

Keith Caswell, Caswell Engineering, builder of sanitary sewer in Brooklyn Park, Interviewer: Howard Heck.

Phil Cohen, School Board Member, Village Council member 1963-1965, Mayor of Brooklyn Center 1966-1977, City Council member, Interviewer: Eileen Oslund.

Ron Dow, Brooklyn Park Council member 1971-1976, 1979-1982, Interviewer: Bill Schreiber, March 27, 1999.

Marge Dupont, Daughter of former Brooklyn Center Mayor Merton Lane 1917-1921 and 1939-1948, Interviewers: Ernee McArthur, Kay Lasman.

Gordon Erickson, Mayor of Brooklyn Center 1962-1965, Interviewer: Phil Cohen.

Bill Fignar, Brooklyn Center Council member 1973-1981, Interviewer: Ernee McArthur.

Wilbur Goetze, Great-grandparents and potato growers, Brooklyn Park Village Trustee 1961-1962, Interviewer: Bill Schreiber, February 6, 1999.

Dale Greenwald, Owner and partner of Cass Screw Machine Products, Chamber of Commerce leader, Interviewer: Phil Cohen.

Bill Hannay, Brooklyn Center Volunteer Fireman 1956-1978, Chamber of Commerce president, Interviewer: Ernee McArthur.

Baldwin Hartkopf, State Representative, first Mayor of Brooklyn Park.

Howard Heck, Brooklyn Center Village Trustee and City Council member 1960-1971, Interviewer: Ernee McArthur.

John Helling, North Hennepin Community College president, Interviewer: Bill Schreiber.

Gwen Joyner, Daughter of founder of Joyner's Silver Plating, retired Methodist minister, Interviewers: Bill Schreiber, Ernee McArthur.

Orlyn Joyner, founder of *Sentinel Newspaper*, Joyner's businesses, civic leader, Interviewers: Bill Schreiber, Ernee McArthur.

Myrna Kragness, Mayor of Brooklyn Center, 1995 to present, Interviewer: Bill Schreiber.

Jim Krautkremer, Brooklyn Park Mayor, eighteen years, 1973-1990, Interviewer: Bill Schreiber.

Tony Kuefler, Brooklyn Center Council member 1973-1981, Interviewer: Ernee McArthur.

Art Kvamme, Brooklyn Park Trustee 1961, Mayor 1962-1963, Brooklyn Park Lions, Charter Commission, Interviewer: Bill Schreiber.

Louie Larson, Songwriter: "Take Me Back to Minnesota," Interviewer: Ernee McArthur.

John Leary, Brooklyn Center Trustee and City Council member 1962-1972, Interviewer: Phil Cohen.

Art Lee, first Brooklyn Center Village Administrator 1955-1966, Interviewer: Ernee McArthur.

Leonard Lindquist, Chair, Railroad & Warehouse Commission 1949-1952, State Representative 1955-1959.

Jerry Marshall, Brooklyn Park Councilman 1976-1990, Interviewer: Bill Schreiber.

Ernee McArthur, Chamber of Commerce executive, State Representative, community activist, Interviewer: Barbara Sexton.

Dean Nyquist, State Senator, Brooklyn Center Mayor 1978-1990, Interviewer: Eileen Oslund.

Don Poss, Brooklyn Center Village Engineer, Administrator, City Manager 1960-1977, Interviewer; Ernee McArthur.

John Reilly, North Hennepin Community College administrator since 1987, Interviewer: Bill Schreiber, August 17, 1999.

Joe Roche, Aviator, longtime north area resident, Interviewer: Ernee McArthur.

Don Rosen, Founder of Pilgrim Cleaners and "Coats for Kids" program, Interviewer: Phil Cohen.

Evelyn Schmidt, Brooklyn Park developer, Interviewer: Bill Schreiber.

Darrel Schneider, employee of Caswell Engineering, builder of the Brooklyn Park sanitary sewer, Interviewer: Howard Heck.

Bill Schreiber, potato grower, Brooklyn Park Councilman 1967-1972, State Representative, Metro Council member, Interviewer: Phil Cohen.

Ed Shimek, potato grower, Brooklyn Park Village Trustee 1957-1959, Mayor 1959-1961, Village Manager, City Manager, Interviewer: Bill Schreiber.

Glen Sonnenberg, Brooklyn Center School Board, Brooklyn Center Village Trustee 1953-1954, northside community educator, Interviewer: Ernee McArthur.

Alice Tessman, pioneer potato growers family, resident Brooklyn Park since 1908, interviewers: Jane Hallberg, Ernee McArthur.

Eldon Tessman, Life-long Brooklyn Park resident, potato grower, Brooklyn Park Planning Commission, community leader, interviewer: Bill Schreiber.

Ed Theisen, Charter Commission, Republican Chair, CEAP president, Jaycee leader, Interviewer: Ernee McArthur.

Jack Umland, Brooklyn Park Council member 1970-1984, visionary of Edinburgh Golf complex, champion of the common good, Interviewer: Bill Schreiber.

Jack Vaughn, Brooklyn Center Civil Defense leader, discusses his World War II battlefield experiences, Interviewer: Ernee McArthur.

Donald Weesner, Friend of Earle Brown, Interviewer: Ernee McArthur.

Ted Willard, Brooklyn Center City Council member 1966-1971, Interviewer: Ernee McArthur.

John Wingard, Potato grower, Justice of the Peace, State Representative 1963-1972, Interviewer: Bill Schreiber.

Ann Wynia, North Hennepin Community College president, Interviewer: Bill Schreiber.

Chapter Fourteen

BROOKLYN HISTORICAL SOCIETY HALL OF FAME

THE BROOKLYN HISTORICAL SOCIETY HALL OF FAME was founded in 1988. Recognizing that the cities of Brooklyn Park and Brooklyn Center had its separate "celebrities," each city has its own Hall of Fame. Brooklyn Center's Hall of Fame has been in existence since 1988. The idea of a Hall of Fame was inspired by the retirement of Brooklyn Center's Post newspaper Editor, Mary Jane Gustafson. She had been an icon in the communities' news and in their hearts for twenty-seven years.

Then Mayor, Dean Nyquist's recognition committee thought a fitting highlight to her retirement celebration would be to honor Mary Jane, by inducting her into the Brooklyn Center Hall of Fame. It was a celebration of her commitment to Brooklyn Center and her outstanding service to the community. Thus began the Hall that has honored thirteen members of the community since 1988. Brooklyn Center's Hall of Fame Inductees photos are hung on the wall outside City Council Chambers. The "wall of fame" was officially dedicated June 27, 1993. All living members attended the dedication.

With a strong desire to honor their treasured community members, Brooklyn Park opened the doors for nominations to its Hall of Fame in 1998. In the inaugural year the Brooklyn Park inductees were Evelyn Schmidt and Eldon Tessman on June 13, 1998.

The Brooklyn Historical Society

Hall of Fame Purpose & Criteria

PURPOSE:
The principle purpose of the Brooklyn Park and Brooklyn Center Hall of Fame is to identify, recognize and record for history, persons (living or deceased, resident or non-resident) who have made a significant and enduring contribution in the development of the communities.

CRITERIA:
People who meet one or more of the following criteria are considered to be worthy of nomination:
• A person who has made a significant difference in the community.
• A person who was part of building the foundation or roots of the community.
• A person who has made a unique contribution to the community.
• A person who has served as a model to the community/area.
• A person involved in or responsible for 'cutting edge' progress or projects.
• A person whose contributions have had or will have a cumulative (lasting) positive effect on the community

1988
BROOKLYN CENTER
INDUCTEE

Earle Brown

EARLE BROWN was the owner of Earle Brown Farm since 1905, inherited from his grandfather, John Martin. Being active in his community and politically conscious, the meetings to create the Village of Brooklyn Center took place in Brown's garage in 1911. Fearing annexation into Minneapolis, Brooklyn Center incorporated at this historic event.

Brown became Hennepin County's Sheriff in 1920. In 1926 George Dayton said at "faithful" Sheriff Brown's Testimonial Dinner, "the citizenship of this county unites in appreciation of his duties well performed, this man so firmly entrenched in the confidence of all who know him." His law enforcement success led to his draft to start the Minnesota Highway Patrol in 1929. Earle trained the highway patrolmen on his farm. He converted his buildings into classrooms, mess hall and dorms. Earle and four officers, trained in the east, were the instructors. His first class had thirty-five graduates.

Earle resigned from the Highway Patrol in 1932 because he was drafted to run for Governor that year. He lost the election. Many blamed the fact that it was during Depression times and being a Republican was not popular then.

During World War I, Earle offered his land to the military. It was used by Dunwoody School and the University of Minnesota flight trainees under the direction of the Army and Navy. It was also used by other commercial pilots. Because of this, Brown Field Airport became the first Minnesota Commercial Airport.

Earle's generosity was also felt in the schools. He would let the school district park their bus in his barn. When a tornado struck the area in 1929 Earle welcomed the students into one of his homes to use as a temporary school. Today we see Earle Brown Elementary school, named for him as well as Earle Brown Drive near his former home.

At age forty-one Brown married Gwen Foster. With no children, Earle Brown willed his farm to the University of Minnesota. Garden City School and the Earle Brown Continuing Education Center resulted from the sale.

Earle Brown lived from 1879 to 1963.

Editor's Note: Earle Brown was a man of wealth and means. His joy was derived from sharing with his employees, friends and the greater community. This is profoundly evident while reading the Family Stories within this book. So many memories and good deeds involving Earle Brown are mentioned, it would seem that he had touched everyone's life during his time, in one way or another.

Mary Jane was proud of her Polish heritage and was a world traveler. She worked for twenty-seven years at the Brooklyn Center Post as editor and reporter. Her beat was the Brooklyn Center city hall and city council meetings. She had built in radar reading the pulse of the community and reporting on it. Mary Jane took great pride in keeping the community she loved informed. She especially enjoyed the "people" side of every story. Mary Jane made sure those that deserved a pat on the back got it in print. She also took great joy in giving those who deserved a "kick in the butt" their name in headlines.

Mary Jane was named an honorary member of the Brooklyn Center Rotary; the first woman to receive the honor. She also received a Paul Harris Fellowship Award from the Rotary District Governor.

As founder and president of the Brooklyn Historical Society, her greatest endeavor was to work for the preservation of the Earle Brown Farm. She lived to see the grand opening of the renovation of the farm on April 22, 1990. Mary Jane was a contributing writer on a book about the farm's history, published in 1983.

In March 1990 Mary Jane was coaxed out of retirement by the invitation of the NorthWest News staff, a new community newspaper for Brooklyn Park and Brooklyn Center. The thought of reporting on events in the community she loved was just too much for Mary Jane to pass up. Her contribution to the new newspaper gave the Brooklyn Center/ Brooklyn Park tabloid immediate credibility. "If Mary Jane was writing for this paper, it had to be worth reading," thought the residents.

Mary Jane served on the Charitable Foundation Board, Earle Brown Ad Hoc Committee, worked with the Community Emergency Assistance Program (CEAP), the Crime Prevention Committee, the Brooklyn Center All-America Award Committee, and she served on the North Hennepin Community College Foundation Board.

Mary Jane died November 27, 1990, at the age of sixty-nine. She and her husband, Arthur, raised their three children in Brooklyn Center.

1988
BROOKLYN CENTER
INDUCTEE

Mary Jane Gustafson

1989
BROOKLYN CENTER
INDUCTEE

Phil Cohen

PHIL COHEN was Brooklyn Center's Mayor from 1966–1977. While Mayor, the city of Brooklyn Center was at a high growth and developmental stage. Projects such as Brooklyn Center High School, North Hennepin Community College, the Community Center, City Hall, the expansion of the parks system and Twin/Palmer Lake were all brought to reality under Cohen's watch. Interaction and communication between State and Local government was greatly inhanced by Cohen due to his political savvy and the respect he had gained from our state officials.

He served on the village council from 1963–1965 and on the District 286 School Board for two and one half years. Phil was on the staff of the Metropolitan Council 1978–1979 and was Legislative Assistant to Senator Dave Durenberger for ten years, 1979–1989.

Phil was reapppointed to the City Council again in May of 1989, serving to December 1990 and again from 1991–1992.

Phil was a Vice-President of Goff-Wilkie & Associates of Brooklyn Park, St. Paul and San Francisco.

Known for his clowning, Phil contributed his pink polyester suit as his momento to the Brooklyn Historical Society. No one near Phil is ever safe from his ever-present water pistol, usually in the form of an easily concealed pen, to be showered upon any unsuspecting guest.

Cohen's contributions to the community go beyond the political arena. He has been an active member of the Earle Brown Days committee. He has been in charge of many of the events which the community has enjoyed through the years. He was also a member of Brooklyn Center's successful committee bidding for the All America City award. He served on the Brooklyn Historical Society Board and several of its committees, the Peacemaker Board and the North Hennepin Community College Foundation Board.

Phil has also been active in the Brooklyn Center Baseball program, volunteering endless hours, including organizing the annual 4th of July Senior Babe Ruth Tournament each year in Brooklyn Center. In the summer of 1998, the baseball field at Grandview Park was named "Cohen Field" and dedicated for his contributions to youth baseball in Brooklyn Center.

2000 update: Phil chaired the Year 2000 Celebration in Brooklyn Center on February 11th. It's 89th Birthday, Anniversary, Dinner, Dance and Fireworks was a gala kicking off the many events planned for the coming year.

JOHN MARTIN DRIVE in Brooklyn Center is named for a man who was very prominent in Minneapolis in the second half of the 1800s. Captain John Martin, an early Brooklyn Center resident, was the grandfather of Earle Brown.

With capital from a successful visit to the California Gold Rush of 1849, Martin came to settle in the Minneapolis area in 1855. He was born in Vermont in 1820. He was captain of industry, involved in river freighting, flour milling and lumbering.

In 1875 Martin bought 140 acres of the Earle Brown farm site in a bankruptcy sale. At first his family, including grandson Earle, used the farm as a summer retreat. On May 25, 1905, Martin died. He had sold the farm to Earle in 1901 for one dollar. Grandson Earle received the major part of Martin's estate in a trust fund. Martin was said to be one of the richest men in Minneapolis at the time of his death.

Earle Brown made the farm a landmark with the white-trimmed buildings, green pastures and grazing horses. For years, the scene was a treat for passing motorists.

Today the farm is preserved as an inn and business and convention center called the Earle Brown Heritage Center and is owned by the city of Brooklyn Center.

Captain John Martin

MERTON LANE served as President of the Brooklyn Center Council from March 13, 1917 to March 8, 1921. He served again 1939 to 1948. In 1951 the term "Mayor," replaced the title "President" on the village council.

Lane was born in Maine in 1880. He married Mae Craemer of Baring, Maine and the newlyweds moved to Hennepin County. Their vegetable farm was on the west side of Brooklyn Boulevard (old Osseo Road) at 62nd Avenue, where Bridgeman's stands at this time. Lane was active in the Minneapolis Market Gardener's Association from 1903 to the early 1930s. He was a charter board member of the association and served on the board for fifteen years he also served as the board's chairman. Active in many facets of agriculture, Lane was involved with the Farm Bureau and with the State Conservation Board.

Merton not only served his community, but his country in many ways. He was on the Minnesota Selective Appeal Board during World War II. He received a medal and a Certificate of Merit from the U.S. Congress under the Truman administration and a Certificate of Appreciation for Faithful Service from President Roosevelt.

Merton was a member of the original Brooklyn Center School Board.

Merton and Mae had nine daughters and one son.

Merton Lane

1990
BROOKLYN CENTER
INDUCTEE

Madeleine Roche

MADELEINE ROCHE is the founder of the Community Emergency Assistance Program, known to the community as CEAP. The idea started in 1968, when she and friends saw unmet human needs and responded to them. Soon church groups, volunteers and communities joined hands with Madeleine in support of the program. In April 1971 CEAP incorporated as an exempt charitable organization and elected its first Board of Directors.

CEAP'S first office was in St Alphonsus Catholic Church's rectory. With the help of the Brooklyn Center Jaycees and the Bicentennial Commission CEAP moved into the old City Hall. Madeleine saw her dream in ashes, when that first CEAP building burned New Years Eve 1977. With fundraising and a land donation, a new building arose. She served CEAP from 1970-1980 and then worked to develop the Minnesota Temporary Food Assistance Program under Governor Quie.

Madeleine's contribution to the communities in need with the founding and growing of CEAP offered area residents a food shelf, clothing, furniture, babysitting and shelter. Her mission, it is said, began as one of "social love."

Born in St. Andre-Avellin, Quebec, October 22, 1927, Madeleine was educated in French. Welcoming guests and a happy heart are part of her heritage; traits that helped inspire CEAP and her family. The Roches have opened their own home to Foreign Exchange students, who have become extensions of their own family through the years. Madeleine has served on the Board of the Brooklyn Historical Society, serving three years as its president.

Madeleine made the U.S. her home with her Navy pilot husband, Joe. In 1949 Madeleine became a naturalized United States citizen. The Roches raised their eight children in Brooklyn Center.

GWEN FOSTER'S FAMILY ROOTS were in Maine. The family moved to St. Paul where she was born. Shortly after her birth, they moved to Minneapolis. Gwen met Sheriff Earle Brown while she was a secretary at the Radisson Hotel. They married at his Brooklyn Center farm in 1921.

Gwen Brown was on the boards of Asbury and Maternity Hospitals in Minneapolis and the Jean Martin Brown Children's Home in St. Paul, where she served for twenty-five years. Some of the causes that she worked for were orphans, working women, unprotected children, the "old Trails" chapter of the D.A.R. (Daughters of the American Revolution), The Republican Workshop, Women's Club, P.E.O. and North Methodist Church.

Gwendoline and Earle Brown had no children of their own. They both put their heart into many worthy causes. They touched the lives of the community of Brooklyn Center beyond what they could ever dream. They let all people, little and big into their royalty like lives. The moments they shared, gave many memories to treasure for a lifetime.

Gwen died in Vermont in 1947.

Gwendoline Brown

Dr. Duane Orn

DR. DUANE ORN was called, by then Mayor Phil Cohen, "the most civic minded Doctor in Brooklyn Center." Though a resident of Golden Valley, Duane has been considered a beloved and respected resident since the day he came to town. He hasn't missed many major events in Brooklyn Center, and you will find his name on most of the event lists of volunteers or supporters helping make them happen.

Duane served as Brooklyn Center's Community Health Officer for many years. A popular Master of Ceremonies for many events, Orn has been an officer, committee/or Board Member of the Ad Hoc Committee to develop the Earle Brown Farm, CEAP, Brooklyn Historical Society, Northwest Community Cable Board, Chamber of Commerce, Hope Ministries, Peacemaker Center, Crime Prevention Fund, North Hennepin Leadership Academy Committee, Northwest Human Services, the Autism Home and the Brookwood housing development.

In 1963 Dr. Orn was part of the first organizational meeting of the Brooklyn Center Chamber of Commerce. He served two terms as its president. Under his leadership, the Chamber grew and prospered. The city of Brooklyn Center was promoted as the "Something More City." As Chamber president, Orn led the gathering and presenting of a 4,000 signature petition to Congress for a full post office to be located in Brooklyn Center. During Orn's time as president, the Chamber was also active in promoting the building of the new city hall and civic center, which opened in 1971. Ice Days in Brooklyn Center was a Chamber sponsored event in the 1960s. It was a winter celebration with many family events. Over the years, Dr. Orn has been actively involved with Brooklyn Center High School and has been their physician. Orn is a charter member of Brooklyn Center's Rotary International. He is a senior partner at Northport Medical Center in Brooklyn Center. Doctor and Karen Orn have one son, Charlie.

SIGURD EDLING SERVED on the Brooklyn Center Council and Planning Board for many years during the time the city was emerging from an agricultural community into a vibrant reidential and commercial city. As a member of the original Planning Committee (now Commission) from June 1942 to 1960, he was on the "cutting edge" of Brooklyn Center's progress during 1954–1959, the peak home building years.

The Edling farm was located on the site of the present day Marquette Bank in Brooklyn Center (57th and Brooklyn Boulevard). Sig was a vegetable farmer and truck gardener until his farm was sold to the Dayton Company for Brookdale Center. He helped put the Brookdale deal together during the lengthy planning stage from 1955–1960 and saw the new shopping mall through its opening in 1962.

Edling was one of the charter members of the Brooklyn Center Fire Department. Described as "wise and kind," he also served on the Board of the Brooklyn United Methodist Church. Sig and his wife Sylvia had two children.

KERMIT KLEFSAAS taught at Brooklyn Center High School for thirty-two years. He coached football, golf, Jr. High basketball and varsity track for twenty-five years. For eighteen years, he taught summer school. He also worked at Camp Nathaniel, a Christian Service Brigade boy's camp. Kermit came to the new Brooklyn Center High School in 1961 and was hired while working overseas at the American Community Schools in Beirut, Lebanon.

Fans say Kermit is a quiet giant, with the gift of accepting people where they are and then encouraging them to grow. His willingness to help people is based on his belief that "Only one life will soon be past; only what's done for Christ will last." He is remembered by many of his students as an outstanding mentor who helped them on their way to productive lives. His contributions will have a lasting effect on our community, and mold the future...our children.

Kermit is a member of the Hope Chapel Alliance Church. He and his wife, Marilyn have five children.

DEAN NYQUIST has given time, energy, money and most importantly vision to the city of Brooklyn Center. Not only as Mayor for thirteen years, but as a dedicated resident, he instilled in the community a "can do" attitude.

Dean led the committee vying for, and winning, the distinguished honor of All America City in 1986. An honor celebrated far into the future.

As Mayor, Dean was instrumental in creating the Brooklyn Center Community Prayer Breakfast. In 2000 it celebrated twenty-two consecutive years, the longest running prayer breakfast in the state. Dean has been the leader on the committee since its inception. Major projects during Dean's term involved I-94 Freeway, Central Park, Centerbrook Golf Course, the commercial and industrial areas, Earle Brown Farm purchase and Shingle Creek Trail System, plus many more.

Dean's willingness to serve led him to a two-year presidency of the Brooklyn Center Rotary. A priority for Dean, he assisted with several club local, national and international projects of good will.

In 1990 Dean received the Brooklyn Center Police award for leading Brooklyn Center in mediation proposals and for starting the Peacemaker Center in 1983. His outgoing commitment to families and youth of the community has been proven numerous times by the list of organizations Dean has either founded or been instrumental in starting. These organizations all focus on helping families survive, live better lives or giving someone a second chance. The Dean's List includes: Peacemaker Center, Brooklyn Center Mediation Project, Juvenile Diversion Program, Family Conflict Resolution Center and the Brooklyn Center Charitable Foundation.

Dean contributed to the Brooklyn Center general fund his Mayor's paycheck for thirteen years. He believed in volunteering and felt if the baseball coaches and scout leaders weren't being paid, neither should he be.

Dean was elected the area's State Senator from 1967–1972. His feeling while Senator as well as Mayor was that there was no limit to what could be accomplished if we don't care who gets the credit. In 1968 he received a Distinguished Service Award from the Brooklyn Center Jaycees. In 1970 Dean was listed in that year's edition of "Outstanding Young Men of America."

Dean and his wife Marie raised three children in Brooklyn Center.

1996
BROOKLYN CENTER
INDUCTEE

Tom Shinnick

TOM SHINNICK's spirit of volunteerism has touched thousands of community members. The uniqueness of it is, the effects have been appreciated by youth and adults alike.

In 1983 Tom became a member of the Brooklyn Center Lion's Club. Tom has served as Lion Director, Treasurer, Vice President and President. In 1993 Tom received one of the highest awards given to a Lion member, the "Melvin Jones Fellowship Award." In 1996 Tom was elected to become Vice-District Governor and later Governor of the Lions of Hennepin County, overseeing forty-three Lions' Clubs.

Tom's twenty plus years with the Brooklyn Center Little League, along with numerous volunteers, has transformed the program into one of the finest Little Leagues in the state. Through Tom's efforts with the city, a former ballpark is now Centerbrook Golf Course. In turn, two ball fields, a concession stand, playground and a parking lot were built for the league. More than 500 boys and girls each year enjoy playing ball thanks to his leadership. In 1991 Tom was honored for his commitment to youth. One of the fields was renamed "Shinnick Field." Though now retired as league president, Tom is still actively involved in overseeing the baseball program.

In 1996 Tom had served on the Brooklyn Center Park and Recreation Commission for seven years. He also is a member of the District 286 School Board.

Tom and his wife Lorraine of forty years, have resided in Brooklyn Center since 1961, where they raised three children.

Tom is a member of the board of the Brooklyn Historical Society, and recently he was inspired to name the organization's new headquarters, "The Brooklyns History Center."

As a youth, Henry Dorff worked on the Brooklyn Center garden farms. He served his country and his community in World War II, 17th Airborne Division. He graduated from the University of Minnesota in 1949 and as a CPA, became Administrative Manager for Packaging Corporation of America. Henry moved to Brooklyn Center in 1954. He retired in 1985.

From 1961–1964, Henry was Brooklyn Center's Village Clerk, serving as a member of the village council. He was then appointed to the city's first Charter Commission and served for eleven years, five as chairman.

Henry provided leadership for sixteen years on School District 286 Community Education Advisory Council and played a major role in Kaleidoscope. He chaired a unique and successful City/School committee to install lights on the high school tennis courts for the community to use.

Henry's extensive group affiliations show his dedication to the community. They include: Charter member of the Brooklyn Center Chamber of Commerce, Citizens for Better Government, Brooklyn Center Rotary, Knights of Columbus Council #435, American Legion Post #0251, Cub Scout Troop #147 and North Suburb Kiwanis. Henry has served on the Earle Brown Day Festival Committee since 1986, several years as its chair. He is one of the volunteers responsible for creating and organizing the new family events added to the celebration in the early 1990s.

Henry also has served on many committees at his parish, St Alphonsus Catholic Church. His commitment to Brooklyn Center will have a lasting positive effect on all who benefited from Henry's gift of time, energy and wisdom.

Henry and his wife, Emily have raised four children in Brooklyn Center.

Henry Dorff

1998
BROOKLYN PARK
INDUCTEE

Evelyn Schmidt

EVELYN SCHMIDT has been one of the guiding hands in the development of the city of Brooklyn Park since the early 1950s. As one of the city's more prominent developers, she was part of building the foundation and roots of the community as it is today.

Evelyn and Herman Schmidt and Tom and Vivian Thompson bought the Back Way Motel on Highway 81 in 1950. When they sold the motel in 1951, Evelyn kept part of the land, bought five acres to the north, and platted and developed lots and built her first homes. Evelyn continued buying, developing and selling lots until 1959. She built the Villa Del Coronado apartments (192 units) in 1968. At this time she met Fred M. Seed, Vice President of Cargill, Inc. and she, her son Bob, and Fred entered into a partnership to buy many farms in Brooklyn Park for future development. She and Bob formed Brook Park Realty, Inc.

After thirty-four years, Brook Park Realty, Inc. has successfully developed several thousand lots for single family homes, townhouses, apartments, commercial and industrial use. A few years after they started working with Fred Seed, he died of cancer. They have worked with Fred's son, Jim, since then. They are especially proud of the part that they played in the development of Edinburgh Golf Course and the beautiful homes around the course.

Evelyn has been especially involved in the development of the parks in Brooklyn Park. Developers are requested to donate 10% of the land for Parks and Trails. From the time that Dennis Palm became Park Director she worked closely together with the Park Department in the development of the Historical Farm.

She was selected as a member of the North Hennepin Community College Foundation when it was formed. She was chosen to be Grand Marshal in the 1971 Tater Daze Parade. In 1998 Eldon Tessman and she were Grand Marshals of the Tater Daze Parade in honor of of their induction to the Brooklyn Park Hall of Fame. Evelyn received the Paul Harris Award, the Rotary's highest honor for volunteerism.

Her family and company have been very active in the Dinner Auction held each year by the North Hennepin Community College Foundation to raise funds for scholarships.

Evelyn participated in the development of the Community Emergency Assistance Program (CEAP) in its early years.

ELDON TESSMAN'S ROOTS are deeply woven in Brooklyn Township. His family has resided in the community since the 1870s. Working on the family farm, he was one of the potato farmers who made the area famous as the largest supplier of potatoes in North America in the 1950s and 1960s. As a widely respected alumni of the University of Minnesota, Eldon offered part of his land as research test plots for studies and helped in furthering development for advanced potato farming techniques.

Eldon has given much of himself to his city, as one of his supporter's states, "He lives with the philosophy that it is our individual responsibility to make a difference in bettering our world. His world centers on family and the community of Brooklyn Park."

Eldon served on the Brooklyn Park Planning Commission (1960-1972) in the crucial developmental years. He was chair of the commission during the years the site was selected for North Hennepin Community College. He was a dedicated supporter and was committed to bringing the college to Brooklyn Park. He served on the Economic Development Commission from 1972-1977 and the Brooklyn Park Charter Commission, 1992-1997. Eldon was a charter member and has served as President of the Brooklyn Park Rotary Club; as one of its most active members, Eldon has received seven Paul Harris awards, the Rotary's highest honor for volunteerism.

Eldon has been honored twice by his community by serving as Tater Daze Grand Marshall in 1968 and 1998. He was chosen as a respected member of the city of Brooklyn Park who has contributed endless energy, hours, wisdom and vision to the City. Eldon was also honored for his part in the great potato producing heritage the city lays claim to.

Eldon, in 1981, was one of the charter members of the successful North Hennepin Community College Foundation. He now serves as a Director Emeritus and is a member of the College Advisory Board. He and his wife June received NHCC's highest honor in 1996, when they were presented the Presidential Medallion in recognition for their exceptional service on behalf of the college and its students.

In addition to many other commitments to the community, Eldon has been an active, highly valued member of the Brooklyn United Methodist Church since 1942. Eldon and June Tessman raised their five children on the family homestead on 85th Avenue in Brooklyn Park just down the road from their good neighbor, North Hennepin Community College.

1998
BROOKLYN PARK
INDUCTEE

Eldon Tessman

Chapter Fifteen

FAMILY STORIES

THE HISTORY OF THE BROOKLYNS is woven together from the rich tapestries of the lives of the individuals and families who made their home in these two cities. In this chapter, we share some of those stories.

Although our daily lives rarely change the course of history, our stories can inspire others and make a difference. This letter, written by a young Brooklyn Park woman to her grandmother, suggests the influence that our personal histories have on future generations.

Dear Grandma Klohs,

No generation has given more of themselves to make their families, their country, and their world a better place to live than yours, and I wanted to let you know how thankful I am to have you as a grandma. As a survivor of the Great Depression, World War II, and other hardships, the sacrifices you were asked to make and contributions you gave were tremendous. I am very appreciative of all you do for me and of all the memories and wisdom you share with me from your many past experiences.

I commend you on the good job you did in raising a very proud, successful family. I certainly couldn't imagine myself raising four energetic boys alone, while my husband worked all day. You described this time as just plain survival, but I think that inside you knew what you were doing, and worked hard to give those boys everything you possibly could. You provided my father and uncles with the knowledge and a positive outlook to live a prosperous life along with the inspiration that they could be anything they wanted to be in this world. I am sure you are very proud of where they all are today, and I want to let you know, they sure couldn't have done it without you.

You and your generation's contributions to your families and our world have impacted both my generation and me so I want to make a commitment to preserve your legacy. It is amazing all of the things you have actually experienced and lived through. They include wars, fighting for women's rights and black equality, putting a man on the moon, countless inventions, breakthroughs, events, and disasters occurring during your life. Your generation's contributions to better our country and the world are endless! I don't know where I would be today without a television or automobile.

All of these contributions should certainly never be forgotten, and I plan to tell my children and grandchildren all of the stories you have told me, and how you, my grandmother, lived through the Great Depression and World War II. I respect you a lot and admire all you have gone through to make you the strong, generous, and caring person you are today. Your outlook and knowledge about life is not only intriguing, but also inspiring. I look upon you as a role model, and I couldn't dream of having a better grandmother.

Love,
Jennifer Klohs

My GRANDPARENTS, Harry and Hilda Alford, moved from North Minneapolis to Brooklyn Center in 1922 upon their doctor's recommendation. Their infant son, Ray, seemed frail so the doctor advised them that it is healthier for children to grow up in the country. They built their new home at 5334 Camden Avenue North. They raised their five children and spent the rest of their lives there.

Harry Alford worked as Traffic Manager for the Illinois Central Railroad. Legend has it that on returning from work on most Saturday afternoons, he could be seen walking from the bus stop with a brand new piece of glass. His three sons, Sidney, Roger, and Raymond were baseball fanatics and when they were young, played ball in the fields surrounding their home on Camden Avenue. Hence, the need for new glass to replace the windows damaged by their errant line drives. They continued playing baseball together throughout the North side and at Parade Stadium into adulthood.

The three boys, along with their sisters, Lillian, and Joyce, attended Earle Brown School. The Alford family became members of Harron Methodist Church on 55th and Dupont in 1932.

The Alford Family

Harry and Hilda Alford's fortieth wedding anniversary: Roger, Harry, Hilda, Lillian, Ramond, Joyce and Sidney

Harry and Hilda's children grew and married. Joyce moved to Golden Valley and Lil to St. Louis Park. All three boys and their families settled in Brooklyn Center. In fact, for most of my childhood they all lived on the 53rd block of Camden and 4th Street.

My name is Jeanne Larson and I am the daughter of Roger and Marion Alford. I moved to Brooklyn Center in 1948 when I was four years old. I remember playing baseball, kick the can, and flying kites with the neighborhood kids in the field between Camden and 4th Street. We'd roller skate on Camden Avenue because it was the only street in Brooklyn Center with a sidewalk. We called that street "Dirty 4th Street" because it was a dirt road until sometime in the 60s.

I attended Earle Brown School. We rode the bus for first and second grades. There were two buses—the "orange bus" and the "yellow bus." I don't remember which color bus I rode but do remember the competition as to which bus would arrive at school first. The next four years I walked or biked to school. Although homes were taking over some of the open space in Brooklyn Center, we still were able to walk in a nearly straight line through several fields to get to school.

I was a member of the first graduating class of Brooklyn Center High School in 1962. It seemed traumatic at the time to leave North High School and spend our senior year at a brand new school. On the other hand, it was fun to reunite with the 100 or so kids that had begun school together at Earle Brown.

Marion Alford, my mother, still lives in Brooklyn Center and continues to attend Harron Methodist Church. She is the last connection to the Alford family still there.

Submitted by Jeanne Alford Larson

John and Pat Amundson

JOHN AND I MET in September 1966 at Fargo North High School in Fargo, North Dakota. We attended the Fargo High School in our senior year. We were married in June 1969 and have lived in Brooklyn Center for more than thirty years.

My husband, John, is employed as a project manager for States Electric and Manufacturing. The company manufactures high and low voltage switchgear and computer controlled soft loading generator switchgear for emergency back up to utility systems. I was employed at Western Insurance for seventeen years before the company merged with American States Insurance.

I have become involved in the community affairs of Our Lady of Victory Catholic Church. My duties are President of Council of Catholic Women (CCW), helping to serve funeral luncheons and Lenten soup suppers. I also am a member of the choir.

We have two daughters who attended Earle Brown School and graduated from Brooklyn Center High School. Schanna is married to Andre Sherbanenko. Tawna works for Brooklyn Center Municipal Liquor Stores. We have been blessed with three grandchildren, Ali, Amy, and Aaron.

One of our favorite summer pastimes is to go boating down the St. Croix River in our Glastron Boat.

The Amundson family enjoys family barbecues in the back yard.

Submitted by Pat Amundson

John, Andre, Schanna, Pat, and Twana Amundson

I CAME TO BROOKLYN CENTER in May of 1973. The first thing that happened to me was to be stuck on a congested highway. My husband Frank came here from Bloomer, WI, and I came from Eau Claire, WI. We were married in Menominee, WI, on September 8, 1973.

We lived in the Willow Lane Apartments for six months before Bob and Marie Hanley helped us to find our new home at 7206 Halifax Avenue North. We have lived in our home for over twenty-five years. We had three children: John, Joan, and Julie. They all attended Palmer Lake Elementary School, Brooklyn Junior High School, and then graduated from Park Center Senior High in 1993, 1995, and 1999. John has since graduated from Bethel College in 1997 and is now working on his Master's Degree through the same college. Joan graduated from Concordia College in Moorhead, MN, in 1999 and is now working through Office Team at PUR Products in Brooklyn Park. Julie attended Crestview Elementary School, Groves Learning Center in St. Louis Park, and is now enrolled in the Horticulture Program at North Hennepin Technical College. She also is working for the Brooklyn Center Target Store between classes.

While living in Brooklyn Center, Frank worked for WCCO Television (Channel 4), WFBT-TV (Channel 29), COMB later known as Cable Value Network, and QVC, and is now working for the University of Minnesota. Janet worked for K-Mart before being a full time mom, and later worked for Bill's Superette.

Submitted by Janet Anderl

How is your journey, oh weary traveler?
The sun doeth set upon our ocean,
Storms are calming and night is coming.
Crisp cool air is whispering and blowing.
What say you, oh spiritual earth-walker?
Will the dust greet you when the light no longer flickers?
Or will it reject your celestial frame,
And leave you naked before an eternal day?
How are your travel, oh aged journeyman?
Did the day crown you with glory and might?
Or has this night skies brought bitterness to sight?
Answer me this oh wondrous wonderer. . .
As you gaze at the raising moon,
As all nights fall on us so soon
What stroke of color has your brush performed
On this vast canvas which our Father formed?

by John C. Anderl

Frank and Janet Anderl

Frank, Janet, Joan, Julie, and John Anderl (1987)

Gail (Bakken) Andersen

I, GAIL BAKKEN ANDERSEN, graduated from the University of Minnesota in 1940, with a B.A. degree in Journalism and Creative Writing. During the years 1940-1957, I combined homemaking and mothering two children with freelance writing and part-time reporting for Post Publishing Company, a string of Minneapolis suburban newspapers. A major assignment was city council reporting for six growing suburbs. I learned much about civic affairs and property development.

My husband, Lester Bakken, and I built a large home overlooking the Mississippi River in Brooklyn Park. As he had full-time employment elsewhere, I contracted the job under the direction of a registered architect, and did most of the stone and brick work, as well as other manual construction work.

From 1957-1960 I was News Editor for the *Brooklyn Center Press*, combined with home duties. I left editing in 1960 to do special assignments for Post Publishing and freelance magazine articles.

Lester and I were divorced after eighteen years of marriage. I was very active in early Brooklyn Park government and in 1962 was elected City Clerk-Council Member for Brooklyn Park during its rapid growth period, and served until 1966. I gained further experiences in property development, building requirements and related subjects.

In 1968 I married Alf Anderson, an electrical salesman. During the next two years I subdivided nine-lot residential addition to Brooklyn Park. I designed, built and contracted four homes therein. I did the stonework on three of them, in addition to other manual construction work. I operated these activities under the name Birma Development Company, which I use for my building and property development activities.

In 1971 I moved to the Jordan, Minnesota area and presently own the former Jordan Brewery Building that dates from 1870. I also was mayor of Jordan from 1980-1983.

Submitted by Gail Andersen

Gail Andersen

IN 1946 we moved from Minneapolis to Groveland by Wayzata Hwy. 101 and Minnetonka Boulevard. On the property that we bought was an old farmhouse, a barn and a big shed, located on eighteen acres of land. On it was a small lake named Shaver's Lake. At that time we had two small boys, David three years old and Steven six months old. Effie's father, Olie Olesen, who lived with us was in the construction business. The shed was perfect for a shop. Ivan and Dad could "fix" up the house.

Ivan and Effie Andersen

In 1949 Ivan was building a house in Osseo. Everyday he would go past two acres of land with a basement house. It had two acres of sandy soil, weeds, not a tree, and a cow farm next to it. The basement house was very nice looking, with all knotty pine walls, casement windows all around, and it was farm country — potato farms, and nice country people. The price was $6000. "Our first home!" Ivan could build a house on the basement, someday. The boys could go to a country school! In March 1951 there was a bad snowstorm that almost covered the windows. That night Effie's father passed away in his sleep. What were we going to do? Those good farm neighbors, the Goetzes, Schreibers, Johnsons, and Neddersens came to help. The county snowplow cleared the road.

Ivan worked for Pearson Brothers as foreman. They built hundreds of homes in Brooklyn Center and Brooklyn Park. They also built Cross of Glory Lutheran Church. The Andersens were charter members of this church.

In 1955 the Andersens had baby boy, Jeffrey. In 1961 baby boy Craig was born. All of the boys went to Osseo Schools. Steven and Craig went to North Hennepin Community College. David and Steven joined the Navy after graduating from high school. They were on the Aircraft Carrier Forrestal. Steven was on the carrier in 1967 when it caught fire in the Gulf of Tonkin off the coast of Vietnam.

David worked for Northern States Power and retired after thirty-four years, in 1998.

Craig, David, Jeffery, Steven, and Effie Andersen

Steven graduated from the University of Minnesota with high honors and is married to An Nguyen. He has a lithography studio in Minneapolis named Akasha. He taught printing in New York and Paris as a master printer.

Jeffrey worked at Northern States Power for many years and for Steven at the studio.

Craig is a writer and loves books; he has a large collection of books.

Ivan lost both of his legs in 1981 but the Andersens managed to visit and travel by themselves. Ivan died of a heart attack in 1989.

Effie worked as a hostess for the Lincoln Del West for eighteen years. She worked with and met many nice people.

The Andersens sold their property in 1986 and hoped they could live there ten more years. In 1999 Highway 610 came through their backyard.

Submitted by Effie Andersen

Ike Anderson

THIS IS WRITTEN to honor a great friend of the Brooklyn Historical Society. Ike Anderson was born in 1891. He lived his earlier years near the Mississippi River in Camden in north Minneapolis and later on 49th and Newton Avenue North.

As a board member of the Brooklyn Historical Society, he sometimes invited us to have our meetings in his basement amusement room. The room had a chair railing topped by historic logging and horseracing pictures. He paid a lady friend of his to bake a high and light angel food cake, which he served at coffee time.

Over the years, Ike was a harness maker, a horse trainer and racehorse driver for M. W. Savage during the years of Dan Patch. He had a short movie of Dan Patch, which he contributed to the Minneapolis History Museum. Ike Anderson had also been a professional wrestler, until he received an arm injury. He had been a lumberjack. At one time he raised show chickens at 53rd and Lyndale Avenue North. It was because of a mutual interest in prize poultry that he became acquainted with baseball great Babe Ruth. The "Babe" had asked Ike to sew a loop on his "demo" baseball. Before World War I, Ike made saddles for the English government. He used his leatherwork skill as a trimmer and foreman in the upholstery department for the Ford Motor Company.

Working the Logjam in 1908-09 at 57th and Lyndale Avenue North on the Mississippi by Brooklyn Township. Ike Anderson, third from right.

Ike's most colorful descriptions were of working (during the logging boom) for the Mississippi and Rum River Boom Company at about 56th and Lyndale Avenue North on the river during 1908-09. He wore a yoke on his shoulders to deliver water and chewing tobacco to the "River Pigs," or lumberjacks. He was soon promoted to be a catch marker, assigned to sort and mark logs for specific mills as they floated down the Mississippi in the warmer Minnesota months. In the winter, he worked as a harness maker in the Minnesota north woods at a lumber camp. From his experiences, Ike contributed valuable information for the Brooklyn Historical Society booklet, "Tales of Local Minnesota Lumberjacks."

Ike was a widower when we first knew him. He said he seldom needed a doctor in his ninety years, but he became ill and died in his nineties. His second marriage lasted less then a year before he died.

Members of the Brooklyn Historical Society fondly remember Ike's memories of history and bright spirit. He had a saying, "Hope for the best, but be prepared for the worst, and whatever comes, take it with a smile."

Submitted by Jane Hallberg

SWAN ANDERSON was born October 6, 1859, in Upsaala, Sweden, and came to America in the late 1870's, working at Minnegasco, and later on the railroad. He returned and purchased about 300+ acres from the Mississippi to Newton Avenue, 77th to 73rd and 69th. In 1886 he married Amelia Engstrand from Alexandria, Minnesota. They had three sons: Arthur N., 1888: Carl W., 1892; and Edon W., 1896. They had approximately fifty cattle, milking thirty to forty, selling to north Minneapolis boarding houses. Swan retired, 1920, moving to their four-plex at 30th and Washington N.; they lived there until their deaths, Amelia in 1932, Swan in 1955.

Swan August and Amelia (Engstrand) Anderson

Their eldest son, Arthur, died in 1916, age 28. He and wife, Emma Peterson, had three children: Shirley—married Albert Rydeen, they had 6 children, Rodney, Sharon, Marilyn, Carol, Nancy and RuthAnn; Lilias—married Rolland Holmberg, they had 5 children, Glenda, Gayle, Darryl, Richard and Bonnie; and Glen, who died at age 17 in 1932. Edon died in 1959, age 63. He and wife, Gay Lamb, had two children: Vonda Gay, who married Pastor Donald Lichtenfelt, and Eleanor. Son Carl took over the farm, selling milk to Ewald Creamery. Carl married Blanch Leckvold in 1920; they had two sons, Harvey, 1921, and Earl, 1925. In 1928 he sold the cows and machinery, moving to Minneapolis. Carl did factory work until he was laid off in 1930, then built a small house on 73rd Avenue and moved back out. During the 20s & 30s neighbor Malcolm

Carl, Edon, and Arthur Anderson

Moses, owned a steam engine and threshing machine, he helped area farmers with threshing. Osseo was the "shopping center." Keiffer's Butcher Shop used their horse-drawn ice-wagon to bring meat products to your door!

Harvey & Earl attended Benson School at 73rd & West River Road. Miss Weithoff taught grades 1-4, Miss Miller 5-8. There were two basement lunchrooms: north/girls, south/boys. During the winter, mothers took turns making Friday hot dishes. Al Theorin, School Board Supt., farmed on 77th, and came annually to count next year's students. Every year Al's mother brought orange slice candy for each student. 73rd was "washboard"—chuck-holey, dirt, and rarely graded. Brooklyn Center graveled their half; the rest remained dirt until the early 60's paving!

Harvey joined the Navy in 1941. Home on leave in 1942, he married Estella ('Stella) Holmberg. Their daughter, Darlene Joanne, 1943, a Registered Nurse, married Norman Gregornik in 1963 (he died November 1994). They have two sons: David, a pharmacist at St. Jude's Hospital, Memphis, TN; Daniel, a Pharmacist Tech at Mercy Hospital, Anoka. Daughter, Barbara Jeanne, 1947, has had a long career at "the arsenal", later Honeywell. Earl joined the Navy in 1943, then married Caryl Quinn in 1951. Their son, Brian, a truck driver, married Debra Vanilla. They have four children and live in Chester, South Dakota. Brenda married Wes Hein. They have two children and live in Nisswa, Minnesota.

After World War II, Carl built several houses on 73rd. Harvey's and Earl's first houses (Girard & Fremont); all but Carl's first house still stand. Blanche died in 1974; Carl, almost 100, died in 1992.

Submitted by Harvey Anderson, Grandson

L. J. (Bud) and Marge Andrewjeski

Andrewjeski basement home, 1950

AT THE END OF WORLD WAR II, we, L. J. (Bud) and Marge Andrewjeski, looked for property to build a home. An army friend of Bud's knew of property across the street from them. We checked it out and bought it. Two brothers bought property on either side. In 1949 we built our basements. After a day of trying to lay blocks, we decided to hire another friend to take over that job. The Block Layers finished the three basements. Next came capping, pouring the floor, putting in windows, etc., to get it ready to live in. After World War II basement homes were allowed. Bud and any available friend spent the summer completing it. September 1949, we moved in. Electricity was not in yet, so we had a long electric cord laid across the street from our friends' basement home. We used that for about two weeks until we got our own electricity. We had a card table for the kitchen table, a living room set, and a bedroom set. Bud built the kitchen cabinets, divided the rooms, put up wallboard, and tiled the floors. With time and money it became very comfortable.

We had one son (a year and a half old) when we moved into our basement home, and two more before we finished our home above ground. We moved upstairs in 1952. When we moved into our basement home, we sat on our back steps and watched traffic on Highway 100, ten blocks away. Now we cannot see traffic on the next block. I took our boys out for trick or treating on Halloween and walked in plowed cornfields. Our transportation was either our one car or walking to the streetcar on 52nd and Bryant Avenue. That was six long blocks, and especially so on a cold winter day. Bud built a sleigh that our three sons rode, making it much easier. We left it at the corner store. That store is still there.

Our three sons went to Earle Brown Elementary School and Brooklyn Center High School. Our oldest son was in the first class in the new high school in 1961 as a seventh grader and finished there. Our youngest son graduated in 1970. Bud worked in the truck body industry, building, designing, and repairing truck bodies, and semi-trailers. I, Marge, worked as a checkout cashier in grocery stores until 1972, then stayed home for three years, and began work at Brooklyn Center High School in 1975. I worked in the laundry room, washing dirty football uniforms, other uniforms, mending rips and tears, and washed towels for Physical Education classes. I had Special Ed. students work for me as aides. They are still very special to me. I was also in two Drama Classes. I retired in 1989. About three years later I came back and worked part-time to keep the uniforms mended and sew costumes for Drama Productions, a job I thoroughly enjoy.

Our children and I have been members of Hope Lutheran Church for many years. I have also helped there with costumes for Sunday School programs, and for the Easter and Christmas productions. We have had our trying times living so close to the river, having three sons, but we enjoyed living in Brooklyn Center. I cannot imagine living anywhere else. We have friends dating back to 1949 here. I know the day will come soon when we will have to move and that will be a sad day.

Bud died in November 2000.

Submitted by Marge Andrewjeski

THE 26TH OF DECEMBER 1958 brought the signing for and moving into my very first home and last, to date. I now considered myself a "homeowner," even though there was a 4½% mortgage on close to thirteen thousand dollars that was still to be paid. It was like every other home in a two square block area, a three-bedroom rambler, located on a corner lot, I loved it.

Grace Arbogast

Ronald MacLeod was born in 1959. Randal MacLeod arrived in 1962 and Sheryl MacLeod completed our family in 1966.

The years to follow were filled with family times, as well as being a Mrs. Jaycee, Brooklyn Park Firemen's Auxiliary member, co-coach of girl's softball along with a close friend Marilyn Borgen, and a Brownie Leader. The children attended Lincoln Elementary, Hosterman Junior High and Cooper High School in School District #281. At that time kindergarten was held in other schools, as there were so many young children. Today Lincoln Elementary is closed and houses a day care center.

Twenty years later I married Leo J. Arbogast. In 1991 there was earnest talk of reconstruction of 63rd Avenue, the street we entered into from our driveway. We now enter our driveway off Sumter Avenue and have a sidewalk along 63rd as well as concrete curbing. Back in the fifties the houses not only were built alike but did not have sidewalks, only rolled asphalt curbing, and each had its own cesspool and well.

Leo and Grace Arbogast

It was now time to become involved once again in the community. After going to the council meetings regularly to keep a close eye on, and give my input on the 63rd Avenue Project, I decided to run for the West District Council Seat. In 1992 there were many council meetings that completed the planning and approving of the 63rd Avenue reconstruction, campaigning and winning the election. Mid-term the position for Mayor was now on the ballot. Once again I campaigned and won the election. In January 1995 I was sworn in as Mayor and am in my second four-year term.

My husband, Leo, passed away on September 11, 1999.

In forty-one years I have seen potato fields blossom into homes, apartments, industrial and commercial businesses, highways, parks, churches, ice arenas, Senior Center and golf courses.

Submitted by Grace Arbogast

Gene and Rita (Laumeyer) Ascher

On May 3, 1927, Henry B. Laumeyer married Barbara Cecelia Drajna at St. Peter's Catholic Church in Browerville, MN. Henry's parents, Ben and Mary (Stephan) Laumeyer and Barbara's parents, George and Margaret (Motzko) Drajna were farming families from Long Prairie and Browerville. Henry had three perfect cribbage hands, enjoyed hunting, fishing and card tricks. He was a member of St. Mary's Catholic Church. Barbara was a VFW President. She enjoyed gardening, crafts and crocheting.

On April 20, 1920, Louis J. Ascher (born in Germany) married Everett (Effie) Carroll from Erie, PA, at St. Joseph's Catholic Church in north Minneapolis. Louis worked for Grain Belt Beer and Glueks Brewing Company for forty-five years. Both were members of St. Anne's Catholic Parish. Their hobbies included card games, house parties, piano and gardening.

Dallas, Gene, Richard, Debra, Donna, Rita

Rita (Laumeyer) Ascher was born April 9, 1936, sister of Leo, Norman, Walter, James and Philip. School days were spent at country school, Todd County District #48. She graduated from Long Prairie High School in 1954 and worked at Geo. T. Walker as an Inventory Control Bookkeeper until marriage. Gene Ascher was born February 29, 1932, at Maternity Hospital on Glenwood Avenue. He was the youngest brother of Dorothy and James. Gene attended St. Anne's and Lincoln grade schools and graduated from Vocational High School. He served in the Korean War as a Military Policeman in Yokohama, Japan. Gene retired from the Holdahl Company after forty-two years as a Formica fabricator.

Gene was a Star Tribune newspaper carrier for 8 years as a youngster. His hobbies are fine, old music, cards and woodworking. He is a member of Veterans of Foreign Wars, the Brooklyn Center American Legion and St. Alphonsus Catholic Church Senior Club. He was secretary for fifteen years and board member for twenty years for the Brooklyn Center American Legion. He is also a member of the Palmer Lake VFW. Rita has been a volunteer at Community Emergency Assistance Program (CEAP) since 1972. She has been Mrs. Claus and Mother Nature since 1977 at the Brooklyn Center Women's Club. She enjoys crafts, sewing, picking strawberries and going to coffee parties. She is a member of the Palmer Lake VFW, Brooklyn Center American Legion auxiliary, St. Alphonsus Catholic Church Senior Club, St. Alphonsus Ministry, Catholic Council of Christian Women (CCW), and Brooklyn Historical Society.

Rita and Gene are the proud parents of four children and eight grandchildren: Debra and (Marc Palmquist), Nicholas, Colin, Chloe and Christian, Richard and (Annie Evans), Levi and Geneva, Dallas, Donna and (Rick Bever) Kyle and Braden. The Aschers have exchanged the "same" Christmas card with old friends since 1958. They enjoy the State Fair every year, and witnessed immigrants becoming United States citizens. They have lived at 7236 Oliver Avenue North in Brooklyn Center, since 1963. The Ascher family received the "WCCO GOOD NEIGHBOR" Award in 1970. The Ascher children, along with neighborhood children, put on carnivals to raise money for the Muscular Dystrophy Association.

Submitted by Rita Ascher

VERN AUSEN was a charter member of the Brooklyn Historical Society. He served as its president as well as president-treasurer. He revived the Society after the death of its founder, Mary Jane Gustafson.

Vern was born near Pine Lake, Wisconsin, delivered by a neighbor woman on August 25, 1917. He grew up on a farm by the Apple River, near a natural swimming hole. Vern said, "No TV, no radio, no telephone at our place. . . no indoor plumbing." In the spring of 1940 he graduated from the University of Wisconsin with a major in economics and a minor in history. He met his wife, Marvel, in Amery, Wisconsin where she was on vacation from Minneapolis. They met in August and were married the following January, 1941. He worked at Marquette Bank. Fans were used to blow across cakes of ice to cool the lobby, because at that time there was no air conditioning in the building. A civil service test led to a move to Washington, D.C., where Vern worked for the War Production Board for five years.

Vern and Marvel returned in 1947 to Minneapolis. They bought a small house in Richfield, followed by a large older one on 41st and Pleasant Avenue South in Minneapolis. The older home needed repairs, which Vern did not enjoy, so they bought in the Brooklyn Center Garden City Addition on O'Henry Road for a family of six. They could look from the upstairs window of our home across a swamp by Shingle Creek and see the Earle Brown Farm.

Vern immediately joined the Brooklyn Center Planning Commission and served for twelve years; then was elected a Brooklyn Center Councilman in January, 1970. The night of the big tornado, which hit Fridley so hard, Vern was at the Planning Committee Meeting—the only one present—faithfully waiting for the others. He was treasurer at one time for Cross of Glory Lutheran Church, and earlier served as a Boy Scout leader in Minneapolis. Vern was a volunteer for Community Emergency Assistance Program and Peacemakers. He was not a person with just "nine- to- five hours." He worked at the University of Minnesota for thirty-eight years—allocating space for classrooms and offices. He was in charge of real estate, including acquiring property on the West Bank. Locally, his name is on the cornerstone of the Brooklyn Center Community Center.

Vern researched his family, to Norway in the seventeenth century. Three of the couple's four children graduated from Osseo schools, and the youngest from Park Center High School. Son Michael works in photography in Billings, Montana; son Bruce is a printer and lives in Shorewood; daughter Gale lives in Edina is married, is a singer and volunteer; and daughter Deborah lives in Littleton, Colorado and is a soccer mother and volunteer. In addition to the four children, the Ausens have six grandchildren and four great-grandchildren.

Vern passed away on June 11, 1998. Marvel now lives in the senior apartments on the Earle Brown Farm in Brooklyn Center.

Submitted by Marvel Ausen
through oral interview

Marvel and Vern Ausen

Marvel and Vern Ausen

Blanche Anderson Austin

Blanche Austin

BLANCHE AUSTIN was born to Martin and Ida Reynolds on February 12, 1907. The Reynolds farm was in Champlin, near the Brooklyn Park border on Douglas Drive. Blanche and her brother Melvin "Bud" went to the Dunning Elementary School in Champlin. She graduated from Anoka High School and took teachers' training in Anoka. Starting in 1925, Blanche taught in one-room Berg School, on Xerxes Avenue in Brooklyn Park, for two years. While teaching there she met her future husband, Donald "Red" Anderson. They were married in 1930 at Brooklyn Methodist Church on Brooklyn Boulevard.

During the first year and a half of their marriage, her father-in-law, Magnus Anderson, died, and her husband became seriously ill, and was paralyzed for several months. After a lengthy recovery, Red was able to do only light work. In 1931 when their son Kenny was born, Mrs. Alma Anderson asked them to come and live with her and run the farm. Blanche lived in that house on 85th between Noble and Humboldt Avenues from December 1931 to November 1973. Thirty-six of those years were with her mother-in-law, Alma.

Blanche Anderson recalls the old "Riverlyn" (now "Rum Runners") Dance Hall. It began as the West River Road Farmers Improvement Association "Community House." The men of the community, including her father built it. It was an important center for the community during the Depression Era. Another landmark building Blanche attended was the Bragdon Church on Noble Avenue in Brooklyn Park.

A daughter, Dawn, was born in 1941. In 1956 Blanche's husband, Red, died. Red had been on the Brooklyn Village Town Board for many years, and did street and road work for the village. Later that year the Village Town Board hired Blanche to work on the assessments. Her office was in the old, unsuitable (mice in the drawers and no rest rooms) Town Hall on Zane Avenue and Brooklyn Boulevard.

Brooklyn Park was growing rapidly, and with the high assessment for the sewer project, Blanche needed to sell her farm. In 1965 Lyman Lumber Company bought the land. She was allowed to live in the house until it was sold for development (1967). In 1968 Evelyn Schmidt hired Blanche to be her private secretary at Brook Park Realty, Incorporated. She did the bookkeeping for twenty-two years. In 1969 Blanche married Ed Austin. Ed died in 1975. Blanche's family now consists of two children, two stepdaughters, four grandchildren and four step-grandchildren.

Blanche taught Sunday School at Brooklyn United Methodist Church for thirteen years and was Circle Chairman seven different times, the last time for fifteen years. Blanche also did private tutoring in the area.

The first time Blanche went to visit the newly-restored Brooklyn Park Historical Farm, she was looking through the old accounting record book of former owner, Chris Eidem, and saw the name of her Grandfather John Reynolds and her father in payment for digging potatoes. It was like visiting old friends of the past.

Submitted by Blanche Austin

The Robert Sr. and Muriel Baglo family lived at 8301 Westwood Road in Brooklyn Park for thirty-four years. Robert's family lived in Fergus Falls, Minnesota and Muriel was born in St. Croix Falls, Wisconsin.

They met at Sibley Park in South Minneapolis when Muriel was 14 years old. Muriel and her friend were visiting the park and Robert was there with a friend. Muriel said Robert pushed her on the swings and merry-go-round and told his friend, "Someday I'm going to marry that gal." Robert was two years older than Muriel. They dated occasionally over the years. She graduated from Roosevelt High School and they married in 1931. They lived in a small apartment in south Minneapolis and paid $19.00 per month rent. Robert earned $12.50 per week salary. They paid $1,800 for the first house they bought. Muriel said of their first home, "We were lucky to have what we had. We were able to buy groceries and pay the rent, that's all we needed."

Robert worked for Dietene and Delmark Company as a production supervisor. Muriel was a stay at home mom. They had three children, two sons and a daughter, four grandchildren and eight great grandchildren. They raised one of their granddaughters until she was twenty-one years old.

Robert and Muriel were both active in the Brooklyn Park Senior Citizens Club and were some of the earliest members. They celebrated their 55th wedding anniversary in 1986. Robert died in 1987. Muriel moved to senior housing at Brookwood in Brooklyn Center. She continues to be an active member with the Brooklyn Park Seniors.

Robert Sr. and Muriel Baglo Family

Muriel Baglo with two great-grandchildren

Douglas and Betty (Hopwood) Barker

My PARENTS were Art Barker, born in 1899 in Courtney, North Dakota, and Margaret E. Holmberg, born in 1909 in South Minneapolis. Art left Courtney at 14, and came to Minneapolis to work. The Holmberg family had moved to Brooklyn Park about 1916. Art and Margaret married and had four children: Douglas (myself), Donna, Sally and Margaret.

I was born June 14th, 1929, in North Minneapolis. Our family moved to Brooklyn Park in the very early 1930s, to a small home on 81st Avenue, before Highway 169 (now highway #252) was even blacktopped!

I remember big snow storms, drifts four feet high; all the men and boys grabbed their shovels and worked hard clearing the road enough so we could get to 169, which the State plowed. After a few snowstorms, the bigger farmers, like Bergs, hitched up an 8 to 12 horse team to a "V" plow and cleared some of the key roads.

Every fall, farmers helped each other with threshing. They'd bring a big steam engine tractor (or two) and went from one farm to the next harvesting the oats, rye and barley until everyone's fields were done.

I went to school at Benson School (a man named Benson donated the land) on 73rd and Highway #169, graduated 1943; and Anoka Jr. /Sr. High, 1947, after which I enlisted in the Air Force, during the Korean conflict, and was discharged in 1950.

While I was in the service my family moved to Courtney, ND, where Dad and Mom opened a restaurant in 1947. My father died in 1968. Mother married Jacob Bartkowski in 1969; they moved to Minnesota, near Ottertail Lake, where they also ran a restaurant, retiring in 1980. He died, and Mom moved to Mesa, Arizona, where two of my younger sisters live.

Doug and Betty Barker with their family:

On leaves home (while living in Courtney) from service, I met my bride, Betty Hopwood. We married in 1951, and first lived in a mobile home on my Aunt Stella and Uncle Harvey Anderson's property at 73rd and Girard Avenue North. We bought our home on Girard in April 1955.

Fleishman Malting Company employed me from February 1951 (purchased by ADM, 1968) until my retirement in 1994. Betty, after kids were grown, housekept at the Clover Motel on 65th and Lyndale Avenue North, and then worked at what is now Stewart Sandwich, retiring in 1986.

I have three sisters. Donna and Robert Hopwood (also brother to my wife, Betty) live in Phoenix, AZ, have three children: Steven, Susan, two children each, and Bob; Sally and John Boyle, of New Freedom, PA, have three children: Patrick & wife, Diane, living in Alice Springs, Australia, have four children, Carole and James Childs, New Freedom, PA, have one child; Margaret (called Midge) & husband, Tom O'Dell, living in Mesa, AZ, have four children.

Betty and I have three sons: Michael and wife, Jackie, who have sons: Jesse & Christopher, and live in Brooklyn Park; Jeffrey and wife, Ramona, with daughters, Katrina (Katie), Elizabeth (Betsy) and Ryan, living in Dayton, Minnesota, and Timothy and wife, Kathleen, with Sandra, James and Phillip, living in Champlin, Minnesota. It looks like "my crowd" has enjoyed staying in the north Metro area!

Submitted by Douglas Barker

WHEN ROBERT AND ADELINE BARTH moved to Judy Lane in April 1954 there weren't too many people living in Brooklyn Center. By that fall, most of the houses were finished on their street and from their front yard they were able to watch the traffic flow by on Highway 100. At the time, the highway had two lanes with many traffic lights.

At one point, within the next couple of years, they counted sixty children on their block, but nobody ever worried about safety. People didn't lock their doors. Robert and Adeline had two girls, Vicki and Kathy, when they moved to Brooklyn Center and Chris was born in 1959. The children attended Brooklyn Center High School and live in Minnesota again after many years of moving about the world.

The Barths retired to Florida in 1990 and return at least once a year to keep in touch with everyone. Bob was in sales during his working years and Adeline was a typesetter for twenty years.

Vicki is a Photo Stylist, Kathy is a CPA, and Chris is an Air Traffic Controller (after a stint in the Navy).

Bob and Adeline have four grandchildren—the oldest granddaughter will be married in April. Their only grandson was married in October 1989 in Hawaii (he's in the Marines), and their two newest granddaughters, Martha and Elizabeth, live in Northfield, Minnesota with their parents Chris and Barb.

The Barths have many fond memories of Brooklyn Center. It was a wonderful place to raise a family.

Submitted by Adeline Barth

Robert and Adeline Barth

Robert and Adeline Barth with Vicki, Kathy, and Chris

CYRUS AND RUTH BECK are living on land that was originally bought from the United States Government in 1856. The original landowner was Lewis Atkinson.
The Becks bought the home when it was still a part of Osseo, Minnesota but is now part of Brooklyn Park.

Ruth was born in Erskine, MN, and Cyrus in Lancaster, MN. The Becks have six children: Ronnie, Alwood, Gary, Renee, Steven and Judy, all of which attended Champlin and Riverview Elementary Schools. Then they attended Anoka Jr. High School and Jackson Jr. High Schools. They then graduated to the old Anoka Sr. High School and the new Anoka Sr. High School.

They have ten grandchildren: Clifton, Kristina, Daniel, David, Amanda, Kathy Ann, Jake, Christopher, Paul and Michael. They also have two great-grandchildren: Sean and Nikolas.

The Becks have lived in their house since 1955.

Ruth's mother was born in Sweden in 1898. She came to northern Minnesota when she was three years old. She is still living at this time.

Submitted by Ruth Beck

The Cyrus Beck Family

Jean Beck

My Grandmother Emma May Miller came from Lima, Ohio and married Grandfather Joseph Brown who had come from New York, in about 1900. They had five children, the oldest being my father, Robert Wm. Brown, born in 1901. They lived in a small house with five acres of land at 5300 Emerson Avenue North in Brooklyn Center. They had a cow named Daisy, two sway-backed white horses, Nelly and Dolly, a dog, a cat, two pigs and a few chickens. Grandpa worked twelve hours a day, six days a week, while grandma took care of the children and raised a large vegetable garden. They then moved to a larger house at 5426 Fremont Avenue North.

My grandparents started an Episcopal Church in their own home. Later, with the help of the Bishop of Minnesota and a "big" church, they were able to have a little white church moved on to a lot at 53rd and Emerson, and St. Stephan's Mission was born.

Grandma Emma died in 1915 and left five children, three to fourteen years in age.

My father, Robert, was about fifteen years old when he was sent to North Dakota to work on a ranch. Robert came back to Brooklyn Center and met Clara Nyberg Oliver, a childhood friend, and they became sweethearts. They married about 1925 and lived in the old house at 5426 Fremont North. They moved to West Allis, Wisconsin for several years, returning to Brooklyn Center about 1930, moving into a small house at 5410 Girard Avenue North. They lived there for the next forty years and raised three children.

Beck Family: Al, Steve, Gary, Ron, Judy, Ruth, Renee, Cyrus

Robert was a master electrician and worked at that trade most of his life. He and his wife Clara were members of Harron Methodist Church. Robert was also on the Earle Brown School Board for many years. He taught electrical code at Dunwoody Institute in Minneapolis. Clara was active in church, school, and Red Cross during World War II. Robert and Clara lived in Brooklyn Center most of their lives and had four children.

My sister, Lenora and her husband, Walter Klesk, lived in Brooklyn Center until 1955. They had two sons.

Robert O. Brown, my brother, and his wife Marilyn had four children. He has passed away.

I lived in Brooklyn Center, attended Earle Brown Elementary School and then Patrick Henry High School and graduated from Minneapolis Vocational High School. I became a Registered Nurse, taking my training at Minneapolis General Hospital (now Hennepin County Medical Center). In 1962 I married Ken Hornibrook. We had three children, Howard, Cindy and John.

I worked as a RN all my married life but also worked in our Sign Shop with my husband Ken. We had a Redwood Sign Shop at 3445 Penn Avenue North in Minneapolis. We made many commercial and residential signs all around the state.

Kenneth died in 1988 and I then married Kenneth A. Beck, we have lived in our new home in Brooklyn Park for the past nine years.

Submitted by Jean Beck

ARNEUWELL (ARNIE) was born and raised in Wheatcroft, KY, and Doris was born in Edwards, MI, and raised in Indianapolis, Ind. After returning from the Army, Arnie moved to Indianapolis and that is where we met. We were working for a department store at the time. We later married and started a family. Arnie went back to engineering school and was hired by IBM In 1964 Arnie was transferred to Minneapolis, MN.

We moved to Brooklyn Center in 1969, and had another child. Our children went to Earle Brown and Brooklyn Center High School. We also raised two nieces who also attended Earle Brown and BCHS.

After leaving IBM, Arnie was an electronics instructor for the TCOIC program and also was a manager for Minneapolis Elect Steel Co. before being employed for the Airports Commission in accounting. Doris worked for Honeywell two years before being employed by Northwest Airlines for 31 years.

For recreation we enjoy traveling. We have been to such places as Hawaii, Mexico, Haiti, Puerto Rico, St. Thomas, St. Croix, Canada, Bahamas, and many parts of Europe. We also took a family vacation this year to Jamaica. We like visiting with families and friends. Our children, Rodney, Larissa, and Ebony have traveled many places with us, and we all have traveled in many of our states.

Arnie is involved in many community activities, such as being on the Brooklyn Center District 286 School Board, board member North Hennepin Leadership Academy, Co-Chair Brooklyn Center Family Resource Center, Co-Chair of The Alliance For Families and Children, Treasurer for the Hospitality House Boys and Girls Club, and board member for The Right Step Academy. Doris loves to cook, and do church work. She has been a choir president, and a trustee for a number of years, and loves to work with children.

Submitted by Arneuwell and Doris Benifield

Arneuwell and Doris Benifield

Doris and Arneuwell Benifield

The Robinson and Bennett Family

ROBINSON BENNETT was born in 1825 and died in 1912. He homesteaded in 1852 at about 103rd and West River Road. Elisa, his wife, was born in 1827 and died in 1902. They had Dorcasanna, George, and John.

Dorcasanna likely was one of the first white children born in the area and died of "membrane croup," no doctor, no church, no undertaker. For a hundred years, a small marble stone marked the lone grave on West River Road, where her mother could see it each time she looked out the window:

Dorcasanna Bennett, Born May 1, 1856. Died October 30, 1857.

In 1852 Silas Merrill homesteaded in the area now known as Brooklyn Park Historical Farm. From 1894 to 1975, it was known as the Eidem Farm. The City of Brooklyn Park purchased the farm in 1975.

Selling pumpkins

Silas and Margaret Merrill's daughter Florence married John Bennett and their children were Maud and Robinson Silas, who was born in 1895.

Robinson married Pearl Haven (1896-1975) from Fonda, Iowa. They purchased land in 1918 on 101st and West River Road and bought themselves a wanagon to live in while building their home. A wanagon was a traveling shelter on a barge that was often placed along the river for loggers. They had four sons: George, Glenn, Royce and Jerry.

Robinson and Pearl would open their home to travelers to water their horses and rest. When the Farmers Market opened In Minneapolis, he secured a stall where he sold produce six days a week. Winters were spent cutting wood for neighboring farmers.

In my teen years I remember going to market on Saturdays, helping my dad George with the selling. This time was special because my grandparents and Uncle Royce were there with their families. They had stalls on the other side of the aisle and we would talk during the slow times.

I saw my grandparents at church on Sundays, and Grandma sometimes had the families over for dinner. When I was little, we celebrated sometimes in the basement because she had not completed her canning.

I grew up one mile north of my grandparents' farm and rode my bike or horse to visit them. Grandpa always had stories to tell. One was about the "Dead Man's Curve," a sharp turn on West River Road. People drove too fast, miss the curve and end up in the Mississippi River. The Bennetts helped move the cars out of the River.

I am now married to Curt James Kummer. In 1979 we purchased my grandparents' home from the Bennett family. The home still had the wood-burning furnace, pump house, root cellar, chicken coop, silo, chickens, roosters and a dog. We have a 2.75-acre hobby farm raising mostly fall vegetables, squash and pumpkins. We still heat with a wood-burning furnace, but do have a gas furnace as a backup heat source.

Curt and I hope to be living here for years to come and have memories of our own that will be cherished.

Submitted by Jerry Bennett and June (Bennett) Kummer

WHEN I ATTENDED RIVERVIEW SCHOOL in 1938 it was a one-room schoolhouse. Thirteen pupils attending then and four of them were in my grade. The school had a library, one schoolroom, and a restroom with a chemical toilet. The teacher, Miss Barnes, lived in the little old white school up the road. The old schoolhouse was very primitive and Miss Barnes lived there with her mother.

In 1940 I went to school in Minneapolis, to Jordan Jr. High, and to North High School. I rode to school with my parents and sometimes had to catch rides home from school. Sometimes the ride home was a little scary. After high school I went on to the University of Minnesota. After finishing my schooling at the University of Minnesota, I married Bill Berg. We have three daughters and seven granddaughters.

As a child, my folks had a cow, a calf, and many chickens; they also had a pet crow, dogs, cats and some mink. One day her uncle came out to visit and my mother sent him to kill a chicken. He killed a chicken, but he killed the wrong one. He killed Tizzie Loo, our pet blind chicken, by mistake. We ate the chicken not knowing it was our pet. We searched for our pet chicken but never found it.

In the summer we canoed, fished and swam in the Mississippi River. In the winter we would clear a space for skating. The river supplied us with many hours of entertainment. We lived at 8900 West River Road while we were growing up. As adults we built a home next to that lot and we are surrounded with all of the gorgeous natural nature.

Submitted by Betty Berg

Betty Berg

River View School 1938-39: Laverne Zimmerman, Gladys Perry, Laverne Zachow, Betty Blesi

The Ken Berglund Family

THEY MET IN JANUARY 1947 at the Varsity Cafe. She was the waitress and he the fountain boy. His name was Kenneth Berglund, born and raised in the Lindstrom, Minnesota area. Her name was Lillian Torkildson, and she came from Madelia, in southern Minnesota. She was attending the University of Minnesota, and he went to the Minnesota School of Business.

As time went on, they were engaged, got married, and were blessed with three sons, Bob, Dick, and John. They moved to Brooklyn Center from NE Minneapolis in 1954, and lived at 5812 James Ave. North for twenty-eight years. The boys all attended Earle Brown School. Lillian sang with the "Mother's Singers" for a number of years, under the able direction of June Scofield. What a fun time, with our spring concerts and all.

The three boys were confirmed at Hope Lutheran Church. They were Boy Scouts for many years where their Dad, "Mr. B.", was Scoutmaster for about twelve ears. Dick went on to be an Eagle Scout. Those were fun years: camping, earning merit badges, Rum River Court of Honors, and even a trip to the Big Horn Mountains.

Ken was Traffic Manager at Hoffman Engineering in Anoka for twenty-five years. He retired the day he turned sixty-five, which was June 24, 1988. He has been heard to remark, "My wife finally let me retire. She was afraid I wouldn't find enough to do."

In March 1962 Brookdale Mall opened. There were three big stores, Penney's, Sears, and Dayton's. There was even a grocery and dime store. Lillian got a job at Brookdale. Her application was accepted at Penney's, and she began work at $1.25 an hour. She spent thirty years in the Bedding and Bath Department, and enjoyed the work immensely.

By December 1992 Ken had already been retired for over four years, and Lillian decided she should be home baking Christmas cookies. In January 1993 she too retired. Now she worried how she would keep busy. In February, they took a two-week vacation to Hawaii with Tom and Ruth Vincent. That got her out of the working mood, and into a more leisurely life style. She became involved with singing in the choir at church, and other women's groups.

Ken spent a lot of time on his lawn. The first summer after retirement, he spent two months putting in an automatic sprinkler system (and it worked). He also likes to golf, and is on a league at Hayden Hills.

May 30, 1998, Ken and Lil celebrated fifty years of marriage with a party at Hope Lutheran Church, put on by their children and five grandchildren. What a good time to gather old friends and relatives.

They like to travel, and in July 1998, they and three other couples, took a wonderful trip to Alaska. It was a Holland-American line, and they spent three days aboard a wonderful, huge ship, the "Niew Amsterdam." They traveled then by rail, coach, and boat to see the many faces of Alaska and the Yukon. Alaska is full of trees, rivers, mountains, glaciers and ice fields, and many other wonderful sights. We had a wonderful time.

Submitted by Lillian Berglund

Kenneth and Lillian Berglund (1989)

MY GRANDFATHER, Carl John Bergstrom, Sr., moved from Menominee, Michigan to Brooklyn Township around 1915. He settled on the Mississippi River near 85th Avenue North where he operated a truck farm for more than thirty years. He and his wife, Regina, raised eleven children on that farm, five of who went on to own Brooklyn Center Hardware and Implement Co. The store was located on what is now known as Brooklyn Boulevard and 69th Avenue North. Brothers Carl, Edward, Arnold, Theodore, and Phillip Bergstrom were well-recognized and respected business owners who served many of the farmers in the area.

In 1937, my father, Carl J. Bergstrom, Jr., and his wife, Esther, purchased eighty acres of land on 85th Ave. No. between Xerxes and Regent Avenues in Brooklyn Park. They began truck farming on the side with the help of their growing family, which eventually included seven girls and three boys. In the mid-1950s, Carl devoted his efforts to full-time farming. The land was rich and fertile, some of the best tillable soil in the region. Carl and Esther managed to raise their family off the income from farming.

During these years, Carl was active in local government and in his church. He served as the Justice of the Peace for Brooklyn Park from 1954 to 1965, and was active as a deacon, Sunday School teacher, and a charter member of his church. He and three of his brothers, Edward, Theodore, and Phillip, sang in the Bergstrom Brothers' quartet. They performed at a variety of churches and special events, and often their children were invited to sing with them. Carl also sang as a soloist and performed at numerous weddings, funerals and church services.

In 1962 Carl decided to again sell farm equipment while still maintaining his truck farm. He established Bergstrom Tractor and Implement Sales, which he and Esther operated from the 85th Avenue location for the next twenty years. As their children grew up and left home, Carl and Esther had to scale back their farming, and they rented out the land. Then Carl sold and repaired garden tractors, snow blowers, tillers and lawnmowers.

By the late 1970s, land in Brooklyn Park had become a hot commodity and property taxes were forcing many of the older landowners to sell to developers. My folks sold the bulk of their property, retaining the original farmhouse and business and five acres. When my parents retired in 1982, my brother, James P. Bergstrom, retained part of the family business, moving it to Albertville, Minnesota, St. Michael, and finally, Becker, where he operates Bergstrom's Lawn and Garden Equipment today. My father entered a nursing home in 1983 and passed away in 1987. My mother sold the farmhouse and remaining property in 1984.

Today, Edinburgh USA Golf Course lies on the eighty acres that I helped farm as a kid! Some of the original lilac bushes are still there, as well as some evergreen trees my dad so lovingly planted.

Submitted by Adele Bergstrom

The Carl Bergstrom Family

Carl Bergstrom, Justice of the Peace in Brooklyn Park (ca. 1965)

Wallace and Elaine Bernards

NINETEEN-SIXTY WAS A BIG YEAR for Wallace "Gunnar" Bernards and Elaine Nelson. Gunnar and Elaine got married in Blue Earth, MN (Gunnar's home town), accepted a new job, and moved to the Twin Cities.

Gunnar had been an educator in Olivia, MN, since 1952, first as a teacher and coach, then as principal (1954-1960). He came out of Blue Earth High School (1944), served twenty months in the U.S. Air Force at the end of World War II, attended Augustana College, and graduated from the University of Minnesota in 1950. Gunnar then spent two years teaching and coaching in Chamois, MO. At the time of their marriage, Elaine had taught home economics for two years at Olivia, Minnesota after having graduated from Augsburg College in 1958.

Phil, Neal, Wallace, Elaine, and Jefferson Bernards

Early in 1960 Gunnar received a call from Superintendent Ralph McCartney encouraging him to apply as principal for a new school being built just north of Minneapolis, Brooklyn Center High. In May 1960 school board chairman Manfred (Ben) Davidson called to offer Gunnar the job. He readily accepted.

After the nuptials in Blue Earth, the young couple headed north to start a new life, and a new school, in the Cities. But first they took a honeymoon detour to Canada and spent the summer at Carleton College with the National Science Foundation summer program. The newlyweds moved into school board member Dr. Robert Veneer's home at 5413 Oliver Ave. No. while Dr. Veneer was on sabbatical.

In the fall of 1960 Gunnar and Superintendent McCartney went to work creating the foundation of Brooklyn Center High School. The scheduled fall 1961 opening was affected by a sheet metal strike that caused the school to open without all of its classrooms. Undaunted, staff and administration alike did their best to make do. Stories of improvisation are legendary with the vanguard of Brooklyn Center High School.

Both Gunnar and Elaine are extremely proud of the fact that all three of their boys graduated from BCHS: Jefferson in 1979, Neal in 1981, and Phil in 1984. During their tenure as parents to school age children, Gunnar and Elaine also took in three foreign exchange students: Misami Ieda (Japan), Lars Normann (Sweden), and Rolf Solem (Norway). During their retirement, Gunnar and Elaine have visited them all.

In 1983 Gunnar retired from BCHS after thirty-three years in education. Since then he has shared his experience with countless student teachers as a supervisor for young educators at St. John's and St. Benedict's Colleges. He also currently serves as executive secretary for the Tri-Metro Conference.

Shortly after Gunnar's retirement from BCHS in 1983, Elaine began a second career in real estate. She has also volunteered as a Peacemaker, supported Augsburg College through alumni work, and served on the Brooklyn Center Prayer Breakfast Committee. Elaine is now retired from real estate and spends her time tending to eight grandchildren and various home improvement projects. In 1999 Gunnar and Elaine surround themselves with family, travel when possible, are active at Hope Lutheran Church, and still live in Brooklyn Center—a city they love to call home.

Submitted by Elaine Bernards

I REMEMBER when there was so much space between farmhouses that Halloween trick or treating on Osseo Road was slim picking.

I remember putting on our ice skates and trudging with shovels down to Shingle Creek to shovel off the snow. Then skate and trudge home again, exhausted.

I remember the wonderful soil for growing melons and potatoes. And the asparagus field that we went scurrying down to, to cut asparagus for dinner.

I remember flooding the garden to make a skating rink.

I remember the Bookmobile (a mobile library) coming to the farm, tooting its horn and all of us clambering aboard to get lots of books to read.

I remember us kids playing "bird dog" for Uncle Roy, walking ahead to scare the pheasants, then "hitting the deck" when we flushed out a bird.

I remember walking across the field to Osseo Road and down a quarter of a mile to catch the bus for school.

I remember the beautiful sound of the cottonwood trees surrounding the house, as the leaves rippled in the wind.

Submitted by Virginia Bistodeau

Virginia Wheeler Bistodeau

Mary (Smith) Blesi

Mary Blesi

Nathaniel Smith was a veteran of the War of 1812. He served with the 21st United States Infantry of Maine. His grave in the Brooklyn Crystal cemetery has a marker placed there by the Minneapolis Chapter of the Daughters of the War of 1812. This was the first such marker that the Chapter placed in Minnesota.

The family moved to the Minnesota Territory in 1850. The Minnesota Territorial Census listed the family as Nathaniel, his wife, Anna, their children, Harris Nathaniel, Debora, Mary, Esther and Laura.

The Smith family homesteaded near what is now Crystal Airport. Mary Jane was only seventeen years old when she taught in the first school near Shingle Creek. The school was a very crude structure with dirt floor.

In 1857 Harris Nathaniel Smith married Mary Jane Flanders. She had moved here from New York in 1853. They were the parents of three sons. The oldest son, Harry Herbert, became my grandfather. He married Nettie Smith, a daughter of another pioneer family.

Nettie Smith's father, George Hoshel Smith, was born in New York in 1843. His father, Horace, moved the family from New York in 1854 and homesteaded near Osseo in the Brooklyn Township. George was a farmer and also a pioneer railroad builder. He worked on the Great Northern and Canadian Pacific Lines. He was also involved with building and maintaining roads in Hennepin County for more than thirty years. In the winter he worked in the pineries (the forests) in northern Minnesota.

George had also served in the Civil War. Having served in twenty-five battles he was discharged after the Battle at Fredericksburg with a Citation for Bravery. Harry Herbert and Nettie Smith raised five children on the eighty-acre farm between 62nd and 63rd Avenue North. After the death of my grandfather, Harry A. Smith (my father) moved to the farm and continued farming the land.

My mother, Anna Claus, was born in Illinois. She married Harry A. Smith in 1924 on the farm. They had three children. . . Harris Nathaniel, Mary Jane and Thomas. Mother became severely handicapped with rheumatoid arthritis and was bedridden for seventeen years. She passed away in 1947 after coming down with pneumonia.

I grew up on the farm, attended Abraham Lincoln School, at 62nd and Broadway, and Robbinsdale High School. Our father sold wild horses and sometimes got a semi-trailer load, twelve to fifteen horses. The horses had been caught in the North Dakota Badlands. It was quite a sight to see all the neighbors gathered around to view the horses.

David Madigan and I were married right after high school. We had one child, Kathleen. David passed away soon after from a malignant brain tumor. John Blesi and I were married in 1949 and recently celebrated our golden anniversary. John grew up in Dayton, MN. He was a construction worker all his working years.

We had one daughter, Janet. The two girls and spouses have given us seven grandchildren and seven great-grandchildren.

Submitted by Mary Blesi

Janis Blumentals was born in Riga, Latvia and came to the United States after World War II with his parents and sister. We came as political immigrants called displaced persons and settled in Minnesota. After graduating from the University of Minnesota School of Architecture, I worked for several architecture firms in the Twin Cities. In 1972 I was assigned to be the project manager for an apartment building in Brooklyn Center and so started a twenty-seven-plus year affair with Brooklyn Center and Earle Brown Farm.

I had to first find Brooklyn Center on a map and then create a building that everyone would like—Mayor Phil Cohen, City Manager Don Poss, and building owners Deil Gustafson and Cy Sheehy. After a few changes the building became a reality and Shingle Creek Towers stands just south of City Hall.

In 1973 I went to work as staff architect for the Brooklyn Center Industrial Park. In 1976, together with my partner and wife Susan, we established Blumentals Architecture, Inc. Our first office was located in the Farm's administration building until 1988 when we designed ourselves out of the building. After a temporary office in Palmer Lake Plaza, we moved back to the Farm. As part of the design team that renovated Earle Brown Heritage Center, we had the opportunity to design a new lofted office suite in the H-Barn.

Susan and Janis Blumentals

In 1998, once again, we designed ourselves out of our offices. The expansion of meeting facilities included renovation of the H-Barn. We are now located in the D-Barn, the two story barn next to the water tower, in a unique, open, two story office with exposed post and beam ceilings.

Over the years, our eight person architectural office has designed over 100 projects in this community. Some of our projects include multi-tenant buildings in the Industrial Park, Super 8 Motel, Earle Brown Lanes, The Crossings at Brookwood, Brookwood Townhomes, Earle Brown Terrace, Woven Hearts Assisted Living, Sunlite Multi-Tenant Building, addition to Creative Carton and New Horizon Child Care In Brooklyn Park. Our special project is Earle Brown Farm. After the City of Brooklyn Center bought the Farmstead in 1985, we became part of the architectural team that transformed the Farm into the Earle Brown Heritage Center.

Eleven years later we designed the Heritage Center building additions and renovation. The construction is just being completed for this final phase that creates a Heritage Center that will serve even better the ever-mushrooming convention market.

These years have been very productive for Blumentals Architecture. We expect to continue our practice in the community. We have designed projects in nineteen states, with overall construction value over $200,000,000, but projects in the Brooklyn community will always be closest to our hearts. We want to do our part to maintain and improve the Brooklyn Community. We are very active in the Brooklyn Community Chamber of Commerce and participate in Chamber activities to help strengthen the community. We like it here!

Submitted by Janis Blumentals

Blumentals Family

Melvin and Alice (Roers) Boesen

MELVIN PETER BOESEN was born on July 11, 1931, to Clarence and Adelheid (Lenarz) Boesen in Little Falls, Minnesota. Melvin's parents and he moved to Millerville, Minnesota in 1934. He attended St. Mary's Parochial School in Millerville, grades one through eight and Brandon High School, graduating in June of 1949. He enlisted in the U.S. Navy on October 11, 1949, and was honorably discharged in September 1953. He enrolled at the College of St. Thomas, St. Paul, Minnesota and graduated with a BA degree in June of 1957.

I, Alice Emma Roers, was born on July 14, 1936 to Hubert and Anna (Kuhn) Roers at their home in rural Garfield, Minnesota. I attended Hillsdale School District #37 grades one through eight, a one-room, country school, and Brandon High School, graduating in June of 1954.

Melvin and I were married on August 18, 1956. We initially lived in Minneapolis, and moved to Brooklyn Park in April 1958. The CPA firm of Peat, Marwick, Mitchell & Co. employed Melvin from 1957 to 1964. In 1964 he went to work for Investors Diversified Services, Inc. (IDS), now known as American Express Financial Advisors, Inc., and retired in August 1993. Maico Co. Inc. employed me in the home office from 1954 to 1957.

We have three living children and one deceased child. Daughter, Marcia Kay, was born in 1957. Our son, Thomas Melvin, was born in 1958. Daniel John was born in 1960. Melvin Peter Jr. was stillborn in 1962. Each of the children attended Park Brook Elementary School, St. Alphonsus Catholic School, North View Junior High School and Osseo Senior High School.

Marcia graduated from Osseo Senior High in 1976 and from St. Cloud State University in May 1980. She married Brian Dale Johnson, a 1979 graduate of St. Cloud State University in August 1980. She worked for the Prudential Insurance Company of America for ten years before becoming a full-time homemaker. Brian is presently employed by Volunteers of America National Services. They have two daughters: Leah Mary, born in 1986, and Dana Alice born in 1990. They reside in Brooklyn Park.

Thomas graduated from Osseo Senior High in June 1977 and graduated from the University of Minnesota in 1981. He obtained his M.B.T. in 1983. He is presently a tax partner in the CPA firm of Simma Flottemesch and Orenstein, Ltd. He is single and resides in St. Louis Park, Minnesota.

Daniel graduated from Osseo High School in 1978, and attended SCSU for two years. He subsequently attended St. Cloud Vocational Technical College. He is presently employed by the City of Preston, Minnesota and is in charge of its Waste Water Treatment Plant. He married Joan (Terwey) Loso in 1987, and became a stepfather to Joan's children: daughter, Adrienne Grace Loso, born in 1978 and son, Aaron Joseph Loso, born in 1980.

Submitted by Alice E. Boesen

In 1942 while working at Northern States Power in Minneapolis, I dated a man who was in the United States Navy during World War II. He was teaching hydraulics. His name was Walt Boone. On October 10th we had our first date and on October 17th I married him. He was transferred to San Diego, California on October 19th. In 1945 he received a medical discharge and we settled back in Minneapolis. For the next two years we lived in a Quonset hut. In 1948 we purchased a home at 5958 Camden Avenue North in Brooklyn Center.

We both worked at Earle Brown School and then went on to help all the World War II vets in the area build Brooklyn Center High School, where Walt drove a school bus for twenty-five years. There has been a member of the Boone family in that school for thirty years, from 1963-1993.

In 1986 our son was driving Walt to his home in Kentucky for the Kentucky Derby. Walt suffered a heart attack and died during the trip.

In 1991 I went to the fiftieth anniversary of the Pearl Harbor Survivors in Hawaii. Walt had always said he would never go back because it would be too painful. He was off the U.S.S. San Francisco at Pearl Harbor. I laid a wreath above the U.S.S. Arizona in honor of one of the members of the organization, who had died a month before the anniversary. A sea diver placed his ashes inside the Arizona. While at Pearl Harbor, I had the privilege of meeting President George Bush.

One month later, the St. Alphonsus Catholic Church choir was invited to sing for the Pope in Vatican City in Rome, Italy, for New Years. I accompanied them and met the Pope. Meeting those two world leaders a month apart is not something one does regularly.

Submitted by Vinnette Boone

Walt and Vinnette Boone

Walt and Vinnette Boone

Earl Bernard and Evelyn Luella (Stephens) Borgen (now Berkman)

Earl was Minneapolis born and raised, served in the Navy during World War II; upon returning home studied typewriter repair under the GI Bill. I, Evelyn, was born in Montevideo; I lived there through 10th Grade, 1934. Our family moved to Osakis; it was three years before we could afford my finishing 11th-12th grades, graduating in 1939. I came to Minneapolis, attending "College of Commerce" business school on LaSalle Avenue.

In 1950 we purchased our little one-bedroom house on 73rd Avenue North from Tony and Gert Bach, who fashioned it around an old chicken house. When we remodeled, there were little drop-down doors hidden in a wall. We were elated to move in with our 70-pound Airedale-cross, Sam, a broken down sleeper, nail kegs for chairs, and an outdoor lawn chair we used indoors! Our children were born there—Jack in 1953 and Julie in 1957. We lived there until Earl's death in 1983.

The Little Borgen Hacienda (May 1950)

Due to rapid population growth and development around us, the kids attended three different elementary schools: Riverview, Monroe and Jackson Jr. High and briefly Jackson couldn't take all of its 8th Graders, so Julie attended the newest elementary school, Evergreen Park. Both graduated from Anoka High School. Jack has one daughter and two stepchildren. He lives in Oakdale and manages a liquor store in Lexington. Julie has one daughter. She works for Miracle Ear, Inc., in St. Louis Park.

We had a beautiful yard, neighbors called it "Borgen's Park", those days you purchased acreage, not "a lot." When assessments (water, etc.) came through, we learned we had two lots. We built a neat tree house, an exciting addition, also a favorite stopping-spot for walkers to and from school. Eventually police classified the tree house a public hazard and it had to come down.

Fremont Avenue North at 73rd was but a path to undeveloped property; our children had unrestricted play space. When building began all around us, Fremont became a street; our children had to learn this was no longer their private playground.

Our "little town," as we called it, roughly encompassed property between Humboldt and Dupont from 73rd to 70th Avenue. Early neighbors included the Bachs, Pedersens, Scharbers, Weltes, Walt and Harriet Grabor, Nick and Marcie Beumer, Len and Birdie Besnett, Harry and Beverly Green, Abe and Ceil Magnan, Chuck and Cathy St. Mane, Art and Ruth Ziesmer, Carl and Blanche Anderson, Harvey and Stella Anderson, John and Dagny Clark, Mavis Huddle, Pete and Ardy Fiebiger

In 1960, at Lutheran Church of the Master services at Brooklyn Center High School, I filled out a volunteer slip for part time office help and began a wonderful association with Mavis Huddle, Parish Secretary, Pastor Swedberg, and all. This led to a part-time job, with pay, continuing to 1990.

Rekindling a pre-World War II friendship, a second marriage was imminent. Kenneth Berkman, Winthrop, Minnesota, also widowed, and I were married July 28th, 1990, and moved to Winthrop, where things are a bit less hectic. A fine young man named John Wright purchased the house on 73rd, and takes excellent care of it.

Submitted by Evelyn Berkman

KAREN CARLSON grew up on a farm at 55th and Humboldt Avenue North in Brooklyn Center. Our father was a gardener and a carpenter. Our mother was active in church, civic, and school events. Children, school, and church were the center of their lives.

My four siblings and I attended Earle Brown School. Bean suppers and carnivals at school brought the entire community together. The first and second graders (there was no kindergarten then) were bussed to and from school. The rest of the children walked. In the spring of the year, streets flooded because there was no storm sewer system. The walkers waded to and from school. The playground was any open space where they could play ball. The nearby woods gave them an opportunity to play "hide and seek," or climb trees.

In 1959 Floyd Bouley and I were married. We continued to live in Brooklyn Center until two of our five children were born. The Bouleys moved to Minneapolis, then.

We have watched the area of Brooklyn Center change from small farms and a few homes to industry and many homes and parks.

Submitted by Karen (Carlson) Bouley

Floyd and Karen Bouley

Alpha and Howard Carlson, the parents of Karen Carlson Bouley

ADOLPH BOYSON moved to the Brooklyn Center area when he was eighteen months old. Adolph's father had dairy stores on 69th and Humboldt Avenue North and on 47th and Humboldt Avenue North. He peddled milk in the North Minneapolis area. Adolph was educated at the Cap Martin School on the Earle Brown farm. Cap Martin was Earle Brown's grandfather and Earle and Adolph were raised together.

Earle Brown and Adolph used to go on picnics, parties, and trips and they hunted together. Mr. Boyson said that Earle was "a common man."

Adolph's father also owned a farm on Logan Avenue North and 55th. Mr. Boyson bought the old Hamilton School and built a home from the lumber. The home still stands at Emerson and 55th North. He also had a farm where the Northport Clinic is located. He raised vegetables on this farm. When Adolph visited the Northport Clinic he told the nurses in the office they were sitting where the dining room once was.

He can still envision his mother along the Mississippi River catching the logs for firewood as they came down the river from the logging camps.

Adolph feels that he must be "the most popular man in Brooklyn Center" because he still has many friends that come and take him out. When asked to what he attributed his long life, he replied, "I worked hard and lived moderately." When asked what does he think of men going to the moon, he replied, "It's all right, but the money could be better used here. We need things in this country."

The clipping was found in a Bible of one of our early residents.

Adolph Boyson

David and Jody Brandvold

IN 1934 DAVID'S PARENTS, Ragnar (ScKeiver) and Verna Brandvold moved to Brooklyn Center from 44th and Penn Avenue North where they lived behind ScKeiver's Barber Shop. Dave was 3 years old. He attended eight grades at Earle Brown School and graduated from Minneapolis Vocational High School where he studied architectural drafting.

As a young teenager, Dave helped his Dad build the house at 55th and Girard Avenue that is still affectionately referred to by the family as "the brick house." Later they built and moved into the house at 57th and Humboldt Avenue where Verna still lives.

Dave and I met in 1949 when I came to Minneapolis from Williston, ND, to attend Medical Technology School. We married in December 1950 and moved into our first house at 57th and Irving Avenue where the only finished room was the bathroom.

David, Belinda, Paul, and Jody Brandvold

Our refrigerator was a sheet of plywood loosely nailed over the front doorway. The closer the food was to the door (on the floor), the colder the food. Many times during that winter we woke to frozen milk and eggs. The inside of this home was pretty much finished by the time our daughter, Belinda, was born in 1952. Our son, Paul, was born in 1955. We moved to the suburb of Fridley in 1958, but by 1960 the hometown atmosphere of Brooklyn Center called us back. Since then we have built and lived in six more homes in this school district. None, however, have had the rustic "charm" of that first house. Dave was a "quality first" home builder who specialized in building on vacant lots and who also built several homes for alumni of the school district who wanted their children to attend small schools like those in District No. #286.

Our ties to this school district run deep. As a member of the District #286 School Board from 1971 through 1995, I was honored to serve eight years on the Minnesota School Board Association Board of Directors and six years on the Minnesota High School League Board of Directors.

Our feelings of loyalty for and pride in Brooklyn Center have grown even as the "burbs" have grown around us. Dave and I spent the last three winters in Arizona where Dave died in February 1999. As I now prepare to move on, I know that wherever I may be, Brooklyn Center will always be my true home.

Submitted by Jody Brandvold

Loyd and Laverne Brandvold

LOYD WAS BORN in 1935 shortly after his parents, Ragnar and Verna, moved to Brooklyn Center. He attended Earle Brown Elementary School, Our Lady of Victory Catholic School, Patrick Henry High School and Minneapolis Vocational High School. He met his future wife, LaVerne Ericson, on the school bus when they were in eighth grade. LaVerne was born in Isanti and moved to Brooklyn Center with her parents, four brothers and three sisters in 1947. She also attended Earle Brown Elementary and Patrick Henry High School.

After graduation, Loyd joined the Army and a year later, in 1955, he and LaVerne were married. Shortly after Loyd was discharged in 1956, he and LaVerne bought a house at 57th and Dupont Avenue in Brooklyn Center and opened Loydy's Diner at 52nd and Lyndale Avenue North in Minneapolis. There they served hamburgers for a quarter and coffee and donuts for ten cents each to many, many Brooklyn Center residents until about 1969. During that time they had three children: Kari–"Dolly" (1957), Kristi–"Babes" (1958), and Guy (1960).

After they sold Loydy's diner, they bought Breezy Point Lodge in Brainerd and operated it for two years before they sold it to Hopkins House. In about 1969, they opened the Chuck Wagon Inn in Northbrook shopping center at 57th and Logan Avenue North in Brooklyn Center.

During the next few years Loyd and LaVerne sponsored a very successful woman's softball team, "The Americs." LaVerne's brother, LeRoy Ericson, managed the team and in 1971 they won their way to the National Competition in Florida. Loyd was also president of the Brooklyn Center Little League for two years and managed the umpire programs for two years. Tiring of the long late hours, they sold the Chuck Wagon Inn in the mid-1970s and Loyd went on to learn the glazing business. He presently owns and operates the "Easy Does It" Glass Company.

Submitted by Loyd Brandvold

Branvold Brothers David (9), Loyd (5), and Donnie (7)

Ragnar and Verna Brandvold

RAGNAR (SCKEIVER) BRANDVOLD was born and raised in Stanley, Wisconsin. He migrated to Minnesota in 1925 where he went to work as a barber in his brother's barbershop in Spring Park.

Verna Dunn was born in Rhinelander, Wisconsin and moved with her family to northeast Minneapolis in 1914. She graduated from Edison High School in 1927.

In the summer of 1929, Verna and a group of friends rented a cottage on Lake Minnetonka. When "the group" needed haircuts they went to Tom's shop where ScKeiver cut Verna's hair. They met again that fall when Verna went to a party hosted by mutual friends. Love blossomed and Verna and ScKeiver were married on March 4, 1930.

Shortly thereafter, ScKeiver opened his own shop at 44th and Penn Avenue North in Minneapolis. In 1934 they moved to a small house at 54th and Girard Avenue with sons David (3) and Donald (2). Son, Loyd, was born in 1935. A few years later the family built and moved into what would eventually be the garage of the "Brick House" at 55th and Girard Avenue. After two more children, Jerry (1944) and Kathleen (1946) were born, the family built and moved into a house at 57th and Humboldt Avenue where Verna still lives. ScKeiver retired in 1970 and died in 1991.

Submitted by Loyd Brandvold

Loyd Brandvold and friends in the first phase of "The Brick House" at 55th and Girard with 1930s Austin

MY FATHER, OSCAR BREKKE, second generation Norwegian immigrant, married Hazel Olson. They farmed in western Minnesota at Canby where I was born in 1925. I am the oldest of their six children. In 1930 our family moved to Albee, near Milbank, South Dakota. I attended elementary school in Albee and Revillo High School. We had a graduating class of twenty-eight students.

Math was my favorite subject in school. I played center on the high school basketball team; we didn't have a football team. During 1943-1945 I served as a flight cadet in the Navy. After serving during World War II, I chose to stay with the Reserves. Later, while attending Brookings, South Dakota State College studying engineering, I was called to serve in the Army during the Korean conflict. Honeywell employed me from 1952-89. I retired just two months short of thirty-seven years with the company.

I met my wife, Doris Jensen, in 1950 and married her in 1952. Doris was born and raised in Sioux City, Iowa. She was the older of two children born to Arthur Jensen from Norway and Martha Hannemann, a pastor's daughter. Martha was born in 1900 and still lives in her own home. Doris graduated from the University of Minnesota as a dental hygienist. She retired from that profession in 1987.

Doris and I drove around looking at houses in 1955. We had $600 as a down payment and bought our home at 5536 Irving Avenue for $12,900 with a GI mortgage.

Our family consists of four children: Karen, Paul, Carol and Curt.

Karen married Martin Frusti and they have two children, Carrie who is married to Curtis Yoder, and Eric who graduated from high school in 1999. They live in Menominee, Michigan. Paul is married to Kitty. He is a painter and with his family lives in north Minneapolis with our step-grandchild, Gina. Carol lives in Bloomington and manages Personal Decision, Inc. Curt lives in West Monticello and is a partner in a home-building corporation.

I was chairman of the Brooklyn Center Committee for Better Schools when Brooklyn Center High School was being built. I was a member of the school board for twenty-one years. Ralph McCartney and Wallace Bernards were in office at the time. The hardest part for me in being a school board member was the length of the meetings. I was honored in 1977 to be one of six, out of seventy-five nominations from two thousand and fifty school board members in the State, to the "All Minnesota School Board," recognition of contributions to public education.

It was my opinion that the year they sold the country on the "new math" concept, they turned things backwards and it cost a lot of money. Now they are finally getting back to teaching basic math concepts.

In 1968 I was appointed to Intermediate District #287, Suburban Hennepin County Area Vocational/Technical school board and still serve there. Currently I am a math tutor at Brooklyn Center High School.

Submitted by Byron Brekke

Byron and Doris Brekke

Byron and Doris Brekke
August 1999

Britts Family

Maurice was born in Alton, Illinois. Therese was a native of the St. Paul/Minneapolis area. Maurice attended St. John's University and Therese attended St. Catherine's in St. Paul. Both received BA Degrees in Education in 1950. While Maurice served in the U. S. Navy aboard the carrier U.S.S. Antietam in the Korean Conflict, Therese studied Medical Technology in Battle Creek, Michigan. They married in July 1951.

In 1955, Maurice received his Master's Degree in Education from the University of Minnesota. For the next 30 years, he served at various times as a teacher, counselor, Director of Human Relations, and principal in the Minneapolis Public School System. During summers, Maurice was a Camp Director servicing inner city youth. He received a Doctorate Degree in 1970 in Education Administration from the University of Minnesota. Therese worked as a Medical Technologist at various hospitals and later, Group Health in Brooklyn Center. In 1973 she left the medical field for teaching. She taught at Osseo Senior High School, Sacred Heart, Robbinsdale and religious education at St. John's, New Brighton. In 1989 St. Thomas University granted her a Master's Degree in Religious Education.

Therese and Maurice raised nine children. As of 1998, all but one of the children lives in the Minneapolis/St. Paul area. Johnice, her husband Jim, their two children live in Brooklyn Park; Louise lives in Brooklyn Center; Lorraine, her husband Jim, their four children live in Brooklyn Park; Agnes, her two children live in Blaine; Cathy, her husband Phil, their two children live in Illinois; Maurice Jr., his wife Betty, their six children live in Ramsey; Theresa, her husband Ron, their two children live in St. Paul; Mary and her daughter live in Brooklyn Center; Dannielle and husband Carl live in St. Louis Park.

The Britts family moved to Brooklyn Center in 1959. They became active in church, school, scouting and sports. Maurice has been a volunteer, delivering food to the needy; Chairperson, Minneapolis FoodBank; Chairperson, Black Voice Channel 2 TV program; Member Knights of Columbus, Brooklyn Center DFL; and a Brooklyn Center City Council member. He is a published writer and poet.

Retiring in 1985, Maurice and Therese spend much time with their children and grandchildren. Maurice is active with the Minneapolis FoodBank, Retired Principals Association, and writes and teaches classes for Metropolitan State University.

Submitted by Maurice Britts

Front row, Cassie, Rita, Jayda; second row, Britni, Cathy, Krista, Kellen, Agnes, Robbi, Mary, and Tanni; third row, Jim, Lorraine, Dannielle, Therese, Johnice, Maurice, Therese, Louise; fourth row, Maurice Jr., Jim; at the peak, Nathan, Jordan, Joshua

THE DICK BROBERG FAMILY rented a farm on 69th and Humboldt North in Brooklyn Center. Their land extended to Bassett Creek. There was just one farm that separated their farm from the Earle Brown Farm. At this time people from Minneapolis and Camden would come out and dump their garbage along the road. Dick's dad picked up some papers among the garbage with a name on it. He took this to Earle Brown, who was sheriff at the time. Earle Brown dished out some good old-fashioned justice. The word spread quickly and the garbage was no longer dumped there.

Dick Broberg

Dick Broberg's great-grandfather owned a farm which ran from Osseo Road to Bassett Creek, where Brookdale is now located. In 1910 his great-grandfather paid $4,900 and sold it for $51,000 a short time later.

Great-Grandpa Burquist owned an island on Twin Lake in Brooklyn Center. In order to get to the island they had to build a log road. They had built a cottage on the island. Great-grandpa had bought that island in the early 1900s.

Dick Broberg went to Abraham Lincoln School located on 62nd and West Broadway. The school has since been replaced with a new school. His teacher for three years was Thora Thorsen. She was later honored by having the school named after her.

Oral interview with Marian Klohs

Paula Brodin

I WAS BORN IN 1920 and have lived in Brooklyn Center since the age of two. I attended Earle Brown School through 8th grade, Patrick Henry High School for 9th and 10th. I graduated from North High School in the June 1938 class.

I married John Szabla in 1940, and we had four daughters. Wendy graduated from Moorhead High School and lives in Colorado. Our second daughter, Paulette was in the first graduating class of Brooklyn Center High School and lives in Arizona. Jean and Linda graduated from BCHS and Jean lives in Brooklyn Park, and Linda in Minnetonka. Our daughters attended Earle Brown School, and two grandchildren also attended Earle Brown. On July 3, 1958, I married Rodger E. Brodin and we moved to Moorhead, MN for three years. We returned to Brooklyn Center in 1961. My husband passed away October 17, 1989.

My father, Charles Havill, was born in England and came to the U.S. at the age of seventeen, settling in North Dakota. My mother was born in Missouri but moved to Minot, North Dakota at the age of three. They met and were married. My father went off to World War I and my mother stayed in North Dakota teaching school. After my father returned, they moved to Minneapolis. In 1922 they purchased a home at 5450 Bryant Ave. North. My father hiked to 49th and Lyndale Avenue to take the streetcar downtown to Minneapolis Milling Co. where he was an accountant/bookkeeper. He kept this job through the Great Depression. It later became Archer Daniels Midland Co. My father served on the School Board for many years along with Frank Smith, Sr., and John Ryden.

Paula (Havill) Brodin, Patty Havill, and their parents, Charles and Florence Havill

We used a kerosene-cooking stove and wood cook stove in the kitchen. We had a coal furnace. Coal was delivered by a horse-drawn wagon. Coal was put in our basement through a chute in the basement window to the coal bin. Ice for our icebox was brought by horse-drawn wagon, and Franklin Milk Service delivered milk.

I walked to Earle Brown School at 59th and Humboldt Avenue from my home on 55th and Bryant Avenue in good weather, rain, and blizzards. When I was in first or second grade there was a big blizzard. No one was dressed for winter. An eighth grade boy carried me the last few blocks. The snow was deeper than knee-high and we could hardly walk. Our legs were bare and nearly frozen. This was probably in 1928. We lived through sand storms and tornadoes. A tornado hit Earle Brown School, destroying the one-two room original schoolhouse at 59th and Humboldt Avenue.

We attended North Methodist-Episcopal Church and Sunday School. Then neighbors began Harron Methodist-Episcopal Church in Brooklyn Center. While they were building the church basement, we met in the homes of Mrs. Perkins at 55th and Lyndale, and Mrs. Shirleys, at 53rd and Camden. When the weather was warm, we met under the oak trees on the vacant lot at 55th and Bryant. We had a portable organ, and the Sunday School classes sat on Indian blankets under the trees.

I like to write poetry and often wrote for the *Brooklyn Center Post* newspaper. Mary Jane Gustafson, Editor of the Post, would call me "The Brooklyn Center Poet."

Submitted by Paula Brodin

MARLENE WAS BORN in a house in Brooklyn Park in 1939 and spent fifty years of her life there. She was raised on a dairy farm and as a teenager worked for the truck farmers picking and sorting vegetables. Many Brooklyn Center and Brooklyn Park farmers raised potatoes and vegetables that were sold to processing companies or at the Minneapolis Farmers Market, to grocery stores, or to individuals for personal use.

When Marlyn graduated from Osseo High School in 1957 she went to Minneapolis to work for a couple of years. After marrying, she moved back to Brooklyn Center. With a blended family the house soon became too small. They moved to a farm with a large house, which was only one half mile from where she had been raised.

With their love for farming they soon started truck farming. They raised cucumbers for the Gedney Company and planted sixty acres of many kinds of vegetables that were trucked to the Minneapolis Farmers Market to sell. They raised their plants for the field in a greenhouse, which soon turned into a spring plant business.

With eight children, they were all busy and worked very hard to keep up with the crops as they came into harvest time. Their days started at four in the morning so they could get to the market and have everything unloaded by five to sell to the grocery store buyers and to individuals as they came to shop. Most of the family was home weeding or picking and sorting to get another load ready for the next morning.

Marlene became a single parent in 1978. She moved to a smaller farm one mile down the road in 1980. She still had four children at home, so they built more greenhouses and continued the plant business and also raised vegetables and more cut flowers to sell. Most of the potato and vegetable farm fields were sold out to developers, so the farmers re-located farther out. Marlene and family remained until 1992 when they also sold to developers.

Marlene now lives in Elk River with a greenhouse and two acres of cut flowers that are sold at Minneapolis Farmers Market. She promotes farming as a very good healthy way of life to everyone and sincerely hopes the family farm will always stay alive in Minnesota. One son still has a vegetable farm in Brooklyn Park on the family farm among all of the roads and projects. Another son is farming vegetables in Elk River.

Submitted by Lorraine Senlycki Spears

The Brooks Family

Roy Brunsell

THERE AREN'T MANY OF THEM around anymore—former truck farmers who were born in Brooklyn Center after the turn of the century and still live there. Roy Brunsell is one. His grandfather, Lars Magnus Brunsell, came to Minnesota from Sweden. His father, William Brunsell, was born in Minneapolis about 1880 and served on the Brooklyn Center Village Council for thirty years, as mayor, 1923 to 1937, and as clerk.

"My grandfather and father operated a store in the Riverside and Cedar area over by the University of Minnesota," Brunsell said," and when my grandfather bought forty acres, where Brookdale is today, my father came out here to farm."

His oldest brother was four when the family moved into the old farmhouse at what was then 53rd and Osseo Road. There were four Brunsell boys and all joined their father in truck farming.

A baby sister died at six months. Roy Brunsell is the youngest and lives with his wife, who is the daughter of Mert Lane, who was Brooklyn Center mayor from 1939 to 1950.

The Brunsells raised radishes, carrots, lettuce, peppers, eggplant, tomatoes and a few potatoes. Roy remembers when his father would leave Brooklyn Center with horse and wagon at two A.M. to sell vegetables in the Minneapolis market.

"I rode with him more than once," he said. "Dad would have to get up even earlier to feed the horses. He'd come back to Brooklyn Center about noon."

Brunsell went to Twin Lake School on Brooklyn Boulevard, when the school was only one room. That was before the present building, now occupied by the Alano Society, was built. "When we had to have two teachers, a curtain went up to divide the room," Brunsell remembered.

Brunsell's father served on the Twin Lake District #25 School Board when the frame building was moved to 57th and Colfax Avenue North.

Brunsell was on the school board when Twin Lake School joined Robbinsdale School District #281, about 1946, because Robbinsdale had a better tax base and could offer the children a better education.

Brunsell's father was one of the first to own a Staver car, purchased in 1912. "It was a big trip to go fishing at Pulaski Lake near Buffalo," Brunsell said. "We'd go about 30 to 35 miles an hour on the gravel roads." The Brunsell brothers were deferred from service during World War II because they were farmers, but Roy started flying in 1941, learning at the Old Robbinsdale airport. He said, "If I was going to be drafted I wanted to be a pilot." He owned a three passenger Piper Super Cruiser and flew until 1956. In the wintertime he often flew to Canada to fish on skis. He was also a member of the Brooklyn Center Volunteer Fire Department for nineteen years.

Born and raised in Brooklyn Center, he expects he'll probably be buried in Mound Cemetery in Brooklyn Center.

Information taken from article printed in Brooklyn Center Post,
written by Mary Jane Gustafson

SKIP AND JANELLE McCOMBS built the Burley's home in Elsen's City View Second Addition in Brooklyn Center in 1961. Clark and Caroline became the second owners in October 1968.

Clark was born in Aberdeen, South Dakota, in 1930 to Alva and Icie Burley. He grew up in Guelph, North Dakota and graduated from Guelph High School in 1947. After working in Bismarck, North Dakota and Aberdeen, South Dakota, Clarke entered the army and served from 1951-1953.

After being discharged from the army, Clark moved to Minneapolis and worked for Juster's clothing store while attending Minneapolis Business College. Clarke started working for International Multifoods in 1956 until he became disabled in 1987. He worked in various accounting positions.

Caroline was born in Littlefork, Minnesota in 1940 to Carl and Iva Kjemperud. She graduated from Littlefork–Big Falls High School in 1958. She then attended Concordia College in Moorhead, Minnesota from 1959–1961. Caroline then moved to Minneapolis where she worked for Lutheran Brotherhood from 1961–1992. She started working as a typist, became a programmer and was promoted to Senior Systems Analyst in 1968.

Clark and Caroline were married in 1962. They lived in an apartment in south Minneapolis until moving to Brooklyn Center in 1968. They were members of Central Lutheran Church in downtown Minneapolis from 1963 until the mid-1970s.

Craig, their son, was born in 1971. He attended Garden City Elementary, Brooklyn Junior High and Park Center High School. Following graduation in 1990, he attended North Hennepin Community College and Dunwoody Institute where he studied to become an automotive technician. He has been employed at Sears Automotive in Brookdale since 1991. He married Cyndi Hirt in 1996 and they live in Corcoran, Minnesota with their two sons, Austin and Nicholas.

While Craig was in grade school, the family was active in Brooklyn Center American Little League. He also played football, basketball and house hockey. He was confirmed at The Lutheran Church of the Master in Brooklyn Center in 1987.

Clark and Caroline are active members of The Lutheran Church of the Master and have served in various capacities, including council, since they joined in the mid-1970s.

Caroline went back to school and graduated from the University of Minnesota in 1978 with a degree in Business Administration. She has been employed at LifeUSA Insurance Company since 1993. She is currently a systems analyst.

Submitted by Caroline Burley

Clark and Caroline Burley

Clark and Caroline Burley (1999)

Robert and Betty Cahlander

BOB CAHLANDER was born and raised in Brooklyn Center, attending Twin Lake School, Lee School and Robbinsdale High School. At the tender age of seventeen, he started working for the Brooklyn Center Street Department. He worked his way up to the supervisory position. He worked for the City forty-one years—forty-one years of order changes, record breaking snowfalls, billions of pot-holes that had to be patched, thousands of acres of park grass that had to be cut, opportunities, responsibilities and accomplishments.

Bob "the Bear" spent twenty-six years as a volunteer fireman with the Brooklyn Center Fire Department. Assistant Fire Chief Bob Cahlander was interviewed by the news media that was on the scene of the Howe Fertilizer Plant fire in 1979. He was asked, "Isn't it dangerous to store dynamite in these buildings?" After a long pause in the freezing cold and with a deadpan look on his face, he slowly replied, "Only if it explodes."

In the last two years Bob enjoyed quite a reputation as "King of the Keyboard." His personal E-mail messages became not so personal when they were mistakenly sent to *everyone*. And then there was the "smoking keyboard" incident. While Bob was busy typing and planning one of his projects the computer burst into flames. Relying on his firefighting expertise, he was able to quench the fire in time without much damage to his office.

After hounding city officials many years for a Bobcat they finally relented in 1995 and let him have it.

During the years he worked for Brooklyn Center he rarely missed a "painful Wednesday dental appointment" on those beautiful spring and summer days. Could it have been that he was out playing golf?

Betty (Nashholm) Cahlander was born in Baudette, Minnesota. She grew up in Minneapolis and graduated from Patrick Henry High School.

Front row, Bob Cahlander and granddaughter Bailey; back row, Tim, Karla, Britt, Jon, Betty, Sue

Bob and Betty are the parents of four children, three sons and one daughter and two granddaughters. The Cahlanders lived in Brooklyn Center from 1958 to 1986. They lived in Bob's parent's old house. His parents lived next door. In 1986 Bob and Betty moved to Brooklyn Park.

Betty has worked for the Hennepin County Services Center for twenty years.

It was at the retirement party on February 8, 1996, that Bob's co-workers and friends roasted and toasted him at the Brooklyn Center Holiday Inn.

It was Betty's inspiration that brought about the metal sculpture of a bear. It had to be a bear! That is what Bob was. A bear is committed and loyal to his family and work. Thus, "Bob the Bear."

The bear found his home at the Cahlander Park at 65th and Brooklyn Boulevard. The park was dedicated to Bob because of his many loyal years of work for Brooklyn Center and his work as a volunteer fireman. The Cahlander family donated the bear.

Bob Cahlander died in 1996 of brain cancer.

Submitted by Betty Cahlander

ROBERT CAHLANDER was the first police chief in Brooklyn Center. He was born in Minneapolis in 1897 to Axel and Anna Cahlander. He was raised on a farm in what was at that time the Village of Brooklyn Center. Bob began his career with Brooklyn Center in the 1930s. He was elected to one of two part-time constable positions. He was appointed to the job of Marshall in 1932. Bob purchased his first uniform in 1935. It consisted of dark blue trousers, a gray shirt, a dark blue cap and a leather jacket. He provided the uniform, as well as his gun, ammunition, handcuffs, Billy club and his car. The only thing the village provided was his badge and reimbursement for gas.

Robert Cahlander

There were two constables working on a part-time basis. The other constable was Elzie Nelson. They normally worked at night patrolling in their own cars. The village didn't have a station to car radio system to notify the constable of calls, so they would drive past their homes several times a night. If they needed to answer a call the wife turned on the front porch light and the driver knew to stop and find out where to go.

Bob married Julia Wherry in 1935. Julia had been married before and therefore provided him with an immediate family. Bob later adopted Vern, Darlene, and William. In 1937 Bob and Julia were blessed with Robert Lee, who became known as Little Bobby. Bob and Julia built a home by the family farm. They felt fortunate to have a home of their own in which to raise their family, especially with times being so hard and money so scarce.

By 1942 Bob was working as constable, dogcatcher, weed inspector, as well as doing the snow plowing and grading the roads for the village. He was earning the enormous wage of $150.00 a month. By 1953 Bob was hired as a full-time police officer and was appointed to the position of chief. They received no training or first aid instructions at that time. The officers finally received training in the 1960s. Bob was a charter member of the Brooklyn Center Fire Department.

The most common crimes of the time were domestic disputes, thefts, suicides and window peeping, although potato thieves were not unheard of.

One of the major events in Bob's law enforcement years was the liquor store robbery of 1954. Bob and the liquor store manager were returning from the Camden Bank with money for the weekend check cashing business. Three armed gunmen wearing disguises with false noses and glasses held them up. Two of the three were said to have 45-caliber automatic guns and the third was armed with a machine gun. They not only got $5,000 in cash, but they also stole the chief's 38-caliber pistol and his 410-shotgun. The case was never solved.

Bob retired in 1962. They moved to a hobby farm near Big Lake, Minnesota in 1968 where he enjoyed gardening and playing cards.

Submitted by Betty Cahlander

Howard C. and Alpha L. Carlson

HOWARD C. (1911-1986) AND ALPHA L. (1910-1999) CARLSON lived on the corner of 55th and Humboldt Avenue for over forty-seven years, watching their neighborhood change over the years from a rural farming district of gravel roads and scattered houses in the 1930s to a thickly populated community of paved streets and closely spaced wood frame homes that characterized a good portion of Brooklyn Center in the post World War II era.

Born in Sweden, Howard, with his mother and father, immigrated to the United States in 1928. He lived with his parents for a time in Brooklyn Center and worked on area farms before acquiring his own place. At the same time he studied the craft of being a carpenter, a trade he made his own as suburban sprawl reached his farmlands, first in Brooklyn Center and later east of Johnsville.

Alpha was born in Northeast Minneapolis to parents who, like Howard's, had come from Sweden. She graduated from Edison High School, played the piano professionally, and worked during the Depression years of the 1930s at Northrup King and Company. Later, in the 1960s and 1970s, she worked at Dayton's Department Store in downtown Minneapolis. After her marriage to Howard in 1937, she settled with her husband into the home at 55th and Humboldt Avenue, North.

Here, and on their property near Johnsville, Howard and Alpha raised a large variety of vegetables for sale in Minneapolis. They built barns and sheds to wash and prepare their produce for market, and over the years they remodeled their Brooklyn Center home in response to their growing family.

The couple raised five children at their corner lot home: Karen, Paul, David, Jean, and JoAnn. All five children attended Earle Brown Grade School. The three older children attended North High School before moving on to careers in nursing, higher education and business. Jean and JoAnn attended the then recently built Brooklyn Center High School before embarking upon education and business careers.

Howard and Alpha attended Harron United Methodist Church, where Alpha was a Sunday School teacher—something she did for fifty years, and Howard served on the board of directors.

Indeed, much of their social life centered around the church and their family. They hosted large family gatherings at Easter and Christmas and at such secular holidays as the 4th of July and Thanksgiving. Often during the summer months they hosted large outdoor gatherings on their spacious, tree shaded lawn, and many times in attendance at these barbecue picnics were relatives visiting from Sweden.

After Howard's death in 1986, Alpha moved into an apartment building just a few blocks from the spacious home she had shared with Howard and their children. At the time of Alpha's death in 1999, the couple had seventeen grandchildren and twenty-nine great grandchildren.

Submitted by Paul Carlson

JOHN CARLSON WAS BORN in Minneapolis and later moved to a farm in Luck, Wisconsin. He graduated from Luck High School in 1959. Patricia was born and raised in Minneapolis, graduating from Washburn High School in 1959. It was at a pizza party that John and Pat met in 1960 and two years later were married.

John David and Patricia J. Carlson

We have been residents of Brooklyn Center since 1972. We have two children. Brent Edward was born October 15, 1967, and Wendy Sue was born October 30, 1970. They both attended Earle Brown Elementary School and Brooklyn Center Junior-Senior High School. Brent graduated in 1986 from Brooklyn Center High, and Wendy in 1989. Both children attended Sunday School at Lutheran Church of the Master and were confirmed there.

Brent graduated from Northwestern Electronics Institute in 1990. He has been an Electronic Technician for twelve years. He is now furthering his education in the electronics field. In August 1998 Brent married Susan Klein. She is employed by a firm of lawyers and is taking paralegal courses at North Hennepin Community College.

Wendy attended Lakewood Community College for two years. She is now a Marketing Service Representative (MSR) for a computer company. In June 1997, Wendy married Tony Jacobsma, a graduate of Park Center High School and Hutchinson Technical College. He is also an MSR for a computer company.

John worked for the Soo Line Railroad (CP Rail) for thirty-two years and has just recently retired. Patricia has always been a homemaker.

Submitted by John and Patricia Carlson

Mark and Kathleen Carmody

As I LOOK AROUND THE CITY of Brooklyn Center, I am surrounded by places that mean so much to me. It astonishes me because I grew up not being familiar with places for any length of time. By the time I was eighteen, I had lived in eight different houses in four states and seven cities. My father worked for the Pillsbury Company and with every promotion came another town and a new city. Mark grew up in St. Joseph, Minnesota. His parents still live in the same house that they lived in when he was born.

I moved to Brooklyn Center in 1984. It was my first apartment and I relished being able to have a place of my own. I met Mark at a Christmas party in Mendota Heights. We started talking and discovered we both lived in Brooklyn Center, and decided to meet at Perkins Restaurant in Brooklyn Center for a late night breakfast.

After our marriage we moved into his house and have lived there since.

I claim Brooklyn Center as my hometown now because I have lived here longer than anywhere else. I enjoy the feeling of driving around seeing places that are important to me. There is St. Alphonsus, our parish church where Mark and I were married and our two children were baptized and are now altar servers. There is the Shingle Creek Apartment building with its flashing red light on top. Our daughter at the age of two was convinced that was where they set off the fireworks at the end of Earle Brown Days. It has been the "Ba-Boom" building ever since. There is Evergreen Park Elementary School, where our children attend and where I have become a "professional volunteer." There is the bridge that goes over Shingle Creek just as it starts out of Palmer Lake by 69th Avenue. I stand on it when I go for walks and think it is the prettiest site in the city, no matter what the season. The new police station on Humboldt Avenue and the fire station on 63rd and Brooklyn Boulevard that were started when I served on the City Council are particularly pleasing because of the lengthy work involved by many to get the bond ready and passed. City Hall is one of my favorite places. The new housing development on 53rd Avenue on the southeast corner of the city is the one with the most meaning because it was a long process that was successfully completed just after I left office. It is one thing that I accomplished while in office that I do believe will have a lasting impact on Brooklyn Center.

One day as I was driving around, I realized that this was home. I have long-term friends that I have invested in and don't want to lose. So we found a house in Brooklyn Center that fit our needs and we stayed. It is nice to finally have a hometown.

Submitted by Kathleen Carmody

WHEN I WAS A KID, my family moved around quite a bit. My parents, who were Canadian, lived in England for several years where I was born in 1953. While I was still a baby, our family moved back to Canada, where we lived in Ottawa and Montreal. In 1962 my dad took a job with Honeywell and we moved to Minnesota. I remember as an eight-year old crossing the Great Lakes in a big ferry boat as our entry to the United States.

As a child I heard President John F. Kennedy speak about public service and he inspired me to get involved in government. While in school I had internships with a state senator, a congressman and at the county attorney's office, which furthered my interest in public service. In 1983 I was appointed by Governor Rudy Perpich to serve on the Metropolitan Council and then, in 1986, with the retirement of State Representative Bob Ellingson, I ran for and was elected to the Minnesota House.

Issues I have worked on in the House are crime issues such as the legislature passing tougher laws for violent criminals and drunk drivers, consumer protection, education improvements, and property tax relief. Among the laws I enabled the legislature to pass are Taxpayer's Bill of Rights, expansions of Minnesota's open meeting law, vehicle forfeiture for repeat drunk drivers, Minnesota's Racketeer Influenced and Corrupt Organizations Act, truth in auto insurance coverage, and the opening-up of felony conviction records.

Greater equity for the Brooklyn Center and Brooklyn Park area in such issues as education funding, highway construction, economic development and college building improvements are important issues to me. I was able to have the legislature pass funding for new and remodeled buildings at

Phil Carruthers

Rory, Phil, and Alex Carruthers

North Hennepin Community College and at Earle Brown Heritage Center. Other projects I worked on are water quality improvements to Shingle Creek (the Shingle Creek Stormwater Ponding Project), the construction of Highway 610 and upgrades to Highway 100.

In 1993-96 I served as House majority leader and in 1997 I was elected speaker of the House, a position that I held from 1997 through 1998. These positions were great opportunities for me to work on issues important to citizens. As speaker of the House, I worked to bring more nonpartisanship and cooperation to the House.

When I'm not working, I enjoy playing ball, fishing, hiking, nature watching and camping with my two boys—Rory, age 7 and Alex, age 10.

Submitted by Phil Carruthers

The Robert Cashman Family

ROBERT CASHMAN AND MARILYN CHRISTIAN had their first date the night they graduated from Earle Brown School in 1942. Robert joined the navy later and served in the Philippines during World War II.

Robert and Marilyn were married in 1947 and in 1949 moved into a small house near Robert's parents. Robert worked on the railroad while Marilyn stayed at home and was a homemaker. Robert was a volunteer fireman for Brooklyn Center for eighteen years. Serving as Chief of Bureau of Fire Prevention was his last position there.

In 1973 Robert left the fire department and the railroad and worked with the State of Minnesota as a Fire/Arson Investigator. They had to move three times in three years and in 1976 moved into the original Roy Cashman home in Brooklyn Center where they remain to date.

They have two children, Sally (Paul Fischer) of Zimmerman and James of Brooklyn Center. There are four grandchildren and four great-grandchildren.

Robert and Marilyn enjoy their summer place in Tenney, Minnesota, the smallest town in the state with a population of three.

Submitted by Rob and Marilyn Cashman

The Roy Cashman Family

IN 1927 ROY AND IVA CASHMAN and sons Paul and Robert moved from Robbinsdale to Brooklyn Center. Roy worked seven days a week on the railroad and Iva was a homemaker. They had three more children, twins Beverly and Barbara and then Roy.

All five children graduated from Earle Brown School. It was hard to concentrate as they looked out the windows and saw all the animals at the Earle Brown farm. Every car on the road was familiar. There were few houses then. Many of the houses had double lots. There was a ballpark on 54th and Emerson. The boys that Robert chummed with had a swimming hole on Shingle Creek just north of 57th Avenue. The Brooklyn Center tool shed was nearby.

Bob Cahlander, Sr., would grade the streets with a horse-drawn grader and was police chief at night.

Iva's name is in the cornerstone at Harron Methodist Church. The church is on 55th and Dupont Avenue North. All of the Cashman children went to Sunday School there and to the Young People's Group.

The Cashman children; Paul (Veryl) is deceased, Robert (Marilyn) live in Brooklyn Center, Beverly (James Madden) live in Brooklyn Center, Barbara Little in Brooklyn Park, and Roy (JoAnne) live in Mora, MN.

Submitted by Rob and Marilyn Cashman

ALICE (McLEOD) CASWELL was born in August of 1865 in Brooklyn Township, Minnesota. She was the daughter of Alexander and Annie (McConnell) McLeod. Both of Alice's parents were born in Nova Scotia, Canada.

Arthur Donald Caswell, Alice's son, resided in Anoka and founded the Caswell Target Carriers of Anoka. He designed the ROTC indoor range, which included the Caswell target carrier, in 1926 for the Military Department at the University of Minnesota. The Caswell Target Carriers are still in use today, (1999)

Taken from the Brooklyn Historical Society Archives
"Tales of Local Minnesota Lumberjacks"

Alice Mabel McLeod Caswell

IN 1955 when we first moved to Brooklyn Park from Minneapolis, the West River Road was Highway 169. Our house at 8545 West River Road was only three years old. We bought the house from Bob Johnson. Mr. Johnson had built the house. This was farm land owned by Al and Pearl Mattson with only one large oak tree on the lot behind theirs, owned by Bob Nelson.

The mornings out there were beautiful. Looking out our picture window we could see Mattson's sheep grazing across the road often with deer among them.

There was no lawn, only black dirt. We were told that this used to be Mattson's watermelon field.

Our two boys and the neighborhood boys would gather in our back yard and play baseball or football. This wasn't the best for a developing yard but it was great to see all those young boys playing and getting along so well.

My husband, Ray Chamberlain, passed away in 1983. I am still living at the same place and have been here for forty-three years.

I did re-marry to Harold Lindstrom. We enjoy the neighborhood. It is still a good neighborhood although it has undergone many changes in the later years.

Submitted by Tess Lindstrom and Arelen Westberg

Chamberlain and Lindstrom

Ron and Betty Christensen

RON AND BETTY CHRISTENSEN and their first daughter, Kari, moved to Brooklyn Center in December 1961 when Brookdale was in the planning stages. Their second daughter, Nancy, was born in 1961 and their son, Kurt, was born in 1971. The three Christensen children attended Orchard Lane Elementary School, Northview Junior High, and Park Center High School. Ron served in Korea as a Lieutenant in the Air Force in 1956 and 1957. One of his main duties was to command the Air Control Center that controlled military flights over South Korea. He also traveled with the Air Force Inspector General group to air bases in Japan and Okinawa.

Betty and Ron both grew up in Duluth, Minnesota, graduated from Duluth high schools, and were married in April 1959. During their first year of marriage Ron was employed as an Electrical Engineer for General Electric Company. He was selected to participate in the General Electric Engineer in Training Program. This program provides three to six month assignments in various General Electric facilities. They used this time to travel and stay at cities in Virginia, Illinois, Pennsylvania and Minnesota. They decided to return to Minnesota where Ron was employed as an Electrical Engineer in the Aerospace programs. He worked on some of the instrumentation that was installed on the moon-landing spacecraft.

Betty, Kurt, Ron, Nancy, and Kari Christensen

Betty worked as a secretary for various companies in Brooklyn Center and Brooklyn Park. She spent most of her time raising their children during their school years.

In 1972 Ron and two partners started an electronics manufacturing business. During the business venture, Ron and the partners invented and patented a new type of electric motor. The business was sold in 1980.

Ron and Betty considered moving in 1975, but the children wanted to stay here to be close to their friends. So they added 1000 square feet to their house, which made it very adequate and comfortable. They have lived in the house for nearly forty years.

In 1975 Ron became very active in Osseo School District activities at the request of the superintendent. For five years he served as a leader on school bond election committees and school district boundary committees. He was elected to the Osseo District School Board in 1980. He served in this capacity for fifteen years. During that time the student population more than doubled. The number of schools also doubled during that time. These were busy times for all of them. He also served on the Hennepin Technical College School Board.

Ron also was involved in Brooklyn Center City activities. He was a leader in the Park and Recreation Bond election in the late 1970s. He was involved with the development of the Earle Brown Heritage Center. He served several years on the Brooklyn Center Finance Commission. At the present time Ron is the owner of an Electrical Engineering Consulting business. Betty is employed as a secretary for an injured workers job placement company.

Submitted by Ron and Betty Christensen

WE CAME TO BROOKLYN CENTER in 1959. Along with us came our three children, Sherry, Roger, and Sue Ellen. Penny was born later.

When Penny was fourteen, she bought a raffle ticket from her teacher at Regent Junior High School for one dollar and won an Arabian horse. John Davidson, the singer, pulled her name out of the bucket at the raffle held in California.

Roger worked for Western Electric for thirty-seven years and retired at the young age of fifty-six. I worked at Brookdale Daytons for twenty-five years.

When we moved here in 1959, the Brookdale parking lot was a wild asparagus field. At that time the children would pull a red wagon up to Brookdale and fill it with asparagus. At the time of our transfer, Brooklyn Boulevard was still named Osseo Road. The closest grocery store was a National Tea Store located at Sixty-eighth and Brooklyn Boulevard, the space now used by Iten Chevrolet.

Sorrow hit our family in December of 1955 when our twin girls died at birth and then it hit again in 1994 when daughter, Sherry, died from breast cancer after fighting it for five years.

Roger and I took many trips over the years. . . to England, Switzerland, Paris, Austria, Amsterdam, Italy, Germany, Poland, Russia, Finland, Sweden, Norway, and in the United States and Hawaii.

Roger was a lover of old classic cars. He owned a 1962 red Thunderbird and took it to many shows.

Roger passed away in October 1998, at the age of seventy years. He is buried at Fort Snelling and the twin girls, Jean and Joan, are there with him. At this time I am still in the family home with Roger's faithful dog, Brittany.

Submitted by Phyllis Christenson

Roger and Phyllis Christenson

Roger and Phyllis Christenson and their grandchildren, Michael, Charles, Spenser, Sara, and Marc

IN 1939 Henry and Lillian Christian, and their daughters Marilyn and Joan, borrowed an unfinished trailer and moved one mile north into Brooklyn Center from Minneapolis. They had two lots and could use the neighbor's water and outhouse. Henry and his friends dug the basement by hand. Before winter set in they were able to move into the basement house. People lived in basements or garages that had been placed in the back of lots in hopes of building up front at a later time. The basement roof leaked and they often slept with pans on the beds to catch water.

When World War II broke out, Henry worked at Onan's until he retired. Lillian went to work in Minneapolis department stores. She volunteered for many years at a Lutheran Book Store on Chicago Avenue South in Minneapolis.

Marilyn and her five girlfriends went skating or to the movies at the Camden Theater in North Minneapolis. Summer evenings they walked the streets with no problems. Two of the girls were relatives of Earle Brown. They could go into all of the outbuildings and sit on the carriages. There were peacocks wandering around.

Marilyn (Robert Cashman) lives in Brooklyn Center, Joan (Charles Bloom) also lives in Brooklyn Center and grandson James Cashman lives in the original Christian home place.

Submitted by Marilyn Cashman

Henry and Lillian Christian

Elaine Tessman Christiansen

I WAS BORN in 1930 and for the first sixteen years of my life, my home was 'on the farm' where my brother and sister-in-law, Eldon and June Tessman reside. My earliest memories of the farm are the hot, dry summers of the early 1930s. My parents, Albert E. and Esther Tessman, were working tirelessly to save their potato and vegetable crops with newly installed irrigation.

During the spring planting season, I remember my mother spent hours in the granary cutting the seed potatoes for planting. I can't remember that she ever cut her fingers and I can only imagine how her body must have ached! After planting, Daddy took my hand and we walked through the fields, looking for the potatoes to sprout and grow and later, for potato bugs and any evidence of disease. It was always a special event for me when I went with him to the Minneapolis Farmers' Market. When there was snow to be used for freezing it, my mother and Alice Tessman were masters at creating new flavors of ice cream.

Fond memories of my grandparents and Uncle Edmond Tessman are many. My Grandpa Hildebrandt would come to help hoe the small crops during the summer. Grandpa Hildebrandt and Grandpa Tessman would often sit on the back porch, swapping stories of their younger days. My Grandmother Tessman demonstrated her talent for color and design in handcrafts and rugs she created. Uncle Ed and I played card games together. The Brooklyn Center 4-H Club and Ellen M. Bohanon, our club leader, were important to Eldon and me. We enjoyed trips to Hennepin County and Minnesota State Fairs with project exhibits and demonstrations, and each of us earned a trip to National 4-H Congress in Chicago.

Joel, Jim, Dave, John, Grandson Will, and Elaine Christiansen

After I graduated from Arizona State at Tempe, my first work was in Martin County, MN as Extension Home Agent. The 4-H Club program was also part of my responsibilities and, in 1953, I joined the Minnesota 4-H staff in St. Paul

I met Martin Christensen on the St. Paul Campus, and we married in 1955 and made our home in Falcon Heights where we raised our four sons, John, David, Jim and Joel. Martin worked in the Department of Agricultural and Applied Economics before his untimely death in December 1982. For more than thirty years, I managed the 4-H Cafeteria in the 4-H Building at the Minnesota State Fair. After Martin's death, I was employed as editor for Pillsbury Publications.

In my retirement years since 1994, my interests have turned to the Hamline Church Dining Hall at the State Fair and the Minnesota 4-H Foundation. Life is rich and full with the joy of five grandchildren. John and Catherine have two little boys, David and Jill have a daughter and Jim and Sue are parents of twin daughters. My youngest son Joel lives in Montana. In July 2000 a new dimension begins as I marry Hal Routhe, a longtime friend, and also the father of four sons. My life since age sixteen has been away from Brooklyn Park, but it is Brooklyn Park and 'the farm' that will always be my "home-home."

Submitted by Elaine Tessman Christiansen

I, Richard Christofferson, grew up in Brooklyn Center. In 1936 my parents moved into our new home on 54th and Girard Avenue that had been built with the help of a crew of relatives. I was nine months old.

53rd Avenue was the boundary line between Minneapolis and Brooklyn Center, as it is today. When it snowed, the south half of the street was plowed by Minneapolis and the north half was plowed by Brooklyn Center. Police authority had the same demarcation line. Russ Gilbertson was Brooklyn Center's first Chief of Police. Many still-familiar names lived in the neighborhood, names like Brandvold, Duoos, Brueninger, Nyberg, Johnston, and Gilbertson. Everyone helped one another out, the doors to homes were unlocked, and our friends' parents were like second parents to us. At the Brueningers house I was always welcomed and I knew where the cookie jar was. Roy Duoos was my Sunday School teacher at Harron Methodist Church and in later years, he was my foreman at Northwestern Bell Telephone Company.

Earle Brown Grade School was a two-story building located at 59th and Humboldt and we walked to school each day. As you looked west, you could see from Girard Avenue to Osseo Road, now Brooklyn Boulevard. The only thing in between was truck farms. Humboldt Avenue was covered with cinders from coal stoves. It made for tough times on bicycle tires. As kids, my friends and I hunted pheasants where Brookdale now stands and we swam in Shingle Creek. This was especially nice on a hot day after a grade school ball game. A person can still see the area that we had cleared and cleaned for the swimming hole, but the trees are gone.

We lived in an area that welcomed the energy and curiosity of kids. Just about every Saturday I walked over to Earle Brown's farm where I sat by the white fence, ate a picnic lunch, and watched the white-faced cattle graze. Once in a while Mr. Brown picked me up and took me to his office. He let me sit on his silver saddles. I was six or seven at the time and it was many years before I realized the thrill of these experiences and knowing Mr. Brown.

Another time, I was sitting in the same place having my Saturday picnic when a "big" car stopped. A very big man stepped out and talked to me for three or four minutes. He got back into the car and left. Years later as I was watching TV I realized the person that day had been Burl Ives.

I grew up in a place that was safe and nurturing. It was a time of individual wells, out houses, unlocked doors, vegetable gardens, alleys, cinder streets, and caring neighbors. Time brings change and progress is good. With lots of emotion, I walked out the door of the house on 54th and Girard for the last time in 1996. Mom and Dad were gone. The house had been sold. But, sixty years of fond memories remain.

Submitted by Richard L. Christofferson

Richard L. Christofferson

The Chubbuck Family

IN 1870 ROBERT JOHNSON, along with his pregnant wife Sophie, and a two-year-old son, John, left Norway in a sailboat for America. They homesteaded in Brooklyn Township. Their address was Camden Station Rt. 5. They cleared the land and farmed. The kids did chores before dark because they were afraid of the howling wolves at night.

A Norwegian Lutheran Church was built on a parcel of grandpa's land at Brookdale Drive and Sheridan Avenue North. They raised a family of thirteen children. The youngest child, Annie, married Samuel Chubbuck, a handsome young man from Iowa (much to her father's disappointment because he was not Norwegian).

Sam and Annie and their family lived in North Minneapolis. He worked at the Ford Plant. Apparently there was reconciliation in their relationship because when grandpa was no longer able to farm, he offered the farm to Sam if they could live with them until they died (which they did at age 92). Sam then quit his job and moved his wife and three pre-school daughters, Shirley, Ruth and Vida, to the farm.

Sam was a dairy farmer and shipped milk. He butchered a cow, a calf, and a pig each fall so that the family had meat for the winter. All parts of the animal were used. They made blood sausage and head cheese, rendered out lard, ate the tongue, heart, liver, pickled the pig's feet, etc. Once a year they had a special goulash that included beef, pork and kidney, along with vegetables. Annie canned fruits and vegetables. During the Depression, the family never felt poor because they always had enough to eat.

Sam always did the chores but the children worked in the fields weeding onions, picking potatoes, etc., each day, and swam in the Mississippi River every evening after chores. When worship services were no longer held in the Norwegian Church, the Chubbucks used the building for sorting and storing onions.

The federal government issued an agricultural program called the Agriculture Stabilization Conservation Service (ASCS). The farmers were permitted to plant a certain amount of acreage into prescribed products while maintaining other land for pasture.

Sam, along with a few other farmers, measured fields of participating farmers in Brooklyn Township, kept records, and corresponded with Washington, D. C. regarding the program.

Sam was also involved with the Berg School Board and occasionally our family supplied board and room for a teacher.

Shirley married John Leitzke, grandson of Oscar John, the Osseo, Minnesota blacksmith. They have lived in the same house in Osseo for fifty-eight years. John continued the business in his grandfather's shop and his sons, Robert and Richard, run the business. Their daughter, Joyce Miller, lives in Eden Prairie, Minnesota.

Ruth married Ray Zopfi of Osseo and lived on a farm north of Osseo for many years. The Zopfi family originally came from Swanden, Switzerland. They have four boys: Ken of Osseo, Tom of Worden, Montana, Arn of Maple Grove and Ron of Champlin. Their daughter, Rikie Falck, lives in Osseo.

Vida, the youngest of the Chubbuck children, married Rex Dorn and they farmed and raised their family of four children (Jan, Jill, Jeff and Joe) in Brooklyn Park. They have been members of Brooklyn United Methodist Church for fifty-four years.

The family has lived, loved, laughed and died in Brooklyn Park for four generations.

Submitted by Vida Dorn

Sophie and Robert Johnson, who homesteaded in Brooklyn Township in 1870

JOHN AND DAGNY CLARK have resided in Brooklyn Park for fifty years, from 1949 to 1999. They were married in Minneapolis in August 1947 and lived in the city for two years before deciding to buy a house. John wanted to raise chickens so they looked for a chicken house and found one at 7301 Humboldt Avenue North on an acre and a half of land. They said, "We have had good times and bad times here." They had four children, twin sons passed away the day they were born. John was born in 1949 and Constance was born in 1957.

The house was cold. They didn't have a furnace, just a little oil stove. When Dagny sat and held the bottle to feed the baby she had to put her feet in a pan of warm water or they would have frozen. After two years we finally could afford a furnace. What a difference! A warm house at last!

The Clarks bought two hundred chickens. They were hybrid and very excitable. John had to knock on the door before entering their domain and if anyone else tried to enter they went berserk. One year of that was enough. No vacation, just egg picking. Eggs sold for nineteen cents a dozen—not very lucrative.

Sometime along the way a streetlight was installed on their corner. Dagny stood and looked at it until quite late the first night and her husband said, "Don't worry, it's not going away." They couldn't get a telephone when they first arrived in Brooklyn Park and spent months on a waiting list.

The Clarks have seen a lot of progress through the years. New churches, schools, Brookdale Shopping Center, City Hall, Edinburgh Golf Course, blacktop roads to name a few.

When it rained hard their cellar filled with water, as did the street. They jokingly called it lakeshore property. Finally, storm sewers were installed, so that problem was solved. Before improvements were put in, the taxes were nine dollars a year, then they jumped to fifteen dollars, then to thirty, and have been on the rise ever since.

The Clarks planted over one hundred trees and bushes on the property and it was fun to watch everything grow.

The change of Humboldt Avenue from a cow path in 1949 to a major thoroughfare caused a big change in traffic conditions. Thousands of cars use the road today.

They had to sell their house because of the road, so they bought a house on the freeway in Camden in north Minneapolis and had it moved to their adjoining property. It was moved about three A.M. and people going to work were surprised to find a new building where none had stood the day before.

The Clark children are married. They have a wonderful daughter-in-law and son-in-law and one grandchild with another due in January 2000. The Clarks feel their family has been blessed.

Submitted by Dagny B. Clark

John and Dagny Clark

Wilfred and Gladys Clasemann

WE BECAME RESIDENTS of Brooklyn Center in 1963 when we purchased a new home on Newton Avenue. Wilfred worked for the bus company downtown at that time and we were also the parents of four small children.

Gerard, the oldest, was four years old then and started school in 1965 at the brand-new Monroe School. Later Evergreen School was constructed for our neighborhood. Gerard now works for Dain Rauscher as a vice-president. He and Mary have five children, including a set of four-year old triplets. Gregory was three in 1963 when we moved here and now is living in Prescott, Arizona and installs cable for communications. Linda was two in 1963, and now is an engineer for the State of Minnesota. Daughter Louise was the baby then and is now a medical secretary. All four are happily married today and busy raising the ten grandchildren. Twelve years later, Kevin arrived in 1975. Raising a son when we were in our forties kept us busy and young. Kevin is a draftsman, and is having a lovely new home built in Elk River, Minnesota near Lake Orono.

Wilford, Gladys, and Kevin Clasemann

In 1972 Wilfred joined a German singing group, The Happy Wanderers, as their accordion player. Many of the members lived in Brooklyn Center. They did a great deal of entertaining and providing music at many of the major establishments in the Twin City and rural areas. They became quite famous and loved at celebrations like the St. Michael German Festival and endless other festive events. People really enjoyed their records and tapes. In 1990 it was time to retire.

Wilfred retired in 1996 from Honeywell, and each day, he practices his accordion and keeps taking advanced lessons to increase his expertise. He also enjoys frequent carving and painting classes. Gladys has been taking many computer classes at North Hennepin Community College and finds this new technology very fascinating. We are also very active at St. Alphonsus Catholic Church assisting as Eucharistic Ministers and helping in the other works of the Church. I, Gladys, am an election judge, and we both have worked tirelessly for pro-life candidates in our area.

We are grateful for the trails near our home and spent happy hours walking and biking around Palmer Lake and into Brooklyn Park. We are taking advanced dance lessons given by our community. Brooklyn Center's close proximity to downtown, with the Community Center and Brookdale Shopping Center expanding is really terrific! Even a new police station is being built nearby on Humboldt Avenue! Wilfred assisted with the COP program for youngsters for some years. The city surely offers endless possibilities for education, recreation, and service.

We are truly enjoying our retirement years right here in Brooklyn Center. It is a good city to work, and retire in.

Submitted by Gladys and Wilfred Clasemann

THE CLEMENSONS moved to 8200 97th Avenue North in Brooklyn Park in 1971. They purchased, what was known as the Bud Fair Farm and before it was known as the Ball Place. The abstract for their place goes back to 1858, when Minnesota became a state.

They moved here from Golden Valley. Darlene and Lyle both were raised on farms in northern Minnesota, in Clearwater County. They had moved to the Twin City area in 1964, living in north Minneapolis for several years. The realtor who guided them to buy the property had looked at the future zoning and noted that his area would be future industrial. The plan also showed the route where Highway 610 would likely go through. In 1974 zoning took place and their property was grandfathered in.

They purchased the place because they owned a construction business and needed more room for their equipment. In 1978 they got out of the construction business. Lyle became an inventor engineer and invented many things for sale, which still sell today.

When people came out to visit they always commented that we lived way out in the "boonies." At that time 97th Avenue ran all the way through to Highway 152, that is now the route of Jefferson Highway. Highway 152 was later changed to 169.

One time a potato farmer, who no longer lives in the area, left his water sprinkler for irrigating his potatoes, run up almost onto the road on the south side of our house and it sprayed into the kitchen. That did not set well with my wife—it never happened again. In the fall after the potato harvester had gone through, the kids used to pick potatoes that were left in the field.

The Clemenson children really enjoyed this place. They were able to have dogs and had plenty of room for them to roam. One time they purchased a female and a male Norwegian elkhound so the children would have puppies to sell. The dogs did have puppies and the children were able to sell them. But the female dog had a habit of roaming. One night she went over to Fischbach's and killed a few geese that belonged to Lulu Fischbach. After paying Lulu for the dead geese there wasn't much money left over from the puppy sales.

The family went skiing in Elm Creek Park and swimming and had many picnics in the summer in the Brooklyn Park parks.

We were told Highway 610 was to be built in the early 1980s. The thought was at that time, it would take about fifteen years, when we first moved to Brooklyn Park. However, there never seemed to be enough money from the State Highway Department to fund it. In 1990 we purchased the Hilmer Guntzel place on the east side of Brooklyn Park and moved there in the fall. The house was built in 1917, according to city documents.

Submitted by Darlene and Lyle Clemenson

Lyle and Darlene Clemenson

The Clemenson Family

Jack and Eileen Clifford

WE MOVED into our Brooklyn Center home on August 1, 1955. The yard was full of tall weeds and the daytime temperature was in the '90s. Both remained about the same for two weeks.

We joined Our Lady of Victory Catholic Church and our four children attended grade school there, followed by Brooklyn Center High School.

John (Jack) worked for Honeywell for thirty-seven years at various locations and in a variety of jobs in Production, Quality Control and Engineering Management, retiring in 1987.

Eileen was a stay-at-home mom until the youngest child was in high school. At that point Eileen went back to school achieving a Bachelors degree, a Masters degree and a Doctors degree in Health Education and related fields. She taught at North Hennepin Community College, retiring in 1995.

Jack and Eileen Clifford

Their children have embarked on a variety of careers. Mark, the oldest, lives in California and works as an Engineering Manager. Charles graduated in Biology and works as a computer Analyst Consultant. Greg works at Honeywell in Production. Christine is employed by Prudential as an Accounting Manager. We have thirteen grandchildren.

We split our year between Lakeland, Florida and Brooklyn Center. We enjoy the best of both areas. Dogs have been a big part of our lives in Brooklyn Center. Fritz was our first dog. He was a dachshund and a wonderful pet for the family in the fifties and sixties. Gold, Heidi and Archie (two goldens and an Irish setter) were our companions in the sixties and seventies. They gave us wonderful moments as upland game hunters. Tasha and Bandy were with us in the eighties and nineties. They were both hunting breeds. Bandy is the last survivor at thirteen years and doing well despite arthritis.

Both of us became pilots at Crystal Airport following retirement. Much of our time has been spent on flying activities in Minnesota and Florida. Eileen is a member of the 99's and flies blood for the Red Cross from rural Minnesota to Saint Paul for processing. The 99's mark town names on local airports. Each summer they attend airshows, breakfasts and lunches on fly-ins. We have our plane hangared in Plant City, Florida in winter. The local EAA Chapter sponsors an airfest in October and works on SUN-N-FUN in Lakeland in the spring. We work both events each year. On at least one Sunday a month the Plant City pilots called "Munchers," fly to different Florida cities for lunch. Their motto is "Eating our Way across Florida."

We have watched Brooklyn Center change considerably over the forty to fifty years of residency here. Brooklyn Center never got much of a strong industrial base so taxes were always fairly high.

Overall we have found Brooklyn Center to be a safe and satisfying place to raise our family and to live in retirement.

Submitted by Jack and Eileen Clifford

PHIL COHEN AND BEVERLY WARGIN fell in love, and married in November 1949. Our first residence was at my parents' home. My father was wonderful in welcoming Bev into the family and counseled me "Not to rent! Only with a home you can call your own would you be able to have a life of your own."

We bought our first home at 5353 Dupont Avenue North in 1950. We will forever be thankful to a fine neighbor, Bill Doane, who gave me a quick education and valued help with the well, pump and cesspool.

Our daughter, Deb, was born in November 1950. My brother, Saul, drove the newborn home in his big Buick, stopped at my parents' house so they could see the first girl in two generations born into the family. Although we had a small house, it rang with excitement with our first child. The house was brightly lit up for our first Christmas in our first home. Stephen was born in August 1954. Nancy arrived in December 1956. And then it was time to look for a new house, which we found at 5302 Humboldt and moved into on March 1, 1957.

The Phil and Bev Cohen Family

Bev and Phil Cohen Family

Deb, Steve and Nancy attended Earle Brown School, and all graduated from Brooklyn Center High School.

Deb went on to graduate with honors at the University of Minnesota with a degree in teaching the learning disabled. In 1972 she married Dick Shultz, who holds degrees in Music Education. They live in Mora, Minnesota with their two sons, Zachary, 16, and Nick, 14. Deb teaches in Princeton, Minnesota and Richard is a realtor in Mora.

Steven has excelled in sports, both as player and coach. He was the head baseball coach from 1981 to 1995 at North Hennepin Community College. Steve married Colleen Gaffeny in 1978. They have a daughter, Anna, 15, named after my mother and she attends Cooper High School. Steven and Colleen are divorced but remain good friends. Steve was selected to be the Staff Director of the Senior National Team. Steve's wonderful companion, Annette Towne, is pursuing a Doctorate in Child Psychology at Fresno, California.

Nancy married Gary Anderson in 1978. They live in Brooklyn Park with their two boys, Brian age 17 and Ross now 14. Both boys are open enrollment students at Brooklyn Center High School. Nancy works at Park Brook Elementary School as an Administrative Aide. Gary is plant manager for Leef Brothers.

My wife, Beverly, was the mainstay of the Cohen family. She was lost to us on September 4, 1995. She was diagnosed with cancer earlier that year but was determined to make the best of the situation and wanted to live out the rest of her days in the home she loved at 5501 Humboldt Avenue North, which was built in 1988.

Over the forty-five years of our married life, Bev was a devoted wife, mother and grandmother. Her only sorrow was not being here physically to see her grandchildren grow up. She is best known for her "culinary arts."

Submitted by Phil Cohen

Peter and Shirley Cook

PETER AND I (SHIRLEY) graduated from Edison High School in 1947 and 1948, respectively. After graduation Peter went into the army. After being discharged from the military, he enrolled in the Minnesota School of Business. While he was going to school, I went to work for Ministers Life Insurance.

On September 30, 1950, Peter Cook and Shirley (Koehler) were married at St. Mary's Orthodox Cathedral located in northeast Minneapolis. Shortly after our marriage Peter was recalled to the Korean Conflict and decided to join the Navy instead of the Army. He was immediately sent to the Great Lakes and then on to Norfolk, Virginia where I later joined him. We lived in Norfolk and then returned to the Twin Cities where we bought a three-bedroom stucco rambler. This was in an area of Brooklyn Center that was referred to as Hipp's Fourth Edition.

We moved into our new home on May 1, 1956, with our first daughter, Constance who was born in March of that year. Our second daughter, Christine, was born in the fall of 1957. Two years later, in 1959, our son Thomas came into the world, and in 1961, our last child Tamara was born.

Our home is located at 5837 Washburn Avenue North. There were no streetlights, just open fields. At one time corn and asparagus grew here. It was a very unique, tight-knit community. After living here for forty-eight years we still have many of our original neighbors.

Pete went to work for Sperry Rand and later worked for Hennepin County in the Finance Department for more than thirty-five years. In 1973, after being a stay-at-home mom for seventeen years, Shirley went to work for Steven Fabrics in the Accounting Department.

Our family has watched Brooklyn Center grow from a small community into the city that it is today.

Connie, our daughter, married Thomas Gorham and they are living with their two sons, Gregory and Brent, in Brooklyn Park.

Chris married Scott Nelson and they live with their children, Jonathan and Julie Ann, in Maple Grove. Our son Tom married Dr. Kae Ferber and they reside in Madison, Wisconsin. Tamara married John Bauers and they have made Howard Lake, Minnesota their home.

Peter retired from Hennepin County in 1986. Shirley continued working at Stevens Fabrics until 1996. Today they still find themselves enjoying summers at their cabin on Cedar Lake near Annandale, Minnesota.

After fighting a battle with cancer, Pete passed away on October 16, 1999.

Submitted by Shirley Cook

Peter and Shirley Cook

IN MARCH 1955 our family moved to Brooklyn Center. Osseo Road was then just a dirt road. Frank Howe built the homes on our block. There were many asparagus fields on 69th and France Avenue in the area where the water tower is now located. Many years ago Grandma Lane had a truck farm where Pilgrim Cleaners is now located. The grandchildren helped to pick vegetables for market.

On 63rd and Osseo Road, Karl Cahlander had cows. Every once in a while they got loose and were in our area. There were many pheasants and other wild life where we lived. I used to get upset when people from the city dropped cats and dogs off, expecting other people to pick them up and take care of them.

My oldest son went to first grade in a school that was located where the old city hall used to be. The school was also a voting place at election time.

One memory is going to the Starlight Drive-In Theater. Across the road from the Drive-In was the Hartkopf turkey farm. If the wind was blowing in the right direction the odor was not a pleasant one. An annual thing in the spring or summer was the burning of the Palmer Lake basin. The kids thought that was just great! We saw all kinds of wildlife come out of the grass.

The Mound Cemetery at that time was open to Swedish people only. But things have changed since then and it is now open to all nationalities.

Submitted by Deloris Cooper

Deloris J. Cooper

THE BENNET FAMILY built our home in about 1860. The Countrymans purchased the home in 1949. It was an old farmhouse with an outside toilet, and water was attained from a pump outside of the house. They still use the same well but had all of the plumbing brought into the home.

We are very happy with the location by the Mississippi River. We have traffic in front of our home, but it would be lonesome without the many cars that pass by.

Brooklyn Park built a pond in our back yard and it didn't take long before ducks and geese discovered a nice peaceful place to raise their young. In the spring many little ducks and geese hatch and when the little ones are ready, the mothers march them across the road to the river.

The West River Road is sometimes dangerous. One spring a boy drove his car over the riverbank into the river. He wasn't found until the next fall after the leaves fell from the trees. The river is beautiful, but one must be careful when driving near it.

Submitted by Martin Countryman

Martin and Deloris Countryman

The Deloris and Martin Countryman home

Alcid Joseph and Mary Magdeline (Pumarlo) Couture

ALCID JOSEPH COUTURE was born November 15, 1892, near Loretto, MN, to Joseph and Madeline Dupont, Couture. Mary Magdeline Pumarlo was born August 15, 1897, daughter of Frank & Mary Desjardins, Pumarlo of Hamel, MN. Both families originated from Canada. (The teacher where Mary's mother, Mary Desjardins, attended school had such difficulty pronouncing their last name, she convinced Mary to change it to Gardener!)

They began their life together in the Hamel area, moving in the early 1920's to north (40th) Minneapolis. In 1927 they moved to Brooklyn Park, first renting 20 acres on 77th Avenue North, raising vegetables, livestock (cows for milk, calves for meat, horses to work the land), chickens, necessities for what was becoming a large family.

Alcid and Mary Couture, family and friends

They relocated to a home with acreage for raising their own food and meat, adjoining 77th, down to the Mississippi River. Later, the parents older, most children married and gone, they moved again on 77th, purchasing two lots from Fred Peterson, then building a smaller "retirement" home. Dad worked at General Mills for more than thirty years.

All seven children attended Benson School at 73rd and West River Road. Descendants include the following:

Eleanor, born August 26, 1922, and husband, Irvin Dehn, live in Elk River, MN. They have twelve children: Deanna (Conchignano) of Maui, Hawaii; Steven, New Brighton, MN; Jeannette (Maruska), Shoreview; Linda (Phillips), Roswell, Georgia; Donna (Praught), Buffalo, MN; David, Rockford, MN; Donald, Minneapolis, MN; Judy (DeMars), Otswego, MN; Kenny, Osceola, WI; Barbara (Ayers), Coronado, CA; Robert, Chanhassen, MN; Lloyd, Otswego, MN; plus twenty-five grandchildren, two great-grandchildren (by Deanna) for Irvin and Eleanor Dehn. Earl, born April 24, 1924, died May 1, 1979, major heart attack. Earl's wife, Marge, lives in Robbinsdale, MN. They had two daughters, Jean (Cvetich), and Jill (Anderson); each had two children, making 4 grandchildren for Earl & Marge Couture. Allen, born May 12, 1925, and wife, LaVerne, now live in Deerwood, MN. They have three daughters: Nancy has two children; Cindy has two children; and Kathryn. This gives four grandchildren for Allen and LaVerne Couture. Beatrice, born October 4, 1926, was married briefly, no children. She lives in Glendale, CA. She enjoyed a full life working for the City of Los Angeles, in defense plant work and real estate. She is in a convalescent care center with Alzheimer's Disease. Leona, born February 7, 1929, and husband, Jack Hannick, live in Burbank, CA. They have five sons: Robert has two children; Steve has two children; John; Ronald has threee children; and Brian. There are seven grandchildren for Leona and Jack Hannick. Donald, born February 7, 1929, died February 4, 1998, of a heart condition. Donald's wife, Pat, lives in Minneapolis. They have three children: Leona, who has 3 children; John has two children; and William; making five grandchildren for Donald & Pat Couture. Walter, born October 17, 1938, and wife, Ursula, live in Champlin, MN. Wally has worked at Northern States Power since Anoka High School graduation in 1956. Walter has five children by a previous marriage: Daniel, Steven, Ronald, Julie and Kristen. Alcid and Mary were married October 26th, 1920. They enjoyed nearly sixty-nine years together before Mary passed away November 15, 1989. Alcid stayed on for another three years, he died March 3, 1993.

Submitted by Mrs. Eleanor Dehn, Eldest Daughter

DOUG AND KARLA were married in 1967 at LaPorte City, Iowa. They were high school sweethearts and had dated for seven years.

Doug started attending the University of Iowa in 1964 and Karla started in 1965. Doug graduated with a degree in physical education and was hired to teach in Brooklyn Center High School in 1969. They then moved to Brooklyn Center in the apartments just west of the school.

Karla student-taught in Iowa in the fall and graduated in November with a degree in physical education. Karla was finally able to make the permanent move to Brooklyn Center that fall. They moved from the apartments to their current residence in 1972 and have lived there ever since.

Doug has worked for Brooklyn Center School District for thirty years, the first twenty-three as a physical education teacher and the last seven as the Coordinator of Community Education and Student Activities.

Karla began working for the Brooklyn Center School system in 1983 in the food service. Currently she is the head cook at Earle Brown School.

They have three boys that graduated from Brooklyn Center High School. Dray, the oldest, lives in Brooklyn Center and works for the Bureau of Engraving in Minneapolis. He has one daughter, Alecia. Bryce graduated from the Missouri Southern State College with a degree in Social Studies. He and his wife Pam live in Joplin, Missouri. Bryce teaches Social Studies in Webb City, Missouri; Pam is currently completing a bachelor's degree in nursing. Flave has one more year to finish his degree in Social Studies. He graduates in the year 2000.

The Darnell family attended Brooklyn Center Baptist Church for twenty years, until it was sold. They now attend Brooklyn Park Evangelical Free Church.

Submitted by Karla Darnell

Doug and Karla Darnell

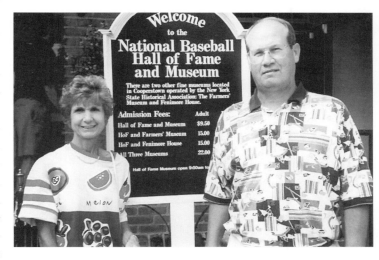

Doug and Karla Darnell

Manfred G. (Ben) and Shirley Davidson

I, MANFRED, was born June 14, 1918, at Balsam Lake, WI, the only child of Anna and Henry Davidson, a village merchant. My father died when I was seven years old. I attended Balsam Lake High School, and graduated in 1935. After World War II, I attended the University of Minnesota, Extension Division.

My wife is the former Shirley French. She was born in Austin, MN on January 5, 1918, and moved to Frederic, WI, in 1919. She graduated from Frederic High School in 1935. We met in 1939 and were married on June 14, 1945. During the World War II years, she was employed at Frederic, WI; Barrington and Chicago, IL; Spokane, WA; Los Angeles and Oakland, CA.

We have three children and seven grandchildren: Dennis (1947) married Ruth Johnson—Children: Cory and Leigh. They live in Phoenix, AZ.

Neil, Dennis, Deborah, Ben, and Shirley Davidson

Deborah (1951) married Donald Jacobs—Children: Matthew and Evan. They live in St. Louis, MO; Neil (1954) married Deborah Kessler—Children: Lindsay, Hannah, and Morgan. They live in Brooklyn Park.

Prior to World War II, the Agricultural Adjustment Administration at Balsam Lake and the State Bank of Centuria, WI employed me. After WWII, I worked at Simonsen Lumber Company in St. Cloud, MN; and from 1947 to 1983 at Our Own Hardware Company in Minneapolis and in Burnsville, as Treasurer and Securities Administrator. Shirley served as mother and homemaker.

I was inducted into the U.S. Army at Ft. Sheridan, IL, on November 5, 1941. I received Corps of Engineer training at Ft. Leonard Wood, MO. I left the U.S. June 3, 1942, aboard the Queen Elizabeth and arrived in Scotland June 9, 1942, then to the Midlands of England, Algeria and Tunisia in North Africa, Sicily, Corsica, and Italy. I was awarded battle stars for seven campaigns including assault landings in Algeria, Sicily, (under the command of General George Patton, Jr.), and Salerno, Italy. After three years of foreign service I was honorably discharged in October 1945. After returning stateside, I was assigned to the Air Inspector's Office at Geiger Field, WA, to inspect military facilities at Geiger Field and Fort George Wright.

With the support and help of Shirley, I have been involved in community and church activities: Scoutmaster, Business Advisor for Junior Achievement, member of the Brooklyn Center District School Board from 1959-1968 (Clerk and Chairman) at the time when the first High School and Kindergarten were constructed; member of Mayor's Liaison Committee; School District representative on Twin City Metropolitan Planning Commission; Hope Lutheran Church Treasurer for twenty-three years and an usher; I served as Trustee and Deacon at Hope and on various committees; involved in building program at Hope Church and School District #286 referendums since 1958; volunteer with Short Term Evangelistic Ministries; former member of BC Southeastern Neighborhood Council; Earle Brown Days Ambassador; Park Crest Baptist Care Center since 1981; first Treasurer of the Lutheran Youth Encounter; and recognized in 1960 by the Brooklyn Center Education Association for the Minnesota Education Association Distinguished Service Award and was the first person from the School District to be nominated for this award.

Submitted by Manfred (Ben) Davidson

Don Davis was born May 15, 1942, and raised in north Minneapolis, the oldest of three children, the other two being twins.

I, Marie Hogoboom, am one of three children. I am of Dutch and Norwegian heritage, born and raised in south Minneapolis. My father was from Michigan and mother was from Wisconsin. I attended Macalester College and graduated from the University of Minnesota.

The Don and Marie Davis Family

My husband and I met at Macalester College, married, lived in St. Anthony and then Chicago while he worked for the railroad. He became a Brooklyn Center Police Officer in 1967. He worked full-time while taking advantage of a city program, which allowed him to finish his education. Don graduated from the University of Minnesota in 1971 with a degree in Criminal Justice. He was a Law Enforcement instructor at North Hennepin Community College for twenty-three years and instrumental in training more than one thousand officers.

We moved to Brooklyn Center in 1967 and to Brooklyn Park in 1978. Don was a Brooklyn Center Police Officer; Hennepin County Criminal Justice Coordinating Council member; Chief of the Department of Public Safety for South Lake Minnetonka; Brooklyn Park Police Chief, 1978-1995; Deputy Commissioner and Minnesota State Commissioner of Public Safety; presently he is Public Safety director of the Suburban Hennepin Parks District.

I am an x-ray technician and have always worked part time. I worked for the Columbia Park Medical Group for fifteen years.

We have two daughters, Nancy and Lori, and one grandson Brandon Davis Cichy. Nancy and her husband Dean Cichy live in Becker, Minnesota. Dean is a Deputy Sheriff for Sherburne County. Nancy is employed by Coborn's in St. Cloud, Minnesota. Lori lives in Maple Grove, Minnesota and is a registered nurse at North Memorial Medical Center.

When our girls were growing up, I read to them nightly. Don coached their sports. I feel lucky to have been mostly a stay-at-home mom. I now have time for golfing, playing bridge, bowling and reading. Don is a workaholic, but he enjoys yard work, civic activities, ironing shirts and reading.

Donald and Marie Davis

Submitted by Marie Davis

Ed and Dorothy Decker

ED DECKER WAS BORN in Little Falls, MN, on March 9, 1928 and grew up on the Tony Decker farm north of Swanville. Dorothy Axel was born on a farm in Parkertown near Randall, MN, on March 4, 1934. Dorothy and Ed met in 1949 and were married at St. Peter's Lutheran Church in Randall in 1952.

Ed was working as a depot agent for the Northern Pacific Railroad in Swanville when Uncle Sam called him into service in 1951. Ed spent two years in the Southeast Signal School at Camp Gordon, GA. He was a Radio Operation teacher teaching International Code and Teletype to recruits and veterans alike.

In March of 1953, the Deckers returned to Swanville, where Ed resumed the duty of depot agent. In 1954, an opening occurred for a telegrapher in the "MS" office in the former Great Northern Depot on Hennepin Avenue.

Ed and Dorothy Decker (1987)

The Deckers relocated to a small apartment in Robbinsdale at $75.00 a month. They moved to a new home built by Russ McChesney & Sons at a cost of $13,995, in 1954 and continue to live there now.

The four Decker children, Dave, Dana, Denise, and Daniel, were born and raised in Brooklyn Center and attended Brooklyn Center High School. Due to job demands they all moved to other places but return to Brooklyn Center quite often.

Ed worked as a telegrapher and train dispatcher in the Great Northern Depot until 1974 when the depot was closed. Ed was promoted to Chief Dispatcher at the Burlington Northern Office in Fridley in 1976. He retired as Manager of Train Operations in the Burlington Northern General Office in St. Paul in December 1983.

Dorothy worked for over thirty years as District Manager for Santa Photo Company. While doing this she covered numerous shopping malls, including Brookdale Shopping Center. She retired in 1993.

The Deckers traveled over 150,000 miles in their motor home. They have also visited ten countries. They have no immediate plans to leave Brooklyn Center, but as the saying goes, will "follow the bouncing ball."

Some of the biggest thrills in raising their family have been watching their sons do well in sports, and their daughter excel in music. They are hoping their grandchildren Jaclyn, Alyssa, Amanda, Kristin, and Derek will all have the same opportunities.

Submitted by Ed Decker

THE LAMONTE DEHN FAMILY moved from north Minneapolis in February of 1956 to Brooklyn Center. Our family consisted of Lamonte, Donnette, and our three children, Robert, Richard and LaDonna. When Lonnie (LaDonna) was four years old a new neighbor moved in across the street. She went over to their front door, put her hand and head up to the screen and hollered, "Do you have any kids?" and they of course didn't because they were an older couple.

As the years passed all of the children were involved in school activities and very busy. In the summer time the boys were involved in Little League and Babe Ruth baseball. All of the parents helped out wherever they could. My wife, Donnie, helped the other mothers working the concession stands.

Lonnie, not to be outdone by her brothers, was a member of Bluebirds, and then flew up into Campfire Girls. Later on in high school she became a Centaurs cheerleader for Brooklyn Center High School.

I worked for the Hennepin County Sheriff's Department and worked all different shifts, so I would help by acting as umpire whenever I could. I remember when the Little League first started, the fathers got together with the priest at Saint Alphonsus Catholic Church and talked about playing our games on their ball field diamond. We offered to lay the sod, put up the bleachers and the cyclone fencing around the field. The priest said that would be just fine and that is how our Little League got its start. We played that way until land was obtained for our own ball fields. Those were the 'good ole days', and will not be forgotten. They were very enjoyable.

Our children are married with their own families, but still live in the immediate area of Brooklyn Center.

In 1981 I retired from Hennepin County after working there for thirty-five years. Donnette and I did some traveling, but never wanted to move from Brooklyn Center, as we enjoyed the comfortable life-style here.

In 1987 after forty-two years of married life, Donnette died of cancer. I then decided to make himself more available to the Brooklyn Center Lions Club, the Crime Prevention Program and three to four bowling leagues. I not only participate in the leagues, but also I am secretary for three of them. In the summer I am involved in playing and working at the Hampton Hills Golf Course.

I have always liked living in Brooklyn Center, as it is more like a small city rather than a Metro City.

Submitted by Lamonte Dehn

The Lamonte Dehn Family

The Denn Family

Brooklyn Center and Brooklyn Park are prominent in the memories and experiences of our family over the past thirty-three years. Despite family changes and four fairly significant career moves during that period of time, the "Brooklyns" have remained our hometown area of choice.

In December 1965, we moved into our first home at 3024 Quarles Road, Brooklyn Center. At the time we had two daughters, Theresa and Jennifer. We actually were directed to this particular house by a friend, another Brooklyn Center resident, who thought we would not only love the house and neighborhood, but also the community. He was right.

Almost immediately we joined St. Alphonsus Catholic Church, and quickly became involved in many of the activities of the parish. Then came participation in the Jaycees/Mrs. Jaycees, PTA, Girl Scouts, the Brooklyn Center capital building program, Community Emergency Assistance Program, a few election campaigns, etc. Along the way, in 1970, we welcomed our son, Michael, into the clan.

Jim and Rose Denn

In July 1975 we relocated to Brooklyn Park. This allowed us to maintain our affiliation with St. Alphonsus and to stay in contact with our many friends in both communities. In 1978 we increased our family size with the birth of our second son, Brian. This was also the period of involvement with kids hockey, baseball, football, as well as band, science field trips, summer camps, and other sundry activities. A few years later, we were privileged to play a role in bringing the amazing Habitat for Humanity program to this part of the Twin Cities region.

Throughout our years in the communities of Brooklyn Center and Brooklyn Park we have always felt "at home," and pleased that in some small way we were able to contribute to the growth and development of these thriving cities.

While we cannot lay any claim to the memories or history of the early years, we do recognize that we have greatly benefited from the vision and hard work of the many individuals and families who were here, and who laid the sound and thoughtful civic foundation the cities are able to build on and enjoy today.

Submitted by Jim and Rose Denn

I, BARBARA, GREW UP in Minneapolis and attended North High School. Ed grew up in the Robbinsdale and Brooklyn Center areas. He attended Anoka and Robbinsdale High Schools.

Ed and I were married at the Brooklyn Center Methodist Church in 1950. We built our first house in Brooklyn Center on 58th and Regent Avenue North, a short distance from the Crystal Airport. In 1953 we purchased a home at 809 56th Avenue North and lived there for twenty-six years.

We had one son and three daughters. Things were quite different then. In our area there were few homes per block. The roads were still dirt roads; each family had its private well, and its own sewer system. Then the housing developers came in and soon the area was filled up. Brookdale Shopping Center had not been developed yet but Brooklyn Center was becoming a city.

Our children attended Earle Brown School and Brooklyn Center High School. At the time, Earle Brown School did not have kindergarten. Part of the building was an old two-story structure. In 1967 the old part burned. The fourth, fifth and sixth graders were bussed to other area schools for a couple of years.

There was a dairy store located on 53rd and Bryant Avenue North for daily groceries. The store always had a large selection of penny candy for the children.

The children were in Boy and Girl Scouts, 4-H Club and the Brooklyn Center School Bands. I was a member of the League of Women Voters. Our family attended the Lutheran Church of Triune God.

We had wonderful friends and neighbors. Brooklyn Center High School, with the purple and white Centaurs, was a great place to raise a family.

Michael is married. He and his wife have four children and live in Wayzata, Minnesota. Lynn is married and they live in Wyoming, Minnesota. Kris is married, with her husband and two children lives in Cokato, Minnesota. Jean and her husband and one child live in Faribault, Minnesota.

We have many happy and pleasant memories of Brooklyn Center, a small town, now a big city.

Submitted by Barbara Dilley

Ed and Barbara Dilley

Louis Dinzl Family

IN 1937, when I was about fifteen years old living in north Minneapolis, my Dad bought a 100-foot lot on the Mississippi River at 78th Avenue North in Brooklyn Park. This area was the Shoop farm where I had been invited out to ride horseback when I was about twelve years old.

One winter day my Dad and I were clearing brush along the riverbank and I was skating, as the ice was smooth and free of snow. A little later we were amazed to see a truck with a load of logs driving down the middle of the river. I believe these were the Scherer Brothers, who started their lumber business selling lumber cut from logs buried in sand since the early 1900s when there were saw mills along the river in north Minneapolis. The Scherer Bros. Lumber Company is still a family-owned business on the Mississippi River in North Minneapolis.

The years flew by and I found myself sitting behind twin 50-caliber machine guns in the tail of a B26 on bombing missions over Germany during World War II. Fortunately, I survived that ordeal and returned to Minneapolis.

In 1947 our family moved from the city into a small home we had built on that river lot just two lots from where the Shoop homestead had been. There were still several large elm trees from the Shoop homestead there. Sadly, we would lose them and about a dozen other elm trees to the disease that came long in the 1970s and 1980s. Victory Airport was a grass strip at Newton and 77th Avenue North (Brookdale Drive). In 1949 I received approval to take flying lessons under the GI Bill. I took my flight training with Clark Flying Service at Victory Airport. I obtained a private license but did not pursue a flying career, as there were many ex-air force pilots competing for jobs at that time.

Farms along the Mississippi River, taken in 1949 by Lou Dinzl, flying out of Victory Airport

I served on the Brooklyn Park Town Planning Commission for about seven years or more with Abe Zimmerman and others when "Baldy" Hartkopf was mayor.

One summer I observed a tornado coming toward our home but it turned and went north and demolished part of Riverview School at 93rd and West River Road. It also pushed Mr. Warner's garage over the riverbank with his new car in it. He just purchased it the day before and had no insurance. He was our tax assessor at the time.

In 1951 I spent the summer on construction of a secret air base at Thule, Greenland. In 1952 I married a great girl (LaVonne Wire) from South Dakota. We lived at 79th and West River Road until 1965 when we built a home on Mississippi Lane where we raised four children and are retired there. Our children are:

Carol (Bill) Sabetti — three children — Brooklyn Park
Curtis (Cris) —three children — Brooklyn Park
Connie (Jerry) Schultz — two children — Mora, MN
Cathy Dinzl — Minneapolis

Submitted by Louis Dinzl

KAY AND I CAME from rural Minnesota, having grown up on small farms in western Hennepin County. After high school we moved to Minneapolis for continued schooling and employment. We met in 1948 and were married in 1950.

Our first home was a two-room 3rd story attic apartment in south Minneapolis. After a few months, we moved to the suburb of Columbia Heights where we rented the upper floor of a house, consisting of three bedrooms and a bath. These three rooms became our kitchen, bedroom and living room. In 1952 we bought our first home, a small three-bedroom rambler in Brooklyn Center. We wanted to buy in Brooklyn Center because of its proximity to our families and friends and its convenience to work. This first home, on Brookview Drive, though it had no garage or landscaping except a boulevard tree, was like a palace to us. All of the houses were newly built on a former asparagus field. The neighborhood families were growing, similar in age, employment, and income.

Our family grew in size to five children; Jeanne, Steven, Michelle, Laurence and Mary Beth. Because of the need for a larger home, we moved in 1971 to our present home at 61st and Emerson Avenue North. Our family did not want to leave Brooklyn Center or School District #286. We are fortunate again in having good neighbors and neighborhood.

During the years we lived in Brooklyn Center we were active members first at Our Lady of Victory Catholic Church and later, at St. Alphonsus Church. Our children attended elementary school at Our Lady of Victory and at Earle Brown, and high school at Brooklyn Center High School. All five children went on to earn college degrees. Two daughters, Jeanne and Michelle, live in California; our two sons, Steve and Larry, live in Arizona, and our daughter Mary Beth lives in Brooklyn Center.

I have worked in the structural and reinforcing steel phase of building construction from 1949 to retirement in 1996 consisting of drafting, engineering, estimating/bidding, and project management.

Kay was a homemaker during the growing-up years of our children. Later on she did office work until her retirement in 1990.

We now are enjoying our retirement and are busy with our church, volunteer projects, travel and our lake cabin.

Our hobbies have been a big part of our lives. For me it is music (piano, organ, choir), gardening, and building things. Kay enjoys playing cards (Bridge, 500), gourmet cooking and Mary Kay cosmetics. We were active members of Citizens for Better Government for several years and worked on many local election campaigns. I have co-chaired a successful District #286 school bond referendum, and we both participated in several school board campaigns.

Being residents of Brooklyn Center for forty-seven plus years entitles us to say that the city has many good citizens, a knowledgeable and caring city government, good schools and is a wonderful place to live.

Submitted by Paul Ditter

Paul and Kay Ditter

Henry and Emily Dorff

I WAS BORN in north Minneapolis in October 1922, the fourth of five boys of Emma and Henry Dorff, Sr. . At age twelve, I biked up the Osseo Road to help the Brooklyn Center garden farmers dig and pick potatoes for a nickel a bushel. I made twenty cents that day. I also delivered the Minneapolis daily newspaper. I graduated from North High School in 1940 and in 1943 joined the 17th Airborne Division during World War II, becoming Staff Sergeant, a paratrooper and glider man. The 17th played a major role in the Battle of the Bulge. In March 1945 we crossed the Rhine River, landing behind enemy lines in gliders. I returned home January 1946 and, with the help of the GI Bill, enrolled in the school of business at the University of Minnesota and graduated in 1949. After graduation I went into public accounting and passed the CPA examination. In 1957 I went to work as comptroller for Northwestern Corrugated Box Company in NE Minneapolis where I retired after twenty-eight years of service.

Henry and Emily Dorff Family

My wife, Emily, was born in North Prairie, Minnesota in 1920. She was one of six children, three boys and three girls. Emily walked four miles to school, crossing woods and fields to get there. Later Emily attended St. Francis in Little Falls, an all-girls high school. After three years of nurses training she became a registered nurse. Following graduation Emily worked at the University of Minnesota Hospital during the polio epidemic. Emily loved working in the nursing field for ten years.

Emily and I met at a dance in March 1951 at the Prom Ballroom in St. Paul. We were married in September. In April 1954 we moved to Brooklyn Center at 53rd and Irving. We brought our two sons with us: Burton, age 2½ years, and Dennis, one month. In 1955 we had our daughter, Mary, and in 1957, Carol. All our children attended Our Lady of Victory and Brooklyn Center High School where they lettered in such sports as football, golf, wrestling, track, and gymnastics. In addition, Mary and Carol were cheerleaders and Athena award winners—Mary in 1973, and Carol in 1975. In 1966 we moved to an acre of land on the Mississippi River, south of Durnam Island. There was an abundance of wildlife including deer, rabbits, gophers, ducks, and geese. We enjoyed it there for twenty-two years. Emily and I continued to be involved in community life, Cub Scouts, community education, church activities and civic organizations and clubs. I was elected to the Brooklyn Center Council in 1960 and served two terms. Later I served as chairman of the Charter Commission and on the Conservation Commission. Currently I am serving as chairman of the Earle Brown Days Festival. In 1988 we moved to a twin townhouse in another part of Brooklyn Center. We continue to be active in the community that we love and cherish. In 1998 the Brooklyn Historical Society elected me to the Brooklyn Center Hall of Fame.

Submitted by Henry Dorff

My wife Beverly (Busch) and I grew up in south Minneapolis. I am the oldest of nine children. Beverly is the second youngest of five. Beverly is of German descent and I am of Swedish and Scottish descent. Beverly graduated from South High School and I graduated from Roosevelt High School. We met in 1952, and were married in 1955 after my discharge from the army. We moved to Brooklyn Park in 1961 into a $15,000 rambler. The population of Brooklyn Park then was about 10,000. Beverly worked for Northwest Bell for twelve years.

Ron and Beverly Dow

Our daughter Beth was born in 1965 and Missy in 1968. Beth married Keith Taylor from England. They have two children: Miles and Mason. Missy married Jim Hopp of Brooklyn Center. They have three children: Adam, Alyssa and Aaron. I worked for Honeywell Inc., for forty-three years and retired as Manager of Corporate Photographic Services in 1995.

In response to the political turmoil that existed in 1964, I encouraged the formation of Northtown/Lynbrook, a Civic Association in our housing area, and was elected president. Over the years we fought and won against the first Townhouse Ordinance. We fought for property tax equity and the policies were changed. We merged with Brookdale Estates Civic Association in opposing and closing a city dump. We organized a local celebration called "Funarama" and dedicated twenty-five acres as Norwood Park. We were able to get members appointed to the Planning Commission, Parks Advisory and a City Hall Study Committee. One Northtown/Lynbrook Civic Association president, Bjorn Rossing, was Planning Commission chairman, and eventually mayor. I was a member of the Planning Commission in 1967, Brooklyn Park Athletic Association president in 1967, Tater Daze Chairman in 1968; Outstanding Young Man in 1968 and elected to the city council in 1970. Lost an election in 1976 and was re-elected in 1978 and lost again in 1980.

Ron Dow

In the 1960s and 1970s, Brooklyn Park Junior Chamber of Commerce members were an active and dedicated group of young men. At one time or another they had two members on the Osseo School Board, five city council members and two were Brooklyn Park mayors. They were also members on various city commissions. The Jaycees helped pull the community together by starting "Tater Daze" and uniting the homeowners with the potato growers. The growers put on a tractor pull that brought participants from around the state. Working with interested residents, Jaycees, city staff and the growers were the best of times in our family's community life.

Brooklyn Park was one of the fastest growing suburbs in the metropolitan area in the 1970s and 1980s. The city council held countless well-attended public hearings for the rezoning of open land and extension of public utilities. There were endless arguments in the East District about the need for the new utilities and the financial burden on existing residents. Our family enjoyed the opportunity we had to participate in the growth of Brooklyn Park. We had fun, met life long friends and assisted in creating a unique place.

Submitted by Ron and Beverly Dow

Dolores Duoos

DOLORES MOVED to 53rd and Camden Avenue in Brooklyn Center from north Minneapolis with her parents, Otto and Velma Wyttenbach, in 1922. Her husband, Roy Duoos, moved with his family from a farm near Shell Lake, Wisconsin, in 1926. The Duoos family lived on 53rd and Emerson. As a young girl, I attended Sunday School at the home of Mrs. Shirley on 53rd and Camden, later at the home of Marianna Perkins on 55th and Lyndale, and from there to a grove of trees on 55th and Bryant. That was the beginning of Harron Methodist Church. Roy Duoos' family was a member of Hope Lutheran Church. When a tornado caused destruction at Earle Brown School, they attended classes at Harron Methodist Church until all was repaired.

Both Roy and Dolores went through eighth grade at Earle Brown Elementary School, on to Patrick Henry High School, and then to North High School in Minneapolis. To get to North High from Brooklyn Center, they would catch the streetcar on 52nd and Bryant Avenue.

The Dolores Duoos Family

At that time Brooklyn Center was still largely a rural area so all of the streets were dirt. In 1937, though, Camden Avenue became the first and only street in Brooklyn Center to have sidewalks. As a child, Roy worked on farms during the summers for Howard Carlson at what is now 55th and Humboldt, and also for Erick Rydeen near 56th and Logan.

Roy and Dolores started dating after an Earle Brown reunion dance, May 17, 1941. They were married on October 25, 1941. After service in the armed forces and short stays in Austin and Duluth, Minnesota, they moved back to Brooklyn Center. They lived on 54th and Dupont Avenue, next door to Roy's parents, and raised three children—Judy, Jim, and Larry there. Dolores worked at Earle Brown School for seventeen years selling lunch tickets. All three children went to school there and graduated from Brooklyn Center High School. Roy died in 1980 from non-Hodgkin's disease.

They have three granddaughters, Ellie, Amy, and Molly Duoos, who are the second generation to graduate from Brooklyn Center High School. Her daughter-in-law, Joan, has worked at Earle Brown for twelve years. Two grandchildren, Brett and Scott Anderson live in Texas.

In all, Dolores has lived on 53rd and Camden for twenty-one years, on 54th and Dupont for twenty-five years, and for eighteen years on 54th and Fremont. (64 years)

Two-and-a-half years ago, she joined a few of her Earle Brown classmates by moving into the Crossings Apartments at Brookwood. Brooklyn Center has been a wonderful home for Dolores and her family since 1922.

Submitted by Dolores Duoos

My parents married in Maine and came here on their honeymoon to visit Dad's sister, Emma, and her husband Everett Howe. My father, Merton Lane, was Mayor of Brooklyn Center from 1917 to 1921 and again in 1938-1948. My mother is Mae Craemer. I was born in 1910 at our home on Osseo Road, about where Brookdale Chrysler Dealership is today. There are nine girls and one boy in my family. When a baby was born Aunt Lizzie came from the East to help out, so my mother never left her bedroom for six weeks. Dr. Lockwood came from Camden in north Minneapolis by horse and buggy, but if he didn't arrive in time, one of the neighbor ladies acted as midwife. When my brother, the ninth child, was born the doctor took a bushel of peas as payment.

Marjorie Dupont

As a small girl, the Indians sold us woven baskets; mine even had a cover. It wasn't too long ago that I put mine in a garage sale but was sorry afterwards that I did.

I attended a two-room Brooklyn School. I had excellent teachers including Thelma Howe, Mrs. Brown and Jeanette Fair. We took the streetcar to high school at a Girls' Vocational School located about where the Minneapolis Convention Center is now. When the Depression came along and things got tough, we had to leave school and work.

While my parents were in Maine they attended the Catholic Church. When they moved here they attended the First Baptist Church, then switched to the Methodist Church while Henry J. Soltau was there. Mother went to church with us, and then we'd come home and tell father

The fiftieth anniversary of Merton and Mae Lane

what the sermon was all about. My mother would cook on Saturday for Sunday. They didn't believe in working on Sunday.

My Grandmother Lane was real little and feisty. Grandmother Craemer was the big, quiet type. When we would get noisy in the house and run around, she would sit back and say, "Well, the very idea."

I met Hector Dupont at the Ascension Club in Minneapolis and we were married in St. Anne's Church. At twenty-seven and a half years I was considered an old maid.

We were in Wayzata, where my husband was tap dancing in a show, when we heard about the bombing of Pearl Harbor. During World War II we knitted scarves an hour every day to send to the boys in the service.

My husband owned and operated a filling station on 26th and West Broadway in Minneapolis for forty-eight years. We have four children: Diane, Renee, Gideon and Tom. Diane lives in Buffalo, Renee in Rogers, Gideon in Coon Rapids and Tom lives in northeast Minneapolis. We have ten grandchildren and ten great grandchildren.

Men of today don't take responsibility for raising a family like our parents did by making decisions together. Talking things over makes for a successful marriage. My definition of success is character.

Hector, my husband, died during the Halloween blizzard of 1991. I have lived in my house in North Minneapolis for fifty-five years.

Submitted by Marjorie Dupont

Julia Dussault
"The Pillow Lady"

JULIA WAS BORN in Budapest, Hungary in 1910. She arrived in the United States in 1920. Julia and her husband, H. A. Dussault had fourteen children, thirty-one grandchildren, and twenty-nine great grandchildren. They moved to Brooklyn Center, to a house near 57th and James Avenue in 1949.

Christmas was Julia's favorite time of the year. Many of the family members crammed into the little house. "It was wall to wall people", her daughter, Midge, claims. Julia always had a beautiful village on display, with many of the items made by her in a ceramics class. She always made sure that Santa Claus came to visit the little ones who showed up at grandma's house.

Julia loved dogs, flowers, birds and the trips she took to Red Wing in the fall to see the colors of the changing leaves. And she liked hats. She had a hat to match almost every outfit she owned. "She was a very classy lady", remarked a friend.

Halloween was Julia's second favorite holiday. For nearly thirty years she made pillows from quilted fabric scraps donated by Modern Quilters, a former employer of hers. Each child that came to her house to "trick or treat" was given a pillow instead of candy. She made between 500-600 pillows every year. She had pillows stacked everywhere. The children came for a pillow year after year. She even had second generation children come to get a pillow.

After Julia died on October 29, 1997, it was decided that a poster was needed so the trick or treaters could read. . .

"The angels came and took the pillow lady.
Sorry no more pillows."

Thanks to the donation from her family to the John Ireland Memorial Fund, a red maple tree will grow near Julia's resting place at St. Mary's Cemetery. "A tree is special because it will always be there", said her daughter, Virginia.

Submitted by Midge Eggert

Julia Dussault
"The Pillow Lady"

JAMES EBERT is the fourth of six children. . . three boys and three girls. Their parents were Oscar and Tillie (Schmidt) Ebert. Tillie was born in Brooklyn Township. Oscar and Tillie each had one brother. Oscar was born in Maple Grove, Minnesota in a log cabin that sat on one hundred sixty acres of land that Oscar's father, Conrad, had homesteaded. Conrad died in 1950, and his wife Minnie (Cornelius) died before Jim was born. Jim's parents met while attending a little red brick one-room schoolhouse, two miles north of Osseo, Minnesota. The school was Turgeon School, which is now a home and barber shop.

After attending Turgeon School, Osseo High School, and the University of Minnesota, Jim served in the Army from 1954 to 1958. He then joined the Army Reserves until 1974. While he was stationed in France, he visited Germany, the country of his origin. He discovered the main street of Frankfurt was named Ebert Avenue after a fourth cousin.

His family and childhood were close, loving and caring. Jim says his father and mother never had a bad word for family members or others; they observed and found reasons to praise others. His father "would take his shirt off his back" for others. His mother and father were very active in 4-H for many years.

Jim liked his education in a one-room school. It was a positive, one-teacher experience where he could learn everything from one class. Older pupils tutored younger pupils. His favorite subject was math, taught by his dad sitting around the kitchen oak table using the kerosene lamp. When he asked his dad how to spell a word, he was told to "Sound it out and look it up in the dictionary." His father taught him how to learn.

Rose was born in Hastings, Minnesota. She and Jim met at the University of Minnesota. She was trained as a nurse. Osseo School District 279 employed Jim for thirty years. They had four children, two boys and two girls. Their three living children, Lynn, Bob, and JoAnn live nearby; Laura died in a car accident in 1981.

There are seven grandchildren, ages three to thirteen years — Jennifer, Bob Jr., Andrew, Nicole, Heidi, Alex and Alycia.

The Eberts have passed on to their children the same values they were raised with, including the importance of respecting others, courtesy, and treating others as you would want to be treated. Jim considers that his greatest contributions to society are his family, his volunteering and helping people. He admires his wife Rose. She is the most loving, caring, cooperative and encouraging person. He and Rose have lived in the same house in Brooklyn Park since 1966. "I would like to be remembered as having helped someone each day of my life and made them smile." Jim remarked.

From an oral interview by Ernee McArthur

The Jim and Rose Ebert Family

Jim and Rose Ebert

John and Electa (Cotton) Eidem

John Eidem Jr. and Lectty (Electra) Cotton Wedding (April 29, 1892)

DELEVAN H. COTTON (1826-1917) came to St. Paul in 1850 from New York. He purchased land in Hennepin County in January 1860. After Delevan's first wife died, he married Sarah Jane Merrill (1838-1896). They had seven children. Delevan and Sarah Jane are buried at Mound Cemetery in Brooklyn Center.

Delevan and Sarah Jane Cotton's daughter, Electa, married John J. Eidem, Jr. in 1892. John Jr. was the third of fourteen children and the first born in the United States to John J. Eidem, Sr. (1842-1928) and his wife Ingaborg (1846-1921) who came here from Eidem, Norway. They changed their name from Johnson to Eidem when they arrived in America. Both are buried at Mound Cemetery.

In 1894 John Jr. (1869-1956) and Electa (1872-1950) Eidem purchased the farm at 4345 101st Avenue North from Julia Bragdon, widow of Willard H. Bragdon. The 1900 census lists Delevan Cotton as living with the family at the above address.

The farm consisted of forty acres on which there was a large house, large barn, outbuildings, windmill, granary, milkhouse and machine shop. Livestock included Holstein cows, four or five workhorses and chickens. They sold eggs and milk. John had a tractor in later years. John raised potatoes and onions, which he took to the Farmers Market in Minneapolis. In the fall they had sheep shipped in by rail, then herded them by foot to the farm. They fattened them over the winter and sold them in St. Paul in the spring. A hired man slept upstairs.

Electa loved flowers and had flowerbeds all over her yard. Her specialty in the kitchen was apple coffee cake and chicken potpies. She especially liked pretty dishes (cut glass). She had Haviland China with a gold band. She enjoyed needlework and won a blue ribbon at the Chicago World's Fair in 1935 for a braided rug. She also loved quilting and embroidery. Her favorite colors were peach and orange.

Electa was a schoolteacher and drove a car. She loved to entertain, play the piano and dance. On their fiftieth wedding anniversary she wore her wedding dress and danced every dance at the Riverside Restaurant where they celebrated.

They always celebrated July 4th with fun and fireworks. Thanksgiving was a very special family day also.

John Jr. and Electa had two sons, Archie (1893-1977) and Leland (1897-1977). Archie worked in the harvest fields out West, and in 1918 bought the Silas Merrill farm at 4201 101st Avenue N. He moved his new wife, Anna Sachs (1893-1974), into the home in 1925. After Anna's death, Archie lived there another year. They are both buried at Mound Cemetery.

John Jr. and Electa lived on their farm from 1894 until John's death in 1956. Archie's grandchildren, Marlys (Eidem) Johnson and Tyrus Eidem, retained ownership of the property and rented it out until 1975, when it was purchased by the City of Brooklyn Park. It is now the Brooklyn Park Historical Farm.

The two surviving Eidem Grandchildren are Marlys (Eidem) Johnson, New Ulm, MN, and Leland's son, Robert (Bud) Eidem, who has lived in California since the 1970s. Tyrus passed away on August 5, 1999. He lived his entire life within one mile of the farm in Brooklyn Park.

In 1986 the City purchased the Archie and Anna Eidem farm to the east.

Submitted by Marlys Johnson, Vella Zimbrick and Carol Seppa
Edited by Marlys Eidem Johnson

IN 1862 my maternal grandmother's father's Norwegian family immigrated, including my great-great grandfather and grandmother: Guldbrand Dahl (originally Guldbrand Botolfson, son of Botolf Peterson & Maren Kirsksena Magnusdotter, Dahl of Nitterdahl, Norway). They left Bergen, Norway, May 22nd, 1862, on the Sleipner (first passenger boat through the St. Lawrence Seaway) with their first four children, his three brothers and two sisters. August 2nd, 1862, the Sleipner, seventeen passengers and 350 tons of cargo, met a full gun salute, City of Chicago officials and Captain Jenning's Marching Band! The local Nora Lodge (gave travelers money, food & care) Norwegian residents greeted the weary travelers after their 71-day journey. My great-great grandparents moved from St. Paul to Gennessee, now Atwater, MN, in 1870, becoming the town's first blacksmith.

Lillian Dahl, born March 31, 1906, to Gilbert Dahl (born 1866, St. Paul) and Emma Person (born 1873, Skonia, Sweden, immigrated 1888) attended primary school in Atwater, District #75, and a half year at Atwater High School. At 14 she assumed full household responsibilities (her mother had died) and with brother, Albin, stayed home running the farm, keeping the family together. Their father was bedridden for 2 years before he died. Hardship was no stranger here.

Lillian came to Minneapolis in 1925 to earn money to send home. She attended American Business College (Mpls.) & Business University for Girls (St. Paul). She earned room, board and streetcar fare by childcare & housework. The winter that Sears & Roebuck opened on Lake Street she went to apply; the line stretched for two blocks! The next day, 37 below zero, she went again, wearing all her warm clothes. This day only twelve hardy people came! All were hired! She studied piano and violin several years at Minnesota College of Music and MacPhail. After the Market Crash, 1929, she did housework for Dr. Moir, also served as second maid for Ellis Rose in his 18-room mansion. In 1934, Lillian met and married Harold Eisenbrand (April 3, 1900). A $20.00 gift from her parents was used to buy silverware. A family tradition began: she gave both daughters and two granddaughters silverware as they married.

Grandmother's eldest, Donna Augusta, born November 7, 1934, died August 6, 1985 of cancer, married Constantin Topoluk (Ukrainian refugee). They had three children: D'Ann (1953); Sherry (1955) and husband, Mike Stidd, in Utah; and Scott (1960) and wife, Beth, three children: Nicholas, Natasha, Tatiana. Daughter, Jeanette Laura, born November 27, 1936, is married to Kenneth L. Ready, Jr. (Irish descent). They have four children: Kathleen (1954) and husband, K. Michael Brown, have three children: James, Christopher & Eric; Colleen (1957), and husband, Dirk Marshall, have two children: Rochelle & Damian; Patrick (1948) and Kenneth, III. (1965). There are three great, great-grandchildren.

My grandparents bought their Brooklyn Center home in 1936; the house was simple, but grandmother loved the ten acres of land. I remember climbing the beautiful plum trees as a child. My brother, Patrick, owns the house presently. Grandmother began a twenty-five-year career with Honeywell in 1946, retiring in 1971. In 1960 she sold nine acres of her land, located an eighty acre farm near the Mississippi River in Dayton, MN, and had it paid for by 1965! (Grandfather died February 22, 1964.) I will always remember her as a very sound-minded businesswoman. The land was the treasure! In my grandmother, I see my ancestors' dreams to acquire land. At 93 she lives on her farm tending her house. My best childhood memories are there; we still plant a garden together each spring. That Scandinavian farming blood runs strong in our veins!   *Submitted by Granddaughter, Colleen Marshall*

Lillian Rosalie (Dahl) Eisenbrand

The Eisenbrands

Ruth Elias

In 1962 my husband and I were looking at houses to buy. We were not approved for a loan on a house we liked because the wife's income was not considered. We were advised to look at some less expensive houses in Brooklyn Center. We moved into our house on 68th and Emerson Avenue North in December of 1963.

There were vacant fields around us to the west. We could see our dog's tail wagging above the tall weeds where she was so happy to have room to romp. It was quite a few years before it started looking homier with attractive shrubs and trees. I bought two lilac bushes and planted them by the driveway next to the neighbor's house. The builder mowed them down when pushing dirt around on the neighbor's lot. I asked several times for the builder to give us more fill dirt for the back yard, but it never came. The builder just ignored my calls. Finally I had to ask a dirt hauling company for truckloads of fill dirt so the backyard would not be a big hole.

We only had one car so I walked to the bus line on 69th Avenue North. All the childhood years of ice skating, sliding down hills and skiing in Farview Park in Minneapolis prepared me for the tough life as an adult. I finally managed to get a used car after my husband and I parted ways. I had to put a trickle-charger on the battery for the car to start in the morning. I wore out several snow shovels before I got modern and bought an electric snow blower. A neighbor installed an outdoor outlet for me to use for the snow blower and trickle charger.

Thanks go to a couple of former neighbors who helped get the car off the hard-packed snow ridges made by the snow plows. They helped in many small disasters.

Gradually the shopping center on Humboldt and 69th Avenue North was built. The condominiums went up, and the empty lots were filled.

As I viewed the new houses being built, I wondered why the homeowners were getting asphalt driveways when I thought concrete was the way to go. I hired a man to do the concrete work. When I came home one evening, kids had thrown rocks into the wet cement. It did not harden smoothly; it cracked and crumbled. When I had the posts put in for my cyclone fence, a neighborhood "bad" girl worked them loose. One of the "bad" boys set fire to my bushes. These incidents required police calls. But, I'm still here and the "bad" kids are long gone!

In the summer a person can relive the excitement and sounds of the games being played at Brooklyn Center High School. From my back yard one can view the Earle Brown Days parade coming down Dupont Avenue. I had the privilege of an "all-day" sucker, a Holloway by golly, at the band concerts when I was a kid. These concerts are as American as the old Sears and Roebuck catalogue.

I have driven a small motor home since 1985 around the U. S. When I retired in 1990 I searched for a place to move to which was warmer and kinder to "oldies." But no place was ideal, so here I am.

Submitted by Ruth Elias

THE FIRST MEMORY I have of Brooklyn Center comes from the summer of 1955, when I was four years old, standing with my sister, Lynn, on top of the pile of dirt that had been excavated to build our new home at 5406 Morgan Avenue North. Our parents, Edwin and June Ellingson, moved to the suburbs after World War II. Just moving one block out of the city limits made all the difference in our lives, determining where we would go to school, who our friends would be, etc.

My Dad was born in South Dakota on April 15, 1925. His mom was from Norway and his dad had been born in Dodge County, Minnesota, of Norwegian parents. My Dad's grandfather's name was Ole Rutland. In Norway, the children's last name would have become Olson, meaning "son of Ole" but because there were too many Olsons in Minnesota, the family picked the last name of Ellingson for the children. Dad left his parents during the Depression and moved in with relatives in the Blooming Prairie area. He graduated from Austin High School in 1942 and immediately joined the Navy. He served in the South Pacific and ended the war in Shanghai, China.

Dad and mother met in Minneapolis. She, too, had grown up on a farm, near Gaylord, Minnesota. She was descended from German Lutherans named Kusske on her father's side and Jahns on her mother's side, which arrived there around the time of the Civil War. She had been shot in the lower back when she was fourteen which paralyzed her legs, making it necessary to use crutches the rest of her life.

My dad was an assembler at Northern Pump in Fridley, Minnesota and my mom worked as a secretary for Miles Homes at 4500 Lyndale Avenue North.

Lynn graduated from the University of Minnesota with a degree in History. She is now working in Turin, Italy for the International Labor Organization, which is a part of the United Nations.

I attended Carleton College in Northfield, Minnesota. In 1975, I graduated from the University of Minnesota with a law degree. At the University, I met Carol Grams, my wife; we were married in the fall of 1975.

I was elected as a Representative to the State Legislature for Brooklyn Center in 1976. I served in that position for ten years, and then decided to take a job as the Government Relations Manager for the Minnesota Board of Public Defense.

Carol and I have three children: Neil, Amy and Kristina (nicknamed Daisy after her great-grandmother). Carol is an elementary art teacher at Breck School in Golden Valley. We live in Minnetonka, in a home built with a kit bought from Miles Homes.

Pastor Roger Carlson, formerly of Hope Lutheran Church, came back to do the memorial service for June Ellingson when she passed away in 1996. My parents are buried at Ft. Snelling Cemetery.

Submitted by Bob Ellingson

The Ellingson Family

Gil and Marion Engdahl

Gil Engdahl

GIL ENGDAHL WAS BORN in a Douglas County, Minnesota farmhouse that had no electricity or running water. Gil was the sixth of eleven children born to Edwin and Ada Engdahl. Gil's father abandoned his wife and family when Gil was eleven years old, so his early life was a challenge as they moved from rented farm to rented farm scratching out a living.

When the Japanese attacked Pearl Harbor, starting World War II the family was certain the draft would take at least one of the boys. Gil, insisting that it be he, volunteered for the draft and entered the navy in September 1942. Gil spent forty months aboard a heavy cruiser in the Pacific Ocean, whose engagements in battle included Iwo Jima.

After his discharge in January 1946, Gil planned to utilize the GI Bill to get a University of Minnesota Accounting Degree. However, before classes started, he heard about a public accountant who was looking for a young man to help him. After a brief interview, Gil took the job and went to work immediately. While working at this job, Gil met Marion Scofield, a beautiful young lady from North Minneapolis. Gil and Marion dated, fell in love and were married in July 1948.

Obviously Gil enjoyed the accounting profession, as he spent his entire career in the public accounting field, specializing in various types of business and income tax accounting. Gil was involved with Earl Bakken and Palmer Hermundslie, in the early days of Medtronic Corporation's founding. In 1953, the Engdahl's bought a house at 59th and Dupont in Brooklyn Center, well beyond the paved streets of Minneapolis. Gil and Marion not only raised their three children in that home, but also as of this writing in 1999, still live in the same well kept home.

From the very beginning, Gil has been involved in his church and community. His community service includes charter membership of the District #286 School Board, the Earle Brown Farm Restoration Committee, the Brooklyn Center Jaycees, the Chamber of Commerce and the Rotary.

He spent seven years on the City Planning Commission, including serving as Chairman. He is a long time member of the Methodist Church, including long stints as Treasurer and Auditor. As of this writing, Gil is 76, is still active in the church, the Rotary, the Charitable Foundation, and in other community and church capacities.

Gil's well-known accounting expertise and sound business judgment made him a highly sought-after person by many boards and foundations. Bakken Museum of Electricity in Life; Hermundslie Foundation: Medical Plastics: Arrowwood Lodge: Sports Craft: S. C. Distributors; Brooklyn Center Charitable Foundation; and Medtronic are some of the organizations he has been involved with.

Gil's community service has earned him recognition and many community service awards including the Rotary's coveted 'Lifetime Achievement Award'. Mr. Engdahl is known for utilizing his expertise in the financial aspects of projects and organizations and for having done so with honesty, trust, integrity and vision.

Submitted by Gil Engdahl

WE HAVE LIVED in Brooklyn Center for thirty-six years. We thought that we had moved a long way out from south Minneapolis. We moved in July, so one of the first things we noticed was the nice cool nights. In Minneapolis we had so much cement that held the heat of the day, so the nights didn't cool off much. Another thing we were very pleased with was our large lot. Here we were able to have a garden. The bellowing of the white-faced cattle on Earle Brown Farm made us think that we really were out in the country.

In the winter our streets were plowed wide and clean, unlike the streets in Minneapolis. In the spring we picked wild asparagus where Brookdale Ford is located.

My husband, Don, and our sons Roger and Dale trapped muskrats along Shingle Creek. Many mornings they got up before school and work to check their traps. They were pleased when they caught something. They were paid fifty to seventy-five cents for a skin. It was hard work but they enjoyed it.

Roger and Dale played in many sports events with the Park and Recreation or high school teams. They had great programs in baseball, football and hockey. Many of the parents participated. We made lifetime friends. Don was umpire for many of the games in the early years. In fact, Don and Harry Roberts built the dugouts at Grandview Park.

We enjoyed Grandview Park. It gave the boys something to do all of the time. I still like to see the lights at the ice rink. There used to be many children skating.

We watched the big fire at Earle Brown School in 1967. Don helped the firemen. The fire was a sad time, but the boys thought it was great not to have school for a few days. Roger and Dale graduated from Brooklyn Center High School, in 1973 and 1978. We liked the small school district. It was similar to the country school, people knew everyone else.

Don passed away in January 1978.

Roger lives in Colorado Springs, Colorado, and Dale lives in Clarkfield, Minnesota. There are four grandchildren: Donald, Nickolas, Michael and Sean.

We have had many enjoyable hours in Brooklyn Center. They were great years. We watched Brooklyn Center change and grow and grow some more. Many businesses have come and gone.

Time moves on. . . .

Submitted by Marge Engstrom, Roger, and Dale

The Engstrom Family

Dale, Donald, Marge, and Roger Engstrom

The Gordon and Grace Erickson Family

My father was twenty-one years old when he came from Sweden to Saint Paul, Minnesota. My mother was born in Wisconsin. My birth year was in 1920 in Illinois. Our family moved to LaCrosse, Wisconsin and then migrated up the Mississippi River in the 1930s.

I was raised in a small town, Plum City, Wisconsin and lived there until I enlisted in the Navy in 1942. After World War II, I completed my education in engineering in Chicago and worked in LaCrosse.

My wife, Grace, and I met in 1942 at a Naval Training Center in Michigan. Grace was from Detroit and we were married there in 1944 while I was on leave.

I moved to Minneapolis to work in 1956. We then moved our family to Brooklyn Center in 1958. We had four children at the time and became actively involved in school and community issues. We came to know a lot of people. I was encouraged to be a candidate, and was elected Mayor in 1961. I credit the Citizens for Better Government organization for my success in being elected and my neighbor, Ed Burt, who "launched me."

I served Brooklyn Center from 1962 to 1965 as Mayor. Later, there was a resignation from the Council and I served a one-year term. We immediately started some mammoth projects, including completely rezoning Brooklyn Center. We worked to change the Village into a City, and the voters approved this. The bedroom community expanded into a large residential-commercial area, and in four to six years the whole complexion of Brooklyn Center had changed.

I had the pleasure, after leaving the Council, to serve as the Chairman of the Capital Long Range Improvement Commission. That study and work gave us a new city hall, community center with inside pool, equipment garage, fire station and more.

After Earle Brown passed away in 1963, we were given the opportunity to plan the Earle Brown Farm area and zone it properly.

After serving four years as Mayor, I decided I needed to spend more time earning a living for my family. The Council had been meeting every Monday night for two or three years to accomplish all of their work.

I feel that I had a major part in the 1960s at a time of crucial development. I would like to be remembered as somebody who answered a call to be involved in local government. It was a great experience, and what I learned served me well for the rest of my life.

In 1972 our family moved to San Diego, mainly for business reasons. After retiring in 1990 we moved to Tucson, Arizona. On May 15th, 1992 my wife, Grace, passed away. I continue to be active in my church, artists' associations, and visiting our children: David Lee in San Diego, Charles Edward in Los Angeles, and Debra Jean in Illinois. Judith Ann and Jeffrey Allen live in Tucson. There are seven grandchildren and two great-grandchildren.

Submitted by Gordon Erickson

IN THE LATE 1950S AND EARLY 1970S the area of 56th to 57th Avenue of Dupont was noted for its many activities. The many children on this block were very resourceful kids. Very few mothers on this block worked in those days, so they were treated to various activities. The children put on magic shows that made our hair stand on end. Things were really magical. It made mothers wonder how they could cut off a victim's leg without the person even crying out. There were many other plays the children acted out. They even put on a Mary Poppins show. With the help of a pulley up in Fink's big tree Mary Poppins was able to fly through the air.

Judy (Erickson) West

One summer Mr. Fink had set up his big eight-man tent in the back yard. The gang camped out in the back yard for a week. They washed their paper plates and clamped them out onto the clothesline to dry. Thank goodness the mothers, especially Mrs. Parent, were very generous and snuck food out to the campers.

And, of course, there were the endless games of green light, red light, cops and robbers, and Simon says, etc.

In order to make money the kids sometimes charged the mothers admission to see some of the plays, a very high fee of maybe three cents. But after they had saved enough money to buy a box of cake mix they would treat the mothers to a piece of cake and a very diluted glass of kool-aid. Sometimes the frosting on the cake seemed like it was just sugar and water spread on and then it soaked into the cake. But, oh, it tasted so good.

The kids also had a neighborhood paper that they printed themselves. Sometimes it was done on a dilapidated old typewriter and other times it was hand printed. It had recipes and always a little neighborhood gossip and sometimes it even included some cartoons. The kid responsible for financing this paper went for blocks selling subscriptions for as little as three cents a copy. Of course most housewives ordered several subscriptions at once, never knowing if there would be another printing.

Many of the children belonged to 4-H. This caused a lot of commotion about the time the Hennepin County Fair approached. That last garment had to be completed. Were those tomatoes going to be ready to show? Was that pie crust done to perfection? How about the jam, did it look good in the jars? Are we ready to put on that play? Am I ready to read "Casey at the Bat in Mudville"?

Then there were religion classes, Bluebird Meetings, the Indian Guide Meeting, the Pine Car Derby, the Indian Princess Meetings. The Brooklyn Center High School Band marching in the Aquatennial Parade, marching in full dress wool uniforms. How they ever lived through that long march in the July heat is still a mystery. We have to admit none of the kids raised on Dupont Avenue then, ever got into serious trouble.

Submitted by Judy (Erickson) West

Maynard and Barbara Erickson

AFTER SERVING in the Civilian Conservation Corps (CCC) at Medora, North Dakota, Maynard, joined the navy in 1943. The CCC was a program set up by the federal government to provide work for young adults during the Depression. The worker received one dollar a day. At the end of the month he was expected to send home twenty-five dollars to help support his parents and he was allowed five dollars for the month. Of course they didn't need much more because everything was provided: clothes, haircuts, medical help, as well as on-the-job training.

He served four years in the navy during World War II, mostly in the South Pacific. After the war, he was assigned to further testing of the atom bomb at Bikini Island. Having moved all of the inhabitants off the island, the navy personnel moved animals and plants onto the island. After the bomb explosion, they retrieved everything to determine the effects of the radiation fallout.

Maynard and Barbara Erickson Family

Maynard and I, Barbara, met at Dickinson State Teachers' College at Dickinson, North Dakota, which we both attended. Having been raised in the mid-western part of North Dakota on farms during the Depression, we had much in common. In the fall of 1950 Maynard came to Minneapolis to further his education while I taught all eight grades in a country school in North Dakota. We were married in 1951 and moved to Brooklyn Center in 1957. We had six children and all attended Earle Brown School and Brooklyn Center High School, and then went to higher education.

In the first few years we lived in Brooklyn Center, we could hear the cows and calves kept at Earle Brown Farm. There was no water or sewer service at the time. There were no streetlights for a few years. The children had open fields of weeds where they played "hide and seek" and searched for insects for their science projects or for 4-H Club displays.

Maynard worked for Food, Machinery, Chemicals (FMC) for thirty-three years. I was a "stay-at-home" mom until the children started school. Then I worked part time at Minnesota Fabrics for twelve years, and as a receptionist at St. Bridget Catholic Church for the next nine years.

Both Maynard and I are retired. We are members of Clarence LaBelle VFW Post and Auxiliary and Brooklyn Center American Legion Post #630. I spend much time volunteering at church, helping with Lenten Soup Supper, funeral luncheons. I am a member of Brooklyn Center Women's Club, and a member of the Brooklyn Historical Society helping with the printing of this book.

All our children have traveled extensively, to Cambodia, Australia, Thailand, Vietnam, European countries, Mexico, sailed along the Mediterranean coastline, Hong Kong, Hawaii, Alaska, Fiji Islands, Greece, as well as the United States.

Judy and Jay West live in Bloomington with Nick, Emma, and Nora. Jon and wife Stacey, Patricia, and Nancy live in Minneapolis. Linda and Fred Unmack live in Lewistown, Montana, and Bernice and John Gillespie, along with Megan Rose, live in Billings, Montana.

Submitted by Maynard and Barbara Erickson

HARRY ERICSON married Daisy Dahlin in 1933. When they moved from Minneapolis to Brooklyn Center in 1947 they had eight children: LeRoy, Harriet, LaVerne, Bonnie, Darrell, Janice, Chuckie, and Denny. Harry built and moved the family into a small house at 59th and Dupont. This building was intended to be the double garage for the house he planned to build. However, those plans were sidetracked when Daisy died in 1953 and Harry in 1955. The children continued to live there until they graduated from high school. Harry, a roofer, taught his sons the business which LeRoy operated until he retired. The Ericson children spent many Sundays at the Earle Brown Farm visiting their Uncle Carl Swing who was the farm foreman.

LeRoy and wife, Millie; Denny and wife, Debbie; and LaVerne and husband, Loyd, still live in Brooklyn Center or Brooklyn Park.

Submitted by Loyd Brandvold

The Ericson Family

WE MOVED to the Eldon and Virginia Tesch house on 55th Avenue in Brooklyn Center in 1972, one year after our marriage. I was born and raised in the Lake Nokomis area of south Minneapolis. Although Dell grew up in Los Angeles, his family was originally from the Keewayden neighborhood east of Lake Nokomis. He spent many summers at his grandparents' home there and moved in with them after high school. Dell and I are graduates of the University of Minnesota.

In 1974 we spent two months traveling by bicycle through northern Europe, including our ancestors' homeland in Sweden and Norway. Since then our family has studied Swedish. I have become quite proficient in it. This trip kindled our interest in our family roots. I researched our genealogy, which goes back to the 1600's in Sweden, Norway, England and France. In 1994 we again traveled to Scandinavia with our two sons, Karl and Dean, visiting relatives and the home country.

Our family is comprised of outdoor enthusiasts, participating in Scouting, camping, canoeing and gardening. Karl is a budding horticulturist and a graduate of North Hennepin Community College; Dean presently is a junior at Brooklyn Center High School and is becoming a computer whiz kid. I work in the sales and marketing department of a mid-sized company, headquartered in Minneapolis. I enjoy gardening, nature and cross-country skiing. Dell is a professional asset manager and an avid writer, working to educate the public on economic issues, the need for environmental preservation and the specter of overpopulation.

The Dell (Wendell) and Linda Eriksson Family

Linda and Dell Eriksson and sons

We chose our home because of its proximity to services—bus, freeways, shopping, its abundant natural areas and the high quality of the local school system. We also liked the relatively large lot with mature trees, close proximity to parks and Shingle Creek, and an affordable, safe and stable neighborhood.

We have seen many of these attributes that attracted us in the early 1970s diminish over the years. We need to work to re-establish Brooklyn Center as a highly desirable community, focusing on improvement of its schools, significant reduction in crowding and congestion, and re-establishment of its natural areas.

Submitted by Linda Eriksson

The Donn H. Escher Family

Donn Escher

DONN ESCHER, his wife Eileen (Ludtke) and two children (Gary and Dawn) moved to Brooklyn Center in February 1960 from St. Paul. Donn was born and raised in Hopkins, and Eileen was born and raised on the family farm in Kimball, MN. Donn and Eileen met while attending Gustavus Adolphus College, St. Peter, MN, and were married in 1954.

Two additional children were born to the Eschers in Brooklyn Center: Sandra and Christine. All four children attended Garden City Elementary School, Brooklyn Junior High School, and Park Center High School.

Donn worked in personnel management and labor relations for the State of MN in St. Paul and served as Assistant Commissioner for the Department of Employee Relations and Director of Employee Relations for the Department of Education. Eileen was a Medical Technologist and worked in various hospitals in the area, including the Golden Valley Health Center and the University of Minnesota Hospitals. Both were charter members of Lutheran Church of the Master in 1960.

Eileen was active in various charities, including the Girl Scouts. Donn served on the Government Study Commission in 1962-63 that led to a referendum, changing Brooklyn Center from a village to a city. He also served ten years on the Charter Commission from 1978-1988 as a member and Chair of the city's Financial Commission from 1992 through the present (1999).

The Escher family traveled throughout the nation with their four children, covering forty-four of the fifty states. After the children were grown, Donn and Eileen traveled extensively in Europe.

Donn retired early in 1990 to be a caretaker for Eileen who had breast cancer. Eileen died in April 1991. Since that time, Donn devoted his time and talents to the Minneapolis Synod of the Lutheran Church, Luther Seminary in St. Paul, Peacemakers in Brooklyn Center, and President of the MN Retired State Employees' Association. Following Eileen's death, Donn has continued his European travels and now has many friends in several European countries.

The Escher family remembers when Osseo Road had only two lanes with graceful elm trees providing an umbrella over the road. We also remember the fields where a freeway now runs and the picking of asparagus from those fields. In 1960 there were no trees or shrubs or fences on 65th Avenue North and all the residents had the opportunity to get to know and share with one another. Now, all that has changed and there are a very few of us original residents living in the Garden City Addition of Brooklyn Center.

Submitted by Donn H. Escher

My FAMILY MOVED to Brooklyn Park in 1963 when I was eighteen months old and my sister, Laura, was a newborn. Our father, Lance, was a lineman for Northwestern Bell. Our mother, Judy, worked as a secretary for Dean Nyquist and Honeywell. Our parents grew up in the Minneapolis area. Brooklyn Park was an outer ring suburb then. It seemed like the country because there were so many open fields and very few businesses. West River Road was the main road then. There was a little drive-in hamburger joint at 73rd Avenue and a vegetable stand run by our neighbor, Mr. Thompson. River Road Foods was the neighborhood store owned by two brothers, Ed and Harry Burns. All of us referred to it as "the little store" and made several trips a day there. The staff knew everyone by name and if you were short of money you could pay the next time.

Benson School sat abandoned, across the street from us, for many years. It was a great place for us to explore. We'd find old books there. We liked playing softball in the yard behind the school.

Our parents bought the original Benson School for $10,600 and had it moved to its present location at 216 73rd Avenue and converted it into a home. The school had been built in 1872.

As children we loved looking at photographs of the pupils in their long dresses and serious faces. Our living room was the classroom, where behind the paneling remains the original blackboard. Our laundry room had been the boys' cloakroom. The girls' cloakroom became the kitchen. Our bedroom was so large we could ride our trikes around in it. In the winter our parents set up the swing set in it. Playing school was one of our favorite pastimes. I liked being the teacher. We had some school desks in our bedroom.

Our mother decorated the house in an early American style. The Tribune Newspaper did an article on our house in 1969.

There was an old red tool shed out back where our dad kept an odd assortment of critters. . . weasels, minks and chickens. We'd burn leaves behind the shed. I really liked the smell of burning leaves.

We had a terrible problem with bats getting into our house and had to call the police many times to help. My sister and I still sleep with our heads under the covers.

There was a tiny dirt floor cellar under the kitchen where dad kept his tool bench. We were afraid to go down to the "dungeon." The house made so many creaks and moans but we loved living there.

We were free to wander all day, making forts in fields or playing at Riverdale and Evergreen Parks.

As teenagers we'd "hang out" at Brookdale Shopping Center, Lynbrook Bowling Lanes, and cross the Mississippi River in waist-high water to Durnam Island to sun bathe and meet boys.

I now live in the Stratford Crossing neighborhood, staying home full time to raise my two daughters. They also like growing up in Brooklyn Park.

Submitted by Jean (Nelson) Estenson

Jean (Nelson) Estenson

Marie Estenson

I AM AN ELEVEN-YEAR-OLD GIRL who lives in Brooklyn Park near Edinburgh Golf Course. I go to Jackson Middle School in Champlin. Before that, I went to Monroe Elementary and Palmer Lake Elementary. My favorite school subjects are: music, and cooking classes. Our homework consists of reading for twenty minutes a day. But there is much other homework too! The Drug Abuse Resistance Education (DARE) Program at school was a highlight of fifth grade. We learned to say "no" to drugs. I really like having seven different classes in a day.

We go to Brooklyn United Methodist Church on Sundays and every year we are in the Christmas program. Afterwards the whole church has a potluck dinner.

I was in Girl Scouts for five years. Many good friendships were made. I remember that we went to a nursing home and gave people cards that we had made and sang to them. We also went to the Mall of America for our own pleasure! Girl Scouts was a fun time!

Michelle and Marie Estenson

We like to go to free and fun things. . . concerts in the park, puppet shows, and story time at the library and swimming at the Civic Center. We go to the Brooklyn Park Historical Farm every time there is a special occasion. I like getting the samples of food (Yum!).

We like to make crafts with our Grandma Judy, who also lives in our neighborhood. We paint, make tassels, sew, weave, make clothes for our dolls and many more things.

Our house is in the Stratford Crossing neighborhood north of 85th Avenue. We have a creek in the backyard that flows into the Mississippi River. We've seen many wild animals back there—deer, mink, fox, beaver, blue heron and ducks. There are so many kids in the neighborhood to play with and we all do a lot of things together. I have a cute eight-year-old sister named Michelle. Mom used to dress us alike until I was ten years old. My mom, Jean, stays home full-time with us. She has lived in Brooklyn Park for thirty-seven years and went to the same schools I do. My dad works at U.S. Food Service as a sales representative. He gets lots of prizes from his work each year. My dad is in Fargo; we like to go there.

When I grow up I want to be a singer or a music teacher! I enjoy living in Brooklyn Park.

Submitted by Marie Estenson

JOHN, OUR SON DAN (1963), AND I moved to Brooklyn Park in May of 1964. Vern Donnay had completed the Brookdale Estates subdivision about eighteen months earlier. So for the most part our neighbors were other young families, many of who became life-long friends.

Osseo Road was undergoing major construction on its way to becoming Brooklyn Boulevard. Shopper's City in Brooklyn Center on 63rd and Brooklyn Boulevard was the store of choice as a grocery and department store. There was little or no development north of Brookdale Drive.

Many winter fun outings were spent pulling a sled behind our neighbor's dune buggy on land that is now Central Park.

Our family grew, Anne (1966) and Mary (1970). We moved from our home on Noble Avenue in 1971 and spent one year in Wayzata and six in Champlin—finally "Coming (back) Home to the Park" in 1978.

Upon our return we became very involved in school activities and community organizations. The children graduated from Park Center High School.

I had the ultimate privilege of giving back to the community by serving on the City Council for three terms.

Submitted by Sharon Feess

John and Sharon Feess

Dan, Mary, Anne, Sharon and John Feess

Peter Harold and Ardis Evelyn (Peterson) Fiebiger

Peter and Ardy Fiebiger

PETER WAS BORN October 14, 1906, in Faribault, Minnesota, to German parents, Joseph & Theresa (Schmidt) who immigrated as children about 1860. Joseph died in 1918, leaving Theresa with 10 children. Gardening was vital; preserving food critical! The six sons, supplementing family needs, hunted rabbits, squirrels, pheasants and walked railroad tracks gathering spilled coal. Pete left home young, bummed about, working in Eastern auto plants, then Midwest harvest crews, before returning to Faribault.

Ardis was born July 14, 1912, in Belfield, North Dakota, to Norwegian parents, Oscar & Minnie (Englehartson) who were hailed out twice, denied rain a third year, and returned to farm in Kenyon, Minnesota. Ardis loved farm life, though difficult, and enjoyed 4-H Club activities. She and sister, Doris, sang duets at Hegre Lutheran Church, amid the farm fields. She left Faribault High School for Billings, Montana, helping her older brother's family, graduating there, later returned to Faribault.

Mom and Dad (Pete & Ardy) met and danced regularly to big band music at Faribault area lakeside ballrooms. They married, had daughter, Mavis, moved to St. Paul, then in the summer, 1939, Brooklyn Park. They bought (from Carl Anderson) a little house (no basement, timber foundation) four rooms (and a path) with barn, chicken coop, brooder house, garage & five acres on 73rd, a sandy, dirt, washboard road, wide ditches loaded with sandburs and lovely pink wild roses. At 73rd, northward (later Humboldt) were two well-worn paths legally identified as a cart trail. Following snowstorms, this two-block trail would be hand-shoveled by elderly Millard Crandall who lived midway between 73rd and 77th Avenues, with wife, Eva, in the Anderson farmstead, raising zillions of strawberries every summer.

Dad left Murphy Motor Freight Co., St. Paul, to work at the Century Theater, downtown Minneapolis, where air conditioning was huge fans blowing over giant ice blocks. World War II began; he went to Northern Pump, spending twenty-nine years in the Weldment. He played on their softball team, bowled one or two leagues every winter, and has trophies and bowling shirts to prove it!

Mom was a waitress at Kenny's Coffee Shop (in Camden, N. Mpls) and Jack's (downtown). She loved growing things, especially flowers, all varieties (plus fifty varieties of chrysanthemums!); having farm animals was her passion. She loved cooking, canning (annually preserving some 200-300 jars, even chicken and rabbit) and Christmas baking. Wartime rationing didn't bother us much, except for occasional extra sugar needs for canning and baking.

Their early years' experience in gardening and farm work proved valuable to Benson 4-H Club; Mom loved 4-H, proudly earning her fifteen-year Leader pin! Dad coached the Benson 4-H Softball Team to five consecutive Hennepin County Championships, earning them a permanent trophy.

Summer, 1958, Pete and Ardy built their new house, right where the old one stood. Dad retired from FMC in 1971 and painted apartments 5-6 years, keeping busy (out of Mom's hair!). They were also busy with granddaughters, Teresa's and Valerie's many activities.

March 28th, 1984, the Fiebigers marked fifty years of marriage. Sadly, April 15th, their Golden Wedding celebration, Mom was hospitalized due to complications from pain medication; she died April 25th. Dad turned 93 October 1999, he died October 23, 1999. Governor and Mrs. Ventura graciously honored my father with their presence at his reviewal.

Submitted by Mavis V. Huddle, Daughter

OUR ANCESTORS MOVED to Montgomery, MN from Czechoslovakia looking for farmland between 1857 and 1888. Clarence and Evelyn both grew up on farms near Montgomery. Clarence was in the Army Air Corps during WWII between 1942 and 1946. In October 1946 we were married.

Clarence worked at the Commander Milling Co. until it closed down and moved to Kansas. This put eighty families out of work. Clarence tried different jobs but none really worked out. Clarence's brother was working at Land O'Lakes in Minneapolis so Clarence applied and accepted a job in the plant.

After selling our home in Montgomery, we moved to our 1½ story home at 5420 Colfax in July 1953, living in the same house since. We bought the house for $12,500, which isn't even a down payment today. When we came to Brooklyn Center, we had four young sons: Ronald (5½), Clarence (4), Richard (2½), and Russell (10 months).

Most of our friends and relatives thought that we were "nuts" for moving so far away—out in NO-MAN's land. When we moved here the area where Brookdale Shopping Center is now located was cattle pasture, and north of Interstate Highway 694 was farmland. We went to Camden in north Minneapolis for groceries, banking, and other things. Now we look at Brooklyn Center with all the different kinds of businesses. We have so much here within a short distance.

Our sons went to Earle Brown Elementary School and then to Brooklyn Center High School. I (Evelyn) started to work outside the home after our youngest son started school. I first worked at Dayton's department store downtown and then I got a job as a cook and baker for Earle Brown School. I worked for the school district for twenty years, working at both the elementary and high school. It was great for me to work there as I could be home when the boys had holidays and summers off.

During the Viet Nam War all of our sons served in the military (two in the Marines and two in the Air Force). Our sons have all grown up and are married with families of their own. At the present time they all live in Minnesota and Richard lives a few blocks from us in Brooklyn Center with his wife and children. Our oldest son, Ron, lives in St. Peter. Clarence lives in Coon Rapids and Russ lives in Wayzata.

Clarence worked for Land O'Lakes for twenty-eight years. When we retired we spent quite a few winters in Texas. It always was good to come back to Brooklyn Center. Clarence passed away on October 15, 2000.

Submitted by Clarence and Evelyn Fierst

Clarence and Evelyn
Fierst

Clarence and Evelyn Fierst's fiftieth anniversary with their sons Ron, Russell, Clarence Jr., and Richard (October 28, 1996)

Linda and Richard Fierst

MY ANCESTORS came from Germany, Norway, and Poland in the late 1800s settling in the U.S. looking for a better life. My grandparents (Herman and Olga Korthals) purchased a home in Brooklyn Center in March 1934. My dad was fourteen at the time and attended Vocational High School. In 1948 my parents (Arthur and Bernice Korthals) bought half of the lot and built a home on the land. Since they were building the home themselves, they lived in just the basement part of the home until they could afford to finish the upstairs portion in 1953. This is the same house that Richard and I live in now. We bought the house from my parents in 1980, remodeled it, and moved in with our three children: Eric (5), Ryan (3), and Andrea (1). Our children are actually the 4th generation that have lived on this land.

Richard and Linda Fierst's house, built by Linda's parents in 1948

Richard grew up two blocks away at 5420 Colfax Avenue North. We met in 1967, dated in high school, and married in 1974. Our first house was in Brooklyn Center by 53rd and Xerxes. We lived there for four years until we built a new home in Brooklyn Park. When our oldest son was nearing school age, we decided to move back to Brooklyn Center and School District #286. We liked the small school size. We both went to Earle Brown and Brooklyn Center High School and our children had some of the same teachers that we did. It did make going to the conferences a little weird, being the parent and not the student. Our neighbors are most of the same ones that were there when we grew up. Everyone keeps an eye out for each other and our children always felt safe going to any of them if needed. We always liked the feeling of a small community within the big city. We have close proximity to the freeways, but we also could walk a few blocks and be right at the Mississippi River. It was also handy having Richard's parents a few blocks away.

Our three children graduated from Brooklyn Center High and decided to go into the military before continuing their education. Eric, in the Marines, has served in Cherry Point, NC, and had two deployments in Italy. Ryan, in the Army, served in Germany and Bosnia. Andrea, in the Army National Guard, did her basic training and mechanics school at Fort Jackson, SC, and is assigned to the Brooklyn Park Armory.

One of the many reasons we like Brooklyn Center is that the streets are always plowed quickly in the winter. With all the changes that are planned, Brooklyn Center's future looks bright.

Submitted by Linda L. Fierst

I WAS BORN in Upper Darby, Pennsylvania, a suburb of Philadelphia. My father, George, is descended from Irish immigrants who came to this country in 1723 and settled in southeastern Pennsylvania. There is some evidence that my father's mother was a Delaware Indian. The parents of my mother, Anne Marie (McCallum) Filson, came from Ireland as children at the turn of the 20th Century. Grandfather McCallum was a doughboy in WWI.

The Walt and Anna Filson Family

My most memorable boyhood vacation was a trip with my family to California in 1966. I was the second oldest of seven boys and my parents took us across the country in a station wagon and travel trailer. While in Anaheim I spent time swimming with a cute little girl whom I knew I would never forget. We separated and although I promised I would write, I didn't.

After graduating from high school in 1970, I joined the U. S. Navy, and while in boot camp began to write to Anna Marie Triggs, the sister of one of the guys in my company. While in training at Great Lakes, I flew to Minnesota to meet the girl I had been writing to. We met on February 20, 1971, and were engaged a month later and married January 29, 1972. While engaged we looked through some photos of a vacation her family took to California in 1966, and there in the album was a picture of us together. I guess if God wants it to be, it will be, no matter what. While still in the service we had two children, Wesley, in 1973 and Charles, in 1974.

After I left the service we moved to Minnesota and I went to work for NPS. When winter arrived and the ground became too frozen to dig, I was laid off. With nothing better to do, I joined the Champlin Police Reserve. I never intended to become a "cop" but when the opportunity presented itself in 1975, I took a job with the Dayton Police Department. In 1977 I took a job with the Appleton Police Department. I thought that a small town would be a great place to raise my sons—it wasn't. There were very few opportunities.

I applied with the Brooklyn Center Police Department, and on July 9, 1979, was hired and we moved here.

Having grown up in and near Philadelphia, Brooklyn Center seemed like a small town to me. What I liked was the small town friendliness and the big city opportunities. I knew that I had found a good place to raise a family. In 1981 Josiah was born.

We have three grandchildren. Wesley and Karrie live in Texas and have two daughters; Alyssa and Ashleigh. Charles and Kathryn have a son, Daniel, in Brooklyn Park.

For almost twenty-one years, I have lived and worked in Brooklyn Center, and have seen changes and growth in the city. And, like the city, I have grown. I have earned three degrees and a teaching license. I have worked and volunteered in Brooklyn Center because volunteers have made this a great place to live.

Submitted by Walt Filson

The Filson family. Back row, left to right: Charles, Walt, Josiah; Front row, left to right: Kathryn and Daniel, Anna, Kerrie and Ashleigh, Wesley and Alyssa

Margaret Ione Finch

My Mother, Margaret Ione Finch, (1897-1979), born in Brooklyn Township, MN, related the following information to me:

Her father was Elias W. Finch (1855-1928), who came to this area from Patten, Maine. He married Iona E. Merrill (1868-1909) born in Minnesota. They had three children, one being my mother. Elias Finch was an election judge for Brooklyn Township. As a child, my mother would be awakened in the early dawn by the jingling of the horses' harnesses as her father returned into the farmyard after delivering the votes to the Hennepin County Court House in downtown Minneapolis.

My mother also told that as a child she remembered a hotel (near the present Northern States Dam), and at this hotel many dances were held. This hotel later burned down. She told too, how as children, they played in the stagecoach tracks at that place.

My mother often told me of a time when her father was taking her to hear a famous speaker, and he said to her, "I want you to remember this man." My mother said that all she could recall was that this man had white hair. This man's name was Mark Twain.

Another interesting story my mother told was that as a young girl she and some of her friends, worked at the Gedney Pickle Factory near Camden in North Minneapolis. At the end of the day their hair had a strong vinegar smell and if they were going out on a date, they really had to work at getting the vinegar smell out of their hair.

Submitted by Shirley Small

Margaret Finch Bowers with Elias Finch (her father) and Shirley Bowers Small (her daughter)

AFTER GRADUATING in 1941 from Becker High School in Becker, MN, I, Ruth, moved to Minneapolis. I met my husband, Fermon "Tex" Finley during World War II. He was born and raised in Texas, but moved to Minneapolis. We married in 1946 and six months after we married, we bought our first house in Brooklyn Center at 5343 Emerson Avenue North. We knew very little about the area; we had seen the house for sale in the Minneapolis Star newspaper.

The Finley Family

There were many potato farms beyond us and the streetcar only came to 53rd Avenue North. Black people could not go any farther than 53rd Avenue North at that time; they could not buy or rent in Brooklyn Center. Things have certainly changed for the better now.

Three children were born to us while at our first home: Wayne, Gary, and Susan. We then decided we needed a larger home, so we bought one at 6006 Bryant Avenue North. By now, two were in grade school at the old Earle Brown School. Two more sons were born to us, Daniel and David. All five children attended Earle Brown Elementary School and all graduated from Brooklyn Center High School. Three of our grandchildren graduated from BCHS, Tane, Michelle, and Deke Finley. Our oldest son, Wayne, has taught at Earle Brown Elementary for almost thirty years. My husband, Tex, ran Christy's Auto Service Station at 53rd and Dupont Avenue for ten years.

Ruth Finley and her children Wayne, David, Dan, Gary, Ruth, and Susan

By this time, a new high school had been built and he heard they were hiring custodians and bus drivers. He applied and got the job. He worked there for 20 years before his retirement. Everyone knew Tex Finley—especially since he was the only person wearing a cowboy hat at hockey games—long before "country" was popular. He loved Brooklyn Center people, especially the young people.

We had great times attending sporting events at BCHS; all four sons played hockey and football. I am sure if there had been girls' sports, our daughter would have played also. We spent many Saturday evenings at Twin Lake boating, swimming, and water skiing—it was so convenient.

Brooklyn Center was a great place to raise children. It was kind of a small town atmosphere with most of our children's friends living within two miles of our home. Our children could walk to school, and go to Grandview Park for ice skating and sledding, and to the "Corner Store" on 59th and Lyndale to pick up bread or milk. Our two oldest sons have made their homes in Brooklyn Center.

After my husband's death in 1986, I continued to live in my home. However, in June of 1998, I decided to sell and I moved to a senior apartment at 6201 North Lilac Drive. I just was not ready to leave Brooklyn Center after 52 years so I feel right at home in my new apartment, especially since there are so many people from Brooklyn Center who live here.

Submitted by Ruth Finley

Wayne and Nellie Fischbach

WAYNE AND I were married at Hill City, Minnesota in 1948. I (Nellie) met Wayne while I was working for the Forestry Station in northern Minnesota. My job was to collect a two-cent tax on Christmas trees. We met when Wayne had to come to the Forestry Station, and were married in June. We lived with Wayne's parents for a while. Grandpa Fischbach added a section to his house. That section happened to be part of the former Osseo jail.

We built our house, which stood where Highway 169 now passes by. That house was condemned because of road construction, so we moved it to 8300 93rd Avenue North. The highway wasn't built for another twenty years.

Our family consisted of seven children, five girls and two boys. They all attended the Osseo School District.

The former Fischbach home, part of which was the former Osseo Jail

We raised potatoes and corn. We owned about eighty acres of land, some of which we sold to St. Vincent's Catholic Church for a cemetery.

In 1945 the area experienced the devastation of a cyclone. It took everything but the two houses on the site. The barn, corncrib, machine shop, ten pigs and all of the chickens were destroyed.

At one time we had a swamp behind the house. We counted as many as one hundred twenty white swans. The water level has now dropped because of all the city wells that were installed in the area.

One of our sons now lives in the grandparent's home and has a very successful garden store. From this store he sells potatoes and corn. He raises his own produce and sells it himself.

Wayne and I had a strange, but similar experience. We each had a leg amputated. Wayne had a blood clot behind the knee that necessitated the amputation. He worked for many years after the surgery but passed away in 1982. I lost my leg due to diabetic complications. I am able to live a good life at home where I keep busy baby-sitting our grandchildren and also do a lot of work for the Brooklyn Park Senior Club.

Submitted by Nellie Fischbach

ON JUNE 9, 1990, Chris met Janet and began a relationship that will last a lifetime in such a wonderful city. They were married on June 10, 1994.

Janet is from Fridley, MN and says that she moved from the 'Other Side' of the Mississippi River to the West Side, a move that was for the best to start a whole new life. Chris has some family from this area and has lived here since 1983. He has memories of attending Osseo High School and graduated in 1985. Chris worked in the earlier years for "Mr. Steak" that is now "Blondies" on Brooklyn Blvd. He started his hobby of bowling at Village North Bowl that is still a favorite spot to many.

Janet graduated from Coon Rapids High School in 1988 where she grew up in the nearby area. She moved to Brooklyn Park knowing hardly a single soul. Janet got involved and started volunteering in several places in the city and has represented Brooklyn Park on many levels. Her one favored memory was the building of the local Wal-Mart Store where she loves to shop.

Chris and Janet work at the same company in the Northwest area. The Brooklyn Park community has had many changes and new places built in the area. Chris and Janet have made many memories of the changes from collecting 'Precious Moments' figurines to sharing a friendship with a couple in England. Sharing the joys of living in Brooklyn Park across the sea has been an experience that will last a lifetime.

As we reach the New Millennium, more memories will be made in the 'Fletcher' Family. Chris and Janet are proud to be a married couple in the wonderful city of Brooklyn Park. May the love continue to grow more with each passing year and with many 'Precious Moments.'

Submitted by Chris and Janet Fletcher

Chris and Janet Fletcher

Chris and Janet Fletcher

Jean Forrest

HOWARD CARSON came from Sweden in 1928. He moved to 5455 Humboldt Avenue North in Brooklyn Center and lived there until his death in 1986. My mother lived there one more year after his passing.

I was the fourth of five children born to Alpha and Howard Carson. I was born in 1949 and lived at the above address until I was nineteen years old.

As a child, I remember open spaces and very few houses. Behind our house were a large barn, a chicken coop and ducks running around. Houses were built on the land that my parents sold. My brothers had a special place like a large tree house that I would sneak up to and hide in. The land south of the house was converted into a large skating rink where kids from around the area came to skate. Some of the boys that worked on my parents' farm would skate there also.

I was in the first seventh grade class that attended Brooklyn Center High School. When math classes became too boring, I watched the cows move about on the corner of Earle Brown's farm. At that time the farm extended to 65th and Humboldt Avenue North. The father of one of my friends worked for Earle Brown. During school breaks we went over to the farm, explore and play. Eventually, the land was sold and a large hotel went up. No more cows there. I had really enjoyed them.

It was progress happening in Brooklyn Center when Brookdale Shopping Center was built "Our own Mall"!

Ericon Drive and Judy Lane are two streets in Brooklyn Center named after relatives on my father's side.

Life, as I had known it, changed. Our farmland turned into yards with houses, a high school was built, Earle Brown Farm was sold. Hotels were added, huge offices and stores were built, sidewalks and curbs were put in.

I always felt safe while growing up. We never locked doors and things could be left out in the yards. It was a safe, fun place to live.

There was a little grocery store across the street from us which was owned by Rose and Elmer Sandholm. I could go in with ten cents and come out with a bag full of candy. I could go in and buy a loaf of bread and Mr. Sandholm would give me a free treat. People knew each other and looked out for each other.

Submitted by Jean Forrest

WHILE I WAS GROWING UP in the Camden area near Brooklyn Center, everyone knew Earle Brown. He was a hero, a celebrity. He was particularly well known to our family because a close friend of our family, Aaron Carlson, had been Earle Brown's baby sitter when he was growing up. Aaron had told us much about Earle's childhood. Earle Brown was so respected in our family that my brother was named after him, "Earle" spelled with two e's just like Mr. Brown's. I followed the creek from the Camden area up the Mississippi River to Earle Brown's farm and hide in a ditch just over a knoll, watching the airplanes take off and arrive at the small airstrip on Brown's property.

The Minnesota Highway Patrol was established in 1930 and Earle Brown was a very important part of its organization. I joined the patrol in 1931. The military style training for the patrol recruits was held on Earle Brown's farm. A converted barn became the barracks and was also home for the recruits. We trained, studied, worked, ate, and slept there. The recruits were required to earn their own keep so we cut wood, carried water, and cleaned the barracks and equipment. We did our laundry and ironing.

As part of our police training, we were required to behave like gentlemen, treating everyone with respect. Earle Brown insisted that we use no foul language or behave in any improper way at any time and that our uniforms be impeccable. Our conduct was to be a tribute to the State of Minnesota.

We learned to drive cars, ride motorcycles, handle weapons, becoming Minnesota's law on the highways. At that time there were no driving manuals or behind the wheel training. We just got behind the wheel and drove. My first driving experience was disastrous. I drove right across the pasture directly into the creek. I had no idea how to stop the car, no one told me and I hadn't asked. Mr. Brown was NOT impressed.

During my thirty-five years with the patrol, Earle Brown became a personal friend. Through those years I had been privileged to meet presidents, governors, and many dignitaries, but not one could compare to Earle Brown. He was a leader, my chief, my friend and the most highly respected person I had ever known.

Earle Brown was Brooklyn Center's number one son. It was my humble privilege to serve as an honorary pallbearer at his funeral. There was never anyone like him, before or after. His name was Earle, spelled with two e's.

Submitted by Rosemary (Forsberg) Jackson
from conversations with my father

Russell T. Forsberg

The Edward and Geraldine Forystek Family

AFTER HE SERVED in the army during World War II, our dad, Edward Forystek, returned to the Twin Cities. Though he worked for the Pillsbury Company at the "A" Mill in Minneapolis, he met our mother, Geraldine Sturdevant, and by 1950, was building a home in Brooklyn Park. He built it on a former cornfield on part of the land he had farmed as a young man growing up just west of Newton Avenue, south of 77th Avenue North. While we were growing up we had a dead furrow across our lot from the last time the field was plowed during the war.

For most of the Forystek family children, early memories include working in farm fields. In the early 1960s I started working for John and Doris Pavloff on their farm directly across the street from our home. Before I went to work there, for about ten cents an hour, my older sister, Ruth and brother, Bruce, had been working there for some years. We planted onions in the spring, weeded the fields, then picked and packed vegetables through the summer.

When I was growing up, the families on our little strip of houses, from Newton Avenue going west, were Kruse, Meyer, Halvorson, Rudolph, Forystek, Adams, Becker, and then the Lazaroff farm. Those few houses made up our neighborhood. My brothers and sisters worked with other neighborhood children on the Pavloff and Lazaroff farms. I worked on those farms for many years and eventually for Wilbur Goetze on Regent Avenue. Forystek children baby-sat for others. We walked with neighbor kids to the school bus stop for many years. When the housing development started just north of 77th and Newton, we eventually had

Tenting in the backyard: Wesley, Ruth, Niles, and Bruce Forystek (1958)

paper routes with the *Minneapolis Tribune* and the *Star* newspapers. There were separate morning and evening editions in those days.

When I started kindergarten in 1960, I was bussed all the way to Osseo Elementary School. Ruth and Bruce attended Our Lady of Victory Parochial School in Minneapolis, but by the time I went into first grade we were all attending Ascension School just off West Broadway Avenue. We later attended Osseo School District schools. There seemed to be a new elementary school each year in the 1960s. We also spent a few years at St. Alphonsus Catholic School.

After decades of work and study in Brooklyn Park at the end of the century the eleven Forystek children are, for the moment at least, scattered. Ruth is in St. Paul and Bruce is in Iowa. I am with the Army Reserve in Japan. In Texas are Niles and Michelle, while Renee and Nathan are in South Minneapolis. Vincent and Martine are in Mound, Minnesota. Anthony is in Rosemont and Roger is in Indiana. We still get back to Brooklyn Center to visit our mother who now lives near Park Center High School. We can also drive past our former home and see the now huge trees planted by our father a half century ago.

Submitted by Wesley P. Forystek

ARNIE FOSLIEN, was born into a Norwegian-Lutheran Minnesota farm family of thirteen children near Alexandria, MN. June Foslien (Arnie's wife) was the daughter of an Irish-Catholic railroad family from St. Paul.

Arnie and June moved their family into Brooklyn Center in 1955 — a place they called home for the rest of their lives. It was a move that greatly blessed the community because it opened the door to their more than thirty years of commitment and dedicated service to their adopted 'home town'. Their marriage was blessed with six children: Arnie, Mike, Johanna, Tim, Mary and Patrick.

Arnie and June became deeply involved in church and community leadership and activities. Arnie who converted to Catholicism, jokingly said he wanted to be the first Norwegian Pope. Arnie provided leadership in many capacities at St. Alphonsus, including Parish Trustee and a number of years as a member of the Parish Council. Adult Education was June's primary interest at St. Alphonsus.

Arnie was one of the Founding Members of the Citizens for Better Government, which was an organization of Independents, Republicans and Democrats whose mission was to search out and support candidates for City Council, who would commit to serve in a non-partisan manner.

Another organization near and dear to both June and Arnie was Community Emergency Assistance Program (CEAP), an organization they worked hard for in fund raising events and many other capacities.

Both Arnie and June enjoyed music and the arts. Arnie possessed a strong bass voice and loved to sing operettas. Arnie also was a poet of sorts and authored a small book of poems for their grandchildren, titled 'Hocus Pocus Poems'. A popular speaker because of his wit, Arnie often served as Master of Ceremonies.

Arnie Foslien and Dr. Duane Orn

The Arnold (Arnie) and June Foslien Family

By vocation, June was a devoted wife and mother, and Arnie was a trucking industry leader, this following ten years as a MN State Patrol officer. Arnie was founder of the Minnesota Motor Transport Council of Safety Supervisors and spent most of his career in the trucking industry working on safety matters. At the time of his retirement in 1975, Arnie was Vice President of Personnel and Safety for Hyman Freight Lines. Arnie was also considered a highly effective lobbyist for the trucking industry.

Arnie was considered a colleague, mentor, friend, and a man as good as his word by all who knew him. At Arnie's retirement, his close friend and trucking industry associate Jim Denn, said, "Arnie's interest in trucking, as great as it was, was secondary to his interest in people and life in general. He had a gift for bringing out the best in everyone he came in contact with — a man with a vision of what others could be. He was simply one of a kind."

Arnie died on November 22, 1986, at the age of 74, and June died on January 21, 1988. Brooklyn Center was blessed for many years by the care, commitment and service given by this outstanding couple.

Submitted by Jim Denn and Tony Kuefler

The Freeman and Chowen Family

I AM KATHYRN CHOWEN. I was born in 1920. We lived in north Minneapolis. My grandmothers were of Scottish and Irish descent. My parents bought the house in 1920 for $2,900, paid in cash. I remember my mom baking extra bread, and then sending us kids with some to the neighbors who had little food. My father took some of the needy kids to Schuler's Shoe Store for shoes after the parish priest had alerted him that they needed help. There wasn't any welfare then. People helped each other.

My dad, Gilbert Lewellyn Chowen, was born in 1880. His uncle was George S. Chowen, one of the first representatives in Minnesota. The street "Chowen Avenue" was named after him. My dad was an engineer on a dredge that he and another man built. He worked on Lakes Minnetonka, Calhoun, Powderhorn, Camden and Shingle Creek where he became acquainted with Earle Brown. Two of my brothers worked on Earle Brown's truck farms when they were young.

Dad had a chance to teach horse farriering (horseshoeing) at the University of Minnesota, but he liked dredging the lakes much better. He built all the tools that he needed.

I remember watching the Millers play baseball in Nicolet Park. One year I received a bike for Christmas. My dad gave me the job of riding my bike downtown to the main post office to purchase Postal Saving Certificates.

Rose Ann, my sister, was in second grade at St. Bridget's Catholic School, when she got her head stuck in a desk. Needless, to say the room was in an uproar and Rose Ann could not stop laughing.

I met my husband, Bill Freeman, at the Lowry-Emerson Bowling Alley. In 1941 he began working for the Northern Pacific Railroad as a switchman, then brakeman and then yardmaster. Bill and I were married in November of 1942 in Camp Bowie, Texas. Two weeks later he left for the South Pacific during World War II. We didn't see each other for over three years. But, it worked out. We had six children: Sue and Jean live in Minneapolis; Bill and Patty live in Brooklyn Park; Tom in Napa, California; and Bob in Billings, Montana.

In 1969 the railroad moved us to Billings, Montana after offering Bill a promotion. We took our three youngest children and Grampa Bill Freeman. Grampa lived with us because he was blind. We had a record player from the Minneapolis Library for the Blind. I heard many sports stories while I was doing the housework. Our children were in competition swimming and in baseball. They had many records pertaining to sports. Bill had a massive heart attack and had to retire at the age of fifty-one. He liked fly-fishing. He died in 1984 from a stroke. I moved back here and eventually moved into the Realife Cooperative Apartments of Brooklyn Park, near St. Alphonsus Catholic Church.

We had forty-two years together. I am grateful for our children and for the wonderful times with our nine grandchildren. With quilting as a hobby, swimming and Tai Chi as exercise and many friends from St. Alphonsus, I am a grateful senior citizen of Brooklyn Park.

Submitted by Kathyrn Freeman

Patty, Kate, Bill, Sue, Jean, Bob, Tom, and Bill Freeman

On April 1, 1961, Ralph and Kathleen (Kitty) Gagnon moved their family to 5649 Colfax Avenue North, Brooklyn Center. The young couple grew up in Red Lake Falls, MN, married and moved to the cities to find work. During their first few years of marriage they lived in Minneapolis. As their family continued to grow they felt the need to find a permanent home and safe community to raise their children. They found the Brooklyn Center home and determined it would meet their needs.

Ralph worked for Armco Union Wire in Bloomington, Minnesota. It took years for Interstates Highways 94 and 35w to be completed, which made for a long daily drive. Kathleen stayed home raising their children, Jed and Shelby. Time went by quickly as the children were involved in park ball and scouting. When Jed started school at Earle Brown, Kathleen was pregnant with their third child, Sharon. Kathleen and Ralph worked hard to provide for their family, but with the support of good schools, dependable friends and a strong faith community, they completed their family by having two more children, Elaine and Carol.

As the family grew older they enjoyed annual camping trips across the nation. Vacation time was always a special time to be together as the children all had such diverse interests during the school year. Ralph and Kitty spent many hours watching sporting events in which Jed, Shelby, and Carol participated. They also spent a great deal of time enjoying musical performances, as all of the children were involved in either band or choir.

As time passed Jed married Katie Fianzzo and moved to Alaska. Shelby married Kevin Manion and lives in Chanhassen, MN. Sharon has pursued her career and is currently living in the Minneapolis area. Elaine married Doug Gifford and lives in Ham Lake, MN, and Carol married John McLain and lives in Brooklyn Park.

Ralph and Kitty have been blessed with seven grandsons and two granddaughters. The couple has enjoyed their retirement by traveling across the country together to visit family. Ralph has found hours of enjoyment carving, and Kitty spends a great deal of time volunteering for church activities.

Submitted by Kathleen Gagnon

The Gagnon Family

Front, Jed Gagnon, Shelby Manion; back, Elaine Gifford, Sharon Gagnon, Carol McLain

Robert and Vivian Gale

THIS IS OUR 45TH YEAR in our home on West River Road in Brooklyn Park. We previously lived in Fridley for three years and prior to that we lived in North Minneapolis where we both were born and raised. I, Vivian, attended North High School and Bob attended Patrick Henry High School.

We were married in Calvary Presbyterian Church in Minneapolis. After making our home in Brooklyn Park we became charter members of Trinity Presbyterian Church in Brooklyn Center until it dissolved. We later attended Our Saviors' Lutheran Church in Brooklyn Center.

Our two sons were four and six when we settled here. One attended first grade at Benson Elementary on 73rd and West River Road, and the younger boy went to nursery school in North Minneapolis, while I worked a four-hour day at Curtis Publishing Co.

The Gale Family: front, Bob, Vivian, Tim, Chris; back, Vicki, Bev, Tom, Lori

Bob was employed at Arbor Tree service several years and then started a job at Cargill Incorporated (Northeast location) and retired from there aftertwenty-seven years of service. At the time he was also a volunteer fireman for Brooklyn Park. Orris Aldrich was Fire Chief, with two assistant chiefs, two fire marshals and approximately thirty volunteer firemen. In those early years, several of the charter members built one of the first fire trucks in our front yard. Bob retired from the Fire Department in 1976 after nineteen years of service.

Our sons graduated from Anoka High School. Tom attended Metropolitan Junior College before being inducted into the U.S. Army with service in Viet Nam. He married Bev Sutter in 1971 and lives in Robbinsdale with their two daughters, Vicki and Lori. Tim worked in Rochester at a garage and expected to be drafted but was injured in a fall and paralyzed. He spent four months at St. Mary's Hospital there and then was transferred to the University of Minnesota Hospital for rehabilitation. He married Chris Monson in 1979; they have one son, Michael, and live in Brooklyn Park.

After our boys were in high school I returned to Government service and had a total of fifteen years with the Federal Government.

We have been members of the Clarence LaBelle VFW Post and Auxiliary for forty-nine years. I have worked on various election boards since 1947. We are members of the twenty-five-year club with Cargill, Inc.

There have been many changes in the city in our forty-five years and at this time we plan to remain residents in "this old house."

Submitted by Bob and Vivian Gale

WHEN ERNEST AND I met he was working at the Twin City Arsenal in New Brighton, Minnesota. I was working at the restaurant in downtown Dayton's Department Store. We were married in April of 1947. We rented a one-room apartment in a private home. After a year we were ready to look for our own home. We had not built up a large bank account yet so it was almost impossible to get a loan. We went to Camden Bank for help. They had a proposition for us. Patrick Henry High School PTA would build a basement home to our specifications if we would buy the lot. That is what we did.

The men on the Northside went to work. W. J. Corah did the excavating and back-fill free of charge. Jack Rozawich dug the cesspool, furnished and installed the blocks and pipes. The Dahleen Building Company did all of the carpenter work free of charge. Miller Pumarlo, LaVon Brothers, Walter DeLong and James Wunderlich provided the material at cost and did the work.

We had our own home and Patrick Henry PTA had $700.00. We had a garage built soon after, but continued to live in the basement for several years. This area was known as "Gopher Town" because so many neighbors started out with basement homes.

We have one daughter, Brenda. She attended Our Lady of Victory School and graduated from Brooklyn Center High School. She is employed at the Department of Motor Vehicles in Robbinsdale and now lives in Maple Grove with her three children: Becky is a freshman at North Hennepin Community College, Angie is an eleventh grader, and Keith is in fifth grade.

Ernest retired after working for the Twin City Arsenal ammunitions plant for twenty-eight years. I retired then also and started doing volunteer work. I work for the Leisure Age Center at Elim Lutheran Church in Robbinsdale. I help with the school lunch program at Our Lady of Victory School. I supervised the funeral luncheon committee there, and also help with the fund-raisers for the church.

After retirement, Ernest and I did much traveling. Ernest passed away in June of 1995 after a four-year illness.

Submitted by Florence Gardner

Ernest and Florence Gardner

The Gillespie Family

I AM THE THIRD GENERATION of Gillespies in the Brooklyn Township vicinity. My grandfather, James I, homesteaded here before the 1855 United States Census. The Gillespies came from Maine by covered wagon, leading a fresh cow. Grandpa's 65-acre farm reached from below 44th Avenue North and Humboldt Avenue in north Minneapolis to the Mississippi River.

Grandpa was a founding father of Crystal Lake Cemetery and the first services for North Methodist Church were held in his barn. A circa 1900 plat map shows "James M. Gillespie's First Addition."

Near 46th Avenue, a plat is marked "Gillespie's Camden Park Addition." I, James II, grew up there. My old, oilcloth plat map, No. 67, shows a "Garbage Crematory" inland from the river above 49th Avenue North. The City of Minneapolis Workhouse and Hopewell Hospital are shown east of the garbage facility on Lyndale Avenue. East of the workhouse and hospital, on the river and extending south, were four brickyards. My grandfather retained an access to the river, and below that Smith and Pillsbury were lessees. There was a flourmill northeast of Camden, between Lyndale Avenue and the river. My dad said a waterwheel turned by Shingle Creek waters ran it. Some of the old mill foundations still remain on Shingle Creek. Between 44th and 45th Avenues, the C. A. Smith Lumber Company rented land from James Gillespie I, for their sawmill. A narrow-gauge railroad hauled fresh lumber to dry. There were acres and acres of drying lumber. Playing on the logging booms in the river a Smith boy drowned. His family set up a memorial fund for a Camden swimming pool.

Joanne and Jim Gillespie

My father, Hugh, continued on the farm and I grew up there. The usual farmer's garb was bib overalls. I remember the brickyard companies that obtained high quality clay near the river and used it to make firebricks for the lining of boilers. My pals and I would fish in the two clay pools that were left after the removal of the clay. I would take the tiny sunfish home and after we cleaned them, mother would fry them for dinner. They were only about two inches long.

I developed polio in 1940. Doctor Ike, from Lowry and Central Avenue, treated me with some little white pills obtained from New York. I recovered with no permanent disabilities, but I had to learn to walk all over again. During World War II, I served in the Air Force working on B-26 airplanes. In civilian life I worked for Cummins Diesel, repairing huge over-the-road trucks and stationary engines.

Joanne Salinger and I were married in 1950. We bought a lot on 84th Avenue North and Fairfield Road in Brooklyn Park and built our house. We raised our son James III, and our three daughters, Janna, Jill, and Julie there. The water level was high there. During construction I found three feet of water in the basement, and a wall caved in. I pumped it out and installed a sump pump.

Submitted by James (Jim) Gillespie

JOHN AND RUBY GODDARD moved to their new home in Brooklyn Center in 1955 with their two children, Lynne and Bruce. There were still wide-open spaces and asparagus growing in the yards. Joanne, the youngest daughter, was born a few years later.

John's home state was North Dakota and Ruby was from Northeast Minneapolis. John was an over-the-road truck driver and died in a truck accident in 1973.

Ruby has been a stay at home mother and volunteered at the Earle Brown Elementary School for a number of years.

Lynne and her husband, Len Kohut, live in Brooklyn Park.

Bruce and his wife, Julie, live in Blaine. Bruce is an over-the-road driver.

Joanne has been a community volunteer for years and presently serves on the Brooklyn Center School District #286 school board. She received the Brooklyn Center Rotary Volunteer of the Year award in 1994. She is employed at North Memorial Hospital and works in the Post Coronary Care Unit.

Ruby has two granddaughters. Jill works for Michael Foods and lives in Wayzata, and Kellie is a student at Prince of Peace Lutheran School.

Ruby and Joanne make their home together in the family home on 55th Avenue.

Submitted by Ruby Goddard

The Goddard Family

Joanne in Taylor Tot, Bruce on tricycle (1959)

The Goetze Family

In 1870 my great grandparents, Rudolf Goetze and Francissca (Cannes) Goetze, moved to Brooklyn Township from Carver County with their family of eight children and purchased eighty acres (located at the present day address of 91st and Regent North) that became the Goetze family farm.

My grandparents, Herman and Minnie (Schreiber), took over this farm in the mid 1890's and raised two children, Harvey Goetze and Irene (Goetze) Zopfi.

Harvey Goetze and Elsie (Deisting) took over the farm in the early 1920s. They had two children, my brother, Everett, and me, (Wilbur).

During the drought years in the 1930s, Brooklyn farmers were severely tested, but they were hardy souls and developed individual irrigation systems with numerous innovations, which allowed them to compete nationwide in the growing and distribution of their potato crops.

The original eighty acres was enlarged by my grandparents and also by my parents to 160 acres.

In 1956 my wife Carol (Kraft) and I took over the operation from my parents. We raised four children, Karen, Jane, Linda and Steven, on this same farm. Karen married Ordell Dreessen; they have two sons, Eric and Scott and live in Osseo, MN. Jane married Peter Williams; they have three children, Laura and twin boys, Ross and Jeff, and live in Maple Grove, MN. Linda married Thomas Webb; they have two sons, Joseph and Daniel, and live in Portland, Oregon. Steven married Heather, and they live in Rogers, MN.

The Goetze House (1900)

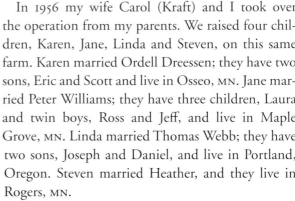

Throughout our farm's history the raising of potatoes for the commercial market was the main crop until 1984. Being a typical Brooklyn farm, a variety of other crops were raised, such as corn, soybeans, rye, cows, chickens and vegetables. We remained on the farm until 1988 when the farm began to be developed into home sites as part of the Edinburgh Golf Course.

Our family has been active in the community of Brooklyn over the years. My father, Harvey, was Brooklyn Township clerk for many years. I served on the Brooklyn Park Planning Commission and on the City Council, as well as being one of the founders of the first bank in Brooklyn Park.

Carol and I are very proud to be members of a family with a long history in this community.

Submitted by Wilbur Goetze

I WAS BORN February 17, 1959. My parents, Bruce & Mavis Huddle, moved into the almost-finished upstairs of my grandparents' (Peter & Ardis Fiebiger) new home ten days earlier. My grandparents moved in downstairs shortly after. The first grandchild, I received abundant attention in our young, three-generation household; sister, Valerie arrived five years later.

Monroe Elementary School's first year, 1963, I entered kindergarten. One special activity I enjoyed was Monroe Melotones Grades 5-6 Choir, directed by Principal Roy Humbert, a wonderful man, dear friend; he made a big difference in many lives.

I was active at Lutheran Church of the Master, Sunday School, Choirs & Confirmation, also dancing/modeling lessons, Bluebirds, Camp Fire Girls and 4-H Club membership — earning blue ribbons sewing a prom gown with a full-length, hooded satin-lined velvet cape, which I wore to my senior prom.

Anoka Senior High School was exciting! Because of my interest, Mom engineered bringing Navy Jr. ROTC to Anoka. I had classes in Naval Science, took part in Rifle Team ("Marksman" here, also later at the Academy), Color Guard and Drill Team. One summer day, waiting for the Anoka Bus going to drill practice (with plugged rifles), another cadet and I suddenly had Brooklyn Center, Brooklyn Park and Hennepin County Sheriffs cars coming at us from all directions! Someone had called in "two teens with guns on the highway!" They escorted our bus from 73rd & Lyndale Avenues to the Anoka field! (Thereafter, we cased the rifles!) I marched in lots of parades, attended Great Lakes boot camp, and was Unit Commander 1976-1977, my senior year. This background, and Commander Schaefer's recommendation, prompted a year's Naval Academy Prep School scholarship in Newport, Rhode Island, followed by a Naval Academy appointment. After two years, choosing to discontinue, I entered Navy Reserves (six-year enlistment), returned to Minnesota, and studied drafting at Hennepin Vo-Tech. I married a Navy man in 1981, traveling to Pensacola, FL, San Francisco, CA, Hawaii and Houston, Texas, for ten years, divorced, continued Navy Reserves, a Hull Technician (metal worker/welder).

In 1991 I returned home to Brooklyn Park with Max, a magnificent New Foundland/Retriever, and Mini, a beautiful Labrador. In 1993 I married a fellow Reservist met at Ft. Snelling activities. Now, twenty years in Reserves, I'm a Senior Chief Petty Officer and Damage Control Instructor. I'm also a six-year member (Captain) Minneapolis Police Reserves, Hennepin County Volunteer Mediator, CPR Instructor, and work Twin City Federal Security full time.

My husband, Michael Good, Minneapolis-born, raised and schooled, has three children: a medical intern daughter in California, a flight attendant in Boston, an architect son in Minneapolis. Mike is a fourteen-year "Star-Tribune Newspaper" driver. His hobbies/sports include running, biking, fishing and yard maintenance at our home and city relatives.

My hobbies include target/pistol shooting, rubber stamp arts and crafts, woodworking, growing water plants and lilies, wildflowers, and perennials — many continuing from 1983 — my Grandmother's last garden.

We live in the same Brooklyn Park house where I grew up, with my Grandfather, nearing 93, and my Mother; we're an older three-generation home now, with two new dogs: Bear, a Lab, and Sparky, a Schipperke, both much loved and full of fun, as we all try to be.

Submitted by Teresa B. Huddle-Good

Teresa Bernadette (Huddle) Good

Teresa B. Huddle Good and Michael Good

Alfred and Marian Graser

ALFRED GRASER was born and raised in Harvey, North Dakota. He graduated from the Harvey High School, and then came to Minneapolis in 1941. Because of leg surgery he did not pass the physical exams required for the armed services in World War II. Marian (Bueghly) Graser was born in Minneapolis. She was raised in Orchard Gardens, Minnesota and moved to Brooklyn Center, Minnesota, where she attended the Old Brooklyn Center School on Osseo Road. She and Alfred were married in 1942. In 1949, they moved to 57th and Knox in Brooklyn Center. Marian said that at that time there were many vegetable farms in the area. Except for a short time when Alfred was transferred to Milwaukee, they have continued to live in Brooklyn Center, in three different homes.

The Graser children: Warren, Kenneth, Jim, and Catherine (1955)

Alfred and Marian raised three boys and one daughter. Kenneth graduated from North High School. He served in the Air Force. Kenneth married Pamela Mitchell from North Dakota. They have one son, Steven, and live in Georgia. Warren attended Lincoln Jr. High and graduated with the first class at Brooklyn Center High School. He also was in the Air Force. Warren married Ann Derthick of Salem Oregon, and they have two children, Karen and Andy, and live in Elkton, Maryland. James graduated from Brooklyn Center High and was in the Army in Vietnam. James married Nancy Engdahl of Brooklyn Center. They have two children, Heidi and Darwin, and live in Maple Grove. Catherine graduated from Brooklyn Center High and married Russell Dahl of Osseo. They have two children, Nicole and Thomas, and live in Mankato. Having raised her family, she is now attending school at Mankato to further her training as an artist. She now does ink painting.

Alfred worked for the Soo Line Railroad for thirty-two years. Maybe it was because of his profession that he became an avid model railroad enthusiast. His wife, Marian, said that he had trains and tracks all over the basement floor. He had her so interested that she would sit alongside him making boxcars. Alfred also was a stamp collector.

Marian was a "stay-at-home mom" for many years, taking in typing for businesses. In 1961 she started working outside the home. First, she worked for Munsingwear, then the Greyhound Bus Lines. For eighteen years, she worked for Powers department store.

She and her husband were involved with activities at Brooklyn Center Baptist Church. Eventually Marian gave up working with the "little ones" at church because she was apt to bring home germs that could adversely affect her husband's health. Alfred battled leukemia for five years. When he passed away in 1992, Marian sold just about all of his collection of model railroad equipment and his magazines.

Now, Marian's time is taken up by traveling, going south for the winter, knitting, walking, and being a Keen-ager at church. In 1995 Marian was one of the chaperones for a Girl Scout Troop that traveled to England, France, Germany Austria and Switzerland. "A unique experience," Marian said.

Submitted by Marian Graser

THREE BROTHERS of Dutch and Norwegian descent, Russell, Warren, and Neil, sons of Harrison and Isabel Gray, moved to Brooklyn Park from Wisconsin in 1904. Two were farmers in the Brooklyn Park area—Russell and Neil. Warren retired from Howe Fertilizer. Neil farmed in the area that is now Candlewood.

Russell purchased the farm at what is now 89th and West Broadway from Otto Setzler in 1929. Otto founded the First Bank in Osseo. The same year Russell married Otto's daughter, Marie. I was Russell and Marie's only child. I was born and raised on the farm. Mom and Dad were charter members of the Osseo Methodist Church.

My family raised winter wheat and potatoes as our main crops. On the side, we fed pigs, chickens, and sheep in the winter. My father helped drive sheep from the railroad to the farmers who fed them for the manure for their crops. DDT was also used on their potatoes that doubled their crops. The barn on our farm was built in 1906. It has wooden pegs instead of nails.

The Calvin and Janet Gray Family

I attended Smith School and graduated from Osseo High School, was drafted and served in Korea during the Korean War. I was a farmer, an only son, have only one eye (blood pressure rupture as child took one eye) yet, I knew if I were drafted, I would serve, and did.

I met and married Janet, one of six children of Vic and Aggie Aydt. Vic was an implement and Chevrolet dealer in Rogers, Minnesota. Janet and I met at a dance hall in Rogers. We have three daughters: Lisa who married Craig Beigert from Osseo, and they have three children, Vanessa, Mallory and Adam. Jill married Paul Reichel from Brooklyn Center and they have two children, Hannah and Chloe. Mona is married to David Smith. There are two grandchildren, Jamison and Harrison. All three daughters and their families live in Maple Grove.

The Calvin Gray Family

I took over the farm in 1965 when my father retired. My mother, Marie, died in 1983, and my father, Russell, died in 1994 at the age of 94. I still farm in 1999 with the help of my two sons-in-law, Craig Beigert and Paul Reichel. When we quit raising potatoes in 1994, we were the last potato farmer in Brooklyn Park. My co-potato farmer and friend, Eldon Tessman, and I were honored for once contribution to the potato farming heritage when we served as Grand Marshalls in Brooklyn Park's Tater Daze Parade in 1994. We are farming approximately 900 acres and grow corn and soybeans. The Christmas trees I planted in 1989 are now ready for cutting.

Submitted by Calvin Gray

Editors Note: The farm, homestead of Calvin Gray, is completely surrounded by new homes, separated by a wooden fence; there remain the buildings and reminder of a great working farm of the 1900's. Each fall the community looks forward to the day the "Sweet Corn for Sale" sign goes up. As winter arrives the Christmas tree sign replaces the corn sign and once again area residents visit the farm in the heart of progress.

Dorothy Greb

DOROTHY IS ONE OF TWO DAUGHTERS of the town doctor from Kasson, Minnesota, which is now like a suburb of Rochester.

Dorothy graduated from the University of Minnesota as a psychiatric social worker. She met her husband, Fred, while they were members of a hiking club. They were both in their middle forties. Fred had grown up on a farm north of Jamestown, North Dakota. He liked the farm and bought and sold farms in northern Minnesota. Dorothy continued to work as a social worker in Wadena County and for the Lutheran Social Services in North Dakota.

Dorothy said, "My first visit to Brooklyn Center was in early 1961 when my husband and I went north on Osseo Road, a dirt road, and later to Shopper's City to buy our first dinette set."

Then, when moving from their farm in 1967, they chose a house in Brooklyn Center at 5408 Queen Avenue North to be closer to Fred's brother and mother in North Minneapolis. They would look out over a wildlife area that later became Lion's Park and Centerbrook Golf Course. They also had a big back yard that was a part of five unfenced back yards so it was like a park.

Fred and Dorothy Greb

They found themselves surrounded by neighbors the same ages and with similar interests. There was much going back and forth and mutual enjoyment, especially of the gardens, flowers and birds. In the early years many pheasants and ducks visited them. For Dorothy it was like a continuation of the small town life she had enjoyed as a child, and for her husband it was a little like the rural life he so much enjoyed.

Dorothy says, "I felt extremely happy married to Fred. We couldn't have been more alike in so many ways. He was the love of my life. We traveled, visiting friends in the United States and Europe."

In his later years, Fred worked for the Park Board and the Baptist Home in the old building on 49th Avenue North. The new Baptist Home (Parkcrest) was built when he himself was a patient there and died.

Dorothy has since sold their home and appreciates senior housing that is available in Brooklyn Center, close to her old neighborhood and friends.

Submitted by a BHS Volunteer from an interview

WE BOTH GREW UP on farms near a small town north of Minneapolis called Mora, the home of the Vasaloppet ski race. We married right out of high school and moved to Minneapolis to find jobs and start our lives together.

I, Dale, had worked at a small machine shop, called Cass Screw Machine Company before I graduated from high school. My brother was employed there and thought it would be a nice start for his little brother. I wasn't so sure yet that that was my passion, but now with a wife and a child, I wanted a steady income. Soon we found a house to buy in Robbinsdale. We lived there with our two children, Debra and Rex. In 1978 we moved to Brooklyn Center. By that time, I was working toward ownership of Cass Screw Machine Company, which had moved to Brooklyn Center in 1965.

So it was a good fit for our family. My wife, Louisa, worked during this time. She worked at the Ambassador Hotel on Highway 394 for seventeen years.

Our children grew and graduated from Robbinsdale High School and later went to North Hennepin Community College and the University of Minnesota. Our daughter, Debra, resides with her husband and family in Brooklyn Center. Our son, Rex, and his family reside in Andover, Minnesota. We have four grandchildren.

We now live in Brooklyn Park and I am President of Cass Screw Machine in Brooklyn Center. I am active in the Brooklyn Communities and have a sincere passion to keep our hometowns a very good place to live, work, play, go to school and to worship.

Dale and Louisa Greenwald

Submitted by Dale Greenwald   *The Greenwald: front, Chelsea, Randy, Dale, and Louisa; back, Leah, Teresa, Nicholas, Debra, Gina, and Rex*

Robert James and Delores Jean Gross

My GRANDPARENTS, William and Marie Clemens, moved from Minong, Wisconsin, to Cumberland, Wisconsin, where I, Robert, was born to their daughter, Edith Ellen and Francis Gross on March 17th, 1933. In 1936 we moved with Grandma & Grandpa to a small (ten acre) farm in Brooklyn Park.

Grandma Marie worked for the Earle Browns at their big Brooklyn Center farm for many years until Mrs. Brown's death. In the summer I'd go along with her and trap gophers for Mr. Brown for five cents each.

Mother worked at Setchel-Carlson in New Brighton where she met William Bursell; they were married in 1940. Shortly thereafter, he enlisted in the Army and was soon very involved in World War II. Mom and I remained here, while Dad went on to Normandy, France, earned a battlefield commission and served all across Europe through five campaigns. After the war he stayed on in the military. Mom joined him for some stations, but I stayed on with my grandparents.

I attended Benson School (73rd & Lyndale Avenues) from Grade 1 through 6-7, then left to join Mom and Dad, stationed at Ft. Sill, Oklahoma, attending Freshman High School in Lawton, OK. Dad was re-assigned to Erlangen, Germany, and Mom and I went along and I continued school, graduating from Nuremberg High School. I then returned (1952) to the U.S. and enlisted in the Navy.

I met Delores Sison while at Great Lakes Boot Camp, Chicago. She is the daughter of Victor Posadas Sison, who was a multi-lingual student in Chicago from Luzon, Philippines, and Celia Sussman, a Chicagoan whom he met while there. Celia was from a strong Jewish background and Victor Catholic; but they overcame family difficulties and married. Delores attended St. Malichi's and St. Jaralath's Elementary Schools, and was a junior at Lucy Flower High School when she and I met.

William and Marie Clemens with their grandson Bobby Gross

Following my Boot Camp "graduation," I was immediately shipped overseas to Guam and other Pacific points for two years. While home on leave in August 1954, Dee and I were married, and I sent her home to live with Grandmother (Grandpa had passed away). I was then shipped out to Korea until my discharge in 1956; I continued on in the Navy Reserves, retiring after forty years of service.

I returned home to Brooklyn Park and moved into the same house, where (following a couple of remodeling efforts) I still live. For forty years at this same address, I ran a very successful taxidermy business, from which I've now retired.

Delores and I have three children, five grandchildren: Debra Lee Gross (Lyman) and son, Maxwell Gross Lyman, who live in Fridley; Robert James Gross, Jr., wife, Kim, and daughters, Jessica and Meshell, son, Robert James, III, who live in Zimmerman, MN; and Sandra Lyn, and husband, Robert Wachsmuth, their son, Cody, and Robert's son, Justin and daughter, Christina, who all live In Palisade, Minnesota.

My childhood here with my grandparents in Brooklyn Park, and my life raising a family in the same location, have been filled with many great experiences and lots of wonderful memories Dee and I now share with our grandchildren.

Submitted by Robert J. Gross

ARTHUR GUSTAFSON was born in 1917 in Two Harbors, Minnesota. His parents were Fred and Lily Gustafson. Fred had come to the United States in 1911 and settled in Two Harbors. Lilly was born in Duluth, MN to Swedish immigrant parents. Art had an older brother, George, and a younger brother, Paul. Art studied business at the University of Minnesota, graduating in 1941. He served in the United States Navy as an officer on a minesweeper during World War II. After the war he married Mary Jane Sokolowski. Art was a manager at Dayton's department store for thirty-six years before retiring in 1985. He kept close to his Swedish roots. He spoke the language and visited his relatives in Sweden several times.

Mary Jane was born in Minneapolis in 1921. Her parents were John and Marie Sokolowski. John was a professional boxer and owned a bar on University Avenue. Marie received a law degree from William Mitchell College of Law and was a leader of Polish-American organizations. Mary Jane had two younger brothers, Jack and Spencer. After graduating from the University of Minnesota, Mary Jane had a degree in journalism. She worked for Herberger's in St. Cloud, Minnesota and had her own radio show. She met Arthur in a speech class at the University of Minnesota in 1939 or 1940. They dated while students and were married in 1946.

In 1957 Mary Jane went to work as the editor of the *Brooklyn Center Post* newspaper. She wrote stories and a column, covered city council meetings, took pictures and helped compose the paper every week. The paper offered Mary Jane an outlet for her creativity and energy. She was proud of Brooklyn Center and never missed an opportunity to promote the city. Her greatest joy was telling people something new.

Mary Jane traveled to Poland often to visit her relatives. She spoke Polish and was a leader of many Polish cultural organizations in the Twin Cities. When the phone rang at her house, there was a good chance the caller would be speaking Polish. Arthur and Mary Jane had three children, Frederick (1949), Gretchen (1951), and Gail (1953).

I, Frederick, received B.S. and Ph.D. degrees in chemistry from the University of Minnesota and the University of Wisconsin. I work at the 3M Company and live in Bloomington, Minnesota. I am married to Nancy Fellger Gustafson and we have two children. Gretchen attended the University of Minnesota studying International Relations and graduated in 1973. She spent her junior year in Singapore attending the University there. She studied Chinese at Cornell University for one year and then married Kishore Mahbubani. She is now married to Thai Ker Liu, an architect in Singapore. They have two children. Gretchen edits books and also works for a company that restores historic hotels.

Gail attended Boston University, graduating in 1975 with a degree in social work. She completed a Master's Degree at Simmons College in Boston. Gail works as a therapist. She and her husband, Jan Hardenbergh, have two children and live in Sudbury, MA.

Submitted by Fred Gustafson

The Arthur and Mary Jane Gustafson Family

The Arthur and Mary Jane Gustafson Family

The Dale Gustafson Family

BROOKLYN PARK has been the Gustafson's home for forty-four years. How the community has changed! Their house and one other were the only homes in the neighborhood and were right in the middle of what was Panchyshyn's vegetable garden.

Brooklyn Park has been a great place to raise a family. The eldest two children, Larry and Sue, moved here with them. With the birth of Lee and Scott, the Gustafson family was complete. The school district in 1955 consisted of Osseo Elementary and Osseo Junior and Senior High Schools. Brooklyn Park grew rapidly as did the number of schools. The four Gustafson children graduated from Osseo Senior High School.

Iris Park, now Striefel Park, was just across the way. It gave the neighborhood kids something to do summer and winter. In the summer there were supervised activities, baseball games, turtle races, and many other events in which kids could participate. In the winter the baseball field was flooded for a skating rink and they even had a warming house with someone in charge. Neighborhood activities made life a lot easier for parents than the constant car pooling that is necessary today.

Dale Gustafson's house

Dale became active in community affairs. His first interest was starting the Brooklyn Park Snow Patrol in 1972. Snowmobiling was popular and by enforcing the speed limit on city streets, snowmobiling was allowed. Also the patrol started holding classes for children to teach them how to ride and obey the laws.

In 1973 Dale helped organize the Northwest Trails Association. Trails were established and groomed giving snowmobilers great places to ride. Also in 1973, Dale started serving on the Park and Recreation Commission. He kept his position for thirteen years. Dale's last and most important job was being a West District City Councilman for thirteen years. It was a wonderful opportunity to be involved in the growth of the city. Dale continues to be active as President of the Brooklyn Park Development Association and also serves on the Charter Commission.

Brooklyn Park in many ways does not resemble the small community in which they originally made their home, but what has remained steadfast is the small community feeling of warmth and welcome.

Submitted by Dale and Janice Gustafson

Eugene and Mary Hagel moved to Brooklyn Center from Waterloo, Iowa in 1957. He had been employed by the city of Waterloo as Assistant Director of Parks and Recreation. Mary was a registered nurse and had worked at the city hospital. In April of 1957 Eugene was appointed Brooklyn Center's first Director of Parks and Recreation.

Eugene and Mary Hagel

At that time the Village Hall was located at the corner of 65th and Lyndale Avenues and was shared by the police, fire, park and recreation, street department, a liquor store and all administrative personnel.

In 1957 Brooklyn Center had no parkland. Brookdale Shopping Center existed only on paper and miles and miles of open land were still evident in every direction. The view was broken only by the beginnings of several housing developments. The population then was 14,000.

While seeking to buy a house, the inevitable question asked the realtor was, "What's going on across the street?" and almost unfailingly came back the answer, "The city is going to build a park there." A goodly amount of stammering and stuttering followed when the realtor was informed that I was the Park Director and knew nothing of such plans.

The next twenty-eight years consisted of the joyful task of building a park system and providing a wide variety of recreation activities for every member of the family. From virtually no parkland, the system grew to over five hundred acres including a pattern of neighborhood parks, a Central Park with a Plaza, an arboretum, a trail system, a nine-hole golf course, and the first Community Center with a year-round swimming pool in the entire metropolitan area. The Brooklyn Center Arboretum was named the Eugene Hagel Arboretum in his honor. Remarkably this was accomplished with a minimum amount of resistance. Only a few attempts were made to stop or delay the proposals. With a vast amount of support, the park and recreation system was built.

Eugene Hagel at work

The Hagels lived on the corner of 59th and Colfax Avenue North for thirty-seven years. There they raised a family of two boys and two girls. The children attended Our Lady of Victory School, later transferring to Earle Brown Elementary School. They all graduated from Brooklyn Center High School. Mary Hagel died January 8, 2001.

Submitted by Eugene Hagel

Gene and Donna Hageman

WE MOVED to Brooklyn Center in January of 1977 from St. Cloud, Minnesota, when Gene was transferred with United Parcel Service (UPS) to the Minneapolis center. After looking at houses throughout the northern suburbs, we finally found a house in our price range, near a park, on a quiet street and in a good school district.

When the children were young, they took swimming lessons at the Civic Center and we parked at the end of Shingle Creek Parkway on the gravel before the overpass was built. When Derek was five and wanted to play ball we went to the neighboring suburb of Mounds View for T-Ball and 8-Ball, because those programs were not available in Brooklyn Center. Later he played Little League on a field that is now part of Centerbrook Golf Course. The Little League Complex (Shinnick Field) is at the end of our block.

At Brooklyn Center High School, Jill and Derek were in sports, band (Jill was band major), student council, etc. We are all pleased that they had many opportunities to be very involved because the school district is small. Jill and Derek graduated from the University of St. Thomas. Jill was a Public Relations major and is now a u. s. Army Captain stationed in South Korea. After graduating in Finance, Derek volunteered for the Peace Corps and worked in a village banking program in Senegal, West Africa. He is now employed in the Minnesota State Auditor's Office.

I have been an Elementary School Media Specialist at Our Lady of Victory School and in the White Bear School District. I enjoy my job and am not sure when I will retire. I find it difficult to fit in all the traveling I like to do.

Gene retired from United Parcel Service in 1988 and has been busy volunteering at Brooklyn Center High School and in the community. He likes hunting, so, in the fall, pheasants, geese, elk and deer become a priority.

We have now lived here for twenty-three years and continue to enjoy the small town atmosphere.

Submitted by Donna Hageman

Jill, Donna, Gene, and Derek Hageman

I WAS BORN and raised in Mankato, Minnesota as one of seven children. Until I was eight years old, we lived in a house with cold running water. We had to heat water for dishes, washing clothes and the "proverbial" Saturday night bath in a tin tub. Everyone took a bath in the same water, occasionally more hot water had to be added. Children who had not taken their Saturday night baths were lined up for showers at school on Monday—a very humiliating experience. At that time children did not have their own bedrooms or even their own beds. Many times children had to sleep three in a bed.

I lost one brother because of otitis media (middle ear infection). There was no penicillin then or any other antibiotic. I lost another brother when he was sixteen to bone cancer. Otherwise we were not sick too often, only with communicable diseases—whooping cough, measles, chicken pox and a cold.

When I was a senior in high school a government representative came to the school offering the Cadet Nursing Program. The government would pay for everything needed for registered nurses training. We were even paid fifteen dollars a month while training. When the training was completed we were to join the armed forces for one year. By the time I had finished my training the war was over so I didn't have to commit to the armed forces. This was a wonderful opportunity for me because my parents could not afford to send me to college and at that time there were not too many nurses. I graduated from nursing school in June of 1947.

Before getting married, I worked at the University Hospital between 1949 and 1950 with polio patients during the epidemic. Many patients were in respirators; at that time these were called the "iron lung."

Wallace Hagen and I were married. Wallace was a manufacturer's representative. He traveled much of the time. We spent thirty-eight years living in Richfield and Golden Valley. We had six children: Tom, Jan, Steve, Linda, Peter and Rick.

I worked at Northridge Nursing Home for fourteen years. I have now lost my central vision due to macular degeneration, so am unable to drive or read.

I had been going to Brooklyn Center Community Center for water aerobics so I moved to an apartment in Brooklyn Center to be close to the center, which enables me to take part in the wonderful programs offered.

Submitted by Shirley Hagen

Shirley (Mabee) Hagen

Shirley Hagen in Cadet Uniform

Edward and Della Ham

In the early 1850s James Leander Ham, from Portsmouth, New Hampshire, and Francelia Electa Nichols, his wife, came westward to Minnesota. Their homestead was bordered on one side by Shingle Creek and by an old Indian trail, which is now 73rd Avenue North. The Sioux and the Chippewa still roamed the land. Other pioneers came and joined them in establishing a growing and livable community.

James and Francelia had four children: George, Mary, Edward and Alfred. The Hams worked to establish the Brooklyn Baptist Church, on the corner of 69th Avenue North and Brooklyn Boulevard.

Francelia sent to Massachusetts for a church bell. In later years, for lack of members, the two churches merged and the Baptist bell was put up on the Methodist belfry. It is still there.

Brooklyn Methodist Church, 1925 Sunday School Class: Sylvia Lane, Jean Mumm, Marian Arnlund, Blanche Norris, Hazel Green, Arletta Soltau, Janet Lane, Marjory Ham, Dorothy Turchek

In 1912 Edward Ira Ham and his wife, Della Ethel MacFall, came to manage the farm. They then had two children, Marian and James, now deceased. Four more were born on the farm; Marjorie, Edward, Jr., George, and Philip. Farm life, on the edge of a big city, was ideal! Shingle Creek was a great source of enjoyment. Just walking through the meadows was adventurous. There were frogs, snakes, and a wealth of wild fringed gentians, violets, and pink, white and yellow lady slippers. It was dangerous too; often an explorer had to be "fished out", carried home, spanked and saved for "posterity."

Edward became involved in community affairs. He was active in the Baptist Church and the school board. He was secretary of the Brooklyn Town Board, the Minneapolis Market Gardener's Association, and the Mound Cemetery. In the 1920s he helped organize the Farmer's Club, which met in the hall above the Howe Store. It was the place to hold community meetings, plays, potlucks, oyster stew suppers and dances. He lent his talents to entertainment at the Methodist Church, and sometimes wrote poetry for special occasions.

During the Great Depression, young people in the community with time on their hands started a Drama Club. The plays began in the Ham home and eventually moved to the gymnasium, where admission was charged for the benefit of the Methodist Ladies Aid. They sponsored the "Club" for several years, and a succession of "Home Talent Plays." Among the actors were: Marian Ham, Director; Robert Hamilton, Charles Bohanon, Edward Ham, Jr., Albert Purdham, Clarence Moulton, George Ham, Vernetta Bohanon, Marjory Ham, Martha Norris, Clyde Lane, Anne Swan, Dick Pingelly, and Helen Leathers.

Edward died in 1949 and Della in 1954. Edward Ham, Jr. came back and lived on the farm from 1949 to 1964. He was there when the Minnesota Centennial Committee honored those who owned and were living on the one-hundred-year-old family farms.

The building boom caught up to the Ham Farm in the 1960s. All that remains now are new homes, new families, the old oak trees, and happy lifetime memories.

Submitted by Marjory (Ham) Hamilton

LINCOLN, also known as Link or A. L., was born and raised in the deep valley of Cow Run near Marietta, Ohio in 1861. He was born during the Civil War period and most likely was named after President Abraham Lincoln.

The Hamilton family was farming in the hills suited for coal mining rather than raising crops.

Olive (Ollie) Davis was born in 1862 in Lowell, Ohio. Her mother died when Olive was quite young. Her father, Daniel Davis, remarried. He did not spend much time at home because he was working in the coalmines in Virginia. Olive's brothers, Rex, James and George, left Ohio to work in the oil fields in Tulsa, Oklahoma.

Olive and Link had known each other for many years. When they decided to get married, people asked her, "Why are you going to marry that little Hamilton boy?" She replied, "Because he is the best there is and I love him." Olive was then only eighteen years of age and Link was only twenty-one.

Soon after their marriage Lincoln and Olive Hamilton came to Minneapolis by train. They had five dollars left. They went to Brooklyn Center to work for his brother, David, on a farm. They soon rented a farm close by. While living here six children were born, Charles, Frend, Grace, Neva, Carrie and June. Florence was born soon after the Hamiltons moved to a farm that they had bought. There were only ten years between the oldest and the youngest child. Oh, what fun they had! Dad disciplined by giving stern looks, but mom believed in spanking. So the offender would be sent to the woodpile to fetch just the right stick for her to use.

The parents of Link, William and Hannah Hamilton are buried at Mound Cemetery in Brooklyn Center, Minnesota. Link and Olive are buried there also.

"The Hamilton Link" Leone Wadsworth Howe

Abraham Lincoln Hamilton

Ollie Davis and Lincoln Hamilton's wedding (1882)

The Frend Hamilton Family

Frend Hamilton

ANNA'S HUSBAND, Frend (Hammy), drove Earle Brown around when he was sheriff. He was not really a chauffeur but a deputy sheriff. He became a deputy in 1910, ten years before Brown became Hennepin County Sheriff. Hammy was a small but strong man who could handle any prisoner. His brother, Charles Hamilton, was a jailer in downtown Minneapolis for over twenty-three years.

At the time of the June 1929 tornado, Brown called Hammy and asked him to come over, it was important! Just as Hammy arrived, a tornado hit, and Brown's shed blew away and smashed the windshield on Hammy's car, cutting his face. Hammy crawled to the house, but all were in the basement and couldn't hear his knock. Finally, they came up and called Doctor Kramer of Camden. The doctor only got part way to the farm and had to walk the rest of the way because of downed trees. He sewed up Hammy's face and called Ann, his wife, and they all stayed at the farm that night.

When old Ev Howe, Brown's friend and neighbor, died they were at a party at the home of Ann and Hammy Hamilton. Hammy drove Earle over to the site, and they shoveled their way up to the Howe place. She recalled that on another occasion, Earle put on and paid for a dinner and dance at the Columbia Heights Chalet for all deputies and their wives.

Mrs. Anna Hamilton was a slim little lady, who lived in a Brooklyn Park Senior Apartment. She was ninety-six years old in 1981 and attributed her long life to belief in God, no smoking or drinking, only ordinary food and a lot of bread—either home-made or commercial. Her long life may also have resulted from hard work. She started work at eight years old when she took care of and played with a baby, with the mother at home, over a period of two years. Then the young couple and their baby went to the Klondike, where the baby caught pneumonia and died. Anna grieved because she had become very attached to the child. At eleven years of age, Anna worked in a cookie factory, taking cookies out of the oven, but six months was all she could endure. At age twelve, Anna worked for a laundry, ironing stiff shirts with pleats down the front and stiff, separate, starched collars. Then she had to polish the collars with a polish iron.

When she married Hammy in 1917, he was a widower as his first wife, Edith, had died, leaving two boys; so she helped raise the boys and four children of other family members. She was too small to carry a child full term, but she raised six children.

Anna Hamilton lived in Brooklyn Township from 1918 to 1965 at 8101 Zane Avenue North. Her husband, Hammy, died in October 1965, about two years after his good friend, Earle Brown.

From an interview with Anna Hamilton in 1981

AN OLD BROOKLYN TOWNSHIP MAP showed that an area called "Poverty Hill" where Zane Avenue North and 80th Avenue merge.

Addison Hamilton and his wife Mary Hamilton, from Ohio, settled there in the 1860's. They had three children: Clara who married Dan Norris, and lived close by; Blanche, who married William Lawrence and lived in Brooklyn Center; and John, who married Olive Edwards and settled right there on the "Hill."

John and Olive had nine children: Mae—Mrs. Vern Lennartson; Gertrude—Mrs. MacCrary; Ruth—Mrs. Harold Eckberg; Alice—Mrs. Walt Brunsell; Myrtle—Mrs. Caesar Copeland; Joseph, Robert, Barbara, and John Wesley. Some of them lived in the neighborhood. Gertrude lived in Wisconsin, Joseph in Mississippi, and John Wesley in Washington. Barbara drowned at the age of nineteen.

The Hamiltons built a big white house on the corner large enough to hold all of the family plus Grandmother. There was a "bunkhouse" for the hired hands. The farm was quite extensive, and they raised potatoes as most farmers did in that area.

The Hamiltons were steadfast members of the Methodist Church. Olive, a very altruistic woman, was an ardent worker in the "Ladies Aid." John moved about the neighborhood. He was the first to know the newborn babies, the sick and the dying, helping those in need. He was very civic minded; he loved people and had a great sense of humor. He was always on the church board, was involved in Mound Cemetery in Brooklyn Center and the Masonic Lodge. He spoke at graduation ceremonies and even made a "run" for the Legislature. Olive died in 1945 after a long illness and John lived until 1951.

Robert W. Hamilton and Marjory Ham were married in 1938 and lived on the Hamilton Farm until it was sold in 1957. They had two children: William Edward and Marcia Marjory. William married Sheery Curtis. They had two children, Lisa and William, Jr. Marcia and Dan Kaliher had two daughters, Michelle and Carmel.

In 1950 Robert and Marjory built Hamilton's Drive Inn on the corner of Brooklyn Boulevard and Zane Avenue North. It was there for ten summers.

When the farm was sold, they moved to their home on 80th Avenue. Robert served as the Assessor for Brooklyn Park. Marjory went to work at Osseo School District's Crest View School, which was built on the Hamilton farm's old asparagus patch.

Robert and Marjory said "good-bye" to Brooklyn Park in July 1965, and moved to Bemidji to run their Travel Trailer Resort. They had many happy years seeing the U.S. in their Avion Travel Trailer.

Robert died May 1988. John Wesley is John and Olive's only living child. Marjory, the only living spouse, is home in Brooklyn Center enjoying her "Golden Years."

Submitted by Marjory Naomi Hamilton

John and Olive Hamilton

Granddaughters of the Pioneers: Blanche (Hamilton) Norris and Marjory (Ham) Hamilton

Craig and Linda Hanka

WE WERE SO EXCITED to move into our two-bedroom starter home on Labor Day weekend of 1975! We felt as though we were blessed to be moving into Brooklyn Center. Both of us had been raised in the North Minneapolis area, and knew Brooklyn Center as a neat suburb where Brookdale Shopping Center was located. We purchased the house from a widower named George Andrusko. He and his wife raised their children in that house, and we could tell that he was a bit reluctant to leave. We understood why, once we moved and began to raise our family there!

I remember being so impressed by the large yard that was "our very own." We'd sit out in our lawn chairs, and watch little Heather toddle through the grass. There was even a white picket fence! A dream come true! One funny thing is that the master bedroom had been used for a dining room for some time before we moved in. We slept under a huge crystal chandelier for quite awhile before we were able to convert it completely to a real bedroom.

Craig worked in the security department of what was then called FMC. It was just across the river, so it took him only about five minutes to get to work. Craig celebrated twenty-six years on the job at that location, which is United Defense now.

I worked at Abbott Northwestern Hospital until Brian was born in the fall of 1977. I was then able to be an "at-home Mom" until 1981 when Brian started pre-school at Cross of Glory Lutheran Church, and Heather was in second grade at Earle Brown Elementary School. At that time, I was hired as the After School Program Coordinator at Earle Brown School. I liked that job because it really opened doors to get to know families in this wonderful community! Linda remained at Earle Brown until February of 1996, when she was hired as the Coordinator of the Brooklyn Center Family Resource Center located in the Humboldt Square Shopping Center.

They say, "It takes a community to raise a child." We want to thank the Brooklyn Center Community for helping us to raise our two wonderful children, Heather and Brian. We had so many affirming experiences in the Brooklyn Center community.

We were involved in the annual PTA talent shows at Earle Brown School. Heather was in the Brooklyn Center High School marching band. Brian enjoyed the choir at the high school, and especially liked being a member of the track team. They received much support and help with values clarification by their participation in clubs and organizations that are such an important part of Brooklyn Center. Special thanks go to those adults who give their time and effort freely to children, whether it is Boy's Brigade, Scouts, Pioneer Girls, youth groups or sporting programs.

Our "starter home" has turned out to be our "ender" home as well. Because we like Brooklyn Center, we have never wanted to leave.

Submitted by Linda Hanka

OUR FAMILY was somewhat connected with Brooklyn Center, at least back into the 1920s, perhaps even farther. My mother's uncle was a deputy under Earle Brown and was killed in a gunfight up by Elk River, Minnesota. I remember, as a lad, visiting Earle Brown with my father. In 1944 my father, Harold W. Hannay, bought seven acres along the Mississippi River north of the I-694 Bridge. In 1945 he built his home at the present 6440 Willow Lane North.

After my release from the Navy my wife, Twila, and I purchased an acre lot from my father and started building our home. As I recall the population of Brooklyn Center was around 2200 at the time. Most of the people were living in the southeast portion of Brooklyn Center adjoining Minneapolis.

My father had been involved with Civil Defense during World War II and created Brooklyn Center's Civil Defense organization in 1946. He was also one of the organizers of the Brooklyn Center Volunteer Fire Department in 1949. People who were active in both organizations were the ones who took over the local government and brought Brooklyn Center from a farmer-oriented village to an urban city.

I joined the Fire Department in 1956 and served twenty-two years. During those years, I established an insurance agency, actively promoted the building of Brooklyn Center High School, was organizational chairman of the Brooklyn Center Chamber of Commerce and also served as its president (1974-75) and served on its Board of Directors. I served as founder, Scout Master and Explorer Advisor of Troop #410 of Earle Brown School. I served five years on the Selective Service System (1970-1975). In 1972-1973 I was Junior Citizen of the year. From 1976-1984 I served on the Brooklyn Center Charter Commission (I had been active in writing the original charter).

In my more private life I was one of the founders of Lutheran Church of the Master and was president of the congregation for twelve years. I am a charter member of the St. Andrew Society of Minnesota and served as its president for a number of years. A group of people of Scottish Heritage formed the organization in 1976.

Active in the MN Association of Mutual Agents, I was also one of the founders of the Metropolitan Insurance Agents Association.

Currently my community involvements are with American Association of Retired Persons teaching the 55 Alive/Mature Drivers Course and working with North Hennepin Chapter #1370 of AARP. I am also Chairman of the reunion committee for the North High School Class of 1939.

We have four children, all of whom graduated from Brooklyn Center High School. Our oldest son, Bill, was also a member of the BC Fire Department in the late 1960s. His son, Bill, now lives on Regent Avenue North. Our great-grand children living on Regent Avenue represent the fifth generation of Hannays to live in Brooklyn Center.

Submitted by William Hannay

William and Twila Hannay

Bill and Twila Hannay

George and Bessie Hanson

GEORGE AND BESSIE HANSON moved to Brooklyn Center in 1934 living at 58th and James Avenue North, which was a farmhouse and lived there for fifteen years. In May 1948 the old farmhouse burned down. They then built a new home next door to the farmhouse and lived there for forty-eight years, until their death. Their grandson, who is still living there today, then bought the house.

Submitted by Ilene A. Hanson

Baldwin Hartkopf Family

Baldwin Hartkopf

GERMAN FARMERS began settling the prairies of what is now Brooklyn Park in the mid-1800s. The grandfather of Baldwin Hartkopf left his hometown of Danzig, Germany after seeing letters from relatives who had settled in the Minnesota town of Osseo. In 1862 Karl Hartkopf and his wife, Amelia, with their four small children arrived in Prairie du Chien, Wisconsin. (They eventually had thirteen children) They took a steamboat up the Mississippi River to St. Paul, Minnesota where they stayed until 1865. By the time they arrived at their home site in Brooklyn Township, they had five children. Henry, the father of Baldwin, was their first child born in this country. They chose forty acres for their home at what is now 73rd Avenue North and West Broadway, because they needed Shingle Creek to water their livestock. Henry, with the help of a dog, was in charge of herding cattle. There were no fences then and only the herd leader had a cowbell. In later years he told his son, Baldy, that it was a difficult task.

German was the only language spoken in the home of Henry Hartkopf and Alma Goetze, whom he married in 1891. Baldwin and Florence (Mrs. Bruce Russell) of Golden Valley were their two children.

As a youth, Baldwin and his buddies associated with Brooklyn Township boys and girls more than Osseo young people because very few of the Brooklyn Township area youth smoked or drank. "Baldy" usually avoided alcoholic drinks throughout his life. Many Brooklyn Township people were against liquor. The population was mostly English and Scandinavian and belonged to Methodist or Baptist churches.

Baldy received his early education in one-room schoolhouses. For fourteen months he attended District #32 School on West Broadway and 89th Avenue North. The school was sometimes referred to as Skunk Hollow School. He remembered walking with a friend to Coulter School in all kinds of weather. He later attended District #43 School in Osseo. It took him an hour to walk to school. At age fifteen in 1907, Hartkopf enrolled at the School of Agriculture at the University of Minnesota. The Agriculture School provided room and board along with strict discipline.

Baldwin married Obeline Paul of Osseo and inherited the Hartkopf family farm. He and Obeline had four children: Whalen, Audrey Alford, Murlin and Baldy, Jr. They have eight grandchildren and eight great-grandchildren.

Hartkopf remembered the old days when delivering a load of potatoes or other produce to Minneapolis took about three hours. Farmers got up at 1:00 A.M., tended their horses, packed and arrived at the market about 5:00 A.M. for deal making and exchange of produce. He also lived to see housing developments engulfing southern Brooklyn Park and discipline problems for today's youth. He recalled the fun of old-time parties with popcorn, chocolate cake and apples, cards, chatting and games.

Submitted by Jane Hallberg

MY MOM AND DAD met at the United Service Organization (USO) in Albertville, Minnesota. When Dad brought Mom home, they liked to stop by Victory Airstrip and look at the stars, so when he brought her as his fiancée to a "bomb shelter" house (capped basement) in Brooklyn Township, she knew this was the place she wanted to live, because it was right across from the airstrip! In 1948 the newlyweds moved into the "bomb shelter." With family and neighbors' help, they added two stories, expanding upward. Dad was handy with car repairs and clever at trading his skills with others for tips and help in house building. For auto repair, an electrician neighbor showed Dad how to wire the house; another helped with the plumbing. Of course, my carpenter grandfather showed Dad many carpentry tricks. The 77th Avenue (now Brookdale Drive) home still stands strong.

Teresa Ann (Kruse) Hassell

We had seven houses on our street. We had goats and horses, and it was always exciting when either horses or billy goats were loose. We had baseball games in the field, always challenging who was to be on which team. Baseball was officially over when we went to the bonfires at Pavelok's truck farm.

Mom was always an active Democrat, as was her father. Dad stayed home with us kids while Mom went to the City Council meetings. She brought home the news on all of the issues: she told my Dad when the Council decided to change our address, not once, but twice! And it was a big deal when Mom came home and told Dad they were putting in sewers. What had begun as an idea, and argued before in the Council, had become a reality.

The Kruse Family: front, Edwin and Mary; back, Dick, Terry, Rosemary, Loretta, and Tom

Whether my parents agreed or didn't, it was always fun hearing the discussions! We understood the power of the town Council, especially when big trucks came and diggers started digging up the streets, piling dirt up on our property. Workers came to the door one day, advising that they were shutting off our water. A large water truck came by daily and we'd fill up several gallon containers to carry us through. At first this was exciting, then it became quite tedious! We were happy we did not grow up when it was normal to carry water by buckets from the nearest river or the outdoor well every day!

When they were working on the streets, construction noise put me to sleep in the afternoon; once they were done digging sewers, Mom couldn't get me to sleep! Next they were paving our street; then they started building houses where the airstrip and potato farms had been. These were the first steps of Brooklyn Township becoming Brooklyn Park and Brooklyn Center.

After high school graduation, I married and had two children: Woody and Rose Ann. My brothers, sisters and I (Thomas, Richard, Rose Mary and Loretta Kruse, Swedberg) still live in either Brooklyn Center or Maple Grove. I am a Home Health Care worker, working with physically challenged children. I also belong to Liz's Challengers in Brooklyn Center.

Submitted by Terry (Kruse) Hassell

Ralph and Dolores Hastings

Ralph Hastings

RALPH HASTINGS and his brother, Maurice, were both born in Gresham, Oregon. They were raised on Grandfather George Smith's eighty-acre farm. The farm was located east of Osseo, the southern boundary of which is now across the road from North Hennepin Community College.

After Grandfather George retired, Ralph and his brother helped Uncle Jess Smith and son with the farm work. They farmed an additional eighty acres with horses. They raised potatoes, corn, wheat, rye, oats, and hay. They churned their own butter. Although Uncle Jess had a Fordson tractor and a truck, most of the farm work was still done with horsepower. Uncle Jess also had some dairy cows.

The house Ralph was raised in was fairly modern. It had electricity and an indoor bathroom. The family owned a 1918 Studebaker car.

Osseo was a famous potato market area. The boys earned two cents a bushel while picking potatoes. Ralph said he remembers one truckload of potatoes was bid at twenty-five cents a hundred pounds. That load of course was taken back home and used as hog feed.

Ralph and his brother attended a one-room school in District #32. After graduating from there they started high school at Monticello, Minnesota but graduated from Osseo High School.

Ralph and Dolores met soon after he graduated from high school. They dated for nine years before they were married.

Grandfather Smith was in active service during the Civil War, and fought in the Battle of Gettysburg. Maurice served during the World War II. Ralph worked at the Ford Plant during the war making tanks for the war effort. Ralph and Dolores have four living children with spouses, ten grandchildren, and sixteen great-grandchildren.

The Hastings were very much involved with Our Lady of Victory Catholic Church, as Eucharistic Minister, as ushers, and helping with fund raising which enabled Fr. Musch to build the big complex of buildings. One Sunday as Ralph was distributing communion, his grandson turned to his dad and said, "I didn't know that grandpa was a priest."

Dolores and Ralph were involved with Cub Scouts. They were Watkins Products distributors for many years.

Dolores was a former president of The League of Women Voters of Brooklyn Center. She was a member of the Housing Commission for Brooklyn Center, and a member of the Brooklyn Historical Society. Dolores enjoyed working with the different commissions. When she believed in something, she would fight to get things done that needed doing.

In the late 1950s, at a time when retarded children did not go to school, she enrolled her youngest son in a school for the retarded in Minneapolis.

She was always a good friend and a caring person. When it was necessary for Ann Jarvimaki to get to the hospital, Dolores drove through an ice storm to get her there.

Dolores passed away in May 1999.

Submitted by Ralph Hastings and JoAnne Jackson
Lucy Her, Star Tribune Writer

HOWARD AND ANNE have been residents of Brooklyn Center and Brooklyn Park since 1955. They moved to Brooklyn Park in 1984 and presently live in the ReaLife Cooperative Apartments of Brooklyn Park. Howard was born in 1925, in Northfield, Minnesota. Anne was born in 1925, in St. Clair, Pennsylvania. They met after World War II while working for the U.S. House of Representatives in Washington, D.C. Anne was a secretary in the office of Jay LeFevre, a Congressman from New York. Howard delivered mail to his office. They were married in Washington, D. C. on November 28, 1946.

Howard graduated from North High School in Minneapolis. He earned a letter in track and ran the mile event in high school. He served in the Infantry in World War II, from 1944 to 1946. Howard saw combat with 85th Regiment, 10th Mountain Infantry Division in Italy, and was awarded the Infantry Combat Badge.

They moved to Minneapolis in 1948, where Anne worked as a secretary for the Nash-Kelvinator Corporation in Minneapolis. Howard graduated from the University of Minnesota in 1952, with a Bachelor's Degree in Civil Engineering. He then worked for the City of Milwaukee as a Project Engineer in the Street Construction Department. Then, the University of Minnesota Plant Services Division employed him until his retirement in 1988 as Manager of the Civil Engineering Section.

Howard was a co-founder of Citizens for Better Government, a non-partisan local political organization in Brooklyn Center in 1960, and served twice as President. Citizens for Better Government were successful in electing local candidates to the city council for twenty-five years. He was elected as a trustee (now called councilman) to the Brooklyn Center City Council and served from 1959 to 1971. During his tenure he served as Mayor Pro-Tem. Howard and Anne were active in the Democratic Farmer Labor (DFL) party in the 1960s. They were elected as delegates to the 1966 State Convention. In 1976, the Brooklyn Center Jaycee's honored Howard with the "Brooklyn Center Outstanding Citizen" award. Howard has served on the board of directors of four homeowners associations and served four terms as president.

Howard and Anne were active at St. Alphonsus Catholic Church in Brooklyn Center. Howard was an usher, a lector and chaired a committee to design and construct the grounds for the new church in 1969. Howard was active in the Community Emergency Association Program (CEAP) for many years and served two terms on the board of directors. Anne was very active in the church Rosary and Altar Society and served twice as chairperson of her guild. She was a Brownie and Girl Scout leader. Anne was one of the founders of the first Brownie and Girl Scout troop in the north half of Brooklyn Center. Anne was also active in school and community activities.

Their children are Karen Marie Karbo, Susan Mary Heck and Dianne Elizabeth Fischer. They have one grandchild, Allison Anne Fischer.

Submitted by Howard and Anne Heck

Howard and Anne Heck

The Heck Family: front, Corky Fischer, Allison Fischer, Dianne Fischer, Anne Heck, and Karen Karbo; back, Susan Heck, Howard Heck, and Skip Karbo

The John Helling Family

John F. Helling

THE JOHN HELLING FAMILY moved to Brooklyn Park in June of 1967, after I had been selected as the President of the fledgling North Hennepin State Junior College.

The college had been in operation since the fall of 1966, but the acting Dean had been transferred to Minneapolis Junior College in April, and I was asked to take over on a part-time basis until I could complete my present job responsibilities at the University of Wisconsin, Madison and assume full-time status on July 1st.

Our family consisted of my wife, Edwina, daughter Lisa and sons Erik and Leif. We purchased a home at 7841 Georgia Avenue that was just one and one-half blocks north of Brooklyn Boulevard (Osseo Road). Shingle Creek ran through a large field behind the house. The field belonged to A. M. Hartkopf who still farmed it, but it was a great place for children's games and snowmobiling in the winter. Eventually the northern eighty of that parcel became the permanent campus of North Hennepin Community College when we moved it out of rented facilities in Osseo in the summer of 1969.

I had been born in Rochester and lived in Minnesota nearly all of my life, except for a couple of years in the army and two more years as a professor at the University of Wisconsin. I remained President of North Hennepin Community College for twenty-three years until my retirement in 1990.

The college grew from a student body of 414 in 1966-67 to one of more than 7,000-head count by the time I retired.

Those years in Brooklyn Park were exciting and filled with activity.

My young people all graduated from Osseo High School, which was also being inundated with children from the burgeoning population of Brooklyn Park and other North Hennepin suburbs. The boys were active in interscholastic swimming with Leif taking a first place in the 1976 statewide meet. Lisa participated as a pom-pom girl, played in the band and grew more beautiful every day.

Edwina, who had a B.A. from Hamline University, took classes at St. Thomas and obtained a M.A. in community relations, which she utilized in her job as Community Liaison person with the Osseo Schools.

My schooling included high school at Rosemount, Minnesota, a BS from Hamline University, a M.A. and a Ph.D. from the University of Minnesota.

My forebears immigrated to America from Norway in 1835. The community they left was called Hollingdahl so when they arrived in America they were labeled "Hollings" which eventually changed to Helling. Most Hellings were farmers who homesteaded land in southern Minnesota. My father left the farm to enter the business world in the Twin Cities where I grew up. I began my professional life as a teacher, but didn't really find my true calling until I took the job of starting and running the college in Brooklyn Park.

Submitted by John Helling

THE LIVING ROOM in the Hamilton house was never used. It just sat there looking clean, neat and elegant. All discussions and all work were done around the dining room table. When Olive went to Minneapolis to do her shopping by horse and buggy, the children would play in the living room and get it all messed up. But they knew just about what time she would be expected home so one would keep an eye out for her. As soon as she was spotted they would get busy and clean up the room. When mother arrived home the room was spic and span.

Carrie Henry remembers her mother shopping in Minneapolis for materials to make the girls' dresses and the boys' shirts. Olive Hamilton could do anything she set her mind to. She knit the long black stockings the girls had to wear, the socks that the boys wore, and even made suits for her husband, Link. Grandpa Davis gave Olive a six-month-old racehorse. She and Frend trained him to be driven. All the girls knew how to handle horses.

Carrie Hamilton Henry

Mr. Hamilton liked to go to the Farmers' Market to sell produce. Carrie remembers peeling onions for market. The first few days they would cry, but eventually the eyes got used to the fumes and the peelers had fun singing and teasing each other about boys. They also had to cut and bunch the asparagus for market.

Carrie had the chore of cleaning the chimneys for the kerosene lamps and keeping the lamps filled. The Hamiltons had a woodshed attached to the house. In the summer it was cleaned so that the food could be cooked there, but it was eaten in the house.

Florence Hamilton with nephews Gordon Hamilton, "Bud" Dorn and his Mother, June Hamilton Dorn

There was a span of ten years between the oldest and the youngest in the Hamilton family. Carrie said, "Boy, did we have fun!" Their parents were very strict. Their father just gave them his look and they knew what he meant. Mother believed in a stick so she sent them to the woodpile. The children were not to quarrel and if they were caught at it, mother made them say, "Dear little sister I'm sorry and I will never do it again." About that time they were ready to spit at each other.

Mother could do anything, but father was equally as good; he was a director of the Osseo Bank and the Camden Bank. When the Depression came he lost all his money. All he had left was their eighty-acre farm.

Leone Hamilton Wadsworth Howe said that her grandmother, Ollie, made quilts, raised canaries, played the Jew's Harp, wrote plays and acted in them.

Out of the seven Hamilton children, Carrie was the only one who moved away from the Brooklyn or near by area. She lived on a big farm in southern Minnesota with husband, James and their five children.

Submitted by Leone Howe

Joel and Debra Hilstrom

DEBRA CARDINAL was the third of four girls born to Dennis and Gloria Cardinal on June 21, 1968. Debra attended Garden City Elementary School in Brooklyn Center. During junior high Debra enjoyed math and speech as her favorite subjects at North View Junior High School. There she participated on the synchronized swim team, competitive swimming and diving team, and gymnastics team. Debra graduated from the Park Center High School in 1986 with "B" honors.

On July 26, 1986, Debra Cardinal and Joel Hilstrom were married at Calvary Presbyterian Church in Minneapolis. Debra and Joel Hilstrom moved to Columbia Heights while Debra attended the University of Minnesota. Their first child, Stephanie Marie Hilstrom, was born in 1989.

Joel and Debra moved from Columbia Heights to Brooklyn Center in 1990, purchasing their home in 1991, where they continue to raise their family.

Debra graduated from the University of Minnesota with a Bachelor of Arts, majoring in Sociology, minoring in Speech Communication in December of 1990.

Jeremy Cardinal Hilstrom was born in 1993. Until January 1997, Debra stayed home to take care of the children, working part-time as a bookkeeper and doing volunteer work. Joel works as a tow truck driver for a family towing business.

Having demonstrated her interest in the community and public policy, Debra was encouraged to apply to serve on the Planning Commission, and was appointed to serve from 1992-1994. She ran for the Brooklyn Center City Council in 1994 and received the highest number of votes of seven candidates in the primary and of four in the general election. As a City Council Member, Debra has worked to preserve Brooklyn Center neighborhoods, reduce crime, provide affordable and accessible services, and promote long-range planning, accountability and fiscal responsibility. Debra was re-elected in 1998 and continues to serve Brooklyn Center on the City Council.

Submitted by Debra Hilstrom

THE HOHENSTEIN HERITAGE in Brooklyn Township, began in 1856 when my great-grandfather, Adam Hohenstein (1832-1919), came up the Mississippi River along the east side of Brooklyn Township on his way from St. Anthony to the Crow River. He followed the river to the area near Hanover where he found Matthias Harff and said, "If the water gets high, we'll get wet feet." Then he went about a mile and one-half farther and made his claim near the head of a spring-fed creek in the northeast quarter of Section 11 of Greenwood Township. He arrived on June 10, 1856, and the farm was in the family nearly 92 years until it was sold to State Senator Welsh.

Adam Hohenstein had been born at Himbach, Kreis Bedingen, Oberhessen, Germany, in 1832, and sailed from Antwerp on the boat E. Z. and arrived in New York on August 18, 1852.

On October 28, 1858, Adam married Caroline Glaser, at St. Anthony. Five sons and two daughters grew to maturity: Karl, Emilie, Henry, August, Louis, Emil, and Lena.

Adam's grandson, Carl Hohenstein (oldest son of Karl), and his wife, Agnes, (Haar), lived on a truck farm near the Earle Brown farm at 6425 Colfax Avenue North from the late 1920s to the early 1950's. In 1909 Carl was sponsor for my father, Immanuel (1909-1999), son of Emil (1876-1960). After graduating from Dr. Martin Luther College at New Ulm, Minnesota, Carl taught in Lutheran parochial schools in Weyauwega, Wisconsin, and Gibbon, Minnesota before settling in Brooklyn Center. Carl and Agnes had one son, Edmund Werner Hohenstein, born August 18, 1917, at Gibbon, Minnesota.

"Werner" grew up in Brooklyn Center and entered the service of his country in World War II. He was serving as a tail gunner in an airplane over France on November 30, 1944, when his plane was shot down and he gave his life for his country. His body was never found.

Carl and Agnes moved to Rockford, MN, and later to Belle Plaine where they were living in 1967. Finally they moved to Beloit, Wisconsin, to be near her sister, and Carl died there in 1972. Agnes died in 1984, at Watertown, Wisconsin.

Rev. Lloyd and Virginia Hohenstein moved to 7749 Newton Avenue North, Brooklyn Park, MN, in September of 1987. He is associated with the Lutheran Institutional Ministry Association. Pastors of the Wisconsin Evangelical Lutheran Synod refer their hospitalized members to him for spiritual care. He makes regular trips to the Hennepin County Adult Correction Facility in Plymouth to conduct Bible classes at the Women's building and to conduct devotions at the Work-Release Building. He conducts occasional services at the Minnesota Correctional Facility at Oak Park Heights. The Hohensteins were married August 3, 1958, at Oconomowoc, Wisconsin, and have six children and sixteen grandchildren. Most of them live in Wisconsin. The Hohensteins are members of Brooklyn Evangelical Lutheran Church at 69th and Zane Avenue North.

Submitted by Pastor Lloyd A. Hohenstein

The Hohenstein Family

Pastor Lloyd and Virginia Hohenstein

Abraham Herbert and Hulda Louise (Erickson) Holmberg

A. Herbert and Hulda Holmberg at their golden wedding anniversary (Spring 1957)

MAY 1903, Dad, 17 — youngest of four sons and four daughters — left Sweden for the U.S., with $6.00 and a train ticket to Minneapolis. He worked through Fall harvest at an uncle's farm, learning enough English to return to Minneapolis where he worked digging and laying storm sewers, then as a carpenter's helper.

July 1903, Mother came from Sweden, via Minneapolis, to family friends in Wisconsin for a year, returning to Minneapolis doing housework.

They met at seventeen, both playing in the Salvation Army Band, Dad clarinet, Mother guitar. Dad did custodial work downtown for $10.00 a week. He got a $2.00 raise when they married. He accepted the Reinhards' work offer at their battery store on Hennepin Avenue.

They bought a South Minneapolis house with no basement and the upstairs unfinished. Mother's brother, Claus, immigrated; he stayed with them, finding work: tenhour days, six-day weeks back then. He and Dad found time to jack up the house, locate timber and slide a foundation beneath the floor. By hand, they dug a basement, built forms, mixed cement, poured both the floor and walls — then finished the upstairs! Carl, Margaret and Rolland were born in that house; it's still standing!

Grandpa Peterson (Mother's dad) homesteaded on Little Fork River near International Falls, MN, building a huge log cabin on a beautiful high bank. The folks rented out their Minneapolis house to go live with Grandpa Peterson, who wanted them to stay, work and inherit his land. Twins, Estil (Dick) and Estella (Stella), were born there. Things didn't work out, Dad and Grandpa had differences. In 1921, Dad returned to Minneapolis, sold the house, bought a house with five acres in Brooklyn Township (Park), and sent for his family.

In 1927 I was born on our farm; we had cows, chickens, and "Suzie", a white horse. One day Dad put me on Suzie's back, leading her to Mazurak's to team her with his horse for fieldwork. Enroute she reared up, striking Dad's leg. I hit the ground hard, taking a general, lasting dislike for horses!

Winters and summers, Dad and three neighbors walked to the streetcar line (51st & Lyndale Avenues) to work downtown until Dad got his first automobile, a Model "T." I remember going along Saturdays and Sundays to Reinhard's, checking out the building.

Mother's was also a life of hard work. Mondays a copper boiler was on the wood stove — wash day! Dad got home 6:00 P.M. — suppertime! Friday's beans were put to soak overnight for baking with bread and buns every Saturday. Summer's work added vegetable gardening and canning. An expert regulating its temperature, Mother did everything on/in the old wood-burning stove, especially great cream puffs, angel food and sponge cakes — No stomping or door slamming, a cake might fall! She had an electric stove; primarily used for brewing quick pots of coffee for evening company who enjoyed a table of goodies.

Dad's uncle's surname was "Magnuson." Dad explained that upon entering Swedish military service, they took an assumed surname. Returning to civilian life, they could keep that one, or take back their original. Grandpa Karl Holmberg kept his chosen name, thus began us Holmbergs.

Submitted by Robert E. Holmberg

ROLLAND, son of Herbert and Hulda, and Lilias, daughter of Arthur and Emma Anderson, were married March 1st, 1934. Like many contemporaries, they married someone from "the neighborhood." Rolland lived on 81st Avenue, Lilias on West River Road. Grandpa Anderson gave them twenty acres (at 73rd & Dupont) as a wedding gift. With family and friends' help, they built a house, still standing, almost sixty years, and with same color.

Their five children: Glenda, Gayle, Darryl, Richard, and Bonnie, all attended Benson Grade School and Anoka Junior-Senior High School.

Money was scarce; gardening wasn't a hobby, but a necessity. Raising vegetables for eating and canning was essential. When fruit became available each summer, it was bought and canned for winter consumption. We raised chickens for eggs and dinner meat—fried, baked, roasted. We'd get fresh milk daily from Grandpa Holmberg's cow, Mother would spoon the cream off the top for baking, or butter, or coffee. We kids got older; Grandpa sold the cow; Franklin Creamery filled our milk needs.

Rolland served in the Marines in Nicaragua before World War II and during WWII he was stationed in San Diego, CA. When he came home, he returned to work at Reinhard's (where Grandpa H. also worked), then drove truck for Knowel Trucking. Lilias worked with Caterers, Inc. for many years, serving elegant meals to some of the elegant people in the high-class homes of the Metropolitan area.

Glenda and Gayle had a paper route to make some money as kids. The "Star and Tribune Newspapers" didn't want to let "girls" peddle papers at that time, but said they'd give them a trial. They were successful. They had a long route for only thirty-five deliveries. The route was passed on to neighbor boys, brother, Darryl, and myself—through Jr. high school.

We grew up to go our own ways: Glenda has a son, Mark Schultz, by her first marriage, and three grandchildren; she worked several years at Minnegasco, and met Duane Roepke—they married, settled in Robbinsdale and North Minneapolis until retirement. They now live at Browns Lake by Eden Valley, and winters with other "snowbirds." Gayle also has a son, Robert Curtis, from her first marriage; she worked with her husband for twenty-five years in Alaska running a lodge and game/outfitter business. She now lives on the Island of Kona, Hawaii, with husband, Ralph Hind. Darryl has daughters, Jodi, Darci, Glenda and June, and son, Darren, by previous marriages; he drives an over-the-road truck; he and wife Judy, have daughters, Jennifer, Sheryl & Pamela and live in Illinois. Richard has worked at Northern States Power since the Air Force; he and wife, Gayle, a teacher, live in Corcoran, MN, have a son, Nathan, and a daughter, Erica, and a granddaughter. Bonnie had lived in Alaska with Gayle; she married Orville Proctor, they were owner/managers of several large markets there. Orville died in June 1992; Bonnie died April 1994.

Rolland and Lilias lived to celebrate their Golden Wedding Anniversary in March of 1984. Lilias born 1913 passed away 1989 and Rolland born 1911 joined her 1989. That was a very hard year.

Submitted by Rick Holmberg

Rolland Herbert and Lilias June (Anderson) Holmberg

Rolland and Lilas Holmberg on their fiftieth anniversary with Richard, Gayle, Glenda, and Bonnie

The Paul W. Holmlund Family

THE HOLMLUND FAMILY arrived in Brooklyn Center in July of 1959 when they moved into their new home at 6536 Indiana Avenue North. Paul, Shirley, and daughter Kathy (who was four years old at the time) had moved from northeast Minneapolis. Daughter Julie was born in 1961.

The family joined Cross of Glory Lutheran Church in Brooklyn Center and became active members. Both girls played in the Park Center High School Band and also participated in many other school activities. In 1973, daughter Julie helped dad design the City of Brooklyn Center logo, which is still being used twenty-six years later. Both Kathy and Julie graduated from Park Center High School and went on to college. They are now married, have children, and live in Prior Lake and Lakeville.

When the family moved to Brooklyn Center in 1959, Osseo Road (now Brooklyn Boulevard) was a two-lane, tree-lined road. A truck farm was located between our home and the National Tea Grocery Store in what is now one of the Iten Chevrolet buildings. We cut across the field to get to the store. Each spring, we were faced with blowing topsoil from freshly plowed fields. Shortly after we moved to Brooklyn Center, Interstate 694 was constructed through the farm and cut off our route to the store. About the same time, Osseo Road was upgraded to a divided highway and renamed Brooklyn Boulevard. Paul remembers being at the opening ceremonies. He also remembers attending the opening ceremonies for the new Interstate 94 from Minneapolis to Brooklyn Center, and for the Brooklyn Center Post Office.

Paul was an auditor with the certified public accounting firm of Peisch and Peisch in Minneapolis when the family moved to Brooklyn Center. Shirley also worked in downtown Minneapolis for Northwestern Bell Telephone Company.

One of Paul's audits was at the Earle Brown Farm for the Brown Holding Company. Earle Brown lived there at that time, and the audits were conducted in a room just outside his office. Paul delivered the completed audit report to Mr. Brown's home.

In August 1964 Paul was appointed director of finance for the then Village of Brooklyn Center. The village hall was located on Osseo Road, which is now Brooklyn Boulevard. When the village became a city in December of 1968, Paul retained his position of director of finance and, in January of 1969, was also appointed city treasurer. The city moved its offices to the new civic center complex in 1971.

Paul was a long-time member of the Rotary Club of Brooklyn Center, and was a past-president. Paul retired in 1993, after being employed by the City of Brooklyn Center for twenty-nine years. After making their home in Brooklyn Center for thirty-five years, Paul and Shirley moved to Burnsville in 1994 to be closer to their grandchildren. The family has many fond memories of life in Brooklyn Center.

Submitted by Paul Holmlund

HAVING SERVED AS A NAVY PILOT during World War II, Ken Houchins attended the University of Minnesota under the GI Bill. He graduated from the Institute of Technology with an Aeronautical Engineering Degree.

Unfortunately, after graduating, jobs in Aeronautical Engineering were scarce. When he was offered a job at the University Book Store, he accepted. He served in this position for nineteen years, then on to B. Dalton Book Store and Montgomery Ward. He worked at St. Gerard's Catholic Church in Brooklyn Park. In his retirement years, he is now working part-time at Brookland Executive Golf Course in Brooklyn Park. Alice worked at the Minnesota and Coop Bookstore during the years of 1947 to 1950. She started work at seventy cents an hour and moved up to ninety cents an hour.

Alice and Ken were both raised on farms near Randall and Pierz, MN. Ken and Alice were married in 1946. They bought their first house in 1951 at 73rd and Dupont North in Brooklyn Park. In February of that year they rented a trailer, loaded it with half of their possessions, and drove to their new home only to be confronted with five-foot snowdrifts in the driveway. They shoveled out the snow, thinking that next weekend they could bring in the rest of their goods. Sure enough next weekend another snowstorm came and a repeat performance of shoveling had to be done.

The Houchins' raised two boys, Thomas and Jeffrey, and one girl, Mary, in this house.

Ken was a charter member of the volunteer fire department in Brooklyn Park. He helped with the Boy Scouts and 4-H Clubs. Alice served with the Fire Department Auxiliary. She helped with the Camp Fire Girls, and volunteered in the schools their children attended. To help with the family income without taking much time away from their children, she sold Sarah Coventry jewelry, worked at the Palace Inn in Crystal and worked part-time for a catering service for twenty-eight years.

When St. Gerard's Catholic Church Parish was founded in 1970, Ken was one of the trustees on the steering committee. Alice did much volunteering for the parish. She served on many committees. She served as a lector, on the finance committee and the parish council. She started serving on parish committees right after Vatican II, at a time when women were entering the more "assumed" roles of men. Alice also served on the board of the Archdiocesan Council of Catholic Women.

When St. Gerard's celebrated its twenty-fifth anniversary, Alice was awarded the coveted plaque of "Volunteer of the Year" award for twenty-five years of volunteering at the parish.

Ken retired in 1986. He and Alice then started traveling in their RV. They travel to warmer climates in the winter and spend their summers in a condo in Maple Grove. They play golf at Brookland Executive Golf Course in Brooklyn Park where Ken still works on a part time basis.

Submitted by Alice Houchins

Ken and Alice Houchins

The Ken and Alice Houchins Family

Leroy Merton Howe

THE FIRST FAMILY OF HOWES came to America in 1635 on the ship "Truelove", from London. They settled in the Boston area but many began farming in Maine. The lineage on record begins with Asa Howe, born in 1778, who married Susan Fisher, born in 1791. Asa came from Merrimac, Massachusetts to Cooper, Maine, where he built a log cabin and began to have a family.

In 1882, David Howe, Roy's grandfather, was born in Cooper, Maine. David married Charlotte Green Brown of Princeton, Maine and they had ten children—five daughters and five sons. One of their sons, Everett Edward, was the father of Roy.

Everett Howe married Emma Dora Lane. The Lane people also were early settlers in America. Daniel, born in 1796, married Temperance Pettigrow, born in 1800. They had twelve children. Their youngest child, Francis Lane married Eliza Strout; they had eight children, one of which was Emma.

The Howes settled in Brooklyn Township in the early 1850s. They started the first store and post office; one of the Howes helped organize the cemetery, and was the first Mound Cemetery president. The Howes were farmers and appreciated the sandy soil after farming the rocky land in Maine.

Everett and Emma had four children: Frank, 1893; Charlotte (Lottie), 1895; Vera, 1899 (died at age 16); LeRoy (Roy), 1901. The children went to school in Brooklyn Township. Roy always said his favorite teacher was Mrs. Brown. He was grateful for her stern, good teaching which taught him the value of education. He went on to North High School in Minneapolis and the University of Minnesota's Farm School.

Taken from "Our Heritage" Howes and Lanes by Lottie Howe Stole, 1974.

Ralph and Leone Howe

LEONE WADSWORTH HOWE was born in Maple Grove, Minnesota in 1924 on a farm three miles south of Osseo. She came from a long line of pioneers to Minnesota. Her paternal grandmother, Nancy Potter Wadsworth, was a southerner, who came to Minnesota because she sided with the North during the Civil War. Leone's grandfather, Charles Wadsworth, was the auctioneer of the area. He cleared the land on the Brooklyn Park-Maple Grove border (on 77th Avenue North). Leone's maternal grandparents, Ollie and Lincoln Hamilton, came from Ohio in the late 1800s and settled in Brooklyn Township (81st Avenue between Regent and Zane North).

In 1943 Leone married Ralph Howe of Brooklyn Center. Their grandparents, Howe and Hamilton, were in business together and also were best friends. The business was in Minneapolis where they sold seed and were potato brokers.

The Ralph Howe family lived in Brooklyn Center, Brooklyn Park, Maple Grove, and Champlin during their marriage. They have two sons, Mark, and Dale, and two daughters, Merrily Heyn and Jeanne Newstrom. The family includes ten grandchildren and two great-grandchildren.

Leone Howe is the author of *Once Upon a Farm*, *An Album of Brooklyn Centre*, *History of the Earle Brown Farm* with two other authors and *The Hamilton Link* with help from all of her cousins. She took an active part in group writing, *A Church Grows in Brooklyn*, the history of Brooklyn United Methodist Church. In 1997 Leone edited with the family members the history of the Myrtle and Roy Howe Family, a two-hundred-page book, *Best Bet*.

Ralph was a corporate officer of Howe, Inc. He retired in 1986.

Submitted by Leone Howe

Ralph and Leone Howe

ON MAY 16, 1940, John Huberty of Lakeville, MN, married Loretta Sakry of St. Cloud, MN in the Church of St. John Cantius, St. Cloud.

Sandra, their only child, was born at Northwestern Hospital on May 26,1943. Shortly after she was born her father was sent overseas to serve in the Seabees in the South Pacific during World War II.

After his return to Minneapolis, in 1945, they continued to live on the third floor of the Delano Apartments at 11 Spruce Place. The apartment was located two blocks from Loring Park and three blocks from the Basilica, where Sandra attended school through the sixth grade.

Soon after, John Huberty went to work for the Northern Ordinance Plant (aka "The Pump") in Fridley, MN. He worked there for thirty-seven years, retiring in 1982. He passed away in 1985 at the age of 62.

In 1955 they moved to a brand new pink three-bedroom Marv Anderson rambler at 5347 Morgan Avenue North in Brooklyn Center, MN. There were no trees, no grass and dirt roads. The houses were built on farmland and for several years they had asparagus growing up through the grass.

The Hubertys joined Our Lady of Victory Catholic Church in North Minneapolis and Sandra attended school for her seventh and eighth grades there. Because there was no high school in Brooklyn Center, students from there were bussed to North High School in North Minneapolis. The students were known as the "kids from the country." During high school Sandra worked part-time at the Bridgeman fountain located inside the Merwin Drugstore in Northbrook Plaza.

On October 23, 1965, Sandra married Ronald J. Cich from St. Paul, MN. They were married at Our Lady of Victory Church and moved into their first home on Rice Street and Larpenteur Avenue in St. Paul, MN.

In December 1966 their first child, Peter, was born. Paul, Mary, Michael, and Timothy followed him.

The Cich family moved six times over the years and in September, 1986, they moved back to Sandra's childhood home at 5347 Morgan North. They added three more bedrooms, another bath and a family room to the house. All the children have left home. Peter is a career Air Force personnel and lives with his wife, Anna, and children, Alex and Rita at Hill AFB in Utah. Paul and wife, Andrea, live with their three children, Elaine, Kristofer, and Jordan in Woodbury, MN. Mary has an apartment near Lake Calhoun in Minneapolis. Michael attends school at St. Cloud State College. Timothy recently joined the Air Force and is in training in Texas.

Ron retired in February 1998 after thirty-three years with 3M Company in St. Paul. They continue to live in the house at 5347 Morgan Avenue North with Sandra's mother.

Submitted by Sandra (Huberty) Cich

John and Loretta Huberty

Mavis Valerie (Fiebiger) Huddle

IN THE SUMMER OF 1939, Mom and Dad (Peter & Ardis Fiebiger) and I moved "to the farm." We had chickens, ducks, geese, Guinea hens (great "watch dogs"), and dumb turkeys. During one freezing rainstorm they stood, wings freezing to the ground. Mom and Dad gathered them in bushel baskets to carry inside! I remember a nasty rooster gleefully chasing me every time I went to the "facilities," 100 feet from the house; Dad ended his fun with a hammer one day! We had a cow (home-made butter and ice cream); raised a calf and hog annually (filling rented freezer/locker). During World War II we raised rabbits to sell and eat. Meat rationing wasn't a problem!

One summer I weeded onions at Clausen's, for ten cents an hour. Dad made me quit—couldn't break even on soap to clean me up afterwards! All seasons I walked a half mile to school on dirty, muddy, icy 73rd Avenue! Mrs. Yaklich's corner store, at Lyndale Avenue, carried penny candy, school supplies, pop and "off sale" beer; working men gathered regularly, sitting on beer cases, relaxing, watchfully!

Refrigeration? Iceman, Winnie LaCrosse, came three days a week! Window cards told our needs; he'd cut the block with huge tongs, throw it onto his leather-caped shoulder, and carry it to our icebox! Cloverleaf & Franklin Dairies delivered, with premiums. The Watkins man brought Mom her favorite vanilla; other "vendors" provided "home shopping."

Special pets include Rex, my English Shepherd, and our black cats, Tom & Mitzi. We hatched pigeons; they "boxed" wing-to-paw with our cats—great entertainment! I had two horses: Scout, and Boots, and raised two champion hogs and two lambs in 4-H Club.

Mavis Huddle and her Harley at Roamin' Wyoming Rally in Cody (1988)

In July 1951 I met biker, Johnny Carroll; he loved that motorcycle! An October 17, 1951, accident took him, and roughed me up. I bought my first Harley after graduating Anoka High School in 1952! My present "Hog" was a gift from fiancé, Walter Misjak, who died December 4, 1985. I organized MRMTC (Minnesota Rider Motorcycle Touring Club) and have AMA, MMRA, and Travelers Club memberships.

I married Bruce Huddle in 1954, divorced, 1964: I have two married daughters: Teresa and Valerie. Besides participating at school and with all their numerous activities, I also solo-chaperoned busloads of 30-50 teens to the Medina & Marigold Ballrooms so they could experience true ballroom atmosphere. This kept me occupied several years!

As Dyckman Hotel Reservationist 1952-57, I met Eleanor Roosevelt, Tyrone Power, Adlai Stevenson and Joe Lewis. I was Parish Secretary, Lutheran Church of the Master, twenty-two years; Secretary-Treasurer 1982-88 of two companies owned by my former ('57-'59) 3M Super, E. Wayne Bollmeier.

I worked local politics with Brooklyn Park's famous Tuffords & Helen Rosing for Flora Rogge, BP Mayor; several years DFL for Hubert, Fritz, & Orv—fathers of Campaign 98s "Our 3 Sons." I was Campaign Secretary to Jesse Ventura, and hold Reform Party office. I belong to the Lincoln and Continental Owners Club (LCOC). I'm also a member of the National Rifleman's Association's, "Silver Bullet" Club.

I survived some fine "Old School" teachers! I was blessed with wonderful, loving parents who helped teach my girls and me what's important in life, supporting us in all of our endeavors. We've enjoyed many rich experiences prior to the "progress" (?) in these northern suburbs.

Submitted by Mavis Huddle

My parents married in Faribault, MN, and shortly thereafter moved to Minneapolis, where they lived for many years, and where I was born. My two sisters were several years older than I, one of whom died at age eleven from a scarlet fever and diphtheria epidemic. At the time I was one year old and unfortunately never knew her.

When I was two years old my parents returned to Faribault for a few years. We lived in a large house high on a hill, and I cherish the memories: awakening to the delightful smell of fresh bread baking, picking bouquets of violets in the woods near us, walking down the road by myself (it was safe then) to visit my grandmother nearby.

Faribault was always my second home. While I don't visit there very much any more, I still have a fondness for the city and my many relatives there.

One day I fell down the basement stairs, screaming and crying. My mother and sister ran down the stairs, found me sitting on the cement floor, and asked, "Did you hurt yourself?" Still screaming, I cried, "NO, I LOST MY GUM!" Then on my first day of school I displayed my stubborn side. I refused to go to school because I didn't like my new shoes. (Even then I was clothes-conscious) My mother prevailed, of course, and I went to school, shoes and all. I remember those shoes and still don't like them.

My sister was eighteen-years old when she married, and I was then five years old. I always felt that her fiancé didn't like me. Consequently I didn't like him until one day he gave me a little black baby doll. That changed everything. I still have that doll and recently learned it is valued at $500. I think he paid twenty-five cents for it.

After returning to Minneapolis, I attended schools in North Minneapolis, and graduated from North High School at the height of the Depression. I was fortunate to get a job with Federal Housing Administration where I worked many years, ending up with an Underwriter's Rating, the first such rating given to a woman in any of the FHA offices throughout the country, a minor accomplishment compared to today's women executives, ceos, etc. Eventually seeking a change, I went into private industry as a real estate closer for several more years.

In 1956 I purchased my current home in Brooklyn Center. I married late in life to a very fine man who agreed to live in my house although he himself owned a few houses. I then worked with him in his canvas business until he retired, two years after which he passed away. My life then changed considerably.

At the suggestion of a friend, I joined the Golden Valley Garden Club and later became its president. I joined the Brooklyn Center Women's Club, and will have completed my second year as its president. This has been a rewarding experience, and I feel that in some small way I finally have contributed something to the community.

Submitted by Beatrice Humbert

Beatrice Humbert

The Larry and Helen Ingalls Family

In June 1964 the Lawrence (Larry) and Helen Ingalls family (including children, Rebecca and Steven) moved from Lakewood (a suburb of Denver) Colorado, to Brooklyn Park, Minnesota where Larry would be working for General Mills.

The Ingalls family had been living in the Jefferson County School District in Colorado, which was one of the top districts in the nation, and wanting to maintain this level of education for their children, chose the Robbinsdale District #281 which was also considered very good.

Soon after locating in Brooklyn Park, Helen obtained employment at North Memorial Hospital. She later spent many years in the home mortgage business doing processing, closing, and underwriting. Both Helen and Larry are now retired.

Larry and Helen Ingalls

The Ingalls' place of residence in Brooklyn Park was a rather new home located at 7317 64th Avenue North, where they still reside. Both Helen and Larry are natives of Wisconsin, Helen from Menomonie, and Larry from near LaCrosse (Onalaska). The Ingalls children, Becky and Steven, graduated from Cooper High School, Becky in 1969 and Steven in 1972.

Larry and Helen are the proud grandparents of six grandchildren and one great-granddaughter, Ashley Kate.

Becky is married to David Miskowiec and they now reside in Moline, Illinois. Her three children by her first marriage are Ed Otterness married to Staci (Zemek) and their child, Ashley Kate. Other children are Melanie and Kristine Otterness, both unmarried.

Steven is married to Carol (Ewy) and lives in Rogers, MN. Their children are: Daniel, Jennifer and Erik.

Larry and Helen are members of the Church of Jesus Christ of Latter Day Saints (Mormon) and brought with them from Colorado their desire for family history research. In tracing their lineage they found a common ancestor nine generations in the past. Both Larry and Helen are actively engaged in volunteer work at their family history center.

Some interesting discoveries in tracing their lineage were: Helen is a descendant of the DOANE family which have been in this country since the early 1600s. A college at Crete, Nebraska is named after this family. It is interesting to note as well that the famous "Doan" pills for backaches can also be attributed to this family.

Another discovery is that a member of the Narragansett Tribe of Native Americans, living on the east coast in the 1600s, married into the Doane family. Helen's paternal side is all Scandinavian, immigrating to this country in the late 1800s.

Larry's ancestral line dates back to about the 12th century, or, into the Viking era. The original "Ingalls" name is believed to be Old Norse, "Ingvaldr." Over time it has evolved to the now Ingalls spelling when two brothers, Edmund and Henry, immigrated from England to Lynn, Massachusetts, in the early 1600s. Larry is a descendant of Edmund and related to Laura Ingalls Wilder.

Submitted by Larry and Helen Ingalls

CHARLES WILLIAM JACKSON, an orphan, was born in 1862. At about age thirteen he came to live with Charles Reuel (C. R.) and Clara Howe and help out at the C. R. Howe Store. C. R. Howe was born in Washington County, Maine in 1848. He moved with his parents to Brooklyn Center in 1853, was appointed postmaster of Brooklyn Center in 1873, and opened a stock of general merchandise at that place in 1875. In 1871 he married Clara M. Butts and they had two daughters: Retta and June.

Charles Jackson graduated from the University of Minnesota in 1896. In 1907, he was tired of teaching (he was a school principal) and bought the store from the Howes. Retta Howe (Mrs. Adolph Beckum) played the organ at the Anoka MN church attended by Catharine Williams, a nurse of Welsh descent. Retta asked Catharine if she would help her mother take care of her father who was very ill. This is when Catharine met Charles Jackson.

Charles and Catharine were married in 1908. Their living quarters included bedrooms above, and a kitchen and parlor behind, the Store. Also above the Store was a hall where community suppers and other events were held.

Charles and Catharine had seven children: Clara Elizabeth, John Reuel, George Edward, Charles David, Mary Catharine, William Adolph, and Llewellyn Lloyd. The first six children were born at home at the Store. Their daughter, Mary Catharine Jackson, worked for the Corp of Engineers for thirty years.

By 1921 the business climate had changed. With more people having automobiles they travelled to places like Camden to buy their groceries. So the Jackson's sold the Brooklyn Center Store (formerly the C. R. Howe Store) at the SW corner of 69th and Osseo Road to Bill and Doris Gadow who had a barbershop.

The Jackson's rented a thirty-acre farm in Brooklyn Center from 1921-1925. Llewellyn was born in the rented farmhouse they called the "Little Gray House by the Creek." In 1924 a smallpox epidemic quarantined Catherine in North Minneapolis caring for Clara who was attending school there. Retta (Howe) Beckum cared for the other Jackson children, who attended school in Anoka during the epidemic. In 1925 the Jacksons purchased a forty-acre farm in Maple Grove. Charles died in 1926. Sons George, Charles and William served in the Armed Services in World War II. Catharine then rented out the farm and later sold it. She continued her nursing career. Catharine, born in 1881, died in 1976 at the age of 95.

The Jackson' oldest son, John Reuel, married Thelma Greninger and moved to South St. Paul. Their daughter Karen is married to Dr. Duane Orn. Their son is Carl "Charlie."

Submitted from an interview with Mary Catharine Jackson

Charles William and Catharine Jackson Family

Grandmother Catherine Jackson

The Jacobsen Family

HELEN GRADUATED from Patrick Henry High School and Mel graduated from North High School. We bought a Franson home in Brooklyn Center in 1955. How exciting it was when streetlights were put in. There was an abandoned asparagus field where Brookdale shopping center stands. Christmas trees were collected after Christmas and put in a pile there and then burned in one huge bonfire. As a small child I remember going to the Earle Brown Farm to see the animals on a Sunday afternoon and to the Camden Drug Store in north Minneapolis for a triple-decker ice cream cone.

Our daughters, Pamela and Nancy, went to Brooklyn Center schools, which were small with wonderful devoted teachers—it was like going to a private school.

When we moved to Brooklyn Center, Mel had a wedding photography business.

Mel, Nancy, Helen, and Pamela Jacobsen

He built a dark room in our home, did his own film processing and print making, and worked full-time at Daytons department store. He loved it so much that he got a job at General Mills in the photography department and went into commercial photography. The wedding business kept growing and he made the decision to leave General Mills and have a full-time business. He started doing commercial jobs and this grew to the point that he gave up weddings.

A fire station was built near Mel's house when he was growing up. He spent a lot of time there playing ping-pong and other games with the firemen. He thought it would be really nice to be a fireman. When he stayed home full time they recruited him to be a volunteer fireman, which he loved. He fulfilled both of his dreams. He also was a charter member of the Brooklyn Center Chamber of Commerce and later he joined the Brooklyn Center Rotary.

We just moved into our home in June 1955 when it was announced that Brookdale shopping center would be built. There were hardly any stores in Brooklyn Center so this was great. Mel took pictures from the first groundbreaking shovel full of dirt until its completion.

Mel developed lung cancer and died in August of 1980. I always helped run the business, so when Mel died I hired photographers. Then I had to go out and promote the business. I started out by visiting the companies we had done business with over the years. The business grew. I sold it in 1990 to Drew Trampe.

When I took over the business, I became active in the Brooklyn Center Chamber of Commerce, Earle Brown Days and the Brooklyn Center Prayer Breakfast Committee. I especially remember the preparation for and receiving the award, "All American City." About twenty people from Brooklyn Center went to Cincinnati, along with about fifteen other cities, to tout why we should receive the award. We had a lovely booth and things to give out and we took turns manning the booth.

Pamela married George Toper and they live in Greenwich, CT. Nancy married Tom Brandon and they live in Maple Grove with their two children Jonathan and Becky.

I moved into a town home in 1994 in Brooklyn Park. I do a lot of volunteering and enjoy playing bridge.

Submitted by Helen Jacobsen

DAVID AND DONNA JARL and their six children, Debbie, Kim, Pam, Sandy, Mark and Brian moved into Brooklyn Center in 1969 to a home located at 55th and Girard Avenue North. They remember the horses on the Earle Brown Farm and thinking that they lived in the country.

David and Donna Jarl

David graduated from the University of Minnesota. He worked for Kraft Foods and then worked for Land O' Lakes until his death in 1984. He was active coaching Little League, Youth Football, and was very much involved with the Babe Ruth League. He served seven years on the Brooklyn Center School Board.

The Jarl children graduated from Brooklyn Center High School. Three still live in Brooklyn Center, and have children attending schools: Earle Brown Elementary, Brooklyn Center High School and Evergreen Park Elementary.

Donna worked at Earle Brown School for twelve years until her retirement. She now resides in a senior highrise apartment in Brooklyn Center. She is happy to be a part of this great city.

Submitted by Donna Jarl

The David and Donna Jarl Family

ROBERT AND MARY JENSEN purchased a newly built home on 63rd and Humboldt Avenue North across from the Earle Brown farm in 1959.

Robert and Mary Jensen

They had a great view of the farm. The open pasture land made it easy for the children to make friends with the horses by feeding them apples.

Mary had known Phil Cohen from her high school days at North High School. He was then a member of the school board. She introduced him to Robert.

Robert served one term as President of the Earle Brown Elementary School Parents Teachers Association (PTA). Phil Cohen introduced him to Mayor G. Erickson, who then appointed him to the Planning Commission. Robert served in this capacity for twelve years. This was a period of heavy growth, with strong pressure for housing and commercial development. The need for a comprehensive land use plan was critical. The Planning Commission, under the direction of the city council, prepared such a plan with the assistance of professional planners, city staff and neighborhood advisory groups. The city council formally adopted this plan that continues in place today with current updates as required.

The Jensen's oldest son, Steven, had to attend school at Lincoln Junior High in Minneapolis, because Brooklyn Center had no Junior or Senior High School at that time. Four of their children did graduate from the newly built Junior and Senior Brooklyn Center High School.

The Jensen home was close to the freeway system. They watched the construction of the overpass on Highway 100 and Humboldt Avenue. The city was divided by four school districts and a freeway system that cut them in half. The city, however, has maintained its cohesiveness and reputation as a "Something More City."

Submitted by Robert Jensen

Mayor Phil Cohen and Bob Jensen viewing the Senior High Rise Housing

David Johnson

Born in 1909, Howard Johnson was raised in Mitchell, South Dakota, hometown of former Senator George McGovern. For a time Senator McGovern's father was Howard's pastor. Howard's mother, Clara Todnem, was born in a sod shanty in the wilds of South Dakota in 1884. Clara's father changed his name from Lars Tobias to Louis Todnem when he arrived from Norway. Howard's grandfather, Wilford Johnson, was a guard at the execution of the Lincoln conspirators.

Magnhild Hauff was born and raised in Huron, South Dakota, which is the hometown of the former Vice President Hubert Humphrey. Samuel Hauff and Ragnihild Edlund emigrated from Sweden, met and married in the Twin Cities, then moved to Huron, SD. While working for the Huron Parks Department and attending a church there, Howard met Magnhild. They attended Miltonvale Wesleyan College in Kansas. After marriage and graduation they founded a church in Sioux City, Iowa. For more than forty years they pastored Wesleyan churches in Iowa and Minnesota. Mom passed away in 1988. Dad later married Vivian Bardsley who passed away in 1999.

The David Johnson Family Reunion (August 1999)

I am the sixth of seven children born to Howard and Magnhild Johnson. As a PK (preacher's kid) we lived in parsonages next to the church. Dad had to maintain the church, house and car, some of his skills rubbed off on us kids. I graduated from high school in Albert Lea, Minnesota and attended Technical School in Austin. I served four years with the Army, including three years in Frankfurt, Germany. In the late 1960s, Germany was divided between the free Western part and the Soviet-controlled East. West Germany was about the size of Minnesota, but with over sixty million people. Being so crowded, most people lived in apartments and traveled by streetcar, train, bus, bicycle or motorcycle. Personal automobiles were considered a luxury and highly taxed, as was gasoline.

After release from the Army in 1970, I lived with oldest brother Howard's family in Crystal. In 1971 brother Ed and I bought a house on Georgia Avenue in Brooklyn Park and invited our sister Carolyn to join us. Ed later went to college, married and never returned to Brooklyn Park

In addition to having a full-time job with a medical company, I volunteer with several organizations. I have served on the board of Roslyn Park Wesleyan Church in Fridley for more than twenty years. A personal relationship with Jesus is the only thing of eternal value. I am newsletter editor for the Twin Cities Creation Science Association. TCCSA educates people on how the Bible's account of creation is more logical and scientifically sound than evolution. I serve as co-chair of Senate District #47 Republicans because the U.S. Constitution gives individuals and states certain rights, privileges and responsibilities but also limits government. It is my belief that the federal government has usurped responsibilities the Constitution gave to states and individuals and has grown too large. I am Treasurer of the Brooklyn Historical Society and help with the Heritage Millennium Book project.

Submitted by David Johnson

AFTER THE 1929 TORNADO, Lavern Johnson found himself helping Edwin Nelson remove pieces of roof blown from Earle Brown School off the land on which their house now stands. Lavern grew up in Minneapolis and attended schools in this city. He joined the Civilian Conservation Corps (CCC) in Ely, Minnesota.

Marjorie attended a one-room school, first through eighth grades. She graduated from Winthrop High School and attended Mankato Business College. After college she worked for Office of Price Administration in Nicollet and Sibley Counties, and held office jobs in Minneapolis.

Lavern and Marjorie were married on June 27, 1948, at Bernadotte Lutheran Church east of Lafayette, Minnesota. They moved to a new home on Emerson Avenue North shortly after their marriage. Except for the years he spent in the army during World War II, Lavern worked for Mereen Johnson for forty-five and a half years. He headed the night crew.

The Johnsons have three children. Dennis is a lawyer and married to Shelly Arnold. Shelly is from Alabama and works for North Memorial Hospital as an IV therapist. Their children, Katie and Richie, are from Korea and are attending Junior and Senior High Schools in Hopkins.

Deanna (Johnson) Sjogren is a senior youth leader and a marketer in New Ulm, MN. Dennis, her husband, farms near Lafayette, MN. He runs Agra Placements Services in New Ulm. They have two children. Melissa married Curt Henderson. Their wedding took place forty-eight years after Lavern and mine at Bernadotte Lutheran Church. They now live and work in Bloomington, Minnesota. Eric farms at home, raising beef and sheep.

Wayne lives in north Minneapolis and has worked for U.S. West for twenty years. The Johnsons are members of Triune God on 59th and Humboldt Avenue North. Marjorie taught Sunday School, Crusaders and helped with the Women's Group. She organized quilters, who began making walker/wheel chair bags, and now they make napping quilts for Crest View and larger ones for Lutheran World Relief, Trinity First and Salvation Army. Marjorie has put in over four thousand hours at Crest View with Helping Hands. They organized the Earle Brown 4-H Club. Marjorie was leader for several years. Many of its members won prizes at both the county and state fair levels. They built a circular four-sectioned display at Brookdale Shopping Center.

Our block had about sixty children. Because we lived on a dead-end street, they played ball in the street. They had parades, amusement shows, dug holes in the driveway. They had small swimming pools during the hot weather in which to cool off.

A few years ago we joined "National Nights Out" organization. We all get together for a potluck supper at various houses.

We had tragedies in our neighborhood. Two-second graders drowned in the Mississippi River trying to retrieve mittens. That "unloaded" gun shot one senior boy. Another sad incident was Linda, married one Saturday, and three weeks later was buried because of heart problems

Submitted by Marjorie Johnson

Lavern and Marjorie Johnson

Neil and Mercedes Johnson

THE JOHNSONS first became associated with Brooklyn Center and Brooklyn Park in 1962 when Mercedes took a job as parish worker at the Lutheran Church of the Master in Brooklyn Center.

In 1963 Neil took a job as assistant engineer for the City of Brooklyn Park, which was just starting its own engineering department. Neil was attracted to the job by Mavis Huddle, secretary of Lutheran Church of the Master. Soon after, they moved their family from an apartment on 19th and Park Avenue in Minneapolis to the upstairs of a farmhouse on 85th and West Broadway (the Theresa Schmidt farm).

The Johnsons claim they were so poor prior to Neil's new job that they ate venison for weeks. Neil would come home from work with expectations of something different but the cooking odors betrayed the venison, even though it was in a different form.

Neil and Mercedes were married on January 19, 1963. They believe that day is the coldest day on record—29 degrees below zero. (Neil had always said that it would be a cold day before he gave up his bachelorhood) It was so cold people had to stay over with one of the families in that farming community of Providence, Minnesota.

Their lives throughout the thirty-six years of marriage have been very much church-oriented. They are still members of Lutheran Church of the Master even though they moved out to a small farm twenty-five miles west of church. Their children, grew up at this church, wouldn't let them change churches. Their decision to stay was based on their wanting them to stay active even though with choir, high-league, etc., they drive 60,000 miles or so each year.

Mercedes became Children's Ministries Director for a number of years and Neil served for many years on the church council and now retired as city engineer.

Neil and Mercedes Johnson and family

In 1999 all four children have married and have blessed Neil and Mercedes with twelve grandchildren.

Submitted by Neil Johnson

IN AUGUST OF 1919 John and Edna Santee and their four children moved to Brooklyn Township where they had purchased a nine-acre farm at 5520 Old Osseo Road, which extended east to Shingle Creek.

Mr. Santee, my father, a science teacher at North High School, earned $90 a month nine months of the year. With his farming background, what better way to supplement his income to provide a better living for his family? A large garden provided year around vegetables, chickens supplied eggs and Sunday dinners, and a cow was the source of our dairy needs.

I have fond memories associated with Bessie, our Jersey cow. In the summer we rode with my father in his Willys Knight touring car to a rented pasture on the shore of Twin Lake. He would sing favorite songs and identify wild flowers and birds while milking the cow. One of the saddest recollections of my childhood was the demise of Bessie. One summer our beautiful cow broke through the fence, not for "grass that was greener" but for fermented corn from a still. Corn mash was the basic ingredient for illegal liquor produced during Prohibition. Bootlegging was a lucrative business on secluded acreage that bordered Twin Lake adjacent to the pasture. Needless to say, our beloved Bessie died of alcohol poisoning.

The loss of our supply of milk, cream, cottage cheese, and butter increased the cost of food for our family. Mother increased the size of her flock of chickens and sold eggs to help pay the grocery bill. Fresh eggs in the winter sold for as much as ninety cents a dozen, the equivalent of three pounds of round steak.

Moving from Edina to Brooklyn Center was advantageous from a transportation standpoint. Father had a much shorter drive to North High School. In the winter when the road was impassable, he would ski two miles to 44th and Fremont Avenue North and board a streetcar for the ride to school on 18th and Fremont.

We children walked three-quarters of a mile to the one-room school. We received a good basic elementary school education. Mother, an education major, class of 1904, University of Minnesota, supervised our homework and made sure we passed the required state board examinations. When we graduated from the eighth grade, we went on to North High. The transition from a country school to a city school was difficult. When I entered 9th grade my parents moved to Minneapolis, and, in 1933, returned to their Brooklyn Center home where they resided for fifteen years.

I have a wonderful heritage of devoted parents who celebrated fifty-seven years of marriage. Father died at age eighty-six and mother lived to be ninety-eight. My brother, John, the eldest, and Wallace, the youngest, are deceased. My sister, Mary Santee Weise, lives in Oregon. Francis Johnston, my wonderful husband of sixty-four years and I, moved to ReaLife Cooperative Apartments in Brooklyn Park in August 1998. So you see I have come full circle in Brooklyn Township.

Submitted by Helen Johnston

Helen and Francis Johnston

Francis and Helen Johnston

Harvey and Marie Johnston

Harvey Johnston and Marie Fournier were married at Ascension Church in 1931. They moved to Brooklyn Center in 1954. Harvey's life work was Acme Metal Spinning Co., Inc. He started working at Acme at age seventeen. During the war years he put in many long days and weeks on war-related contracts. He retired as owner and president after forty-seven years there. Four of their five sons worked at Acme. Tom owns Acme today.

Marie worked at the telephone company before she married. When the children came she became a stay-at-home mom, caring for Tom, Lloyd, Larry, Phil, Lynn, Harv and Fran. Harvey and Marie were charter members of Our Lady of Victory Catholic Church in 1946. They were very active in the early years of building the church, school, rectory and convent. Both were active in various clubs, guilds, and circles. Harvey was a trustee for over thirty years, and ushered until five years before he died. Their five youngest children are OLV grade school graduates. Larry was in the first graduating class (1949).

Harvey and Marie were very proud of their home. When they bought it, the interior was unfinished. That was no problem for Harvey, as he was quite handy. With five children still at home they finished off the bedroom downstairs first, then a bath, amusement room, workroom and a room for the pool table. The lawn and yard were always beautifully manicured. In the winter you could see Harvey plowing snow, pipe in his mouth, the smoke mingling with the blowing snow!

Harvey and Marie Johnston with Harv, Phil, Lloyd, Tom, Fran, Lynne, and Larry

Marie enjoys raising dogs, canaries, and flowers. Quite often you will find a strange plant growing that Marie has come across while traveling, or from the woods at their lake place.

They were proud to have their twenty-seven grandchildren come to visit and stay at their home. They have been joined by forty-six great-grandchildren and three great-great-grandchildren.

Harvey had a wonderful spirit of sharing and generosity. One of his favorite charities was featured on the front page of the newspaper: Marie was advised to "hide the paper before Harvey sees it, or there won't be any retirement money left!" Their closest involvement to political activities, besides voting regularly, is displaying political signs in the yard, usually at the request of their good friend, Ernee McArthur.

Many changes have occurred in their forty-four years there. The farmhouse became a four-plex and Madsen Floral made way for townhouses. There is city water and sewer, and mailboxes are on the houses.

Excerpts from "Hero Speech" by Brandi Midkiff, age twelve: "My hero is my great-grandma Johnston. She is ninety years old and her husband, my great-grandpa, died about four years ago. They were married for sicty-eight years. Just because she is old doesn't mean she can't have fun; she can have fun! Even though there are bad times… she is still there for whoever needs a little talk. The qualities she has are: courageous, brave, honesty and kindness. She is a great role model for me and other kids."

Submitted by Lynne Johnston

ANDREW AND LYLIS JONES moved their family from the Mississippi Court in north Minneapolis to the present address, 54th and Penn Avenue North in Brooklyn Center, in April, 1955. Their children wanted to remain in the Our Lady of Victory parish and school. When they moved to Brooklyn Center they moved to a dead end street, with farmland across the street. There was no city water, no houses. They did not have junior or senior high schools in the area. Brookdale Shopping Center had not yet been established.

Their son Lyle, graduated from Patrick Henry High School. Mary Margaret graduated from Holy Angels, Eugene graduated from North High School and Ronald and Timothy graduated from DeLaSalle.

Andrew is now deceased, but before retirement he worked for Honeywell Local 1145 as Business Agent. After his retirement he worked as Sergeant-at-Arms at the House Chambers.

Lylis did much volunteer work at Our Lady of Victory Senior's group, the Funeral Lunch Committee, and the school lunch program. She also delivered communion to shut-ins and served communion at the five o'clock mass on Saturday evenings.

Andy and Lylis have five children, fifteen grandchildren and twenty-six great-grandchildren. Lylis is kept busy attending special functions for children, grandchildren, and great-grandchildren.

Submitted by Lylis Jones

Andrew and Lylis Jones

The Joyner Family

THE KOTTKES AND KRIENKES, mom's parents, came from Germany in 1873 and 1875. The Joyners and the Fosters came from England in the 1600s, to New York and then southern Minnesota. Their motivation to succeed and fully enjoy life was passed on to future generations.

In 1931 mom, dad and the three children moved from North Minneapolis to mom's (Krienke) family farm in Maple Grove. Mom's parents died leaving several minor children for their oldest child, my mother to raise. There were ten around the table during those Depression years. There was no electricity or running water. The water would be frozen in the bucket in the kitchen in the morning.

Mom and dad were active Farmer-Laborites, supporters of Floyd B. Olson. Mom had a political job in St. Paul during those years, and worked other jobs during the war. Mom supervised many volunteer activities in north Hennepin County, touching many people's lives. Gwen, my sister, said mom was ahead of her time. She wasn't fazed by a male-led society.

The Joyners: front, Gwen and Victoria; back, Lyn, Albert A., and Albert K.

Our family attended the Osseo Methodist Church. Dad was Sunday School superintendent, taught first aid during World War II, and served on Draft Board Number 25. He and mom were 4-H Club leaders.

In 1940 the family moved into Osseo. Dad worked in Minneapolis until 1943 when he started his silver plating and refinishing antiques business in our home and garage. In 1947 mom and dad moved the business to property purchased from the Hartkopf family at what is now Brooklyn Boulevard and Highway 81.

Albert, Gwendolyn and I (Lyn) graduated from Osseo High School and Hamline University. Our dad, Albert A., died in 1953.

Our family businesses included the Silver Shop, the Sentinel Newspaper in 1956; Joyners Bowling Lanes in 1957; Brooklyn Park Golf Course in 1963; Silver Springs Golf Course in Monticello in 1974; and Joyner Bowling Lanes in Monticello in 1976.

Our mom, Victoria, was Mayor of Osseo from 1954 to 1977, and sought Republican endorsement for Congress in 1956. She died in 1981.

Al was Brooklyn Park's township clerk for eight years. He was a charter member and president of the Brooklyn Park Lions and, along with me, served on the Minnesota Chamber of Commerce Board of Directors. He married Lorraine Connelly, a registered nurse from Arkansas. They had three children: Pam, Nancy and Jay, and six grandchildren: Julie Ann, Adam, Jenny, Joey, Tony and Nellie. Lorraine died in 1993 and Al died in 1994.

I was a member of the Brooklyn Park Planning Commission for four years, President of Brooklyn Park Chamber of Commerce and the North Suburban YMCA.

I am presently married to Bonnie Larson. I have five children from a previous marriage: Cynthia, Blake, Claudia, Heather and Dwight, and six grandchildren: Brandon, Ryan, Raymond, Olivia, Veronica and Gabriel. I also have four stepchildren and six step-grandchildren.

Gwen married Elmer Christensen, resides in California and is a retired diaconal minister in the United Methodist Church. They have four children.

Joyner's Die Casting and Plating Inc. continues to be a Brooklyn Park business in 1999. My son Dwight and I are partners in the business.

Submitted by Lyn (Orlyn) Joyner

My PARENTS, Joseph and Thora Kamedula, moved to 73rd and West River Road in 1936. We lived in a three-room house that had an outhouse and a pump. The cellar was located outside of the house and was made out of hard packed dirt. I remember many good times in our little house. It was a simple home, but it had everything we needed. We had our Saturday night baths in the old washtub. A pail and dipper stood on the cabinet in the kitchen.

The Kamedula Family

My Pa built a combination garage and shed for our animals out of lumber from an old railroad car. It had a dirt floor and a hayloft up above. We raised a cow, a goat, chickens, a pig, and a dog. We always had a garden of vegetables and berries. My first selling job was when I was five years old. Ma built a stand and we sold big juicy, ripe strawberries and raspberries for ten cents a box or two boxes for fifteen cents. The little house was sold in 1948 and was moved to Champlin on the West River Road. The house was added on to and still stands today. Dad built us a new home with two bedrooms and inside plumbing. Doris and I both attended Benson School on 73rd and West River Road, two houses away from ours. Across from the school was Yaklich's Store, later West River Road Foods.

Ma Kamedula with Betty and Doris in front of "The Little House" (1940)

The funniest thing that I remember was the day Ma went up into the attic to get some canning jars. The attic didn't have a floor so one had to hop from one rafter to another. My friend, Janice, and I were having toast and cocoa in the kitchen when we heard a big noise and all kinds of jars came down from the ceiling. When I looked up, there hung Ma by one arm and she was swinging from the rafters! My Mother was a little chubby, and every time she yelled her tummy would shake and more jars would fall down around Janice and me. We laughed so hard we were weak. Every time she yelled more jars would fall. I still laugh when I think about it.

The scariest time I remember was in the year 1941. I was in the second grade when I heard over the radio, that we were at war. I asked Pa what is war. He said it's when people kill each other. I remember the blackouts we had. A siren sounded and everyone had to put out their lights, and cars had to pull off the road and shut off the motor and lights. This was in case enemy planes came to bomb us. Everywhere it was so dark and quiet, I was scared.

My parents are deceased now, and the house has been sold. I drive by there once in a while and all the memories come back to me. A freeway now cuts through what once was a potato patch, and the gardens that used to be full of berries and flowers are gone, but the memories will always linger.

Submitted by Betty (Kamedula) George

David and Vi Kanatz Family

DAVID AND VI KANATZ were among the earliest settlers in the new Garden City addition of the Village of Brooklyn Center, which had been developed by the University of Minnesota. They raised their three children, Stephen, Kathy, and Timothy, in their new home on O'Henry Road.

The University connection was an important factor in this decision. They met at the University where Vi interviewed David for a job at the Student Activities Bureau. David continued his career at the Saint Paul Campus, stating that "working with students kept him going." David did his undergraduate work at the University of Wisconsin and pursued graduate studies at the University of Minnesota. Vi, a native Minnesotan, graduated from Washburn High School in Minneapolis and the University of Minnesota.

David and Vi Kanatz and friends

David and Vi almost immediately became involved in civic activities and were leaders in the newly formed Brooklyn Center DFL Party.

Vi was a driving force in developing a political consciousness in the community, particularly for women, and helped form the local chapter of the League of Women Voters in 1958. She served as the Brooklyn Center League of Women Voters' first president and later was appointed to the Minnesota League's Board of Directors. Vi claimed she "loved the League" as it provided a forum for women to study in depth, to discuss, and to act on issues in government. Her keen interest in equal rights led to appointments on the Brooklyn Center Human Rights Commission, the Charter Commission, the Minnesota Fair Employment Practice Commission and the State Commission Against Discrimination. Vi's commitment to change attitudes about discrimination, combined with her logical thinking and marvelous speaking ability, made her a strong voice on this issue. Brooklyn Center leaders called upon Vi to arbitrate a local racial discrimination issue.

In 1968 Vi started law school at the University of Minnesota and earned her law degree in 1971 with a specialty in Labor Relations. She spent the next eight years as a labor mediator for the State of Minnesota. Later, she was a partner in a private law practice in Saint Paul.

Vi always wanted to be a judge. She was an arbitrator in labor disputes and a judge in the Hennepin County Conciliation Court.

David's strong support for Vi's many activities was one of the greatest factors in her many achievements. David spent thirty-five years at the University of Minnesota. The last fifteen years before his retirement in 1986 were served as Assistant Director in the Office of Student Financial Aid.

David served as a Page for the Speaker of the House, Phil Carruthers, for the 1997-1998 legislative sessions. Presently, David is a volunteer for the Cancer Society, led into because Vi had cancer of the vocal cords. He served on the University of Minnesota Regents Candidates Advisory Council of the State Legislature from 1988 to the present.

David's hobbies are trout fishing, gardening, tennis, and is devoted to Vi. The Kanatz house is a house of many books. Vi is an avid reader.

Submitted by Eileen Oslund and Phyllis Owens

THE KEMPPAINEN FAMILY moved to 60th and Aldrich Avenue in Brooklyn Center on February 2, 1951. The house wasn't quite finished and we had to wait until spring to get the outside stuccoed but it was snug and warm and had all that room! We had four rooms, a bath and a full basement, a typical GI bungalow. There were only five other houses on the block and several capped basements when we moved in. We had no landscaping, no garages, no driveways, no trees, and no street except a dirt road that became a mud road in the spring. The families were busy the first years building garages, landscaping, putting in driveways and gardens.

That first year, 1951, there weren't any homes between Aldrich and Emerson. I would sit in my living room rocking my baby, or reading to my three-year old and watch the cars whizzing by on Highway 100.

We had two little girls, Karen and Gayle, when we moved to BC and that fall a little brother, Robert, was added to the family. As they grew, "all that room" got pretty crowded. We added a full dormer across the back making two bedrooms and a bath, room for everyone.

Before we had city water we relied on the well and worried what we would do if the electricity went out. We soon learned to fill the water jugs and the laundry tubs at first sign of a storm and not worry.

Children grow and soon ours were in school. Earle Brown was an excellent school and they got an excellent start there. Our oldest daughter, Karen, went to Jordan Jr. High for the 7th and 8th grade and then our own high school was finished. All three children got a good education at the high school where they participated in many extra-curricular activities as well.

Old Highway 100 was still there when the high school was built. Then the plans for the freeway came out with no plan for a safe crossing between Lyndale Avenue and Humboldt. We will always be grateful to our School Board and Superintendent Ralph McCartney for insisting vehemently that a bridge be built over the freeway at Dupont Avenue.

My husband, Arthur, an electrical engineer, worked at Northern States Power Co. for over thirty-seven years, retiring in 1987. For the last seventeen years he was General Manager of Substation Engineering and Construction. I spent my time being a home-maker doing volunteer work at the schools, working with Blue Birds and Cub Scouts. We both are active at Hope Lutheran Church.

Brooklyn Center has been a good place to live for nearly fifty years. It was a great place to raise a family. We always had good schools and a caring municipal government.

Submitted by Mrs. Arthur O. Kemppainen

The Kemppainen Family

Karen, Gayle, and Robert Kemppainen Children (1961)

The Ketter Family

I WAS RAISED near 57th Avenue and Lyndale Avenue North. We lived along the Mississippi River. We played on the river all summer. About a mile from our house was an island called Durnam Island. During the Depression four or more homeless men lived on the island in shacks made out of cardboard. They cooked chicken, pheasants, carrots and potatoes. We had no fear of them. We ate with them. Nobody knew where these men went in the winter.

The Scherer Brothers Lumber Company sawed logs across the street from our house and the lumbermen let us play in the large pile of sawdust; we did not know of all the dangers in those days. When we played on the river, my mother gave each one of us a whistle. When she whistled we answered her and she knew that all was well. We saw no danger in those days. When I was a little older we would paddle up north beyond Durnam Island. On the west side of the river, we found another small island and a house on it. We called it the "funny house." It was built with concrete and had a stairway leading to the second floor. It had only the one room. To get to the house you had to sit in an iron chair and glide over the river. During prohibition days there were parties up there at night. We never did figure out how the inebriated people returned to the shore.

Betty Ketter with canoe and trailer

When the Armistice Day storm on November 11, 1941, hit Minneapolis my dad was called by Earle Brown School to pick up the children and take them home. North of our place was an open area. There were eight or ten cars in the snow bank covered with very hard snow. It was so hard we were able to walk over the top, right up to the car windows. We cleaned off the windows and looked to see if anybody was inside. Most of the people had left their cars and walked two blocks back to the Babbling Brook, a dance hall and beer parlor. The place was full of people. It took three hours to dig cars out of the snow. It took three or four days for the snowplow to come and clear the street.

When the Earle Brown School was hit by a tornado, we all went to see the school. The roof and papers were all over. There was no school for a few days.

When Mrs. Fischer was a little blonde girl, she lived on 76th and Lyndale North. She would play on the riverbank. The Indians had a walking trail that they used to go from the north to the south. They always stopped and talked to her and touched her blond hair and called her "white angel." In those days no one was afraid of Indians.

My husband and I had two sons, Karl and Kenn Ketter. We ran a canoe business at 79th and Lyndale Avenue North.

Submitted by Betty Ketter

My husband, Kermit, and I (Marilyn) served in an orphanage in Beirut, Lebanon from 1959 to 1961. I was the nurse and Kermit taught and coached in the American Community School. While we were living there, Kermit's sister, Virginia Tesch, who was on the charter commission in Brooklyn Center, informed us of a new school being built and of the possibility of applying for a teaching position. When the application was sent, Ben Davidson, head of the school board, recognized the name and recommended Kermit to the board. Ben had been Kermit's boss at "Our Own Hardware", where he had worked while attending the University of Minnesota.

The Kermit Klefsaas Family

Kermit was hired as a Social Studies teacher and a track coach in the fall of 1961. He taught Brooklyn Center Junior High social studies, and Senior High physical education. He also coached golf, track, football and Junior High basketball for twenty-five years. He taught thirty-two years in all and retired in 1993. He was a sensitive and caring teacher. Since retirement he continues to drive bus charters for Brooklyn Center High School and enjoys the contacts with students and school personnel.

Kermit's sister, Virginia, told us of a home for sale in her neighborhood. The Sherwoods were selling their three-bedroom rambler. We looked at it in the evening and decided to buy it the following morning. We felt that God directed us to this house and neighborhood. We have had no regrets. Our family has lived in the present home at 5443 Oliver Avenue North since 1963.

Karin, Kermit, Kraig, Krista, and Kim Klefsaas

Our five children attended Earle Brown Elementary School and Brooklyn Center High School. They enjoyed school and its many activities, the Honor Society, music, art, sports and other activities. We felt these activities were as important as their scholastic accomplishments, all working together to help them become well-rounded adults.

Our oldest daughter Kim, taught for ten years at Earle Brown School. She and husband, Terry Westra, live in Lexington, MN., with their three children.

Krista is an artist. She and her husband, Tom Ottoson, live in Robbinsdale with their three children. Kermit is an Assistant Principal in the Staples-Motley School system. He and his wife, Lorna, have two children. Kraig teaches Special Education in the Mankato East High School. He and his wife, Talarie, have two children. Karin works for a homebuilder and lives with her husband, Aaron Schulz, in Lakeville.

As a family, we have attended Northbrook Alliance Church in this community for over thirty-six years. We served the church in many capacities, and as the children grew up, they also took responsibility to help and serve others.

The faith has been an important part of our lives. We have tried to live in a way that reaches others with the love of Christ, and to give Him the glory for anything that has been accomplished in or through our lives.

Submitted by Marilyn Klefsaas

Matthew Klohs

WHILE GROWING UP in Brooklyn Park, Minnesota I met one person who stood out from everyone else. The person that I am talking about is Jesse "the body" Ventura.

My reason for knowing Jesse so well is because I was best friends with his son, Tyrel. As life went on Mr. Ventura became a coach and an inspiration at Champlin Park High School, at Champlin, Minnesota. If there is one thing I know about Jesse it's that whatever he does or whatever he is a part of, it is going to be the best and done right. He used to tell son, Tyrel, and me stories about his Navy Seal experience and how there was no room for error. He said that is one of his reasons he has always strived to be the best. I have learned along with his son and many of our friends that no matter what happens don't let anyone get to you. If someone doesn't like you or says stuff about you, don't let it bother you. If you let someone get to you they'll be able to razz you for the rest of your life.

Jesse was about standing up for not only yourself but for anything you believe in. "The Body" is proving this to the entire state of Minnesota right now. Nobody thought he had a shot at winning the 1998 election to become Governor. He believed in himself and his politics, knowing the people of Minnesota would do the right thing and put him in office.

There are many things that Jesse has done and will do, but there is one thing that everyone has to remember, he started in Brooklyn Park.

Submitted by Matthew Klohs

IN THE SPRING OF 1947 my uncle heard my husband and I were looking for a home. At that time Ted and I had two sons, Dick, three years old and Ted, Jr. who was one.

Uncle Joe suggested a small home at 9110 North Irving Avenue. It had two acres and a nice little building, all for the price of twelve hundred dollars. Even my mother thought it was a great idea, and loaned us the money to make the purchase. So off to Brooklyn Park we went, as innocent and trusting as the day was long. We took everything in stride, even when it was discovered that the well only gave two pails of water at a time and then we had to wait until more water accumulated.

When Ted and I moved on to the land, there was high, dry prairie grass surrounding the house. We had no garbage service so we had to burn it. One day as I was burning garbage a spark escaped and very quickly turned into a wild fire. I grabbed a rug and started to beat out the fire. As quickly as I blotted out the fire in one area it started up someplace else. It was a good thing I had a strong heart and could move fast. I was able to put out the fire but after that, believe me, I was very cautious with fire.

We didn't have a car, so we used the bus that ran on West River Road. Telephone service didn't reach our home for several years. All in all we were quite isolated.

In the next four years we had two more wonderful sons, Dennis and Joey. When our boys were growing up they had many live pets—goats, rabbits, dogs, cats and little

Ted and Marian Klohs Family

Jennifer, Matthew, Judy, and Joe Klohs

chicks. They were familiar with all the wild creatures that roamed the land. They steered clear of one thing, snakes.

All of the boys attended Riverview School, then on to Anoka Junior and Senior High School. Dick graduated from the University of Wyoming. Ted, Dennis and Joey graduated from the University of Minnesota. During their school years they were very active in sports and in the summer they worked on potato farms. The hard work in the potato fields made them realize an education was necessary.

Our sons are now all married with families of their own and because they enjoy nature, they now live by open space and water: Dick by Cedar Island Lake, Ted by Rice Creek, Dennis by Lake Minnetonka and Joey by the Mississippi River.

Ted died in 1987. I still live in the same house. The little 12 x 24 house has been built onto four times. I keep busy volunteering, at Eastman Nature Center, Como Park, Brooklyn Historical Society, and the Girl Scouts.

"Life goes on and on and on."

Submitted by Marian Klohs

William Knight Family

WILLIAM KNIGHT was born in England in 1815. He married Bridget in 1845 in Machias, Maine. They had nine children: five born in Machias and four in Minnesota. They were some of the first settlers in this area, homesteading on the east shore of Twin Lake in 1856 (north of the Minneapolis city limits). In 1866, he added eighty acres to his acreage in the vicinity that is now the flagpole on Victory Memorial Drive. The land was used for truck farming.

William M. Knight, born in 1850, son of William and Bridget, was a farmer, stonemason, well digger, worked in the lumbering business for fourteen years, and from 1906-1910, was a Hennepin County Commissioner.

William M. Knight married Mary Ann (Fewer) from St. Anthony. Their children who survived are Walter, Knight, Everett, Otis, Richard E., Willis, Eleanore, and Mae. They grew up on a twenty-acre Brooklyn Center farm. The Knights owned the farm from 1856-1925. The Twin Lake School (now the Alano building on Brooklyn Blvd) was built on part of the farm. The old farmhouse is still in use at 49th and Washburn Avenues North, just a few feet inside the Minneapolis city limits.

The Knights: front, Willis, Otis, and Everett; back, Clement, Walter, and Richard E.

Their son Walter was Deputy Clerk of District Courts. Clement when he retired was Vice President and General Manager of the St. Paul Store of Maurice L. Rothschllds, Young Quinlan. Everett was a Minneapolis Fireman, Otis worked for Minneapolis Gas Company, and Willis worked for a furnace company.

Richard E. Knight was born in Brooklyn Center in 1879 and died in 1956. He married Ethel M. Fleming and they had five sons: Leo, Richard R., Earl, Willard, and Frank. They raised their family in north Minneapolis. Richard E. was the chief accountant for the Minneapolis Gas Company and retired in 1935.

As a young man, Richard E. Knight, with F. D. Huff as publisher, were owners of the first regularly published Brooklyn Center newspaper called *The Sun*. There were four persons on the staff of the four-page paper: Knight, Huff, Dan Libby and W. S. Randal.

The paper was first printed October 21, 1898 from Camden Place and the price was three cents. They proclaimed a subscription goal of 1,500 copies at 3-cents, but one month later set the actual number of subscribers at 100 for 1-cent a copy.

The Sun knew how to boost its community. A story in the 1898 Christmas edition read: "Howe's immense auditorium was overwhelmingly crowded with the elite and conspicuous aristocracy for the multitudinous labyrinths of the prosperous town of Brooklyn Center, to witness the marvelous animatography, presented by the Novelty Company Saturday evening Nov. 13."

The *Chicago Tribune* recognized The Sun by printing: "… It is certainly a great thing for its size." *Brooklyn Center News* in the November 1898 newspaper was as follows: "Our Reporter in this section has been ill with a tumor on his big toe. He reports that the people are as sleepy as usual and not any news to be found."

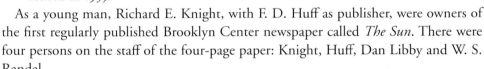

Information from Mrs. Richard R. (Ollie) Knight, age 90,
and Mary Ann (Knight) Anderson, age 80

MY HUSBAND, CARL, AND I (EVE KOEGL) were looking for a house that was large enough for our family of five, as well as one we could afford. We had three children, Charles, Mary and Michele. We found our house in Brooklyn Center on Colfax Avenue in the Bellvue Addition. We purchased our unfinished house from Russell Gilbertson and his wife. Mr. Gilbertson was constable in Brooklyn Center and one of our neighbors, William Gallien, had previously been mayor.

The gas for heating our house was piped in from Bryant Avenue. Years later the gas line was put down Colfax Avenue as well. Our streets were dirt and we had a cinder driveway. Now everything is blacktopped. We didn't have cement curbing on our street until 1998. We had our own well over one hundred feet deep, a sand point for watering and our own three-tank septic system. No city water and sewer back then! Our taxes were $66 when we moved in; now they are sixteen times greater.

The buses didn't run into Brooklyn Center and when they did, we'd still get off at 52nd and Bryant Avenue to avoid the extra nickel charge for the bus crossing into the suburbs. There weren't any grocery stores in Brooklyn Center then. We had our groceries delivered from Ruff Brothers in north Minneapolis. Shopping was done downtown; no suburban shopping centers back then. There was much excitement when a major shopping center (Brookdale) was coming to Brooklyn Center.

When we moved to Brooklyn Center our older children, Charles and Mary, were transferred from Jenney Lind Elementary to Earle Brown Elementary with the unpleasant foreboding of being "kept back" at the end of the school year "because Minneapolis Public Schools were so far behind Earle Brown." I explained that I was a teacher and if they gave me the qualifying factors they needed to keep up with their classmates, I would tutor them. They passed. In the fall Our Lady of Victory Catholic School opened and we decided our children would attend there. We looked forward to Brooklyn Center having a high school even though our children attended parochial high schools.

Earle Brown Farm, with its equipment, carriages, horses, buildings and even the animal cemetery, were all excursions for our family.

The Civic Center was the best. The grandchildren all enjoyed swimming there. I have taken "Exercise and Dance" and progressed to "Low Impact Aerobics" for approximately twenty years with Bev Wilson as our faithful teacher. I also have belonged to Brooklyn Center Women's Club almost since its beginning except for a two-year break.

Carl passed away January 28, 1985, and I have managed to continue to live in my home ever since. I appreciate the many improvements and amenities from the City of Brooklyn Center and hope to live in my house until I die.

Submitted by Eve Koegl

The Carl and Eve Koegl Story

Eve and Carl Koegl

The Paul and Cindy Kopacz Family

PAUL KOPACZ was raised in north Minneapolis and is a 1968 graduate of De LaSalle High School. Cindy Hill is from Brooklyn Center, and a 1970 graduate of Brooklyn Center High School. We were married in 1974.

In 1976 we moved to Brooklyn Park and lived in the old homestead of Victoria and Paul, my great-grandparents. This house was built in 1921 on twelve acres of land.

Peaceful, good neighbors, acres between houses, country atmosphere right in the city, and lots of room to plant beautiful gardens. Our children loved working in the garden and riding on the tractor with Grandpa Harry.

We have two children. Jason was born in 1977 and Elizabeth was born in 1979. Our children have been fortunate enough to be raised on their great-grandfather's land. Jason and Beth went to elementary school at Monroe Elementary in Brooklyn Park. Both graduated from Brooklyn Center High School.

Beth, Jason, Cindy, and Paul Kopacz

In 1983 we built a new house next to the original homestead. Jason's heart was broken when the land was divided up. He just couldn't understand why Grandpa couldn't keep the tractor and all the land to plant the gardens every year. Beth just wanted to put baby oil on our dog, George, and suntan under the elm tree with him. They adjusted to a small back yard garden and sunscreen.

We continue to support the great communities of Brooklyn Center and Brooklyn Park. This really is home to us. We have tried to teach our children that family and community are important.

Submitted by Paul Kopacz

MY PARENTS, PAUL AND VICTORIA KOPACZ, purchased land on 79th Avenue North in 1914. I was born in 1915 and I had a brother, John, born in 1912, who passed away at the age of six from the outbreak of influenza in 1918.

My dad worked for Archer Daniels during the winter months. At that time, work was only seasonal. In the summer he farmed his land in Brooklyn Park and took his produce to the Farmers Market. Truck gardening was necessary to augment their living. Prices of produce were fluctuating. The first crop of melons would bring $5.00 a bushel the first few days and by the end of the week it would be $1.00 a bushel.

In 1922 my father built a house on the land with the help of one of his neighbors. He continued to farm ten acres until he passed away in 1945. My mother rented the land out for farming. She continued to live in the farmhouse until she passed away in 1969. The old farmhouse is still standing. My son, Paul, lived there with his family and now has a new house on part of the original homestead. My grandchildren are being raised on their great-grandfather's land, which since has been named Victoria Acres. It is hard to believe how the area has grown. Even in 1975 this area was still like being in the country. We farmed a couple of acres, rode my tractor and sold our produce. One mile away it was residential. My daughter Kathy and her family also live in Brooklyn Park.

I attended Benson School, which was located at the northeast corner of Lyndale and 73rd Avenue North in Brooklyn Village. This school was grades one through eight. The school had two classrooms.

I remember those snowy winter days, blowing snow all the time. Once my dad went to work on Monday and couldn't get home until Thursday night. He was only fourteen miles away, but with so much open space, the snow drifted over.

South of 79th Avenue there were three farms. The Theorin brothers owned one. They raised mostly potatoes, which they shipped out of Camden. This farm would have been across the street from the now Monroe Elementary School.

Fred Peterson owned the next farm, also a potato farmer. He loved horses and used them in all of his farm work. He had one special horse that he used for showing. Mr. Peterson also shipped potatoes from Camden. Sometimes when Lyndale was too muddy he would use four horses to pull the load of potatoes to Camden. Fred loved to have barn dances. He had them in the spring and fall when the hay was gone.

Then there was Fischer who had land at the southwest corner of 77th and Lyndale North. He was an onion grower and he was the only farmer who owned an onion-topping machine.

Submitted by Harry Kopacz

The Paul and Victoria Kopacz Family

John and Harry Kopacz

Marsh and Dee Korvela Family

WHAT SEEMS LIKE FOREVER to a youngster is but a blip in time as we become older. Remember the "olden days" back in the early 1960s when there were more fields than houses in and around Osseo. My friends from Brooklyn Center who were bussed to Lincoln Jr. High School in North Minneapolis talked about going to work on the "truck farm" during the summer. The kids in North Minneapolis hadn't an inkling as to what a truck farm was. I remember a friend expressing her desire to work at her dad's auto parts and salvage shop before she'd ever work on a "truck farm"! Most students living on the North side never ventured into the country. No reason to, because all their activities were tied up in the big city.

I met Dee during my senior year at high school. She was quite a catch! I liked her spirit from the start. She was "street-smart" but with a certain innocence about her. We rode up to Osseo on my motorcycle, just to get away from the hustle and bustle of the city. Little did we know that some day we would be married and living in the area.

Marcel, Marsh, Karlin, and Dee
Korvela

We were married in 1968, lived in Brooklyn Center by Zayre's Shoppers City for a year and then moved to South Minneapolis. Ten years later we moved to our new home in Brooklyn Park. Not being able to have children, we adopted Marcel and Karlin when they were babies. What a great life-changing experience! We wanted the most for our sons and I'm glad we were able to provide it for them. Dee became active in the community because of them. Both Marcel and Karlin were and still are active in sports. Dee poured her energies into them and their friends within the community. It has always been very important to our family that we have close relations with friends across culture lines and she has put her heart and soul into her involvement by supporting the youth sports programs in Brooklyn Park. She became involved with the Cooper Brothers, Lerris and Lamar, when they put together the "Brooklyn Park Bulls" AAU basketball team. This team of mainly minority youth was good! They took second in state the first year and went on to Memphis to play in the nationals. We wouldn't say that the parents for this team were wealthy folks; they just had a strong desire to see their sons earn the opportunities they deserved. Dee and her comrade team moms raised the funds within a few weeks to send them to Memphis on a first class trip.

One of the most challenging and interesting experiences for our family was to support Dee in her run for the House of Representatives during the 1998 election. It was a very positive experience getting to know the pulse of our community. It gave us good insight into local politics.

Brooklyn Park is where the hopes and dreams of our people beat to the rhythm of a vibrant community.

Submitted by Marsh and Dee Korvela

THE KRAGNESS FAMILY moved to Brooklyn Center in 1967. The family consisted of John (Ron) and Myrna, their children, Glen, Karen, Laurie, and Cindy plus three foster children. Ron was an over-the-road truck driver, and Myrna was a stay-at-home Mom. With seven children, the house looked like a mansion compared to the small rambler in Brooklyn Park where we had previously lived. We were all excited about the big, beautiful, white house on the corner. It was especially exciting for me, as I did not drive at that time. Shopper's City was across the street. The doctor and dentist were only two blocks away, and Brookdale Shopping Center was within walking distance. I was in heaven.

The Kragness Family

Foster care was an ever-changing situation for us. Through the years there were fifty-plus, mostly teen girls, which lived with us. Park Center High School had many graduates from our household.

Steven was born in 1969. When he started school in 1974, I decided to go back to school myself and enrolled at North Hennepin Community College. It had been many years since I had worked in an office and wanted to upgrade my skills for full-time employment. I wouldn't know until many years later what a wise decision that was.

Ron continued to drive truck and finally purchased his own semi. His dream was to be an owner-operator. He was able to live his dream for a few years anyway. He had a heart attack on December 26, 1979, and passed away on December 29th.

After twenty-three years of marriage, I now had to make many adjustments for my family and myself. Two of our children were in the Marine Corp., the two youngest, plus a foster child, were at home. It was my doctor's advice that led me to get involved with my city. I was having difficulty with the adjustment. He told me to get busy, volunteer, find things I was interested in and get involved. That led me to the Earle Brown Days Committee.

I met the nicest folks and felt I was able to return a little of my time for the benefits my family received while living in Brooklyn Center. I was appointed to the Charter Commission.

The Kragness Family: front, Laurie, Myrna, and Karen; back, Greg, Cindy, Glen, and Steve

In 1993 the Brooklyn Taxpayers Association contacted me and asked if I would be interested in running for City Council. After much discussion with my family and close friends I agreed to run for Mayor, never thinking that I would actually win. What an exciting time that was, so much to learn and do. With support from the Brooklyn Center Taxpayers Association and my family, we were successful. The first year was very stressful with changes in city management and council members. I'm thankful to say things have been going smoothly since.

On April 25th, 1998, I married Theodore Kauth, a childhood friend.

In November 1998 I was re-elected to another four years. I am looking forward to exciting changes for our city.

Submitted by Myrna Kragness

The Krambeer Family

OUR FAMILY ARRIVED in the Brooklyns in 1987. Our first residence was on 68th Avenue North in Brooklyn Center.

Rich Krambeer began working for a law firm in the area in 1985 and the daily commute from Apple Valley was just too much. We have now lived on Zealand Avenue North in Brooklyn Park since 1990. Our family includes seven children: Joe, who lives in Plymouth; Sarah, who lives in Minneapolis with her son Joshua Kauck; Matt, who lives in Plymouth and Adam, Katherine, Rachel and Mary.

My parents, Howard and Agnes Krambeer (both now deceased), were natives of New Ulm, Minnesota. Their German ancestors immigrated to the United States in the mid-1800s, settling in the New Ulm area.

The Rich and Marilyn Krambeer Family

About 1940 my parents moved to Saint Paul, where I was later born. I am the youngest of six children. I attended St. Agnes Grade and High Schools, obtained a degree in Political Science from the University of St. Thomas in Saint Paul, and a law degree from the University of Minnesota Law School.

Dr. Fred and Charlotte Hass, my parents, were born and raised in North Minneapolis. They lived in Jordan, Minnesota, when I, Marilyn, was born. Eventually they settled in Golden Valley, Minnesota, where they are today. I am the second of five children. I attended public schools in Golden Valley and received a degree in Elementary Education from Augsburg College.

My paternal ancestors immigrated to the United States from Germany and Sweden, respectively, in the mid-1800's, eventually settling in the Zimmerman, Minnesota area. Both of my maternal grandparents immigrated to the United States from Norway in the early 1900's. They first met on a boat coming over from Norway as teenagers. Years later, they married and raised their family in Minneapolis.

Rich has been an attorney since 1974. I served in the United States Army 1970-1972, including duty in Viet Nam with the 173rd Airborne Brigade. I was elected to the Minnesota Legislature in a special election in December 1991, only to be defeated in the general election in November 1992. Marilyn has been an elementary school teacher, licensed daycare provider, and registered nursing assistant.

Our family served as emergency shelter home foster parents for adolescents in Dakota County, caring for over 100 children during the years between 1981 and 1987. We have provided respite foster care for a mentally challenged high school student in Hennepin County from 1991 through 1999.

Our children have attended schools at Edgewood Elementary, North View Junior High, and Osseo Senior High. Rich has served on the Osseo School Board since 1993, including a term as Chair.

Our family has been active in North Heights Lutheran Church for many years. Another long-time family interest has been soccer. Our children have been involved at many levels, from park and recreation to traveling, high school and the state and national Olympic Development Program.

Submitted by Rich and Marilyn Krambeer

DON GREW UP on a farm ten miles southwest of Strasburg, North Dakota. He went to a one-room country school and Strasburg High School. His parents, Ludwig, and Odelia, moved to Strasburg when he was a sophomore. He went to St. John's University in Minnesota. In 1962 he graduated with a BA in biology and natural science.

After college graduation, Don and two of his friends went to a dance at Herried, South Dakota. Nothing exciting was happening, so we went to a Centennial celebration in Hosmer, South Dakota. While at the carnival it started to rain so we started back to our car. At a street crossing, a car with six girls and one guy stopped at a stop sign. They asked them for a ride. They didn't get one, but later saw them at a dance. Whoopee John's band was playing. Don asked Sylvia to dance. The girls were nursing students who were out with a local friend. Sylvia had a date that night with a medical student but he never came. Later it was discovered that Sylvia's date hit a cow on a South Dakota road and never made it to the dance. For me, the cow was in the right place at the right time. I ended up taking Sylvia back to her friend's house. The rest is history.

Sylvia, daughter of Fred and Lydia Boeshans grew-up on the family farm in rural Beulah, North Dakota. She went to a two-room country school for the first eight years and graduated from Beulah High School. She earned a BSN degree from Jamestown College in North Dakota.

Don and Sylvia were married in 1964 in Minneapolis, where Sylvia was a pediatrics RN at North Memorial Medical Center. Don taught high school science in North Dakota between 1962 and 1969, taking fifteen months off to earn a MST degree in 1967 from the University of North Dakota.

In 1969 we moved to Brooklyn Center with our children Steve, Doug and Debbie. Don took a job at Target Stores as a programmer trainee and was promoted several times. His first supervisor ended up being one of his programmer analysts before he left Target as a project manager.

Together Don and Sylvia spearheaded the formation of the Twin Cities NFP Center, Inc., in 1975 where Don served as the Executive Director while Sylvia volunteered her time there. Meanwhile, Kurt, Paula and Mary were added to the family.

In 1987 we started a home-based family business remanufacturing toner cartridges for laser printers. Steve, Doug, Debbie and Kurt all worked full time for at least one year in that business. When the business took up too much space, we leased space in an industrial complex.

In 1994 Don was elected to the State Senate. He was named "Legislator of the Year" in his first year by ABC Minnesota. He lost the election in 1996 with the President Clinton sweep.

Don now works in preventive health care with Rexall Showcase International. After the children were grown, Sylvia started working in the hospitality industry using one of her special gifts, hospitality.

Submitted by Don and Sylvia Kramer

Don and Sylvia Kramer Family

Sylvia and Don Kramer

The Jim and Shirley Krautkremer Family

SHIRLEY AND I moved to Brooklyn Park from Omaha, Nebraska in 1964. I was born in Jordan, Minnesota and moved to Papillion, Nebraska in 1942. Shirley was born in Storm Lake, Iowa and moved to Omaha in 1953. Both of us worked at Mutual of Omaha where we met. We were married in June of 1957 when I returned from the Army. I received my college degree during six years of night school while holding a full time job.

We have four children. All graduated from Osseo High School. Daughter Julie married John Sirianni of Eau Claire, Wisconsin, where they now live. They have two children. Dan lives in Plymouth, Minnesota. Paul married Tammy Johnson of Brooklyn Park, Minnesota. They live in Champlin, Minnesota. They have three children David

was married to Katie Barnhill until her untimely death. He then married Amy Heiskala and they live in Brooklyn Park, Minnesota. They have three children.

Julie, Dan, and David graduated from the University of Minnesota. Paul graduated from Brown Institute. Julie works at home. Dan works at Boston Scientific as a technician. David is a CPA working at CP Railroad. Paul works at Greentree Financial as a computer specialist manager.

Shirley did not work outside of the house until the children were in school. She worked at various part-time jobs until she started working at Medtronic, Inc. in Brooklyn Center. She worked there for 21 years until she retired. I worked at Sister Kenny Foundation, Midland Cooperatives and for the State of Minnesota. I also had my own computer and consulting business for a period of time. I worked in the computer business for most of my career.

The Krautkremer Family

I worked on the Transportation Advisory Board of the Metropolitan Council as a charter member and served for seventeen years. I was appointed to the Metropolitan Council by Governor Arne Carlson and served for two years. I served as Mayor of Brooklyn Park for eighteen years (1972-1989).

While I was Mayor, I created the Brooklyn Park Community Organization, with members representing all Brooklyn Park community organizations. I worked for twelve years to get approval for the Boone Avenue interchange.

Brooklyn Park Community Organizations took over the Tater Daze Festival when the Jaycees were looking for another sponsor. The Krautkremer family and some young friends did most of the work. Bill Schreiber donated many pounds of potatoes to be used as prizes the first years. The Park Department had to tow the trucks with rides to the site because they had problems.

We spent hundreds of hours to get approval for the 610 Highway and bridge, and Highway 252.

Brooklyn Park received the designation as one of the best-planned communities in the United States for its development policies. I received recognition as WCCO Good Neighbor and was Knighted by the King of the St. Paul Winter Carnival.

Submitted by James Krautkremer

DAN MET SUSAN GROVES at Brooklyn Center High School and found that her family lived just down the street. Dan's older brother, Jim was a friend of Susan's oldest brother, Rik. She is the daughter of Hollis (deceased) and Arlene (Lommen) Groves who moved into the 55th Avenue residence at 2312 in 1954. The Groves family moved in with Richard, January 1947, Barbara, April 1948, and Susan, November, 1953. A son, Kevin was born in July 1960. All the children graduated from BCHS. Dan and Susan were married in 1972 and lived in Duluth for three years while Dan finished his tour with the U.S. Air Force, as a ground to air electronics technician. They moved to Minnetonka as Dan pursued his education in Bio-Medical Electronics, purchased their first home on 44th Avenue in North Minneapolis in 1978, and then purchased the family home in Brooklyn Center in June 1982.

The Dan and Susan Krekelberg Family

Dan is the Director of Engineering and Housekeeping at Saint Cloud Hospital. Susan is Operations Manager at Bearcom Wireless Worldwide. Dan and Susan were blessed with three children: Timothy (March 1977), Christian (February 1980), and Kelly (September 1982). The family is involved in music with barbershop quartets, church choirs, high school band and choir, as well as musical productions at BCHS.

Tim and Chris are graduates of BCHS and Kelly is in the junior class. Tim is married to Jill (Weathers) from Santa Anna, Texas and they have a daughter, Madeline, two years and a son, Hayden, two months. They live in Misawa, Japan, where Tim serves as a Russian Linguist for the U.S. Air Force and continues to pursue his education at the International School there. Christian works as a Security Officer for Talisman and is pursuing his career in Law Enforcement in Alexandria, MN. Kelly hopes to pursue Musical Theater when she leaves high school and is currently singing with a professional girls choir, Partners in Praise.

Tim, Christian, Kelly, Dan, and Sue Krekelberg

Submitted by Susan Krekelberg

The Warren and Connie Krekelberg Family

WARREN JAMES KREKELBERG was born in January 1923 and raised in North Minneapolis by Joseph and Dora (Pouliot) Krekelberg. His father worked for the Soo Line Railroad and met Dora in Hamel, MN. They were married and had five children: Jules (deceased), Betty, Dolores, Warren, and Joyce. All, but Warren, still reside in the Metropolitan area. Warren attended North High School. He joined the Reserves in January 1940, but before he had a chance to make any decisions about his future, he was called to active duty in the U.S. Navy, at seventeen years of age. He was on the Sands Destroyer when Pearl Harbor was bombed and served in the South Pacific Islands, New Zealand, and Australia during World War II.

Constance Helen Manske was born in August 1922 and also grew up in North Minneapolis with her parents Reinhardt and May (Pettit) Manske and two brothers, Donald and Tom, and one sister, Barbara (deceased). The Manske household was always filled with many additional foster children. Connie attended North High School and was a close friend of the Krekelberg sisters. She soon met their handsome brother and became his wife.

Warren and Connie Krekelberg

In 1946 Warren and Connie were married and lived in University Village while Warren pursued his education. During these years, two children were added to the family: Warren James, Jr. (Jim) in May 1947 and Joseph in July 1948. They moved to other locations in Minneapolis and by the time they heard about the new housing development going up by the Earle Brown Farm, they had added two new sons to the family: Daniel in March 1952 and Kevin in January 1954.

They officially moved into their rambler at 2201 55th Avenue North in 1955. Warren landed a job at Ford Motor Company and Connie worked for Red Owl on 63rd and Osseo Road and later for Kroger Grocery on Penn and Lowry, leaving for work as soon as Warren arrived home from work.

In July 1963, a girl, Colleen was added to the family and the boys were already approaching graduation from Brooklyn Center High School. Jim, Dan and Kevin were known at BCHS for their participation in choirs and musicals and Joe for his participation and talent in gymnastics. Colleen attended and graduated from Totino-Grace High School. The family faithfully attended Our Lady of Victory Catholic Church, where Warren sang in the choir and served as a soloist. Music was prevalent in their lives with the boys singing in choirs, Colleen playing the piano and Warren and Dan singing for years together in the Minneapolis Commodore Chorus and in a barbershop quartet called "Sounds of Music."

Connie died in February 1980 of cancer. Warren retired from the Ford Motor Company in 1984. He married Karen Lund from St. Cloud, and they now live in Green Valley, Arizona, where they spend most of their time singing and playing golf. All the children are married now. Jim and Dianne have two boys and live in Shoreview; Joe and Annie have four boys and two granddaughters and live in Blaine; Kevin and Lauren have two children, by Lauren's previous marriage, and two grandchildren and live in Alpine, California; Colleen and Chris have four daughters, one from Chris's previous marriage, and live in Zimmerman.

Submitted by Susan Krekelberg

Mom didn't know too much about the Redemptorist Priests, but she knew she wanted her church closer to home. Going to church "at the Priests' house" was very different than going to Our Lady of Victory. Each week more people came to Mass; everyone knew the money collected was for building a church.

Mom was on the committee to determine how to raise money for the new church; a long-standing idea was born! A five-year-old was intrigued by the talk of a "Fun Fair"; I was for anything that sounded like fun—the fishing booth was my favorite, and the doll I got was perfect! And the great music of the Happy Wanderers that had everyone dancing was wonderful. We were there Thursday night putting up booths, and each day and night until Sunday night when they announced the winner of the new car!

When there was enough money and the church was built, Mom took us to the corner-stone sign, stating, "This church wasn't built in 1959. Buildings don't build or make churches, people do. This church was built in those committee meetings and every week in Mass at the priests' house." She meant that "we can't do everything, but we have the power to do something." It is our responsibility to make a difference.

Being seven years old and knowing "what I wanted" was sometimes a problem for Mom and Dad. Mom was a Den Mother for Cub Scout Troop #454 and couldn't be a Brownie Leader. Even though Dad didn't know the leader, he agreed to let me try Brownies. One day he was furious. "How could a leader let a seven-year-old child walk five miles in a blizzard because I was forty-five minutes late, stuck in traffic?!" All I could think of was losing all my pencils walking over Shingle Creek! I still think there might be a troll under the bridge, like in the story of "Billy Goats Gruff."

My parents' dilemma: how could they give me the same sense of accomplishment that the Cub Scouts gave my brothers? Who could they trust? Mom brought this up to Mavis Huddle at a Brooklyn Park Council Meeting two years later, and she suggested a solution they could live with. Dad and Mom agreed, there wasn't anyone who could take better care of me (away from home) than Ardis Fiebiger.

Ardy and Pete Fiebiger had been involved in 4-H Club work for several years. She built a group of kids who really looked out for each other and had fun. There wasn't much that Ardy or Pete couldn't help us to learn: self-accomplishment and pride in workmanship were the cornerstones of all projects, whether for meetings, County or State Fair exhibits.

Edwin and Mary Kruse's Wedding

These lessons have helped me be successful in my life. After my Anoka High School graduation I went on to become a computer programmer and then a business analyst. I'm very grateful for my loving Christian family and many good, dear friends.

Submitted by Rose Mary Kruse

The Tony and Joanne Kuefler Family

TONY AND JOANNE KUEFLER came from Wadena, Minnesota farm families. Tony served in the U.S. Army during the Korean Conflict, working as a Security and Legal Clerk at Fort Richardson, Alaska. They were married in June 1957, when Tony was a student at Dakota Business College in Fargo, North Dakota.

Following graduation in 1958, Tony began his thirty-five year career with Northern States Power, as an accountant in Fargo, North Dakota. In 1963 Tony transferred to the Minneapolis corporate headquarters, where he spent twenty-five years, working as a Computer Programmer, Systems Analyst, Supervisor, Manager and General Manager in Computer Systems. He spent his last five years as Northern States Power Project Manager, in Eau Claire, Wisconsin.

The Tony and Joanne Kuefler Family

Joanne and Tony raised five children. Joanne was a dedicated, stay-at-home mother until all five children finished high school, and then she became a merchandiser for American Greeting Cards. Joanne, a super bargain shopper, also has skills in haircutting, wallpapering, oil acrylic painting and gardening, in addition to having excellent listening skills.

As of this writing in 1999, Joe, his wife, Pam and their six children live in Ferron, Utah; Steve, his wife, Jane, and their two children live in Plymouth, Minnesota; Kathy, her husband, Jim, and their two children live in Rogers, Minnesota; Ken, his wife, Karen and two children live in Calgary, Alberta, Canada; Carol and her husband, Emilio, live in Madrid, Spain.

The Kuefler family has been active in church, school, sports and camping since moving to Brooklyn Center in 1963. Tony has been a particularly active volunteer in his church and community and has also served as a leader in many organizations. He has served as President of the Jaycees; the first St. Alphonsus Catholic Church Council president; St. Alphonsus Fun Fair Co-chair; Knights of Columbus Committee Chair; Brooklyn Center Republicans; Campaign Manager for two state legislator campaigns; Treasurer and Director of Brooklyn Center Historical Society; Citizens for Better Government and the Brooklyn Center Taxpayers Association; Northside Life Care Center Board; Earle Brown Days Festival Board; and nine years Brooklyn Center Council member ('73-'81). Tony was also active in his profession, serving as President of the Twin Cities Association of Systems Management.

Since retiring in 1993, Tony and Joanne travel (mostly in their motor home) about three months each year to see their children and grandchildren, friends and sights in all fifty states and beyond. When not traveling or enjoying his hobbies of fishing and golfing, Tony continues with a heavy schedule of volunteer activities. It helps to keep him young and out of trouble, he says.

Submitted by Tony Kuefler

My wife, Dolores, and I, Arthur, moved into Brooklyn Park in September 1956, after building our own home in which we still reside.

Dolores is the daughter of John and Olga Madsen of Madsen Floral Shop. I am the son of Carl and Hilda Kvamme who came from a Red River Valley farm at Ada, Minnesota. I graduated from the University of Minnesota as an engineering student. I spent thirty years as a sales manager for Armco Steel Corporation. Dolores was a medical technician and employed at the University of Minnesota Hospital.

We have two children. Diane Oliveira is a Metro Transit driver. Dan Kvamme is a registered mechanical production engineer for Federal Cartridge. We have two grand-children, Sharon and Eric Kvamme.

We were both active in local politics. I was Mayor of Brooklyn Park, 1963-1964. I am a charter member of the local Lion's Club and as of this time have had thirty-eight years of perfect attendance and was given a Life Membership by the International Association. Dolores also was a Charter member of the Lioness Club and is active in many charitable organizations.

Submitted by Arthur Kvamme

Arthur and Dolores Kvamme

Arthur and Dolores Kvamme

Richard and Patricia LaBelle

RICH AND I met in typing class at Robbinsdale Senior High School. We went to prom together with a large group of friends. We had a great time going to Twin Lake Beach, riding the streetcars down to the Radio City Theater and dancing at the Prom Ballroom in St. Paul.

We were married June 10, 1950, at Sacred Heart Church in Robbinsdale. We drove to the north shore of Lake Superior in our 1948 red Ford convertible for our honeymoon. We lived in Robbinsdale the first five years of our marriage. Our goal was to settle in a home by the time our first child entered school. We wanted to stay in the same School District #281, so in 1956 we bought our first rambler home in Brooklyn Center. Our wonderful neighbors were the Woodys, the Elmers, Dennis' and the O'Briens. Our parents thought we were crazy to move so far out of town, but we found that the three-bedroom home on Admiral Lane worked out for our growing family of four children. Our house payments were $87.00 including tax. Yes, those were the good old days!

We still did all of our shopping in Robbinsdale stores because there were no large stores in Brooklyn Center. We also went to church at St. Raphael's Catholic Church in Crystal because St. Alphonsus had not been formed yet. The first ten years in Brooklyn Center were very busy years raising our children, which grew to be seven—five girls and two boys. Our neighborhood was our source of friendship and entertainment. Building a garage meant that all the neighbors helped and it was a good excuse to have a party. The area was filled with children. My father-in-law always said, "It looks like recess time at school around here", thus there was always a birthday party, a circus or a bike parade to watch. All the children attended Northport Elementary School so we were actively involved in PTA, Girls Scouts, Boy Scouts, music and dance lessons, Little League and then catechism classes.

We watched Brookdale Shopping Center being built, with SuperValu being our grocery store, along with Sears and Dayton's Department Stores. Big time shopping now! Shopper's City was our Target in the 1960s, everything from groceries to furniture. The Starlite Drive-In Theater was our family outing. We popped popcorn, made Kool-aid, put the pajamas on, all stuffed into our ten-passenger station wagon (with wood grain sides), the minivan of the 60s. Going out for a family treat was driving to 69th and Osseo Road to visit Roy's A&W for a root beer float.

In 1965 we moved to a new home large enough to accommodate nine of us. Finally we were able to seat nine people around the kitchen table and we had 2½ baths. Guess who got the half? Rich and I did.

In 1969 we installed one of the first in-ground pools in the area. It was our "vacation spot." Who could afford to take nine people, a dog and a cat on vacation?

Submitted by Pat LaBelle

WHEN MY HUSBAND was discharged from the Navy in 1951, we bought a small house on the edge of north Minneapolis. After living there for eight years we looked for a lot to build on in Brooklyn Center so that our children could continue to attend Our Lady of Victory School. We bought the last vacant lot on the Edling/Ryden farm and built our home on it. We have seen forty years of growth and changes in Brooklyn Center and for many years prior to that as we both grew up and lived on the north side of Minneapolis.

My father-in-law often traded chickens and ducks with Earle Brown in the 1940s. As a young boy, my husband would visit the Brown Farm with his Dad. The Farm contained a logging camp building, which Earle Brown brought down from northern Minnesota. This long building was a cook shack, dining and bunk-house all in one. It was like a museum, with skids and many logging tools used for cutting trees.

We remember when the fields on both sides of County Road 10 were tomato fields. This was before Brookdale Shopping Center was built. As I recall, Bill West's gas station was the only business on the corner of 57th and Highway 100. It was moved slightly to the east to build the 57th Avenue Bridge across Highway 100. We were introduced to "discounting" when Shopper's City was built. This was a new way of doing business for grocery and department stores.

Our oldest son worked on Edling's potato farm in Brooklyn Park during the summers of 1966 and 1967. All five of our children graduated from Brooklyn Center High School. We were introduced to an innovation in schooling when our second son attended the Vo-Tech School part time while attending Brooklyn Center High School. Our children took swimming lessons at the Civic Center pool and enjoyed many hours there during the summers.

We have enjoyed seeing the area along Highway 100 develop into a beautiful golf course from the marshy area it had been. Many people at that time were afraid it would present a traffic problem, which I don't believe it proved to be. It has been a nice enhancement to the community.

Submitted by Donna Laberda

Editor's Note: Donna died on January 12, 2001, but before she died, she was able to see a nearly completed copy of this book, to which she contributed so much.

The Ed and Donna Laberda Family

Ed and Donna Laberda

The Cliff and Gen Lane Family

CLIFF LANE was one of twelve children born to Dan and Irma (Woodman) Lane. Cliff was born in 1917. The Dan Lane family home was on Osseo Road in Brooklyn Center. Dan came from Maine and is a brother to former Brooklyn Center Mayor, Merton Lane. Dan Lane was a truck farmer.

Cliff Lane left home to work for Roy Howe in the potato business, driving truck and going to the market.

Gen Ernst, was born in Plymouth, Minnesota one of seven children. I brought produce to the market, and that is where Cliff and I met.

We were married and have five children: James lives in Columbia Heights, Virginia lives in Brooklyn Center, Barbara lives in Wayzata, Anne Marie lives in Corcoran, Linda lives in Brooklyn Park. We have eleven grandchildren and ten great-grandchildren.

Glen and Cliff Lane with Barbara, Anne Marie, James, Linda, and Virginia

My husband worked for a grocery wholesale supply company; where he received his grocery business experience. In 1949 we built a grocery store on 69th and Osseo Road. We owned and operated the largest Red Owl Agency at that time. In 1969 we sold the grocery store and leased to others. We had partnerships with Richard Ernst, and later, Dorothy Ernst. In later years, Art Noel had the meat department. All our children worked in the grocery store.

We remodeled and extended our strip mall to the north, which included a pharmacy, dry cleaners, barber shop, dental office, paint and wallpaper and beauty shop.

When Loring Lane was ready to sell the DX Station, we purchased it. The station later became a Tires Plus store. The Laundromat east of the Station was divided. It had a television repair shop and a flower shop.

The old Sinclair place on 65th in Brooklyn Center was our home for a time before we moved to Medicine Lake.

Cliff died in July 1990 after having open-heart surgery and lung cancer. In August of 1999 I sold my property on 69th and Brooklyn Boulevard to the City of Brooklyn Center. I am now eighty years old and am active with the seniors, do church work serving funeral luncheons and continue my work of nineteen years at Adult Corrections at Parker's Lake.

Submitted by Gen Lane

DANIEL AND IRMA LANE lived on the corner of 69th and Osseo Road. This family consisted of twelve brothers and sisters; Joyce, Doris, Maurice, Clyde, Beatrice, Clifford, Ronald, Loring, Phyllis, Lawrence, Jack and Jerry.

Their daughter, Phyllis, and her husband, George Ste. Marie, had six children: Dennis, Sandra, Susan, Kathleen, Judith and Janet. Growing up, the Ste. Marie family lived in a chicken coop on the farm of an Aunt and Uncle. Work started at four or five in the morning and ended at four or five in the afternoon. There was no grass to play in, only sand and dirt. They had homemade toys to play with. A trailer that was used on the farm was a playground to them when not in use.

Susan, one of their daughters, did not like school when she was in kindergarten so she would run home only to be banished to a bushel basket at the end of the field. There she would stay until her mother finished her work around four or five in the afternoon.

Eventually, the Ste. Marie family moved to a big house on 69th and Osseo Road. There was no bathroom in the house so their father made a shower in the garage. This house was taken down in 1965 and a Pure Oil Gas station was built next door.

The family had owned a 1930 car that the father, as much as he hated to, had to sell in order to pay for his wife's hospital expenses after just having delivered a baby.

The Ste. Marie family purchased its first television set in 1950—a 21-inch model. This was the highlight of the 1950s.

Susan Ste. Marie still lives in Brooklyn Park. She has seen many changes over the last fifty-five years. She likes fishing, bowling, cards and most of all her children: Kim, Kelli, Karen and her six grandchildren.

Submitted by Phyllis Ste. Marie Pomerleau and Susan Ste. Marie

Daniel and Irma Lane

Denny, Sandy, and Sue Ste. Marie on their favorite plaything—the trailer

The Burnett and Larson Families

On June 10, 1939, Warren and Opal Burnett, along with their children Lloyd and Margie, moved into a home with 3½ acres located at 801 65th Avenue North, Brooklyn Center. Janney, Semple, Hill & Co., employed Warren and Opal was a homemaker who put their acreage to good use by planting huge gardens. They also raised chickens and sold the eggs. Our next-door neighbors, Sonnenbergs, were truck farmers and had some farm animals.

Lloyd and Margie attended Earle Brown School and their parents soon became active in school and church activities. Opal was treasurer of the PTA when Cedric Adams was guest speaker at one of the school's famous "Bean Suppers." The walk to school was a mile of dirt roads that sometimes proved to be a challenge, in winter with too much snow, and in spring with too much water. Earle Brown School was a two-story structure at that time, accommodating grades 1 through 8. The hot lunch program was started at the school sometime in the early 40s.

Margie Burnett and her Second Grade classmates at Earle Brown School (1940)

Opal and Warren's home was always open to visitors and sometimes renters who, during World War II, were desperate for housing. Shortly after the war they decided to take in foster babies from Lutheran Social Services. They received an award from Governor Wendell Anderson for twenty-five years of service in caring for 160 babies. In 1978 Opal was presented with an "Outstanding Senior Citizen Award" from the Brooklyn Center Jaycee Women for her many acts of community service.

In 1952 Margie married Bill Larson at Harron United Methodist Church in Brooklyn Center. Following Bill's discharge from the Navy in 1955, they purchased a home on the 5900 block of Colfax in Brooklyn Center. Their first son, Daniel, was about six months old when they moved into their home, and a second son, James, was born in 1958. Both boys attended Earle Brown School. Daniel was in 6th grade when the school burned down in the winter of 1967. His classroom was in the same two-story structure that his mother had attended. Margie was active in many volunteer activities at Earle Brown. Both boys graduated from Brooklyn Center High School and were active in band and gymnastics during their high school years.

Margie and Bill Larson reside in their home on Colfax Avenue. Over the years they have remained active at Harron Church. Bill was a member, and served a term as president, of the Brooklyn Center Community Band. They hosted two high school exchange students and Margie was a volunteer Braillist for several years. Both Margie and Bill deliver meals for Community Emergency Assistance Program and volunteer in the Aquatic Program at Courage Center.

In June 1999 it will be sixty years that Margie has lived in Brooklyn Center. There are now apartments on the land where her home had been in 1939. It has been a community of good neighbors and great friendships, and has grown to have many conveniences. We have enjoyed our many years here.

Submitted by Marjorie L. Larson

DURING THE DEPRESSION, in 1936, Anna Wiezsorek (meaning evening) came from Poland. She was raised in a sod house with a straw roof and a dirt floor in Poland. Anna immigrated to Flint, Michigan and stayed with her godfather and his family. She had been educated in Poland and did not speak English. This presented a problem in finding work and socializing and the only work she could find was housework. She cleaned houses, receiving only five dollars a week. Later she found work in a pickle factory in Chicago. The old lamplighter was a familiar figure in Chicago. He came down the street carrying his ladder, leaning it up against the lamp post, going up and lighting the gas lamp. In the morning, he came back and put all the lamps out.

Anna met Glenn Larsen in Chicago. They were married and already had their two children, Glenn and Gloria, when Glenn started working for Frye Roofing Company in Minneapolis. At that time there were no houses available for purchase in Minneapolis so they lived with Glenn's mother in Wisconsin. In 1948 they moved to Minneapolis. They were able to buy two lots at 54th and Colfax Avenue North and build their house.

Glenn and Anna Larsen

Anna remembers when Father Musch held mass in the Army barracks on 52nd and Dupont. She cleaned the barracks, by sweeping the board floors, putting fresh flowers on the altar and helping Fr. Musch in many ways. Their children went with her being pulled by mom in their little red wagon.

After the children started Our Lady of Victory Catholic School, Anna went to work at Christman Sausage Factory on 13th and Marshall. She worked there for twenty years.

Glenn died on November 30, 1975. Anna still lives in their house, filled with her special bottle collection and the cups and saucers that are on display. Her yard has a colorful display of flowers in the summer and fall. She now actively takes part in an aerobics class taught by Beverly Wilson at the Brooklyn Center Community Center. She still has Polish friends in northeast Minneapolis that she socializes with.

Anna Larsen with Lindsey, Charlie, and Corisa Larsen

She is the proud grandmother of five grandchildren and three great-grandchildren.

Submitted orally by Anna Larsen

The Louie and Everiel Larson Family

LOUIS (LOUIE) FREDERICK LARSON was born in Wisconsin in 1918. His parents, John and Hannah (Pederson) Larson, knew each other in Norway, then met in United States and were married. Louie is the youngest of seven children. Louie grew up on a farm by Duluth and around Elbow Lake, Minnesota. They walked four miles to the one-room school they attended. The teacher came early and fired up the stove.

Louie met his wife Everiel at a favorite dance hall on 27th and Lake Street in Minneapolis. They were older and it was the second marriage for both of them. They moved to Brooklyn Center in 1952 with their son, Everiel's son from her first marriage (the son has since died).

Louie was a Brooklyn Center volunteer fireman from 1954 to 1969. After twenty-five years of employment by Mobil Oil Corporation, he retired in 1980.

Louie and Everiel Larson

There was music in Louie's home while he was growing up. His father played the fiddle, but music wasn't a way to make a living; it was a hobby. His stepson was into music and the teenagers' rock and roll band practiced at the Larson home. Jon Vezner, who became a Nashville songwriter, was the band's band boy (gofer).

Louie's hunting and fishing buddies died and that left him alone and this brought him back to his hobby, music. The first song he wrote was, "When I Think of You It Brings a Tear." There were many other songs, but the song that continued to develop was a song he wrote about his experiences hopping freight trains, looking for work during the Depression. "Nearly fifty years after returning home, Larson put those haunting images to words and music, crafting his tribute to the state, "Take Me Back to Minnesota." The Minnesota House of Representatives commended Louie for writing the song in honor of "Celebrate Minnesota 1990." Marilyn Sellars ("One Day at a Time" is her signature song) and the Minnesota Boy's Choir recorded the song.

Louie said, "I'd like to be remembered as one who likes to pay back to a State that has been very good to me. We live in the greatest country in the world and I think a person, who has gotten so much, should remember to pay back."

Louie's advice to those in the future who read this: "Live your life to the fullest, enjoy the things you have around you and work toward something that you love."

Submitted from an interview

Kay was born in Thompson, North Dakota, and spent a sheltered childhood in that small farming area. Her father was a business owner, so they lived in town. She left Thompson to attend the University of North Dakota and Grand Forks School of Hair Design. After that she moved to Minneapolis where she lived and worked for about two years, then moved to Robbinsdale, where she lived for five years. During those years she met her husband to be, Len Lasman, an electronics technician, who was a Minneapolis native. On June 28, 1975 Kay became Mrs. Lasman, and the stepmother to Len's two daughters, Randee and Debra. One year later they shopped for a house.

The Lasman Family

Where??? Brooklyn Center??? But that's out in the *boonies*! That was their first response when the real estate agent suggested looking for the kind of home they wanted, in their price range. Brooklyn Center could give them more house for their money than any of the other areas they looked at—so Brooklyn Center bound they were. That was back in 1976, one short year after Kay and Len Lasman were married.

Brooklyn Center was attractive to them for many reasons. It had a "small town" feel to it and they felt welcome in the neighborhood immediately. There were neighborhood gatherings that reminded Kay a lot of her childhood life. They also enjoyed the proximity to city life that was just a short twenty minutes away in downtown Minneapolis. They felt they had the best of both worlds.

Kari, Len, Kay, and Jarret Lasman

Kay worked as a self-employed cosmetologist until 1979, when she quit work to become a "stay-at-home" full-time mom after the birth of their first child, Kari Lynn. Life changed a lot and they moved into a "voluntary simplification" mode, as they went from a two-income to a one-income family. Their second child, Jarret Joseph, was born in 1982. When Jarret entered kindergarten, Kay went to work in the school that both children attended. She still kept summers open so she could be with her children. During those years, she served on many school and school district volunteer committees. Her first volunteer city involvement was co-coordinating a cleanup effort of Shingle Creek Trails which became an annual event for three years until the "Adopt a Park" program came into being.

Later she applied for and was appointed to a position on the Parks and Recreation Commission for a three-year term, after which she ran for City Council and was elected in November 1996. She thoroughly enjoys being on the council and has met people from all over the country as a result of it. The next couple of years were full of changes as Len retired, Kari went off to college and Jarret began high school.

Life here in Brooklyn Center has been good to them. It is where they plan to live out their autumn years—in the place they love.

Submitted by Kay Lasman

The Bev and Dick Lawrence Family

Bev and Dick Lawrence

WE MOVED TO BROOKLYN CENTER in 1961 when Dick accepted a position as a Business Educator in the brand new Brooklyn Center High School and Bev accepted a Home Economics position at Robbinsdale Junior High School. We were born and raised in rural Minnesota settings (Bev on a farm outside Clements and Dick in Kasson, having met at Mankato State College), but we adjusted to suburban life. They found Brooklyn Center a great place to live, raise a family, and pursue a career.

After Bev had taught for two years in Robbinsdale, she resigned to become a full-time homemaker. Our two daughters, Karen and Jeanne, were raised in their home on Poe Road and they too have fond memories of the community.

When the girls were older, Bev returned to the job market and she became the full-time director of Children's Ministries at Brooklyn United Methodist Church. She enjoyed thirteen years in this position while working with many wonderful people and children. In this capacity Bev developed many new opportunities for the children. With the assistance of a great staff, Bev coordinated the largest Methodist Sunday School in the Minnesota Conference. Later she served Brooklyn Methodist Church in a part-time capacity as coordinator of volunteers, which gave her additional opportunities to work with many talented people, for the last four years.

Dick enjoyed working with the students, staff, administration and community while at Brooklyn Center High School. He began Business Internships Program at Brooklyn Center High School in 1967 and served as coordinator of this program until he retired in 1993. He also served as the school's Vocational Director for a number of these years. Dick had the very good fortune of teaching many highly motivated students in the Business Internships Program. The Office Education Association Club, which later became the Business Professionals of America Club, was an integral part of this program. Brooklyn Center students exhibited excellence by achieving many region, state, and national honors. Beginning in 1977, the Brooklyn Center Chapter was named the State Chapter of the Year five of the next six years and National Chapter of the Year in 1978.

In addition, during the decade of the 1980s, five times a Brooklyn Center High School student was named the top Business Professional of America Student of the Year in Minnesota. During these years, the local Business Professional of America Chapter began and continued the annual rocking chair marathon to raise money for Special Olympics, a service project which received state and national recognition.

When we moved to Brooklyn Center, the Brookdale Mall was just being built; now it is being remodeled. They like the way our inner-ring suburb continues to work at being a good place to live.

In retirement they remain active at Brooklyn United Methodist Church. In addition, Dick volunteers at North Hospice and French Regional Park. They enjoy the additional opportunities retirement provides to spend time with their hobbies and with their families.

Submitted by Dick and Bev Lawrence

NICK LAZAROFF came to this country from Bulgaria in the early 1900's. He wanted to be a farmer and bought some land in Minneapolis between Camden and Lowry Avenue North. There he raised different kinds of vegetables: onions, radishes, peppers, etc. He hired children who came from northeast Minneapolis to bunch the vegetables that were taken to the city market. Because they didn't take orders beforehand they had to guess how much produce they needed to get ready for the market. What they didn't sell had to be discarded.

Ann Warhol, one of the girls who worked for Nick Lazaroff, married him in 1924. Their first son, George, was born in 1927. They farmed by the Mississippi River and then purchased a farm in Brooklyn Park. At that time the street was called Camden Station Route #5, which was changed to 77th Avenue North and later to Brookdale Drive.

The Lazaroff Family

Their land contained a lot of peat in which they planted radishes. They had stringer lines that went along the fields and dug ditches to irrigate, pumping water from Shingle Creek.

There were many Bulgarians who settled around that area but most of them are now gone.

George Lazaroff married Harriet Reed. They made their home with George's parents. This couple had two daughters.

Nick passed away in 1952. George and family took over the farm. They developed the farm by building several greenhouses and raised flowers. Flowers are a big seller to this present day. They also built another building for retail business.

The Lazaroffs eventually sold some of this land to the city for parkland. As time goes by, all of the land on which they planted and later rented will be developed into homes, which won't leave much land in Brooklyn Park to farm. The Lazaroffs still raise crops in other parts of the area, near Andover and on land by Highway 65.

When they started their farming business the roads were not developed yet. It was all dirt roads. Harriet remembers taking sleigh rides down 85th Avenue North. Their daughters rode their horses on the dirt roads.

The old Lazaroff Farm House

Their two daughters have decided to keep what they have left in Brooklyn Park and keep on selling to local friends and neighbors.

From an oral interview by Marian Klohs

The Art and Ruth Lee Family

As THE OLDEST OF FOUR SONS born to Frederick Wilhelm and Myrtle Lee from South Dakota, I, Art Lee, was raised in Rapid City and graduated from South Dakota School of Mines and Technology. The Lutheran faith was important in our family life. I met my wife, Ruth, at church.

I had different kinds of employment such as working for Boeing Aircraft in Seattle, Washington during World War II. My ambition was to be a city engineer. I was interviewed in three Twin Cities communities, the third one being Brooklyn Center.

Brooklyn Center hired me to be Village Engineer in 1955. At the first council meeting I attended, the Dayton Company announced the building of Brookdale Shopping Center. The University of Minnesota, or Winston Brothers, let it be known at the second council meeting that they had development plans in progress. All of these developers needed sewer and water, which we didn't have.

I was then appointed the first Village Administrator. The population in 1955 was about 8,000 and by 1960 it was over 24,000. The first year I asked about a budget. They brought out two sheets of paper and the total budget for that year was $60,000.

Art and Ruth Lee celebrating their fiftieth anniversary with their family (1992)

The first four years, every Council vote was unanimous. Development was progressing so rapidly and there was so much work to be done in such a short time, the Council met every week. The dedicated, unpaid Planning Commission also met weekly; then there were Park Board and Charter Commission meetings. I would be at the office at 8:00 A.M. go home for dinner, and then be at meetings until midnight or 1:00 A.M. One of the main reasons I left is that I had allowed meetings to take over my life.

Ruth and I have three children, Marsha, Jim and Mark. Marsha is married to Mansfield (Donald) Dillon, they have one son, Dana, and live in Texas. Jim is married to Bettie, and lives in St. Paul with their two children, Kristen and Ryan. Jim is Compensation Manager for the State of Minnesota. Mark married Randee. They live in Plymouth with their two children, Steve and Marija. Mark is Deputy Director of Hennepin County Health Department. It pleases me very much that our two sons have followed with work in public service.

I was employed by Brooklyn Center for eleven years. I then took a job as Administrator of the Hennepin County Highway Department. After retirement in 1984 we moved to Tulsa, Oklahoma and Arkansas, then moved back to the Twin Cities to be closer to the family. We continue our membership at Cross of Glory Lutheran Church in Brooklyn Center.

I would spend more time with my family if I were given a chance to live my life over again. Ruth did a very good job with the children and I'm proud of them and what they have accomplished.

Submitted by Art Lee

KAREN AND I began "going steady" in our junior year of high school. Ten years later we were married and moved into an apartment on the southwest corner of 65th and Beard Avenue in Brooklyn Center. We lived there for six years and in 1973 purchased a home on 60th Avenue and Lyndale North. We still live in this house. Three years after moving there I served on the City Council and for the next thirteen years, I did my best to represent the working men and women of this community.

Karen retired from the telephone company in 1985 after working there for twenty-eight years. She has been employed at Malmborg's Garden Center and Greenhouse part-time for the past four years. The Lhotkas both like flowers and take pride in how colorful their yard is. I plan to retire from Target Stores, after working there for twenty-two years. We plan to do more gardening, golfing, entertaining, and more traveling in the winter.

Submitted by Gene Lhotka

Gene and Karen Lhotka

Robert and Rose Lillestol

WITH FOUR CHILDREN, Bob and I knew we had to have a larger home. In 1958 we started searching for one in Bloomington, but found none that we could afford. We went to what I thought was a foreign country—Brooklyn Center. There we found a four-bedroom rambler on Paul Drive in a Vern Donnay development on the west side of what was then just a village. There was nothing familiar and it took several years to become comfortable in our new community.

Brooklyn Center was beginning to grow rapidly at that time, although there were not many places to shop. We did our grocery shopping in the neighboring suburb of Crystal and other major shopping back at Southdale, which we were familiar with. It was many years before Brookdale Center opened.

Robert and Rose Lillestol and family

We had been married in 1944 at Central Lutheran Church in Minneapolis. We lived in Minneapolis until November of 1952 when we moved to Bloomington. We had two daughters at the time. Lauri was born in 1945 and Kim in 1948. A son, Corey, was born in 1954 and another daughter, Lynn, in 1958.

Lauri was in eighth grade when we moved to Brooklyn Center. She attended Osseo Junior-Senior High School. At that time it was the only secondary school in the district. The other children went to several elementary schools, as the district added new ones each year to accommodate families moving into Brooklyn Center and Brooklyn Park. Bob and I were active in Parent-Teacher Associations and chaired two school carnivals, one at Edgewood and one at Fair Oaks. Bob was also PTA president.

During our years in Brooklyn Center, Bob was active in Cub and Boy Scouts and served on one of the city's commissions. I remained a "stay-at-home-mom", volunteering as a den mother in Girl Scout activities, room mother and nurse's helper at school. I returned to the workforce and learned to trim dogs at the Brookdale Center Pet Shop. Later I operated a dog grooming business at home.

Lauri married Wesley Winters in 1965. They have two children, Peter and Sarah. They live in Crystal, and she has been community editor of the *Brooklyn Center Sun-Post* newspaper since 1995. Kim married Jack Bird and lives in Texas. They have three sons, Robert, Andrew and Eric. Corey married Leslie Swan and lives in Minneapolis. They have one son, Daniel. Lynn married Frank Stone. They live in Blaine and have two sons, Nicholas and Anthony.

After retiring from almost thirty-seven years at Honeywell as an industrial engineer, Bob was a volunteer driver for "Meals on Wheels" sponsored by Community Emergency Assistance Program, and made adaptive items to enable people with disabilities to remain employed. He enjoyed fishing and loved to sit in the backyard watching birds come to the feeders.

Bob died of kidney failure in 1992. I am still living in our home and am an active member of the Brooklyn Center Women's Club.

Submitted by Rose Lillestol

IN 1951 the Lindblads left northeast Minneapolis and moved to Brooklyn Center. There were just a few houses west of Humboldt Avenue, but rows and rows of lilac bushes. The land was flat as a pancake and stubbles from the cornfields dotted the area. On 57th and Highway 100 there was just a stop sign. There was only one telephone and that was at Casey's grocery store. As more houses were built a four-party-line telephone system was installed.

What once was a wild asparagus field became Brookdale Shopping Center.

It was country living, with wild pheasants and the Earle Brown farm birds and animals clucking and mooing. Muriel's grandpa lived with the family. He, Barbara, Sandra, and Debra took many walks over to see the animals, antique carriages, fire trucks and saddles—items that Mr. Brown was collecting.

This area of Brooklyn Center developed rapidly. In no time there was a nice shopping center with two grocery stores, bakery, hardware, liquor store, dry cleaner/laundry and a doctor.

In 1958 Muriel joined the Earle Brown School cooks and among the appliances she operated was the potato peeler. The potatoes tumbled in the container with its rough interior with water running through taking out the peelings. Then, of course, the potatoes were cooked and mashed. This was a heavy job but the children loved mashed potatoes and hamburger gravy. Eventually the school bought a commercial mixer that did the job so much faster. Life got better. With the big mixer the cooks started making caramel rolls and French bread.

As the years went by, a hill for sliding was developed in the park and the high-in-the-sky freeway bridge was built.

School District #286 became a town inside a town and it was as one large family. The citizens are friendly and became involved. Muriel is still happy that the family moved to Brooklyn Center.

Submitted by Muriel Lindblad

Muriel Lindblad

Everett and Ruth Lindh

Everett and Ruth Lindh

EVERETT AND RUTH LINDH and their two children, Sharon and Allen, moved to Brooklyn Center in the Southeast neighborhood from Fridley in 1955.

The Lindhs say, "When we came to Brooklyn Center, we moved into an area that had earlier settlers and new families with young children. It was a nice mix, combining the groundwork of the early residents with the dreams of the new families. It was a happy experience."

On Sunday mornings the Lindhs can be found at the Harron United Methodist Church worshipping God with the faith community. This is the church where their two children received their Christian formation and were confirmed.

Sharon and Allen attended Earle Brown Elementary School and graduated from Brooklyn Center High School.

Sharon married Charles Brenner. They live in Carbondale, CO. She is a CPA and Charles is an architect. Everett and Ruth travel to Colorado often, especially during peach harvest season.

After graduating from the University of Minnesota as an electrical engineer, Allen married a Brooklyn Park resident, Nancy Pfaffe. They have three boys, Michael, Matthew and Peter. 3M has employed Allen for twenty-one years. He and his family recently completed an assignment in Belgium and reside in Shoreview. Ruth and Everett enjoy attending their grandson's geography bees, concerts and baseball games.

Ruth's family roots come from the Lake Pepin area and they return there often for family and community reunions. Everett has fond memories and learned values under the care of his grandparents on the farm. Everett retired from Harvest States after 34 years of employment. His present hideaway for fishing with his son and grandsons is a cabin on Snake River.

Texas has been the Lindh's resting place in the winter for many years. Everett finds the golfing to his liking there also.

Everett and Ruth have a calling to assist older family members and friends without children move from their homes into assisted living places. Ruth says, "Emptying houses is our specialty." The neighborhood children consider them concerned and caring grandparents. Everett served on the SE Neighborhood Association. The Lindhs deliver, through Community Emergency Assistance Program, "Meals on Wheels" to the elderly and shut-ins.

Everett and Ruth describe raising children and growing old together as "The Good Life in Brooklyn Center."

Submitted by a Brooklyn Historical Society Volunteer

LEONARD LINDQUIST was born September 5, 1912, a first generation Swedish American. My father Axel, who constructed Catholic churches and parsonages in North and South Dakota, died in 1926 when I was fourteen years old. I had two sisters and one brother. My mother opened a boarding and rooming house at Pillsbury Avenue and Lake Street in Minneapolis. At fifteen years of age, I rode freight trains to the wheat fields in Montana for work.

In 1931 I graduated from West High School, after dropping out for one year to help my family. During the Depression I had a newspaper route with 550 customers. Once again I rode the rails to the west coast for work in lumber mills. I worked on construction as I attended the University of Minnesota in 1933-1937 and the University of Minnesota Law School in 1937-1939, and was admitted to the bar in 1939.

Elsie Kelly was one of five children, and grew up in Minneapolis. She was a 1939 graduate of the University of Minnesota in Theater where she was one of the leading actresses on campus. We met at the University and married in 1934. We lived in Washington, D. C. from 1939-1941.

During World War II in 1942-1946, I was in the Navy Air Corps in North Africa. Elsie worked with the Red Cross in Ireland and England.

In 1946 I formed a law firm with Earl Larson. We built our home in Brooklyn Center at 6940 Willow Lane after living at 5706 West River Road. We had three boys, Lowell, Lawrence and Kelley. I was a member of the Earle Brown School Board, a member of Duoos Brothers American Legion Post. I was Justice of the Peace, Brooklyn Center Village Attorney, member of VFW and Isaak Walton League, active in Community Fund, Sister Kenny and Boy Scout work.

I was appointed Chairman of the Railroad and Warehouse Commission where we got rid of the racketeers trying to take over the streetcar company. Our family had to leave our home in Brooklyn Center for a time, because of threats, and for safety. I served four years in the Minnesota House of Representatives. I became a National Labor Board mediator and arbitrator. My wife, Elsie, died in 1979. We sponsor the Elsie Kelly Lindquist Scholarship at the University of Minnesota Theater group.

I officially retired in 1988, but never ceased working. In 1993 I joined a new organization, Professional Sports Linkage, to bring at-risk youth, professional athletes and business professionals together. It provides inner-city kids hope for the future by improving life skills enabling them to recognize their identities and to realize their potential as human beings.

Son, Lowell, married Judy Kindlein, they have four children: Rachael, Becky, Nathan and Daniel. Lowell is a clerk for a federal judge and lives in Cottage Grove, Minnesota. Lawrence (Larry) married Jackie Chalmers and they live in Brooklyn Center. He is in the antique retail business. Kelley is director of art space studio homes for struggling young artists and lives on Park Lane in Minneapolis. In 1995 I moved back to Brooklyn Center, next to my son's house on Willow Lane.

Submitted by Leonard Lindquist

The Leonard and Elsie Lindquist Family

The Leonard and Elsie Lindquist Family

Warren & Cari Lindquist

A LONG TIME AGO, the 10th of March 1922, in a flat very close to the railroad tracks at 127 West Broadway, a beautiful (according to his mother Alma Bye Lindquist) baby boy was born. "Maybe he will be President someday," said his father Edwin. "Let's name him Warren, after President Warren Harding." (Incidentally, a young girl named Alma and her brother lost their father unexpectedly. Their mother did housekeeping to help the family survive. Alma picked up coal along the railroad tracks to keep the home fires burning.)

This was the beginning of a full life for Warren Lee Lindquist. He did not become President of United States. He does recall being president of the following organizations: Minneapolis North Suburban Kiwanis Club; Brooklyn Center Crime Prevention Fund; University of Minnesota Education Alumni Association; and Minnesota Elementary School Principals 25 Year Club. He was proud to receive the Lifetime Achievement Award from the Brooklyn Center Rotary Club for his volunteer work.

Kevin, Robert, Amy, Peggy, Cari and Warren Lindquist, Claudia Olson, Colleen, Christina, Mike and T. J. Loth

In Warren's early years he lived in Northeast Minneapolis. This was during the Depression and his dad drove a Bambi Wagon (bread, sweet rolls, etc.) pulled by a horse. He attended Whitney and Prescott Schools. The family then moved to the north side where he went to Jordan Junior and North High Schools. By the way, this is where he picked up the name "Link"—some said he was late for graduation and the question was asked, "Where's the missing Link?"

Money was needed if he were to go to college. The Twin City Furnace Company was looking for a draftsman. He worked there for over a year before enrolling at the University of Minnesota. The Naval ROTC also helped pay for his education. Calculus, Physics and Chemistry were not his favorite subjects, so on to Great Lakes Naval Training Station, quartermaster training at Bainbridge, Maryland, and Submarine Base at New London, Connecticut. Stops aboard the U.S.S. Proteus sub tender included Pearl Harbor, Guam and finally Tokyo Bay for the signing of the Treaty. The Second Class Quartermaster arrived home after World War II and continued his education under the GI Bill.

Link switched from The School of Engineering to The College of Education and received his Bachelor of Science Degree in Industrial Arts and Elementary Education. He also earned a Masters Degree in Education.

Warren met a wonderful girl, Cari Ermatinger, at a twilight dance. They tied the knot in 1950 and moved to Brooklyn Center in 1957. Warren is very proud of their three beautiful children, Claudia, Kevin, and Colleen, and their five grandchildren: Christopher, Amy, T. J. (Timothy Joseph), Christina and Robert.

Warren found a second home at Earle Brown Elementary School in 1950 where he taught grades three through six for six really fun years and served as principal for the next twenty-eight years (he says he would love doing it all again). As Warren tells his story, he looks out his cabin window at beautiful Lake Alexander and says, "It's been a wonderful ride!"

Submitted by Warren Lindquist

JIM LINDSAY was born in 1932 to Margaret and Joseph Lindsay, whose families migrated from Luxembourg and Germany. He has lived within five miles of his birthplace, Robbinsdale, Minnesota, for the first sixty years of his life. Jim has fond memories of his childhood home overlooking Twin Lake in Robbinsdale. His home sat on top of a big hill. The area between the home and lake was the site of an annual picnic held in conjunction with the Lion's Club harvesting and destroying wild marijuana. The hill was cut down and used to fill in the lake when Highway 100 was extended across Twin Lake after World War II.

James P. Lindsay

Jim and his family moved to north Minneapolis. He attended Ascension Catholic Grade School, graduating from Minneapolis Vocational School. He worked for a wholesale hardware for nine years. In 1951 he married Gloria Johnson before being inducted into the Army. Basic training was served at Fort Sill, Oklahoma. Jim was assigned to the 24th Division, 52nd Field Artillery Btn. After serving one year in Japan his unit was transferred to Korea. In Korea he was assigned to a Prisoner of War camp holding Chinese and North Koreans and as a prime mover driver in the artillery.

Returning from service Jim moved to Brooklyn Center in 1954. In 1958, along with 700 candidates, Jim tested for the Brooklyn Center Police Department. Being one of two people appointed, he became the fifth officer with the department on January 10, 1959. In October 1960 Susan Marie Lindsay was born. Jim chose the police profession for his lifetime work. He served three years each as a Patrolman, Sergeant and Lieutenant before being appointed Deputy Chief for ten years. He completed his service as Chief of Police for fourteen years. The last ten years also included being Emergency Preparedness Director for the City.

James Lindsay

Taking advantage of the GI Bill, he obtained a degree from North Hennepin Community College in law enforcement. In addition to attending upper level classes at the University of Minnesota, Jim obtained a Ford Foundation Grant to attend a fourteen-week police administration course with the Southern Police Institute at the University of Louisville in Kentucky in 1965. Jim was an active member of many service clubs including Brooklyn Center's Rotary Club, Lion's Club and Taxpayer's Association. With the Police Department he helped to organize many programs: Crime Prevention Fund; Peacemaker, a juvenile diversionary program; a domestic abuse program; DARE program, among others.

He assisted in the department's growth from a five-person department to over 70 employees. The agency developed into a full service department with its own radio dispatch center, jail and investigative unit.

In 1973 Jim married Marilyn Zimmerman, a lifelong resident of Brooklyn Park. They made their home in Brooklyn Center until they retired in 1992. They split their time between Plant City, Florida and Brooklyn Center until becoming permanent Florida residents in 1994. They continue to spend summer months in Minnesota.

Submitted by Jim Lindsay

Marilyn Fischer Lindsay

MARILYN FISCHER LINDSAY was born November 1931 into the Fischer family, longtime residents living near 75th and West River Road in Brooklyn Park. Grandparents William and Emma Fischer resided next-door operating an eighty-acre farm. Marilyn, first of four girls of Helen and William Fischer, attended all eight grades at the Benson two-room school located at 73rd Avenue North and West River Road. High School was completed attending Anoka High School.

Her sisters Janice, Virginia and Carolyn, share fond memories with her. Early years involved farm life, as her father worked the homestead with his father. Grandma cooked in the summer kitchen for family and hired help. Grandma made all the butter, jellies, jams and sausage after the cattle were slaughtered. Marilyn enjoyed the wonderful smell of hams and bacon that lingered for weeks.

At the early age of five, while playing with her collie dog Lucky, Marilyn followed him onto the ice in the Mississippi River. The ice gave way, dumping her into the frigid water. Lucky was a hero, barking feverishly drawing the attention of a neighbor, Albert Fisher (no relation), who came to investigate and pulled her to safety. One time Marilyn was so proud to find a garden snake, she took it to a neighbor's house to show her. The lady immediately fainted. Believing the neighbor died, she hid for several hours before discovering she was still alive.

Marilyn's work career started at age thirteen, working for Pete's Grocery part time in northeast Minneapolis. The work involved whatever was needed: cleaning, stocking shelves and waiting on people. At age sixteen Marilyn started part time at the Minneapolis Star complaint desk until graduating from high school. She then took advantage of a full-time position in the Circulation Department working with mail subscription customers.

Marilyn married Calvin Zimmerman in October 1951. Calvin also grew up on a farm in Brooklyn Park operated by his parents Abe and Elsie Zimmerman. Darcy, the only daughter, came along in September 1952. Darcy, like her mother, graduated from Anoka High School. Darcy married and became the mother of Nick, born in December 1978. Nick is a graduate of Park Center High school in Brooklyn Park.

In 1965 Marilyn applied for and was accepted for a position with the City of Brooklyn Park. She worked as special assessment clerk for two years before accepting the same position in Brooklyn Center.

Marilyn and Jim Lindsay married in July 1973. Lindsay was Deputy Chief of Police for Brooklyn Center. They resided in Brooklyn Center near Shingle Creek and Brooklyn Boulevard. In 1980 Marilyn left Brooklyn Center to join ex-city engineer, Jim Merila, in his engineering firm. She retired in 1992 as office manager after working with Merila for twenty-five years.

In September 1992 Marilyn and husband took up winter residence in Plant City, Florida. The Brooklyn Center residence was sold in 1994 and they became permanent residents of Florida. They continue visiting relatives and friends in Minnesota on a regular basis.

Submitted by Marilyn Fischer Lindsay

ONE HUNDRED YEARS AGO Isaac and Jane Littell and their son, Floyd, then seventeen, immigrated to Minnesota from Vernon, Indiana. An old personal property insurance policy suggests they lived for a time at 49th and Humboldt Avenue North in Minneapolis. Then in June 1900, they moved "near Camden Place" to the old house still standing today at 55th and Emerson Avenue North. Adolph Boyson's father built it fifteen years previously with lumber from the old Hamilton School on 44th and Fremont Avenue North. The house and four acres of land were purchased for about $800 from Paris Reidhead.

In 1904 when Jane was forty-five years old, she took the buggy to Anoka to the doctor because she thought she had a tumor. He informed her she was pregnant and she fainted dead away. Alberta "Bertie" Littell was born on May 20, 1904, and lived there all her lifetime.

The Littell and Dunn Families

When Bertie was eleven, Jane was confined to a wheel chair, probably with MS. Isaac continued to farm the land and acquired twelve acres total along the way. Their son, Floyd, worked for Earle Brown, and died in 1920. Jane died in 1928, right after Bertie married Orville Dunn. In the early 1930s they had two children, Carol and Marilyn. Bertie and Orville were charter members of Harron Methodist Church on the corner of 55th and Dupont Avenue. Isaac was the janitor there until his death in 1945 at 89 years of age. Orville was the choir director for many years, and Bertie the pianist. The tradition continues. Their daughter, Carol Dawidowicz is the organist and their granddaughter, Pamela Wrolstad, is choir director. Marilyn Barland is in the choir.

Alberta Littell Dunn with Jane Littell (her mother) and her Aunt (1909)

Bertie went to Earle Brown School, as did her daughters, and also Marilyn's children, Pamela and Arnie. When Marilyn and Jack married, he built them a house next door. They lived there until after Orville died in 1967, and shortly after sold it and lived with Bertie in the old place.

When Brooklyn Center celebrated its 75th anniversary in 1986, Bertie was to be honored at the celebration as one of the oldest residents. She was interviewed by a reporter from the *Brooklyn Center Post*, but died a few days later before the celebration. The article appeared in the *Post* on the day of her funeral, February 13.

Marilyn and Jack lived in the old house until 1995 when they moved to Wisconsin. The house is still standing and a new family now calls it "Home."

Submitted by daughters Carol Dawidowicz and Marilyn Barland
Exerpts taken from Brooklyn Center Post—1986

The Samuel and Sarah Locke Family

MY GRANDFATHER, Samuel Locke, lived in Brooklyn Center most of his life. He was born in a log cabin at Silver Creek, Wright County, Minnesota, in 1856. His parents were Jonah Britton Locke, born in 1823 in Wadesville, Virginia (the old Locke farm) and Sarah Brooks Locke, born in 1828 in York County, Pennsylvania. They moved to Silver Creek, Minnesota from Tremont City, Ohio in 1855. In 1875 Jonah and Sarah purchased a home and acreage in what is now Brooklyn Park at approximately Brooklyn Blvd. and Hampshire Avenue North. My father, Donald Locke, was born in that house in 1898. That house, incidentally, is still there and occupied at this writing.

Samuel's grandparents moved from Virginia to Ohio in approximately 1834. On January 13, 1881, Samuel married Sarah Kathryn Green, daughter of Mahlon and Margaret Green of Brooklyn Township. Mahlon and Margaret moved from Belleville, Illinois in 1860. Sarah's brother, Duff Green, was the Brooklyn Center Village Clerk in 1876.

Samuel and Sarah purchased a home at 7015 Osseo Rd. (now Brooklyn Blvd.) He and grandma lived in that same house for nearly 50 years. They raised four children— Olive, Fred, Amy, and Donald. Olive and Amy both taught school for a number of years. Samuel worked on his farm and did carpentry. He also served as Brooklyn Center Village Clerk and Assessor for twenty-five years. He was well known and well respected in the community.

Grandma died in 1940 and Grandpa in 1946. After my Grandpa died, my parents, Donald and Emma Locke and family, moved into that house and lived there for about 8 years. At that time the houses were far apart and in that area were many truck farms. Brooklyn Center was just a beautiful, quiet countryside.

I remember well the old Brooklyn Center store, run by Mrs. Howe and her daughter Edna; the "Lane and Ernst Red Owl Store"; the Loring Lanes DX station on the corner of 69th and Osseo Road (now Brooklyn Blvd.); and the old Brooklyn Center Methodist Church, where we held our Boy Scout meetings. I have many good memories of the many good neighbors and friends that I knew there.

I attended the old Brooklyn Center School (four-classroom school), when they only used two of the classrooms. First through fourth grades were in one room with one teacher; and fifth through eighth were in another room, with another teacher. There were five of us in my class when I graduated from eighth grade. Those were wonderful days that I will never forget.

Submitted by Everett J. Locke

THERE MUST BE a first time to everything, as there was in our family leaving Maine and coming way out west to Minnesota.

The family consisted of father, mother, and four children. I was eight years old and the proud possessor of a little tin trunk. One day, father said he would give me ten cents for my trunk. I asked him why he wanted it. His answer was that he was going to save money to bring us to St. Anthony, and he wanted the trunk to keep our money in. I was so pleased with the idea that I willingly gave up the trunk and contributed my dime. It took us three years to save enough money for the journey.

One bright day in June an oxen team drove to the door and took us and our baggage to Grandmother Longfellow's and then to the boat. The boat left on Monday morning at four o'clock. We arrived in Boston on Tuesday morning. We took the train to Albany, New York and from there went by canal boat to Buffalo and steamboat to Chicago. There we hired a man and his team to drive us across the prairies of Illinois, to Galena. From Galena we came by boat to St. Paul, Minnesota.

Among our baggage was a red chest (every family in those days had one). When unloading it from the boat the bottom fell off the chest. Men, women and children scrambled to pick up the things, but mother said she never got more than half of the things back again.

Arriving in St. Anthony on July 2, 1851, we decided to stay for a year and a half.

One day in the early spring, a little barefooted boy came to our house to live. We named him Daniel Webster because he could not give us his name.

In the summer of 1852 father made his claim to a piece of land in Brooklyn and the next winter built a log house from trees cut in the tamarack swamp about a mile east of here. In February 1853 we moved in. We arrived about four o'clock in the afternoon. Father had the oven full of baked potatoes, and even now in imagination I can smell those potatoes. That winter was a severe one. The Indians liked to visit, sit around the stove and warm themselves.

In February 1855 a little barefooted girl came to live with us. One day when father and mother were gone I was left to care for all of these children. I missed one of the children and ran to the creek. Using my arm for a fish line and my hand for a hook, I drew out a new kind of fish. The fish happened to be Daniel Webster who had strayed away. The other children were overheard to say, "Some of us have to emigrate because the pie won't go around." Like the pie the house was too small for all of us, so I decided to emigrate and have a home of my own.

Written by Mary A. Getchell and read at the
50th anniversary of the arrival of the Jacob
Longfellow family to Minnesota.

The Jacob Longfellow Family

Vern and Ortrude Ludescher

VERN LUDESCHER was born and raised in Rockford, Minnesota and graduated from Delano High School. After high school he worked on a farm for ten dollars a month, plus having to furnish his own clothes.

He was a member of the Civilian Conservation Corp. (CCC) for six years. He received thirty dollars a month. Out of the thirty dollars he had to send home twenty-five to his family. He got pay raises as he worked his way up and then was allowed to keep more money for his own use. While in this service he learned cooking for a large mass of people and worked in the mess department.

After the CCC he went to work for Northern Pump. From there he was drafted into the Army during World War II. While in training the regiment, with a Forest Ranger's knowledge, adopted a deer. The deer slept in the barracks with the recruits.

Vern was in service with Dave Moore, the Twin Cities radio and TV personality. He also served under General George Patton in Luxembourg. His commanding officer was in the Women's Army Auxiliary Corp. (WAAC). This was rather unusual for that time.

Returning home from service, Vern went back to work at Northern Pump for a short time before he started at General Mills in the mechanical division. He then went to work for Research, Incorporated in the purchasing, consulting and plating departments. Vern had a lot of hands-on training and he also taught himself by studying at the library.

Ortrude (Trudy) Hill was born and raised in the Caladonia, Minnesota area. She graduated from high school there in 1934. In 1939 she came to Minneapolis, and worked for Gross Industrial (garment rental). She lived in a converted garage on Memorial Drive while she was waiting for her husband's return from the service.

In 1948 they moved to Brooklyn Center where they built their own house. They lived in the basement for a while. They cooked on a kerosene stove and watched pheasants right outside their windows.

While Trudy worked for Gross Industrial on 15th and Nicollet Avenue, she took the bus to 52nd and Bryant Avenues North at night and then walked from there to 61st and Camden Avenue if Vern wasn't there to pick her up. She claimed it was real scary. There were no streetlights and no roads from 52nd on. She said there was one house on the whole route that had a light on, and to her it was very comforting as she walked through the knee-high grass towards her home.

Trudy and Vern are both retired, but very busy. Vern is a beekeeper and processes his own honey. He is interested in photography, and likes to go mushroom hunting. He also goes portaging and camping in the Boundary Waters Canoe Area (BWCA). Trudy likes baking cookies. She bakes cookies for friends, neighbors and her family. She likes making "care packages" for her college-age grandchildren. With Vern's help, she has a garden and freezes the produce.

From an oral interview by Barbara Erickson

Vern Ludescher on a bridge built by CCC

DARLENE DUNPHY was born in Cloquet, Minnesota and moved to White Bear Lake as a teen-ager. Bill Luther was born and raised on a farm in the Fergus Falls, Minnesota area. He moved to the Twin Cities to attend college at the University of Minnesota.

Darlene and Bill Luther

Bill and Darlene met while Bill was studying at the University. After their marriage, Darlene and Bill lived in an apartment in New Hope. When it was time to purchase their first home, they chose to stay in the developing northwest suburban area and settled in a home on Dallas Road in Brooklyn Center. In 1978 Bill and Darlene built a home on Shingle Creek Drive in Brooklyn Park. They were attracted to the growing family-oriented community. In the meantime, their own family was growing—Alex was born in 1977 and Alicia in 1981.

Darlene worked as flight attendant for Northwest Airlines and Bill started a law practice. In 1974 he successfully ran for the Minnesota State House of Representatives from Brooklyn Center. In 1976 Bill was elected to the Minnesota State Senate from the Brooklyn Center/Brooklyn Park area, where he served until 1994. He also served as the Assistant Senate majority leader during this time. Bill now represents the 6th Congressional District in the United States House of Representatives. Darlene received her bachelor's degree in Business Administration from the University of St. Thomas. In 1992 she was elected State Representative from the Brooklyn Park area and continues to serve District 47A in the Minnesota House of Representatives.

The Luthers have been involved in the area for many years. Darlene served on the Community Emergency Assistance Program Board and is past president of the Northwest Road Runners Special Olympics Bowling Team. The family belongs to St. Alphonsus Catholic Church. Alex is a 1995 graduate of Park Center High School.

Alex, Alicia, Darlene, Bill and Crystal Luther

The Luthers have watched Brooklyn Park and the surrounding communities grow and thrive in the twenty-five years they have lived here. What started as a second tier suburb dotted with farmland has grown into one of the largest cities in the state. Darlene said, "The Brooklyn Park/Brooklyn Center area is a wonderful place to raise children. It is an honor to live in this community and represent it in the Legislature."

Submitted by Darlene Luther

John & Christine Magnusson

JOHN ANDREW AND CHRISTINE MAGNUSSON arrived in Brooklyn Center in 1893 and resided on 221 acres of farmland located at 4014 69th Avenue North. The farmhouse was torn down to make way for road construction about 1993. At that time, it was the second oldest home still in existence in the Brooklyn Center community. Gladys Pully, their granddaughter, managed to rescue the etched glass window from the parlor, and it now hangs in her living room with the farm picture under it.

Gladys' grandparents emigrated from Sweden, coming to this country in 1864 and 1888 and lived in Indiana before coming to Minnesota. They were married in 1890. Eight children were born to this couple:

Delbert was born in 1892, Lillian in 1894, Emma in 1896 (died at age 15). Jennie was born in 1899 (Gladys's mother), Signa in 1899 (Jennie's twin who died at 5 months of age), Sigrid in 1900, David in 1903, and Alice was born in 1905.

After searching Hennepin County Registry of Birth they were able to solve a mystery as to why Jennie's birth was never recorded, thus leading to great difficulty when applying for a passport to visit Sweden. They found that Jennie's twin sister, Signa, was listed twice.

The Magnussons raised vegetables, mainly potatoes, on the farm until they retired and turned the farm over to their son David and his wife, Maude. They continued farming until David's death in 1971. Maude sold the farm in 1973.

Jennine Serafina Magnusson spoke Swedish while growing up, attended the old wooden one-room school where Mrs. Saddie Brown was her teacher, and later went into Minneapolis to attend West High School, graduating from there in 1917. Even though she spent time helping with the farm work, she studied piano and never forgot how to play. She even managed to get to Sunday School during the snowy winters. Gladys has a lovely hand painted bowl Jennine's Sunday School teacher gave her for perfect attendance.

The Magnusson Family

Jennie Magnusson and Knute Nelson from Anoka, Minnesota were married after his return from serving in France in World War I. They were married on November 14, 1920 at the farmhouse and immediately left for a honeymoon to California.

Because of rainy weather and very bad roads, they only made it as far as Texas, where they planned to stay for the winter. However, they built a home in Dallas and raised five children there. Gladys's first trip back to the farm was in 1930 when she was four years old, and she remembers the big house and great barn where they fed the horses.

Her grandparents, John and Christine, are buried just a few blocks from the old home at Mound Cemetery on 69th Avenue along with Signa, Emma, David, Delbert and members of their families. Now all that is left of the old place is a huge tree that stood in the yard.

Submitted by Gladys Nelson Pully

My husband, Dale, and I moved to Brooklyn Park in 1971. We were searching to buy a home with three bedrooms, a garage and trees in the Robbinsdale School District. It was not an easy task because we had about $25,000 to spend. We found our home at 7300 64th Avenue North and moved in on September 21, 1971.

Our three children, Scott (class of 1990), Sara (class of 1992) and Peter (class of 1994) grew up in Brooklyn Park and all attended Lincoln Elementary, Hosterman Junior High and Cooper High School. I was a "stay at home mom" until 1987, therefore our yard was a meeting place for the neighborhood kids. A sand box, swing set, balls, bikes and sprinklers were the usual agenda. Contrary to what we always heard about Lincoln Elementary School being the smallest in the district and nothing good comes from that, our children all graduated with honors in high school and college. Scott and Peter were state chess champions in elementary school and I was the coach for two years.

On June 1, 1987, I began my career as City Clerk for the City of Brooklyn Park. Jim Krautkremer was the Mayor and Richard Hennebergrer was the City Manager. Both were gone shortly after I started. The City grew and we built a new City Hall in 1991. Those of us who had been with the City for many years remembered events by "were we in the old city hall then" or in the "new city hall."

We have hosted many students from foreign countries in our home from 1991 to 1999. It gave us a great opportunity to show them our city, state and share our culture, as well as learn from them. Our first student was Fernando from Spain and he was here for one month. We also hosted Saulo from Spain, Alexandre from France, Sergio from Italy, Juho from Finland (1995-1996), Mustafa from Turkey (1995-1996), Joe from Brazil (1996-1997) and Rodrigo from Brazil (1998-1999). On the first day of school in 1996, Joe went to the corner to catch the school bus and one of the students asked, "Do you live there? Is that a hotel?" Joe has returned "home" and now attends Music Tech in Minneapolis. He has become our fourth child.

Brooklyn Park has been a wonderful place to raise a family. When I go to the big new Cub Foods Store, I recall how it was when I started shopping there. It was small, located on County Road 81 (where Carousel Bingo is now) and you used a mini flat bed to put your groceries on and you marked your prices with a red grocery marker.

Submitted by Myrna Maikkula

Dale & Myrna Maikkula

The Maikkula Family: front, Joe, Myrna, Pietro, and Sara Serazzi; back Peter, Scott, Sergio Carboni, and Dale

Diane M. Mattson

HER MOTHER was in the hospital, suffering from anemia, expecting Diane, on December 7, 1941, when Pearl Harbor was bombed. Diane was born on June 27, 1942, on her grandmother's birthday.

Her parents bought six acres in Brooklyn Park when she was one year old. They were told then that the state would build a highway to make a new bridge between Anoka and Highway 100 north in front of their property. But thirty-seven years later, right after her parents sold their land, a highway was built right behind the property and even used a small part of it.

Many families moved to Brooklyn Park and Brooklyn Center to build their own houses to make a better life for their families. There was a small school at 73rd and West River Road, the Benson School. They had a store "Yaklich" across the street where the young people could buy penny candy.

Diane's parents built a basement house when her father was discharged from the Army. Her grandfather, who worked for a lumber yard, didn't think any of the houses they looked at were built well enough. The Mattsons paid cash, as they built the house on top of the basement. They moved into the upstairs for Christmas when she was in seventh grade. They had a two-acre lawn. Her dad was the only one who could start the lawn mower. Then the three of them took turns pushing the mower. It took three evenings after supper to mow the lawn. In the summer they had an acre planted into garden and Diane had the job of pulling the weeds when she wasn't in school. Her mom canned every summer until the one year that Diane's dad was on vacation at the time the peas were ready. He helped shell the peas and decided that for three people it wasn't worth doing all of that in the heat. But mom continued to can other things.

The summer after second grade her dad planted 4,000 tomato plants. He took her to Mississippi Court Housing complex along Lyndale Avenue North. She sold tomatoes individually, or as many as people wanted, sometimes a bushel basketful. Years later someone asked her how much money she made. Her answer was, "I didn't expect to get paid. The money just went the into family piggy bank."

Submitted by Diane "Dee" Mattson

Diane Mattson, Glen Carlson, and Gary Carlson

I WAS EIGHT YEARS OLD when my father died. I had an older sister, Lucille, who was twelve, a younger sister, Bernice, who was six and a younger brother Len who was four years old. We inherited property across from the Mattson Halfway House, but had to sell it because our mother, Grace, had to find other work to support her children.

We as children used to go to the Riverlyn and sit on the sidelines to watch our dad dance. It was a big deal to get to go somewhere off the farm.

When Len was two years old he accidentally hit me on the head with the corner of a hoe. Dad just got a bottle of iodine and poured it on my head. People didn't go to the doctor for something as trivial as a cut on the head from a hoe.

When I was in seventh grade I was able to rent a trombone. After practicing at home for some time Lucille became frustrated and threw the trombone out of a window where it landed in a tree. The trombone was straightened out and I still have it.

Uncle Charles helped me get into the Civilian Conservation Corps (CCC) when I was only sixteen years old. I received thirty-five dollars a month. Of this, thirty dollars was sent home to my mother and I was able to keep the other five. As a joke I wrote home to inform them that I was getting married. Lucille wrote me a letter in answer to that which was a tearjerker. After I left the CCC I went back to school and graduated from Osseo High School. Even though I was older, the teachers were wonderful to me.

Submitted by Gil and Helen Mattson

Gil Mattson

The Mattson Family: front, Len Mattson, Virginia Mattson, Helen Mattson, Glen Carlson, and Diane Mattson; back, Gil Mattson, Grace Mattson, Lucille Carlson, Gary, and Sis Simmons

Grace (Hamilton) Mattson

Grace (Hamilton) Mattson ready to go visiting

GRACE HAMILTON was born in Brooklyn Township in 1887. She married Raymond Mattson, whose family owned the "halfway house" and farm. The "halfway house" was just that, halfway between Minneapolis and Anoka. People needed to stop there for the night to get their horses fed and rested before continuing the journey. The house is still standing there on the West River Road between Mattson Brook Lane and 85th Avenue North.

Ray and Grace had an eighty-acre farm on 93rd—now 95th Avenue. They had four children: Lucille, Gilbert, Bernice and Leonard.

Ray died in 1926 at forty-two years of age. Earle Brown furnished cars for the pall-bearers and family members going to the services at Brooklyn Methodist Church, then to and from Mound Cemetery.

Grace tried to stay on at the farm with the children but she finally had to sell it. It has since then been re-sold for development.

Grace was the first female to be licensed as a boiler attendant. She worked at this job for Twin Lake School.

In 1941 Grace began work at the Earle Brown Farm. That summer she went to Vermont to train the staff on Burklyn Farm, another one of his estates, so it would operate like the Earle Brown Farm House. In 1947, health problems forced her to take a leave. She returned to Brooklyn Center with her sister Florence, who was widowed. They stayed at the Earle Brown Farm until Mr. Brown died in 1963. They had their own house and were expected to feed all the farm hands. They worked Monday through Saturdays, and took turns cooking on Sundays. Grace was a wonderful cook and made an especially good chicken.

Grace was loved by everyone and was always willing to help all. When someone was picking her up, she dressed up, including her fur stole. People called her "Mrs. Brown", because she looked like a millionaire.

The "Bed and Breakfast" on Earle Brown Farm has a room named after her and one for Frend Hamilton, deputy sheriff under Earle Brown.

Submitted by Gil and Helen Mattson

MY PARENTS, Edward and Louis (Ducharme) Mavis, settled in Milwaukee, Wisconsin, where my father had grown up. My mother Louise was from Crystal, Michigan. My father was a long-time employee of A. O. Smith Company, maker of hot water heaters. During the war they made landing gears for airplanes.

I grew up in Milwaukee, the oldest of two children. I graduated from Bay View High School and the University of Wisconsin in Milwaukee. I graduated with a degree in sociology.

Carol Kepner, one of six children of Neil and Alice (Anderson) Kepner, was born in Rochester, Minnesota. Carol's father was transferred to Milwaukee in 1941. Arnie had graduated from high school before Carol began at Bay View High School. Arnie and Carol met at church and were married in Milwaukee in 1951.

Carol and I have three children: Ann, Dennis, Bruce and fourteen grandchildren. Ann works for Children's First, lives in Rockford, Minnesota and has three children. Dennis worked for Burlington Northern Railroad. He lives in Hungry Horse, Montana and has six children. Bruce is a financial analyst for U. S. Bank, lives in Maple Grove and has five children.

Employment at the Northside "Y" on 33rd and Penn North brought us to this area. Gary Rolek, the Executive Director, lived in Brooklyn Center and helped us find our home at 6006 Halifax Place. I was employed at the Northside "Y" from 1964 to 1969. I then came to work for the City of Brooklyn Center, under Gene Hagel, in the Parks and Recreation Department. Don Poss was the City Manager at the time. When Gene retired in 1985, I became the Director of Recreation. I retired January 1997 but continue to manage the Centerbrook Golf Course. I enjoy golfing and it was exciting to have had six of our grandchildren playing in the Junior Golf League at Centerbrook this year.

Carol is a dressmaker, and has sewed for fabric departments both here and in Milwaukee. Presently she works only at home. Carol's hobbies are golfing, bowling and sewing. She has been an active member of the Brooklyn Center Women's Club since 1985 and served as President from 1988-1990.

Submitted by Arnie and Carol Mavis

The Arnie & Carol Mavis Family

Carol and Arnie Mavis

Ethel McArthur

THIS IS THE STORY of a teacher, Ethel (Moore) McArthur. Ethel was of English, Scotch and Irish descent. She was raised near Milaca, Minnesota and had three sisters and one brother. Her father played just about every musical instrument that there was to play. Her mother played the piano. Ethel taught herself to play the piano and continued to play for school programs. Their family almost never missed a fair, circus, parade or any other celebration within a fifty-mile radius.

Ethel was trained to be a teacher, the profession of her Grandmother, Lauretta Wellcome. Lauretta said, when writing about teaching in 1874, "Let the little ones go out often and play among the butterflies and make mud pies."

The first school Ethel taught in was a one-room schoolhouse on the prairie near Aberdeen, South Dakota. There were eight grades and forty-five pupils in that one room. At first she was scared to death. Some pupils were as big, if not bigger, than she was and some were almost as old as her nineteen years. She was afraid that she would have a problem with discipline. She had an idea, if she could get the kids to like her, they wouldn't cause her problems. She found this philosophy was successful. In those days the teacher did everything from being the janitor to playing with the children during recess. Some pupils lived as far as five miles from school and rode horseback. The school had a barn to keep the horses in during the school hours.

Ethel McArthur

Later, Ethel met a Native American man at a dance who would become her husband. They lived in Callaway, Minnesota on the White Earth Indian Reservation, where she was teaching. Her husband passed away at age thirty-nine leaving her with nine children. It was during the Depression and times were rough for everybody. She said it was easy to raise children then, because hardly anyone had a car so they were always at home. Children went tobogganing and skating during the winter. During the summer there was always kitten ball and croquet.

To feed her family, Ethel went back to substitute teaching, harvesting her large garden and canning for the winter months. In later years, there was an opening in the Callaway post office. She retired after twenty years as postmaster.

Three of Ethel's boys and two girls served in the military.

In 1972 Ethel moved from Callaway to Brooklyn Center to be closer to her children. She was one of the first tenants in Shingle Creek Towers. She loved to travel and visit her children in and out of the United States. One of her grandchildren wrote, "When the McArthur clan gets together for some fun and dancing, she is right on the floor whirling with them. She is in her prime at eighty years. . . and there won't be another one like her." Ethel lived to the age of ninety-four.

Submitted by Ernee McArthur

THEY CALLED IT the "City of Hope" in 1957 when Don and Ernee McArthur moved to Brooklyn Center. They had lived at Olson Highway and Humboldt Avenue North for five years, where they were able to learn the richness of the Jewish faith from their landlady, Sarah Rozman. Ernee and Don had been married at Camp Rucker, Alabama, and lived in that state during the Korean Conflict. They decided to look north when buying their house because they were both northern Minnesota people, having been raised on the White Earth Indian Reservation at Callaway, Minnesota. Don was a proud Native American of 1/3 Ojibwe descent. Ernee is of German decent.

Don liked the construction of the $16,400 Marvin Anderson house which they purchased on 55th Avenue North, assuming a GI mortgage. They could not have qualified for financing on their own. At that time banks considered the husband's earnings only. In the 1960s Don and Ernee were to adopt two children, Neil and Amy.

Neil married Maria from Honduras; Amy married Paul Sass from St. Paul. They are raising their families in Cottage Grove and Oakdale, Minnesota. There have been eight grandchildren: Andrea, Neil Jr., Jean-Luc, Monique, Andrew, Cassandra, Tyler and Mikkaela.

In 1988, after a six-year two-month silent battle with cancer, Don died. Before he died he built his vision, a tribute to his Native American people, a half-log cabin on Leech Lake where he, his family and friends had fished for thirty-five years, all the years he had been employed by Minnegasco.

Ernee continues to be a volunteer in the community, as she has been for forty-three years. She identifies herself as an Ambassador for Jesus Christ, following a conversion/reborn again experience in 1973 driving to St. Paul while serving in the Minnesota Legislature.

In June 1995 Ernee found a new life with husband Joseph Lampe, who grew up in St. Louis Park. Joe is the oldest of six children born to Alois and Margaret Lampe. He had also lived in Winona, and Rochester, MN, San Antonio, TX, Riverside, CA, Washington, D. C., St. Anthony and Shoreview, MN.

They chose to sell Joe's Shoreview home and live in Brooklyn Center. They are often drawn to the peace, quiet and renewal they find when spending time at "His place" on Leech Lake, so needed in their active lives.

Joe and Ernee met while working on Senator Don Kramer's volunteer campaign committee in 1994. Joe subsequently was Ernee's escort to the Governor's 1995 Inaugural Ball. They found they had much in common: German, Catholic, pro-life, history buffs and political animals. They feel most fulfilled in their volunteer work with Our Lady of Victory Catholic Church and the local Republican Party. Their "Focus on Jesus' Ministry to the Suffering" is based on a painting of Jesus by Native American, Joe Redboye, and ministers to cancer and Aids patients, alcoholics and other hurting people.

Brooklyn Center continues to be a CITY OF HOPE, because of the abundance of affordable housing. The new century brings new hope, new beginnings and wonderful challenges.

Submitted by Ernee McArthur and Joseph Lampe

The McArthur and Lampe Families

Ernee, Joe, and Family

The Ray H. McArthur Family

AFTER HIGH SCHOOL Ray McArthur from Callaway, Minnesota served in the United States Air Force during World War II, and later with Strategic Air Command in the Korean War. He married Jeanine Wiederholt of Aitkin, Minnesota in 1953.

In 1957 Ray and I moved from Aitkin, Minnesota to Brooklyn Park on 68th Avenue North and Bethia Lane. We had two small children at the time; Gregory was three and Michael two. Kimberly and Jeffrey were born in Brooklyn Park and all of our children attended Osseo District #279 schools, along with some private schooling.

Ray worked for an automobile agency as a fleet manager. His hobbies are travel, hunting and fishing.

I was a stay-at-home mom but was involved in various activities with school and church. Crafts and travel are my hobbies.

Ray and Jeanine McArthur and their grandchildren: Ray, Trevor, Kalee, Jeanine, Ryan, Jeremiah, and Ashley

We did a lot of traveling in the United States, covering the east, west and northwest. Many of these trips were when the children were younger and it was a good learning experience. Today, we often laugh as we share many of those special times.

Because we were one of the first families to move into our addition, we watched all of the homes go up around us. The cornfield was becoming a part of the city. We have many fond memories of those days when all of the neighbors knew one another, watched out for each other, and often in the summer, gathered together for an early evening coffee and cake party in someone's backyard while the children played.

As the children entered high school they became more involved in various sports. Greg took part in gymnastics. Mike was a wrestler, Kim was a cheerleader and Jeff played some baseball.

We lived in the same home for forty-one years, making lifelong friendships as we worked together building on to our homes with garages, driveways, patios, pools, and so on. We watched our children grow up, marry, leave home, and branch out on their own. Soon the little ones (grandchildren) came along. We have eight grandchildren.

Kim and Dennis King, reside in Owatonna, Minnesota. Kim is employed by the school district. Dennis is with Federated Insurance Company of Owatonna. They are the parents of Ryan, Trevor, and Ashley.

Mike lives in Colorado with his children, Jeremiah, Kalee and Jonathan. He is now with the Fellowship of Christian Cowboys as National Chapter Director. He was formerly with Campus Crusade for Christ in the athletic division working with wrestlers, and continues to be involved as a coach for the U. S. Wrestling Federation. Jeff and daughter Kayla live in Colorado also. He is with a construction company and is also in the Colorado National Guard. Jeff served in the Army during Desert Storm. Greg lives in Maple Grove with his little girl, Austyn. He owns his business, "Auto Trends and Van Conversion." He still plays softball and their team is still winning national titles (at their ages!).

Ray and I have moved into ReaLife Cooperative Apartments in Brooklyn Park. Ray is semi-retired while I am Activity Director at ReaLife.

Life goes on—God has been good.

Submitted by Jeanine McArthur

CARMELITA WAS BORN in Saint Paul in the early 1900s to a strong German family by the name of Venne. She was the youngest of ten children. Carmelita went to business school in Saint Paul. She gave piano lessons as a side business.

Ralph was born in Northfield, Minnesota, in the early 1900s. He came from a family of seven sons and one daughter. In his mid-teens the family moved to Ogilvie, MN, where he finished his school years.

While going to the University a friend fixed Ralph up with a blind date. The date happened to be Carmelita. The rest is history.

Ralph's first teaching job was in a one-room school in Montana. After Ralph and Carmelita were married, his first teaching job was in Mora, MN. There he taught math and science. He also coached track and started Mora's first Hillbilly Band, which was a huge success.

Clay was born while they were in Mora. They lived in a converted chicken coop, on the Mora Golf Course, which Ralph took care of. Ralph later became the principal of Mora High School.

The next move found the McCartneys in Pemberton, MN. Ralph was superintendent of schools. They remained here for three years.

Ralph's next superintendency job was at Mabel, MN. After two and a half years there Ralph took a job at Olivia, MN.

In 1960 the McCartneys moved to Brooklyn Center, MN, where Ralph took on the job of being superintendent of the new high school being built here.

Carmelita was the kind of woman Ralph needed for a superintendent's wife. She was a wonderful hostess at home and at school gatherings. She was a woman who made you feel as if you had known her all your life, after just a few moments.

Ralph retired in 1971. Both, he and Carmelita liked the Brooklyn Center School District. Many of the trees planted around the high school came from Ralph's boyhood farm by Ogilvie. We all know a part of Ralph is always watching over Brooklyn Center High School.

Submitted by Clay McCartney

Ralph and Carmelita McCartney

Alexander and Annie McLeod

ALEXANDER AND ANNIE (McCONNELL) McLEOD were born in Nova Scotia, Canada. Their daughter Alice was born in 1865 in Brooklyn Township. The farm was located on the west side of the Mississippi River near 85th Avenue North.

Alexander died of injuries sustained while he was lumbering in the Big Woods, circa 1870. The Big Woods was described as a 5000 square mile hardwood forest on the west side of the Mississippi River from the Crow Wing River south for more than one-hundred miles.

Annie then married John William Pride, Jr., a decorated Civil War veteran who saw action in several battles, was wounded and captured by the Confederates. He was held prisoner and suffered ill health as a result of his treatment in the notorious prison, Andersonville.

Alice McLeod Caswell and Arthur Donald Caswell

ARTHUR AND ALICE CASWELL FAMILY

A young man, Arthur Anson Caswell, living on Mississippi River, observed Alice across the River and was attracted to her. After meeting and courting her, they married and had six children: Mildred, Keith, Robert, Arthur Jr., Leigh and Elizabeth.

Arthur was a law enforcement officer and inventor. One of his inventions was a target range system for law enforcement training. The system is in use yet today. Arthur is one of three lumberjacks written up in the Brooklyn Historical Society publication "Tales of Local Minnesota Lumberjacks."

Arthur and Alice's son Keith was a construction engineer. He married Dorothea Wilberg of Anoka. They had eight children; one of the children is Keith P. Caswell of Maple Grove.

Submitted by Jane Hallberg

ROGER McCORT was born and raised in Seattle, WA until his mid-teens when his family was transferred to Manteca, CA. Roger is the oldest son of three children born to Robert and JoLynn McCort. Robert McCort worked for AT&T for over thirty years and made several transfers within the company. He retired in June 1998 in Marietta, GA. JoLynn McCort was a devoted homemaker and mother through most of her children's lives. August 2, 2000, will be Bob and Lynn's 32nd wedding anniversary.

The McCort Family

After completing high school early in an accelerated program, Roger enrolled at Delta San Jouquin College in Stockton, CA. During a trip with the InterVarsity Christian group to Urbana, IL, Roger felt called to leave college and join EPPIC Ministries in Richfield, MN. EPPIC was a pantomime group that re-created the word of God through mime. During his first few weeks in Minnesota as a young man of seventeen, he met Bridget Bjerke, a girl of fourteen, who was active at Bethany Covenant Church in Richfield, which had become Roger's home church.

Bridget was the oldest daughter of two children born to Howard and Mabel Bjerke. Howard Bjerke is a Vietnam veteran of the U. S. Army and native of Rugby, ND. He has worked most of his life as a welder and is very active in the Machinist Union. Howard was the youngest child born to Helen and Henry Bjerke. Mabel Budrow was born in Fort Knox, KY, and was the youngest child of Howard and Irene Budrow. They moved to Baudette, MN, in the early 1950s, and in 1969 Mabel moved to the Twin Cities to begin her career in the mortgage arena, spending most of her career with Midwest Federal Savings and Loan. Mabel Budrow and Howard Bjerke married in July 1970, and have lived in Richfield, MN, for more than twenty-two years.

Roger McCort and Bridget Bjerke were married in June 1991, only nine days after her graduation from Richfield Senior High School. They made their home in Hopkins, MN, for six years before coming to Brooklyn Park, MN, in August 1997.

Howard and Mabel Bjerke, Bridget Bjerke and Roger McCort

After years of work in the retail industry, Roger found his technical niche, and works as a computer hardware technician for Now Micro in New Brighton, MN. Roger currently serves as President of the First Minnesota Historical War Gaming Society.

Bridget began work for AAA Minneapolis in August of 1991, and is employed in the public relations, government affairs, marketing, and traffic safety side of the business. Bridget works closely with local law enforcement in both Brooklyn Park and Brooklyn Center through the Minneapolis Auto Club Foundation for Safety (a part of AAA Minneapolis) to provide school safety patrol items and other traffic safety materials to students in Brooklyn Park, Brooklyn Center, and all over Hennepin County.

Since moving to Brooklyn Park, Roger and Bridget have taken a special interest in the historical and tourist attractions of the northwest suburbs, and have finally become involved in politics at the local level.

Submitted by Bridget McCort

Greg and Chris McGeary Family

GREG AND CHRIS ARRIVED in Brooklyn Center in April of 1969. Greg's job as Assistant Store Manager of the new Goodyear Service Store at Brookdale brought them to Brooklyn Center. Before coming to Brooklyn Center, they lived in a two-bedroom apartment in Elmo Park in Hopkins, MN. With the fourth child on the way, something had to change! They bought their first house at 3007 Thurber Rd. and live there. As the years went by, the house at 3007 Thurber Rd. became too small, but it was made to work as they chose to send each of their six children through sixteen years of private, Catholic education. Their children, spouses and grandchildren are:

Anne Marie McGeary, Sharon Lynn McGeary Kehn (husband Kevin Kehn) and children John and Allison, John Patrick McGeary and son John Charles (J. C.), Janet

Greg and Chris McGeary

Mary McGeary Litwin (husband James Litwin) and children Laura and Timothy, Mark Thomas McGeary (wife Molly Schwalbach McGeary), and Thomas Gregory McGeary.

All of the children live in the Twin Cities metropolitan area.

Greg grew up on a farm near Danvers, MN, in the western part of the state (Swift County). He is the son of John and Susan McGeary. He attended a one-room country school for seven years and graduated from Benson High School where he was co-captain of the football team. Chris was born in northern Wisconsin but moved to Bismarck, ND, with her parents, LeRoy and Alice Hall, when she was three. Her father owned the Hall Funeral Home in Bismarck from 1946-1972. Chris graduated from St. Mary's Central High School in Bismarck.

Greg and Chris met at a college mixer in the old gym at St. John's University in Collegeville, MN, where Greg was a student. He came to St. John's following six months active duty in the U.S. Army National Guard. Chris graduated from the College of St. Benedict in St. Joseph, MN, in 1962 and they were married December 29, 1962, at the Cathedral of the Holy Spirit in Bismarck. Greg graduated from St. Cloud State in 1966.

Much of their life in Brooklyn Center centered around St. Alphonsus Catholic Church where they served on the CCD Board and Greg was president of the Parish Council. They co-chaired the St. Alphonsus Homecoming celebration in 1994. Helping the Boy Scouts of Troop #454 with their Citizenship in the Community Merit badge provided an opportunity for Greg and Chris to learn and appreciate Brooklyn Center heritage. Their most satisfying volunteer effort was the many years spent in marriage ministry through Worldwide Marriage Encounter.

In 1983 when the children started college, Chris went to work for Northern States Power where she manages information technology training. Greg sold Ford heavy trucks for twenty-five years. Following retirement from Minar Ford, Greg is pursuing a new venture in preventative health care with Rexall Showcase International.

Submitted by Greg and Chris McGeary

THINGS ARE CHANGING. I went to school in a one-room schoolhouse in central Minnesota from 1949-1956. One teacher taught grades one through seven; first I had Mrs. Reiten, then Mrs. Carlin, who I had for all seven years. There were six rows of desks and six pupils in a row. There were forty pupils in the school. When it was time to go to eighth grade in the consolidated school, I heard that girls couldn't wear pants. I said that I would wear a dress, but I wouldn't wear a slip.

Pupils didn't take typing until tenth grade. We had spelling every week. In the fall all of the pupils brought rakes to school and raked the schoolyard. We burned the leaves and had a wiener roast. The teacher and the Mother's Club had supplied the food. My brothers and sisters walked the half-mile to school and we cleaned bathrooms before the other pupils came. We were very happy to do it because it was an indoor bathroom — not an outhouse like we had at home.

When I first started teaching in Minneapolis Public Schools on 51st and Irving Avenue North in 1970, I had one class of thirty-five seventh graders. The pupils brought all their materials except for one or two who chose not to work. I taught reading individually so pupils did not come up to the front of the room in groups. I taught spelling and vocabulary every week. The pupils had seven different teachers each year. I remember sending one pupil to the office for aggressive behavior my first year. The most common offense for detention in our school was gum chewing.

Now in the 90s I am still teaching seventh graders. I have thirty pupils in the room and about ten don't do any work or bring their materials.

All of the pupils except for five percent arrive by bus. There are seven hundred fifty pupils in the school. The pupils wear their bra straps and underwear showing. Now my pupils take keyboarding in sixth, seventh and eighth grade.

Pupils know how to correct their spelling on the word processor before turning it in. Pupils use their database on the computer to look up synonyms on the Thesaurus. I send about ten pupils to the office every week for racist or sexist name calling, threatening, hitting and kicking. We have several pupils transferred out each year for bringing weapons, stabbing and hitting a teacher. Now students complain when they are asked to pick up their candy wrappers and waste paper. "That's the janitor's job!" they retort. Pupils vandalize the bathrooms by writing racial and sexual slurs on the walls, urinating on the walls, throwing the soap down the hall and plugging up the toilets with towels. In school, some things stayed the same and some things are different.

Submitted by Joyce McMains

Joyce McMains

The Stan Meyers Family

REPAIRING TELEVISIONS for RCA Service Company, Stanley Meyers chanced on the Gleason homes in the Village of Brooklyn Center. We needed a house but had no money. Gleason required no down payment and we could earn closing costs if we did our own painting. It was an answer to prayer. We moved to 5530 Judy Lane in May of 1954. In August, son James was born. Stanley Jr., was four, John three, and Harvey, eighteen months. Amy was born March 1956, David in August 1957, Ana Lisa, September 1960, and Sidney, February 1964. We now had 10 people in a three-bedroom rambler and one small bathroom. Two sets of bunk beds and a folding trundle (part of a former sofa), accommodated five boys in one room; the girls had bunk beds in the other; Sid's crib was in our bedroom. Income from the *Minneapolis Star* newspaper that the boys delivered from 1960 into mid 1970 helped Stan and the boys eventually add three basement bedrooms and shower.

Meyers Family get-together: front, Sid, Ana, and Dave; middle, Jim and Amy; back, Stanley Jr. (Herb), John, Harvey

After two years in the Navy, son Stanley received a Secretary of State appointment to Annapolis. Now a Captain in the Navy Reserves, he works with the Government's nuclear supply program. He, Nancy and two daughters live in Port Orchard, WA.

After Navy boot camp, John traveled from Gaeta, Italy, on the U.S.S. Springfield and Littlerock as "sound man" for the Sixth Fleet Band and Choir. As an EE he works for Scitex in Atlanta, GA. He, Jan, and their daughter Erin live in Dunwoody, GA.

Harvey joined the Air Force, earned an EE and MBA and now has his own computer company, "Alphaware." He and Mary live in Burnsville, MN. Jim became a jet engine mechanic for the Navy and used his GI bill to earn an accounting degree. He also maintains C-130's for the Minnesota Air National Guard as a reservist and technician. He, Linda, and their four children live at 5530 Judy Lane.

Amy majored in journalism and has an M.A. in Christian Education from Bethel. She, John (Teske), and three daughters live in Brooklyn Park. David, an EE, works for Honeywell. He lives in Brooklyn Park with Renee, their three sons, and daughter. To help skaters develop proficiency, Dave invented the "crossover trainer." Ana Lisa and Mickey (Nelson) live in Ramsey. Ana uses her A.A. in accounting at Medtronics.

With a B.S. degree, Sid works as a computer consultant from his home in Golden Valley. He and Dana have three children, two adopted from Korea.

Totally disabled by rheumatoid arthritis, Dad Stan was forced to retire from RCA in August 1974 and I returned to Civil Service employment. I continued to serve as secretary to the Minnesota Air National Guard Commanders until I retired in 1985. Stan died February 9, 1979, at age fifty-six. Having served as a Navy Radioman in World War II, he is interred at Fort Snelling National Cemetery. He never saw his grandchildren. Grandmother now to our seventeen, I continue to do laundry and go golfing. (I decided it was better to play golf than remarry.)

Submitted by Ethel Meyers (nee Frobom)

In 1923 George Miller and his wife Anna Kramer purchased a plot of land (2½ acres) in the Brooklyn Township just north of the Minneapolis city limits. They parented thirteen children and raised them in an old two-story farmhouse with no indoor plumbing or insulation, burning wood to heat the house and cook.

In 1941 Ralph Miller and his wife Alvina Roden bought the homestead from his father. They then converted the wood heater to coal heat. At that time, N. W. Hanna, a coal company, employed Ralph. He worked there until he retired.

Mary Ann Stewart, Ralph and Alvina's daughter, was born in 1938. They had one son who passed away in 1985.

The Millers farmed the land, raising vegetables and five hundred baby chicks each spring. On many occasions Alvina cleaned and dressed as many as twenty chickens to be sold. Because this was during World War II, the fresh vegetables of corn, peas, beans, potatoes, tomatoes, and carrots were in great demand.

Three generations of the Miller family attended Earle Brown Elementary School, including Ralph (who remembered the tornado that hit the school), their son, and Mary Ann and her two children, Timothy and Cynthia Bailey. A highlight of Mary Ann's grade school years was the annual field trip to Earle Brown Farm.

In the late 1940s Ralph decided to divide the property and sell the lots for housing. He retained the two lots on 56th and Colfax Avenue on which the original homestead stood. Ralph, who wasn't a carpenter by trade, built a new home for his family. A basement was dug and covered and we moved in. Many families lived in their basements until the upper levels were completed. Ralph, working a full time job, had to build in his leisure hours. He demolished the old farmhouse, salvaging the lumber it was built with. Ralph often commented, "You can't buy lumber like this anymore," as there were no knotholes in any of the salvage. Ralph did most of the work himself and only contracted out the electric and the ceramic tile.

The Millers lived in the basement for about eight years. Mary Ann went off to a private school in Duluth. In 1956 the year she graduated, the three-bedroom rambler was complete and they moved to the main level. After Mary Ann's marriage to Ron Bailey in 1957, her father built a smaller rambler on the adjacent lot, which Ralph and Alvina moved into. They rented out the house on the corner. Eventually, they moved back into the original house where they resided until their passing.

Mary Ann and her husband purchased a home on 60th and Dupont in 1963 where they raised their two children and she has lived there ever since.

Submitted by Mary Ann Stewart

The Miller Story

The Odean and DeLaine Mork Family

ODEAN AND DELAINE (OLSON) MORK are both natives of rural North Dakota. There were nine students in DeLaine's rural one-room school nine miles from Northwood, North Dakota. She attended this school from first through eighth grades. Odean's one-room rural school was near Petersburg, North Dakota.

Odean and DeLaine credit the strict and disciplined English teachers in high school for their interest in reading.

The Morks and their two daughters, Cindy and Collette, moved to Brooklyn Center from Colorado in 1962. Randy and Phillip were born here. All four children graduated from Anoka High School and were well prepared for college. The Morks now have six grandchildren.

Odean retired in 1992 after thirty years of employment with Honeywell. He now enjoys reading, working on his own cars, and spending time in Arizona in the winter.

DeLaine's maternal grandmother was sixteen years old when she came to America from Norway to "a better life here." She had packed all of her belongings in a trunk and brought it with her. Grandmother would cry when talking about Norway because she knew she would never get back there. Her sister and brothers also came to America. DeLaine said that her grandmother stressed going to church, reading the Bible, keeping holy the Sabbath and did not believe in dancing and cards, but she was a lot of fun. Grandmother affected her granddaughter's life more than she realized.

If her mother was not there when DeLaine came home from school she was very upset, so she tried to be there for her own children when they came home from school. Now she finds that their children do more for theirs than she and her mother ever did. They are more involved with their children, taking them to different places, just spending more time with them.

Ingaborg and Gunder Olson were hard working, kind and always willing to help people in need.

DeLaine remembers spending quality time with her dad while planting a tree, and then years later after he died of cancer at the age of seventy-seven years, she saw it in full growth on their second generation farm. She enjoys reading, walking and biking. She is interested in researching and seeking family roots in Norway. She has passed on to one of their children the trunk given to her by her grandmother Ingaborg.

Submitted by DeLaine Mork

GEORGE NASSIG worked for the Cedar Lake Ice Company for fourteen years. He was a young man of twenty-two years when he started in 1922. The next year he was made foreman of the car ice crew, the men responsible for putting ice in the railroad cars to protect perishable food. In the fall and spring of the year he would help the drivers going house-to-house selling ice or service at some of the finer hotels.

Nassig spent winters cutting the ice on the lakes and on the Mississippi River. George said he spent eleven years cutting ice on Twin Lake in Brooklyn Center.

Ice cutting on the lakes began the day after the New Year and continued through February. First they had to scrape the snow off the ice to enable the ice to freeze to a larger thickness. Sometimes they had to scrape three times to get the ice to freeze to the thickness of about twenty or more inches. The cut cakes were about twenty-two by thirty-two inches and weighed about four hundred and forty pounds. The ice, chained in the water, was pushed up on a conveyor and went under a planer where it was cut to uniform thickness. It was then loaded into railroad cars ready to be moved to ice houses.

Bob Cahlander, Brooklyn Center's first police chief, was one of the men at the controls watching for "cripples." A cripple was any cake that was not perfect.

The ice was stored in specially built icehouses, all forty feet tall. Sawdust was packed in between the studs for insulation. Hay or sawdust was put on the top layer of the ice to keep it from melting. The icehouses had separate rooms and you would open only one room at a time.

Cedar Lake Ice Company was started in the 1890s. It was a million dollar business but George Nassig was paid fifty cents an hour for all his work. After President Roosevelt's National Recovery Act (NRA) was put into action, George was paid a straight salary of one hundred seventy-five dollars a month. He then belonged to a union.

Dayton's paid six dollars for a ton of ice, but the railroads paid only two and a half per ton. They could use the cripples.

George quit working for Cedar Lake Ice in 1936. He bought a farm in Wisconsin, where he farmed for fifteen years and then worked for an implement dealer in South Dakota. He moved to Brooklyn Center in 1956, worked for the village on maintenance and dispatching, and then retired when he was sixty-five years old.

Submitted by Barbara Erickson
(Information from "The Iceman Cometh and Then He Fadeth Away")
by Mary Jane Gustafson

George Nassig

George Nassig with Ice Tools

Charles Nassig

CHARLES NASSIG was in the First Minnesota Regiment, Company I. He was one of seventeen men in his Company who survived the Battle of Gettysburg in July of 1863. Seventy-five percent of the men died within fifteen minutes of battle. Charles Nassig was also in the Battle of First Bull Run, Virginia and the Battle at Antietam Creek in Maryland.

Charles Nassig was a stonemason by trade who had come from Dresden, Germany when he was in his twenties. He landed in St. Louis. He had heard so much about St. Anthony that he moved here in the 1840s. He used to say that there would never be anything in this wilderness. He went back to St. Louis and returned to Minnesota in the 1850s, homesteading in Eden Valley, Meeker County.

The Civil War between the states broke out in 1861. Charles joined the Army. After two years and eight months he was discharged because of wounds received in the fighting. He had been wounded at Antietam and Gettysburg, both.

After his discharge, Mr. Nassig drove a team of oxen with supplies to Fort Sisseton, South Dakota from Fort Snelling. The trip took four weeks, one way. They would encounter herds of buffalo going to water. The caravan had to stop and let the buffalo pass. If they shot one or two the rest closed the gap. The buffalo traveled single file with the head on the rump of the buffalo ahead. The calves ran alongside.

Charles Nassig moved to Golden Valley where he farmed and raised a family. He never felt well again after the war. It is believed that his illness developed because of food shortages when the enemy had cut off the food supply line. One time he had come upon a field with potatoes the size of marbles. He refused to sell any to a captain for two and half dollars, saying his stomach came first.

George Nassig's leather scabbard, in which he carried his ice pick when he worked for Cedar Lake Ice Company, was made from his grandfather's Civil War knapsack.

The house that Grandpa Nassig built in 1880 in Golden Valley is still standing.

Grandfather David Bies was in the 8th Minnesota Regiment, Company K. He walked to join the regiment in 1862 when there was an Indian uprising. They walked from Fort Snelling to the South Dakota Badlands driving the Indians back. He also escorted a caravan of Finlanders and families going to work in the lead mines in Idaho before the Civil War.

Submitted by Barbara Erickson
Information from "The Iceman Cometh and Then He Fadeth Away"
by Mary Jane Gustafson.

JAMES NAU was born near Perham, Minnesota and grew up in Saint Cloud. He joined the Civilian Conservation Corps. (CCC) serving in northern Minnesota where the Corp planted trees creating the forests as we see them today. After the CCC, he worked in a defense plant in Detroit, Michigan for a while. He then joined the Merchant Marines serving during the World War II.

I was born in Arvilla, North Dakota. I attended the Arvilla schools through the tenth grade, and finished my high school at Larimore, North Dakota. I then attended Business School at Grand Forks, North Dakota.

Jim and I met at Yellowstone Park. I worked in the main office at Mammoth, Wyoming and Jim did the painting of the Yellowstone Park buildings, etc.

Jim and I have been Brooklyn Center residents for forty-nine years, in the same house for that length of time. When we moved in the land behind us was vacant. There was talk of creating a cemetery on the vacant land, but eventually builders bought the land and houses soon sprung up there.

We have been parishioners at Our Lady of Victory parish for forty-nine years. Our six children attended the parochial school. Dennis went on to DeLaSalle High School, Dale graduated from Nazareth Hall. The other four graduated from Brooklyn Center High School.

Dennis is in the computer manufacturing business. He and wife, Rita, live in Gibbon Minnesota.

Dale went on to become a priest. He is with the Duluth Diocese where he is a Chancellor, a Campus Minister for the University of Minnesota-Duluth and is on the Marriage Tribunal. A few years ago Fr. Dale was invited to Rome. While there he was with a group that con-celebrated mass with Pope John Paul. At the end of the mass Pope John Paul presented each of the con-celebrants with a rosary. Fr. Dale presented his to me. I feel very honored to have this rosary blessed by the Pope.

Stephen is a building contractor. He and his wife, Lorraine, live in Minnetonka. Patrick is a professional photographer. He and his wife, Jill, were just recently married. Mary is married to Mark O'Brien. She is an elementary school teacher in Shoreview, Minnesota. Marcia married Dean Flicker and is a practicing psychotherapist for Wright County at Big Lake, Minnesota.

Jim and I have eight grandchildren and two great-grandchildren.

Jim was self-employed doing painting and paper hanging. I worked for the Sears credit department at the Brookdale store. I worked part time there for twenty-five years. I also volunteered at Our Lady of Victory School and at the parish kitchen helping with the school lunches. I helped at an Adult Day Care Center. After Jim retired he volunteered for Community Emergency Assistance Program for many years.

We celebrated our 51st anniversary in November of 1999. During these years we have seen many changes.

Submitted by Isabel Nau

The James and Isabel Nau Family

James and Isabel Nau on their golden wedding anniversary (1998)

The Ed and Ruth Nelson Family

ON MEMORIAL DAY WEEKEND in 1982, the Ed Nelson Family composed of Edward, his wife, Ruth (Candy), and their two children Carla, age eleven, and Jeffrey, age nine, immigrated back to their home state of Minnesota from Rockford, IL. The Nelsons were again looking for a place that had home value, quality schools, and a stable community, as well as a location near Ed's office in Crystal. They found it in the southwestern neighborhood of Brooklyn Center. They moved in to a home they had purchased at 5236 Great View Avenue North, which had been built in 1962 in the Twin Lake Woods Addition of the city.

During the past seventeen years at this address, the Nelsons have had some major accomplishments. Ed was a seven-year national sales leader for the Presbyterian Ministers' Fund and in 1988 was a top national producer. In 1989 he started his own business, Comprehensive Stewardship Services, Inc., a financial consulting firm. He earned the Chartered Life Underwriter (CLU) designation in 1986 and the Charter Financial Consultant (CHFC) designation in 1988.

Candy has been teaching Spanish in Independent School District #279 since 1983, and at Osseo Senior High School since 1991. She received her Master's Education degree from the University of Minnesota in Second Languages and Cultures in 1997. Carla played basketball and graduated from Cooper High School in 1989 with top honors. She also played basketball and went on to get a B.S. degree in Chemistry from Bethel College in 1992 and a Ph.D. in Analytical Chemistry from the University of Wisconsin in 1996. Motorola in Austin, Texas employs her in microchip technology.

Jeff was involved in sports (football, basketball, and track) and graduated from Cooper in 1991 with top honors, and from Drake University as the top business graduate in 1994. Sterling Commerce in Columbus, Ohio employs him in e-commerce projects. Jeff received his MBA from Ohio State University in 1997.

The Nelson Family also hosted three foreign exchange students: Gerrit from Germany in 1985, Marta from Barcelona, Spain in 1988, and Alex also from Barcelona in 1990. During the children's growing-up years, the Nelsons enjoyed canoeing on Twin Lakes, playing and skating in Northport Park, and participating in the former Brooklyn Center Baptist Church. Ed has served on various church committees, as church chairman, has sung solos, and was in choir. Candy and Ed were on the initial medical and house construction missions team from their church to a war zone area of Guatemala in 1994. They have taught English as a Second Language to global professionals in Guatemala City. They serve on a missions team from their church with the responsibility for communications with about fifteen missionaries in Latin America.

Now that the Nelsons are "empty nesters", they are also enjoying the many activities offered in Brooklyn Center. As the recent motto of the city says, they have found Brooklyn Center to be "a great place to start and a great place to stay."

Submitted by Ed Nelson

GORDON AND EMILY NELSON were born and raised in the Baldwin, Wisconsin area. They moved to Brooklyn Center in 1958.

Gordon was a manager at Northern States Power Company. Emily was a registered nurse at Lutheran Deaconess Hospital. Later she was employed with Lutheran Social Services as a childcare worker with foster care. They had many friends that lived in the area that inspired them to look to the north metro area to live.

In earlier years their sons, Doug and Brent, played on the American Little League team, Malmborg Orioles (Malmborg's Garden Center and Greenhouse). Gordon was a coach for four years. (Tim Laudner started with the Malmborg Orioles and later became catcher for the Minnesota Twins.)

Their children attended a different school each year until Fair Oaks Elementary was built. Doug was with the first graduating class of Park Center High School in 1972.

There are still five families on Toledo and 64th Avenue who are the original owners since 1958. The Nelsons moved in March of 1999 to a one-level residence in Brooklyn Park.

Gordon is one of three people in Brooklyn Center who is a recipient of a heart transplant. The heart was transplanted at the University of Minnesota Hospital in 1986. He is an inspiration to many.

Their daughter Cheryl has helped many of the residents of the area get back on their feet as a physical therapist at North Memorial Medical Center since 1986. She is now Mrs. Cheryl Schlicht and lives in Maple Grove, Minnesota.

The Nelsons have been members of Cross of Glory Lutheran Church since 1959. They enjoyed their years in Brooklyn Center and have watched the many changes of landscape from potato fields to a bustling successful city. They elected to enjoy their retirement years in the area they have grown to love.

Submitted by Emily Nelson

Gordon and Emily Nelson

Emily and Gordon Nelson with Cody

Robert and Maxine (Betty) Nelson

WHEN THE "SENTINEL" — now the "Post" — featured the Nelsons as the largest family in Brooklyn Park in 1965, two year old Leona and her four year old brother, Gordon, were too young to even dream about college. Now they have both graduated from the University of Minnesota.

Leona graduated with a Bachelor's degree in metallurgical engineering. Gordon received his degree in mechanical engineering. Though they never took courses together, Leona and Gordon were able to help each other with schoolwork and emotional support when needed.

After graduation Gordon began a job as an engineering assistant in Minnetonka where he incorporated new technology into existing computer terms. Leona, too, landed a job as an associate metallurgist in East Chicago, Indiana. She helps analyze the quality of the company's products. Leona got a sample of independence when she lived at the University of Minnesota. She says, "It taught me how to budget my time and money."

Maxine (Betty) said she is proud of all of her children. She undoubtedly should get some of the credit for teaching them good work habits.

When the children were growing up they did not have all of the conveniences. They were raised on rummage sale clothes, but in those days you could pick up some nice things.

Front, Rita Nelson, Roberta Sinotte, and Paula Nelson; middle, Leona Hamrock, Amy Trossen, Marilee Nelson, Maxine Nelson, Suzanne Small, and Gordon Nelson; back, Cecelia Keenan

Betty and her children remember how she tended to her garden that spread over the family's three lots. Every year she canned fifty pints each of grape jelly, raspberries and rhubarb, and always with a baby on her arm. "You manage, if you put your mind to it", she said. "The family enjoyed a lot of happy times", Betty said. Holidays always proved special with so many family members around and it seemed it was always someone's birthday. In 1975 the Nelsons saw three of their daughters get married.

Leona and Gordon agreed that the best part of having so many siblings is that they always had a friend. Gordon said, "The neighbor kids thought our house was a great place to be because there were always so many kids around." The Nelson children especially enjoyed making homemade root beer. They could not decide who should be in charge, so they took turns.

With so many brothers and sisters, sharing was a part of life. The children shared clothing through the hand-me-down system. The children baby-sat to earn the clothes they wanted. At one point they had built up a clientele, with eighty-one families demanding their services. With such a demand, the Nelsons could afford to be selective and rated clients on such criteria as whether they had a color television.

Maxine says, "No, I wouldn't recommend such large families today. The rules are different today. Let's just say people cared more about one another before." The older Nelson children went into varied fields—legal, international order specialist, a jewelry consultant, vice president of personnel, one living in Europe with her family, representative for CPT Corp., a postal carrier and one into law enforcement.

Information gleaned from "Brooklyn Park Post" article written by Cathy Schmidtke

CHARLES F. NICHOLS SR. was born in Duluth, Minnesota on October 1, 1924. I was one of two sons born to Edward and Dorothy Nichols.

I attended schools in Duluth, then Dunwoody Industrial Institute in Minneapolis and the University of Minnesota. I received my B.S. in Industrial Arts in 1948, an M.A. in 1956 and my Educational Administrative Certificate in 1957. In 1960 I received a NDEA scholarship, completing this in 1961.

In 1940 I was in St. Paul to play in a basketball game against the Hallie Q. Brown settlement house. At the dance after the game, I spent three hours just sitting and talking with the girl friend of a friend before returning to Duluth. In 1945, as a new student at Dunwoody, I was invited to a party at the Hallie Q. Brown and while there, told a sponsor of the three hour talk the last time I was there. I was told the girl was in the gym. I went down to see if she remembered me. She looked across the floor, saw me standing by the door, came over and said "hello." Six months later we were engaged and married after two years.

My wife, Elizabeth, was one of nine children that were born to John and Aleen Young. She grew up in St. Paul.

We have five wonderful children: Elizabeth, Linda, Charles Jr., Bruce and Nancy. Elizabeth lives in Minneapolis and is employed by Abbott Northwestern Hospital; Linda lives in Robbinsdale and is an executive with Dayton-Hudson (Target) Company; Charles Jr. lives in Brooklyn Center and is manager of inspections for Northwest Airlines; Bruce lives in Golden Valley and is a Senior Field representative for Xerox; Nancy lives in Brooklyn Center and is a nurse at University Hospital. We have ten grandchildren: Tiffaney, Sam, Sasha, Jessica, Stephanie, Martina, Loren, Candice, Arin and Edward.

I have had a long career in education and served on numerous councils and commissions. After leaving the Minneapolis Public Schools, I went into the construction business in the design, manufacture and sales of aircraft hangers, as well as becoming a marketing consultant to various aviation-oriented organizations.

I served on the Brooklyn Center Charter Commission for six years, two years on the Human Rights Commission, and two years on the Planning Commission and was elected to the City Council in 1995. I served one term on the City Council.

My life long interest in aviation has allowed me to fly most types of aircraft. I served on the Tri-Cities Airport Commission and the Board of Directors of the Crystal Airport Aviation Association.

More recently, I have been appointed by Governor Jesse Ventura to serve as chairman of the Metropolitan Airports Commission. MAC oversees the operation of the Minneapolis-St. Paul International Airport and six other airports in the metro area.

Elizabeth died in 1995 after fifty-one years of marriage. I continue to live in our family home with my children and grandchildren close by.

Submitted by Charles F. Nichols Sr.

The Charles F. and Elizabeth Nichols Family

Charles Sr. and Elizabeth Nichols on the forty-nineth wedding anniversary

Kenneth Nordberg

Soon after the Nordberg family moved to Brooklyn Center in 1947, Kenneth joined Boy Scout Troop #299. The Troop met in the basement of Brooklyn Methodist Church, a white, lap sided structure located at the intersection of Noble Avenue (then a sandy trail) and Osseo Road (now called Brooklyn Boulevard). To earn money for Troop equipment and camping trips, the scouts sold bean supper and spaghetti dinner tickets door-to-door, serving their sumptuous repasts to relatives and neighbors in that musty cellar.

Ken Springer was their Scoutmaster. Mrs. Springer, the Scoutmaster's mother, lived across the street in another of Noble Avenue's original homes. Mrs. Springer's cookie jar was always full for visiting Boy Scouts. Her kid-loving black and white Cocker spaniel, Pepper, made every visit a bedlam.

Earl Dorn was a troop committeeman. One of his sons and Kenneth were in the same patrol and they often held patrol meetings at the Dorn farm, located on Noble Avenue a few blocks north of the church. Thus, Kenneth occasionally trod upon the musical floors of the Dorn house (then nearly fifty years old), totally incognizant of the fact that some fifty years later the house would be his beloved home — so much for predestination.

The land upon which this house (purchased in 1974) stands is part of an eighty-acre parcel purchased by Amos Berry from the United States Government in 1856 — two years before Minnesota was granted statehood. Early landowners discovered the soil produced excellent crops of potatoes and for more than one hundred years potatoes were the primary farm crop of this area, originally called "Camden Station."

Early documents reveal the main part of our house was built in 1900 by David Hamilton. Before construction began, many horse-drawn wagonloads of limestone (likely quarried from the banks of the nearby Mississippi River) were hauled to the site to lay a sturdy foundation, one that has settled remarkably little in nearly a century. The house was raised over heavy notched beams and all building materials were secured with square nails. Having discovered photographs of similar houses sold in old mail-order catalogs, the owners believe their home, like many homes and barns of that period, originated as a kit purchased from Sears and Roebuck.

This house continued to be a farm home until 1961 when its last farmer owner (Earl Dorn) sold most of the land to a developer. Restored extensively in 1974 and again in 1996, this wonderful old house survives as a unique reminder of Brooklyn Park's early rural past.

Submitted by Kenneth J. Nordberg

IN 1955 my wife, Alvera (Kozeny) Nordberg and I moved from North Minneapolis into the Cherry Meadows Addition of Brooklyn Park on 63rd Avenue North and Winnetka Avenue, near West Broadway. Along with us came our three small children, Nancy, Douglas and Sandra.

I worked for the Bemis Company, Packaging Service Division, as a design engineer. Soon after moving to Brooklyn Park I joined a group of citizens who were interested in promoting a fire department. The council approved the concept of a fire department in 1957. I became a charter member and secretary of the organization, and remained with the fire department for twenty years, retiring in 1977 at the age of 51.

Alvera Nordberg, was the first president of the Firemen's Auxiliary, and remained a member until her death in 1968. We had been married for twenty-two years. I then married Gladys Wittmer-Armager in 1970.

The Raymond A. Nordberg Family

At the time our family moved to Brooklyn Park, West Broadway was a paved county road, and what is now State Highway 81 was old U.S. Highway 52. The residential streets in Cherry Meadows were not paved, nor did the homes have a city sewer or water system. The roads were gravel and in the summertime had to be graded or leveled.

All three of the Nordberg children attended Robbinsdale District #281 schools. Nancy still lives in Brooklyn Park. Douglas and Sandra, with their families reside in Hanover, Minnesota and Plymouth, Minnesota, respectively. I have five grandchildren.

I retired from the Bemis Company in 1988 after being employed there for forty-two years. I am a member of the Bemis Company Retirees Club, the Elks Club in Brooklyn Park, and the American Legion in Brooklyn Center and am an active member of the Brooklyn Park Senior Club. I still live in the house that we homesteaded in Brooklyn Park.

My second wife, Gladys, died in 1998.

Brooklyn Park Fire Department Members

Submitted by Raymond A Nordberg

Clarence and Alice Nyberg

Dale Nyberg with his granddaughters, Mindy and Ashley

IT WAS ON A COLD DECEMBER DAY in 1934 that Clarence and Alice Nyberg moved their family to Brooklyn Center. Clarence spent several years working for the Works Project Administration (WPA), a government project during the Depression. He also worked for Brooklyn Center as a maintenance man, and was a caterpillar and truck operator. He had a variety of jobs. One job was to pick up welfare commodities at Prior Lake and deliver them to the unfortunate ones, including themselves. He was paid ninety dollars a month.

Politics was an important part of Brooklyn Center life. It didn't matter which party won, there was always a celebration with a house party. The ladies came with their specially prepared recipes to share. The hostess furnished the coffee. If the host family was fortunate to have a basement, an accordion player provided a good time for all.

In the summer the roads had to be graded (bladed was a common term). The roads or streets were all gravel, so had to be bladed — leveling off the gravel. It took two men to do this job, one on the tractor and one on the grader.

Colfax Avenue was a dead end street. The Nybergs had access to their home off Bryant Avenue. Clarence and Bill Doane worked for weeks cutting a road into a street. Colfax was finally completed as a street in 1938. The new street stretched from 53rd to 55th. Soon after the street was completed, new houses began to sprout up. The Nybergs moved into their basement home on Colfax in 1940. They had a cistern pump for water as their only convenience.

They had just settled in when the Armistice Day blizzard of 1941 moved in. Alice and the four children sat in their *hole* in the ground, huddled around the old coal stove and by lamplight watched the snow slowly cover the windows. After several days the roads were opened and Clarence was able to be home with his family.

On Saturday the old bean pot was bubbling away on the top of the heater. Then with a loaf of fresh baked bread and a dish of sauce, supper was ready. Life was great! The Nybergs ate a lot of beans, rice, and onions.

Because building supplies were scarce, it took three years to complete their home. All of the neighbors helped build it with Mr. Strout's supervision, hence the name *"friendship home."*

In the summer the children helped truck farmers. They learned to like asparagus because they were given all of the odd ones.

Harlan and Dale delivered the newspaper to the Earle Brown Farm. At Christmas Mr. Brown gave each boy five dollars and a gallon of maple syrup. That was a generous gift for those days.

Dale went back to visit Earle Brown School with his granddaughter, Mindy. All four of the Nyberg siblings graduated from there.

Dale has retired. Harlan is in Brooklyn Center. Merold is in San Diego, CA. Darlene is now living in Alta Loma, CA. Alice is living at the Maranatha Apartments, in Brooklyn Center.

Submitted by Alice Nyberg

DEAN AND I looked at a house on 53rd Place at the invitation of friends who lived across the street. They indicated that the house was for sale. We liked the house and the neighborhood and subsequently bought it. This was in 1960. We were married in 1961, so we rented it for a year before moving in. All three of our children were born while we lived in that house. They attended Northport School. Lee, our oldest, was in the last class that graduated from Robbinsdale Senior High in 1982. Our daughter, Jeanette, graduated from Cooper and our youngest son, Rick, transferred to Brooklyn Center High School and graduated from there. We had a wonderful camaraderie with that neighborhood that has lasted these past thirty-eight years, even though we have moved twice since then, first to the far western end of Brooklyn Center, and now in the far eastern portion of Brooklyn Center.

The Dean and Marie Nyquist Family

Our lives became involved in the public arena when Dean ran for the State Senate in 1966 and beat the incumbent. He was in for two terms. He also ran for Attorney General, lost that race, but when he ran for mayor in 1977, he won, and subsequently ran for four terms unopposed and was mayor of Brooklyn Center for thirteen years. I served on the Parks and Recreation Commission, on the Brooklyn Historical Society and on the Northport Parent Teachers Association. All the family was involved in Brookdale Covenant Church.

We have seen many changes in the city since we moved in 1961: There were still some farm animals where Brookdale Shopping Center is now, Brooklyn Boulevard was Osseo Road (a two-lane highway), the Earle Brown Farm had the buildings that were unoccupied and becoming run down, Central Park and the Community Center were built, a golf course was built, and we saw the beginning of Community Emergency Assistance Program, to name a few.

Submitted by Marie Nyquist

Marie and Dean Nyquist

The Thomas G. O'Hehir Family

Thomas and Frances O'Hehir

THOMAS G. O'HEHIR was born in Duluth, Minnesota, March 12, 1916. He married Frances McCafferty in 1940. Tom started in law enforcement in Duluth in the 1930s. He then was drafted and assigned to the Navy at Great Lakes Training Center. After four weeks, he was pulled out of boot camp and assigned to help set up the separation center and inform the men about civil service.

Tom attended the Delinquency Control Institute at the University of Southern California, and then returned to the police force in Duluth. He continued his education at the University of Minnesota, and later in his career trained at the FBI Academy. Tom responded to an ad for the Brooklyn Center Police Department, interviewed and began March 12, 1962. Tom sees one of his major achievements as being a member of the steering committee at North Hennepin Community College, molding their Police Science Program.

As Brooklyn Center's Chief of Police, he was a strong advocate for continuing education and saw the importance of writing, English, and science courses. Tom has a strong belief in family values and used to tell his officers, "Don't go stopping for a beer on the way home—go home and have a beer. And don't let me catch you stepping out on your wife. You'll never pick out anything as good as you've got at home."

During his years in Brooklyn Center, Tom continued his work with the Juvenile Justice Program, which began when he was in charge of the Juvenile Offenders Program in Duluth. In the late 50s, he was on the committee that started the Minnesota Juvenile Officers Association, which is still active today. Torn was the associations' first president. He was Vice Chairman of the Governors Committee on Children and Youth under four Governors.

Tom served Brooklyn Center as Chief of Police for sixteen years, and retired in 1978. Tom and Frances celebrated fifty-seven wonderful years of marriage and had seven children. Frances died in 1998. The O'Hehir's seven children are: Thomas Jr., retired from Southern Calif. Edison Power; Michael had his own trucking company and died at age forty-nine of a brain aneurysm; Trisha, a dental hygienist, is a published author, and travels world wide giving seminars; Peggy works for a freight airline; Kathleen worked for Republic/Northwest Airline, and now owns Just Treuffles Candy Shop; Theresa works at General Mills in their Research and Development Division; and Kelly was in the Navy, and now works out of her home as a Web Page designer.

The O'Hehir family lived at 59th and York and has been members of St. Alphonsus parish since 1962. In 1999 Tom moved to a retirement facility in Brooklyn Center. Tom says he needs people around and doesn't want to leave the City. He spends a lot of time traveling to visit his kids, thanks to tickets Kathy has obtained for him by working at the airline. He misses his travel companion, but reaffirms his deep sense of family in each and every visit.

Submitted by a Brooklyn Historical Society volunteer

IT WAS A VERY WARM HALLOWEEN NIGHT in 1964 when Gerald and I and our seven-month-old son, Jerry Jr., moved to Brooklyn Center on 55th Avenue North. We moved six miles north from where we had lived. Winter came before I met any neighbors. That first winter I cried while looking out the windows thinking that we were so far out in the country. I saw no one around. Lions Park was only a promise then—an empty field next to us. There was no Russell Avenue from 53rd to 55th.

About a year later, Jerry and I had a wonderful surprise: twin boys, Paul and Mark. With three boys under two years old, I never had time on my hands again.

Jerry worked in the office for Grain Belt Brewery and worked overtime quite often. Sometimes Mrs. Erma Mero and Jane Nordquist would come over and help feed the twins. Another neighbor, Bill Boris, was also a great help to me.

Jerry and Audrey Olejar

Jerry and I were blessed with three more children, Angela, Timothy and Maria. The empty field was a great, adventurous play area for our children and the neighbors Jim Galvin, Dave Walker, and Jeff Sackmaster.

All the children except Maria went to Earle Brown kindergarten. They continued the primary grades at Our Lady of Victory School. With the grace of God, we were able to send them to Totino-Grace High School.

I was a "stay at home mom", which most of the mothers were at that time. There was much volunteer work for us to do. Only volunteers operated the Our Lady of Victory office, so we took the commitment seriously.

Gerald and Audrey Olejar and family

During the summer months, there was a Park Board baseball program for five through eight-year olds. I loaded up our station wagon with fifteen to twenty kids and drove to other parks to compete in games.

The boys played Brooklyn Center Park Board hockey and baseball. Jerry, Sr. coached baseball with Paul Worwa for years. The moms worked in the concession stands. We met many friends through the sports programs.

Shortly before the 1973 Roe vs. Wade decision legalizing abortion on demand, I became involved in politics. I used to organize the Pro-Life caucus for Precinct 1 for the DFL. After the DFL party left me, I continued my efforts in the Republican Party.

Our children were taught that because all people are made in the image and likeness of God, all life from conception to death must be respected and protected.

Brooklyn Center seemed to be a good place for us to raise a family. We hope that we were a good family for Brooklyn Center.

Submitted by Audrey Olejar

Lelabel O'Loughlin

THE SNOW WAS PILED HIGH that day in 1951, when we drove to Brooklyn Center to look at a new house. Humboldt Avenue was one of the few residential streets that cut through. There sat the small white house, alone on the block amid small farms. The price was right, so after the house was completed, we moved in.

Although this was foreign territory to me, my husband was quite familiar with the area. When he was about fourteen, he lived at the home of Paul and Mary Mogenson, owners of the Brooklyn Center Dairy. Their farm was located on the property now occupied by Northbrook Shopping Center. The dairy tended cows, bottled milk, and delivered to the homes on the route. My husband attended the old Earle Brown School for a while and lived in a big house on 69th Avenue, since then moved.

The old Earle Brown School (1952)

My husband had to take me to the streetcar line at 5:00 A.M. so I could get to my job at Sears. In the afternoon I walked home from 52nd and Bryant Avenue. I remember that a goat from the farm on the other side of Earle Brown School used to visit our garbage can every night.

The nearest stores were Casey's Grocery (57th and Logan) or Clymer's Dairy Store (59th and Lyndale). Our two daughters took the bus to Patrick Henry High School. Because of changes in the school district, one daughter graduated from Patrick Henry, the other from North High School. Our third daughter attended Earle Brown Elementary and graduated from Brooklyn Center High.

A big change in my life occurred in 1957. When I wrote to Manitoba for a copy of my birth certificate, they replied that I was never born! My mother said the courthouse had burned down. After a few months, my uncle informed my husband that I had been adopted and brought to Minneapolis at the age of three months. No more information from Canada could be obtained, although I learned my biological mother's name. I went to the Minneapolis downtown library and searched directories from all over the world. I wrote letters to each person whose name I shared. Because the last name had an unusual spelling, there weren't many to write. Almost everyone responded but no one claimed to know of my mother or me. Happy 40th birthday!

My 75th birthday was even better. When I went to the Brooklyn Center Government Center to apply for a passport, I was asked for my papers or green card. It seems that, having been born in Canada and adopted here, did not make me an American citizen! This was really frightening. Although I had attended school, graduated, married, voted, and worked in the United States, I wasn't legal! I immediately contacted an immigration attorney, and it took over a year for me to become a real American citizen. That was undoubtedly one of the happiest days of my life.

I have seen Brooklyn Center change over the years, and it is a great city in which to live!

Submitted by Lelabel O'Loughlin

I WAS BORN in May 1923 to Judith Carlson and Erick Rydeen. I was their second child, as a son had been born in 1917. Harold, my brother, had been injured at birth and had to wear leg braces as a result. He died in 1926 when he fell from a bicycle. Two more sisters were born to the family, Jean and Doris.

Betty Rydeen Olson

The Rydeens had a vegetable farm in Brooklyn Center. The original farm home is still standing on the corner of Logan and 56th Avenue North. My sisters and I helped out on the farm by bunching onions, radishes, asparagus and carrots after school and during the summers. The main crop was potatoes and we also helped with the harvesting of potatoes and with getting them ready for market. Mr. Rydeen would take loads of fresh vegetables to the Farmers Market each day.

All of the Rydeen children went to Earle Brown School. I went to Patrick Henry and then to Robbinsdale High School at the original Regent Avenue School, from which I graduated in 1940. I then attended Minnesota School of Business and after graduation, was lucky enough to find a job that paid sixty-five dollars a month.

In June 1947 George Olson and I were married in a garden ceremony in front of my parents' home.

My father had a strip of land on Logan Avenue from 56th to 57th Avenue platted. The corner lot on 57th was given to us as a wedding gift from my family. George was a carpenter and built our first home on that lot. It was a basement home, which was quite common then. We lived in the basement until 1950, at which time our first daughter was born. That necessitated the completion of the house.

We sold that house and built another one down the block next to my mother's home, my father having died in 1950. George went into the construction business with Albert Rydeen, a cousin of mine. We sold our home on Logan and moved into one of the homes that George and Al had built on Brooklyn Boulevard.

Basement Home (1947)

It was in this home that George and I raised our four daughters, Georganne, Beverly, Judy, and Janice.

I was born and raised in Brooklyn Center and am still living there, although George passed away in 1984. I still have family in the area, including two sisters, a daughter, a niece, and nephews. The other daughters live in Wisconsin, Georgia, and Tamarack, MN. I have seen many changes in the area that began mostly as potato farms and is now a growing community.

Submitted by Elizabeth Olson

Mike Ondarko

MIKE ONDARKO was a twenty-two year old newlywed when he was drafted into the United States Army in 1942. He carried the radio for the Battalion Commander in the 134th Infantry in the 35th Division. Mike with thousands of other young men was in the battles at Normandy and in Germany. He said he never had to shoot at anyone but was hit with shrapnel twice. The first time he was hit in the back and was in a hospital in England for six weeks. The second time he was sent back to a United States Hospital for surgery and repair of bone and nerve damage to his arm. This time he was hospitalized for eight months.

In addition to all the unpleasant memories, no baths or clean socks for weeks at a time, the loss of so many of his friends, the loss of some of his hearing caused by the noise of land mines and guns, there are many wonderful things to think about. He thinks of all the camaraderie, friends helping each other. He thinks about all the children (orphans) following the men wherever they went, about the little girl who didn't know what an orange was until Mike peeled it and showed her how to eat it.

After his discharge Mike and his wife, Mary Ann, were so busy raising a family that he forgot about the medals he had earned and not received. About 1989 he decided that he wanted the medals due him. The Veterans of Foreign Wars, The Disabled Veterans and letters written by him did not prove successful. He then contacted Representative Jim Ramstad for help. After two years Rep. Jim Ramstad presented Mike with:

- The Purple Heart with Oak Leaf Clusters
- The Bronze Star
- The Good Conduct Medal
- The American Campaign Medal
- The European-African-Middle East Campaign
- The World War II Victory Medal
- An Honorable Service lapel button

Mike just wishes Mary Ann, his wife, could have seen them. She died in 1992.

After all the work Mike went through to get his medals he may have set a precedent that will help other veterans get what is due them.

He wants to build a frame for all his medals and hopes that someday his grandchildren and great-grandchildren will study about World War II and about all the young men who gave up their lives or suffered to protect the rest of us.

From an oral interview by Barbara Erickson

Mike Ondarko at Training Camp (1942)

WHEN WE DECIDED to buy a house we wanted it to be in a northern suburb. Both Arland and I grew up on the north side of Minneapolis. I graduated from North High School and Arland from Vocational High, downtown. We met at Lincoln Jr. High, so we consider ourselves grown where we had been planted.

Arland's grandparents came from Norway, probably in the late 1800's. My mother was born and raised in Minneapolis, but her father came from Quebec, Canada at the age of nine years. He could speak only French, so we do have some history of our family immigrating to the United States for a better future.

In our search for a home, Arland and I had heard of this house in Brooklyn Center. It sounded perfect. It was a two-bedroom house with room for expansion. We visualized what could be done—build bedrooms upstairs, finish the basement, add a bathroom. Arland was a real "handy" handyman. We knew he could do all of those things.

When we bought this house in 1956, it was a quiet neighborhood. There were no sidewalks or curbs and the back yard was full of sand burrs, and there was lots of growing space. The mortgage on the house then was four and a half percent interest. Our monthly home payments went from thirty dollars a month to eighty dollars. A negative thing about buying where we did was the school situation. Earle Brown School was close by, but there was neither a kindergarten or a high school. The high school age children were bussed to Minneapolis.

We had five children: Diane, James, Carol, Kristine and Richard. We were soon busy with Brownies, Girl Scouts and 4-H Club. Arland coached Little League and Park Board hockey. Our boys were busy with football, and hockey, so that kept the Opsahls busy with Athletic Boosters.

The Opsahl Family celebrating their parent's fiftieth anniversary (June 1999)

Arland was given an award in 1971 that read, "In recognition of outstanding service and dedication to the Athletic Department." He was instrumental in getting lights up for the ice rink at the high school and also, with other volunteers, built ticket booths for the football games. He enjoyed sharpening the skates for the hockey players. Jokingly, they claim this is why the team went to the state tournament under the coaching of Paul Bouchard.

I remember my mother saying when we moved out here, "Why do you want to move out so far? There is nothing out there, no stores, no busses, etc." Look at us now! We grew, the city grew and hopefully, we helped shape some of its young citizens.

Our "golden years" are still filled with a busy volunteer schedule including our growing church, Lutheran Church of the Master. We plan to stay in our home, which now has a busy street in front of it.

Submitted by Patricia Opsahl

Arland and Patricia Opsahl

The Orn Family

DUANE ORN was born November 26, 1932, to Ralph August Orn, a Soo Line Railroad section foreman and Eleanor Virginia (Larsen), a schoolteacher at Luck, Wisconsin. I graduated from Turtle Lake High School. My mother insisted that I attend college for at least one year. I attended Billy Graham's Northwestern College and then continued at the University of Minnesota for pre-medicine and medical school. I did my internship at Mercy Hospital in Toledo, Ohio, and spent one-and-a-half years at Olmsted Medical Group in Rochester, Minnesota, before coming to Brooklyn Center in 1962 to Northport Medical Center.

Karen Jackson's grandparents, Charles and Catharine Jackson, owned the C. R. Howe Store in Brooklyn Center from 1907, when Charles purchased it, until 1925. The Jackson's oldest son John was born above the store, became a carpenter, and married Thelma in 1940. They moved to South St. Paul, MN, where their daughter Karen grew up and graduated from high school. Karen then attended the University of Minnesota. Karen and I were married at the Minneapolis Basilica. She is a vice-president in Private Financial Services for U.S. Bank.

Dr. Orn, Karen, Charlie, Are, and Murisiku

Carl August Orn ("Charlie" after his great-grandpa) was born July 14, 1983. He is the focus and the apple of the family eye. He is a handsome 6' 3" teenager with a winning smile, whose interests include the art of negotiation, creative writing, sports and the Chinese language (eight years of study when graduating high school). He has expressed an interest in studying architecture in college.

We had the very good fortune of having two exchange students live with us. They came for a week and have stayed for 10 years. Are Hansen is from Norway, and Murisiku Raifu is from Ghana. They are like two sons to their American parents and a true brother to Charlie. Both completed high school. Muriskiu attended Amherst and is a second year medical student at the University of Minnesota. Are is a third year pre-med student at Augsburg.

Our family enjoys fun and games. Together we sail on our little 19-foot Flying Scott that is docked at Medicine Lake. At least one ski trip is planned annually. A trip to Grand Cayman for swimming, snorkeling and scuba diving was added to help rehabilitate the arm that Karen broke while skiing in 1998. All the family is open water scuba certified.

Christmas Eve with lutefisk, as well as other Scandinavian foods, tends to round out our year. We have all of the family to our house for a Christmas Day celebration and dinner, as well as all of the anticipated exchange of gifts, never to be exceeded by the true gift of Christmas.

The Orn family has been taken into the hearts and lives of the people of Brooklyn Center as well as the Brooklyn Center High School where many of our friends live, work, and go to school. We will always be grateful to them, and with whom we anticipate the future.

Submitted by Dr. Duane Orn

MY WIFE, CAROLYNN AND I moved to Brooklyn Center/Brooklyn Park in 1965 when I accepted the position of the city's first Recreation and Park Director. Since that day we have had a love affair with the community and its people.

I was born and raised in north Minneapolis, Carolynn in south Minneapolis, both of Scandinavian parents. We met at the University of Minnesota and were married in 1962 in Minneapolis, during which time I was completing my Master's degree at the University of Minnesota.

We have three children: Brent, Mark and Roxann. Brent is News Director at a radio station in Estherville, Iowa. Mark has a degree in public parks and recreation. He works for the city of Brooklyn Park as a program coordinator in charge of community recreation programs. Our daughter, Roxann, is a graduate of the Minnesota State University at Mankato and works with teenagers and at-risk children for the city.

The Dennis C. Palm Family

When we moved to Brooklyn Park, the community was basically rural with a small suburban area but it was an exciting place to be Recreation and Park Director. The future potential was tremendous! The community was enthusiastic about having a parks and recreation program. The new young residents of Brooklyn Park, as well as the farming community, embraced us and agreed to build a nationally recognized park system.

The early days were exciting, interesting and even thrilling. Parkland was purchased, recreation programs developed, and public support grew. Success came quickly.

In 1969-1970 the City of Brooklyn Park won the National Gold Medal Award for excellence in Park and Recreation management for the smallest community category in the nation. The next few years were ones of significant population growth and progress. Over a million dollars in government grants were received. Again in 1981 the city received the National Gold Medal Award for excellence in Recreation and Park management in a larger population category. Brooklyn Park was the only community in the nation to ever win the award twice.

Dennis and Carolynn Palm with Brent, Mark, and Roxann

In the 1980s the community grew. The acquisition and restoration of the Brooklyn Park Historical Farm (Eidem farm) took place. Edinburgh USA Golf Course and Clubhouse became a reality. People and businesses were flocking to the community. The community provided for diversity and many options in living styles. In 1997 the voters of Brooklyn Park overwhelmingly approved a sixteen and a half-million-dollar park bond referendum to assure a quality park system into the 2000s.

Brooklyn Park has been a wonderful place for the Palm family to call home. Our children were deeply involved in the community, both as participants and volunteers. Carolynn worked over twenty years on a full or part-time basis both for the Osseo School District and the city. Brooklyn Park will always be "HOME" and I am very proud to have played a role in its magnificent growth and development as its Park and Recreation Director for nearly thirty-three years.

Submitted by Dennis C. Palm

The Victor and Marlene Peppe Family

On November 22, 1963, the Peppe family moved into the Brooklyn Park house on 64th Avenue that was to be home for the next twenty-two years. On that day this growing family of nine planted roots in a community that would become a fundamental part of its very identity.

By that time Victor Peppe was already a man of worldly experience. Raised during the Depression in New York, Vic rushed to beat the conclusion of WWII and joined the Navy just in time to witness the surrender of Japan at Pearl Harbor. Following his tour of duty he traveled west and began attending the University of California at Los Angeles. He had all the markings of a star tailback, until it was learned that a previous stint as a semi-professional football player made him ineligible.

The Peppe Family

Next, he tried his hand in Hollywood and enjoyed some real success. As a stunt man, Vic saw extensive action. In classic productions such as "From Here to Eternity" and "On the Waterfront," just to name two, he stood in for the lead actor.

Fate changed the direction of Vic Peppe's life when, in 1954, he met a beautiful and charming young woman sitting in front of a piano eating bar snacks and sipping soda. Marlene Berg was just 18, a telephone operator for Ma Bell who had just transferred to Los Angeles. A recent graduate of North High School in Minneapolis, she was relishing her first opportunity to be on her own. She had no idea what kind of turn her life was about to take. The next year they were married.

It didn't take long for them to start the family both wanted. Shortly, two children were born. Vic settled down to more traditional work, and soon they were contemplating returning to Marlene's hometown. The children kept coming.

For nearly twenty-five years in Brooklyn Park, this family grew to number twelve children: Kevin, Teri, Michelle, Mike, Bob, Lisa, Craig, Vic, Jim, Chris, John and Angela; and twenty-seven grandchildren. The kids grew up and moved away, but the house on 64th continued to be "home base." Today, a second and third generation of Peppes occupy the house on 64th, and there are twelve Peppe families occupying Brooklyn Park addresses today and three more in Brooklyn Center. As the new millennium dawns for the communities of Brooklyn, you can bet that the Peppe family will continue to hold these communities close to its heart.

Submitted by James W. Peppe

WILLIAM CARL PETER and his wife Gladys and their three-year-old daughter, Bernadine, moved to the Village of Brooklyn Center in 1935. We lived at 718 53rd Avenue North. The city of Minneapolis ended on the south side of 53rd so we lived in the country. There was a dairy store on the corner 53rd and Bryant and a grocery store on the corner of 53rd and Camden. North of 55th was mostly farmland with a few homes scattered here and there.

My brother was born in 1936 and was named after my father. We loved the freedom of walking everywhere day and night. Soon many of our relatives moved into the area: an uncle next door to us, another on Lyndale Avenue, and another on Dupont.

My dad was the Village Clerk and my Uncle Charles Genosky was the Justice of Peace. We had village meetings in our garage.

The Earle Brown School was known as District #118 and housed one grade level for each grade from first through eighth. Our neighborhood was very close and we walked to school together and looked out for each other no matter what our age. There were many fun times playing red light/green light, kick the can, annie, annie over, etc.

When Bernadine was ten and her brother Bill was six, Kathleen, their baby sister was born. She was born in November and they had to learn how to baby-sit.

Their father William became sick the following September and, because of the war, the drugs he needed were not available for civilian use so his infection settled in his kidneys. They operated on him but he had a cerebral hemorrhage and died in December of 1943. He was only thirty-seven years old and without the help of our church, neighbors and close relatives we would never have made it through our grief. Gladys remarried two years later.

After graduating from Patrick Henry High School, Bernadine married her city boy friend, Chet, who lived on 52nd and Camden and followed him during the Korean War. They had their first child, Colleen in 1952, and their second daughter, Roxanne was born in 1954. They purchased their first home in January 1955 in Brooklyn Center on Fremont Avenue North in a new addition named Colleen's Addition.

In 1961 Bernadine went back to her former elementary school, Earle Brown, to work. The girls were in school and she worked at various jobs. After thirty-two years of service in the Brooklyn Center School District, Bernadine retired in December 1993.

Living in Brooklyn Center has always seemed like a small town to the Petersons with everyone looking out for each other. Many caring people have touched our lives—the greatest place to live and raise our children and best of all call "home."

Submitted by Bernadine (Peter) Peterson

Chet and Bernadine Peterson

Bernadine Peter Peterson

Donald and Bonnie Peterson

WE BOUGHT our Brooklyn Center home in the fall of 1969. We bought in Brooklyn Center because Donald's sales territory was mainly north of the Twin Cities and at that time you could get more home for the money.

Donald was born in Minneapolis, MN, in the now-closed St. Andrews Hospital. Bonnie (Foss) Peterson was born in Canby, MN.

At the present time Donald is commissioner on the Park and Recreation Committee. He has done many things to support the family, such as salesman, owner and operator of coin-operated laundries, chain saw repair shop, RV campground and presently a word processing business. The Minneapolis Gas Company, the Federal Reserve Bank, and Aslesen Company have employed him.

He served in the United States Navy during World War II as an aviation cadet. He is a member of The American Legion and Unizar Lodge #347 A.F. & A.M. He enjoys a good game of golf.

Bonnie and I have made two trips to Europe. On our first trip in 1972 we toured England, France, Netherlands, Germany, Italy, and Austria for our twenty-fifth wedding anniversary. In 1998 we made a second trip touring Norway and Sweden.

Submitted by Donald Peterson

JOHN POINTS' PARENTS of German, Irish and French ancestry came from Illinois in 1920. They rented a farm near Mora, MN and worked the farm for fifty years. After John's father retired from farming he sold real estate.

John's mother had an eighth grade education; therefore, she was eligible to teach school. She taught grades one through eight in a one-room country school for four years. After her teaching career she was a "stay at home mom" raising their family of three boys and three girls.

John Points

While going to school the pupils played the usual games such as Red Rover, Red Rover, Jump Rope, Kick the Can, etc. But John's passion was playing with marbles. He enjoyed winning the other kid's marbles and then he lost them again.

John remembers when his parents and his siblings drove to Illinois in a 1926 Model-T Ford. It took them sixteen hours to reach their destination.

John worked in a cheese factory, weighing the milk and putting the cheese into the presses when it was ready. He moved the presses to the aging rooms.

When John was fifteen years old, he was helping his father haul fruit. On the way home an empty tub fell off the trailer. John put the tub into the trailer and was going to ride in the back of the trailer to their home against his father's better judgment. The trailer came loose and after zigzagging across the road it came to rest in a ditch on top of him. He had a fractured skull, a brain concussion, and some broken ribs. Both of his arms and legs were broken. He had injured his eyes and ears. He was rushed to Eitel Hospital in Minneapolis, MN, where he was given a one-in-a-thousand chance of survival. He was unconscious for more than five weeks. It was six months before he was finally able to start walking again and regain his balance. His weight had dropped from one hundred fifty six pounds to eighty-three pounds.

John had an eighth grade education. After working as a welder for a while he attended welding classes and made a career of it. He worked for Spartan Trailer Company. The company made trailers for hauling canoes and boats. John was married in 1960. He and his wife have two girls.

From an oral interview by Barbara Erickson

Sarah Robinson Pollock

WE MOVED TO BROOKLYN TOWNSHIP on March 19, 1950. Our farmhouse was on the corner of County Road 110 and 109th Ave. No., now called Noble Avenue. We moved from a three-room apartment in Minneapolis to this eight room, old yellow brick farmhouse. We rented for $75.00 a month with the option to buy. With only three rooms of furniture and eight rooms to fill, all of our friends used us as a repository for really old furniture. Thirty-five years later, we collected antiques, but we maintained that the antiques collected us.

In the spring of 1954, the people voted that we become the Village of Brooklyn Park. Our first mayor was Baldwin Hartkopf. The first caller to our home was Olaf, the driver of the Bookmobile from Hennepin County. We had bookmobile service for at least fifteen years. This monthly visit was greeted by all of the neighbors. Few phones were available. Ours was in the Anoka phone system; our neighbors were in the Osseo system. It cost twenty-five cents to call Minneapolis and fourteen cents to call our nearest neighbor. Our family includes Manford Robinson, Sarah Nye Robinson, and children, Paul, eleven years, and Elizabeth, seven years.

Our automobiles consisted of two Model A Fords, with one in working order usually. The winter of 1950-51 was a wild one with snowstorm piling on snowstorm. Snowplows came late to the county roads in those days, so the men of the neighborhood shoveled mightily every evening and the cars often were left on West River Road. Manny worked at Honeywell and rode with someone from Monticello. His tactic was to use crutches and propel himself over the drifts to get to the highway. He had polio when he was two, so was very good with crutches and kept them for emergencies. He also wore a brace.

The Sarah Pollock Home

After most of the family was grown, I attended North Hennepin College, which was started in 1966 in the old Osseo High School. I worked part time at Spancrete Co. in Osseo and scooted over to classes and returned to my typewriter afterward. We were a group of Continuing Education women who were the vanguard of the many who now re-enter the academic world. After two years I transferred to the University of Minnesota for a degree in Elementary Education, with a certificate for teaching students with learning disabilities. I graduated in 1970 and was employed by the Anoka-Hennepin District until I retired in 1984. This was a new field at the time, and I found it challenging and rewarding.

The spaciousness of the old farmhouse was great for raising a family. I was widowed in 1978 and often had foreign exchange students stay with me for company. In 1984 I remarried and moved to Brooklyn Center, where my new husband, Everett Pollock, owned a smaller home.

Submitted by Sarah Pollock

ANN AND I, and daughters Vicki and Susan became Brooklyn Center, Minnesota residents in November 1960 when I was hired as Village Engineer by Art Lee, Village Administrator. I was employed by Brooklyn Center from 1960 to 1977, first as Village Engineer, then as Village Administrator and finally as City Manager.

Ann (Johnson) Poss, the younger of two children, grew up in LaCrosse, Wisconsin. I was born in the small Mississippi River Valley town of Onalaska. Ann and I met in college. I am a 1955 engineering graduate of the University of Wisconsin at Madison. I was employed in the city engineering department in LaCrosse before moving to Brooklyn Center.

My mother was a very assertive person for her time. She believed that anybody could be what they wanted to be and had high expectations for her five sons. I had a sister who died at a young age. My father believed in hard work and his passion in life, other than his family, was working. He was a tax auditor for the Standard Oil Company.

Ann and I have three children, Vicki, Susan and Dan. Vicki married Dennis DeLaittre from Brooklyn Center. They live in Phoenix with their son Joseph. Susan married Terry Lucas and now lives in Circle Pines, Minnesota with their two children, David and Andrea. Dan and Lauren and their two daughters, Hannah and Rachel, live in Oakdale, Minnesota.

Ann says, "The nicest gift she could have been given by Don was to be a stay-at-home-mom. I was able to be with my children when they saw their first butterfly and when they walked barefoot in the grass that tickled their toes. Not many moms now get to do that, they have to work or choose to work." It is important to her that all three of the moms, their two daughters and their daughter-in-law, also are stay-at-home moms. Our son, Dan, married a professional woman. When their first child

The Don and Ann Poss Family

Susan, Dan, Ann, Don, and Vicki Poss

was born, he asked his wife what would it take to make her happy, to run the house efficiently, have her pleasures and needs taken care of? Whatever it would take he was willing to work to provide. It was so important to Susan that her mom was always there, and she wanted the same for her children. Vicki works out of her home so she is able to be home with their son.

Ann and I have been married for forty-five years, and have lived in our first house in Brooklyn Center for thirty-nine years. We have enjoyed our lake home near Annandale with our children and grandchildren. We spend part of the year at our home in Phoenix, Arizona that is just a few houses from our daughter, Vicki and family, with whom we share a lake place near Phoenix. We have the best of both places, with grandchildren here and there. My hobbies are reading and fishing. Ann is a reader, also, and a bridge player.

Submitted by a Brooklyn Historical Society Volunteer

The William and Maxine Price Family

WE CAME TO BROOKLYN CENTER in August 1961. Maxine and I moved to our current home on Dupont Avenue North with our four children, Jean Ann, Joan Charlene, William James, Jr., and Janet Maxine. The family had moved from Windom, Minnesota where we had lived from 1944 to 1961. The family relocated to Brooklyn Center so that I, William (AKA Bill), could be the science and educational media consultant for the new Brooklyn Center High School that opened in 1961.

We continued to live in Brooklyn Center after I took a position as professor in the Continuing Education Department (now called University College) at the University of Minnesota. Maxine did homebound and substitute teaching in District 284 and later worked for Dayton's. I retired in 1979 and Maxine in 1980.

Maxine and William Price

Jean and Joan graduated from Windom High School and the University of Minnesota. Joan and her husband, Norman Purrington, have two sons and a daughter and live in Lake Elmo. Joan is a physical therapist and Health and Safety Coordinator for NE Metro 916. Jean and her husband, Gary Hanson, have two daughters and live in Austin, Texas. Jean is a health program consultant in Children's Services at the Texas Department of Health. Bill, Jr. graduated from Brooklyn Center High School, enlisted in the U.S. Navy and served twenty-seven years on submarines and in the Naval Reserve, retiring as a Lieutenant Commander. He and his wife, Kathy, have two sons and live in Williamsburg, Virginia. Janet graduated from Brooklyn Center High School and the University of Minnesota. She is an elementary school teacher in Delano and lives with her husband, Firoz Price, and daughter in Maple Plain, Minnesota.

As a family, we worshipped at Harron United Methodist Church for thirty-seven years. When the children were home the family enjoyed camping in Minnesota, Wisconsin and eastern states. After retirement Maxine and I traveled extensively. We enjoyed trips to France, England, Switzerland, Germany, Austria, Hungary, Sweden, Denmark, Norway, Poland, Czechoslovakia, Spain, Greece, Aegean Islands, Morocco, Turkey, Malaysia, Kenya, China, Japan, and Hong Kong.

We also spent time watching sunsets at our lake place near Willmar and on a creek near Okabena. Boating on Lake Minnetonka and the St. Croix and Mississippi Rivers were part of Maxine's and my life, especially after retirement. Both Maxine and I were active in the Minnetonka Power Squadron, a unit of the United States Power Squadron. Maxine was the Power Squadron's historian for a number of years. I taught many of the member classes in addition to the Public Boating Class. I also served as Squadron Commander, District Commander, and on the National Education Committee. Other public service included original membership on the Brooklyn Center Conservation Commission. Maxine and I were part of the Adopt-a-River Program of the Minnesota Department of Natural Resources for many years.

Submitted by William Price

In the early 1900s Charles and Lunetta Purdham moved to a seventy-four acre farm in Brooklyn Township near what was later 85th and Zane Avenues. They had four sons, Plummer, Harold, Walter and Elbert. By the end of World War I the three older boys had moved to establish their homes elsewhere. Elbert, the youngest, born August 13, 1899, stayed on to run the farm. In 1921 he was married to Anna Feck. To that couple two children were born, Charles in 1922 and Alyce in 1924.

Elbert farmed until 1934. In the years that followed he worked for Hennepin County, the State of Minnesota and Northern Pump (later known as Northern Ordnance and FMC) During that time he and the family moved to the "Chapman House" where Iten Chevrolet is now located, near the intersection of Interstate Hwy. 694 and Brooklyn Boulevard. He retired in 1964 having relocated to 6321 Halifax Drive.

Both children graduated from high school, Charles from North High School in 1939 and Alyce from Patrick Henry in 1942. Following military service during World War II, both attended Hamline University, receiving their Bachelor of Arts degree in 1948. Charles was married to Alice Boquist in June of that year. Alice entered the teaching profession, serving most of her years in Austin, MN.

Upon completion of the Master of Sacred Theology degree from Boston University School of Theology in 1951, Charles began full time ministry at the Nashwauk, Pengilly, and Kelly Lake United Methodist Churches on the Iron Range of northern Minnesota. The first of their three children, Lois, was born in 1951. Two sons followed, James in 1955 and David in 1956.

Other appointments served by Charles include the Proctor Brookston UM churches: North Methodist Church in Minneapolis, Minnesota Annual Conference Council Director, Superintendent of the Metro East District of the Minnesota Annual Conference, and Hillcrest United Methodist Church in Bloomington, MN. After retirement in 1986 he served as Field Director for the Metro West United Methodist Union (new church development), Interim Pastor of First UMC in Lindstrom, MN, Supply Pastor at Central Park UMC, St. Paul, MN, and Coordinator of Pastoral Care and Crisis Counseling for the Upper Midwest Recovery Program following the Minnesota and Red River floods of 1997.

In 1986 Charles and Alice moved to Brooklyn Center, residing first at 7212 Humboldt North and later at 6910 Willow Lane. During that same period, Charles' parents, Anna and Elbert, took up residence at the Maranatha Care Center in Brooklyn Center. Elbert passed away October 13, 1993, and Anna died March 1, 1998.

David Purdham, the younger son of Alice and Charles, lives at 2649 78th Avenue North in Brooklyn Park. He and his wife, Mary, have two sons, John and Michael.

Submitted by Charles Purdham

The Purdham Family

Leona Raisch

It has been three years since my family and I moved to Brooklyn Center. We lived in the Camden area for more than twenty years and decided it was time for a change. Being of Native American descent, when we move back to where we started from we call it "coming full circle."

In the early 1960s, my husband and I lived in Brooklyn Center in a small two-bedroom house on Humboldt and 54th Avenue North. We then moved to the Camden area. Our children attended Our Lady of Victory School until they graduated from eighth grade, all four of them, Roberta, Sharon, Sam and Robert, Jr.

What a happy day when we moved to Brooklyn Center three years ago! The neighbors welcomed us with open arms. They came and introduced themselves to us, brought us homemade cookies and bread. We felt so welcomed to the neighborhood.

Our neighbors offered help with the children if they ever needed a place after school and for whatever reason no one is home; the neighbor will be there for them.

Leona, Sam, and Baby Raisch (1969)

I should explain who resides in our household: Roberta and Bill (mom and dad); three children: Ashley, age eleven, Adrian, age eight and Marcus, age five; then there is me, Leona, mother, grandmother and great grandmother. We are all enrolled members of the Red Lake Indian Reservation in northern Minnesota. We have a home on the reservation where we spend time whenever it is possible. We attend pow-wows and ceremonies. We are very involved in our Indian culture and willing to share it with anyone who wants to learn about us or how we live. My daughter, Roberta, does cultural diversity at Earle Brown School in Brooklyn Center. She also teaches Indian diversity at Head Start in Brooklyn Park. She brings in dancers, a drum and singers that perform for the children. She also teaches the younger children how to make dream catchers and do bead work at Earle Brown School.

We moved here to 55th Avenue North in August 1996. In October 1996 my husband was diagnosed with cancer and passed away in April 1997. He got to know and like the new house and sat on the porch with his coffee and enjoy the scenery. My family and I are very thankful to the "Great Spirit" that we had time for closure with him.

My husband and I have worked hard all of our lives to have and maintain a home for our children. American Indian people have the same needs and wants as other people do. Children are very important to us. If I may quote from Chief Sitting Bull, "Let us put our minds together and see what we can do for our children." This is our philosophy. My family and I continue to enjoy Brooklyn Center and help make it a safe place to live and treat people of every race as we were treated when we moved to Brooklyn Center.

Submitted by Leona Raisch

SHORTLY AFTER WE WERE MARRIED in 1947, Wally and I bought a house near "Schiebe's Corner" on 6th Avenue North (Olson Highway) close to Medicine Lake. Our son Gregory Jon and daughter Jae Suzanne were both born while we lived there. As the children approached school age, we decided to move closer to the city. The traveling time for children in the Wayzata School District was too great for small children.

In 1955 we moved into our home in Brooklyn Center. I grew up in North Minneapolis and Wally was well acquainted with Brooklyn Center. Wally had bunched radishes on one of the many truck farms here at that time (a penny a bunch). The farmers would send a truck over to his northeast Minneapolis neighborhood to pick up the youngsters to work on the farm and return them home at the end of the day. So it was a natural choice for us to move to Brooklyn Center.

There was no kindergarten in the Brooklyn Center School system then, so Greg and Jae attended Mrs. Lund's pre-school at the corner of Fremont and 61st Avenue North. Homes were constructed all around us. It was natural for the children to play in the excavated basements after the workers had left for the day. It is impossible to tell how many sneakers were lost in those basements that summer. If the parents were lucky and only one shoe had been lost, perhaps an identical pair could be purchased, and thus the usage could be stretched a bit more.

The radish fields disappeared and Highway 100 took their place. Then the real excitement came when Brookdale opened and the area residents had their own shopping center with Sears, Penney's, Dayton's, and Donaldsons. About that time the "Beatles" came upon the scene, and many more homes were enlivened by the sounds of the "garage band." Ours was no exception, noisy, but fun.

Wally worked for American Bridge Company until the company moved to Gary, Indiana. He then worked at St. Paul Structural Steel Company until that plant closed. I worked as a checkout clerk at Klines's, Piggly Wiggly, and Country Club Market. These were all located in the same building simultaneously, at 57th and Morgan Avenue North. One summer there was a carnival in the vacant field across from the store. Later, Country Club built their store there.

Greg graduated in 1969 from DeLaSalle High School and Jae Suzanne was in the very first graduating class at Grace High School in 1970. Later on Totino was added to the school name in honor of its benefactor, Rose Totino.

I still live in Brooklyn Center and would never want to move. It has changed drastically, but it's a nice place to live.

Submitted by Doris Ranzka

Wally and Doris Ranzka

The Redburn and Carlberg Families

The Redburn family moved to the Brooklyn Center area in 1939. They lived on 53rd and Bryant Avenues North for about two years as renters. The family included father Winfrey, mother Elizabeth, son Winfrey, Jr. or Bud as he was called then, and daughter, Lorraine.

Our family then bought a home just a few blocks from there at 512 53rd Avenue North, just east of the Baldigo store. While living at this address I attended Patrick Henry High School. The only way to get there was to walk up to 55th and Humboldt to the Jake Woods Store and take the school bus from there each day. Bud attended all grades at Earle Brown School. As a young girl I walked to the Earle Brown Farm. We went through many of his barns and saw his own bank building on the property.

Adar and Lorraine Carlberg (1998)

I married Adar Carlberg from the Cambridge, Minnesota area in 1946. Adar had been in World War II, serving in Europe for three years, in most of the intense battles. In all of that time he did not have a furlough, but he was also the only man in his division to return home.

We lived in Robbinsdale for a few years after we married, but moved back to Brooklyn Center, near 55th and James Avenue. There were potato fields across from our home.

Adar worked for the post office as a letter carrier, mostly on the North side, and later downtown. He retired in 1979. I was fortunate enough to be able to stay home with our two children while they were growing up. When I went back to work in 1966, I started as a billing clerk for J. B. Dain Brokers and retired from there in 1982.

Our son, Leighton, now lives in the Green Bay, Wisconsin area and he and his wife have two daughters. Our daughter, Charleen, lives in Golden Valley. She and her husband have two children, a daughter Kristen and a son Shawn.

Submitted by Lorraine Carlberg

I, GAYLE, AM A DESCENDANT of founding forefathers in Brooklyn. My maternal great-grandparents were Nahum Crooker and Esther Reidhead. They came to St. Anthony in May 1854 and pre-empted forty-four acres of land along the Mississippi River in 1856. The land included the north half of what is now known as Durnam Island. John Durnam, a brother-in-law of Nahum, owned the other half of the island. They had many logjams at the head of Durnam Island.

Nahum and Esther had two sons, John and Charles Jefferie. Gayle's grandfather Charles married Zora Plummer and farmed this land. They raised four children, Charles, James, Clara and Harriet.

My mother Clara recalled how the Indians camped on the island and often rode their horses through the home place. They stopped and looked at them but never bothered anyone.

In 1920 my mother married Warren Green. They had five children, LeRoy, Fern, Ray, Glen and Gayle. For a time they lived in the huge brick house my great grandfather Nahum Crooker had built on the West River Road.

Willard and Gayle Redmann

LeRoy and Fern attended the Benson School. Some of the Green children attended Brooklyn Center Grade School District #28. This school had four large rooms upstairs, with an auditorium, a stage and a lunchroom in the basement. The school was just east of the Methodist Church. I walked one mile to and from school each day.

One day as I was walking home from school on a very windy day, I saw and smelled much smoke. I arrived home to see all of the out-buildings—machine shed, granary, summer home, chicken coop, double barns, double corn crib, garages and machine shop—burned to the ground. Only the two houses were left. The barns had just been filled with hay from the fields. The closest fire station was in Osseo and we felt lucky to have saved the two houses.

Green-Redmann House at 7601 Osseo Road

It was fun having Shingle Creek nearby to play in, and skate on in the wintertime.

I married Willard Redmann from Anoka in 1951. We built our first home on a portion of my parents' property on Osseo Road and this site later became the First Brooklyn Park State Bank in 1969.

Willard remembers while building our house in the evenings, after working all day at the Goodin Company, people drove by and threw potatoes at him. In all, he probably saw five cars drive by all evening. Not much traffic along Osseo road then.

We have two children, Barbara and Gregg. We also have four grandchildren. In 1969 Willard and I moved to our present home, on 86th and Riverview Lane located about three miles north of where Nahum Crooker settled in 1856.

Willard retired from the Goodin Company in 1987. I had worked as a bookkeeper for Bauer Welding and Metal Fabricators, Inc. Since retirement we spend a part of our winters in Arizona.

Submitted by Gayle Redmann

Anton J. (Tony) and Adell (Hansen) Renko

I was born May 9th, 1920, in the town of "Brooklyn", to Anton and Bertha Renko. They were vegetable gardeners. There were five kids; as we grew, we worked beside our parents. As I got older, I didn't always like the work, but I learned a lot. We also had time to play and ride bikes.

I got my schooling at Benson School. That wasn't too bad; I liked it. High school was Patrick Henry in Minneapolis, seven miles from home. On good days, when the tires weren't flat, I'd ride my bike; winters I hitchhiked. When spring 1936 came, 10th Grade, I dropped out, thought I was smart enough, didn't need anymore schooling. That was a mistake! Summers I stayed home and worked for Pa and Ma. Everything was going good, until 1941!

Tony's Garage

I got a "job offer" from Uncle Sam (re: World War II); it lasted a year, for $21.00 a month, providing food, clothing, shelter, and even a big rifle, but no calendar! Soon after came a nice long "cruise" in the Pacific to New Guinea. Sometime later I found myself in a taxi on Lyndale Avenue, and on the seat was a paper dated July 29th, 1945. Lucky me! Home at last!

I didn't want to go back to gardening; I had learned the auto repair trade. In 1948 I built a small service garage at 7959 Lyndale Avenue North; before long I was in the repair business: Tony's Garage!

I'd been sowing a lot of wild oats without a crop — it was time for a wife and family! I bought a Chrysler New Yorker convertible. One day I pulled into a drive-in and there she was! A carhop — and a keeper, Adell Hansen! On June 24th, 1950, a J. P. (Justice of the Peace) in Norwood, Iowa married us.

We bought a small house trailer and lived next to the garage. November 1952, son, Tony Jay was born; what a happy day that was! In 1953 we built a bigger garage and gas station closer to the road. Business was good. I think the only other garage in the township was Libby's on 95th & West River Road. We also did lots of snow plowing and towing. In 1958 our daughter, Robin, was born, but only lived two years. July 12th, 1960, we were blessed with the birth of daughter, Kathleen. Another very happy day!

In 1963 we built a new house across the road from Tony's Garage. Thanks to all of our good customers and employees, we doubled the size of our building in 1964. I was quite lucky; I never had more than 500 feet to go to work!

We also had horses and some Herefords along with the garage business. In 1970 we bought a farm in Princeton, Minnesota. We sold out to two employees in 1972 and went into farming! "Out of the frying pan, into the fire!"

Tony's Garage was good to us, and thanks again to all of our wonderful customers who made it possible.

Submitted by Anton J. (Tony) Renko

Pa, Anton Renko, was born in Austria (now Slovania) and at age fourteen, stowed away on a ship for America. Discovered about halfway across, he was allowed passage to Ellis Island. He spoke no English, but learned quickly, and then traveled to Michigan for two to three years, before coming to Minneapolis in 1912, where he went to work for Minneapolis Moline. Ma, Bertha Gutcasol, was born in Minneapolis to German parents, and worked at Munsingwear as a seamstress.

Early in 1914 Pa and Ma Renko settled in Brooklyn Township, the Sunkist Acres Development, with six-month old daughter, Ceceilia. They intended to raise a family and become vegetable producers, the "going thing" at that time. Before long they learned the skills of growing vegetables and marketing them at the Minneapolis Farmers' Market.

It was time to start growing some helpers for the future: Annette in 1917; Tony in 1920; Frank, Jr. in 1922; finally Verona in 1931. They started out living in a tent, then a very small house. After an add-on, or two, it was time for a bigger house, which they built; it still stands at 8000 West River Road in Brooklyn Park.

The farm size also grew, from three and a half to fourteen acres. We were all kept busy planting, weeding, picking and bunching. Along came the Depression; a lot of veggies didn't sell. That meant another job for Ma: get a big bunch of Mason jars and fill them with those veggies, canning them! That she did! Between the chickens for meat and eggs, a cow for milk and the canned veggies—we ate really well!

During the 30s it was very hot—over 100 degrees day after day! We swam in the Mississippi nearby to cool off and sleep outside at night. In 1934 Pa put in an irrigation system. That meant better crops, more work, and a place to cool off besides swimming in the river.

In the late 1930s Ceceilia and Annette went to work in Minneapolis. Then in 1941 Uncle Sam wanted us boys, leaving Pa and Ma shorthanded again.

Frank was married in 1945 and built a small house on the farm. He also wanted to start gardening and raise a family. He and his wife, Beverly, worked with Pa and Ma while raising five kids: Frank Jr., Patty, Ronald, Chris and Becky. In 1957 the need came for a bigger house; they built next to the old house at 8015 Sunkist Blvd.; it's still there today.

June 11th, 1958, came our first tragedy: Frank Jr. drowned in the Mississippi River at age twelve. By that time gardening was no longer a living. Pa and Ma sold off property, lots, one by one, and quit gardening in 1962. On January 14th, 1965, Frank Sr. was killed in an industrial accident at work in Minneapolis. Beverly raised all of the children to maturity by herself and did a wonderful job.

Pa Renko died in 1970; Ma Renko died in 1971,

Submitted by Anton (Tony) Renko, Eldest Son

Anton and Bertha Genevieve (Gutcasol) Renko

"Ma and Pa" Renko on their golden wedding anniversary (February 1963)

Wendy Richardson

Wendy Richardson

GROWING UP IN CRYSTAL I looked forward to special deliveries of farm produce by my great uncle, Baldwin Hartkopf. Sometimes we visited his farm in Brooklyn Park where I laid in the front yard with my cousins and pretended to watch movies at the Starlite Theater, whether they were playing or not! Other times we might ride one of the horses, chase the cats or marvel at my Aunt Obeline's many pet birds in cages in the front room, while the grown-ups visited. My grandmother and Aunt Obeline were sisters, and grew up on a farm that is now the Osseo Post Office site. Whenever they talked about going somewhere, it always involved Osseo Road. I thought it must be like the "Yellow Brick Road" and it could take you anywhere you wanted to go.

During high school, my parents moved to Brooklyn Park. When I got my driver's license, I went with my friends to the 52 Hi Drive-In for pop, burgers and French fries. We also went to the A&W Root Beer Drive-In on 69th and Osseo Road. I graduated from Osseo Senior High School.

After we were married, we bought a house in Brooklyn Park, where I still live. In 1975, while pregnant, I began making quilts, and in 1976, joined the Brooklyn Center Friendship Quilters. They met twice a month at the Brooklyn Center Community Center, and are still active today. Working with fabric became a large part of my life and I was no longer content to make traditional quilts. I began creating more personal work—art wear and wall pieces of my own design. I took classes, entered contests and began teaching classes at quilt shows. I belonged to Minnesota Quilters, had several committee and board member jobs and was President in 1989. I began selling work at juried art fairs in Minnesota and around the country. The American Quilter's Society Museum in Paducah, Kentucky, purchased a quilt for the museum, and the Minnesota Historical Society has purchased a garment and a quilt for their permanent collection. I have taught and volunteered at the Brooklyn Park Historical Farm and have had my quilts hanging at Brooklyn Park City Hall.

Five years ago, I began dyeing my own fabrics and selling them. This enables me to have more personal choices in the fabrics and colors I want to work with. I have designed garment patterns and now sell these products around the country and in Europe and Japan.

My son graduated from Park Center High School in 1994, and in 1999 from the University of Colorado in Boulder, where he now lives. I walk my dogs at Hartkopf Park, formerly part of Baldy's farm, and drive around and shop at places that looked much different as a child, but have many memories.

Submitted by Wendy Richardson

NORENE ROBERTS was raised in Massachusetts. She said her parents "sort of dragged us, but we went everywhere," and that included historical sites. "I have been to Independence Hall in Philadelphia twenty times." Norene said her mother, Betsy Roberts, does not believe things should stay the same forever, "You can't freeze-dry a city," she said. Thus, came the beginnings of a historian in Norene.

Norene says, "I can't live without knowing the context and continuity of an area, I don't want to live anywhere without feeling plugged in."

Norene "plugged in" when she and her husband Joe, a technical writer, moved to Brooklyn Park at 7800 Tessman Drive. She joined the Brooklyn Historical Society in 1992, served on the Board of Directors, 1992-1995, and was Treasurer, 1993-1994, and President, September 1994 to March 11, 1995. She served the Society in many other capacities, and received the coveted "Mary Jane Gustafson Award" in 1995. Norene has written extensively and her writings and research are well represented in this book.

Norene is a contract historian, and owner of Historical Research, Inc. She says being a historical practitioner for the past twenty years taught her how to learn. Norene says there are lessons children should learn from history: "I would say that every human being who lives goes through the same experiences and feelings that you will go through in your life — the personal challenges, politics and personal development." The most surprising thing Norene has learned from history is, "That human beings are connected, not only through geography, but also through time."

Norene was named 10th Distinguished Alumna of the MacDuffie Prep School in Massachusetts, University of Minnesota Distinguished Alumna for the College of Liberal Arts, and Master Gardener with the Hennepin County Extension Service. She has a Ph.D. in American Studies from the University of Minnesota.

Joe and Norene sold their home in Brooklyn Park in 1995 and returned to Norene's home state of Massachusetts. They built their new home on land owned by her family. Her mother lives near them and they need to be close.

Norene is the elected Goshen, Massachusetts City Clerk with extensive responsibilities. Joe is involved with Veterans Affairs.

Submitted by a Brooklyn Historical Society volunteer from
Brooklyn Center Sun-Post interviews of June 3, 1992, and October 26, 1994.

Joe and Norene Roberts

Jules Louis Rochat

Jules Louis Rochat (1908)

JULES LOUIS ROCHAT, born April 5, 1832, in LePont, State of Vaud, Switzerland, came to America in 1866. He came on the steamer Arago that took fourteen days from LeHavre to New York. Arriving on June 28, 1866. After staying in St. Paul with his brother, Jules Henri, he bought a farm near Osseo—fifty-eight acres for $1,200 and had a house built. The house had three bedrooms and an attic, a stable and fences. He wrote, "There is a road that goes to my farm and cuts through it. The house is on the edge of the road. I will be three to four minutes away from the village of Osseo. The place is called Bottino preyrie." He said the land around there was flat, and he had trees on the non-cultivated land (twenty-five acres were cultivated). In the woods were wild cherries, which came in clusters, and "wild prunes of March raisins," black currants and currants "like the ones we plant in Switzerland."

Jules said, "The ground is sandy and easy to cultivate. We can plough with one horse. One ploughs one time, plants, harrows and harvests with the machine pulled by two or three horses, and five or six men afterwards. . . to gather, tie up and pile up the bundles. . . one harvests five to six acres per day. Afterwards, one gathers the seeds to put them in a pile or to thresh them. We use the threshing machine and eight to ten horses, and seven to eight men." Threshing took one day "without raising the scythe and the flail. Potatoes are picked up with the plough, we plant them in the ground, and everything is done with horses. It is more agreeable than in our mountains of Switzerland where we do everything by hand."

Jules and his wife, Marie, were happy, however, what bothered them the most was the English language. "If I knew German, I would be fine. Where I go, only Swiss German from Glaris is spoken." Jules noted the vegetables grew easier in America than in Switzerland and grew rapidly. After only eight days, "we don't recognize anything because everything grows so fast. The summer is very hot, but it is almost always windy. There is enough air and we breath easier than in Switzerland." He didn't agree with the way farm animals were left outdoors or in an open shed. The cows grew long hair like bears. Milk cost eighty cents a jar, and potatoes sold for fifty cents a bushel. Wheat was $1.40 a bushel—$5.25 for 100 pounds of flour and one half a dressed pig was eleven cents a pound.

At age 78 Jules went back to Switzerland, but returned at age 81. He died in 1915 and was buried in Niggler Cemetery, Osseo.

A George Rochat farmed east of the present North Hennepin Community College, and Eva Rochat Schmidt and her husband, Carl, owned forty acres of farmland on the site of today's North Hennepin Community College. Eva was Jules' granddaughter.

Condensed from an 1867 letter translated from French by a Professor Imhoff.
Furnished by genealogist Dorothy Rochat Weeks of Colorado

In November 1949 Lloyd and Genevieve Rocheford bought a lot in Brooklyn Center that already had a foundation for a home. They joined Our Lady of Victory Catholic Church. The Rocheford family included the two girls, Sharon and Patricia. The following July after moving into the house, Michael was born.

The area was considered "truck farming land." The truck farming consisted of potatoes, asparagus, and rhubarb. Vern Fransen had started twenty-four houses forming a loop from Highway 100 and back again. The Rochefords are the last remaining original owners of their house in the neighborhood of twenty-four. The village of Brooklyn Center had fewer than five thousand people at that time.

In two years there were two more children — the twins, Terry and Tim. Marianne was born three years later and Annette was born eight years after Marianne.

In the years the Rochefords have lived here they have seen many changes. Not long after 1949 the farm across the street in Minneapolis was sectioned into house plats. Many homes were built from Upton to Washburn between 51st and 53rd Avenues. This was no longer a farm area but a residential area of North Minneapolis.

Many big elm trees were cut down to widen what was Osseo Road (now Brooklyn Boulevard). Several truck farms were taken over, and then turned into Brookdale shopping area. A water tower was set up nearly in their back yard and serves as a centerpiece to the nine-hole executive golf course.

Mr. Rocheford was a salesman for A. S. Aloe, a surgical and hospital supply house. His territory was all of North Dakota. After seven years with the company he started a new job at what was Northern Pump. He did a variety of jobs from crane operator to machinist parts inspector. As part of his work, he became a Vice President for the union. He worked for FMC for thirty-two and a half years at a 'temporary job'. He retired from FMC Corporation, the old Northern Pump, in 1985.

After a typical family Sunday dinner in August 1992, all seven children and their families went home. That evening, as they were trying to cool the house, they were running fans and the air conditioner. Genevieve was awakened in the middle of the night by the smoke detector. She went into the living room to see a small flame by the fan on the floor. As she woke Lloyd, the flames went up the drapes and across the living room. They both escaped the house, and a neighbor who is a firefighter helped Lloyd put out the flames. After four and a half months of rebuilding their home, their families rejoined them for the next family dinner right before Christmas that same year. Rebuilding a house was only part of the story. Coming back to the neighborhood and having the kids come back home was the rest of the story.

Submitted by Lloyd and Genevieve Rocheford

The Lloyd and Genevieve Rocheford Families

Front, Sharon Fraser and Genevieve Rocheford; back, Parry Fraser, Marianne Conn, Terry Rocheford, Lloyd Rocheford, Tim Rocheford, Annette Fink, and Mike Rocheford.

The Joseph H. and Madeleine C. Roche Family

AFTER A TWENTY-ONE YEAR MILITARY CAREER in the U.S. Navy as a Naval Aviator, I returned to civilian life in 1964. I brought my family to Brooklyn Township, Minnesota. I was familiar with this territory, having been on the Earle Brown Farm many times with my father Joseph W. Roche. He was a banker in Robbinsdale.

As a boy I worked on many truck garden farms in Brooklyn Center, weeding onions and picking potatoes. On my best day I earned $6.00. Those were good wages during the Depression!

Brooklyn Center was new to Madeleine and our eight children. Brookdale Shopping Center was new. On the farm, horses meandered in a beautiful pastoral setting. We purchased a home on two acres of land at 816 69th Avenue North. We were in the country. The city had a small tree farm west of us and north of us were, what we called, the dirt hills (now Evergreen Park), where the children played safely, the youngest, Gigi, tromping through the tall grasses with only her bouncing "ponytails" showing. It was a safe place to raise a family.

Joseph and Madeleine Roche's fiftieth wedding anniversary with Barbara, Michele, Gisele, Phillip, Denise, Stephen, and Tim

We made friends through our church, St. Alphonsus, and soon we belonged to the community of Brooklyn Center. In the late 60s the Community Emergency Assistance Program, (CEAP), was founded.

The Vietnam War ended. We had an extended family of seven Vietnamese boys. Children everywhere! Those were full years, busy years, and happy years! We purchased a second house west of us, 824 69th. We, the Roches, call the corner "the Roche Compound."

We are now retired and in our seventies. Our family has grown. Two sons and their families live in Brooklyn Center. Our grandchildren frolic in the large backyards where trees abound. We buried a son, John, in Mound Cemetery in 1995.

I, Madeleine, have deep roots in Quebec. I am French and a naturalized citizen of the United States.

We have traveled extensively. We have learned that above all we need roots, a little corner of the earth we can call home—where family, friends and community feed our spirit. Brooklyn Center has changed. Looking back, it was a small jewel in 1964 and is a larger than life jewel for us today. Sitting by the crackling fire, we are HOME at the "Roche Compound" in Brooklyn Center—our first permanent home. May God keep this city safe.

Submitted by Joe and Madeleine Roche

I WAS BORN July 13 1930, and my early years were spent in Osseo, where my father, Matthew Rohe, owned a hardware store and an oil business at the corner of Central Avenue and Third Street where the SuperAmerica gas station is now located. My father was one of seven brothers born in Dushore, Pennsylvania. Two brothers, Lawrence and Fred, also came to Minnesota, and started farming on the northeast corner of Fish Lake in Maple Grove. This area now has many condominiums and is part of the Maple Grove Shopping Center. Fred ultimately became President of Land O' Lakes. My father, mother and sister Mary (Spalding) lived for a time above the business on Central Avenue and then moved to a house a few blocks away. My father died when I was two years old.

After my father's death, my mother, Mildred, married Bert Smith, who farmed with his dad at Winnetka and 93rd Avenues, across from the Mobil Oil pumping station. After selling that farm they moved to a smaller farm at Brooklyn Boulevard and Zane Ave—next to the Brooklyn Township Hall. Across the road—in the area now occupied by Village North Shopping Center—Warren Green, a close family friend, lived. I spent many wonderful hours swimming and fishing there in Shingle Creek. After Bert married my mother, we moved from Osseo to Robbinsdale. Bert worked for Hennepin County and surveyed the centerline for County Highway 18—now Highway 169. He later worked for thirty years as a foreman at Ford Motor Company in St. Paul.

My mother was one of three children (the others were Morris & Muriel) in the Jesse Smith and Mary Bren family of Osseo. Jesse farmed three different farms on 89th Avenue east of Osseo. Two of the farms were east and west of the Smith school at 89th Avenue and West Broadway.

In 1936 we moved to Minneapolis, where I attended kindergarten through high school. About 1948 we bought a basement home on 63rd Avenue near Zane. While living there I attended the University of Minnesota and worked in the local gravel pits. I entered the Air Force and attained the rank of Staff Sergeant.

While in the service in North Africa, I had a pen pal named (Nancy) Anne Toman. We married in 1956 and were blessed with four lovely daughters, Mary Anne, Theresa, Debora and Judith and twelve grandchildren. Nancy's father and grandparents on her mother's side all came from Czechoslovakia.

In 1962 we bought a home on 65th Avenue North in the southwestern part of Brooklyn Park. Having spent most of my youth in the area, I was eager to volunteer in the development of the City. I was a member of the Brooklyn Park Planning Commission from 1967-1974 (Chair 1973-74), West District City Council Member, 1974-1978, and served on the Toward the Year 2010 Task Force in 1988. I continue to attend Council and Planning Commission meetings. The Comprehensive Plan of the 1960s was a giant leap forward for the Village. It was gratifying when, on March 11, 1974, at 11:30 P.M., the Plan's Zoning Ordinance was passed.

Submitted by Jon S. Rohe

The Jon S. Rohe Family

Jon Rohe

The Rorem Family

The Harold Rorem Family: front, Harold, Cynthia, and Betty; back, John, Douglas, Bruce, and Steven (ca. 1970)

In November 1955 we native Iowans moved from New Orleans to Brooklyn Center, renting a home at 59th and Emerson. My husband Harold (formerly an engineer with Shell Oil Company drilling offshore) had accepted a position at Honeywell. Our neighbors told us about new homes being built out near Osseo Road (now Brooklyn Blvd.). We took a drive. It was a scenic, two lane, tree-lined highway with truck farms and greenhouses along the way. We were impressed! Within weeks, we looked at several model homes and chose a Wangstad home (subdivided Magnuson farm west of the present Chrysler dealer). Contractor Andrew Wangsted named the streets after two of his granddaughters, Joyce and Janet, and reserved space for a small park at 61st and France Avenue.

In August 1956 we moved into our house. Friendly neighbors helped to lay sod. Women and small children often "coffeed" in backyards or kitchens. Most were full-time homemakers. Churches and schools were feverishly built to keep up with the influx of people. This first ring suburb was quickly transformed from a quiet rural village into a bustling metropolis. Grocery stores were few and far between. People with a vision developed parks. Soon the promised Brookdale shopping center was built where rhubarb and asparagus once flourished and it was no longer necessary to take the bus downtown to shop. One by one, farm homes were demolished to make room for shopping malls and homes. Trees were cut to widen Osseo Road.

I (Betty) was active in League of Women Voters. Boy Scout work had a high priority for Harold. We volunteered work at our church. The years went so quickly. The Osseo District #279 schools challenged our children (Bruce, Douglas, Steven, John, and Cynthia), who went on to college and pursued careers of their choice. We are enjoying retirement including attending nine Elderhostels from coast to coast.

Submitted by Harold and Betty Rorem

Janice (Green) Rose

Grandma Green's Farmhouse

Janice Rose's grandparents owned the land that is now Village North Shopping Center (76th and Brooklyn Blvd). Her grandmother sold the property there in 1969. Grandmother still has a daughter and son-in-law living in Brooklyn Park, plus two of her granddaughters and their families. Janice's father was born in the old farmhouse.

Before grandmother sold it, the Greens would get in the car, and drive all the way out to Brooklyn Park to visit her.

Although Janice was quite young there are many things she remembers. She remembers the trees that lined the driveway. Most of the trees are still there in front of Circus Pizza in Village North. She happily tells everyone as they go by that those are her grandmother's trees. They also went out to the house for the Brooklyn Park Tater Daze Parade (it went right in front of her house then). As kids playing in the front yard, then wait for the parade to start. There was also a Model T car in the barn that the children loved to play on. The car didn't work but the kids had fun playing with it. There was a creek behind the farmhouse that the children played in.

Submitted by Janice Rose

DOUGLAS AND JOYCE ROSSI were born and raised in northern Minnesota—Mountain Iron and Gilbert respectively. Hard working, iron-mining fathers supported both families. Shift work, long hours in snow or rain or in the damp, dark underground mine made life difficult. Still they were grateful for those jobs and the ability to help their children get an education that would give them choices and opportunities they themselves never had. Their mothers worked hard at home until their later years.

The Rossi Family

Doug and Joyce met in junior college and married after Doug graduated from the University of Minnesota Duluth, majoring in elementary education in 1955. Graduation day was a special day for his parents! Later he earned a Master's Degree in school administration and did post-graduate work at the University of Minnesota, becoming a Gopher fan at the same time.

Doug began teaching and driving the school bus with Warren Lindquist (quite a pair!) at Earle Brown Elementary in 1956. It was the beginning of a happy, enriching teaching experience and life-long friendships. Cyndi, Scott, and Dolan were born during those years. Doug left Earle Brown when he became an elementary principal in the Osseo School District, but the family continued to live in the Brooklyn Center/Park area. They became members of Cross of Glory Lutheran Church on "Old Osseo Road" where both taught Sunday School.

Years later, Doug's work moved the family to Pine Island and Little Falls before returning "home" in 1971 to accept the superintendency at Brooklyn Center School District #286. Later that year their last child, Gina, was born and they built a home on Dupont Avenue North just two blocks from the high school where they lived happily for twenty-five years among good neighbors and friends. It was the "right" decision for them—one that they have

Joyce and Douglas Rossi

never regretted for it was a wonderful place to live and raise a family. The community was and still is unique in its strong, unqualified support of education and all of the other areas children need in their lives: churches, recreation, safe neighborhoods. Doug and Joyce appreciate that truth about Brooklyn Center most of all!

They were active members of Lutheran Church of the Master all those years as well, enjoying the short walks to church and school. All of the children graduated from Brooklyn Center High School and during their college years discovered they were well prepared to compete with students from many schools and backgrounds. All graduated—Cyndi and Gina as teachers, Scott a business major, and Dolan, an engineer. They are all married and there are ten grandchildren so far!

Doug has retired from Brooklyn Center High School and we have moved to a smaller home in Anoka near the Mississippi River, which was especially chosen so we could be close to the Brooklyn Center area, but within walking distance to the woods and water setting of the north country in which we were raised.

Submitted by Doug and Joyce Rossi

Ben and Bets (Beauchaine) Ruffenach

ELIZABETH (BETS) BEAUCHAINE was born in Northeast Minneapolis in 1904. She was the oldest of four children, two boys and two girls. When Bets was about two and a half years old, the tip of her little finger was accidentally cut off when it caught in the water dipper handle. Grandma came over, put the tip back on and bandaged it. The tip grew back on and Bets is rather proud of it.

Bets's mother died when she was ten years old. Their father tried to raise his family properly. He hired a housekeeper and the nuns at the Our Lady of Lourdes School helped. The Turgeon family with fifteen children lived across the street. Mr. Beauchaine thought highly of this family. If his children needed disciplining he used the Turgeons. His children were not allowed to play in their yard, how many days depended on the severity of the crime.

The children attended Our Lady of Lourdes School. The tuition in those days was fifty cents a month per child, twenty-five cents for each additional pupil.

Bets's father and Uncle Joe worked for Schlitz Brewing Company. Occasionally Uncle Joe gave the Beauchaines a ride to school in the beer wagon. The nuns were not happy seeing a beer wagon stop in the front of the school, but that was a way of life for dad and Uncle Joe.

Bets Ruffenach and John Utke at Bets' childhood home

Bets remembers when her mother died. The body was prepared and brought home where it was laid out in the corner of the living room. Relatives and neighbors took turns sitting with the body all night. The casket was opened at the church again for reviewal and then again at the cemetery before it was interred. The body and the family were transported to the cemetery by horse and buggy.

Mr. Beauchaine had a pearl-handled gold-tipped pen he won when he was a student. Bets wanted to use it. He said she could when she was "worthy" of it. She didn't quite understand until she saw a picture in the "Minneapolis Star" newspaper some years later. Governor Floyd Olson was signing into law the state's Old Age Pension bill that her father, with the Eagle's support, worked hard to get passed. Bets' father was Secretary to the Eagles Organization. Governor Olson was using her father's pearl-handled gold-tipped pen. Then she understood what he meant by being "worthy'."

Bets and her husband, Bernard (Ben) Ruffenach were married in 1932. They were together for sixty-five years before he passed on. Ben was in the plastering and stucco business. Bets was his bookkeeper. He did plaster work on the former Rand Estates in Minnetonka, now the Cargill Company.

In 1998 Bets wrote to the address of her childhood home. John Utke, present landlord, welcomed her with a banner across the balcony of the house. She was encouraged to roam about the house. The old woodsided bathtub with the copper lining had been replaced. The pull-chain toilet was gone. The dining room and kitchen floors were the same. She remembers her mother scrubbing them.

She tells of a pot-bellied stove with isinglass sides being moved one block. The fire was still alive inside it. When they got it in place they hooked up the stovepipes and it was ready to heat.

The *Minneapolis Star Tribune* and four television channels covered the story of Elizabeth seeing her childhood home for the first time in seventy-five years.

Submitted by Elizabeth Ruffenach
photo from Star Tribune

DAN RYAN REMEMBERS traveling Osseo Road as a small boy in the early 1950s with his grandfather on their weekend trips to visit relatives in Anoka, Osseo and Dayton. There was always ice cream after collecting eggs at the Joyner farm while the adults spoke of earlier times.

Dan and Karen Ryan

In those days, Osseo Road was not much more than "that road to Osseo." About the only things one noticed from the side windows of a 1950 Buick were trees lining the roadside, farm fields, narrow bridges over Shingle Creek, an old school house, a few older homes and a great deal of dust tossed about on a windy day. A northbound turn onto what is now Noble Avenue was a dirt road trek into wide open farm country.

He remembers observing, one evening in 1958, a new brightly lit service station on Osseo Road. His thoughts at the time centered on why anyone would build a place like that way out here in the country. Little did he know that eleven years later he would be the owner and operator of that same business on Brooklyn Boulevard and Regent Avenue.

The first home Dan and I purchased was on Wingard Lane, right next door to Emma Wingard. The Wingard family had been one of the major potato farming families in the area for decades. Conversations with Mrs. Wingard were living history lessons. One of Dan's many regular customers at the service station was Wilbur Goetze, another of the original families in the area who raised potatoes.

In the early 1970s people still had time to get to know each other, and that included the guy who sold them gas and fixed their car. Dan got to know many of the people in the area and built a reputation as an honest businessman in the community.

As time passed, Dan and I had two children, Erin in 1971 and Adam in 1973. By 1977 a career change was on Dan's mind. The service station business had been good to him and the family but he decided he didn't want to do that work for the rest of his life. Having had two bad experiences in buying and selling homes got him thinking that a good career could be made in real estate if he would simply provide sincerely good, personal service to his customers. As of this writing, Dan Ryan has had twenty-three consecutive successful years in real estate, with the majority of his transactions occurring in the cities of Brooklyn Park and Brooklyn Center.

Dan and Karen Ryan in New Mexico

Today, Dan and I live in a home built on what was once Wilbur Goetze's potato farm. He has a stepson, Steven. I am an active volunteer and a trustee on the District 279 Foundation. I am a mortgage banker and Vice President of Twin Cities Federal Mortgage Corporation. We both love to travel, have been on nine cruises and enjoy winter get-a-ways in Los Cabos, Mexico.

Submitted by Karen Ryan

Erick Rydeen

MY PARENTS, Erick and Judith Rydeen, met in Brooklyn Center and were married in 1916. My father was born in Sweden in 1882 and my mother in 1892. My father came to the United States at a young age, and my mother came in 1906. After they were married they had an eighty-acre market gardeners' farm by 56th and Logan Avenue North. They raised three daughters, Betty, Jean and Doris.

The farm went from 55th and Logan along 57th to Shingle Creek. They grew all kinds of vegetables for the Farmers Market. There were green onions, asparagus, radishes, beans, peas, rhubarb, potatoes, squash, corn, spinach, and carrots, and all of these vegetables had to be picked and bunched daily for the market every morning. If there were any leftovers at market it had to be dumped, as everything for the market had to be fresh. During the summer, potatoes and green onions were the main produce.

Erick Rydeen hauling potatoes (1915)

The three girls helped all summer on the farm, either bunching or driving trucks and tractors. Erick hired men in the summer and local youngsters picked potatoes and bunch radishes down by Shingle Creek in the peat land.

The daughters attended Earle Brown Elementary School; then went to Patrick Henry through 9th grade and finished at Robbinsdale for 10-12 grade. When Doris was ready for high school, Patrick Henry had grades through 12th so she finished high school at Patrick Henry.

In the winter, Erick took sleigh rides with his big team for groups from churches, Scouts and the Stillman Grocery Store families. He was busy Friday and Saturday nights and Sunday afternoons.

A market gardeners' life is busy in the summer because all has to be ready for 5:00 a. m. market the next day.

My father passed away in 1950 and my mother in 1970. They lived in Brooklyn Center from the time of their coming from Sweden until they passed away.

Submitted by Betty Olson

IT HAS BEEN SAID that things are "cheaper by the dozen." . . well, maybe not cheaper, but certainly more interesting, and a lot more FUN, in our case!

I was born on the coldest January day of 1938, the ninth child of a family of twelve in White Bear Lake, Minnesota. There were four boys and eight girls. My father was a mechanic and died at age fifty-six, and my mother was a saint who graced us until her death at age ninety-seven. We eight girls had the unique privilege of doing "Mother-care" for the last five years of her life so she could stay in her own home. We took turns being with her every day, tending to her needs as she had tended ours, until her death in 1997.

My childhood was not always pleasant, but time erases the bad things and highlights the good. I have many fond memories of life before flush toilets and central heat, of family events with the house bursting with relatives. They always liked to visit us although I suspect it was easier to visit us than to have fourteen of us visit *them*, and of the solid relationships that developed among the siblings. We still meet for brunch on the last Sunday of each month at my mother's house, now my brother's house, for "Sibling Sunday."

I met my husband James Sandberg in 1956 on a blind date and we married in 1958. We moved to Brooklyn Center in 1973. James was a firefighter for the City of Minneapolis and I was a mother of three active boys. My outside interests centered on volunteering, including Community Emergency Assistance Program (CEAP) in its very early years. I started my own small housecleaning business in 1979 and continue doing it on a smaller scale even today.

Our sons, Mark, and Alan, graduated from Robbinsdale High School and Hennepin Vo-Tech. Keith went directly into the U.S. Navy after high school. Mark owns and operates Valley Motor Sports in Eagan, MN. He is the father of a fifteen-year-old daughter. Keith spent four years in the Navy aboard the aircraft carrier Enterprise. He is now a Minneapolis firefighter, is married and lives in Rockford, MN. Alan works for Morrie's Imports as a mechanic, lives in Brooklyn Center and is the father of a twelve-year-old son.

James is retired from the fire department and works at his hobby of radio-controlled airplanes. Together, we have enjoyed twenty-five years of traveling the U.S. and Europe on our motorcycle. We belong to three motorcycle clubs, including Minnesota Wings, which was started in our living room in 1982 and has over six hundred members across the state. We are active volunteers in many events—the Minneapolis Aquatennial for fifteen years, Holidazzle Parade for seven years, the Honda Ride for Kids, and many more volunteer opportunities. I am a "people person" and correspond with over thirty people in the U.S., Europe and Australia. I spend a lot of time and energy with my large family, brothers, sisters, and extended. I enjoy the creative domestic lines of sewing, cooking, flowers, and entertaining.

Submitted by Margaret Sandberg

The Sandberg Family

James and Margaret Sandberg

Gerald and Elizabeth (Guiney) Sandvick

BETH AND JERRY SANDVICK moved to the Stonehenge Town home area of Brooklyn Park in 1989. Their attachment to Brooklyn Park, however, began in 1966. Elizabeth was one of the original faculty members of the English Department of North Hennepin Community College when its doors opened to students in 1966. Beth continued as a member of the English Department faculty until her sudden death in 1990. Jerry joined the History Department faculty in 1968, the third year of the college, and its last at the Osseo site.

They were both teaching in October 1969, when the college moved to its present site at 85th Avenue North and West Broadway. The move from Osseo was planned for the summer but construction delays made it in October. The parking lots had not been paved and that autumn brought much rain and a quagmire. Classes were canceled for several days while crushed rock was hauled in to allow use of the lots. That year the classes started in mid-October instead of mid-September.

The Sandvicks both saw the growth of the college through the 1970s and 1980s from the first three buildings (Library, Science, and General Education) to the impressive campus it has become in the 1990s. Faculty grew from twenty-six to well over one hundred and the student body from about three hundred to nearly three thousand. North Hennepin has also become a northwest suburban center for cultural affairs and continuing education and training, as well as an institution offering the first two years of standard college courses.

Elizabeth Sandvick teaching an English Seminar at North Hennepin College the first year the school was in operation (1966)

In the early 1980s a nonprofit foundation was created to raise money for student scholarships. It has become one of the most successful foundations of any two-year college in the country and its annual dinner auction has become a premier social event in this area. The foundation has also helped the college in many ways.

Beth was, and Jerry is, proud to be associated with North Hennepin and to have been a part of its growth and central role in the life of the Brooklyn Park area. Beth taught many English courses, and Humanities, and served on countless committees that are so much a part of the daily operation of a college.

Jerry has taught the History of Civilization, World War II, and Political Science while also doing the other faculty tasks that are necessary for a college to function.

North Hennepin students have changed much over the years but those changes have been mostly matters of style, fashion, and fads that attract late teen and early 20s aged people. No group or institution is perfect but a greatest number of students have goals not dissimilar to those of the time when the college opened its doors. They want to learn, earn a four-year degree, and a rewarding life.

Beth came from Austin, Minnesota and Jerry from Chippewa Falls, Wisconsin. He is sure Beth would hope, and he hopes, that their work at the college has had an influence for the good of Brooklyn Park.

Submitted by Jerry Sandvick

BORN AND RAISED in St. Louis Park, Minnesota, I graduated from Coe College in Cedar Rapids, Iowa, went to Ethiopia as a Peace Corps Volunteer, met Dean Scheid from Sandusky, Ohio, and married him. When trying to decide where we would settle, we went "up north" to my family's cabin. Dean knew he was in "God's Country" and we knew we'd stay in Minnesota.

We wanted to move to a young community where we could raise a family and participate in the city, much the same as our parents had done before. In the summer of 1967 I went to visit an old friend from high school. She and her husband had just bought a brand new house way up north-Brooklyn Park or was it Brooklyn Center? I couldn't believe it! They were in a new neighborhood, few trees, many empty lots and this great big, wide Brooklyn Boulevard that took me there— oh, I thought I'd never get there! Dean and I drove up on Sunday to see the model houses in that new area and when his dad said he'd help with the down payment, we too, were buying a brand new split-level house on a cul-de-sac in Brooklyn Park!

Family and friends found it hard to believe that we would move so "far out" but Dean and I felt confident this was the "smart" thing to do. The neighbors were almost all our ages, with babies and more on the way. There were six houses and twenty-five children in the cul-de-sac! What a place to grow up! We did all the '50's things—stay-at-home-moms, a few part time jobs, taking care of each other's children, helping each other finish the family room or the landscaping. You name it; the neighbors shared it!

We treasure those days. Frankly, I don't know if our children, Scott and Kristofer, will have that same opportunity to experience what we did as a young family, but I think they are better young men for having grown up in Brooklyn Park, Minnesota, in a time when neighbors knew each other and took care of each other.

Today I live with my sister, Rebecca Longabaugh, in Brooklyn Park, in the second house we had built.

Scott is married and now lives in Utah. Kristofer earned a Master's Degree in Library and Information Science and works as a reference librarian at Hamline University from which he graduated in 1994, and also works at a bookstore in Saint Paul.

I have been honored to serve the people of our two communities, for eleven years in the Minnesota House of Representatives and now in the Minnesota Senate. The greatest reward from being elected has been getting to know so many of the wonderful people in Brooklyn Center and Brooklyn Park.

Submitted by Linda Scheid

The Scheid Family

Linda Scheid

Bob and Jean Schiebel

ROBERT DALE was born in 1929 to Otto and Wilhelmina (Rohlfs) Schiebel. Robert had one sister, Betty (Schiebel) Hyatt, born in 1927. Both Robert and Betty were born and raised in the St. Peter, Minnesota area. Their father, Otto, was a rural mail carrier and a mink farmer. Wilhelmina was a homemaker.

Bob attended St. Peter public schools, graduating in 1947. He served in the U. S. Navy during the Korean conflict, from November 1950 to September 1954, and was discharged as a Pipefitter 1st class (FPI). After graduating from Minnesota School of Business in 1956, he worked for the firm of H. J. Flesher and Company in St. Louis Park.

Jean Elaine was born in 1937 to Clinton and Gladys (Trowbridge) Eaton. Clint was employed as security guard and Gladys was an LPN at St. Peter Hospital.

Jean attended John Ireland Catholic School and graduated from St. Peter High School in 1956. She was employed as a Psychiatric Aide at St. Peter State Hospital until January 1959. Bob and Jean married in 1959, moved to Minneapolis, then to Hopkins, finally, settling in Brooklyn Center in 1962.

Bob was employed with A. J. Pederson and Company from 1958 to 1985 as an accountant. He became Controller of Industrial Tool, Inc., in New Hope in 1985. The word "retirement" is not in his vocabulary.

Jean and Bob Schiebel (1984)

Bob and Jean raised three children. Jean was a homemaker and volunteer at schools, church and in the community. Active at St. Alphonsus Church, she has served on the Parish Council, the Council of Catholic Workers (CCW), St. Patrick's Guild and Funeral Luncheon Committee. Community activities have included Brooklyn Center Charter Commission, Crime Prevention Committee, Humboldt Square Substation, League of Women Voters and Community Emergency Assistance Program (CEAP).

Jean, an active Democrat, has served on many political campaigns and committees too numerous to mention. She attended three Democratic National Conventions: 1984 in San Francisco; 1988 in Atlanta, and as a delegate to the Chicago Convention in 1996. Bob has served as Treasurer for State Representative Phil Carruthers and he and Jean are also members of the St. Peter American Legion Post #37 and VFW Post #1220.

Currently, 1999, Bob is still working, Jean is still volunteering, their children, Linda, a graduate of St. Catherine's is a Sr. Buyer at Fargo Electronics in Eden Prairie, has three sons and lives in Northeast Minneapolis. Kurt, a graduate of St. Cloud State is a technology coordinator for Expo for Excellence Middle School in St. Paul where he resides with two of his three sons. Karl completed St. Paul Technical School and is employed with Coca Cola. He has three daughters and lives in Ramsey, MN.

Submitted by Jean Schiebel

My FATHER, Paul V. Schiebold, came to America in the spring of 1902 from the old Kingdom of Saxony. He had a good education in German but could not read nor write in English. He married Margaret Wegner, of Oriska, North Dakota, in 1906 and I was born in 1909.

Karl Schiebold

I started school in Wisconsin and later enrolled in the Minneapolis schools. I left eighth grade in 1923 and enrolled at Dunwoody Institute.

I vividly remember November 11, 1918, when World War I ended. The newsboys were hawking "EXTRAS." The war was over; papers were selling for a nickel each. People had tied tin cans to the backs of streetcars. As the streetcars rumbled on down the cobblestone streets the cans would cause sparks to fly up. The cans made a lot of noise. There was noise of all kinds, fire trucks were blasting their horns, and church bells were ringing. There was a forest fire raging to the northeast. The sky was overcast with heavy smoke from Minneapolis to Duluth.

I left Dunwoody in 1925 to travel with my father. My father was a veterinary salesman. He had to travel eight miles per day, but could not drive because he was so near-sighted. I had to drive to help keep the family in business.

During the 1932 election campaign I voted by "absentee" ballot for Hoover and Curtis for presidential offices, and Earle Brown as governor of Minnesota.

The former Margaret Deck and I were married in 1934. She had grown up in Sheridan County of Montana at Outlook. She had won a scholarship in 1929 to go to the University of Montana at Missoula to major in library economy.

My father's clientele were mostly druggists with whom I became acquainted. That connection helped me receive a position with a division of American Home Products when they needed a representative to cover the Dakotas calling on physicians, hospitals and druggists. After extensive training in Minneapolis I was transferred to Fargo, North Dakota. My wife and I remained there from 1941, until she passed away in 1993. I then moved back to Earle Brown Commons in Brooklyn Center in 1994 to be closer to my family.

Karl Schiebold and Barbara Erickson at Earle Brown Commons

I knew Hubert Humphrey, Sr., who had a drug store at Huron, South Dakota. Hubert, Jr. (the former U.S. Vice President) worked in his father's drug store and I knew him quite well. As an intern, Hubert, Jr. would go to the basement and make a lunch of tomato soup and cheese sandwiches. This gave him the right to tell people that, "Yes, he worked under a pharmacist."

My wife and I had three daughters and one son. After they had grown and left home, my wife took a position as librarian at St. Luke's Hospital School of Nursing in Fargo. She held that position for nine years and had an enviable good record at the school.

Submitted by Karl Schiebold

The Herman and Evelyn Schmidt Family

I WAS BORN December 26th, 1914, in a farmhouse eight miles from Winterset, Iowa. My earliest memory of an event is the end of WWI. In November 1918 the phone rang for a long time. When my mother answered, the operator told her that the War was over. We drove in our buggy to Winterset and rented a room in the hotel facing the town square. There was a huge celebration—parade, fireworks and they pulled a stuffed figure of the Kaiser up on the flag pole and six soldiers lined up and shot the Kaiser.

Several years later, the government ruled that all cattle had to be tested for tuberculosis and destroyed if they tested positive. My parents' herd had to be destroyed. Shortly after that they lost all of their stock, sheep, pigs, horses and farm equipment to creditors. They were allowed to keep their furniture, etc., and one very old team of horses.

Bob and Evelyn Schmidt and Bjorn Rossing

We moved to Indianola, Iowa. My father did handiwork and mother did sewing and housework. We moved several times a year because we couldn't pay our rent.

In 1931 I met Herman W. Schmidt. He worked for Western Electric, installing telephone equipment. On June 30th, 1932, we were married. I was 17½ and Herman was 22. He had just been laid off by Western Electric so we came north to Chisago City and started a produce house. We bought and sold chickens, eggs, and veal calves. In 1934 we had a daughter, Beverly, and in 1939, our son Bob was born.

After three years Western Electric rehired Herman. We bought a 6 by 18 foot house trailer to live in as Herman was transferred from town to town every few months.

In 1942 we purchased a home in Spring Lake Park on an acre of land for $4,500. It was a two-bedroom expansion house with attached garage and breezeway porch. We had sold the house trailer for $2,000 to make the down payment on the house. I had a large garden and raised chickens. In 1947 I took a job driving a school bus eight hours a day for two years.

One day in 1950, Clint Ratfield, the parent of one of our daughter's dance students, suggested that we build some houses. He was a cement block layer and had built his own home. He said that Herman could do the wiring, and I could secure the financing and do the painting. He said we would hire two carpenters and he would supervise the whole operation. We started houses on lots that we bought, cut down the Oak trees and grubbed out the brush. These homes sold rapidly. We named our company North Dale Realty.

In the 1960s the Schmidt family, along with other investors, started Brook Park Realty and in thirty-two years developed thousands of acres of land in Brooklyn Park. The most visible and proudest development is the Edinburgh Golf Course and the beautiful residential community surrounding it.

Submitted by Evelyn P. Schmidt

I WAS BORN in Maple Grove in 1904 and moved to Brooklyn Park in 1924 when I married Harry Schreiber. The following is an account of our family's record and memory of Schreiber family settlement in Brooklyn Park:

Two young brothers, Fredrick and Christian Schreiber emigrated from Germany in 1853. They met two sisters on their voyage to the United States. They were Dorthea and Mary Ann Lendt. The brothers settled in Chicago working in a brick works company and the sisters settled in Chisago County, Minnesota. The two brothers came to Brooklyn Township in 1860 and purchased land. Christian's farm was located across the road from what is now the athletic complex of Edinburgh Elementary School on Zane Avenue. Fredrick's farm was located almost two miles north. The shipboard romance continued, and in 1862, Fredrick married Mary Ann and Christian married Dorthea.

Fredrick and Mary Ann built the brick farmhouse on Zane Avenue across from Oak Grove Park. Eventually their farm holdings totaled 320 acres. Fredrick and Mary Ann had two sons and one daughter. The eldest son, John, married Eda Tessman in 1896.

Our farm is now 143 acres. Fredrick purchased seventy-eight acres in 1867 and another sixty-five acres in 1890. It had a small house located on it. This became John and Eda's home where Harry was born in 1898. They also had three daughters, Nora (Schwappach), Marion (Paul), and Irma (Rochat). A substantial addition was constructed in the early 1900s resulting in the white farmhouse that still stands on Zane Avenue today. The double story house has the original wood detail on the eaves, the cistern in the basement, and attached summer kitchen. The original red granary, barn and pump house also remain. John and Eda raised potatoes, vegetables and grains to feed the cows, hogs, and chickens.

A one-room school was built about one mile east of the farm, commonly known as the Schreiber School, District 31. John Schreiber was the Clerk of the School Board in 1910. Harry, his sisters and my sons attended that school.

My late husband, Harry, was John and Eda's only son. When we married in 1924 we lived in the home south of the farmhouse, which is where I still live. The fieldwork was done with horses and one tractor. There was no electricity to the farm in those early years. There was a noisy generator in our basement that produced energy and charged batteries for use in our house and the farmhouse where Eda and John lived. Our major crop was potatoes.

Eda and I did many chores together on the farm. We would wash clothes together in the farmhouse summer kitchen using water from the cistern and sold eggs in Camden from our chickens. Harry and I purchased the farm in 1947 and expanded the potato production. Eda and John continued to live in the old farmhouse until the mid-1950s when they passed away. My husband passed away in 1958 and my sons, Gerald, Jack, and Bill, continued the potato operation. During the peak years, the Schreiber potato operation produced more than five million pounds of potatoes a year. I have lived on this land for nearly seventy-five years and am grateful that we have preserved the farm in family ownership for over 130 years.

Submitted by Vera Schreiber

The Schreiber Family

Eda and John Schreiber

The Anton and Agnes Senlycki Family

ANTON AND AGNES were raised in the Owatonna, Minnesota area, married and moved to Minneapolis. In 1943 they purchased a five thousand dollar, eighty-acre farm with buildings dating back to the 1800s. The farm was located in Brooklyn Park at 4401 95th Avenue North. The buildings were in great need of repair and there was no electricity, telephone, or plumbing. They did have a pitcher pump on a sand point well in the house. There was an outhouse for a toilet. In the winter, baths were taken once a week in a galvanized tub set up by the stove, and in the summer they were taken out on the porch. At first the house was heated with woodstoves, later by fuel oil and eventually by gas. There was no heat in the upper part of the house, except for what rose up the open stairway. The children kept warm by bunking together under several layers of homemade quilts. They found that the dairy barn was warmer than the house in the cold wintertime.

Field Rock Walls in the basement of the Senlycki house

The ten-room, two-story house was built with timbers and field rock for the foundation. Beneath one part of the house was a dirt floor root cellar used to store food for the family. Old newspapers were used for insulation.

Over the years many changes took place. The family of five children: Anthony, Lorraine, Marlene, Bernice and Clifford were born between 1935 and 1946. The whole family worked the farm, gardening and raising poultry, pigs and cows.

During the 1940s Anton worked as a polisher at the Northern Pump Defense Plant and farmed during the day. The family raised 2,000 broiler chickens every year, most of which were sold to workers at the defense plant. The eighty acres of the farm were planted in grain and hay and provided pasture for the animals. Farming was done with modern equipment for the times, even though some of the neighbors were still using horses. The farmers helped each other on threshing days and silo filling times. The women and girls cooked hearty meals and lunches for the hungry, tired threshers. Beginning in the 1950s Anton and his sons were well known throughout the area for doing custom harvesting with their fleet combines.

Agnes sewed all of the clothes her family needed. She canned between 600 and 700 quarts of vegetables, fruits and meats each year, most of which was raised on the farm. Most of the shopping for other food staples, dry goods, etc., was done in Osseo, and occasionally in Anoka or Camden. Agnes also made rugs on her loom. She had her own business of taking orders and selling rugs to friends and neighbors.

The children walked to the Schreiber Country School. The family attended the St. Vincent de Paul Catholic Church in Osseo. A neighbor would hitch up his horses to the sleigh and take all of the kids Christmas caroling.

Submitted by Lorraine Spears and Marlene Brooks

GEORGE SETZLER married Mary Zahm. Both were born in Germany: George in 1832 and Mary in 1833. At age fourteen they came from Germany with their families, who settled at Monroesville, Ohio. George and Mary married in 1855. They moved to St. Paul, and then took up a homestead at Cedar Island Lake until 1870, when they moved to Brooklyn Township. George was a cooper by trade and sold the barrels to St. Anthony and St. Paul dealers. George and Mary had eight children: George, Pauline, Gus, Rudolph, Charles, Mary, Otto and Louise.

Louise married Edmund Tessman, and one of their children is Alice Tessman. Charles married Carrie Dexter from Maple Grove. When his parents retired, Charles purchased the eighty-acre family farm, located near present day Highways 81 and 169. They had two children: George and Evelyn. George married Helen Young, had three children, and was a banker in Iowa.

Evelyn's father Charles died when Evelyn was six years old. Her mother rented out the farm and continued to live there with her two children. Evelyn attended Country School #32 in grades 1-3, Osseo schools in grades 4-8 and high school. She attended Macalaster College and graduated in 1935 from the University of Minnesota.

When Evelyn began teaching in 1936 she received $80 per month and lived at home. The curriculum was the same in all the schools and there was a state exam to pass before graduation from 8th grade. Discipline at school was not a problem because there was discipline at home. Evelyn then taught at Winthrop and Atwater, MN for five years before returning to the Osseo School District to teach high school science.

Evelyn attended MacPhail School of Music. She played the organ for church services at the Osseo Methodist Church for thirty years.

During the drought in the 1930s the potatoes were long and thin because they grew down to reach water, or they were knobby and farmers would break off the knobs to make them more salable. This was before farm irrigation. The family's first car was a 1920s Grant with side curtains. Because it didn't have anti-freeze, it was used only in the summer and they stored the battery in the basement for the winter. Electricity came to the area in 1936, replacing the icebox, wood burning range, gaslights and gasoline-powered water pumping system.

In 1966 the Highway Department purchased part of the farm, including their 1912 home, although the highway construction didn't occur for another twenty years. Fleet Farm purchased the remainder of the farm.

In 1968 Evelyn built a house on forty acres of farmland on West Broadway. After about twenty years the farm was zoned commercial-industrial. Brooklyn Park constructed an eight-acre drainage pond, much to the delight of ducks and geese.

After forty years of teaching, Evelyn retired in 1975. When invited to a fifty-year class reunion, she was amazed that her former students were all retired. Evelyn has enjoyed traveling, visiting seventy-one countries over the years.

Submitted by Evelyn Setzler

The George Setzler Family

Evelyn Setzler

Russell and Barbara Sexton

Barbara Peterson was born in Minneapolis, the eldest of three children of Edward and Laura (Simpson) Peterson. She grew up in Crystal, about a mile and a quarter from where she now lives. She attended Abraham Lincoln Elementary School, grades one through eight. Grades nine through twelve were spent at Robbinsdale High School. Barbara was active in the 4-H Club and was Hennepin County Style Queen in 1940. She graduated from the University of Minnesota, majoring in Home Economics with a focus on textiles, fabrics, and clothing. She gained the rank of Ensign in the Supply Corps of the United States Navy. During the Korean conflict, she was employed in Disbursing at the Great Lakes Naval Training Center. She met and married Russell Sexton there.

Russell was born in Sulphur Township, Doddridge, Arkansas. He was the fourth of five children born to Charles and Tessa (Courtney) Sexton. He attended Sexton Elementary School. He then attended high school at Ida, Louisiana for one year and graduated from high school in Bright Star, Texas. A friend dared him to enlist in the United States Navy. He didn't think Russell would be able to pass the test. Russell enlisted for four years. After four years in the Navy he was discharged and came home to find work. In the middle of the Depression there were no jobs, so he re-enlisted for four years. Before his second enlistment was up, the Japanese attacked Pearl Harbor and we were in World War II. A torpedo hit his ship, the Raleigh, at Pearl Harbor. The crew threw everything overboard to keep the ship afloat. He was promoted to Ensign during the war and was on the ship, Indianapolis when it was hit by a Japanese kamikaze. The plane slid down the side of the ship into the water, but a bomb hit the deck. He was ordered to close one of the hatches, which he did. He suffered many nightmares in years later for having to shut in some shipmates in the damaged part of the ship. He served in the Mediterranean during the Korean War.

Russell chose to live in Brooklyn Center, near Barbara's home. Six months before he retired from the Navy, they bought a home on Barbara's GI bill. Barbara and Russell reared six children: Thomas, Raymond, Claire, Jean, Drew, and Lynn. Russell was employed as a stationary engineer. Barbara went back to college and earned a Bachelor of Science in Elementary Education on the GI bill.

Fishing, organic gardening, watching television sports were some of Russell's favorite pastimes. He was a life member of Veterans of Foreign Wars Post #494. Barbara was active in the League of Women Voters of Brooklyn Center, Daughters of the American Revolution, General Society of Mayflower Descendants, Daughters of Union Veterans of the Civil War, Ladies of the GAR, Minnesota Territorial Pioneers, Minnesota's First Families, Business and Professional Women, The Minnesota Genealogical Society and the Brooklyn Historical Society. Her hobby, genealogy, began by tracing her own family. Russell and Barbara have six granddaughters and two great-grandchildren.

Submitted by Barbara Sexton

Barbara Sexton

My FATHER HAD COME HOME from the service in World War I, married and moved to this area to farm potatoes. I was born in October 1921 while we were living on a farm along Osseo Road at 49th Avenue north (the present site of The Howe Co.). My brother Harold was born in that farmhouse in January 1923. My parents rented it from the Howe family. My parents soon bought a house on the north edge of Minneapolis where we were raised. Two sisters were born later.

I graduated from North High School in Minneapolis and with help from my brother I went on to do two years at the University of Minnesota. During these years we worked on the truck farms and potato farms of Brooklyn Center and Brooklyn Township. We became well acquainted in the area, and worked for the Ed Tessman family prior to going into service during World War II, Harold in the Infantry and I in the Air Corp.

While in the service I met and married my wife, Maria. We had five children, four sons and a daughter, and have now been married for fifty-three years. After the war we returned to the area and in 1946, I signed a purchase agreement on what was known as the "Merrill Farm" on 97th Avenue in Brooklyn Township. With help from my brother and the Tessman Family (Ed, Raymond, and Alice), I concluded the purchase and went into potato, vegetable, and hog farming. The first few years were rough and tumble, but in 1950, we put in irrigation, and from then on things picked up.

Things were also picking up in the Township with sporadic development and with efforts by adjoining communities to annex part of the land area. This, along with drainage for the new developments, also became a problem to which the Township had no procedures to deal with. As a result, in 1954, the Town Board petitioned for incorporation as a standard plan village, to be called Brooklyn Park. Supporting this movement became my baptism into local affairs. The voters approved the plan, and a new era began. The next seventeen years I spent as a Council Member, Mayor, Planning Commissioner, Administrative Assistant, Village Manager, and City Manager.

I then returned to potato farming and sold real estate for Brook Park Realty until development overtook us and we closed out with a farm auction in March of 1985. That July the bulldozers took down the house that Sam Merrill had built when he returned from the Civil War. About fifty acres of the land now make up the Brooklyn Park Environmental Area and about fifteen will probably be added when the balance of the farm is developed.

My brother, Harold, spent the balance of his working years operating the "Twin Lanes Market" on present Highway 81, along with a truck farm and greenhouse.

Submitted by Edward D. Shimek

The Edward D. Shimek Family

Maria and Ed Shimek's fiftieth anniversary (1994)

Harold Shimek

The Harold Shimick Home

HAROLD SHIMEK'S CHILDHOOD HOME stood where the Howe Fertilizer Company now stands. In his teen years he worked at Edmund Tessman's farm where he picked potatoes. Mr. Shimek attended North High School for two years. After Patrick Henry was built, he transferred and graduated in its first class. Mr. Shimek went into the Army in World War II after graduation from high school, and served in the Philippines where he was wounded. He received a Purple Heart.

When Mr. Shimek lived at 8124 Lakeland Avenue, he had a greenhouse and a vegetable market. There was a section where the public could pick their own produce. He had this market for twenty-eight years, before selling the land to Curt Carlson in 1973. Mr. Shimek then purchased a home at 9204 West River Road. A Swiss Family, the Jentschs, built this home before the Civil War. The house was originally a farm home of 100 acres. Mr. Shimek lived at this house for twenty-five years and every Christmas and Easter he decorated his home beautifully. In the summer his yard was a place of art decorated with beautiful flowers. In the fall of 1998 Mr. Shimek sold his home and moved to Champlin where he now resides.

Submitted by Edward Shimek

Thomas and Lorraine Shinnick

THOMAS AND LORRAINE were married in 1959 at Princeton, Minnesota, Lorraine's hometown. Lorraine was raised on a farm near Princeton, and graduated from Princeton High School in 1956. Northwestern Bell Telephone Company employed her for eight years, leaving in 1964 with the birth of their first child, Lynn Marie. She later worked for Independent School District #286 as a Health Para for eighteen and a half years, retiring in 1998. Thomas grew up in North Minneapolis, graduating in 1954 from North High School. Thomas worked for Northwestern Bell Telephone Company, later U. S. West, retiring in 1993 with thirty-eight years.

When they moved to Oliver Avenue North in Brooklyn Center in 1961, there was no Brookdale Shopping Center, just farms. They watched the neighborhood and community grow. The three Shinnick children, Lynn, Patrick and Daniel, attended Earle Brown Elementary and Brooklyn Center High School, kindergarten through twelfth grade. Thomas and Lorraine have three grandchildren, Steven, Anna and Jessica, attend Earle Brown Elementary School. Daniel and his wife, Andrea, are Brooklyn Center residents. Lynn lives in New Hope and Patrick lives and works in Fargo, North Dakota.

In addition to working for Northwestern Bell and raising children, the Shinnicks are involved with the Brooklyn Center Lion's Club. Thomas claims it's an honor to belong to that organization. They have also been involved with the Little League baseball teams for twenty some years. Thomas is a Brooklyn Historical Society board member and serves on the school board of Brooklyn Center District #286. Thomas and Lorraine feel that Brooklyn Center has been a good place to live and raise a family.

Submitted by Thomas and Lorraine Shinnick

Tom and Lorraine Shinnick

EARL, THE SON OF ARVE AND OLGA SIMONS, was born in Lawton, North Dakota. Their family moved to Minneapolis shortly after the start of World War II. Earl served four years in the United States Air Force during the Korean Conflict. Following his discharge he started his career in the Consumer Finance Company as the Assistant Manager. In 1959 Earl was named Manager of Northtown Finance Company, which had just received its license as the first consumer finance company in Brooklyn Center. He continued in that capacity until 1965 when he became President of Northbrook Industrial Finance, also located in Brooklyn Center. His next undertaking was that as President of Dependable Credit Company of Minneapolis and later of Crystal, Minnesota. Earl is now with Firstar Bank.

The Earl and Ruthanne Simons Family

Ruthanne, whose family owned Nelson Hardware on 36th and Penn Avenue North, graduated from Patrick Henry High School in Minneapolis. After graduation, she began her career with Mereen Johnson Machine Company, located in the Camden area. She worked for Mereen Johnson for twenty-nine years. Presently, Ruthanne is a Child Nutrition Assistant with the Anoka-Hennepin School District.

Dawn, their daughter, graduated from the College of St. Thomas with a B.A. degree in Human Resource Management. Eric is pursuing his degree in business management, is working in Informational Services with the Dayton Hudson Corporation. Children from a prior marriage include Susan, Joni Simons Werner, Michael and Douglas. Susan teaches in the Osseo School District. Joni, with her husband Stuart and children, lives in San Antonio, TX, where Stuart is employed as a sales representative for Trane Air Conditioning. Michael, his wife Dianne and son Tony, live in Brooklyn Park and both work for the Osseo School District. Douglas is employed as a financial planner in St. Paul.

Eric, Dawn, Ruthanne, and Earl Simons

The Simons have all been active in their church, school, and community. They are members of the Cross of Glory Lutheran Church. Earl, Ruthanne, Dawn, and Eric are presently responsible for the Tape Ministry Program, which reaches out to the members unable to attend services.

Earl's involvement with the community began in 1960 when he was invited to join the Brooklyn Center Lion's Club. He has, since then, been involved with various committees in Brooklyn Center. He served on the executive committee for Community Emergency Assistance Program, shortly after its inception in 1970. He also joined the Board of Directors of the Wayside House, located in Saint Louis Park. The Wayside House serves forty women who are chemically dependent, and provides housing for twenty-three families in two apartment buildings.

Over the years, Earl has been recognized for his community activities. He was recognized as the Outstanding Young Man of Brooklyn Center. The Lion's Club presented him with the Melvin Jones Award, the highest award a Lion's Club member can receive. He was also named as the first member of the Wayside "Wall of Fame."

Retirement plans are now being formed!

Submitted by Earl and Ruthanne Simons

The Slovak Family

FRANK SLOVAK, SR., was born December 8, 1908, a son of new Polish immigrants. Frank grew up in North Minneapolis and attended St. Philip's School on 26th and Dupont Avenue North, a facility his father helped to found. In August 1937 Frank married Gertrude Dinzl (born January 7, 1913) whose parents emigrated from Germany. Gertrude, a "Northside girl," attended St. Joseph School on what were then 6th and 4th Streets North, and North High School.

Frank was a foreman of the Machine Shop at Pako Photo. He and Gert lived on the near northside of Minneapolis and began a family: Frank Jr., Marilyn, and Richard.

Frank Sr.'s godmother, Mrs. Sienko, lived on a farm adjacent to the Earle Brown Farm. This farm was purchased by the state in the mid-1940s as part of the Hwy. 100 construction. When visiting as very young children, the Slovak kids played with the farm animals. Marilyn, whose first horseback ride was on the large white draft horse, would years later own and show her own horses.

Marilyn, Gert, and Frank Slovak

When Frank and Gert had the house on 55th and Oliver built in 1955, there was a barn on the lot behind their home, cornfields only blocks away, and the bus line ended at 52nd and Humboldt Avenues.

As a teenager, Marilyn walked her dog to Earle Brown Farm. Crossing the two lanes of Hwy. 100, she watched horses being exercised on the dirt driveway running through the farm. It was a great sight—a smartly trotting, beautiful horse pulling a sulky. Often the pastured horses, liking attention, came up to the fence line bordering the highway to be petted.

In the late 1970s, Marilyn boarded her own horses, Honey and Southern Comfort, at Earle Brown Farm. It was truly a magnificent horse facility. Every part of the barn was designed for the horses' comfort, from the huge, sturdy stalls, to the cool, cement block arena with its beautiful large windows. How lovely it was to ride down the shady, tree-lined road that ran in front of the barn. In exploring the farm, gravestones for Earle Brown's pet dogs and horses were found in one of the barns. The story was that Earle Brown had his pets buried in the yard behind his home. With subsequent owners, the gravestones were removed and stored in the barn. There were also old kennels and a mess kitchen that contained a huge iron stove and oven.

Frank, Gert, and Marilyn still live in this home. Frank Jr., and Richard, both electricians, are married and have children and grandchildren. Attending a business seminar recently at the Earle Brown Center, Marilyn discovered that one of her old stalls is now a men's restroom, while another is an office. Some of the old stall timbers are still in evidence.

The Slovaks are known in the neighborhood for the big white Samoyed dogs. They have had four during the time they have lived in Brooklyn Center.

Submitted by Marilyn Slovak

DeWitt Clinton Smith and Melissa Smith arrived in Minnesota with their young son, Eugene, in 1857. They settled near Osseo, where they reconnected with old friends from Michigan. DeWitt had a keen interest in politics. In 1859 he was elected County Commissioner for Brooklyn Township, and in 1861, he was appointed Postmaster at Osseo. He left this second position after only a few months to join the Union Army.

DeWitt fought with the famous 1st Minnesota Regiment of Volunteers. He was seriously wounded and permanently crippled in 1862 at the Battle of Antietam. After a slow recovery, he returned to Minnesota and sought to reclaim his old position as Postmaster. He was unsuccessful. DeWitt then began a determined effort to be appointed to the Paymaster Corps. In the meantime, an old friend and fellow soldier, Stephen Miller, had been elected Governor of Minnesota, one of whose appointments was that of State Librarian. DeWitt was appointed to this position on January 14, 1864, but his tenure as State Librarian was a short one. His effort to be appointed to the Paymaster Corps was finally granted, and he rejoined the army in April, or May 1864, with the rank of Major.

In October 1864, after making payments to troops in Tennessee, DeWitt and other Paymasters left Memphis for St. Louis aboard the Belle St. Louis steamboat. At Randolph, Tennessee, guerrillas boarded the steamboat. Everyone on board would have been captured, had not the guerrilla officers been killed and their band repulsed, through the heroic efforts of DeWitt and one Major Beeler. They fought side by side, saved the boat, passengers, government funds and the national flag. However, it cost them both their lives.

After the news of DeWitt's death, Melissa faced the responsibility of supporting herself and her son, Eugene. She applied for the position of State Librarian. In his reply, after indicating that the Librarian's position was filled until 1866, Governor Miller said, "I have doubts as to whether a lady could be appointed, tho' if this vacancy existed I would try to have that difficulty removed by law."

With no solid job prospects in Minnesota, Melissa and Eugene moved to her parent's home in Beloit, Wisconsin, where they remained until their return to Minnesota in the winter of 1866. Unbeknown to Melissa during her absence from Minnesota was the effect her application for the State Librarian position had on Governor Miller. Apparently, he found the courage to put action behind his words for he appointed a woman, Louise Goodwin, to the position of State Librarian on March 3, 1865. When she resigned two years later, the path was cleared for Melissa's appointment. She became State Librarian on April 1, 1867, and held the post for six years. Melissa's tenure was characterized by her intelligent and professional approach to librarianship, with a determination to improve the Library's physical space and book collection.

By her second year, she convinced the Governor to seek appropriations for an additional room. Once attained, she also fought for a new stove, chairs, and desks. During her third year, the Library received an appropriation for gas fixtures, new cases and tables, "affording great additional convenience that those visiting the library cannot fail to appreciate." In her final years, the wood-burning stove was replaced with steam heat. Along with the new carpet, new chairs and an increased appropriation for book purchases, Melissa had every right to state: "It affords me much pleasure to be able to congratulate you (the Governor) and through you the people of the State, upon the improvements that have been made in the State Library.

Provided by and used with permission of Marvin R. Anderson, State Law Librarian

Dewitt and Melissa Smith

Melissa Smith

George William Smith Family

THE HORACE HARDING SMITHS and their son George H. came to Brooklyn Township in 1853 from Adrian, Michigan with a colony of fourteen families. Their son Andrew J. came in 1854. They brought farming implements and stock.

Andrew J. Smith was educated in Michigan and Hennepin County. At twenty years of age he was appointed an assistant in the Army's Paymaster Department. He and his brother, George H., formed a partnership, and in 1880, built a railroad spur out of Robbinsdale for the Great Northern Railroad. In 1881 they built roadbed for the Manitoba and Canadian Pacific Railroad. Andrew was elected to represent his district in the State House in 1876, and was reelected in 1878. He was known as one of the most progressive men in the community.

George H. Smith, Andrew's brother, enlisted in the Civil War in November 1861. He served with Company D, First Regiment of the Minnesota Volunteer Infantry, participating in twenty-five battles, including Fredricksburg. He served until honorably discharged at Falmouth, VA, in 1863. Civil War veterans were given land to homestead when they returned from the War. The land he homesteaded was in the area where North Hennepin Community College is now located. He became a prosperous farmer in Brooklyn Township. For twelve winters George worked in the lumbering industry.

The Smith Family at the Berry Farm

George married Frances Thomas in 1863. They had three children: Fred, Alice and Nettie. Frances died in 1876. George remarried and had four children with his wife, Flora Johnson: Jesse, Arthur, Florabelle and Caroline. Jesse's son George William Smith married Laura Jane Hansen and they live in Osseo. Their three children are Bruce, Gayle, and Shelley.

In 1978 George William and his son, Bruce, (both schoolteachers) purchased twenty-six acres at 98th and Winnetka Avenues to develop a "pick-it-yourself" strawberry farm that is still active. They also are truck farmers. They rent surrounding land to raise vegetables, which are sold at the Farmers Market. Interestingly, the land they purchased was originally homesteaded by Andrew J. Smith, and has had several intervening owners.

Bruce married Gwen Wodtke from Crystal. They have three children: Clayton, Amanda and Emily and live in Maple Grove. Bruce is a coach at Park Center High School and taught at Earle Brown Elementary School for twelve years.

Gayle works for School District #281, and is married to Stephen Boldt. They have two sons: Brian and Chad and live in Maple Grove.

Shelley is a teacher and is married to Ralph Lysdahl. They have three sons: Jonathan, Nicolas and Alexander, and they live in Champlin.

Submitted by George William Smith

IN 1929, and possibly before, Julius Soley was a blacksmith for Earle Brown. His shop was in Camden and they brought the work to him, even the big Belgian horses. What a sight that must have been to see the big horses go through to Camden!

Julius Soley

In 1934 Earle Brown wanted him to live on the farm, so in the spring the Soleys moved to North Place on the far end of the farm. It was an old house, no electricity or indoor plumbing. He built a beautiful garage for the Soleys. The garage was in three sections with a large upstairs. One section was for Mrs. Soley's chickens, so they always had plenty of fresh eggs. The center was the garage for their car and a stall for the Jersey cow, which Mrs. Soley milked and staked down by the creek. The last section was where the outside toilet was and also the stairway to get upstairs. Kathryn (Soley) Paulsen had a beautiful playhouse up there where she and her friends spent many happy hours. Kathryn had a wind-up Victrola and many old records. A few particularly good ones were "Laugh and the World Laughs with You", "China Town, My China Town", and "Shanghai Honeymoon."

When the Soleys had company they toured all of the buildings on the farm. They never tired of looking at the old hearses and buggies that were kept spotless. Earle Brown had a huge barn full of them. The guests liked to see the horses and a few other animals they kept, and also the beautiful peacocks. He had two beautiful dogs, a Great Dane and a Chow, that would follow people around and they also walked Kathryn home from Earle Brown School, one on each side. Those were fun days!

The old house is no longer there and the garage has been moved to the "Inn On the Farm." It's still a fun and beautiful place to be.

The house at North Place (1935)

Submitted by Kathryn Soley Paulsen

Glen and Evelyn Sonnenberg Family

Glen and Evelyn Sonnenberg with Scott, Melanie, Karl, and Melissa

I, GLEN R. SONNENBERG, was born in Brooklyn Center in December 1919, and have lived in the Brooklyns all my life. I am the youngest of twelve children born to my German father, Charlie, and Norwegian mother, Bessie. My parents came to Minneapolis from Ettrick, Wisconsin. My father was an "entrepreneur." After working as a streetcar conductor and building houses in Northeast Minneapolis, he bought ten acres and moved his family to "The Farm" at 6100 Lyndale Avenue North in 1918 and started truck farming.

As a child I went with my father to market by horse and wagon, then Model-T truck. He bartered for nuts and fruit at Christmas time with vegetables from the root cellar so he could give each his kids a bag of. My mother was an excellent cook and loved to sing. We gathered around her and requested songs.

I attended Earle Brown School through eighth grade, walked to Patrick Henry for grades nine and ten, then hitchhiked over to Edison High School until I graduated in 1938.

Our family attended Harron Methodist Church where I sang in the choir and the occasional wedding or funeral. Pa and my older brother Cliff helped dig the basement for the church. I married my wife Evelyn there. I continued to sing in church, and Evelyn also was in the choir or accompanying on organ or piano.

My brother Ray and I fished the Mississippi River. Sometimes we'd sell the fish to the merchants in Camden. We also trapped muskrat along the River and Shingle Creek. Pa went with us downtown to sell the pelts to make sure we got the best price.

In the summers during and after high school I worked at Madsen Floral, Joyner Silver Plating and, with my friend Ted Nordquist, helped his dad build houses. I also worked in the Civilian Conservation Corps and at Yellowstone National Park. I went to San Diego, where my sister Margaret and her husband had moved, and worked at Consolidated Aircraft Corp., where I was drafted and then shipped overseas in World War II.

After the War, I attended Hamline University and rode to and from school on the "Osseo Express." I graduated with a degree in science and chemistry. At Hamline I met my wife, Evelyn. She graduated with a degree in nursing. I taught in Tracy, MN for two years before joining the Minneapolis Schools as a teacher, and then became an administrator. I retired in 1979.

In 1952 I was elected a Brooklyn Center Village Trustee, and served 1953-54. I also was elected to and served one term on the Earle Brown School Board.

In 1951 Evelyn and I moved into our home at 6200 West River Road. We lived in the lower level until we finished building the main level in 1958. We were forced to move when our property was taken for the construction of the I-694 bridge over the River. We found a home upstream in Brooklyn Park, moved in September 1962, and are still there.

We have four children: Melanie, Scott, Karl and Melissa, and five grandchildren. Melanie is a mezzo-soprano and lives in New York City, Scott is a painter and lives with his wife and children in Andover, Karl is an RN and lives with his wife and son in Seattle, and Melissa is a pharmacist and lives with her Airedale in Brooklyn Park.

Submitted by Glen Sonnenberg

RICHARD AND JUNE SORENSON were married in Minneapolis in 1956. Their first child, Ellen, was born in 1957. Mother left her job teaching elementary music in Bloomington to raise Ellen, while our father, Dick, continued to work for Northwestern Banks. Gregory was born in 1958.

Father and mother began looking for a new home for their growing family in 1958. and in August bought a new home at 6308 71st Avenue North. The pine trees were torn down when the storm drain was put in. The other mature trees were damaged when the fire department burned down the farmhouse for practice. Father, mother, Ellen and I moved into the new house on March 15, 1959, and in December 1959, Stephen was born, a tax bonus for the family. Mary was born in September 1962, completing our family.

Mother and father were very active in the community. Mother directed the Prince of Peace Lutheran Church choir for nineteen years. We kids and dad went to St. Alphonsus Catholic Church.

Dad sang bass in the choir and served on the parish council. He chaired the PTA at Parkbrook and Zanewood elementary schools. All of us graduated from Osseo High School where we were active in music and drama programs. We attended the University of Minnesota and marched in the band in the 1970s and 1980s, just as our mother had in the 1950s.

In 1976 we opened a store, "Second and Exchange" in the Zanebrook Shopping Center. After two years we closed because of poor profits. Dad went into real estate in 1976, working for Good Value, Pinetree and ERA. Mother began substitute teaching in 1968 when all of us were in school all day. She substituted for Osseo School District until we all graduated in 1982. She also worked for Minnesota Fabrics at Northbrook Shopping Center.

Ellen married Ron Rasmussen in 1982. They live in Mounds View and have a daughter, Kirsten. Ellen works as a Software Design Engineer for Unisys, Ron works as a Community Residential Supervisor with the State of Minnesota.

Stephen married Holly Ward in 1989. They live in Shakopee with their children, Joshua, Elizabeth and Hannah. Stephen works for Scott County Courts and Holly runs a home daycare.

Mary moved to Crystal and works for Norwest Banks in Minneapolis.

I bought a twin home in Brooklyn Park and work for Damark on 93rd Avenue North.

Mother began to show signs of Alzheimer's disease in the late 1980s. She had to quit work and the family kept her at home until 1996 when she was admitted to the Alzheimer's ward at Crystal Care Center. She passed away in September of 1998 and is buried at Ft. Snelling National Cemetery.

Dad decided to sell the house in 1999, and in October, of the same year married Maxine Gillen, also of Brooklyn Park. He works for The Software Library in Brooklyn Center owned by Chuck Zimmer of Brooklyn Park.

Submitted by Gregory Sorenson

The Richard and June Sorenson Family

Donald and Barbara Sorlien

It was 1960 when Donald Sorlien and I decided it was time to become homeowners for our expanding family and, as fate would have it, Brooklyn Park became our home. Interest rates were low at 5½%. We had no down payment but we had the GI Loan. We looked at houses in Richfield and Bloomington (too noisy), Anoka (too far out) and Minneapolis (needed that illusive down payment). Associated Contractors were building houses in areas that were sometimes wooded. For a house in Garden Acres the advertising went like this:

"The Wabasha is an impressive example of spacious suburban living offered at a modest cost. The extra-large living room provides room for all family activities. The larger kitchen boasts a dining area separate from the work area. . . important to every housewife. As in all Associated homes, closet space is plentiful and the price is right."

We found the wooded lot and the house for the price of $16,370.00. Cornfields grew across the road. In order to get two fireplaces, Don did the entire interior painting and staining. It was wonderful but that monthly payment of $87.00 caused us some sleepless nights.

Within a year a grade school was built a block away. We became charter members of a new mission church on 73rd and West Broadway, Prince of Peace Lutheran. We were active in the new church; Don served as president of the congregation and I took my turn as president of the women's organization. All three of our children were confirmed there. The church has continued to grow. In 1998 the congregation moved into the third new sanctuary.

Brooklyn Park was a wonderful place to grow up during the 1960s and 1970s. Everyone in the neighborhood purchased their homes at nearly the same time. The residents were busy raising their children, planting sod, growing flowers, and getting to know one another. There was always someone for the children to play with. There were lots of backyard swingsets, tag games and bicycles. We flooded our backyard a few years for a skating rink so the children could use the new skates without having to go so far. Most of the moms were "stay-at-home moms" until the last child was in school. They oversaw the activities and passed out cookies and Band-Aids as needed.

During those growing up years many of the children played organized ball through the Brooklyn Park Athletic Association. Don served in many capacities—coach, referee and president.

Our daughter, Katherine, her husband Brian, and their two children live in Helena, MT; daughter Rebecca, her husband Ron, and their two children live in Roseville, MN; and son Jay, and his wife, Ginny live in south Minneapolis.

Submitted by Barbara Sorlien

In 1938 Anton (Tony) Spanjers bought several acres of land from Al and Pearl Mattson. This land is located in the block of 85th Avenue North from the West River Road to the Mississippi River. At that time the address was Camden Station Route 5. Our father, Tony, built a house for us on this land on the bank of the river and we moved from the city of Minneapolis to the country.

There are four children, Robert, Leo, Ella, and Lois in our family. To keep us busy our dad had us plant potatoes, beans, strawberries and raspberries. We took our produce to the market and also sold it at the end of our road on the highway. Our dad drove us to school in the city each day until Robert bought a 1930 Model-A Ford and then he took us. Later the Anoka Bus Company started up and we could take the bus, but it had very limited service.

Our father had the A. J. Spanjers Company. They did home improvements, weather-stripping, which the company manufactured, storm windows, caulking and insulation. He moved his business to Brooklyn Center in 1948. He also loved farming and bought a farm on 93rd and France Avenue North. Robert ran the farm and was the first person to raise turkeys in this area. He also raised pigs, cows and potatoes. We all helped him with his various chores. They later sold the farm and today it is part of Edinburgh Golf Course. Robert bought our dad's business and moved it to Boone Avenue in Brooklyn Park and later to 93rd and West River Road. They now restore historical buildings and do other masonry work.

Dad sold our home on the river at the end of World War II and bought several acres of land on the northwest corner of Brookdale Drive and West River Road. Dad passed away at the age of 72 in 1961. Our mother, Anna, lived there until she was 97 and then died at the age of 99 years in 1989.

Our dad was very active in Brooklyn Park and after his death they gave us a certificate of appreciation for his contribution to Brooklyn Park. He was also a charter member of the Isaak Walton League in Brooklyn Park.

Leo became a dentist and set up his dental practice in Brooklyn Center in 1947.

Ella became a medical technologist and worked for the University of Minnesota Hospital. I became a dental hygienist and married Claude Myers in 1949. We moved to Brooklyn Park in 1976 just a block from our home on the river and on land the Mattsons had their sheep grazing on when we were growing up.

Submitted by Lois Spanjers Meyers

The Spanjers Family

Anton (Tony) and Anna Spanjers (1950)

The James M. and Jean Stalberger Family

JAMES STALBERGER was born on October 4, 1951, in Detroit Lakes. His parents are Art and Reine Stalberger. He graduated from Waubun High School and went on to receive a Bachelor of Arts Degree in 1973 from Moorhead State University at Moorhead, Minnesota.

I was born on October 7, 1955, in Bagley, Minnesota. My parents are Richard and Virginia Carter. I graduated from Detroit Lakes High School. Jim and I were married on October 19, 1974, in Callaway, Minnesota. We have resided in the Brooklyn Center, Brooklyn Park area since 1974.

Jim was employed at the Howe Company for twenty years. He now works for J. R. Johnson in Roseville. I worked for Control Data for seven years, and then did day care for five. I then worked for Bachman's at Brookdale Shopping Center and since moved on to work for Rebarfab, Inc., where I now entered my thirteenth year with the company.

Jim, Bob, Becky, Jason, and Jean Stalberger

Our family consists of three children, Rebecca, Robert and Jason. Rebecca is pursuing her RN degree at Anoka Ramsey College, while working in a nursing home. Robert is married and living in Plymouth. He is manager at Pro Sporting Goods in Anoka. Jason is in the Marines and is stationed at Monterey, California, where he attends school.

Jim is active in the Knights of Columbus as well as his church. I do volunteer work with Jim in the Knights activities and both of us have taught religion while our children were in religious education classes. We both enjoy volunteering for the Special Olympics when the events are held here in town.

Submitted by Jean S. Stalberger

THE WAY OF GOD is that "we will be led where we did not plan to go."

A background of critical care, psychiatry, pediatrics, and supervision in nursing led us into a job of our own making. Somehow the job turned into a calling after awhile. We kept our commitment to integrity and to our ideals.

Many people said there would be long hours, and low pay, and our skills and talents would be wasted. *not true!* Almost twenty-five years of caring for one-hundred-eighty-eight mostly terminally ill, profoundly retarded, small children and their families on a 24-hour basis was an enormous challenge and a great deal of work. There are one hundred eighty eight stories here, some to cry over, and some to laugh about. Emotions never rested! Every day brought new challenges. Life was never dull!

The rapport among the families, Hennepin County, and us was superb. We, and Hennepin County, explored other options a few times, but none ever came to fruition. Our calling was where we already were.

People frequently asked us if the job was depressing. How could we be depressed with all the love and the support in the home? Both of us feel that we received much more from the children and their families than we gave.

Hennepin County was our mainstay, a guide when necessary, and they provided the proverbial shoulder to lean on. The medical profession did its utmost to help in all situations. The Brooklyn Center police had a great, positive impact on our lives with their frequent help. We found them to be truly gentle men. Our neighbors, the Ascher's, are wonderful friends who frequently helped in a myriad of ways, many times when it was not convenient for them.

Our greatest love goes with the children and their families. Our lives have been truly enriched by their presence. There was not a lot of happiness, but true joy did reign supreme. "Keep your eyes on the WEAK, THE POOR, AND THE REJECTED. They are the source of peace."

Submitted by Carol Starner and Jean Knapp

Carol Starner and Jean Knapp

Ron and Naomi Stave

OUR MOVE TO BROOKLYN CENTER came with the building and opening of the Brooklyn Center High School in 1961. Ron was employed as social studies teacher, football coach and as an assistant baseball coach.

Ron and Naomi Stave were married on July 1, 1955; both of us grew up in the Cannon Falls, MN, area. After serving as a tank commander in the Korean War, Ron came back to continue his education at Augsburg College. He taught and coached in the Olivia, MN, High School for three years before coming to Brooklyn Center with the family, which now included Cynthia born in 1956, Marcia, 1958, and Todd, 1960. Daniel was born in 1966.

The family lived at 5543 Camden Avenue. Naomi was a "stay-at-home-mom" and remembers the freedom their children had to walk and ride their bikes in that Southeast Brooklyn Center neighborhood, playing at Bellvue Park and in the open lot next to their house where Madsen Floral had at one time grown flowers. Madsens sold their property in 1983, and townhouses now cover the area.

Ron and Naomi Stave with Cynthia, Marcia, Todd, and Daniel

The family was blessed by the ministry of Pastor Roger Carlson and Hope Lutheran Church at 52nd and Emerson North, as that became our church "home."

After fifteen years of teaching, Ron became Administrative Assistant to Superintendent Doug Rossi, from 1976 until his retirement in 1991. Four years after retiring we sold the family home and are presently in a one-level town home in neighboring Brooklyn Park. The children now all married and with families of their own, live in the surrounding communities of south Minneapolis, Forest Lake, Maple Plain, and Shakopee.

Ron has so many good memories of the fine young men and women he was privileged to work with in the classroom and on the athletic fields of Brooklyn Center High School. . . some of which are included in the section on BCHS Centaur history.

Submitted by Naomi Stave

In 1955 my family, consisting of my parents, Bill and Char (Madden) Sullivan and my three siblings and I, moved from northeast Minneapolis to our new house at 9525 Knox Avenue North. Farm fields surrounded this small development called Willow-stone. One farm was owned by the Zimmerman family and was located where the new interchange for Highways 252 and 610 is currently being built. In 1963, when I was in the eighth-grade, Mr. Zimmerman hired me to pick potatoes for fifty-cents an hour. He told me later that he thought I was too small to be a good worker, but when he saw that I could do the work he gave me a raise to seventy-five-cents an hour. We dug the potatoes by hand and then put them in baskets. When the tractor and trailer came by we loaded the baskets on the trailer.

Bill and Lynn Sullivan

The next year, I worked for Ed Shimek who paid me one dollar and fifty-cents an hour. Mr. Shimek had a machine that picked the potatoes and loaded them into a truck. One day the machine broke down and Ralph from Libby's gas station came and rebuilt the engine right in the middle of the field.

When the potatoes arrived at the barn, we washed them and put them in 100-pound rough burlap bags that tore the skin on my hands to shreds. All in all, I sure earned my wages.

I graduated from Anoka High School. Married my wife Lynn from Greencastle, Indiana, and we work together in the real estate business.

Lynn and I were looking for an old house to buy and renovate, but we weren't having much luck until we happened to drive by and there was the "For Sale" sign on a house in Brooklyn Park. I liked the house immediately because it is brick, and Lynn liked it because the style reminded her of houses in Indiana where she had grown up. We bought our house, built between 1875-1880, in 1985.

Potato harvesting crew, 1971

During the renovation process we made some interesting discoveries. We found and saved parts of the original gaudy wallpaper. We found a walled-up pass-through window between the kitchen and dining room. When we took down the ceiling in the living room we found two old calling cards and a photograph, probably put there as a time capsule when the house was built. The cards read "Miss Mary Bragdon, Anoka, Minnesota, Third Avenue Hotel." The photo is of a Victorian lady dressed in a flow-ing robe with huge sleeves and a short, fringed vest.

There are many rewarding aspects to living in an old house. The feeling of history is wonderful. On really hot and humid summer days, Lynn wonders how a family, dressed in Victorian finery, ever survived. We just put on shorts, turn on the air con-ditioning and have a glass of iced tea.

Submitted by Bill and Lynn Sullivan

Cecilia (Scott) and Dwaine Svardal

Cecilia Svardal

My family moved to Brooklyn Center in September 1959 to a house near Twin Lake Beach. I became involved with a group called Northport Citizens Association when the property that is now the Beach Apartments was up for rezoning from public open space to apartments. Through our efforts, Darrell Farr deeded the area that is now Twin Lake Beach open space, to the city for a park and playground. That led to my appointment to the Planning Commission by the then Mayor Phil Cohen. I served as a commissioner and then chairperson until elected to the city council. I was the first woman on the Planning Commission, the first woman chair and the first woman elected to the city council.

When we first moved to Brooklyn Center, the children and I picked asparagus on the site where the Sears store at Brookdale now exists. During my time in public office I saw our city grow and expand, our tax base widen through good planning, Earle Brown Farm change from an operating livestock operation to the warehouse/commercial mix, the birth of the Heritage Center, the growth of our commercial areas, and our residential land fill up.

I raised seven children: Steven, David, Kevin, Larry, Randy, Kenneth and Susan in our home on Lakeside. They all attended Robbinsdale schools. I married my second husband, Dwaine, and became step-mom to his three daughters: Doreen, Diane and Denise.

Dwaine is now retired from the Minneapolis Police Department and is working in the Federal Court system as a court security officer.

We live in one of the oldest houses in Brooklyn Center on Lyndale Avenue across the street from the Mississippi River. The street was once the stagecoach trail from Minneapolis north. We like our old house and the city of Brooklyn Center.

Submitted by Cecelia (Scott) Svardal

CARL SWING was the last foreman on the Earle Brown Farm and served for over thirty years. He had become foreman in 1933 and kept the job until 1965 when the farm was sold because of Earle Brown's death in 1963.

Harriet Swing's family, the Heidenreichs, had lived in the field house farm on the northwest corner of the Brown Farm acreage. Harriet worked part-time at the Brown Farm, and this is how she met her future husband, Carl. He began work there when he was twenty-four years old. When the Swings were first married, they lived in the field house until Carl became foreman, and then they moved to the two-story foreman's house at the northeast end of the group of Earle Brown farm buildings. It is thought that the foreman's farmhouse was the oldest house on the farm complex.

In 1999 the foreman's farmhouse is attached to Earle Brown's house and is part of the "Inn on the Farm" buildings. After purchasing the Brown Farm in 1965, Deil Gustafson moved the foreman's house to enlarge the old Brown Farm home where Gustafson resided.

Harriet and Carl Swing

Harriet and Carl Swing

One can only imagine how busy Carl Swing must have been overseeing farm crops, the livestock, vehicle collection, a lumberjack building display, sheep shearing, horse and buggy rides for Brown's guests and directing a staff of farmhands as well as some responsibility for cooks, housekeepers and a gardener.

One memory Leone Howe has of visiting the farm, was when Carl Swing would hitch up a team of horses, with bells on the harness, and have them pull a bobsled. Leone, the Swing children and other visitors glided over the farm fields singing "Jingle Bells" all the way.

The Swings were extremely helpful when three members of the Brooklyn Historical Society wrote the 1983 book, *History of Earle Brown Farm*. Harriet and Carl recalled, with smiles, farm life and events and allowed the Society to reproduce many pictures for our 1983 farm book.

Both Swings are gone now. Carl died in August 1997 and Harriet passed on in May 1999. They are survived by two daughters, five grandchildren and one great-grandchild and fondly remembered by members of the Brooklyn Historical Society.

Submitted by Jane Hallberg
Leone Howe
History of Earle Brown Farm

August and Henrietta (Hartkopf) Tessman

AUGUST TESSMAN was born May 9, 1838, in West Prussian, Germany. He came to America at age 20 as a ship stowaway, thus avoiding military service in the Prussian Army. His first priorities in his new country were to become a citizen and to learn the English language. He was a great fisherman in Germany, making his own seines for netting fish.

August settled in the Chaska-Chanhassan, MN area where he worked for an elderly owner of a barge. Later he acquired the barge and established his own business of transporting bricks on the Minnesota River. Two events occurred as a result of this business that had an important bearing on his future life. The first was the meeting of his bride-to-be, Henrietta Hartkopf, on one of his many trips to the dock in St. Paul. The second was an accident while loading his barge when two helpers tossed four bricks each to him at the same time. He caught one batch, but the other hit his shin causing a leg injury that later resulted in an exemption from military service in the Civil War.

Henrietta Hartkopf was born in 1835 in Stattin, Germany. Her family came to America in 1862. She married August Tessman and they had four children while living in Chanhassen: Bertha, who died in infancy, Albert, Emma and Adolph. Hearing of a farm available in Brooklyn Township where her brother lived, they decided to move to a log house on the present site of the Tessman homestead. They arrived September 1, 1870, ten days before the birth of daughter Eda. Edmund, Selma and Ferdinand completed the family. Tragedy struck in 1880 when Henrietta was stricken with pneumonia and died when Ferdinand was four years old. The oldest daughter took over the responsibility of the family when she was only fifteen years old.

In upstairs bedrooms of the log house, snow came in under the eaves. After a few winters of shaking snow off the bedding on cold, snowy mornings, August decided to build a new house. In 1883 the family began enjoying life in their new house that proudly displayed the year 1883 on the front gable. August remarried. In 1888 he built and lived in another Tessman home in Brooklyn Park at 6717 85th Avenue North.

Submitted by Alice P. Tessman

Alice Tessman (1915)

EDMUND WAS THE SIXTH CHILD of eight born to August and Henrietta Tessman. He married Louise Setzler who was the youngest child of eight children born to George and Mary Setzler.

Edmund and Louise were parents of Alice P. and Raymond, their two children who survived. Their daughter, Irma, developed diabetes and died at age ten. Three of their sons died in early childhood.

As children, Alice P. and Raymond attended the Smith School, District #32. Alice attended West High in Minneapolis. There were not many horses and buggies on the road when she was in high school. Alice boarded in Minneapolis for a while and graduated in 1925. After her school years, she was a secretary or school clerk for Minneapolis schools. Then she came home to care for her ailing mother and helped with the farm work.

With her help, Raymond kept the farm going. Theirs was a potato farm, with horses and cows, and they were just a little bit in the dairy business. They also raised corn and chickens. There were potato and cornfields all around the house. They did their own harvesting and fed work crews. Alice used to cut potatoes for planting so there would be an eye on each piece.

Alice was in Eastern Star, and Raymond was a Shriner, a Mason and in Odd-fellows. Alice P. 's hobbies included bowling, reading and travelling. Alice, Ray and their family and friends have visited seventy-one countries. Louise, their mother, died in 1932, and Edmund, their father, died in 1955.

Alice and Raymond never married. They discussed what they would like to do for the community; and second cousin Eldon came up with the idea of a carillon. Eldon did all the work and Raymond and Alice paid for it. With appropriate ceremonies, the carillon was in place on the grounds of North Hennepin Community College, Brooklyn Park, on June 21, 1997, dedicated to the area's pioneer potato farmers. Raymond died in July 1993.

The main farmhouse was built in 1897 and added to in 1907. It has been remodeled over the years. There is a 1920s door and the leaded windows have been there since 1920. Electricity came in 1932. Before that the farmhouse had a generator. Alice was born in this brick house and has the bed she was born in, in 1908, and the chair she was rocked in. All four of the Century Farms houses are of brick, and all are stuccoed over. The City calls it the Century Farm Development: Neddersens, Setzlers and Tessmans. The families have been here for more than a century and were potato farmers.

Submitted by Alice P. Tessman

The Edmund Tessman Family

Edmund and Louise Tessman

The Eldon A. and June E. Tessman Family

My GRANDFATHER, Albert "Al", the eldest son of August and Henrietta Tessman, married my grandmother, Leopoldena "Dena" Kimmerle, in 1896 and established their family on the 1883 Tessman homestead. They had seven children: Aaron, Albert "Bert," Elizabeth "Betty," Donald and Wilbur (two sons, Roy and an unnamed boy, died in infancy).

My father, Bert, took over the 1883 Tessman homestead when he married my mother, Esther Josephine Hildebrandt, in November 1927. My sister Elaine and I are their two children. Our parents worked very much as a team. It was devastating to our family and to the entire community when Dad was killed in a deer hunting accident on November 17, 1942, and buried on our parents' fifteenth wedding anniversary. It changed our lives forever and our mother's health was never the same. At the time, I wasn't quite fourteen years and Elaine was twelve years old. An outpouring of love from the community was evidenced the next spring when neighbors, organized by Emery Holmes, came to plow and plant our fields. Mother and we children, with the able and generous assistance of family and neighborhood friends, continued the farming operation.

The Eldon A. and June E. Tessmann Family

My mother made every effort to complete her public health degree; however, poor health dictated that she needed a warmer climate during the winter months. In the fall of 1946, I began my freshman year at the University of Minnesota, and Elaine and Mother drove to Glendale, AZ, where the Everett Howe family had rented an apartment for them. I continued farming and Mother and Elaine came home for the summer months.

Elaine and I finished our college degrees, Elaine at Arizona State College at Tempe and I at the University of MN. It was our joy to celebrate Mother's Public Health Degree from the University of Minnesota in 1956. Her public health career included recruiting nursing students for Hamline University, public health nursing in Dakota County and at the University of MN Student Health Service.

In 1950 I married my high school sweetheart, June Evelyn Oswald who grew up on a farm in Corcoran, Minnesota. We have a daughter, Paula, and four sons: Mark, Thomas, Todd and Robert. Paula married James Borer from Brooklyn Park. They have three sons: Shannon, Justin and Nathan, and live in Watertown, MN. Mark lives in Las Vegas. Thomas married Dianne Blake from Michigan and they live in Edina. Todd married Dawn DesJardins from Brooklyn Center. They have two sons Derek and Jason, and live in Osseo. Robert lives in Brooklyn Park.

June and I continue to live at the 1883 Tessman family homestead located at 6508 85th Avenue North (formerly known as Tessman Crossroad) in Brooklyn Park, a designated Century Farm and truly a historical farm site.

Submitted by Eldon A. and June E. Tessman

ED THEISEN was born in Cold Spring, MN, where he attended St. Boniface Catholic School. As a youth, Ed helped his father in the grain elevator and while attending college he worked in the Cold Spring Brewery. Ed earned a B.A. in Accounting from St. John's University in Collegeville, MN, in 1952. Following graduation Ed enlisted in the U. S. Marines, serving as a First Lieutenant during the Korean Conflict. Ed's small town upbringing, education and military experience ingrained in him a sense of duty and heightened his leadership abilities, paving the way for a successful career in business and as a community leader.

In 1955 Ed married Kathy Hennen of Watkins, MN. They met while Ed was attending St. John's and Kathy was attending St. Cloud State University. Following graduation Kathy became an Elementary School Teacher at Sartell, Minnesota.

The Edwin and Kathleen Theisen Family

In September 1954 Ed began a successful forty-year career with Northern States Power Company. Starting as an accountant, Ed progressed rapidly, being named Vice President of Management Systems in 1970, Vice President of the Gas Utility in 1974, Vice President and Treasurer of Northern States Minnesota in 1978, President and CEO of Northern States Power Wisconsin in 1980, and President and Chief Operating Officer of Northern States Power Minnesota in 1990.

Ed and Kathy moved to Brooklyn Center in 1956, where they raised six children and became very active in community and church work. Ed's community service included many leadership positions such as President of the Jaycees; Chairman of the Community Emergency Assistance Program (CEAP); Chairman of the Republican Party; and Chairman of the Brooklyn Center Capital Improvement Review Board, which led to a successful city bond referendum to build a new city hall and community center, East fire station, and city garage.

The Theisen Family: front Darla, Ed, Kathy, and Lisa; back, Paul, Dean, Keith, and Scott

Kathy was a den mother for both the Girl and Boy scouts; an active Mrs. Jaycee, a delegate to the Republican State Convention, taught religious education classes at St. Alphonsus for ten years, and is still active in her church guild.

Ed continued his community leadership after leaving Brooklyn Center by chairing the Eau Claire United Way, aiding in the formation of Forward Wisconsin, which created over 5,000 jobs in western Wisconsin in the 1980s; being the driving force in formation of Advantage Minnesota, an organization created to attract new business to Minnesota; serving as chairperson of the St. Paul Chamber of Commerce; and as Regent of St. John's University.

Ed and Kathy's six children are all college graduates. Keith's family lives in Apple Valley, Dean's family in Golden Valley, Darla in Maple Grove, Lisa's family is in Little Falls, Scott's family in Plymouth, and Paul is in Minneapolis.

Ed always found time for family, friends and fun. He enjoyed golf, tennis and playing cards with family and friends. Ed and Kathy spent forty-four happy years together. Following Ed's retirement, they enjoyed their winters in Sun City West, AZ. On June 18, 1999, Ed died at the age of 68, after an eighteen-month battle with kidney cancer. Kathy currently lives in Plymouth, MN.

Submitted by Kathy Theisen

Clayton and Mary Thiebault

IN MARCH 1928, with a loan of $500 from his brother, my father and mother, Joseph and Mary Zupko and their two children left Cicava, Czechoslovakia. They took all their personal possessions by train to Amsterdam, Holland. After ten days they landed at Ellis Island by way of the ship, Arabic.

Without funds and not being able to speak the English language, they journeyed to Minneapolis, Minnesota where they were met by my father's sister and husband. After a few days they left by train to Little Falls, Minnesota, where they were met by Uncle Mike Zupko and his family. They lived a short distance from Flensburg, Minnesota.

My parents rented a small farm a half-mile from Uncle Mike. He again loaned my parents money so they could buy farm machinery. The farm was too small to make a reasonable amount of money, so they rented a 350-acre farm adjacent to theirs. By now they had three small children. They planted crops, raised cattle and chickens and managed to survive. In 1934 during the height of the Great Depression my father could not sell his crops, so he stored what he could, but could not meet the $350 yearly rent for the farm. He borrowed $1700 and bought a 120-acre farm nearby.

Mary and Clayton Thiebault on their twenty-fifth anniversary

World War II broke out in Europe and it rekindled the demand for farm products.

When I started school I could not speak English. I sat for three days not saying a thing. One day it started raining and in my excitement I burst out, "It's raining, it's raining," in Slovak. This finally broke my silence. I was the one who taught my family to speak English.

I attended high school in Little Falls. To pay for the bus fare to school, I was lavatory monitor during my lunch hour.

After graduation I met and married a young man stationed at Camp Ripley. Eventually, I became a single mom with two small children to raise. Life was very hard. The children and I stayed with my parents. I worked in a grocery store for $15.75 a week, working five days from 7:00 to 5:00.

When the children were in middle school I came to Minneapolis to find work. I became a waitress. Doing this work I did not have to buy dress clothes and I had free meals. I worked at the Chuck Wagon, Murray's Steak Restaurant, and the Radisson for twenty-eight years.

I met Clayton Thiebault, whose parents, Joseph and Katherine Thiebault, had come from Montreal, Canada. Clayton and his two sons were living with them. He had been in the Navy. He worked for Burgess and Beckwith. With two other people, a husband and wife team, they started Daly Printing. Clayton was the printman, the husband was salesman and the wife was secretary. He worked there for forty-three years, retiring in 1993.

After ten years of courtship Clayton and I were married in 1967. In the interim I bought myself a house in Brooklyn Center. Clayton and I still live there. We have made many changes and many additions.

Submitted by Mary Thiebault

CHUCK AND HELEN THOMPSON bought three acres of land on the northeast corner of Upper Twin Lake in 1957 from Sigurd and Jenny Skurdalsvold. Their three acres were surrounded by undeveloped Brooklyn Center park property. Chuck spent several years designing his dream home. In 1964, he, his wife Helen, and their two children, Terri and Charlie moved in. Both of the children graduated from Robbinsdale Senior High School.

The Charles (Chuck) Thompson Family

Shortly after moving in, Chuck obtained a Federal Game Farm license, the first one in the seven-county Metro area. He obtained two pair of Canadian geese and they multiplied by the hundreds over the years. He raised bobwhite quail, ducks and a few wild turkeys. He loved the wilderness, and this home was ideal for him. Chuck had a floatplane that he kept in front of the house. This made traveling to and from Ontario for hunting and fishing convenient for him.

Chuck was a pharmacist and co-owned Medical Center Pharmacy in Crystal. Dr. Pattee and Chuck built North Ridge Care Center in New Hope in 1966. Chuck was involved in providing health care his entire career. As a side venture he helped establish Sporting Goods, Inc. in Brooklyn Park in the early 1970s. His interest in this venture came about because his son was an avid hockey player for Robbinsdale and very active in local baseball.

Charles P. Thompson homestead on Upper Twin Lake in Brooklyn Center

In 1981 Chuck Thompson married Mary Jane Schrandt. They remained in the house on Upper Twin Lake with Mary Jane's children, Mark, John and Jayne Schrandt. Mark and John graduated from Robbinsdale Senior High School. Jayne graduated from Cooper Senior High School.

At retirement, Chuck and Mary Jane wondered what to do with their house and property on the lake. Because of their love for Health Care (Mary Jane a registered nurse and Chuck a pharmacist and licensed nursing home administrator), it was decided they would donate their house and property to North Memorial Health Care for a residential hospice facility. This new facility opened in 1997 and can serve eight patients in peace and serenity during their last days of terminal illness.

The original Thompson house has been moved to a location in Plymouth. Chuck Thompson died on November 8, 1997.

Submitted by Mary Jane Thompson

Valerie Gene-Annette (Huddle) Thompson

I WAS BORN FEBRUARY 27, 1964. My family consisted of Grandparents, Peter & Ardis Fiebiger, Mom, Mavis Huddle, and sister, Teresa. At age eight, I remember Teresa, thirteen, having fun at the County Fair in 4-H work, and myself being too young! Mom helped enter my floral painting "Open Class" (public, all ages): nothing! She pursued, to "State Fair, Open Class Youth" (under twelve): a blue ribbon! Next year, old enough, I took every 4-H Club project I was qualified for! I learned you got cash for each ribbon, so I demonstrated in every project! Got lots of ribbons and lots of big money at nine!

Our Principal, Roy Humbert, made Monroe Elementary School especially exciting. He took time each winter giving ice skating lessons to each grade. Grandpa, newly retired, came to school to "be sure my skates got laced up right." He became everyone's Grandpa, tying lots of skates! I also loved being in Mr. Humbert's Monroe Melotones Choir!

I participated in Science Fairs, winning District honors with rabbit, plant & mineral presentations, State Champion with Minerals. I participated in church school, choirs & Confirmation at Lutheran Church of the Master; dancing & modeling lessons, Bluebirds, Camp Fire Girls—and 4-H! At Monroe I began flute lessons, continuing with music/band into 11th Grade. Once (practice, thank Heaven!) marching on the football field, suddenly I was all alone! The Band turned; I hadn't! 'Sure got teased for that one!

At Anoka Senior High I enrolled in Navy Jr. ROTC, Naval Science, plus Drill & Rifle Teams (Captain and only girl on the Rifle Team!) and Color Guard. Color Guard could be exciting: once winds were so strong, lightweight me, had to hold Old Glory down like a battering ram to prevent being blown back into the ranks (which happened twice)! I got some teasing on this, too!

I graduated Anoka, 1982, went to the University of Minnesota, working 20-30 hours weekly, graduating in International Business & Industrial Management. In "U" NROTC, I was Captain of the Rifle Team and "Marksman." I worked a year, then went to Dakota County Tech, earning a one-year Interior Design degree in the spring of 1992.

In November 1992 I married, moved to Hamilton, Montana, divorced in 1995. Staying on, I worked in high-end interior design, plus Mary Kay cosmetics distribution, through which I met a neat guy from Kalispell, MT. In June 1997 Alan Thompson and I were married in view of the mountains. This summer, 1999, we left the Glacier Park area for Seattle, finding greater job opportunities and salary satisfaction.

I'm now with Cort, a nation-wide furniture rental organization, their Seattle—Puget Sound Account Executive. My hobbies include ceramics, cooking, growing flowers indoors and out, and getting together with Mary Kay gals. Alan's home-based computer business is re-establishing, while he trains bus drivers and drives for Seattle Tour Coach. He has a commercial pilot's license (studying to re-certify & teach), a 1956 Cadillac to restore, and enjoys woodworking, building things.

We look forward to our Minnesota trips for family visits, keeping abreast of changes in Brooklyn Park and the Metro area.

Submitted by Valerie G-A. Huddle, Thompson

Valerie Huddle and Alan B. Thompson's Wedding

THE JOSEPH TIBER FAMILY moved to Brooklyn Center in the fall of 1939. Joseph had built a small house at 5310 James Avenue North. The house is still standing and occupied at the present time. The Tiber family consisted of Joseph, his wife Ruth, daughters Lois, Judith, and son Jon.

At the time this area consisted of large truck farms where flowers and vegetables were grown to the north and west. The Edlings and Rydeens were the farmers involved with this truck farming business.

The Tibers raised chickens, rabbits, and always had a huge garden that provided the produce that Mrs. Tiber canned each fall. The nearest grocery/meat market was located in Camden, in North Minneapolis, although there were smaller stores referred to as "the milkstores," one located at 52nd and Humboldt called "Millions," and another at the corner of 53rd and Bryant. The third one was located at the corner of 55th and Humboldt, called "Berry's." At that time the nearest public transportation was the bus from Camden to 52nd and Humboldt.

Judith worked at one of the truck farms when she was quite young, around 1946. A truck picked them up and took them to the west end of 53rd where they picked and bunched radishes for twenty-five cents a bunch. Talk about "child labor"!

The first housing development, called "Meadow Lark Gardens" went up from 55th to 57th on Irving Avenue to Logan Avenue. "Victory Airport" was close by. Their dad took them out there one time to see a "blimp" that landed there.

Mrs. Tiber packed lunches and the children either walked or rode their bikes out to the Earle Brown Farm. There they watched the beautiful horses and cows that were kept in the huge pasture. Earle Brown kept a pet monkey up by the main house and the children went to see it also.

Earle Brown owned many farms throughout the area. One could always tell his properties because the house and outbuildings were all painted red with white trim.

The children started school at St. Bridget's on 38th and Emerson. They attended Earle Brown School for one year and finished grade school at Our Lady of Victory. Lois and Jon both were graduates of Patrick Henry High School, but Judith graduated from North High. Due to the growth of high school students in Brooklyn Center, Patrick Henry could not accommodate all of them; therefore, some were bussed to North High School.

Joseph worked for Northern States Power Company as an appliance repairman until his early retirement due to poor health in 1962. He passed away in the spring of 1963. Ruth was a full time homemaker until 1952 when she accepted employment at Northwestern Life Insurance Co. She stayed there until her retirement in 1976.

Ruth Tiber now lives in Ft. Worth, Texas, to be near her daughter, Lois.

Submitted by Judith Tiber

The Joseph Tiber Family

The Wallace H. Tommerdahl, Sr. Family

The Wallace Tommerdahl Family and Grandmother Ethel McArthur

IN 1952 WALLACE AND I (Charlotte McArthur) Tommerdahl purchased a plot of land in Fieldston Acres from Mr. W. Potkamp, a farmer who lived on 85th Avenue North and West River Road. He had platted out his farmland and sold the wooded lots for $600. We purchased our 100 by 555 foot lot on Westwood Road.

Wally commenced building our home himself that summer of 1952. We moved from an apartment in the Loring Park area of Minneapolis with our two-and-a-half year-old son, Wallace, Jr. (Skip). Barry was born in 1953 and Diane in 1958. Our family attended St. Andrew's Episcopal Church in north Minneapolis. All three children attended Riverview School in Anoka-Hennepin School District #11 and all graduated from Anoka Senior High School.

The Tommerdahl children took part in the Park Board baseball program, the swim program in the summer and football in the fall. Wally coached boys' baseball. I was secretary for the Brooklyn Park Athletic Association for a time. Both Wally and I were active Parent Teachers Association members. We also have chaired the Riverview School Spring Frolic.

Wally worked for the Chrysler Corporation and retired at age 55 in 1980. He later worked for Scherer Brothers Lumber Company in Minneapolis and retired in 1987.

I am a proud Native American of one-third Ojibwe Indian descent. I grew up, one of nine children, at Callaway, Minnesota on the White Earth Indian Reservation. My mother, Ethel McArthur, was a teacher and later a postmaster. Five of us siblings, Ray, Don, Gail and Lois have lived in the Brooklyns, including my mother who moved here after retiring. I was secretary for Bemis Company, and in later years was a secretary in the Anoka-Hennepin School's district office and at Monroe School in Brooklyn Park for fourteen years. I retired in 1987. Wally grew up on a farm near Detroit Lakes, Minnesota. He was one of eleven children.

We traveled throughout Canada and the United States. We traveled in Europe for five weeks, and also in Venezuela, South America and Mexico. We wintered in Arizona for seven years. Growing up, our children had 555 feet of oak trees and brush in which to play, build forts, and have a swimming pool. We sold our home on Westwood Road in 1993 and purchased a townhouse in Brooklyn Park in the Glenhaven of Edinburgh complex on Edinbrook Parkway. The townhouse is on the very site where our son Skip hunted deer in earlier days when Mrs. Wickner owned the land.

Wally and I had been married forty-nine years when he died in 1997. I volunteer for the Brooklyn Park Senior Club; I am an active member of the Brooklyn Historical Society, presently working on the Heritage Book.

The Tommerdahl children include: Skip, and wife Karen in Oak Grove, Minnesota with their children Heather, 23; Jessica, 22; Kelsey, 18, great-grandson, Mark (born October 27, 1999). Barry and Tracy reside in Brooklyn Park. Diane, husband, Mike Janikowski, live in Champlin, Minnesota with children Erin, 15; Michael, 13.

Submitted by Charlotte Tommerdahl

OUR HOME WAS BUILT before the turn of the century (we think). We bought the house in 1949 from a farmer on 72nd and Logan Avenue North. He had built a new house and we were required to move our new (old) two-story farmhouse across the field about two blocks away to 1711 73rd Avenue North. We paid $1,000 for the house, $1,000 for the lot, $1,000 for the basement and $1,000 to move it across the field on great big logs as rollers. We really enjoyed a bedroom for each of us kids and the screened porch across three-quarters of the front of the house.

My precious memories mainly involve me with my 4-H Club activities. Would you believe I was permitted to raise a pig, for two consecutive summers, in this area?

Submitted by Gary Trombley

Gary Trombley

IN THE EARLY 1930s my grandmother, Lillian Dawson, bought three acres on the south side of 69th Avenue, just east of Osseo Road. She built a good sized home in the middle of the three acres and used this as a summer retreat from the city heat. My dad, Bob Dawson, became friends with Ed Ham. They went to dances in Champlin where Bob met my mom, Hazel Fawcett, from north of Osseo.

Grandma Lillian gave her sister one acre to the east and gave her son the acre to the west as a wedding gift. My dad built our house himself but only as fast as money would allow. All three homes are still standing. My parents worked hard tending a small family grocery store in Minneapolis and harvesting vegetables for the many small truck farmers in Brooklyn Center. They enjoyed going roller-skating behind the Methodist Church. When my dad worked at Northern Pump he belonged to a dance band. He played every reed instrument, and the violin and piano. My brother and I shared his musical interest and learned to play several instruments. We liked to dance! Our folks were active in the Mother's Club that put on variety shows.

My mom sold boxes of greeting cards to rural home-makers in Brooklyn Center, Brooklyn Park, and Osseo. Word of mouth was her only advertising. She was also a census taker for the school district in the 1950s. I remember the 5 x 8 inch cards she handprinted. Sometimes I waited in the car for mom because the dogs weren't very friendly. Every year mom cooked hot dogs, baked beans and coffee for the Bergstrom Brothers Implement Dealership's open houses on Osseo Road. I remember the day as cold and muddy.

My brother and I walked to the square brick schoolhouse where our dad was the janitor. Our mother worked in school kitchens. We picked vegetables for the neighbors, Dave Magnusson and Bob Holmes. It took forever to fill a bushel of beans! Mr. Magnusson also flooded a half-acre for a big neighborhood skating rink. We used to ski down the middle of the two lane county road with ditches on each side. In the summer time we would play "Starlight, Moonlight" with the Berg kids.

I walked to the Howe store for ice cream when I was little. As a teenager I walked to the new drugstore on Osseo Road by Cliff's grocery store for a coke. I belonged to the 4-H Club with Gen Olson, now a member of the Minnesota Senate.

My husband, Jack, and I now live in Brooklyn Park. I have worked for the Title I Program for School District #279 and as annuity agent for Twin City Federal Banks.

Submitted by Dixie Umland

Dixie Dawson Umland

Robert and Hazel Dawson's homestead, built in 1939 in Brooklyn Center

Don and Anita Umland

DON AND ANITA were the first of the Umlands from the Verndale, Minnesota area to move to Brooklyn Park in 1959. They walked through a field to choose their lot at 6708 and Xylon Avenue North. Modern Road was a dead-end street at Winnetka Avenue. Many homes were built to the west. Interstate Highway 694 was constructed close to their home. The dead end street became an intersection with Modern Road.

Their children, Mike, Steve, Bruce, Dave and Nancy all utilized the parks and were very active in the many activities and sports that were offered. Mike, Dave, and Nancy worked for the Park and Recreation Department in the summers. About 1970 Don and some neighbors erected the first lighted hockey rink at Edgewood Elementary School. Their sons played most of their hockey games on outdoor ice rinks. Northland Ice Arena was a welcome addition in 1970.

The children attended Edgewood, Northview, and Osseo Junior and graduated from Osseo Senior High School.

Don has been active in the Brooklyn Park Lion's Club for more than twenty years. He volunteered in the community and Grace Lutheran Church in Brooklyn Park. Anita was also active at church and in the community of Brooklyn Park.

Don worked for U.S. West for thirty-six years. Anita worked part time for twenty-five years at Brooklyn Junior and Park Center High School in Brooklyn Park.

They like to bike, using the trails in Brooklyn Park, play golf, and travel in their recreational vehicle and socialize with friends and families. Brooklyn Park has been a wonderful place to raise a family.

Submitted by Anita Umland

I was born to Ed and Ruth Umland in 1938 at Fergus Falls, Minnesota. My father was a farmer and my mother was a grade school teacher, teaching country school, when they were married. They farmed one thousand acres near Campbell, Minnesota. After graduation from high school in 1955, I moved to Minneapolis to attend Hamline University. My parents sold their farm in 1956. They then moved to Brooklyn Center where my dad became a construction foreman for Hipp Construction Company. They bought one of the Hipp houses and I moved in with them in order to save money for college. I married Dixie Dawson, "the girl next door," in 1962. Dad, brother Jim, and I designed, constructed and operated Brooklyn Par3 Golf Course at 83rd and Regent North in Brooklyn Park.

Jack Umland

In the fall of 1969, at the urging of neighbors, I ran for city council and won. After serving seven consecutive terms (fourteen years), representing the Central District (of which six were also spent as Mayor Protem) I chose to step down and concentrate on family and business ventures. My campaigns had been well organized by friends and neighbors with my wife, Dixie, being my strongest supporter.

My many activities include coaching youth sports since I was eighteen years old, a member of Brooklyn Center Lion's Club since nineteen years of age, a nominee for Man of the Year in both Brooklyn Center and Brooklyn Park. I was chosen Outstanding Man of the Year in Brooklyn Park. I served in the Minnesota Air National Guard, organized a number of basketball and baseball teams in both of the communities. I served as a charter member of my church, and president of the congregation for three years and was vice president of Crestview PTA. I served many years on the state board of registration for Architects, Landscape Architects, Engineers and Land Surveyors and was a long time office holder in the Brooklyn Park Athletic Association.

Jack and Dixie Umland and sons (1971)

A few of my accomplishments are: playing a major role in extending funding (federal legislation) which added many jobs to the Boone Avenue Industrial Park. I initiated the first golf course referendum in Brooklyn Park, which eventually led to the development of Edinburgh USA.

I encouraged, endorsed and led in the purchase of property that became the "campus" for Brooklyn Park city services on 85th between Zane and Regent Avenues. I was the leading proponent for the city's first Senior Citizen development near Zane and 73rd Avenue North. During the past ten years I have and continue to serve as Executive Director of the Saint Andrew's Club at Edinburgh USA.

I am very proud of these accomplishments but am most proud of my family. Our oldest son Rob is living in Brooklyn Center, married and they are expecting a baby, making this the fifth generation to live in Brooklyn Center. Craig is living in Cleveland, Ohio and is traveling as a very successful golf tournament director for IMG running national PGA & LPGA events.

Submitted by Jack Umland

Perry and Deborah Unruh

Perry and Deborah Unruh

MY NAME IS DEBORAH UNRUH, and I have lived in Brooklyn Center most of my life. My parents, Don and Sylvia Kramer, moved here from North Dakota when I was six months old. My husband Perry and I, and our two sons, Kaleb and Joseph, live down the street from the house in which I grew up.

I have many childhood memories of this area. With three brothers and two sisters, there was always somebody to play with. We loved to ride bikes, fly kites, and pick wildflowers and wild strawberries in the field that stretched north from 73rd Avenue to Monroe Elementary School. On hot days we went swimming at the Community Center. We also walked to the "corner store" to buy treats. That little store on 73rd Avenue North was torn down when Highway 252 was built and was greatly missed by all the kids in the neighborhood!

You could say our family has "wandering blood", because all of my brothers and sisters have traveled outside of the United States on one or more occasions. We must get it from our parents, who have traveled all over the world. I spent my junior year of high school in Belgium as an exchange student. It was one of the biggest learning and maturing experiences of my life. In addition to living with a host family, attending school, and learning to speak fluent Dutch, I visited Holland, Germany, England, and France.

After graduating from Anoka Senior High School, I attended college at the University of Minnesota. I also spent one summer in Honduras, teaching English and working at a veterinary clinic. I met my husband, Perry, while I was working at a veterinary clinic in North Dakota. I had just finished my internship at a large animal practice in Huff, North Dakota, and started working at a different clinic. One evening, after treating a dog who'd gotten sprayed by a skunk, I went into the waiting room to see if there were any more clients. I hoped to sneak out to my car to get some clean clothes (I'd just done my laundry at the Laundromat during lunch), but there was a handsome man standing at the reception desk. Luckily the skunk smell didn't scare him away, because a year and a half later we were married.

We were married on May 28, 1994, at St. Gerard's Catholic Church in Brooklyn Park and had our wedding reception at the Earle Brown Heritage Center. I think my husband contracted some of my "wandering blood" when we went on our honeymoon. We spent six weeks traveling and visiting friends and family in Germany, France, Italy, Luxembourg, Austria, Belgium and Holland. We agree that Germany was our favorite country, which might be because we are both of German descent.

How fitting that we have made our home in "The Garden City", since we both love to grow flowers and vegetables. If only we could find someone who loves weeding!

Submitted by Deborah Unruh

WE MOVED to Brooklyn Center in September 1966, buying our home from Bernice's brother and sister-in-law, Carl and Betty Benson and their children, Ron, Wayne, and Sherry. Our oldest daughter, Julie, was two weeks old when we moved in. Carla was born in 1968, and Jody in 1971. All three attended Earle Brown and Brooklyn Center High School. Julie is an Occupational Therapist in San Diego, CA; Carla with her two sons, Tyler (1992) and Treyton (1994) live in Brooklyn Center. Carla does Home Day Care. Jody received a degree in Social Work but is now attending the University of Minnesota for a degree in Elementary Education.

Wes was born at Oak Park, MN, and attended elementary school there and then Foley High School. In 1944, at the age of 17, he enlisted in the U.S. Navy serving in the South Pacific for 1½ years. He was in the Marine Corps Reserve from 1956 to 1964 and was called to active duty in January 1962 during the beginning of the Viet Nam War and served in Okinawa until October 1962. In January 1966 he accepted a position with the U.S. Department of Agriculture Meat Inspection which he held until he retired in January 1987. Wes bought a small farm near Oak Park, MN in 1956, and in 1965, he sold this farm and bought another farm north of Ogilvie, MN. Wes has been raising beef cattle for the past thirty-four years and still, at the age of 72, enjoys going to the farm and the quiet life.

Bernice was born in Mille Lacs County, MN and attended a one-room school for eight years and then to Ogilvie High School graduating in 1950. She attended the Minnesota School of Business, completing the Secretarial and the Medical Secretarial courses. She became Secretary to the Director of Nurses at Abbott Hospital. After traveling to Sweden and Hawaii she accepted a position at Vanstrum Travel Service in 1955. She was employed there for the next 17 years, working part time after the birth of the children. She made several trips to Europe and in the fall of 1962, traveled around the world. In 1975 she started part time at Brooklyn Center High School and in 1981, worked full time until retirement in June 1997. Bernice received the WCCO Radio Good Neighbor Award in 1985. She was a Girl Scout volunteer for twenty-three years and a Sunday School teacher for thirty-six years. She serves on various committees at Hope Lutheran Church, and does other volunteer service for District #286.

Retirement is great! Wes enjoys working in the yard, meeting friends at the Donut Shop and going to the farm. We spend time with our two grandsons and enjoy them immensely. Tyler is in 1st grade at Earle Brown, and Treyton enjoys spending time at our house so he can "farm" with "Papa." We enjoy going on short trips and visiting with friends and relatives.

Brooklyn Center is a great City and we are proud to have been a part of it the past 32 years.

Submitted by Wes and Bernice Vaillancourt

The Vaillancourt Family

Wes and Bernice Vaillancourt with their daughters Carla, Julie, and Jody, and their grandsons, Tyler and Treyton

Ralph and Ruth Van Beusekom

IN THE SPRING OF 1957 a friend told the Van Beusekoms about a five-year old home for sale in Brooklyn Center. Just three months after their marriage, Ralph and Ruth moved into their home on 5421 Camden Avenue where they lived for twenty-eight years. They raised three sons, who graduated from Brooklyn Center High School.

As their children grew up, they became involved in many activities in the community such as Scouts, Little League, Babe Ruth and Sr. Babe Ruth baseball, youth football, church activities at Our Lady of Victory Catholic Church, etc. Ralph then became involved with Brooklyn Center High School serving on many committees, including over twenty years on the Community Education Advisory Council and seven years as a member of the Board of Education of District #286.

Ralph and Ruth Van Beusekom

In 1984 they read in the *Brooklyn Center Post* newspaper of a new complex being built in Brooklyn Center only a mile and a half from their home, which sounded first-class. After a walk through the development when it was only a shell, they made the decision to buy a townhome at Brookwood. That development was a joint effort by the city of Brooklyn Center and Housing Redevelopment Authority (HRA). They were featured in the *Minneapolis Skyway News* and in an article written by Neil Pierce, a syndicated columnist whose column appears in many papers in the United States. This purchase was ideal for them because they have a place on Green Lake in Princeton, MN, and do not need to maintain the lawns and worry about snow removal in two places.

The basic reason both Ruth and Ralph enjoyed Brooklyn Center is because they both grew up in the small communities of Delano and Buffalo. Brooklyn Center has the same small-town atmosphere, especially at the school district where you know almost everyone.

Though the Van Beusekoms are homesteaded on Green Lake in Princeton, they continue to spend time in their townhome in Brooklyn Center. Their son Randy now lives there. Brooklyn Center was and continues to be a special friendly community.

Submitted by Ralph Van Beusekom

KATHLEEN CLARK and James Vanderheyden were high school sweethearts in Green Bay, Wisconsin. James joined the military in 1952 and was sent for non-combat duty in Ulm, Germany. He wrote to Kathleen in the U.S. to come to Germany and marry him. Kathleen finally agreed and they married in Germany in 1954. Oldest son Michael was born in Germany in 1955, after which the young family returned to Wisconsin where James finished college to become an electrical engineer. Three more children were born by this time, Catherine, Peter, and John. Several moves throughout the east and midwest for jobs comprised the years through 1963, at which time they moved to Brooklyn Park on 78th and June Avenue in a newly-built home. The family was completed by 1966, with four more children Jean, Daniel, Lisa and Thomas, making a total of eight children.

James and Kathleen Vanderheyden

The growing up years for the Vanderheyden family included many memorable activities. Brookdale Park offered summer sports and craft activities, as well as occasional field trips. A yearly carnival in which children decorated their bikes for a parade with such things as crepe paper wrapped around the spokes and playing cards clothes pinned near the spokes to make a rattling sound when the bikes moved was a real highlight. The bikes were also raced while decorated.

The field across the street from the Vanderheydens consisted of long prairie grasses and a particularly large inviting tree. The tree provided a convenient haven for a treehouse. "Homes" were also made by pressing down a square of prairie grasses and leaving taller grass all around the edges of the square for walls. There were also forts and innumerable paths made in this "field of dreams."

The Raths and Olsons on the Brookdale Drive end of June Ave. had green apple trees. Children often picked apples, sprinkled them with salt and ate them while walking to the next friend's house. The children and their friends devised plays and made costumes from materials found around the house. They presented these plays to friends and relatives.

The Brooklyn Park Athletic Association (BPAA) offered organized sports that the Vanderheyden children participated in enthusiastically. Softball, football, and baseball were among those they played. James coached his children in the various sports for many years. He became president of the BPAA organization in 1968. He saw many changes over these years, including the building of the original "storage garage" for BPAA sports equipment on what is now Central Park. The building has been further developed over the years to its current use as a community activity center.

Kathleen worked for twenty-two years as a Chapter 1 teacher in the Osseo School System, putting her ability to work with children to use both in and outside of the home. James worked as an engineer for Honeywell and later Alliant Tech Systems. The Vanderheyden children are all grown, and Kathleen and James continue to live in Brooklyn Park at the turn of the new millennium.

Submitted by Catherine Vanderheyden Trescony,
Daughter of James and Kathleen

The Vanderheyden Family: front, Peter, Lisa, Thomas, and Daniel; back, Michael, Jean, James, Kathleen, Catherine, and John

The Dean Van Der Werf Family

IN APRIL OF 1968 Dean and Mary Van Der Werf purchased their first home at 6736 Regent Avenue North in Brooklyn Center.

They came to the Minneapolis area in 1963 to attend school. Dean was originally from Sandstone, Minnesota and Mary from Madison, South Dakota. They were married in September 1966. When they purchased their home, Dean was an accountant at Gamble Skogmo and Mary, a nurse at Swedish Hospital.

Three children were born: Sara in 1968, Amy in 1970, and Paul in 1971. The children attended school at Willow Lane, Northview Junior High School and Park Center High School. The family attended Brooklyn Center Evangelical Free Church that was only two blocks from their home.

Sara is now a math teacher at Patrick Henry High School in Minneapolis. Amy is an admissions counselor at Northwestern College in Roseville, and Paul is project set up coordinator for a short-term mission organization in Matamoros, Mexico.

After thirty-one years since moving to Brooklyn Center Dean and Mary still live at the same location.

Submitted by Mary Van Der Werf

The Dean Van Der Werf Family

The Vaughn Families

VAN VERNON VAUGHN and Lorena (Langermann) Vaughn were from Rush City, Minnesota. They married, eventually settling in the Camden area in Minneapolis. They had four children: Bill, Jack, Patricia, and Jim.

Van Vernon was a barber and Lorena worked in the local grocery store. The children attended Hamilton and Jenny Lind Elementary Schools and Patrick Henry High School. Van Vernon was killed by a hit and run driver in 1942.

Lorena was known for her sewing. She made dresses, dance costumes, wedding dresses, curtains and drapes. In her later years she made quilts at church and at home. She made many quilts for Lutheran World Relief. She made quilts for her kids, grandchildren, and other family and friends. We were all proud to have one of Grandma Vaughn's quilts.

In 1952 a tragic fire took the lives of Lorena's brother, sister-in-law and niece. Lorena and her sister raised the two surviving children, Janet and Richard. They also took care of their own father who lived to be 91 years old. After the children became adults and their father died they sold their house in Minneapolis and moved to an apartment in Brooklyn Center.

Lorena served on the Draft Board that drafted Bill in 1943 and Jack in 1944 into the Army for World War II. Pat moved to California to become a "Rosie the Riveter" in a defense plant. Lorena began work at Honeywell—ironically taking over Jack's job when he joined the Army.

In 1946, after Jack was discharged from the Army, he and Leona purchased land in Brooklyn Center to build a house. The following year Bill and Muriel purchased the house across the street and they have been neighbors for fifty-three years on Fremont Avenue. There were cornfields to the west and cow pastures to the north.

During the late forties and early fifties Jack and Bill built a stock car which they took to the various area tracks for races. One of the tracks was in Crystal on West Broadway.

IN 1951 Jim and his cousin Jerry enlisted in the Air Force for the Korean Conflict. In 1956, after he was discharged, Jim and Doris bought a house in Brooklyn Center. It was a new experience to have to deal with a well and cesspool, in those years before city water lines and sewer pipes.

Jack was Chief of the Fire Rescue Squad for many years. After a house fire in Brooklyn Center, to which the Minneapolis Fire Department couldn't respond, Brooklyn Center organized the Volunteer Fire Department (1949). Bill was a charter member and served for more than twenty-one years. Bill served as assistant chief for many years under three chiefs. Jim joined in 1960 and served for more than twenty years. He held the positions of captain and secretary of the Relief Association and Fire Department. Muriel and Doris were active members of the Fire Department Auxiliary.

In the late fifties Jack and Bill bought lakeshore lots on Lower South Long Lake in Brainerd to build a double cabin. Lorena bought a cabin on the two adjoining lots. A few years later Jim bought a lot from Lorena to build his cabin. We had many wonderful summers together at the lake when Lorena called out "coffee time" we would gather on her deck for coffee and conversation. In the evening and on rainy days we played cards or board games.

Lorena Vaughn

Honeywell employed Van Vernon, Lorena, Jack, Jim and Doris. Van Vernon was working there when he was killed. Lorena and Doris retired on the same day—Lorena because she was sixty-five and Doris because she was expecting their first baby. When Jack retired from Honeywell, he and Jim were working for the same department at the Ridgeway Plant. Jim later retired from the new Honeywell plant in Camden. Bill worked for Sears Roebuck Co. for twenty-one years and retired from Carter Day after twenty-one years.

Bill and Muriel had one daughter, Darlene, three grandchildren and three great-grandchildren. Darlene attended Earle Brown School and graduated from North High School (Brooklyn Center District #286 only went up to 8th grade at that time). She married Barry Adler from Brooklyn Center, and their three children are Kim, Douglas, and Jason. Darlene is now deceased.

Jack and Leona have two children: Gary and Pamela. Gary and Pamela attended Earle Brown. Gary graduated from Minneapolis Vocational High School and Pam from Brooklyn Center High School. Gary married Pat Sward from Brooklyn Center and they had two children: Lisa (deceased) and Lee. Lee attended Earle Brown and graduated from Brooklyn Center High School and also attended North Hennepin Community College. Lee has a home in Brooklyn Center. Pamela and Henry "Butch" Kloster have two children: Jasin and Shelly. They both attended Earle Brown and graduated from Brooklyn Center High School. Jasin has a home in Brooklyn Center with his wife, Jessica, and daughter, Allie.

Patricia and Jim Glennon (now deceased) moved to Park Forest, Illinois, where they raised their five children. They have ten grandchildren. After his retirement from Standard Oil they returned to Minneapolis to spend time with Lorena.

Jim and Doris have three children: Vicki, Tracy, and Tammy. They attended Earle Brown and graduated from Brooklyn Center High School and North Hennepin Community College. They have nine grandchildren.

Lorena was a true matriarch who kept the family together. We were always together (including uncles, aunts and cousins) for church, holidays, summers at the lake, etc. She lived her faith and cared about everyone. Lorena died in 1986 at the age of 93.

As told to Doris Vaughn.

Verne and Donna Velasco

In the fall of 1954, as newlyweds out for a Sunday afternoon drive pretending to be prospective homebuyers, we came upon a model home on Camden Avenue in Brooklyn Center. While talking to the contractor he mentioned that he was just starting an identical home on Aldrich Avenue and that we could save money by doing our own painting. We managed to save $1000 for the down payment and moved into 5613 Aldrich Avenue in Brooklyn Center, Minnesota on April 24, 1955. The interest on our VA loan was four percent, and our payments were $62.00 a month. We were so sure we would have a lot more money when the mortgage was paid off. Our house was the last one built on our block, now considered the old section of Brooklyn Center.

Just two blocks east of us along Lyndale Avenue were many lovely homes on river front property with beautiful landscaping and long driveways. These are now all gone to make room for Interstate 94.

Verne and Donna Velasco

We budgeted $5.00 per week for groceries and out of that we also would eat out on Friday evenings at the Beacon Cafe, next to the Beacon Bowling Alley on Lyndale Avenue. Across Lyndale Avenue from the Beacon were truck farms. An apartment complex is there now.

These were the days of "stay-at-home moms", however, we were married five years before starting our family. Then I, also, fell into the daily 10:00 A.M. coffee klatch routine with the neighbors. We had many gatherings at each other's homes. We all had finished off "Rec Rooms" in our basements. In fact, neighbors helped each other finish them off. We knew everyone on the block then, and though some of them have moved on, we remain friends with many of them.

The first year Earle Brown School offered kindergarten was the year our son, Gary, was enrolled. His classroom was in the Baptist Church across the street. Fortunately, Brooklyn Center High School was built long before Gary and his sister Anita were ready for junior and senior high. Before this the students were bussed to North High School in Minneapolis.

We had no shopping malls but there was a variety store on 52nd and Humboldt. Occasionally I walked there. Our grocery shopping was done at Casey's on the corner of 57th and Logan Avenue North. Horses from the Earle Brown Farm grazed in the pastures where Target, Brookdale shopping center and K-Mart are located. Brooklyn Boulevard was then Osseo Road, as it was the direct route from Minneapolis to Osseo. It was just a two-lane road and mostly residential and country. I have noticed that a street sign in Minneapolis still reads Osseo Road.

It has been a good life in Brooklyn Center for us. Even though our children have moved on and out of Brooklyn Center, they would not hear of us moving from here. Brooklyn Center is still their home.

Submitted by Donna Velasco

BEING A WRESTLER'S WIFE was excellent preparation to be a Governor's wife! Those anxious moments for your husband's success and well-being, complaints (roars) of dissatisfied masses, adulation (cheers) when the "contest" pleases: a fine parallel of human nature!

Jesse was born in Minneapolis to loving parents, both World War II Veterans. I was born in Mankato, roots deep into farm country with relatives & friends. We later moved to St. Louis Park. When we met, Jesse was a bouncer, a great hunk of man (with long blonde hair, yet!) to bring home to my folks!! Our early marriage years were also Jesse's early wrestling years; for myself these held trepidation and anticipation, excitement and anxiety, thrills and chills! (Big strong guys get hurt, too!) That happened, bringing serious life changes, but for the better. Jesse began announcing for the wrestling circuit, then radio talk shows with KSTP, later KFAN.

We returned from our jet-speed schedule, settled down, and began our family. Jesse, ever the loving, faithful husband, proved an on-the-spot father — right through labor and delivery with both children! Never a happier, prouder look on his face than when he first held Tyrel and Jade in his powerful arms! — a picture, indelibly painted on my heart! We bought our Brooklyn Park home, where the beautiful Mississippi, wood ducks nesting along the banks, birds, rabbits, squirrels, raccoons, even deer, were everyday happenings. The kids attended Riverview Elementary and Champlin Park, both Anoka-Hennepin Schools. Great! Wonderful! Some regularity! A small measure of peace and quiet! A bigger measure of Jesse and family!

Then it happened: the city council proposed filling a natural wetland nearby. All our lives changed! After neighborhood petitions failed to change their plans, Jesse felt the best, if not only way, was to run for Mayor! The rest, as they say, is history!

Over these years, Jesse's father died, and his mom came to live with us. I'd always dreamed of raising and showing horses and operating a riding school. Jesse found the perfect place, with a private apartment; Mom could still be with us; I could raise horses; he could raise hay! Maple Grove, here we come! Jesse completed his term as BP Mayor, remaining in our riverfront home. We began settling in.

Fast-rising property taxes soon burst upon us. Next, following a warp-speed year with perhaps history's lowest gubernatorial campaign budget, we're on stage at Canterbury Park, TV and press cameras from everywhere, and my husband, father of our two children standing with us, was declared winner of the race for Governor of the State of Minnesota!

Son, Tyrel, handsome, 6'7", has Jesse's honesty and respect for everyone. He's directed his first film project: a PSA with Jesse for MNSCU, has begun a radio spot for The Point, 104. 1 FM, as movie reviewer, plus his rock group!

Daughter, Jade, a beautiful Jr. High strawberry blonde, enjoys life as "normally" as possible, considering who Dad is, taking it all in stride gracefully, an endearing young lady! She's also active in 4-H Club work, main project: Horses — of course!

There's never a dull moment with Jesse, and all moments are open, honest and sincere. We are a very lucky and a very happy family!

Submitted by Terry Ventura, First Lady of Minnesota

The Ventura Family

The Ventura Family

The Mary Ellen Vetter Family

AFTER WORLD WAR II many engineer dads and their families were transferred around the country. In 1953 we left Illinois for Minnesota, destined for "the Pump" and a three-bedroom rambler under construction in Brooklyn Center. The scrubby vegetation had been bulldozed off, leaving a yard that grew sand burrs. The yard burrs could be avoided, but not those that blew into socks and washcloths on the clothesline. We enjoyed our enormous wide-open space with the swamp (Palmer Lake) as our backyard and the Earle Brown Farm, with cattle and crop fields across the street. We stalked through the cattails, fished in Shingle Creek and shared our space with all the wildlife. Our Minneapolis Grandma feared for us, lest we sink into the quicksand. We, however, had confidence in our wonderful, intelligent guardian, our white German Shepherd, Silver Duchess. Duchess was a gift from the Winters family, tenants on the Earle Brown Farm. We remember the frightening annual spring fires in the swamp, usually kids with matches. Also, the dismaying litters of abandoned puppies and kittens. Our rescued kitten, Seraphina, lived to be seventeen years old.

The Vetters

Twelve houses rimmed our dead-end street, a playground for the three dozen children on our block. The Thompsons had the phone; we had the party line. The dads went out and in to work, the milkman and cleaners made deliveries. Large trucks got mired in the sand. Taxi Cabs couldn't find us. We once got mail addressed to "The Vetters, County Road 130, Brooklyn Center, MN." We went into Minneapolis for our groceries, the doctor, dentist, church, etc.

We were living the rapid development of a first ring suburb. The city organized recreational activities and we were bussed off to Lake Calhoun for swimming lessons. And, we got an ice rink. A big day was the monthly visit of the Hennepin County Bookmobile. Then came St. Alphonsus Parish, Boy Scouts, Camp Fire Girls, Little League, etc., all welcome rewards of an emerging new town.

As open space sprouted more ramblers, we became the home delivery service of the Minneapolis evening paper. We each had a share of the 125 customers. We took advantage of Minneapolis and St. Paul events. We enjoyed the Twins baseball games, Aquatennial and Winter Carnival parades, Children's Theater, Symphony concerts, the State Fair, sledding at Wirth Park and more.

Of course, school was in the forefront of our growing-up days. Our realtor directed us to Earle Brown School where we learned that we lived in the Anoka-Hennepin School District. Even though all eight of us progressed successfully through elementary, junior and senior high levels, being bussed to another town often made us feel like commuters. We once calculated that our daily travel to Anoka schools equaled enough miles to circle the globe. We, who were suburban pioneers, feel we were in a right place at a right time. The changes in our neighborhood, in Brooklyn Center, have been amazing.

Submitted by Paul, Jo Ellen, Ann, Larry, Greg, Virginia, Tom, Bob, and Mary Ellen Vetter

KEN IS ONE OF SIX CHILDREN born to William and Bertha Vezner of North Minneapolis. Ken graduated from North High School and Dunwoody Institute. He was in the Army Air Corps during World War II and served in Japan.

Harriet is one of five children born to Olga and Ernest Fremont of Glenwood, Minnesota. She graduated from Glenwood High School and the Minnesota Business College. They met while Harriet worked for Ken in the V. J. Engineering Business, a machine and engineering business that he founded. Ken and Harriet married and bought their first house on 61st and Fremont Avenue North in Brooklyn Center. They lived there from 1953 to 1990.

Their son, Jon, graduated from Brooklyn Center High School and Southwest University at Marshall, Minnesota. He worked for his dad for a time, then moved to Nashville, Tennessee where he has continued to be a songwriter. He married singer Kathy Mattea.

The making of a songwriter is a lot of emotion, feelings, pain, joy and hope." It seems Jon gained all of that through trials and successes. His mother said Jon was born with growths in his throat and stomach; he had clubfeet, and had nine major surgeries before age two. All through school, starting at seventh grade, Jon was writing songs and went on to be a national songwriter.

The song, "Where've You Been?" which Jon co-wrote, told the true story of his grandparents. It was honored as the best country song in 1990. Jon's wife, Kathy Mattea, recorded the song and won top female vocalist of the year by Country Music Awards.

Jon and Kathy reside in Nashville, Tennessee. Jon also has a favorite place to be and write. . . at the Vezner lake place near Paynesville, Minnesota. In 1990 Ken and Harriet moved to a townhouse on the golf course in Brooklyn Park, Minnesota, and in 1998 they moved to Nashville, Tennessee. Harriet has not been in good health the last few years, and Jon and Kathy wanted his parents to be closer to them. They spend their summers in Paynesville.

Submitted by a Brooklyn Historical Society Volunteer

The Ken and Harriet Vezner Family

Rozanne Voss

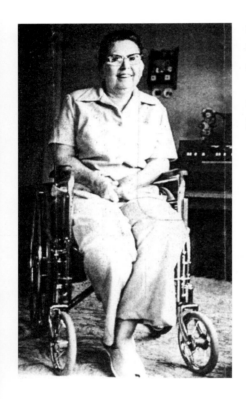

IF THERE EVER WAS A PERSON who was an inspiration to us all it had to be Rozanne Voss. Rozanne had been secretary to former Superintendent of School District #286 Ralph McCartney. She worked at Brooklyn Center High School from the time it opened until she became handicapped with arthritis.

Rozanne was determined to write about her family's history in Brooklyn Township. The family's roots go back to the 1850s. Having a History and English major made her the logical person to write it.

In addition to her arthritis affliction, Rozanne also had to have cataracts removed. She said a whole new world was opened to her after the surgery. Now she was determined more than ever to do more researching and writing.

Her arthritis started in 1962 with a slight pain in her hands and then she became unable to walk. She moved around in a wheelchair. She admitted leaving her job at the high school was very traumatic, but added, "It's like anything else. One door closes and another one opens."

Rozanne said she had many wonderful friends. She had time for them after retirement. When things got really bad, her neighbor, Marilyn Wood would keep her company until Rozanne's husband came home in the evening.

Rozanne has since been relieved of all her pain. She passed on several years ago.

Information from "Brooklyn Center Post" August 29, 1974.
"Life Styles" by Mary Jane Gustafson

Rozanne Voss

BRIAN AND I and our children—Malcolm age 18, Amadi, age 15 and Christina, age 12—moved to Brooklyn Center in June 1990. We moved here from St. Anthony, MN, but our family is originally from the New York / New Jersey area.

We moved to Minnesota in 1984 so I could attend the University of Minnesota Law School, graduating in 1988. After graduation, the Lord told me to get my house in order, go home and raise our children. I haven't yet practiced law.

When we moved to Brooklyn Center the reception was very friendly and inviting. We moved in during the summer and were in the backyard when all the neighbors came to visit. They introduced themselves and told about the neighborhood, the history of our house and how excited they were that we were here. We knew it was a genuine and sincere expression of welcome. We had the same welcoming reception at Earle Brown Elementary School. We have been happy in Brooklyn Center, and have wonderful neighbors.

For eleven years, I have been a homemaker, home schooling parent, and owner of a quilting business called "New Classic Quilts." It was our neighbor, Julie Mastley, who taught me some of the basics in quilting and started me in a whole new career.

We have been Republicans since 1981, became active in 1996, and I was a delegate to the Republican National Convention held in San Diego in 1996. I also co-chair the Heritage Council, an affiliate of the Republican Party of Minnesota.

Brian is an elder at River of Life Christian Church. He also served a year on the Brooklyn Center Planning Commission.

For the last twelve years, we have led the Marriage Fellowship Ministry to couples at our church. In October 1999, we began "Everlasting Light Ministries." Its focal point is ministering the healing power of Jesus Christ to men and women who suffer the loss of children by abortion. Brian has been an employee of FedEx for twelve years, but his heart is to go into full time pastoral ministry.

We have seven children, three living and four deceased. Three died in abortion and one was lost by miscarriage. Our children Malcolm, Amadi and Christina are very active at JC's Place, a youth ministry at Emmanuel Christian Center. Christina is home schooled and Malcolm and Amadi attend Park Center High School in Brooklyn Park.

Submitted by Denise Walker

The Brian and Denise Walker Family

The Walker Family

John Alfred and Axelia C. Holmberg Werner

John Alfred Werner was born in Sweden February 8, 1870; his father's name was also John. His wife, Axelia Holmberg, was born to Karl & Sophia Holmberg, also in Sweden, and is the sister of Abraham Herbert Holmberg of Brooklyn Park.

John Alfred was one of the original assessors in Brooklyn Township — before Brooklyn Center was a Village or Brooklyn Park its own Township. John was an accomplished carpenter, and trained his son, Edwin, in all these skills, who passed them on to his sons, and they to theirs.

John and Axelia built their first home (still standing) on 69th Avenue just west of West River Road. They sold that house to the Lindgren family upon buying the community hall (Riverlyn), and moved into the home beside it. John and Axelia Werner were the first private owners of the Riverlyn Hall and picnic grounds on the Mississippi River at 95th Avenue. Built as a community center / town hall, it was put up for sale when the Depression hit.

John Alfred and Axelia Werner's golden wedding anniversary

John and Axelia had three children: John Edwin (known as Ed), Esther Lucille (known by Lucille), and Evelyn, who has been gone from Minnesota for many years now, to Independence, Missouri. Evelyn had a daughter with her first husband, Wiley Murphy, and 2 daughters and 1 son with her second husband, Everett Meyers.

Son, John Edwin (Ed), (December 3, 1897–June 3, 1961) was known as an outstanding truck gardener, and also as the (only!) paper delivery man, back when Minneapolis had the "Daily Times!" — with quite an extensive route, covering much of Brooklyn Center and southeastern Brooklyn Park. He and wife, Rose Cummers, had three sons: John (Jack), Lorrie and James (Jimmy). Jack and his wife, Priscilla have three sons: Mark, Larry and Curt; Lorrie and his wife, Mildred, have four children: Todd, Tom, Julie and Leslie. Jimmy died of Hodgkin's disease as a very young man, in the mid-1950s, just out of the service.

In the mid 1930s, son Eddie, Rolland Holmberg, Mary Nelson, Ida Anderson, and others combined talents and put on several little stage plays at Riverlyn. They also rented out the hall for church picnics, and held dances on the weekends. The Benson Men's Club held fund-raising dances in the 1940s. Eddie and wife, Rose, and family were among the best dancers. Their son, Jimmy, was accomplished at old-time dancing already in 3rd grade, teaching some girls who thought he was quite the handsome, blonde charmer.

Daughter, Esther Lucille, married Arling Schaefer; they had two sons, Raymond and Roy. Ray and his wife, Lorraine, have four children: Lee — who has three children, Christopher, Jeanette, and Justin; Rex — who has Chad and Christi; Marcie — who has Matthew and Angela — who has Alyssa; and Elaine, who has Aron and James. Lucille's son, Roy and his wife, Shirley, have three sons: Rick — who has Nicole, Martine and Grant; Steve — who has Aaron and Tizah; Hewitt, who has Richard and Michael; and a daughter, April. Ray is a retired electrician; Roy is a retired mechanical engineer.

John A. and Axelia Werner celebrated fifty years of marriage in the mid 1940s. John died February 28, 1959, and was joined by Axelia, November 20, 1959, only nine months later.

Submitted by Ray Schaefer, Grandson

JESSE JAMES AND VIRGINIA WHEELER were residents of Brooklyn Center since the early 1900s. Their truck farm was located behind Evans Nordby Funeral Home and extended from there to Shingle Creek. Their crops consisted of asparagus, potatoes, etc. They had five children, Marcella, Jessie, Lois, John and Margaret. Their farm home built in the 1920s continues to be used.

Jess was named after Jesse James and one of his grandsons was named James Jesse. His granddaughter was named after Virginia. Jess and Virginia had many friends, Burquests, Sparks, Wingards, and Brunsells.

Jess was a member of the Brooklyn Center city council in the 1930s. When Jess died in 1939, Virginia, Stephen Weston's grandmother, sold the farm to her son John who lived on the farm for several years renting out the land. Stephen's mother, Marcella and his dad, Roy, built a house on the farm in the 1930s and lived there until 1962 when they retired.

Truck farming in those days was very different from today. There were no herbicides or effective insecticides, therefore weeds had to be hoed or cultivated and the insects obviously laughed at the ineffective insecticides. It was a hard life. For most of Jess and Virginia's farming life, horses, not tractors, were used and they needed hay all winter and all summer and were very cantankerous, always wanting to quit working and wanting to head for the barn. Sometimes Jess would let Stephen ride Prince, his favorite horse if he hadn't been worked that day. Stephen would sit in the stall with Prince and read books to him and bother him in many ways.

Going to market was tough, too, since it was a long trip with horses. Jess would get up at three in the morning to get the horses harnessed and get to the market on time. In addition to the produce in the wagon, it was necessary to carry water and hay for the horses because they would not be back to the farm until afternoon.

Stephen's sisters Shirley, Phyllis and brother, Roy, with their cousins would always be "cutting up." They would hand churn ice cream and were always told not to sample it when they were finished. Of course, the minute the parents were out of sight they would eat it up.

Brooklyn Boulevard was then named Osseo Road. Stephen would hitchhike. Sometimes he would wait an hour and no cars would come by.

Sometimes Stephen rode Prince over to Twin Lake. They would go into the water as deep as he dared because Prince had never been taught how to swim. They had fun in those days. Now they live within a mile of the old homestead and Stephen is reminded of the "old days." Until now Stephen did not realize he was one of the "old devils."

Submitted by Stephen Weston

Jesse James and Virginia Wheeler

Jesse cultivating with the horses (ca. 1920)

The Joel and Colleen Wiest Family

My wife, Connie and I had just graduated from Brigham Young University in Provo, Utah. We moved to Brooklyn Park on May 1, 1980, after I secured employment in the finance department of Carry's Department Store. Based on my future earning potential, we were able to purchase a small home on 76th Avenue, just off of Humboldt Avenue. All of the roads north of us were still paved with gravel or dirt. I caught the bus at 73rd Avenue and commuted downtown to Minneapolis to work.

When we arrived, our oldest daughter Audrey was nineteen months old. Heather was born about two months after our move. Samuel was born in 1983, and Zachary in 1985. After six years at this address we bought a house on Ashley Terrace, the second house in our subdivision. We enjoyed some notoriety for a period of time, because Kirby and Tanya Puckett had purchased the first house in our subdivision. What a thrill it was to have one of the neighbors on the Twins baseball team that won the 1987 World Series!

Kirby Puckett autographing baseballs for the Wiest Family (1987)

Home sales were slow in our subdivision for a period of time, which was fine with us. The solitude was incredible—our first winter in our new home, the deer would bed down in our backyard for the night. In the spring of 1987, Heather was thrilled to find a rack of antlers in the garden! We enjoyed being surrounded by cornfields and sod farms. For several years we were able to walk through the woods surrounding the golf course and enjoy the rural flavor of the neighborhood. Of particular note were the large trees that still had deer stands in them from the days before 1985 when bow hunting was legal north of 85th Avenue. We always heated our home with wood, and because of the home construction in the area, I was able to haul wood from sub-developments as late as 1992.

In 1990 the Planning Commission granted a conditional use permit for the construction of our church. A large meetinghouse for the Church of Jesus Christ of Latter-Day Saints was constructed on the corner of Edinbrook Terrace and Noble Avenue. We were able to occupy the building in the fall of 1992. Previously we had to drive to Anoka or down to Golden Valley for church services and activities. It was a great blessing to have our church so close to home. The building has been a boon to the community as well, being used as a polling place, a meeting place for the Scout Roundtables and for its Family History Center.

Our children have attended Evergreen, Monroe and Riverview Elementary Schools and have graduated from Champlin Park High School. We have had many opportunities to move, but have always elected to stay in Brooklyn Park because of its fine schools and citizens.

Submitted by Joel Wiest

THE BROOKLYN CENTER COMMUNITY CENTER has been fortunate to have Beverly Wilson as an instructor for children's dance and many adult exercise classes. She is also in charge of the women's "Silver Slippers", a dance group.

The Silver Slippers are often called upon to entertain at nursing homes, the Veterans of Foreign Wars, church affairs, and many more occasions.

Beverly teaches exercise classes for older people, both men and women. She has been teaching at the Brooklyn Center Community Center since 1975.

She started her life work at the age of five years by taking dance lessons. By the time she was ten years old she was off to dance classes three times a week. At the age of twelve she was dancing with the Saint Paul Civic Opera Ballet. She danced with the ballet for two years. She turned professional and joined a dance line when she was fifteen years old.

She graduated from the University of Wisconsin with a major in Physical Education. After college she taught one year at the University of Colorado at Boulder.

She married and had four children, but that didn't stop her life's work. While at home with her children she gave dance lessons to young people and exercise classes for women, and also was able to be a substitute teacher. Beverly has a great deal of energy that she passes on to her participants at the Community Center.

From an oral interview by Marian Klohs

Beverly Wilson

Beverly Wilson

John and Clarine Wingard

THE WINGARD FAMILY first moved to Brooklyn Center in 1918. Arthur and Emma settled on a small farm along Shingle Creek and Osseo Road. They raised fruits and vegetables and sold them at the Minneapolis Market. Cultivation was done by horsepower, until the 1930s when the iron horse, or tractor, was available. Arthur and Emma raised seven children on this farm during the Depression years of the 1930s.

With the advent of World War II the oldest boys went off to serve in the Navy, leaving the youngest to help Dad raise and harvest the crops. They all had to pitch in as the food products were essential for the war effort.

In the 1950s Dad became a State Farm Insurance agent, and the farm was handed over to the boys, Arthur Jr. and John to operate.

John and Clarine Wingard

After WWII the population of Brooklyn Center started to grow. Sewer was extended from Minneapolis and the land was converted to housing. In 1955 Sherburne County became the logical and closest place for farming. The operation moved to a farm between Big Lake and Elk River. It is now nine hundred acres in size and supports five families.

At that time, John, a university graduate and a family man, was asked to serve as Justice of the Peace for Brooklyn Center. He served in that position for eight years and had the honor to unite twenty couples in marriage, plus holding court on traffic offenses and other matters.

In 1962 the suburban communities grew so fast that the Legislature was re-districted to more evenly represent the growth. Robbinsdale, Brooklyn Center and Brooklyn Park became one legislative district. John Wingard was asked by a group of Brooklyn Center citizens to run for the House seat. He received the endorsement of the Republican Party and won the seat in 1963.

John, Clarine and family moved to Champlin in 1965. The farm in Brooklyn Center had been sold to the developers Burch and Wise and Evelyn Schmidt. Osseo Road became a highway and the name was changed to Brooklyn Boulevard. Raising four children on this busy road was not the same anymore.

John and Clarine have four children: John Jr., Tom, Karla and Michael, and ten grandchildren. John Jr. married Catherine Cary and live in Prior Lake with their children: Marty, Daniel, and John III. Tom married LuAnn Hedman, and lives in Elk River with their children: Mark, Melissa, and David. Karla married Charles Miller. They have one son, Charlie, and live in Plymouth. Michael married Elizabeth Beberger, living in Elk River with their children: Matthew, Rachael and Christopher.

Some major pieces of legislation that John worked on which concerned this area are as follows: two vocational schools in rural Hennepin County, cited by legislation a Junior College in NW Hennepin County, worked on Green Acres bill and an eight-million dollar bond issue for Hennepin County Park Reserve system.

Submitted by John Wingard

JIM AND I, PAT WISWELL, hail from the Hill City, Minnesota area. We were married soon after Jim returned home from serving in the South Pacific with the Marines in World War II. We soon decided to move to Minneapolis where job opportunities were so much better. In 1948 we packed up our belongings and moved to a house in Minneapolis just a few blocks south of the Brooklyn Center boundary.

In January 1959 Jim and I bought a new house at 7219 Major Avenue North, where we raised our daughters Mary and Pam and lived many happy years. We were close to church, schools and shopping. It was a great place to live.

The Wiswell family has been a part of the St. Alphonsus Catholic Parish since its formation in 1959, where we were one of the earliest registered families with Envelope #12. Mary and Pam attended St. Alphonsus School through eighth grade.

Our back door neighbor for many years was Reverend Robert Bailey and his family. Rev. Bailey pastored the Brooklyn Methodist Church, a wonderful old landmark on the then Osseo Road. The Bailey's were not only terrific neighbors, but also great friends of the Wiswell family. It was a sad day when Reverend Robert Bailey died at an early age, in 1985.

Two sons-in-law and four grandchildren later, Jim and I thought a one-level home would suit us much better as we grew older. After looking around we located a one-level townhouse complex being built in Brooklyn Park which we found to be very comfortable and eliminated the need for us to shovel snow and do yard maintenance. So, in September 1994, we moved to our present townhouse home at 9109 Yancy Lane.

The Jim and Pat Wiswell Family

The Wiswell Family: front, Mary, Whitney, T. J., Pam, Tyler, and Lindsay; back, Brian, Pat, Jim, and Steve

In May 1996 Jim and I celebrated our fiftieth Anniversary with family, relatives and many friends, at an elegant sit-down dinner in a Champlin, Minnesota club.

I have been a volunteer at the Brooklyn Park Historical Farm, almost since its beginning. My lifestyle fits in with the Historical Farm, because I have been a sewer, quilter, and crafter for many years. I really get into the Christmas spirit after the Christmas Open House at the Historical Farm each year.

The Open House renews many very fond memories. I have been an active member of the Minnesota Quilters, as well as some other clubs. I frequently donate some of my best crafts to charities, such as the St. Alphonsus Annual Auction.

Superior Dairy employed Jim for thirty-two years, where he had a reputation for being very trustworthy. He began as a milkman on a route in Bloomington and Edina, and was a successful Special Account Representative when he retired in 1985. He was very active for many years at St. Alphonsus, serving as Chairman of the Annual Fun Fair, on Building Fund Drives, Usher's Club, and Men's Club to name a few of the volunteer leadership responsibilities he undertook.

Submitted by Pat (Mabel) Wiswell

The Wood Family

HARRY NELSON WOOD was born in 1873 in Bennet Corners, New York. He came to Brooklyn Center in the late 1800s. Here he met Sue Mae Esterbrook who was born in Danville, Vermont. They were married in 1893 in Hudson, Wisconsin and lived on the corner of what is now 57th and James Avenue North in Brooklyn Center.

Harry and Sue Mae had eight children, four boys and four girls. Walter was born in 1895, married in 1919, and moved to California. Margaret was born in 1897 and lived on 54th and Fremont Avenue North most of her life. Mary was born in 1899, married in 1923, and lived most of her life in Brooklyn Center. Cliff was born in 1901 and died at the age of thirteen from kidney disease. John was born in 1904 and lived his entire life in Brooklyn Center. David was born in 1909, never married and lived most of his life in Brooklyn Center. Alice was born in 1915 and left Brooklyn Center after her marriage. Lucille was born in 1918 and lived in Minneapolis for a number of years but has resided in Brooklyn Center for the past eleven years.

In 1910 Harry's house was moved to 54th and Fremont Avenue North and was one of the first homes in that area. Harry was the first to plant trees on the boulevard. He worked on the farm of Earle Brown for many years. He held various positions, but mainly he was a handyman and a groundskeeper, here in Brooklyn Center as well as Earle Brown's mansion in Vermont.

A few years after the Navy discharged John, he met Zelda Dean. They were married in 1927 and purchased a grocery store on the northwest corner of 55th and Humboldt Avenue, owning it until 1948 when they built their home on the northeast corner of that same intersection. They lived at that corner for sixty-three years.

John and Zelda had two children, Eunice was born in 1932 and Dean in 1934. Both children lived in Brooklyn Center their entire lives. After Dean married he moved to the 5300 block of Howe Lane. Dean passed away in January 1996. When Eunice married, she moved to 57th and Emerson Avenue. She lived there until 1985 then moving to 55th and Aldrich where she still resides. John Wood died in June 1990 at the age of 86. Zelda Wood still resides with her daughter Eunice in Brooklyn Center. John and Zelda had five grandchildren and twelve great-grandchildren.

Submitted by Eunice Breuinger

SHIRLEY WUNDERLICH was born in Brooklyn Township in 1925, daughter of Miller and Esther Pumarlo. My parents moved to 57th and Lyndale North in 1924. My sister Betty (Ketter) lives in Brooklyn Park and a brother, Francis, lives in Hamel. My dad, Miller Pumarlo, drilled most of the wells in Brooklyn Center, Brooklyn Park, Osseo, Plymouth, Crystal, New Hope, Anoka, and other areas.

When the Great Depression of the 1930s hit, I was attending the third grade at Earle Brown School. My father and mother were members of the Farmer Labor Group, one of the programs started by President Franklin Roosevelt's New Deal. My father was in charge of distribution of food rations for the Brooklyn Township area. The food consisted of oranges, butter, flour, sugar, raisins and other items. Our home was heated with coal. My mother made all of our clothes, and had a huge garden that fed the family. Our transportation was walking. Our dad had an old beat up truck to go to work. On Sundays, we all piled in the truck to attend church.

Our first home at 57th and Lyndale North was built in 1924. The State Highway bought the home. The land is now part of I-94.

Betty and Francis attended Earle Brown School through the eighth grade. There was no high school in the area at the time, so Betty and I attended a vocational school in Minneapolis, learning commercial cooking. We hitchhiked to Camden, then take a streetcar to school. Returning home, we rode the streetcar as far as Camden, and then hitch a ride home. During the 1940s, the streetcar tracks went as far as 52nd and Bryant Avenue North.

My brother, Francis, completed the 8th grade and was then employed to work on the bridge at Interstate 694.

In 1943 I married a school chum, Clarence Wunderlich. Clarence entered the Army in 1943 and returned after World War II ended.

We lived in the basement for two years while completing the upper portion of our home. When we first started building there were only two other houses on the block. The other land was planted in corn, potatoes and other vegetables. There was a small store that sold a combination of groceries and hardware on 69th and Osseo Road, the only business nearby. The Farmer Labor Group held its meetings on the upper floor of this store.

There were no railroads in this area so Raymond Brothers Trucking did all of the shipping and hauling during the 1930s and 1940s.

I went to school with the Madsen girls, whose parents had the greenhouse on 55th Avenue. All of us girls skated together on the river and had a toboggan-run down the riverbank across the road from our house and we swam in the river every summer.

Clarence and I raised three daughters and a son. I am still very active golfing and ice-skating. I belong to the Fridley Skating Club and skate at least three times a week. The club has been together since 1970. Nine skaters over eighty years old still skate with this group.

Submitted by Shirley Wunderlich

Pumarlo and Wunderlich Families

The Wunderlich House

The Richard Youngberg Family

THE RICHARD YOUNGBERG FAMILY moved into Brooklyn Center in the fall of 1972. Our family consisted of Richard, myself (Karen), Keith and Kevin at that time. Richard was a Vietnam Veteran and had finished his accounting education at the Academy of Accountancy. He worked for DeVac, Inc. I attended Anoka Technical School to become a surgical technician. Keith was in first grade at Earle Brown School.

Our first home in Brooklyn Center was in the new apartments at 53rd and Russell Avenue. We lived in apartment #217, which to this day shows up on the voting registration records for Karen and Richard Youngberg. Richard was active in Clarence LaBelle VFW.

We made many friends in Brooklyn Center and knew that we wanted to live there and especially in the Earle Brown School area. We were involved in Earle Brown PTA and the Little League. At that time there was no golf course—just Lions Park with the Little League Fields. In the spring of 1976 we found our new home at 5419 Girard Avenue North.

The Richard Youngberg Family: front, Kyle, Richard, Melanie, Kevin, Karen, and Ryan; back, Courtney, Kent, and Nancy (1997)

Both Keith and Kevin were at Earle Brown School, and active in the Little League and the Park Board football programs. In February 1977 we were joined by Kent—the new addition to our family.

As the years progressed, Richard went to work for Philips Temro Inc. I spent nineteen years at St. Mary's Hospital as a Certified Surgical Technologist. St. Mary's was bought out by the Fairview system and is known as Fairview Riverside.

The years that our boys spent in the Brooklyn Center Schools were filled with ups and downs. Keith enjoyed sports, especially baseball. In his junior year the basketball team went to the State Tournaments, and was beaten by my hometown team, Barnum. I cheered for Brooklyn Center all the way. He graduated from Concordia College in Moorhead with a physics, math double major. He and his family recently moved from Moorhead to Appleton, Wisconsin, where he is working as an electrical estimator.

Kevin also played some sports, mainly baseball, but he truly enjoyed his experiences in the high school choir. During his teen years he developed an interest in Beekeeping. This interest has provided a life long commitment for him. We originally started with a beehive in the backyard. Working at Twin Cities Beekeeping Supply Store helped him through high school and Hamline University. He is the current owner of Twin Cities Beekeeping Supply and Beekeeper's Candles. The backyard beehive turned into twenty near a field by Hugo, Minnesota. Kevin and his family live in Plymouth.

Kent was a soccer player. He was also very active in the high school choir. Richard and I chaperoned some fun choir trips during his high school years. Kent currently works as a draftsman for a company in Plymouth. He is the newest volunteer member of the Brooklyn Center Fire Department. His fiancée, Courtney Rouschendorfer Hayes, is a Brooklyn Center resident.

Twenty-seven years later Richard and I agree, "this was a good place to start and a great place to stay."

Submitted by Karen Youngberg

I, NOVELLA (ENLUND), was born July 28, 1923, in Freedhem, MN, fifteen miles from Little Falls. My Mom was canning corn on a hot wood stove when she went into labor. Dad went to get my aunt who was helping with haying across the meadow. She delivered me, a healthy eleven lbs. I had two sisters and two brothers at the time. Another sister and three more brothers arrived in our family in later years.

I went to a little one-room school just a mile from our home. When I was thirteen I was confirmed at the Lutheran Church. I soon met Bob Zimbrick who attended the Baptist Church just across the street from the Lutheran Church. Bob was born November 6, 1921, in Brainerd, MN. We started to date.

I worked as a waitress in Brainerd, and Bob went to Minneapolis to drive cab. We planned to get married, but Bob was called into the Army in World War II. I then moved to Minneapolis and worked at the Knitting Factory as a printer while he was in the service.

Two and one-half years later, Bob came home from the service. We were married in August 1945 at my parents home. We moved to Brainerd and Bob worked for the railroad.

Two years later Katherine was born; four years after that, Roberta was born. Bob was transferred to Minneapolis Soo Line and I worked as a waitress again. After a year of Bob commuting between Brainerd and Minneapolis, he said we had to move to Minneapolis. We moved into a house on 60th and Aldrich where we still live today. We had, and still have, wonderful neighbors. Soon after moving to Brooklyn Center we joined Hope Lutheran Church where we are still active members.

Seven years after the birth of our second daughter, we were blessed with a third daughter, Adele. About this time Bob got a job with the City of Brooklyn Center Water Department. He worked there until he retired. I worked at Malberg Bakery for seven years; and Lynbrook Bowl for eight years. Our daughters attended Earle Brown Elementary School and all graduated from Brooklyn Center High School.

Katherine married and has a son; Roberta married and has a boy and girl; and Adele married and has a boy and a girl.

We went on many vacations to Florida, Pennsylvania, Arizona and Hawaii. I joined the Garden Club, Women's Circle at Church, Senior Supper Club, and I bowled three days a week. I enjoy my yard and flowers. We celebrated our fiftieth anniversary at the Historical Farm in Brooklyn Park. I cooked and volunteered there when we had open house during the fall of each year. I thank the Lord for our health, good friends, and our home.

Submitted by Novella Zimbrick

The Zimbrick Family

Novella and Robert Zimbrick's fiftieth wedding anniversary with their daughters Katherine Kyle, Roberta Baker, and Adele Hoffman

The Charles and Eileen Zimmer Family

WE ARE PART of an era known as the Stearns County migration to the Twin Cities. Brooklyn Park became our home in 1966 because it was a new community with good schools, parks, a home we could afford, and a wonderful Catholic parish. Both of our parents came from large families and we had between us about fifty aunts and uncles living in the St. Joseph, Cold Spring and St. Cloud, Minnesota area. Living in Brooklyn Park and near Interstate 94 made attending the weddings, anniversaries, birthdays, parties, and funerals an easy commute. We wanted a reminder of our roots, so the front of our home and a planter are made of multi-colored Cold Spring granite.

Eileen (Dullinger) grew up in St. Joseph and attended high school at St. Benedict's. She completed business college in St. Cloud and worked at the Stearns County Clerk of Court's office until she married her "knight in shining armor." Then it was work at the University, mothering our daughters, and today helping with radiology at North Memorial Hospital.

Julie, Charles, Eileen, and Karen Zimmer

I grew up on a dairy, hog, and chicken farm in Jacob's Prairie, graduating in a class of two from a one-room country school. My education was continued at St. Boniface High School, and then off to see the world of Missouri. . . compliments of the U.S. Army. St. John's University was the next stop for a couple of years and then off to the big city at the University of Minnesota. I had only been to Minneapolis a couple of times before starting school at the University. I remember the first time driving into the city for 10 or 15 minutes, thinking I must have missed the University. After driving another fifteen minutes, there was the campus.

We've had the opportunity to live in Illinois, Utah, and Ohio, and have been fortunate to visit most of the United States and much of the world. We have two married daughters. Karen (Burns) is a ski instructor, teacher and realtor living in Park City, Utah. Julie (Johnson) is a school social worker, and lives in Stillwater, Minnesota. She is the mother of our granddaughters, Natalie (4), Savannah (2) and Rachel (1).

St. Alphonsus Parish is a major part of our volunteer, social, and prayer lives. We have fond memories of the Fun Fairs, Christmas Bazaars, Cana Dinners, Octoberfests and the many educational opportunities.

I worked at the Caterpillar Proving Grounds, designed Flight Control Systems at Honeywell and with Jim Samlaska, co-founded Tele-Terminals (Ameridata). In 1985 Eileen and I started the Software Library to provide software for administrative use by churches and other non-profit organizations.

During our thirty years in Brooklyn Park, it has been transformed from potato and vegetable fields to an area filled with homes, trees, flowers, squirrels, and birds. We feel privileged to have been a part of that transformation, to have many friends here, and to be citizens of this community.

Submitted by Charles R. Zimmer

PETER ZIMMERMAN (1875-1935) married Emma Schreiber in 1898. Peter cleared the land and built a brick home at 2900 93rd Ave N in Brooklyn Park shortly before their son Abraham Christian was born in July 1900.

With the exception of two years that he spent in the state of Washington with his parents when he was nine years old, Abe spent his entire life in the brick home about a mile west of West River Road.

When Abe married Elsie Champlin in 1922, he bought his parents' farm. Their son Calvin was born in 1925, and a daughter, Delores, was born in 1929. Abe was a potato farmer, but also grew some grain and soybeans. They had some cows, but sold them when a tornado destroyed the barns in 1952.

Before they married, Elsie was a teacher at the school on 97th and West River Road. Abe was always very active in the community. He served on the District 30 school board for sixteen years along with Arling Schaefer and Pearl Bennett, who both lived on West River Road.

Calvin and Delores attended Riverview School. At least one of the teachers lived with Abe and Elsie. Miss Einhorn was only nineteen years old when she started teaching and some of the boys were sixteen and got to be a problem to handle, so Abe would go down and straighten them out.

Abe served on the Brooklyn Park Planning Commission and then was a councilman. When Brooklyn Park became a city he was asked to run for mayor, but chose not to and instead served as a Charter Council Member.

Abe died in 1975.

From information collected by Marian Klohs

Abraham (Abe) Christian Zimmerman

The Alvin Zimmerman Family

PETER ZIMMERMAN was born April 25, 1824, in Switzerland. Peter's first wife, Rosine Knobel, whom he married on May 19, 1845, died February 26, 1855 and is buried in Switzerland. In June 1856 Peter married Magdalea Wilheim. She was born January 4, 1836. They came to America from Schwandt, Switzerland in 1862. Magdalea is buried at the German Lutheran Cemetery in Osseo.

While Peter was married to Rosine they had a son named Abraham, who was born September 7, 1848, in Switzerland. Abraham was married twice, to Rosina and Katherine. Abraham and Rosina had a son named Peter, who was born on June 30, 1875.

Peter Zimmerman married Emma Louise Schreiber on September 6, 1898. Peter and Emma farmed on 93rd Ave N, approximately one mile west of West River Road.

Emma's descendants were also pioneers of Brooklyn Park. The Schreiber School was named for Emma's relatives.

Peter and Emma had two sons: Abraham Christian, born in 1900, and Alvin Peter, born September 24, 1903.

One day when Peter went to town Emma decided to drive their new automobile, but soon ran it into the ditch. She had to get her sons, Abe and Al, to hitch up the horses and pull the car out of the ditch before their father returned home. That was the first and last of Emma's driving experience.

Peter lived until April 9, 1935. Emma lived until October 20, 1970. Their son, Abraham died December 24, 1975.

Alvin married Ann Nelson in 1924. They lived on a farm known as the "eighty" which is now Edinburgh Golf Course. Al and Ann had two daughters: Betty Lou and Virginia Ann. Betty married Andrew Hanson on July 16, 1944. They have two children, Mark and Andrea. Mark married Kathleen Marketon in 1974. They were divorced in 1977. Andrea married Wayne Morris in 1978 and they have two children, Amanda and Anthony. Virginia married Robert John Zimmer in 1958. They had two sons, Paul and John. Paul married Ann Hunt in 1990. They have two daughters, Emily Ann and Elizabeth Jean. John married Rhonda Ortscheid in 1992. They have one child, Alexis Mary born in 1996.

Ann Zimmerman died in 1982, and Alvin died January 20, 1989. All their descendants reside in the metropolitan area.

Submitted by Virginia Zimmer and Betty Hanson

Alvin, Abraham, Emma, and Peter Zimmerman

THE ZIMMERMAN HOUSE was originally a Schreiber homestead, built in 1865. The house stood vacant during the Depression, but shortly afterwards Leonard Palmer purchased the house that at the time needed many repairs.

Bob and Connie Zimmerman

Mr. Palmer began the restoration project by putting a basement under the living room and stairway portion of the house. Looking at the house it is quite obvious that the home was constructed in four different stages.

The original part of the house was constructed with limestone from the Mississippi River. The limestone was laid on the ground and the structure built above. Digging and constructing a basement was done at a later date.

In the middle seventies the Schreiber family owned the house once again. Then, in 1979, Bob Zimmerman bought the house from Bill and Jack Schreiber.

Connie and Bob Zimmerman completed the face-lift in the 1980s with extensive renovation. Extensive interior remodeling had to be done, such as re-wiring, plumbing, central heat, and air conditioning. A fireplace was added, in addition to the opening up of a staircase that now has a "spiral" look to it.

The house boasts extensive woodwork with black walnut and cherry being the predominant woods in the older section of the house.

Bob and Connie Zimmerman's House

In 1992 a large "great" room addition was added to the north of the house. Also on the land sets a guesthouse. This house was originally the location of the well for the main house, because, according to superstition, the well could not be located in the house. Years later the well house was made into a milk house. Then it was remodeled and made into a guest or rental house. When it was actually converted into such a house is not clear.

The original four-stall garage was constructed of eight by eight timbers taken from the original barn. Bob and Connie Zimmerman remodeled the garage to its current design in 1988.

The original exterior was wood. At a later date, brick was used for the exterior making the wall very thick.

Bob is a lifelong resident of Brooklyn Park. He was born at home because there was no time to get to the hospital. To keep the other children busy during the birthing process, Grandpa Olson came and took them for a horse and buggy ride.

When Bob rode the bus to school this house was at the end of the bus route. He used to dream that some day he would own it. His dream came true.

Bob went to school in the Osseo District. He graduated from Bemidji State University and now teaches at Champlin Park High School.

Submitted by Bob and Connie Zimmerman

Virgil Zimmerman

MY GRANDFATHER, Abraham Zimmerman, was born in Switzerland in 1848. He farmed the land at 3700 95th Avenue North in Brooklyn Park, Minnesota. His livelihood was raising potatoes, planted and dug by hand and then sold to consumers in Minneapolis. Horse and wagon delivered the potatoes. It was said that two of his daughters, Rachel and Frances, together could dig and pick sixty bushels a day, using a six-tine fork. Abraham died in 1932.

My father, Gabriel Zimmerman, was born in 1878 and grew up on this farm of 150 acres. He followed in his father's footsteps raising potatoes, but had mechanical potato planters and diggers pulled by horses. The seed was all cut by hand. It was a big event when he purchased a truck in 1923 and could deliver the potatoes to markets in the Twin Cities. At that time there were no commercial fertilizers. Ranchers from Montana shipped flocks of sheep to Minnesota to be fattened, and the farmers benefited by using the sheep manure as fertilizer. These flocks were unloaded from the railroad cars and run through the main street of Osseo to outlying farms.

In 1917 potato seed cost $6.50 per bushel, and in the fall after a poor crop the potatoes were sold for thirty-five cents a bushel. Gabriel retired in 1929.

In 1907, after his first wife died, my father married Carrie Heidelberger. I was born on May 21, 1917, in a shed on the farm where we lived because the house had burned in February of that year while my parents were in town. A large home was built in the fall of 1917 for $3,600 and stood until developers demolished it in 1998. Carrie died in 1960.

Threshing with the steam engine on the Gabe Zimmerman Farm (1921)

In 1938 I started to farm, feeding sheep in the winter for fertilizer and raising potatoes in the summer.

In 1943 I married Isabelle Scharber and we had three children: Susan, David and Barbara.

Eventually I had more sophisticated equipment for raising and processing potatoes. In 1947 I installed an irrigation system that increased the yield and the quality tremendously. I sold some of the crop to shippers and some at the Minneapolis and Saint Paul Farmer's Markets. Isabelle died in 1972, and I subsequently married Florene Warner of Osseo. In 1978 I retired and moved to Osseo.

Submitted by Virgil Zimmerman

THE SWISS GOVERNMENt paid their citizens to migrate to the United States. The lack of jobs, farmland and opportunities made this a necessity for the well being of the country and the individuals. As a result, some of the Swiss came to Minnesota to homestead land. Some of these immigrants were from an area near the towns of Glarus and Schwanden. Balthazar Zopfi and Regul "Rachel" Blesi were among these newcomers.

Balthazar and Rachel were married in 1860 and settled on land south of Hayden Lake on Hayden Lake Road. They raised a family of twelve children. All members of the family worked in the fields and with the livestock to make the farm a successful operation. They all had a reputation of being hard, sincere workers. Some of the children attended school in the small brick schoolhouse located north of Osseo on Jefferson Highway. The homestead remained in the family until purchased by Hennepin County. The farm is now a part of Elm Creek Park.

One daughter, Annie married William Wilberg. William was an immigrant from Germany, a harness maker by trade and had a shop in Anoka. The business, with the advent of the automobile, evolved into a tire and service business. William was a musician and was active in organizing bands, including the Osseo and Anoka town bands. He also had a dance band that toured the area. Aaron Tessman, Brooklyn Park, was a musician in one of the bands.

William and Annie had three children: Edward, Dorothea and Raymond. Dorothea married Keith P. Caswell, son of Arthur and Alice Caswell. Keith was a construction engineer. Keith and Dorothea had eight children. One of their sons is Keith P. Caswell, Jr., professional engineer, residing in Maple Grove.

Submitted by Keith P. Caswell Jr.

The Balthazar and Regul Zopfi Family

Index

Eddy, Donna, 14
Edling, Albert, 27
Edling, Sigurd, 2, 26, 41, 173, 177, 200, 205, 209, 244
Edlund, Ragnihild, 396
Edlund, Richard, 127
Egan, Edward, 194
Eggert, Midge, 117, 324
Eidem, Anna, 326
Eidem, Chris, 262
Eidem, John J., 39, 163, 326
Eidem, Tyrus, 326
Eisenbrand, Harold, 327
Eisenbrand, Lillian, 150
Elias, Ruth, 328
Ellingson, Bob and Carol (Grams), 131, 295, 329
Ellingson, June, 329
Ellsworth, Clark, 35-36
Elmer, Dan, 117
Engdahl, Gil and Marion, vii, 14, 330
Engdahl, Nancy, 360
Engh, Erick, 60
Engstrand, Amelia, 257
Engstrom, Marge and Roger, 331
Engvall, Henry, 177
Ensrud, Richard, 98
Erickson, Allen G., 137
Erickson, Barbara and Maynard, xiii-xiv, 130, 139, 334, 446, 465-466, 480, 487, 513
Erickson, Gordon and Grace, 46-47, 119, 203, 209, 235, 332
Ericson, Harry and Daisy (Dahlin), 335
Ericson, LaVerne and LeRoy, 281
Erikson, Bruce, 169
Eriksson, Dell and Linda, xiii, 335
Ernst, Dorothy, 426
Ernst, Richard, 426
Escher, Donn H., 233, 336
Estenson, Marie, 337-338
Estes, Jonathan, 31
Evenson, Rhonda, 150, 154, 157
Fair, Jeanette, 323
Farley, Don, 108
Farnham, Rufus, 27
Farr, Darrell, 534
Fawcett, Hazel, 545
Feck, Anna, 491
Feess, John and Sharon, 339
Fehrman, Darrel, 114
Fiebiger, Ardis and Peter, 132, 278, 340, 359, 390, 421, 542
Fierst, Evelyn, 341
Fierst, Linda and Richard, 342
Fignar, Bill, 13, 138, 235

Fikse, Leon, 109
Filson, Anna and Walt, 343
Finch, Elias W., 344
Finch, Margaret Ione, 344
Finley, Ruth and Tex, 345
Finstad, Gale, 157
Fischbach, Lulu, 162, 305
Fischbach, Nellie, 162-163, 346
Fischer, Allison Anne, 379
Fischer, Corky, 379
Fischer, Dianne, 379
Fischer, Emma and William, 164, 442
Fisher, William A., 42
Flanders, Mary Jane, 30, 274
Fleming, Ethel M., 410
Flesher, H. J., 512
Flesher, Kathy, 118, 128, 132
Fletcher, Chris and Janet, 347
Fogerson, John, 35
Folin, Clint, 190
Fornara, Judy, 113
Forrest, Jean Carlson, 153, 348
Forsberg, Russell T., 349
Forystek, Bruce, 350
Forystek, Edward and Geraldine, 350
Forystek, Wesley P., 350
Foslien, Arnie and June, 233, 351
Framstad, Clarence, 104
Fransen, Vern, 501
Fraser, Don, 45
Frazier, Stanley N., 106
Frear, Dana, 41
Freeman, Bill and Kathryn (Chowen), 352
French, Damon, 177
French, Shirley, 312
Frusti, Martin, 283
Funk, William, 178, 183
Gadow, Doris, 175, 393
Gagnon, Kathleen and Ralph, 353
Gale, Vivian, 354
Gallien, William, 45, 47, 411
Galvin, Jim, 477
Ganzer, Dorayne, 155
Gardner, Ernest and Florence, 355
Garlitz, Mike, 190
Garrett, Lily, 151
Gaslin, W. H., 97
Geissler, Ruth, 118
Gellerman, Chris, 183
Gendler, Neal, 149
Germundsen, Richard, 190
Germundson, Doug, 74, 86
Gervais, Pierre, 30, 94
Gervais, Victor, 160
Getchell, Alva, 37

Getchell, George W., 17
Getchell, Mary A., 28, 41, 445
Getchell, N. H., 42
Getchell, W. D., 29
Getchell, W. H., 42
Getchell, Washington, 27, 29
Getchell, Winslow, 28
Gibson, Elaine, 162
Gilbertson, Russell, 301, 411
Gillen, Maxine, 527
Gillespie, James M., 33, 41, 356
Gillespie, John, 334, 356
Girling, T. F., 209
Girling, Thomas H., 202
Godbout, Roger, 111, 233
Goddard, John and Ruby, 357
Goetze, Alma, 376
Goetze, Harvey H., 183, 199, 358
Goetze, Rudolf, 358
Goetze, Carol and Wilbur, vii, xiii, 13, 53, 56, 65, 181, 183, 198-199, 235, 350, 358, 507
Goldsmith, Don, 102
Good, Michael, 359
Good, Teresa B. Huddle, 359
Goodwin, Louise, 523
Gorham, Thomas and Connie, 308
Gould, Walter H., 156
Graber, Warren, 176
Grabor, Walt and Harriet, 278
Graser, Alfred and Marian, 360
Gray, Calvin, 10, 195-196, 198, 361
Greb, Dorothy, 362
Green, Clara Esther Crooker, 31
Green, Duff, 444
Green, Harry and Beverly, 278
Green, Hazel, 370
Green, Mahlon and Margaret, 67, 444
Green, Warren, 495, 503
Greenland, Carol, 189
Greenwald, Dale and Louisa, xiii, 129, 235, 363
Greenwood, James, 143
Gregornik, Norman, 257
Griggs, Amelia, 33
Grile, Harry, 111
Grile, Patrick, 111
Grim, George, 173
Groenhoff, Ed, 98
Groettum, Carl, 88, 93, 101, 233
Gross, Debra Lee, 364
Gross, Delores Jean and Robert, 364
Grothem, Jean, 41
Guntzel, Connie, 77
Guntzel, Hilmer, 7, 52, 305

Gusdal, Delmar, 98
Gustafson, Arthur and Mary Jane, 13, 40-41, 51, 86, 88, 93, 129-130, 132, 149-151, 175, 183, 190-192, 199, 223, 232, 237, 239, 261, 286, 288, 365, 465-466, 499, 558
Gustafson, Dale, 366
Gustafson, Deil O., 9, 47, 223, 275, 535
Gustafson, Nancy (Fellger), 190, 192, 365
Haas, Bill, 138
Hage, Dave, 13
Hagel, Eugene and Mary, 21, 46, 212, 367, 453
Hageman, Donna and Gene, 368
Hagen, Shirley and Wallace, 369
Hagstrom, Jo Dee, 166
Hajder, Betty, 183
Hall, Alice, 229, 460
Hallberg, Jane, xiii, 2, 13, 40-41, 86, 94, 130, 149, 159, 183, 209, 223, 233, 236, 256, 376, 458, 535
Hallenberg, Ruth, 229
Hallman, Carole, 154
Hallonquist, Mark, 103
Halvorsons, 350
Ham, Della and Edward, 169, 173, 370, 545
Ham, George, 370
Ham, James Leander, 169, 370
Ham, Marian, 370
Ham, Marjory, 370, 373
Hamernick, Ed, 8, 91, 129
Hamilton, Abraham Lincoln, 371, 388
Hamilton, Addison, 373
Hamilton, Anna, 372
Hamilton, Anne, 78
Hamilton, Charles, 370, 372
Hamilton, David, 160, 472
Hamilton, Florence, 381
Hamilton, Frend, 52, 372, 452
Hamilton, Gordon, 381
Hamilton, Grace, 452
Hamilton, Hannah, 371
Hamilton, John A., 166
Hamilton, Marjory Naomi, 373
Hamilton, Mary, 373
Hamilton, Olive (Edwards), 371, 373, 381
Hamilton, Robert W., 370, 373
Hammond, Lynne and Mac, 106
Hampton, Trevor, 71
Hamrock, Leona, 470

Hoisington, Daniel J.   F614.B7
The Brooklyns: a history of H719b
Brooklyn Center and
Bro